COLOUR LIBRARY BOOKS

Atlas of the
OCEANS

COLOUR LIBRARY BOOKS
Atlas of the
OCEANS

ATLAS OF THE OCEANS
has been submitted to the World
Wildlife Fund, who regard it as a
wide-ranging and informative book,
and approve it both as a sound
source of reference, and for general
reading for all age groups.

COLOUR LIBRARY BOOKS

MITCHELL BEAZLEY PUBLISHERS LTD.

Editor — Martyn Bramwell
Art Editor — Pat Gilliland
Cartographic Editor — James Somerville
Assistant Editors — Dougal Dixon
Jinny Johnson
Mike Janson
Cartographer — Anco van den Dool
Assistant Art Editor — Mike Brown
Designer — Ayala Kingsley
Design Assistant — Pauline Faulks
Picture Researcher — Jackum Brown
Editorial Assistant — Pam Taaffe
Production Controller — Barry Baker

Publisher — Bruce Marshall
Art Director — John Bigg
Production Director — Michael Powell

Published by Colour Library Books Ltd, Guildford, Surrey
Original material copyright ©1977 by
Mitchell Beazley Publishers Ltd, London
Also published as The Rand McNally Atlas of the Oceans

Seabed relief maps on pages 114-115, 116-117, 150-151,
156-157, details on pages 158-159 Copyright © Paris Match

ISBN 0 86283 560 7

Printed and bound in Barcelona, Spain by Cronion, S.A.

Dep. Leg. nº B-14181-87

PRINCIPAL EDITORIAL CONSULTANTS

Dr. William A. Nierenberg
*Director, Scripps Institution of Oceanography,
California*

Dr. Henry Charnock
Director, Institute of Oceanographic Sciences

Sir George Deacon
*Former Director, Institute of Oceanographic
Sciences, Surrey*

CARTOGRAPHIC ADVISERS

Dr. A. S. Laughton
Institute of Oceanographic Sciences, Surrey

H. A. G. Lewis
Cartographic Consultant

CONTRIBUTING AUTHORS

Robert Allen
*International Union for Conservation of Nature
and Natural Resources, Switzerland*

Dayton Lee Alverson
*Director, Northwest Fisheries Center, National
Oceanic and Atmospheric Administration, Seattle,
Washington*

Alan Archer
Institute of Geological Sciences, London

Dr. Tim Barnett
Scripps Institution of Oceanography, California

John Bevan
Submex Limited, Submarine Consultants, London

Patricia Birnie
*Department of Public International Law,
University of Edinburgh*

Dr. Quentin Bone
*Marine Biological Association of the United
Kingdom, Plymouth*

Dr. W. R. P. Bourne
Department of Zoology, University of Aberdeen

Dr. David Cartwright
*Institute of Oceanographic Sciences, Bidston
Observatory, Birkenhead*

Dr. David Cushing
*Ministry of Agriculture, Fisheries and Food,
Lowestoft Laboratory*

Sir George Deacon
Institute of Oceanographic Sciences, Surrey

Margaret Deacon
National Maritime Museum, London

Dr. Brian Durrans
*Department of Ethnography, British Museum,
London*

Dr. N. C. Fleming
Institute of Oceanographic Sciences, Surrey

Dr. B. N. Fletcher
Institute of Geological Sciences, Leeds

Prof. B. M. Funnell
Department of Geology, University of East Anglia

Dr. Edward D. Goldberg
Scripps Institution of Oceanography, California

Dr. James Greenslate
Scripps Institution of Oceanography, California

Dr. Roy Harden-Jones
*Ministry of Agriculture, Fisheries and Food,
Lowestoft Laboratory*

Prof. John D. Isaacs
Scripps Institution of Oceanography, California

Dr. E. J. W. Jones
Department of Geology, University College, London

Dr. Niel H. Kenyon
Institute of Oceanographic Sciences, Surrey

Dr. Robert B. Kidd
Institute of Oceanographic Sciences, Surrey

Dr. Alan R. Longhurst
*Deputy Director, Institute for Marine Environ-
mental Research, Plymouth*

Dr. Peter Lonsdale
Scripps Institution of Oceanography, California

Dr. Jerome Namias
Scripps Institution of Oceanography, California

Joyce Pope
British Museum (Natural History), London

G. H. Rhys
Institute of Geological Sciences, Leeds

Dr. David A. Ross
*Woods Hole Oceanographic Institution, Woods
Hole, Massachusetts*

Ann Sayer
*Geological Appraisal Division, British Petroleum
Company Limited, London*

Reg L. Vallintine
Director-General, British Sub-Aqua Club, London

Prof. F. J. Vine
*School of Environmental Sciences, University of
East Anglia*

Dr. Peter Wadhams
Scott Polar Research Institute, Cambridge

Cdr. David Waters
*Deputy Director, National Maritime Museum,
London*

Dr. David Webb
Institute of Oceanographic Sciences, Surrey

8 THE OCEAN REALM

The origin of the seas—changing coastlines and shifting
continents—the structure of seawater—oceans of ice
and the effect upon climate—how the sea moves: currents,
tides and waves—oceans past and future

40 MAN'S OCEANIC QUEST

Ancient fears and myths—the men who discovered the
world: da Gama, Columbus, Magellan—the birth of oceanography—man probes the deep—submersible craft—politics
and the sea—designs for the future

60 LIFE IN THE OCEANS

The pyramid of marine life; from plankton to dolphins—
the structure of sea creatures: vertebrates and invertebrates—living fossils—mammals and reptiles—birdlife
and the shoreline—creatures of the shallows and the deep ocean

90 THE GREAT RESOURCE

Fish, oil, minerals and energy—farming and harvesting the
seas—oceanic reserves of manganese, nickel, cobalt,
copper, gold and titanium—the oil and gas reserve—the
sea as a powerhouse—pollution and the threat to the future

112 THE FACE OF THE DEEP

Unique maps of the world's oceans—physical contours,
submarine features and circulation of each great sea—
the vastness and complexity of the Atlantic and Pacific—
partially enclosed seas: Caribbean, Mediterranean and Red Sea
—polar seas: the Arctic and Southern Oceans—the turbulent
Indian Ocean and the richness of the North Sea—a worldwide
survey of oceanic structure and movement; of marine life and
mineral resources

172 ENCYCLOPEDIA OF MARINE LIFE

A catalogue of the main families of marine life—their form,
anatomy and special adaptations

187 TABLES

191 GLOSSARY

192 INDEX

"Most people like the ocean; they want to live beside it or near it. The conquest of space may be a great national or individual achievement, but it is not a part of the average man's world.

"To oceanographers the sea is an enormous and restless antagonist. The work is nowhere near as glamorous as many would believe; it's tough, rough and very difficult. But, for the average man, there is the ocean—empty, beautiful, available and infinitely appealing."

This statement was extracted from me in 1969 during the course of an interview. My feelings have in no way changed even though much has happened since that could spoil this feeling for the most remarkable reserve on the face of our planet.

The *Atlas of the Oceans* vividly illustrates this contrast. There are images and reminders of the vast beauty of the oceans coupled with the exciting possibility of unlimited resources. But these resources are not boundless—and their careless pursuit could spoil the beauty of the oceans for so many.

This atlas is, in the first instance, exactly what an atlas should be. Pictured here are the component parts of the ocean—its life, its surface, its depths, its islands and archipelagos, and its interface with the continents we live on. But it also portrays man's interaction with, and intervention in, the oceans. This interaction has, in the past, been for pleasure, for food and for commerce: more recently it has also been for minerals, for weather and climate, and above all for science to help in all these pursuits. Just as life on earth is believed to have originated in the oceans, so today the sciences of the earth are elucidated by our study of the oceans.

The physical features of the oceans and their relationships with the continents can all now be rationalized in the new concept of plate tectonics and continental drift. Without this theory we would be unable to understand the simplest processes taking place today, such as the ultimate fate of the huge amounts of sediment carried to the sea by the world's great rivers. Without seafloor spreading, these sediments would level the continents and fill the ocean basins in just ten million years—a span of time far less than the age of the earth.

All are agreed that man's influence on this planet must be curbed and regulated, but we are not always agreed on the means—or the end. Many life scientists feel that the most important goal should be to maintain the variety of life we have on this planet, and it is the precise aim of the science of ecology to explain this variety and its stability in the face of universally fierce competition.

Nothing has illustrated the impact of man on the ecology of the earth more dramatically than the occupation of fishing. In many instances, specific fisheries have destroyed themselves through the inability of society to control fishing in a conservative fashion. Since the total world fishery is now close to the maximum sustainable yield, and since this represents one-tenth of a pound of fish per person in the world, every day, sensible control of fish stocks is of vital importance. A large part of the atlas is devoted to illustrating this all important human activity.

Perhaps most important is the role of the oceans in controlling weather and climate. We are only now beginning to understand the relationships at the air-ocean interface and successful predictions are now being made on the basis of oceanic theories and observations. Further ahead we can look forward to the possibility of weakening that most frightening oceanic phenomenon, the hurricane, and to the effective "steering" of storms to safe areas.

The greed of nations is so great that many of these important considerations are in danger of foundering. Only greater, and wider, public understanding of the oceans can help ensure a sensible and constructive agreement on their future use by mankind.

William A. Nierenberg

Dr. William A. Nierenberg
Director, Scripps Institution of Oceanography,
University of California, San Diego, California.

THE OCEAN REALM

In March 1971, after lying dormant for almost a year, the Mauna Ulu vent of the Hawaiian volcano Kilauea began to erupt, pouring streams of dark pahoehoe lava into a network of hardened lava tubes leading down to the sea. Surprisingly, the entrance into the sea of the hot basaltic lava was not accompanied by vast clouds of steam; the surface of the molten rock cooled on contact to form a brittle tube within which the lava continued to flow. For the first time, erupting lava was photographed underwater, by scientists from the University of Hawaii. Taken through water clouded by fine black sand particles, the photograph shows the incandescent glow of molten lava briefly exposed as the wall of a submerged lava tube cracked open.

GENESIS OF THE OCEANS

The most striking and distinctive feature of our planet, when viewed from space, is the amount of water on its surface. Indeed, because of this the earth has often, and aptly, been called the water planet. Vapor and droplets in the atmosphere, although conspicuous as clouds, represent only a minute fraction of the total volume. Most of the water is contained within the oceans, the remaining few percent being in lakes, rivers and ice caps and in the cavities and pores of the rocks. Collectively the water that is present above, on and within the earth is referred to as the hydrosphere. The way in which this water interacts with the atmosphere and the earth's surface, giving rise to clouds, snow, rain, runoff, evaporation and percolation, is well known. What is less obvious, and much more difficult to study, is the way in which the hydrosphere interacts with the interior of the earth.

There are basically two hypotheses for the origin of the hydrosphere. One is that it formed very early in the earth's history, possibly at the time the earth came into being, and the other is that it has gradually been derived from the earth's interior throughout geologic time. At first glance this second idea seems to be a very plausible one in that active volcanoes are known to

eject water vapor into the atmosphere. The rate at which this is occurring today is difficult to measure, but most estimates agree that with a comparable rate throughout geologic time this process alone would be capable of producing the total volume of water in the oceans. The flaw in this argument is that we cannot be too sure that this water is coming from the deep interior of the earth; much or all of it could be recycled water, which has already been at the surface. Geologists now think that water exists at very much greater depths in the earth's crust than had previously been suspected. Some of this water was incorporated in sediments that were subsequently buried to great depths, some probably percolated downward through cracks in the rocks and the spaces between individual grains. Molten rock, or magma, has a great facility for incorporating water within it and it seems very probable therefore that the magma that rises through the earth's outer layers to produce volcanic activity at the surface absorbs water on its passage upward. The significance of recycled water is even greater now that it has been realized that the majority of the world's volcanoes are associated with the return of oceanic crust to the earth's mantle landward of the deep-sea trenches, notably around the margins of the Pacific.

Water derived from this crust may not only be incorporated in the magmas but may also be crucial to their formation, because its presence will lower the melting point of the rocks at depth.

It is very difficult to assess therefore what proportion, if any, of the water added to the hydrosphere by volcanic activity is new, or juvenile, water derived from the earth's interior rather than recycled from the earth's surface. Recent isotopic studies suggest that some small fraction of this water is juvenile and that ultimately it may be possible to determine just how much. It seems increasingly probable however that most of the water now at the earth's surface has been there since very early in geologic history.

Just as the earth is distinctive in appearance because of the presence of vast areas of water, the solid surface without its thin fluid envelope of atmosphere and oceans would make a similarly striking contrast with that of our nearest neighbors in space. Venus may be an exception, since its surface has been only dimly perceived through its obscuring atmosphere, but it is now well known that the surfaces of the earthlike bodies—the moon, mercury and mars—are very different from that of the earth. This seems to be due to the restless nature of our planet's interior. The earth is a highly evolved planet, the interior having separated into a metallic core and stony mantle, and the surface having been repeatedly renewed and reworked as a result of convection of mantle material. The surface consists of two types of crust—an oceanic crust formed of basaltic material which is constantly being renewed by the convection, and a continental crust of lighter granitic material present in separate pieces forming the continents. Continental crust, like the hydrosphere, has been sweated out of the mantle by the convection process, but one can take the parallel even further in that there is a similar uncertainty as to the rate at which this has occurred throughout geologic time. Again it seems probable that most of the continental crust was formed early on in the earth's history but that it has also been added to gradually ever since. Before considering the early history of the earth it is important to realize that as a result of the earth's dynamic nature and constantly changing face there is no surface record of the early conditions and events. There are small areas on most continents in which the rocks are older than 3000 million years and in these rocks there is evidence for the presence of water at the earth's surface at that time. The oldest rock so far discovered—a sedimentary, or water-formed, rock from West Greenland—is about 3800 million years old, but the earth is thought to have been formed some 800 million years earlier.

It is clear then that our ideas on the age of the earth and its initial evolution are necessarily based on theoretical considerations. We have no direct evidence in the geologic record, nor have we any direct evidence for the composition of the earth's mantle so crucial to an understanding of the evolution of the oceans. Our

models for the age and bulk composition of the earth are derived from evidence from the moon and meteorites. All meteoritic material, and the moon's oldest rocks, yield ages of 4600 million years and this is thought to be the age of the solar system. One of the older theories for the origin of the earth maintained that it had evolved from a very hot cloud of gases from which materials formed at progressively lower temperatures producing the solid planet. Water ultimately condensed from the residual atmosphere to form the oceans. Although modern theories favor a more complex "cold" origin for the earth their implications for the origin of the oceans are not in fact very different.

It is now thought that at the birth of the solar system the material that now constitutes the planets formed a spinning disk of hot ionized gas centered on the sun. As this cloud cooled, grains of solidified material began to condense out and ultimately these began to coalesce to form particles of varying sizes. Some of these particles, or planetisimals, are thought to survive today as meteorites. The composition and texture of meteorites vary considerably, probably reflecting a range of planetisimal sizes or impact histories, but some contain occluded gases and minerals that include water and volatile elements such as carbon, nitrogen and chlorine. Their presence indicates that the meteorites were formed at temperatures no greater than a few hundred degrees above temperatures at the earth's surface today. It is thought that these

The origin of ocean water remains shrouded in mystery, but it seems likely that most was liberated as vapor from newly formed rocks as the earth was cooling and became a major component of the planet's ancestral atmosphere. The vapor condensed when the earth's surface became cool enough to allow water to fall as rain, and the hot pools and lakes that were formed filled and coalesced into the first oceans about 4000 million years ago. Water vapor is still being released into the atmosphere by volcanoes, but only a very small proportion is "juvenile" water, newly released from volcanic rocks; the remainder is groundwater, heated and recycled.

relatively cold particles were the building blocks from which the earth was formed. Thus, according to this model water was incorporated within the earth as it formed. Different theories then disagree in detail. The water may have been released during formation so that by the time the earth had attained its final size virtually all the water was at the surface, presumably in the atmosphere. On the other hand it may have been later that the interior of the earth became hot enough for large-scale melting and volcanic activity to result in an effective degassing of the interior. In either case most of the water in the present-day hydrosphere is thought to have been at the surface soon after the earth's formation. Subsequently, perhaps hundreds of millions of years later, the earth's surface and lower atmosphere would have cooled sufficiently for the water to condense, and torrential rains must have lashed the earth eventually to form the first oceans.

THE CONTINENTAL DRIFT DEBATE

Approximately three-quarters of the earth's surface is covered by water, but only two-thirds by deep ocean basins and oceanic, as opposed to continental, crust. The difference is largely accounted for by the shallow shelf seas that lie between the coastlines and the continental slope, the latter being the true geologic boundary between the continents and the oceans. The extent to which the oceans spill over onto the continental margins has varied considerably throughout geologic time, due mainly to changes in the geometry and mean depth of the ocean basins. During the past few million years, however, it has been determined primarily by the amount of water locked up in ice caps.

As the map of the world's coastlines gradually emerged, scholars were intrigued by the enigmatic distribution of continents and oceans, particularly by the rough parallelism of the opposing shores of the Atlantic and the contrast between the water hemisphere of the Pacific and the land hemisphere centered on Europe. Certainly by the mid-eighteenth century it had been suggested that the Atlantic Ocean basin may have been formed by the separation and drifting apart of the surrounding landmasses. This concept of

Antonio Snider-Pelligrini, in 1858, was the first to reassemble the continents according to geological as well as geometrical evidence. He published these maps that year in his book *La Création et ses Mystères dévoilés* and three years later they were published again by J. H. Pepper in his *Playbook of Metals*, where they were used to account for similarities in the fossil plants of the coalfields of Europe and North America. The idea, however, seemed too farfetched for science or the general public to accept and it was forgotten, not to be revived for 50 years.

The configuration of continents today reflects the movements of the continental plates over the past few hundred million years. The continuation of geological features between continents, the similarities between fossils of different areas and physical evidence such as the natural magnetism of rocks can lead geologists to reconstruct the positions of the continents in times past.

Modern science can predict more accurately the positions of the continents before the last phase of drifting, A super-continent, Pangaea, existed some 200 million years ago and this comprised two parts—Laurasia, consisting of Europe, North America and Asia, and Gondwanaland, consisting of the southern continents. Pangaea was not a permanent mass but had accreted by earlier drifting.

Alfred Wegener, a German geophysicist, astronomer and meteorologist, published a series of paleogeographical reconstructions of the continents in 1915. His evidence was drawn from all the sciences and, although some of it was erroneous, most was quite valid. Despite this his theories were not immediately accepted and his work was not universally recognized until more modern investigations backed them up. He was at a loss to account for the mechanism of continental drift and proposed such unlikely processes as tidal force and variations in gravity at different points on the globe. Although Wegener saw the continents as flexible masses rather than rigid plates and although he was mistaken about the speed of drift, his maps are still acceptable today.

The ring of fold mountains around the continental masses of the Northern Hemisphere gave an early indication that continental drift may have occurred. A continent can be considered to be made up of two components—a rigid interior, or shield, of stable old rocks and belts of fold mountains, usually around the edges. This arrangement led F. B. Taylor, an American geologist, to postulate in 1910 that the shields of the northern continents had moved outward crumpling up the sediments before them. The result was the interrupted ring of mountains consisting of the Alps, the Himalayas, the Pacific island chains and the Rockies. The highest ranges were formed where the moving continents pushed against the static blocks of Africa and the Indian subcontinent.

"continental drift" was revived repeatedly throughout the following two hundred years, but was always largely ignored by the mainstream of geologic thought. Most advocates of the idea, even in the early part of this century, appealed to a catastrophic event to account for the initiation of drift. The earliest proponents associated this with catastrophes documented in the Bible, and later ones with the idea that the moon was formed from a mass of material pulled from the Pacific basin. In the late eighteenth century, however, the first true geologists had enunciated the principle of "gradualism" or "actualism," whereby, they maintained, the whole geologic record could be interpreted in terms of processes occurring today. Since successive generations of geologists were unconvinced that there was any evidence for continental movements in the recent past, there was until quite recently no place for continental drift within conventional geology.

In the early part of this century Alfred Wegener, the German meteorologist, made valiant attempts to document continental motions and supply a mechanism by which drift might be occurring. On these points, however, both his evidence and his ideas were demon-strably unsatisfactory and, perhaps because of this, geologists also disregarded the vast amount of sound geologic evidence that Wegener accumulated.

A basic problem in resolving this debate was that prior to 1950 very little was known about the nature and age of the deep ocean basins. Clearly if one was to distinguish between "drift," which implies that the ocean basins are relatively young, and "permanency," which implies that they are very old, the answers were to be found in the exploration of the deep-sea floor. Only after World War II did the techniques and financial resources become available for this work; prior to this, rather more than two-thirds of the earth's crust was essentially unexplored. By 1960 some remarkable discoveries had been made and the stage was set for a breakthrough in our understanding of the origin and evolution of the ocean basins.

One of the first and most fundamental discoveries was that the earth's crust beneath the ocean basins is much thinner than that beneath the continents and that its physical properties suggest that it is much more closely related to the underlying mantle. In addition, the thickness of the oceanic crust is essentially constant throughout the ocean basins, contrasting with the continental situation in which the crustal thickness typically reflects the topographical relief. Another early discovery was the realization that the Mid-Atlantic Ridge, part of which was encountered by the first transatlantic cable-laying ships, is just one small part of a vast midocean ridge system that encircles the globe and dominates all the ocean basin floors with the exception of the northwest Pacific. If the hydrosphere were removed, this ridge system would be revealed as the most spectacular and continuous topographical feature on the earth's surface. It also became apparent that the crests of the midocean ridges are characterized by a dearth of sediments, by earthquake activity and in places by high heat-flow.

Until quite recently, techniques for sampling the rocks and sediments of the ocean floor were very crude, and by 1960 no material older than 100 million years had been recovered from the deep seafloor. Initial results therefore suggested that the geologic nature of the ocean basins is very different from that of the continents and several factors strongly indicated their relative youthfulness.

The southern continents provide abundant proof that they were once part of a single landmass called Gondwanaland. Apart from the obvious geometric fit of the shapes there are many lines of geological continuity between each continent. These include Precambrian rocks in Brazil and West Africa and a sequence of Jurassic deposits traceable from East Africa, through Madagascar to India. The positions of the earth's magnetic pole can be plotted for any point in geological time by studying the magnetism of rocks formed at that time. Only when the southern continents are placed in the Gondwanaland configuration do the poles coincide during the Devonian Carboniferous and Permian periods. During the Upper Carboniferous and Permian there was an ice age in these regions and the preserved indications of this are continuous between the continents. The distribution of fossils also shows that this was once all one landmass which started to break up in the Cretaceous period about 100 million years ago. Evidence for Gondwanaland was investigated by the South African geologist Alex L. du Toit, in the 1930s.

— Direction of ice flow

Early Permian ice caps

Late Carboniferous ice caps

Fossils of the fern *Glossopteris* from all the southern continents show that they were once joined.

Remains of the freshwater reptile *Mesosaurus* are found in both Brazil and Africa.

The land reptile *Lystrosaurus* lived in Africa, Antarctica and India during the Triassic period.

Hercynian Mountains

Caledonian Mountains

A northern supercontinent called Laurasia existed also until the Cretaceous period. The evidence for this is not so spectacular as that for Gondwanaland, but it can be seen in the line of fold mountains of Devonian age which stretches from the west of North America where it forms part of the Appalachians, through the highlands of Scotland, to Norway and Greenland. A later Carboniferous mountain chain runs from the remainder of the Appalachians and North West Africa to parts of Europe. These chains were formed by the coming together of earlier blocks.

13

EARTH'S MOVING CRUST

The Tonga Trench represents a destructive plate margin, where one oceanic plate is driving into the mantle beneath another. Such a margin is characterized by a deep trench and an arc of volcanic islands formed by melting within and above descending plates.

The East Pacific Rise is a typical constructive margin, where two oceanic plates are being continuously generated. Mantle material is constantly rising and solidifying at the surface, to be added to the trailing edge of the crustal plates as they move apart.

The Peru-Chile Trench is a destructive margin, where two types of crustal plate, one oceanic and the other continental, meet. The oceanic plate forms a trench as it is carried downward, while the lighter continental material is elevated into a mountain range.

The earth is made up of several concentric shells: the core of nickel and iron, existing below about 1800 miles; the stony mantle; and the crust, which averages only 10 to 25 miles in thickness. The mantle is solid except for a layer near the top, called the asthenosphere, which is thought to be fairly mobile. Above this lies a layer about 60 miles thick, consisting of the uppermost mantle and the crust. This rigid outer layer, called the lithosphere, represents the plates that move over the earth's surface. Each plate, such as that centered on Antarctica, is ringed by active plate margins.

In the early 1960s a bold new concept was developed to explain the origin of the ocean basins. In one giant step it attempted not only to accommodate all the new information gleaned from exploration of the deep-sea floor but also to provide a plausible mechanism for continental drift. The basic idea was that the mid-ocean ridges and the marginal trenches are surface expressions of the upwelling and downwelling limbs respectively of large-scale convection currents in the mantle, the thin oceanic crust being derived from the mantle at ridge crests and absorbed back into the mantle beneath the trenches. Clearly these ideas were readily compatible with the earthquake activity and high heat flow associated with ridge crests, and the intense volcanic activity and young mountain ranges which occur landward of the oceanic trenches. Within this framework the continents were considered to be "frozen" into conveyor belts of oceanic crust and upper mantle, upon which they moved passively.

This hypothesis was soon named "seafloor spreading," because it invoked a symmetrical process of lateral spreading about ridge crests. It implied that the deep ocean floor is both young and disposable. Furthermore, if one accepts the geologic evidence for the age of the initial fragmentation of the continents bordering the Atlantic and Indian oceans, then the average spreading rates in these ocean basins must have been 0.4 to 0.8 inches per year on each ridge flank. Initially, most geologists felt that such sweeping generalizations, however elegant, were only possible because at that time relatively little was known about

the geology and geophysics of the deep-sea floor.

Within a few years the basic hypothesis of seafloor spreading had been embellished in a number of ways, two of which in particular led to the general acceptance of the concept and to its reformulation in terms of "plate tectonics." The first concerned the magnetization of the oceanic crust as it forms at ridge crests. The basaltic rocks of the oceanic crust preserve a permanent magnetization, which reflects the direction and intensity of the earth's magnetic field at the time they are formed. If, as now seems certain, the earth's magnetic field has reversed its polarity repeatedly throughout geologic time, then avenues of normally and reversely magnetized crust will be produced parallel to the ridge crests. Thus the conveyor belt of ocean floor also acts as a tape recorder and the detailed evolution of the ocean basins has been revealed by plotting these magnetic growth lines. Since 1968 this sequence of growth bands had gradually been dated: so far no material older than 160 million years has been recovered and it seems extremely unlikely that any part of the deep ocean floor is older than 200 million years.

The other all-important prediction concerned the great fracture zones that traverse the midocean ridges and offset the ridge crests. When these were first discovered they were thought of as faults along which a once-continuous ridge crest had been progressively offset. However, if one assumes seafloor spreading, a completely different picture emerges. The offset of the ridge crest might well be original and permanent; the fault zone need only be active between the offset

lengths of ridge crest and the direction of motion on the fault plane is opposite to that suggested by the offset of the ridge crest. Within two years of these predictions being made they were confirmed by detailed studies of the earthquakes occurring on such fracture zones.

Considerations such as these, together with an improved knowledge of the worldwide distribution of earthquakes, led to the concept of plate tectonics. This maintains that we should think of the outer skin of the earth as being divided up into a relatively small number of rigid plates, which are approximately 60 miles thick and bounded by the midocean ridges, the transverse fracture zones and the deep-sea trenches. The plates are moving relative to each other and the direction of motion between any two plates depends on the type of plate boundary that separates them. Plates separated by a midocean ridge are clearly moving apart; plates separated by a deep-sea trench or an active mountain belt, or both, are coming together, whereas plates separated by a fault zone, as in the Caribbean basin, are moving past each other without creation or destruction of material.

An important corollary of the plate concept is that all plates and plate boundaries migrate with respect to each other in addition to moving across the face of the earth. In theory, just one may be stationary, but on physical grounds it seems more likely that all are moving and that plate motion is indicated by volcanic island chains, such as the Hawaiian Islands chain, which result from the passage of a plate over an essentially fixed "hot-spot" in the mantle.

The surface of the earth can be divided into six major plates and a number of minor ones. Most tectonic events such as earthquakes and volcanic eruptions are confined to the boundaries between these plates and are due either to the destruction of old material beneath trenches or to the upwelling of new material at ridges. The growth of the plates at the margins can be quite accurately measured and ranges from about half an inch every year in the region of Iceland to about three and a half inches a year on the East Pacific Rise. These measurements, made only in recent years, explain observations made over the past century.

Confirmation that new material is formed at ocean ridge crests is derived from the fact that when new rocks are formed, the magnetic particles in them are immediately aligned parallel to the earth's prevailing magnetic field. This magnetic "signature" is locked into the rocks as they solidify and is retained as they move away from the ridge.

From other sources it is known that the magnetic field of the earth has changed its polarity, north for south, repeatedly in the past few million years. When this happens, the rocks subsequently formed are magnetized in the new direction. The resulting pattern of alternately polarized strips is mirrored across the ridge.

The size of the plates is not constant. The African plate is bounded on three sides by midocean ridges that indicate the presence of constructive margins. Since the plate is constantly enlarging from these ridges, and there is no intervening destructive margin; it follows that the ridges cannot be stationary relative to each other but are moving apart as the plate enlarges.

Midocean ridges are formed at right angles to the direction of plate movement. Where the plates have an irregular edge, the ridge between them is offset by a series of faults called transform faults. These are the sites of earthquake activity, but only between the ridge crests where newly formed parts of adjacent crustal plates slide past one another in opposite directions.

The classic locality of the symmetrical arrangement of magnetized strips is Reykjanes Ridge, south of Iceland. This is part of the Mid-Atlantic Ridge studied between 1963 and 1966. The pattern of polarity reversals was found to correlate with those found in the Pacific and with the known sequence of reversals over the past ten million years. Despite the inevitable natural irregularities, the continuity and symmetry of the strips is obvious.

THE IMPERMANENT OCEANS

The Red Sea is an example of the early stage in the opening of a new ocean. An upwelling region in the asthenosphere beneath a continent will set up tensions within the continent, causing it to split. A rift valley such as that found in East Africa today forms along the line of upwelling. As the two parts of the continent move away from each other the rift valley becomes a young ocean basin such as the Red Sea. A midocean ridge forms in the center of it as new material wells up and solidifies. A rift valley at the crest shows that there is constant tension in the ridge as new rocks travel outward.

The Himalayas are an example of an intracontinental range of mountains formed at the destructive margins of two plates. When crustal plates converge they form a trench and island arc. Eventually a continent carried by the subducting plate overruns the trench and merges with the island arc. The other plate then begins to be consumed, forming a new trench and a range of coastal mountains such as the Andes. When a continent carried by this second plate reaches the subduction zone the sediments between them are crushed up into the mountains to form one continent with a mountain range at the center.

The age and mode of formation of the present-day ocean basins testify to the reality of seafloor spreading and continental drift during the past 200 million years. But this span of time is less than five percent of the age of the earth—generally calculated to be about 4600 million years. One is led to ask, therefore, whether these processes have been restricted to this single episode of continental fragmentation, as was implicit in some of the earlier ideas concerning continental drift, or whether continental areas have repeatedly been drifted apart and welded together as a result of the creation and destruction of intervening oceanic crust, presumably by processes equivalent or analogous to the plate tectonic processes we can document at the present day. One of the earliest geologic arguments against a single episode of drift triggered by a catastrophic event was that although it explained quite neatly the distribution and age of the young mountain ranges, such as the Alps and the Himalayas, it offered no explanation for the older ranges such as the Ural, Caledonian and Appalachian mountains, which are not obviously different when one takes into account the much greater degree of erosion resulting from their greater age.

Clearly, in trying to reconstruct the configuration of continental and oceanic areas prior to 200 million years ago, the geologist has only the geologic record locked in the continental rock formations to refer to. However, it is now generally agreed among geologists that there is sufficient evidence in this record to suggest that there were earlier phases of drift and spreading dating back at least 600 million years and probably even earlier.

One of the main techniques used in determining the former geographic position of a continental area makes use of rock magnetism, and, as in the case of oceanic crust, the record one wishes to read is preserved in the magnetization frozen in at the time the rock was formed. Fossil magnetism is most successfully retained in certain igneous rocks, which "lock in" the magnetic orientations as they solidify, but clearly identifiable magnetic signatures may also be retained by sedimentary rocks deposited in water and even in windblown terrestrial deposits. However, whereas large-scale studies of magnetic lineations parallel to ocean ridges must be carried out by ship-borne instruments, continental studies may be carried out by taking a sample of the rock to the laboratory, where its direction of magnetism may be accurately determined. If one assumes that the earth's magnetic field has been dipolar and roughly symmetrical about the rotational axis in the past, as it is at the present day, then the angle that the direction of magnetization makes with the horizontal at the time of formation is directly and simply related to the latitude at which the rock was formed. These fossil compasses also, of course, indicate the direction of the north magnetic pole at this time. Thus it is possible to position continents in the past latitudinally and also to orient them relative to the meridians, but in general it is not possible to deduce their relative position longitudinally. In making reconstructions for times during the past 200 million years, however, one can use the additional information provided by the magnetic growth lines in the ocean basins and the geometric fit of the continents.

Within the framework of seafloor spreading, continental drift and plate tectonics, it is possible to envisage a life cycle for a typical ocean basin. A new ocean basin is formed when a continental area is rifted apart sufficiently for mantle material to well up into the gap and initiate the process of creation of oceanic crust by seafloor spreading. It appears, however, that tensional rifts can form within continental areas without necessarily becoming sites for new ocean basins. In the Red Sea–Gulf of Aden–East African

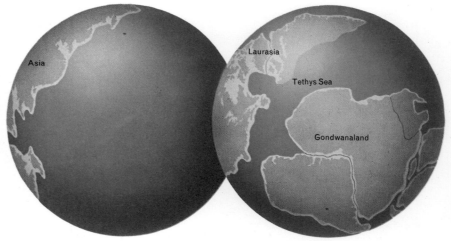

The Cambrian world was an unrecognizable one, with continental plates scattered in a pattern that is very different from that of today. Gondwanaland existed as a single landmass that would not split into Australia, India, South America, Africa and Arabia for another 400 million years. North America, northern Europe and most of Asia were separate continents and were widely spread.

In the Carboniferous, at the time of the coal forests and giant amphibians, North America and northern Europe had closed up forming the range of Caledonian Mountains between them. This landmass was separated by an ocean from Gondwanaland. The South Pole was, at this time, in the southern part of South America and the Asian continent was some distance away.

The Appalachians are a result of a complex history of converging and diverging crustal plates. In Precambrian times North America and Africa were split apart by a spreading ridge, forming an ocean called the ProtoAtlantic. This began to close in Cambrian times with a subduction zone beneath the North American continent. The closing continued until the Devonian, when all sediments between the two continents were crushed up into the Caledonian Mountains, remains of which are found in the northern Appalachians and the highlands of northern Europe. Later, in Carboniferous and Permian times, a further phase of compression produced the Hercynian Mountains, which form the remainder of the Appalachians. In the Jurassic the whole system split apart once more with the growth of the Atlantic Ocean complete with its central spreading ridge.

Rift area for example, whereas the Red Sea and Gulf of Aden are clearly youthful ocean basins, it is a moot point whether the East African Rift will ever become the site of one. Instead it may become the "failed arm" of the rift system. Once spreading has been initiated, the magnetic record confirms that it runs very smoothly, discontinuities in spreading being the exception rather than the rule. Within 50 million years or so an oceanic area such as that south of Australia will have formed and within 100 million years or more a mature ocean basin like that of the South Atlantic will have developed. With time, however, the worldwide geometry of plate boundaries changes, and just as occasionally new spreading boundaries form within continents, presumably new zones of destruction form in the ocean basins. It seems probable that these are typically sited at or near the margins of the basin and in time therefore an Andean or island-arc type of situation, with an offshore trench, develops at one or both continental margins. Thus the passive trailing margins of Atlantic-type are converted into active, advancing margins of Pacific-type. Ultimately, the whole oceanic area may be destroyed beneath the engulfing trenches, and as a result of the ensuing continental collision a mountain belt of the Himalayan type will be thrown up.

Such a sequence of events appears to have occurred in the North Atlantic area during the past 600 million years or so, except that we break into the cycle at its midpoint. Six hundred million years ago there was an ocean in this area, probably not unlike the Atlantic at the present day, but by 500 million years ago it had started to close and was flanked by Andean-type mountain ranges. By 400 million years ago it had closed completely to form the Caledonian Mountains—the northeast–southwest trending ranges joining part of the Appalachians and the mountains of Scotland and Norway. Within the past 200 million years, the present-day Atlantic basin has been formed, the initial splitting occurring very roughly along the original line of closure of its predecessor, the ProtoAtlantic.

When a geologist unravels the eroded remains of collision-type mountain belts he finds that they include great thicknesses of sediment that formed on and beyond the continental margins of oceanic areas and occasionally what appear to be mangled pieces of oceanic lithosphere. It is from such contorted and fragmentary remains that he must reconstruct the grandeur of former ocean basins—gradually decoding the ocean's history on the basis of geologic evidence and theoretical models of tectonic processes.

PERIOD	AGE (million years)	EVENTS
Cenozoic		The continents move toward their present positions.
		India collides with Asia to form the Himalayas.
	65	The Alps form.
Cretaceous		Gondwanaland begins to split to form the South Atlantic and Indian oceans.
	135	
Jurassic		Laurasia begins to break up to form the North Atlantic.
	195	
		Northern Europe collides with Asia to form the Urals.
Triassic		
	225	
Permian		The landmass of North America and northern Europe collides with that of North Africa and southern Europe, creating the Hercynian orogeny that forms the Appalachian Mountains.
	280	
Carboniferous	345	
Devonian	395	North America meets northern Europe, closing the ProtoAtlantic Ocean and forming part of the Appalachians and the
Silurian	430	
Ordovician	500	Scottish and Norwegian highlands by means of the Caledonian orogeny.
Cambrian	570	Considerable plate movement. Details largely obscured by subsequent events.
Precambrian	c.4,500	

The Permian was the time of Pangaea. Southern Europe had closed with northern, destroying the intervening sea to form the Hercynian mountain range. The Asian continent had moved up against

Europe—pushing up the Urals along the line of contact. During this time deserts covered most of the northern landmass, supporting a fauna of reptiles destined to evolve into the dinosaurs.

In the early Cenozoic a great change had taken place in the animals and plants of the world. Modern vegetation had appeared and mammals were becoming the dominant form of animal life.

Pangaea had broken up and the Atlantic Ocean had formed. Antarctica and Australia were still one continent, but India was drifting northward to collide with Asia and produce the Himalayas.

THE COASTAL LANDSCAPE

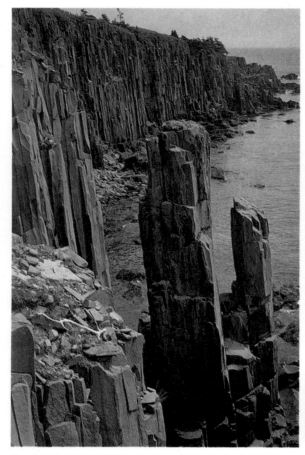

Basalt is a hard rock of fairly even composition, but is often split by cracks called joints. Erosion takes place mainly along the joints, forming cliffs apparently built of individual blocks.

Sandstone and other strongly bedded rocks tend to erode most easily along bedding planes. Very resistant beds such as these iron-rich bands erode slowly, producing a ragged cliff profile.

Chalk often occurs as a homogeneous rock with few bedding planes or joints. A cliff in such an outcrop shows a very even erosion profile with vertical faces and a fairly straight coastline.

Unconsolidated material such as sand or mud breaks up easily when attacked by the sea. Cliffs formed in such deposits are typically of a crumbly texture with slopes of fallen debris at the foot.

Most of the erosive power of the sea comes from the action of the waves. Wind sweeping over the open ocean sets up an oscillation in the surface waters. Although each water particle travels only

An upland area sloping gently into the sea is not a stable configuration. Waves will attack the slope and erode it at the base.

The first-formed feature of coastal erosion is usually a notch in the original slope, forming a small cliff at high-tide level.

The cliff is worn back by the action of the waves cutting into the base and forming an overhang, which eventually collapses.

A wave-cut platform is left below the erosion surface as the cliff is worn back and an offshore terrace is built of eroded material.

a short distance in a circular path, this movement transmits the oscillation many thousands of miles, eventually hurling the near-shore water repeatedly against exposed headlands and beaches.

Small-scale coastal landforms owe their shapes to the local action of waves and tides on coastal rocks and sediments. Large-scale features are the result of relative vertical movements of land and sea level.

The interaction of waves and tidal currents with the land may produce either erosional or constructional features. The former may persist over hundreds of miles, creating dramatic coasts like those of Scandinavia and the American Northwest. The latter may persist over even longer stretches of coast, but generally produce a much smoother shoreline, like that bordering the Gulf of Mexico. Elsewhere, erosional and constructional features may alternate rapidly over short distances to form the attractive and varied coastal scenery typical of the shores of Britain.

When eroding waves attack hard and moderately hard rocks with resistant materials like boulders, pebbles and sand from the beach zone, they eat first into planes of weakness in the rock caused by faults, joints, bedding planes and beds of softer rock. Active erosion is confined to a horizontal band centered on mean sea level. This band is very narrow in tideless seas and broader in seas with a larger tidal range. Progressive erosion leaves a wave-cut platform in front of the cliffs that gently slopes away from the land below mean sea level. This platform is exposed at low tide when it is seen to be littered with pebbles and boulders—the tools of erosion.

Where cliffs are composed of soft materials, such as glacial sands and clays, erosion may proceed mainly by the hydraulic action of the waves operating on sediment at the foot of the cliff. In this case much of

EVOLUTION OF A COASTLINE

When a wave approaches a coast it slows down on reaching shallow water. In this way an advancing wave front is bent as it meets an irregular coastline, turning toward headlands and attacking them first before reaching the bayheads and beaches. Most of a wave's energy is expended on the flanks of the headlands and these are eroded more rapidly than other features. Eventually a straight shoreline will evolve by the destruction of headlands.

A headland or cliff attacked by the sea will first be eroded along zones of weakness such as joints or bedding planes. These then enlarge to form deep clefts.

the sediment may have been contributed by mechanical failure—slumping and sliding—of the upper part of the cliff owing to oversteepening of slopes. Often in these circumstances the rate of retreat of the cliff is limited only by the rate at which longshore and tidal currents can carry away the debris that temporarily accumulates as a protective beach. Average rates of retreat of three feet a year are commonplace along such coastlines, as in the east of England, although in practice retreat takes place intermittently, a few yards at a time, during major storms. Offshore from such soft cliffs the water depth is usually determined by the strength of tidal scour and no wave-cut platform is developed.

In stark contrast, where rock cliffs descend sheer into deep water, as in some fault-bounded Mediterranean islands and some isolated volcanic islands of the open ocean, beach development is very limited and cliff erosion is extremely slow.

While the height of sea cliffs is largely determined by the height of the adjacent land, their form is influenced by a variety of factors: the mechanical properties of the rocks and sediments of which they are composed, the topography of the landscape into which they are cut and the geological history—including sea level and tectonic changes—to which they have been subjected. Great variation is possible, but certain features such as promontories, headlands, caves, blowholes, arches and sea stacks are repeatedly formed in well-jointed rocks, and give rise to some of the most distinctive forms of coastal scenery. Where valley glaciers have previously reached the coast, flooding of their abandoned overdeepened channels produces fjords, and the drowning of folded mountain ranges and river valleys produces ria coastlines and estuaries.

The beaches which form at the foot of cliffs, and in bays between headlands, are mostly transitory accumulations of eroded rock or shelly debris. The amount of material in a beach often varies with the seasons, and with the strength and type of onshore wave patterns associated with them. Most beach material is ultimately removed to deeper water or transported along the coast. However, in some circumstances it continues to accumulate by longshore or onshore movement of sand and gravel, and then forms constructional features such as beach plains, spits and offshore bars. Such features are common around the world, especially where the adjacent sea floor is covered by loose glacial deposits or where large supplies of sediment are provided by major rivers. Often beaches and bars, once raised above sea level by winter storms, will be built even higher by the accumulation of windblown coastal dunes. Behind such structures, in the protected waters of estuaries and even sometimes on the open coast, mud and silt may be carried in on the flooding tide, to be deposited as intertidal sediment flats. As these build up toward high-tide level they are colonized successively by marine and salt marsh plants, which trap more sediment until the land is built up beyond the reach of all but the highest tides. With a continuing supply of mud and silt in the inshore waters there will be a continuous outbuilding of land just above mean high-tide level, forming a potential source of reclaimable land that may be used by man for building or agricultural purposes.

Beaches form in coastal areas where the accretion effect of waves and currents outweighs their erosional effects. Rock fragments and sand eroded from other areas are washed up onto the shore and, when dry, are carried by the wind to form sand dunes, which may then be stabilized, by vegetation, into permanent landscape features.

Ripple marks and other small-scale features form as sediment is deposited by waves in shallow water. The upshore movement of the water erodes material from the seaward face of the ripple and deposits it on the landward face, where the current is slack. In this way, each ripple migrates in the direction of the current.

Path of oblique waves

Longshore drift is the zigzag movement of sand along a beach due to continuous wave action.

Sand-formed features may be moved great distances by longshore drift. In 200 years Sable Island, off Nova Scotia, traveled nine miles eastward. Continuous accretion of sand can easily be seen on this aerial photograph of a sand spit.

Salt marshes form on coasts sheltered from the turmoil of the open ocean. Silt and vegetable matter are brought down by streams and settle when they reach quiet water to form mud flats at low-tide level. The mud may then be stabilized by salt-resistant vegetation forming banks dissected by networks of water channels.

Groynes are walls built out into the sea along beaches to prevent loss of beach material due to longshore drift. The sand tends to accumulate on the up-current side of the groyne, but this is balanced by increased erosion on the down-current side.

Breakwaters are built near harbor mouths to dissipate the force of the waves before they can reach ships at anchor. However, this can upset the local balance of erosion and sedimentation and form new sandbanks where they are not expected.

Seawalls are man-made structures intended to keep the sea away from onshore areas. To do this they must be very strong, as pressures of 340,000 lb/sq. ft. have been measured on some walls. Stone or concrete blocks weighing ten tons have been shifted during storms.

A vertical cleft subjected to constant erosion by the hydraulic action of the waves and repeated impacts of waterborne rocks will eventually enlarge into a cave.

A blowhole is formed when air trapped in a cave is repeatedly compressed by wave action. The pressure is released once it has forced a hole in the roof.

Continued deepening of caves on opposite sides of a headland will cause them eventually to meet in the middle, forming a natural rock arch.

A natural arch will continue to widen until it can no longer support its lintel, which then collapses. The remaining portion is called a sea stack.

CHANGING LEVELS OF THE SEA

Postgracial rebound   Peripheral submergence

• Shells above sea level

Changes of sea level over the past 5000 years are shown by the presence of seashells above high-tide levels and peat bogs that are now submerged. High latitudes have concentric areas of uplift and submergence following the loss of ice caps after the Ice Age.

Raised beaches are among the most spectacular features formed by coastal uplift. A beach that was formed when the land was at a lower level is carried upward as the land rises. The example shown is at Tongue Point, southwest of Wellington, New Zealand.

A glaciated valley has a characteristic U-shaped cross section, as shown in the top picture. A lowering of the coastline will flood this and produce the steep-sided fjord seen in the lower picture.

Although the daily movements of the tides may displace the meeting point of land and sea by nearly 50 feet vertically and thousands of yards horizontally, the average position of sea level relative to the land remains apparently constant over tens, or even hundreds, of years—long enough to provide man with one of his most useful reference points, mean sea level. Over longer periods, however, this average level of the sea is subject to considerable change, due in part to movements of the landmasses and in part to changes in the level of the surface of the sea itself. Landmass movements may be local (tectonic), regional or continental (epeirogenic) or a response to ice-loading (isostatic); changes in water level due to waxing and waning of ice caps are known as eustatic changes.

Perhaps the most dramatic sea level changes have been those caused by changes in the volume of the oceans during the Quaternary period as a result of ocean water being locked in the polar ice caps and glaciers. Precise estimates are difficult to make but at the height of the last glacial period, about 17,000 years ago, the global level of the sea was probably about 400 feet lower than at present. The effects of these oscillations in sea level, which have occurred many times during the last million years or so of the Quaternary Ice Age, are far-reaching and affect the landforms and sedimentary features of every coastline and continental shelf throughout the world.

In the even longer perspective of geologic time it is evident that variation in sea level relative to the continents has occurred not because of changes in the volume of the oceans but because of changes in the shape of the ocean basins. Such changes led to rises in sea level, and consequent submergence of vast areas of low-lying continent, during the Upper Cretaceous period, about 80 million years ago, the Eocene period, about 50 million years ago, and the Miocene period, about 20 million years ago. The precise mechanisms activating these variations are not fully understood, but they have left their mark on the overall geomorphology of coastal regions and on some continental shelf areas.

Where apparent changes in sea level have been caused by tectonic, epeirogenic or isostatic movements of the continental masses, the remnant evidence of former sea levels discloses not only the degree of uplift or submergence but also, by geologic dating of the coastal rocks, the rate at which these events took place. The evidence for past "tidemarks" at the margins of continents and islands is drawn from many scientific disciplines including geomorphology, sedimentology, paleontology and archaeology: beaches and their associated sediments and fossils, cliffs, wave-cut platforms, and man-made harbor walls and seaport buildings are all used to define past positions of sea level. Radiometric dating techniques and archaeological or fossil evidence of age may be used to "fix" the event in time, while comparison with present-day sea level gives the total amount of vertical movement and hence the rate of uplift or submergence.

Raised beaches are a prominent feature of the British Isles and are particularly well preserved around the Scottish coast; "staircase" series of uplifted beaches are common in tectonically active areas such

as New Guinea, New Zealand and California, which are undergoing progressive land elevation, and similar series of raised beaches occur in regions undergoing isostatic uplift following the removal of major ice sheets. Spectacular examples of the latter are found in the Hudson Bay region of Canada and in Scandinavia, where the combination of isostatic uplift of the land areas and eustatic changes in sea level has produced a complex history of alternating marine and freshwater environments in the Baltic region.

Landscapes formed by the normal processes of erosion are also affected by changes in sea level Drowning of river valleys produces ria coastlines, while the inundation of deeply scoured glacial valleys produces the dramatic fjord coastlines of Norway and western Canada. Detailed study of landscapes can therefore give clear evidence of fluctuating sea levels even when the more precise evidence of sea-level deposits has been eroded away.

Along low-lying, predominantly depositional, coastlines even small changes in sea level may cause a large lateral displacement of the shoreline and this may be reflected in an alternation of marine and freshwater deposits. Usually far from spectacular in scenic terms, these deposits often contain a much more complete inventory of events than that retained in large-scale coastal features. In many localities around the shores of Britain, submerged forests occur offshore and marine deposits underlie coastal lowlands. All the major deltas of the world, including the Rhine–Meuse delta underlying Holland, the Niger and the Mississippi, record a prolonged history of subsidence in which the interface between sea and land has repeatedly migrated back and forth across the depositional zone.

SEA-LEVEL CHANGES IN HISTORIC TIMES

The eastern Mediterranean is a tectonically active area and changes in sea level over the past few thousand years are revealed by the elevations of archaeological sites. The Roman harbor at Kenchreai, the Bronze Age harbor at Pavlo and the Turkish–Norman port of Methoni are all now submerged, but the submergence does not extend to the island of Antikythera, where the Roman port of Potamos has been uplifted. Western Crete has been rising for some 2000 years, as shown by the Hellenic–Roman harbor as Phalasarna, now 20 feet above sea level, but the island is tilting and the central and eastern areas are sinking. Southeast Crete, however, shows an uplift indicating the complexity of the system. The floor of the Antikythera Channel is bounded by faults and is subsiding at present.

At the end of the last Ice Age, about 10,000 years ago, the Scandinavian ice cap began to melt. The reduction in weight of the ice led to isostatic uplift of the underlying land and a freshwater lake—the Baltic Ice Lake—formed in the Baltic region south of the ice cap.

The vast quantity of water released by the melting ice sheets caused a rise in sea level that overtook the isostatic rise of the land. The ice lake was flooded about 9500 years ago and became the *Yoldia* Sea, named after the marine mollusk that lived in its salt waters.

Isostatic uplift proceeded apace after most of the ice cap had melted and this overtook the rise in sea level about 8000 years ago. The Baltic area then became a freshwater lake once more, taking its name—the *Ancylus* Lake—from the small freshwater snail that lived there.

The final rise in sea level outpaced the slowing isostatic uplift about 4500 years ago and produced the *Littorina* Sea—named after the common periwinkle—which eventually became the Baltic of today, despite the continuing uplift of land in the Gulf of Bothnia.

River valleys such as those shown in the upper picture have a V-shaped cross section and often have a branching network of tributaries. When a shoreline with these features is flooded, as in the lower picture, the result is a series of branching embayments known as a ria coastline.

21

THE CONTINENTAL SHELF

The active type of continental margin occurs at a destructive plate boundary. Island arcs and basins usually accompany such margins, but along the west coast of South America these have been lifted up to form the Andes.

The passive type of continental margin is merely the sediment-covered edge of the continental element of a tectonic plate. It retains the rift valley structure formed when the continent split away from a supercontinent.

There are two dominant levels in the relief of the earth; the continental terrace—which includes the coastal plains of the continents themselves and their submerged outer zones, the continental shelves—and the deep ocean floor, which lies at an average depth of about 12,000 feet. Between them lie the continental slope and the continental rise, which together mark the true boundary between the upstanding continental blocks and the deep ocean basins.

Continental margins can be divided into two main types. Atlantic-type margins characteristically have broad shelves and gently sloping continental rises, and because of the absence of earthquakes and volcanoes may be called passive margins. Pacific-type margins usually have narrow shelves and deep trenches rather than continental rises, and may be called active margins because they often correspond to belts of deep earthquakes and volcanoes and are backed by young mountain chains. Continental borderlands such as those found off the coast of California are an exceptional type, consisting of a complex of plateaus and basins that may be considered as the broken pieces of nearby continental blocks.

The outer edge of the continental shelf is at a remarkably constant depth of about 450 feet, due to its formation close to sea level between 15,000 and 20,000 years ago. However, the repeated rise and fall of sea level, associated with the waning and waxing of the ice caps, has left its mark on the shelf zones, and relics of earlier, lower, sea levels include submerged beaches and cliffs and ancient streambeds that may be partially filled by deposits containing valuable heavy minerals such as diamonds, gold and tin. Former beach deposits of stones and gravel, submerged by rising sea levels, are increasingly being exploited for constructional materials, and such deposits have been found to contain the fossilized remains of mastodon, mammoth and other large land animals that once ranged the coastal plains in vast numbers—a proof of the dramatic rise in sea level and a source of folklore in many seaboard races.

The relief forms left behind on the continental shelf from times of lower sea level are in many places being actively modified by present-day processes. Waves generated by storms on the surface can transport sands on even the deep outer shelf. On the Middle Atlantic Bight of North America, waves caused by hurricane-force winds erode the sands of the near-shore zone and help nourish a system of long, low ridges, which migrate slowly along much of the shelf. In the many areas where there are strong tidal currents, gravel and sand can be swept into dynamic forms reminiscent of the windblown features of deserts. This mobility of many parts of the seabed poses enormous problems for the maintenance of channels in the approaches to ports and harbors, for the siting of structures such as drilling platforms and pipelines and for the safe disposal of industrial wastes.

The continental slope bounding the continents is one of the largest topographical features on the earth's surface, varying between three and 20 degrees in gradient and rising some 12,000 feet from the seabed. Although present around all the continents, its origins and those of its surface features are varied. Atlantic-type margins essentially have down-faulted slopes formed as the crust was pulled apart, whereas Pacific-type margins are characterized by compressional structures—sediments being added to them by a process akin to bulldozing. Some continental slopes are being actively built outward as sediments are transported across the continental shelf and deposited at the edge; others are being eroded into forms such as submarine canyons, which are the equal in size of the largest cut by rivers on land and may closely resemble the Grand Canyon in appearance. The heads of some submarine canyons have been river valleys at times of lower sea level, but their deeper parts have been cut by turbidity currents—dense mixtures of sediment and water, which flow rapidly downslope under the pull of gravity, perhaps initiated by slumping near the top of the slope. As the turbidity currents slow down they deposit sands, derived from the shelf region, on the deep seafloor, building up a thick wedge of sediment at the foot of the continental slope.

Instantaneous breaks due to shock and slumps

Area of initial shock

Track of turbidity current

Submarine cables

Position and times of cable breaks due to turbidity currents

00.59

03.03

09.01

10.18

13.17

The speed at which material flows down a continental slope was dramatically shown in 1929 when an earthquake shook the Grand Banks area off the east coast of North America. Submarine cables in the area were broken by the slumping of a mass of sediment which then flowed down the slope as a suspended mass of sand and mud particles called a turbidity current, breaking the deeper cables in its path. The times at which the breaks occurred were determined by the times at which transmissions through the cables ceased. Cables were broken up to 300 miles away and the maximum speed of the turbidity current was estimated at about 55 knots.

△ Elephant teeth

▬ Freshwater peats

Delaware Channel

Block Island Channel

Chesapeake Channel

Block Island Shore

Franklin Shore

Shelf

Slope

Rise

Abyssal plain

Hudson Channel: the course of the Hudson River during earlier periods of lower sea level.

Hudson Delta: the depositional fan built out from Fortune Shore.

Hudson Canyon: a deep canyon gouged into the continental slope by debris carried down by the Hudson River.

Active (Pacific-type) margins

Passive (Atlantic-type) margins

Coastal plain

Shelf
Av. width 47 mi.
Av. gradient 10 ft/mi.

Slope
Width 12–60 mi.
Av. gradient 300 ft/mi.

Rise
Width 0–400 mi.
Gradient 5–50 ft/mi.

Abyssal plain

The topography of the continental margin is clearly illustrated when, as shown above, the relief is exaggerated 20 times. The true profile is shown below without vertical exaggeration of scale.

The continental shelf is a submerged part of a continental block while the shoreline is a purely temporary feature. This is well illustrated off eastern North America, where the shelf carries many dry-land features formed when it was above present sea level.

The sonograph above shows gullies at the head of a submarine canyon on the continental slope of the Bay of Biscay. Features formed in these conditions resemble the badlands of arid regions.

Canyon

Shelf

Slope

Suspended material

Rise

Currents are important agents in the transportation of material on the continental slope and rise where the finest particles are present in a suspension just above the seafloor. Coarser debris is carried down the submarine canyons by turbidity currents.

Sand is deposited by the diminishing current in waves as much as 60 feet high.

The finer sands are deposited by the weakest currents in the form of irregular patches.

Where tidal scour is greatest the erosion can sweep large areas of bedrock clear of sediment.

In strong tidal currents, coarse material is formed into strips parallel to the flow direction.

A sequence of sand structures is found on shelves swept by tidal currents. They are seen here on sonographs, each of which covers about one square mile of seabed.

THE FACE OF THE ABYSS

Fossil remains of diatoms are among the most common organic constituents of deep seabed oozes.

These delicate foraminiferan remains, nearly five times life size, were dredged from 4000 feet in the western Atlantic Ocean.

Deep-sea research vessels have for many years carried out sampling surveys of the deep ocean basins, collecting and analyzing the seabed sediments. Although by no means complete, these surveys have allowed a picture, *below*, to be built up of the nature and distribution of land-derived sediments, sediments formed from the remains of marine organisms, and those formed chemically.

Radiolarian tests resemble exquisite glass sculptures.

Manganese nodules photographed with associated seabed sediment.

The surface sediments of the deep ocean floor show great geographical variation and at any one site there is generally a layering of sediments of different types. The two most common sediments are red clay, made up almost entirely of the finest-grained particles contained in the debris washed into the sea from the continents, and oozes, formed from the accumulated remains of planktonic animals and plants inhabiting the overlying water column of the deep ocean basins.

Ooze may be calcareous, if it is composed of the chalky shells of foraminifera and pteropods, or siliceous if it is derived from the remains of the single-celled radiolarians, or diatoms. Hence the distribution of the sediment types partly reflects the pattern of abundance of these organisms—and also the pattern of physical and chemical characteristics of the oceanic water-masses. For example, siliceous ooze is found only beneath the highly productive surface waters of the equatorial and polar regions. However, the dissolution of calcareous shells, which increases with depth, also affects the distribution of sediment types and only red clay survives on the deepest ocean beds.

Sediment accumulating on the floor of the ocean does not merely remain in place as an immobile blanket; on slopes, the slumping and sliding of sediment is common—particularly in areas of soft mud cover in areas prone to earthquake disturbance. On many parts of the deep ocean floor, bottom currents are sufficiently strong to move clay particles in suspension or even transport sand along the seabed. Where strong bottom currents, or midwater currents, interact with a physical obstacle such as the continental shelf, mid-ocean ridge feature or submerged seamount, the channelling and eddying of the water-flow may result in considerable scouring of the seabed in some areas, while sediment may be deposited in great thicknesses in regions of weak current flow. Acoustic maps of the seabed, prepared with the aid of side-scanning sonar equipment, often reveal vast fields of transverse and crescent-shaped sand waves moving across the seabed under the influence of currents in exactly the same way that barchans and linear dunes are swept constantly across continental deserts by the wind.

The rate of accumulation of the fine sediments covering the deep seabed is extremely slow—ranging from a few centimeters per thousand years to as little as a fraction of a millimeter per thousand years—yet such is the volume of the microscopic plant and animal life inhabiting the upper levels of the ocean that in some areas the seabed is blanketed with hundreds of feet of sediment formed from their remains. Terrestrial time scales have little meaning here.

In recent years the detailed study of seafloor spread-

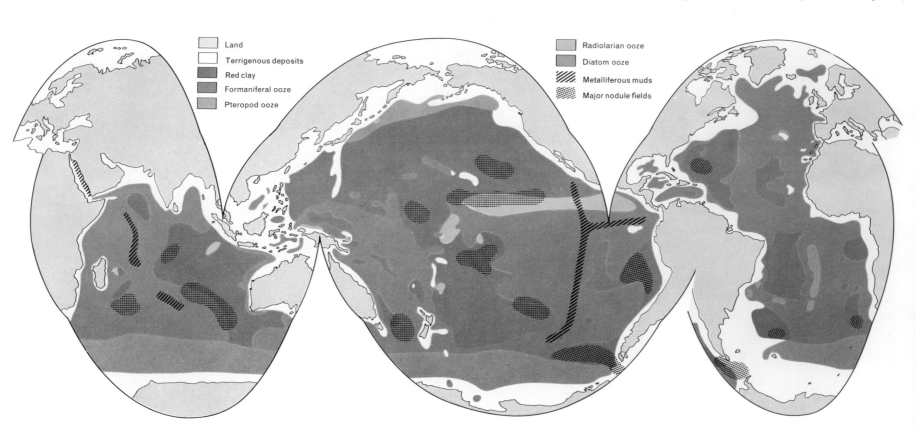

| Land |
| Terrigenous deposits |
| Red clay |
| Formaniferal ooze |
| Pteropod ooze |

| Radiolarian ooze |
| Diatom ooze |
| Metalliferous muds |
| Major nodule fields |

ing centers has shed additional light on the rate of accumulation of sediment and on the relationships existing between ridge activity, sedimentation and the physical relief of the ocean floor. The zone of intense volcanic activity marking the axis of a spreading ridge is completely free of sediment cover, but the flanks of the ridge are progressively modified by sedimentation with increasing distance from the ridge crest. Within two or three miles of the crest, the characteristically bulbous forms of the basaltic pillow lavas become partially hidden beneath accumulating sediment, and at six or seven miles from the ridge crest the seabed may present a flat, almost featureless surface disturbed only by the tops of unusually large lava masses and marked only by the imprints of organisms.

Many other components are added to the constant rain of organic and detrital material falling to the deep seafloor. Volcanic ash may fall into the ocean thousands of miles from the site of the eruption, and for months, or even years, afterward: outer space may also supply material in the form of meteorites. Some minerals are precipitated from seawater as crystals, encrustations and nodules on the seabed and these include the fields of manganese nodules, also rich in copper, nickel, cobalt and other minerals, that may become one of the most valuable future resources of the oceans. Another potential resource of these minerals are the metal-liferous muds found at some seafloor spreading sites. The metals are thought to emanate in hot hydrothermal solutions that have been vented through molten lava beneath the surface and then cooled on contact with the deep seawater—precipitating the metals.

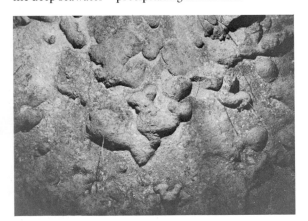

Within half a mile of the ridge crest the young pillow lavas of the seabed are virtually free of sediment cover.

Three miles from the axis the lava is several thousand years old and is being masked by sediment accumulating at 2 cm/thousand years.

Six miles from the active volcanic axis, lava flows are completely covered by sediments showing the tracks of benthic animals.

Inner rift valley
Inner wall
Backtilted fault blocks
Central high (Mt Venus)
Mid-Atlantic Ridge at 37°N
Spreading rate 2 cm/yr

Upwarped rim of asymmetric fault blocks
Central high
Galapagos Rift at 86°W
Spreading rate 7 cm/yr

Crestal rift zone
Marginal graben
Marginal horst
East Pacific Rise at 3.5°S
Spreading rate 15 cm/yr
3 2 1 0 1 2 3 Miles

The shape of a midocean ridge, *above*, directly reflects its rate of spreading. The axis of a slow-spreading ridge lies in a deep rift valley surrounded by faulted mountains; that of a fast-spreading ridge stands much higher than the surrounding seabed terrain.

Seabed spreading centers may be classified according to their spreading rates, and today the East Pacific Rise just south of the Galapagos Triple Junction is the most active part of the world ridge system, adding some 16 cm (6.3 in) per year on either flank.

12 cm/yr
14 cm/yr
COCOS PLATE
6 cm/yr
The Galapagos Triple Junction
5 cm/yr
PACIFIC PLATE
14 cm/yr
Galapagos Islands
NAZCA PLATE
16 cm/yr

The Galapagos Triple Junction is a geologically fascinating area in which the Cocos and Nazca plates diverge both from the main Pacific plate and from each other: the Cocos-Nazca separation is asymmetric and has created the 18,050-foot Hess Deep.

3000m
3500m
Hess Deep; 18,050-foot rift valley of the Cocos and Nazca plates

New crustal material formed at the east-west spreading center

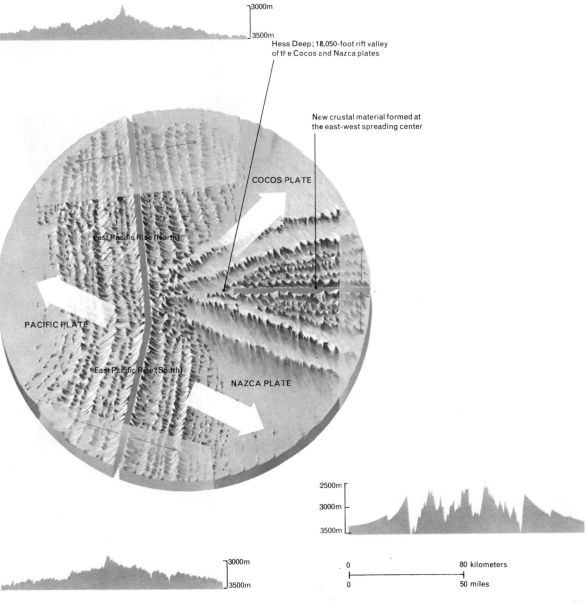

COCOS PLATE
East Pacific Rise (North)
PACIFIC PLATE
East Pacific Rise (South)
NAZCA PLATE

2500m
3000m
3500m

3000m
3500m

0   80 kilometers
0   50 miles

WATER: THE UNIQUE COMPOUND

Water—one of the most commonplace and familiar of all natural substances—is in fact one of the most remarkable compounds occurring in the natural world. Its liquid state, as opposed to the gaseous or solid state, is extremely rare in the universe and only within a relatively minute span of the enormous temperature range of the cosmos can water exist in the liquid state as it does on earth.

Compared with all other chemically similar compounds, water behaves physically in a unique manner, and since approximately 70 percent of the earth's surface is covered by oceans and seas it follows that the physical and chemical properties of this unusual substance play a fundamental role in the basic processes of man's environment.

The freezing point of water should, for example, be considerably lower than that manifest on the earth's surface, and, according to the laws of physical chemistry, the compound should exist on earth only as a colorless gas. Moreover, most materials expand when heated and contract when cooled; water follows this pattern only in part. Cooled down to four degrees centigrade it does contract, but thereafter, with further cooling, it expands, and when it begins to freeze the expansion is dramatic—involving an increase in volume of about nine percent. Were it not for this aberrant behavior, ice would become more dense than the surrounding watermass and would sink. As it is, ice floats at the surface and acts as an insulating barrier— effectively slowing down the cooling of the water and hence slowing down the freezing process. If ice did sink, the polar seas would be frozen solid, permanently, with far-reaching effects on world climates. The polar regions would be characterized by a permanent ice age extending far into the temperate regions.

Another physical property of water which has an absolutely fundamental effect on life on earth is its remarkable capacity to store heat. With the exception of ammonia, water has a greater heat capacity than any other naturally occurring liquid or solid. Land, by contrast, absorbs and loses heat relatively quickly and if the earth's surface were entirely land the planet would be intolerably hot by day and freezing cold at night. The vast volume of the earth's oceans, however, acts as an enormous heat-controlling engine, absorbing and losing heat more slowly and, by virtue of the great current systems, absorbing heat in one area and releasing it again either directly or through evaporation in other areas perhaps thousands of miles away.

The evolution of terrestrial life began in the oceans and here, again, a remarkable property of water would have played an important role. Water has the capacity to dissolve more substances than does any other liquid. The primordial seas would therefore have held a great diversity of elements and compounds, which in time reacted together to form the first basic organic compounds and so start the long process of evolution.

For most practical considerations water may be regarded as being incompressible, but although seawater is certainly less compressible than fresh it does manifest a degree of elasticity. The pressure of water in the deep ocean basins is so great that the water column is estimated to be compressed under its own weight by nearly 100 feet. Although this is relatively small when compared with the depth of the major ocean basins its significance in terms of the position of sea level relative to the continents is of great importance.

Of great theoretical and practical importance in physical oceanography is the molecular viscosity of seawater. The term denotes the relative ease with which a liquid may be stirred or mixed, or the degree of cohesion with which its molecules associate en masse. Were it not for molecular viscosity, turbulent motion of seawater could not be dissipated in heat, with consequent far-reaching effects on the overall heat budget of the oceans and the pattern of world climate. Also, the creation of the small initial waves, capillary waves, at the surface of the sea depends on the combined effects of molecular viscosity and surface tension.

The speed of sound in water is very much greater than in air and increases with temperature, pressure and salinity. In water with a uniform temperature and

salinity distribution the speed of sound increases with depth alone. However, more usually there is a considerable change of temperature with depth, which when combined with the increase in pressure results in a maximum velocity in the region of the thermocline. Sound waves beamed at an angle to the thermocline may be refracted partially or even completely depending on their angle to the thermocline, producing a sound shadow below it.

The optical properties of seawater are of the most fundamental importance to the life processes of the oceans, as all life is based on the minute floating plants, phytoplankton, which inhabit the upper levels of the water column and fix the energy of the sun's rays by photosynthesis. Even theoretically pure water scatters and absorbs light due to the motion of its molecules. When water contains "foreign" matter—either dissolved substances or particles floating in suspension— the effect of absorption is markedly increased. Normally, inshore waters are much more turbid than the open oceans and in them the extinction of light in the shortwave range—blue light—is more pronounced.

Chemically, seawater has an extremely interesting composition. It is, for example, an unusually pure substance, being composed of more than 95 percent water—a degree of purity that exceeds that of a great many commercially produced compounds. It is, however, the many dissolved substances that give seawater its remarkable properties. Every year some 80,000 cubic miles of seawater are drawn off by the process of evaporation, and of this vast quantity of water about 24,000 cubic miles are precipitated onto the continents as rain, sleet and snow. Sometimes made slightly acidic by gases and solid particles dissolved in it, this water attacks the rocks of the earth's surface and combines with temperature and wind to erode the

land. Minerals are carried in solution and as suspended particles as the water makes its way down to the coast to rejoin the sea and complete the basic loop of the hydrological cycle.

Of the enormous range of substances thus found in seawater, the two basic elements—beside oxygen and hydrogen—are sodium and chlorine, which combine to produce salt. They have concentrations of 1.05 and 1.90 grams per liter respectively. Only ten other elements are present in seawater in concentrations greater than one part per million, or one milligram per liter. The remaining elements are present only in extremely minute concentrations.

The total salt concentration of seawater is expressed in parts per thousand (written as ‰ and alternatively rendered "per mill") and for open ocean waters usually has a value around 35. There is a regional variation in ocean salinity between 32 and 37 parts per thousand. Areas such as enclosed basins and landlocked seas, where evaporation is high, may have considerably higher values; salinities of 38 to 39 are found in the Mediterranean Sea, while the northern part of the Red Sea has recorded salinity values of 40 to 41 parts per thousand.

Although seawater exhibits marked changes in salt content with depth and from one area to another, the ratios of the major dissolved minerals remain constant. Beside sodium and chlorine, these major constituents include magnesium, calcium, potassium, sulfur, bromine, strontium and boron. On the basis of their ability to engage in chemical reactions, the elements in seawater are placed in two groups. The so-called "conservative" elements have essentially uniform marine concentrations and are chemically unreactive. The elements of the second group are involved in the life processes initiated in the surface waters through

The hydrological cycle, *above*, ensures the constant recycling of water over the face of the earth. Each year, evaporation removes more than 80,000 cubic miles of water from the surface of the world ocean, and of this some 24,000 cubic miles are carried inland in the form of clouds and precipitated onto the land as rain and snow. The basic cycle consists of this evaporation, transportation, precipitation and runoff cycle, but there are many subsidiary systems within this broad generalization. Rainfall may evaporate back into the air before reaching the ground; return to the atmosphere by transpiration through the leaves of plants, or evaporate direct into a cloudless sky from the barren surface of a desert region.

Constituent	Percent
Trace elements	0.01%
Flouride (F^-)	0.003%
Strontium (Sr^{++})	0.04%
Boric acid (H_3BO_3)	0.07%
Bromice (Br^-)	0.19%
Bicarbonate (HCO_3^-)	0.41%
Potassium (K^+)	1.10%
Calcium (Ca^{++})	1.16%
Magnesium (Mg^{++})	3.69%
Sulfate (SO_4^{--})	7.69%
Sodium (Na^+)	30.61%
Chlorice (Cl^-)	55.04%

Eleven major constituents account for more than 99 percent of the salt content of normal seawater. Many are present in solution in the form of free ions and it is in that form that their relative abundance is indicated in the diagram, *left*. The overall salinity of seawater may vary regionally and with depth, but the ratio of the constituents remains constant.

Penetration of sunlight is attenuated selectively according to wavelength. Attenuation is due to absorption and scattering of the light—scattering being particularly strong in water containing suspended particles.

In a restricted gulf, seawater enters through a narrow opening and spreads out due to surface currents, evaporating as it does so. Thus the most concentrated solutions occur farthest from the sea. If subsidence occurs, vast thicknesses of evaporites may form. As concentrations increase, calcium and magnesium salts form first, followed by the sulfates, sodium chloride and finally the rarer salts of potassium and boron.

▭ Ca and Mg carbonates	□ Sodium chloride
□ Calcium sulfates	▦ Glauberite; polyhalite
▪ Rarer Magnesium, Potassium, Sodium salts, and Borates	

the production of organic matter by microscopic plants. The tiny floating phytoplankton contain the green pigment chlorophyll, by which they are able to take in solar energy and effect the combination of carbon dioxide and water to produce organic compounds and oxygen.

The photosynthesizing plants require a group of dissolved chemicals—nutrients—in order to grow and multiply, and these essential components of the chemical "mix" in seawater include phosphate, nitrate, silicate and small amounts of some metals. The plants in turn furnish the basic food resource for the animal life of the oceans. Plants that sink below the photosynthetic zone, and are not consumed by higher organisms, together with organic debris and dead sea creatures, sink through the waters and are oxidized by bacteria in the deeper layers. These reactions result not only in low values of dissolved gaseous oxygen at depths below the photosynthetic zone but also in high concentrations of the nutrient species. Other substances required for plant growth include vitamins and a number of metals—copper, iron, zinc and cadmium —whose concentrations may be governed by biological activity in the water.

Interactions between the ions of seawater result in the formation of ion pairs of charged and uncharged "species" and these can influence both the chemical and physical properties of the water. For example, the positively charged dissolved calcium and magnesium ions interact with the negatively charged sulfate and bicarbonate ions to produce ion pairs in seawater, and it is the combination of magnesium and sulfate to form the uncharged magnesium–sulfate ion pair that accounts for the marked absorption of sound in seawater. There are many other interactions between the ions of seawater and the dissolved organic matter and many of these interactions produce complex species.

It is only very recently that the remaining 80 elements in seawater—those with concentrations of less than one-millionth that of sodium—have been accurately determined. There are considerable analytical difficulties in this work as well as those associated with recovering seawater samples without introducing contamination from the ship or from the sampling container itself. It must therefore be frustrating for the scientist attempting to isolate minute trace minerals from water samples to know that a number of marine creatures have a remarkable ability, known as bioaccumulation, by which they can effectively extract and concentrate in their body tissues some of the most elusive of these low-concentration minerals. For instance, seawater has a vanadium content of less than one-millionth that of its sodium content, but vanadium is found in the bodies of some tunicates at concentrations 100,000 times greater than that found in seawater. Other tunicate species accumulate niobium, an element with a chemistry similar to that of vanadium, but present in seawater at concentrations 100 times lower than that of vanadium. Oysters tend to absorb zinc; lobsters concentrate copper in their body tissue; other organisms accumulate a variety of other substances. Such findings have led scientists to believe that there will be found at least one marine organism capable of spectacularly concentrating any given element. The affinity some marine creatures show for certain minerals is of more than purely scientific interest. In what later became known as the Minimata tragedy, several hundred people in the Japanese city of that name became seriously ill in 1953 and many subsequently died as a result of poisoning by mercury compounds concentrated in local shellfish species.

The composition of seawater is presumed to be constant over long periods of time, in other words the amount of any given element introduced into the oceans per unit time is exactly compensated by the amount removed from the ocean water by sedimentation on the seabed. The residence time of an element in the ocean, that is the time from its entry from its source on land to its ultimate deposition on the seafloor, is computed on the assumption of this inherent stability of the chemical composition of the seas. The element with the longest-known residence period—sodium— spends several thousand million years in the ocean before being deposited. Other conservative elements like potassium, calcium, chlorine and sulfate have residence times in the range of millions to hundreds of millions of years, resulting from their relative lack of reactivity in marine waters.

At the opposite end of the spectrum are the metals titanium, aluminum and iron, which spend only a century or so in the sea. Such elements enter the oceans in part as rapid-settling solid particles and in part as reactive compounds. Elements with intermediate residence times—periods of thousands of years—are involved not only in the biological processes but also in mineral formation, and this group would include copper, nickel, zinc and manganese among others. Residence time for lead, which is biologically very active, may be as low as a few months in coastal waters.

The concept of residence time is clearly an oversimplification of the picture. In treating the oceans as a simple reservoir, the mixing times of the oceans are assumed to be less than the residence times of the minerals. Yet the oceans are believed to mix in times of the order of a thousand years or less. However, the most important factor is the relationship between residence time and reactivity—the longer the residence time the less reactive is the chemical under consideration.

THE FROZEN SEAS

Ice caps
Permanent ice shelves
Permanent pack ice
Summer extent of pack ice
Winter extent of pack ice
Limit of drifting bergs

The pack ice covering the Arctic Ocean for much of the year is generally thinner but much more deformed than that of Antarctic seas. Fast ice formed against the Arctic shores, and offshore ice formed by freezing of surface waters, rapidly becomes rafted and broken by the ceaseless movement within the enclosed ocean basin. Antarctic pack ice is characterized by much larger floes, generally undeformed except for crushing of the edges and some rafting and pressure ridging where ice is trapped against the coast.

The great ice sheets covering roughly 12 percent of the world ocean have important effects on climate since they act as an insulating barrier preventing the exchange of energy between the atmosphere and the polar seas. Apart from icebergs, all the ice originates in the freezing of seawater—yet seawater freezes much less readily than fresh water, partly because the salt content depresses the freezing point to $-1.9°$ centigrade, but primarily because the water grows more dense as it cools. The result of cooling is that the water sinks and is replaced by warmer water from below so theoretically the atmosphere has to cool the entire depth of the ocean to $-1.9°C$ before the surface water can freeze. In practice, however, the sinking is confined to the upper 300 feet, but even this is sufficient to ensure that the open seas freeze much later in the year than shallow inshore waters.

As the surface waters freeze they undergo a series of distinct changes. Small crystals of ice develop first and these are progressively packed together into a continuous skin or into pancakes with characteristically upturned edges. As the ice sheet consolidates, the sea is covered with a layer of first-year ice six to seven feet thick in the Arctic; eight to ten feet thick in the Antarctic. In summer the continuous solar radiation melts the surface and forms extensive pools of meltwater, some of which extend through the thickness of the floe as thaw holes. If a floe survives it is transformed into multiyear ice—blue in color and exceptionally strong due to the sheets of refrozen meltwater incorporated in its structure. Its prevalence in the central Arctic makes that sea impassable even to the most powerful icebreakers.

During the freezing of seawater, salt is not accepted into the ice-crystal lattice, but is trapped in a network of tiny liquid brine cells each less than one-tenth of a millimeter across. New ice contains some ten parts per thousand of salt in this form, compared with 35 for seawater, but eventually the cells coalesce into brine drainage channels through which the brine escapes into the sea.

An ice floe that begins life as a smooth sheet will become deformed through wind action. The frictional stress of the wind is transmitted over great distance through the ice and a divergent wind pattern will fracture the ice along lines of weakness. The fracture opens into a long narrow lead of open water or into a polynya—a wide pool hundreds of yards across. New ice grows quickly in such openings and when wind stresses later become convergent the young ice is crushed. Broken blocks pile up into a great linear heap above and below the water line forming a pressure ridge which, in the Arctic, may rise more than 40 feet above the surface and have a deep root projecting 150 feet below sea level.

The ice also transmits wind stress to the underlying water, so creating a surface current. Ice drift and water flow are therefore identical over the long term. The Arctic has two major drift patterns; the Beaufort Gyre, in which floes and bergs may be trapped for more than 20 years, and the transpolar drift stream, which carries ice from Siberia across the pole and down the east coast of Greenland. In the Antarctic, winds blowing around the world from west to east generate a northeast-flowing current that constantly carries ice out into the southern oceans.

Perhaps the most magnificent sight in the ocean is that of a giant floating iceberg—one of the huge fragments of ice broken from the end of a glacier or ice sheet on land. In the Arctic some 12,000 icebergs calve annually from the glaciers flowing down to the sea from the Greenland ice cap. They drift with the current up the west Greenland coast and then return down the western side of Baffin Bay and eventually out into the North Atlantic, where, being a hazard to shipping, they are tracked by the International Ice Patrol. Their survival rate is very variable: in 1958 only one reached the Atlantic; in the following year, 693 were recorded. A typical new berg weighs about 1.5 million tons, stands 260 feet out of the water and extends more than 1200 feet below the surface. By the time it reaches the Atlantic it has shrunk to 150,000 tons and erosion may have sculptured it into the form of a castle or cathedral.

Antarctic bergs form in the same way, but are calved from the great floating ice shelves that fringe the continent. They are generally much larger than Arctic bergs—often more than 50 miles long—and usually retain their tabular form. Several thousand calve every year and many drift as far north as $40°S$ before melting away.

Today the polar ice is being studied on a scale undreamed of by pioneers like Nansen, who, in 1893, froze his ship *Fram* into the ice in order to study its drift. Polar ice presents a barrier to man's exploitation of the oil and mineral wealth of the far north—a prize that has given added stimulus to scientific research—and proposals have been made to tow Antarctic icebergs to desert regions such as Western Australia and the Persian Gulf to provide a source of fresh water for irrigation purposes.

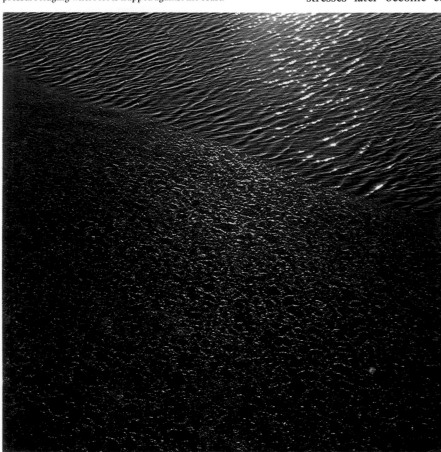

A thickening mass of frazil ice is gradually worked into small pancakes by the movement of the water.

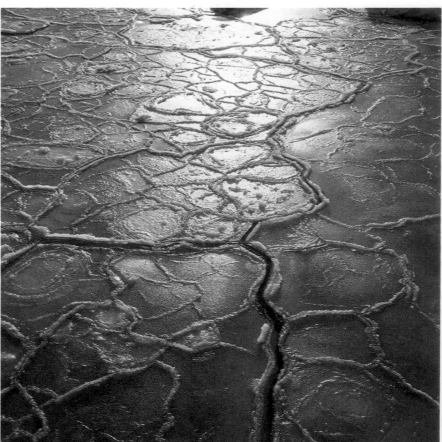

Further freezing below and snowfall on top will convert these rafts of pancake ice into ice floes.

Argus aircraft equipped with side-looking airborne radar and vertical laser profilometer

Side-looking airborne radar

Laser profilometer

Frozen lead

Hummock ice

Frozen polynya: mild pressure has caused thin ice to crack, forming small pressure ridges.

Flat, undisturbed first-year ice, 6 to 7 feet thick.

Upward-looking sonar

Finger-rifting of ice sheet formed by lateral pressure

Heavily deformed pressure ice

Side-scan sonar

H.M.S. *Sovereign* surfaced through a large polynya at 35°N during her 12-day traverse beneath the ice

Polynya: may be several hundred yards in width. Ice thin enough to allow submarine to break through

Frozen lead

Older multiyear ice thickened by freezing and rafting

Small pressure root

Pressure root: may extend more than 70 feet below the surface in the case of a pressure ridge standing 25 feet above sea level

Technology available to the researcher today includes airborne radar and laser profilometers, and submarine-mounted upward- and side-scanning sonar. In a recent joint Canadian–British program a Canadian Argus overflew the track of H.M.S. *Sovereign* so that comparative studies could be made of the upper and lower surfaces of the Arctic ice. The side-looking airborne radar record, *above*, shows heavily deformed ice as white areas; polynyas and leads as dark areas. The upward-looking sonar record, *below*, picks out frozen leads, a polynya large enough to allow the submarine to break through to the surface, and the deep roots of pressure ridges. The reconstruction, *left*, illustrates some of the main physical features in an area grading from undisturbed ice to a region of heavy pressure.

An old berg photographed in the Beaufort Sea shows the characteristic cumulative effects of weathering and melting as it drifts through an area of close pack ice.

The first crystals to appear as the sea begins to freeze are minute spheres, which develop into thin disks, or platelets, known as frazil ice. At a slightly later stage, when the crystals multiply to give the sea a soupy, matte appearance, the effect is called grease ice. In calm waters the ice crystals freeze together into a continuous semitransparent skin called nilas, but if the sea surface is at all rough the skin soon breaks up into individual plates, which acquire raised edges from their constant collisions and hence warrant the attractive name of pancake ice. Finally the pancakes freeze together, or the nilas simply thickens, to form a flat, unbroken ice floe. The floe grows in thickness quite quickly at first, but thickening slows as the ice increasingly insulates the water from the air.

Although icebergs are without doubt among the most impressive features of the polar seas they are not strictly sea ice, having their origins in the glaciers of the Antarctic and the landmasses encircling the Arctic. Ice is a plastic material that flows under its own weight; as the glaciers meet the sea huge pieces "calve" off as bergs to drift out to sea with winds and currents.

THE AIR-OCEAN INTERFACE

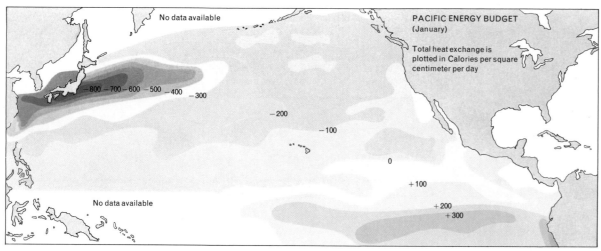

PACIFIC ENERGY BUDGET
(January)

Total heat exchange is plotted in Calories per square centimetre per day

No data available

No data available

The enormous transfer of energy from the ocean surface to the overlying atmosphere in the northwest Pacific is due to prevailing

cold, dry continental air masses flowing over, and extracting heat from, the relatively warm northeast-flowing Kuroshio Current.

Variations in sea-surface temperature distribution can distort atmospheric flow patterns up to the level of the jet stream. The relative positions of these warm and cold reservoirs control the penetration into the continent of cold, dry Arctic air and warm, moist maritime air, so governing climatic conditions over the land.

The fully developed hurricane may extend upward to the tropopause between nine and 12 miles above the earth's surface. Cool, dry air is drawn into the central column of the storm at high level.

Walls of dense cumulus cloud form concentric rings around the eye: they are separated by annular zones of clear air.

Warm, moist air is drawn into the system at sea level, feeding energy into the system as it spirals upward, finally to be dissipated in the upper air.

The strongly rising airflow creates a region of intense low pressure in the eye, often the cause of severe damage to homes, which may explode as the eye passes across them.

Almost every year some part of the eastern American seaboard or Gulf coast is struck by a hurricane with torrential rains and devastating winds. These storms are generated far out to sea off Africa or in the Caribbean, where the surface waters are at temperatures of at least 27°C, and are just one of the many manifestations of air–sea interaction. The hurricanes feed on the warmth and water vapor discharged from the ocean into the atmosphere. As this warm moisture-laden air rises and expands, its stored energy is released as the heat of condensation in high clouds.

The sea, which occupies nearly three-quarters of the earth's surface, acts as a great thermostat, warming air masses in winter and cooling them in summer. In fact, the upper ten feet of water contains as much heat as the entire overlying atmosphere. Along west coasts, maritime influences are obvious, as winds and storms usually travel from west to east: along east coasts, the effects are less readily apparent, but moist winds from the ocean frequently influence both temperature and precipitation.

Ocean currents, and the rate of change of the thermal structure of the upper oceanic layers, are about one order of magnitude slower than that of the atmosphere. Hence, although the atmosphere frequently renders the sea abnormal in its thermal structure, the abnormal temperature characteristic of the sea persists long enough to affect air masses moving over it, often affecting the life history of traversing cyclones and anticyclones. The greatest zones of temperature contrast in midlatitudes usually occur along and adjacent to the east coasts of continents. Storms are frequently born and intensify in these areas, deriving their energy from the land–sea temperature contrast. In this way storms move into the Aleutian area from the Philippines and off Japan, and breakaway depressions move from the Aleutian low-pressure area through North America. Similarly, the thermal contrast between the Gulf Stream and the North American coast is a source of storm generation, and these storms feed into the Icelandic Low, which has a dominant influence upon European weather since it determines the thrust of maritime air into the continent.

Zones of temperature contrasts are not restricted to coastlines. Recent studies have shown that the ocean, like the atmosphere, never has a truly "normal" surface temperature over large areas. There are always marked deviations from normal, often of the order of 1° to 3°C, over vast areas. These "anomalies," which may extend down many hundreds of feet, are often the result of several processes acting simultaneously; the amount of radiation from sun and sky, the loss of heat from the ocean to the atmosphere, the degree of

upwelling or downwelling of water, and the advection of water masses from colder or warmer regions.

Between abnormally warm and cold pools of water, the gradient is frequently and quickly transferred to the overlying air, producing zones of air contrast that can alter the behavior of storms. The vorticity generated is rapidly transferred to higher layers of the atmosphere and ultimately to the jet stream, producing great meanders, which mold the airflow patterns over the continents. In this way a series of similar developments may recur for weeks or months, producing persistent abnormal weather conditions. Extreme dislocations may lead to such abnormalities as the western European drought of the winter and summer of 1976 and the great California drought of the same year. In these cases air and sea patterns were coupled in such a way as to steer cyclonic storms far north of their normal paths, leaving anticyclones with their warm, stable, subsiding air masses to dominate the drought areas.

More recently, recurrent patterns over spells of years have been found in which sea and air cooperate. For example, in the 1970s the eastern United States and western Europe have had predominantly mild winters, whereas during much of the 1960s winters were cold and relatively snowy.

It has been found that sea-surface temperature anomalies are important in generating abnormal weather and climate not only in temperate latitudes but also in the tropics. For example, from the coast of Peru westward to the central Pacific there occasionally develops a pool of abnormally warm equatorial water with deviations as much as three degrees centigrade from normal lasting for many seasons. During these warm-water episodes air over the tropics receives more heat and moisture so the air rises more rapidly than normal, spreading poleward and transporting momentum to the westerly winds.

A number of studies are proceeding in different countries aimed at increasing our understanding of the physics of air–sea interaction processes to improve both short-range and long-range forecasts. These studies involve not only vast observational programs using ships, airplanes, satellites and other sensors but also the most sophisticated high-speed computers and dynamic models. At the same time, empirical studies are being pursued, utilizing historical records and even proxy indicators such as those obtained from tree-rings, ice cores and deep-sea sediments.

Once sufficient knowledge is gained to make long-range forecasts more reliable it may also be possible for man to study the feasibility of controlling weather and climate.

Principal tracks of tropical cyclonic storms.

Storm track

Outer convective cloud band

Eye

Trailing convective cell

Storm tail

→ Low-level winds   --→ High-level winds

The mature hurricane may be 250 miles in diameter and tower upward more than ten miles, its upper layers capped by streamers of cirrus cloud. The dense walls of cumulus-type clouds, which enclose the calm, low-pressure eye, are the region of highest wind speeds, up to 110 mph near the center, and violent precipitation.

Satellite view of a cyclonic storm system 1200 miles north of Hawaii.

- Isobars
→ Wind direction
Warm front
Cold front
Occluded front

Warm

Cold   Colder

Cyclones, or depressions, are responsible for much of the mixed rainy weather of temperate latitudes. They originate as waves in the polar front between cold polar air and warm maritime air. The progression of these weather systems is closely tied to longer waves in the upper atmosphere—the two combining to effect the exchange of heat, momentum and moisture between the air masses. The depression tightens as it develops and eventually occludes as the trailing mass of cold air catches and either undercuts or, as above, overrides the other.

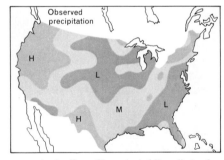

Predicted precipitation

Observed precipitation

Long-range weather forecasting is a fast-developing science based on analysis of past records and on the mathematical probability of a known set of conditions producing predictable atmospheric effects. Charted rainfall prediction for summer 1976, forecast in three ranges—light, moderate and heavy—was generally good, but did not predict the light rainfall of the southeast.

False color photography discloses the internal temperature structure of hurricane Camille (1969). Cool air near the eye shows as gray and blue, increasing in temperature through yellows to reds.

EXPERIMENTAL STUDIES OF AIR–SEA INTERACTION

An understanding of the mechanisms by which atmosphere and ocean exchange heat, moisture and momentum is fundamental both to our understanding of the overall air–ocean interaction and to the further development of medium- and long-term forecasting techniques.

Because of the importance of these basic processes a wide variety of experimental work is now being undertaken at both national and international level. The scale of the experiments varies enormously, from detailed laboratory studies of the "explosion" of fine water droplets into the air as minute bubbles rise to the surface of the water, to major international research programs involving vast resources of men and equipment. One of the largest of these international experiments took place between June and September 1974. Known as the GATE experiment, the GARP Atlantic Tropical Experiment was one major element in an even bigger program, the Global Atmospheric Research Program. GATE set out to investigate the dynamics of the atmosphere over the tropical Atlantic Ocean, deploying scores of oceanographic research vessels of many nations over a carefully measured grid pattern spanning the equator. As each ship recorded critical oceanographic and atmospheric data, aircraft were flown from bases in West Africa to measure temperature, pressure, wind speed and other parameters at predetermined heights above the stationary ships. The enormous volume of scientific data collected simultaneously by the ships and aircraft was radioed back to the mainland for preliminary computer analysis; full analysis of the data will, however, take many years to complete.

31

CURRENTS AND GYRES

Near ports, and around the margins of the oceans, the currents that affect a ship are due to tidal movements in the bays and estuaries along the coast. Once out to sea, however, the marine navigator can forget about these essentially local water movements and must instead take into his calculations the great wind-driven current pattern of the deep ocean.

The winds in each hemisphere are organized into two main systems. Near the equator the trade winds drive the ocean surface waters to the west; nearer the poles the westerly winds drive the waters back toward the east. The combined effect of these winds is to create a broadly circular system of currents known as a gyre. In the North Atlantic, the Canaries Current, the North Equatorial Current, the Gulf Stream and the North Atlantic Current form one such gyre.

The speed of these oceanic currents is generally about six miles a day, but an exception occurs on the western margin of each ocean where a narrower, stronger current is always found. Thus the Gulf Stream and the Kuroshio Current may have speeds in the range of 60 to 100 miles a day. In the Southern Hemisphere the currents in the gyres are generally weaker and the current pattern is dominated by the great sweep of the Antarctic Circumpolar Current.

To understand how the ocean currents behave it is necessary to realize that, like the atmosphere, the ocean is greatly affected by the earth's rotation. Just as an ice skater spins faster on bringing her arms close to her body, so water moving from the equator toward the poles tries to spin faster around the axis of the earth. To a person not aware of the earth's spin, the current appears to be pushed by some invisible force—the Coriolis force. The effect of this force is to deflect any free-moving particle to the right of its intended path in the Northern Hemisphere and to the left in the Southern Hemisphere.

If winds or currents persist for more than a few hours then the Coriolis force acting on them must be balanced by some other force. In the atmosphere this balance is achieved by the winds circulating around regions of high or low pressure: in the ocean a similar balance is created by the currents circulating around regions where the surface of the ocean is slightly higher or lower than normal. The level of the water in the Sargasso Sea, for example, is about three feet higher than in the adjacent coast regions and the outward pressure of this dome of water just balances the Coriolis force in the currents circling the gyre.

The Coriolis force also produces two other very important though rather unusual effects. First, when the wind blows over the ocean for a long period of time the Coriolis force causes a spiral of current directions to develop in the upper 300 feet of the ocean and the net result of this spiral is to transport the overall watermass at right angles to the wind direction. Thus the trade winds and westerlies actually help to pile up water in the Sargasso Sea. Second, the change in the Coriolis force with latitude squeezes the gyres up against the western margins of the ocean basins and results in the narrow and intense western boundary currents typified by the Gulf Stream and the Kuroshio.

A western boundary current such as the Gulf Stream initially flows as a smooth and stable current along the coast. However, as soon as it begins to move away from the coast and swing out across the open ocean, it loses stability and forms meanders. Because of the difference in temperature between the water on the inside of a meander and that on the outside, these structures have proved ideal for study by infrared satellite photography and such studies have shown that the meanders often become cut off from the main current flow to form intense current loops called Gulf Stream rings. Energy from the meander is also transmitted to the rest of the ocean in the form of another type of current loop—the mesoscale eddy. These eddies are about 120 miles in diameter and near the surface the currents within them may flow at up to 16 miles a day. The oceanic eddy structures have been known for less than ten years, but it is now known that they are very widespread and that they may contain more than 99 percent of the total kinetic energy of the oceans.

Tonal variation in this heat-sensitive satellite photograph picks out the turbulent water flow in the northwest Atlantic.

Coriolis force will deflect any free-moving object (air or water particle, or bullet) to the right in the Northern Hemisphere, to the left in the Southern. A particle projected toward the Pole also has an initial velocity eastward due to the earth's spin. To an observer in space the particle would appear to travel A–B; to an observer on earth, who has himself moved from A to A', the particle appears to have curved in the path A'–B.

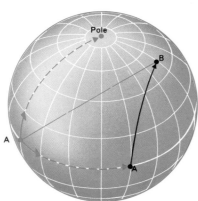

The Eckman spiral causes the water of the oceans' current gyres to be piled up in their centers. The centers are offset to the west by the change in Coriolis force with latitude. A combination of gravity flow down this "hill" and the Coriolis deflection causes a resultant current flow around the hill called the geostrophic flow.

Frictional force of the wind imparts motion to the surface water, which is immediately deflected by the Coriolis force. This layer in turn imparts motion to the water beneath, again with a deflection. As the movement is transmitted downward the deflections form an Ekman spiral. The deepest water may be moving at 180° to the surface flow, but the bulk transportation of the ocean watermass is at right angles to the direction of the wind.

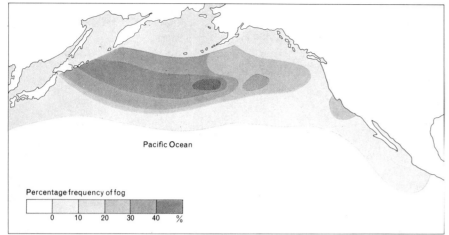

Pacific Ocean

Percentage frequency of fog

0   10   20   30   40   %

Warm southerly wind

Cold Oyashio Current

Warm Kuroshio Current

The manner in which currents and winds interact to create fog is clearly illustrated in the northwest Pacific, where, in summer, warm moist southerly winds blow first across the warm Kuroshio Current and then over the cold Oyashio Current.

Apollo 9 view of the Cape Verde Is. Waves visible in the sun glint beyond Sao Tiago, the upper island, originated far below the surface when the current met the island. The white area in the lee of the island is a calm region of upwelling.

Long-term records of weather patterns over the surface of the globe have enabled the meteorologist to compile maps of the monthly mean conditions of atmospheric pressure and air-mass circulation. The world map, *left*, shows the average world situation for July. The map should be compared with the map of world current circulation, *below*. Winds and wind-generated surface currents are almost perfectly matched— their paths showing the effect of the Coriolis force. Clockwise rotation of winds around the high-pressure zones of the Northern Hemisphere coincide with the clockwise gyres of the North Atlantic and North Pacific, while the counter-clockwise rotation of the Southern Hemisphere winds relate to the counterclockwise gyres of the southern oceans.

Atmospheric pressure in millibars

990
1000
1010
1020

The pattern of the surface currents that pervade the oceans of the world may be classified in 38 major named currents making up five current gyres.

1 East Greenland Current
2 Irminger Current
3 West Greenland Current
4 Labrador Current
5 Gulf Stream
6 North Atlantic Current
7 Canaries Current
8 North Equatorial Current
9 Antilles Current
10 Guiana Current
11 Caribbean Current
12 Equatorial Countercurrent
13 Guinea Current
14 South Equatorial Current
15 Brazil Current
16 Falkland Current
17 Antarctic Circumpolar Ct.
18 Benguela Current
19 Mozambique Current
20 Agulhas Current
21 West Australian Current
22 South Equatorial Current
23 Somali Current
24 Monsoon Drift
25 East Australian Current
26 Humboldt Current
27 Peru Current
28 Equatorial Current
29 S. Equatorial Countercurrent
30 South Equatorial Current
31 Alaska Current
32 Aleutian Current
33 Oyashio Current
34 Kuroshio Current
35 Kuroshio Extension
36 California Current
37 North Equatorial Current
38 N. Equatorial Countercurrent

DEEP WATER CIRCULATION

a   Hydrographic wire
b   Messenger
c   Bottle-tripping latch
d   Valve lever
e   Valve lever connecting rod
f   Stop-cock valve
g   Sampling tap
h   Relay messenger trip assembly
i   Relay messenger to next bottle

The Nansen bottle consists basically of a metal cylinder with stopcock valves at each end linked by levers to ensure simultaneous operation. The bottles are mounted upside down on a long wire; the lower attachment is fixed, but can rotate; the upper attachment can be released by pressure on the top. Initially both valves are open and during lowering water flows straight through the bottle. At sampling depth a weight is allowed to slide down the wire, releasing the first bottle, which overturns, its valves closing to secure the sample. A second messenger is released to trip the next bottle and so on down the wire.

The Ekman current meter is one of the earliest and most effective of the mechanical measuring devices. Once started by a falling messenger weight, the meter records the revolutions of a small propeller kept facing into the current by water pressure on a vane. After a predetermined number of revolutions a metal sphere is allowed to fall from a magazine through a hole in the cover of the direction recorder. The ball lands on a grooved compass needle and is guided into one of the segments of the collecting bin. The compass needle is effectively constant in its orientation and so records the changes in direction of the meter as it rotates around the wire.

Salinity profile across the Atlantic at 36°N in parts per thousand

The pattern of water movement in the deep ocean basins has been worked out from analysis of the physical and chemical characteristics of water samples from depths in excess of 13,000 feet. The primary flow at this depth, indicated by heavy arrows, *above*, is of the cold bottom water penetrating the basins from the Arctic and Antarctic regions. Secondary flow is shown by light arrows.

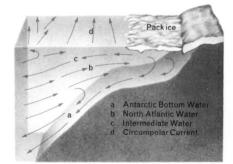

Atlantic water profiles

a Prevailing wind
b Offshore transportation
c Compensating upwelling
d Offshore current

a Antarctic Bottom Water
b North Atlantic Water
c Intermediate Water
d Circumpolar Current

Winds that blow relatively constantly, parallel to a coastline, tend to set up an Ekman transportation of surface waters away from the coast. The coastal flow is deflected to the right in the Northern Hemisphere, to the left in the Southern. The warm, light surface water is replaced by cold nutrient-rich water upwelling from greater depth, often to the great benefit of coastal fisheries.

The most dense water in the oceans, Antarctic Bottom Water, is formed in the Weddell Sea when freezing of the surface water to form pack ice increases the salinity of the underlying water. This cold saline water sinks and flows down the continental slope and is then carried eastward by the circumpolar current, eventually to be swept into the Southern Hemisphere ocean basins.

Profiles of the deep ocean basins may be based on depth, temperature, salinity, oxygen content or on a number of other chemical parameters. The small map, *above*, shows the location of the survey tracks from which the profiles on these pages were plotted. The temperature profile above the map shows the southern Atlantic in three dimensions: the back wall of the diagram shows the vertical temperature profile across the equator, while the side walls represent the vertical profiles of the two north–south survey tracks. The warm waters of the equatorial regions are extremely shallow when compared with the depth of the ocean—the bulk consisting of very much colder middle and bottom waters. The salinity profile, *left*, from Cape Hatteras to Gibraltar, shows the tongue of very saline water spilling from the Mediterranean into the eastern Atlantic.

Throughout the great tropical belt encircling the world, sea surface temperature remains in the region of 25°C. Water collected from about 1000 feet down may still be at a similar temperature, but water from the ocean deeps, perhaps 16,000 feet down, will be near to freezing point—hardly changed since it was formed in some polar sea. From the many measurements that have been made it is known that most of the water in the oceans is colder than 10°C and that on top of this, between 45°S and 50°N, floats the warm water of the subtropical gyres reaching down to a depth of 1500 to 2500 feet. This pattern of temperature distribution affects the distribution of life in the oceans. Tropical fish would immediately die in a polar sea, but Greenland sharks have been found living quite happily in the cold waters 10,000 feet beneath the warm surface waters off California.

The difference in density between the warm and cold waters also prevents the strong wind-driven surface currents from extending down into the cold water. In polar regions the waters are less stratified and consequently the effect of the surface currents can reach down many thousands of feet.

Average speeds of the deep ocean currents can be estimated by following watermasses of known physical and chemical properties. For example, the surface water around Antarctica is unusually fresh due to the addition of melted snow and ice. As this water sinks beneath the warm gyres it can be traced as a layer of low salinity water extending far north into the ocean basins of the Southern Hemisphere.

The densest water is formed on the continental shelves around Antarctica. Here seawater freezes to form pack ice at −1.9°C; salt is left in solution, increasing the salinity of the water, which collects on the continental shelf and then spills down the slope to form the Antarctic Bottom Water. This cold dense water is swept around the southern oceans by the Antarctic Circumpolar Current and can then be traced into the deep basins of the Atlantic, Indian and Pacific oceans. Its strongest flow is along the western side of the ocean basins; in the center and east it becomes progressively mixed by the action of mesoscale eddies.

From following such watermasses it was initially thought that the mean speed of the water in the deep oceans was about 100 yards per day. However, in 1957, when neutral buoyancy floats were first used to measure currents at a depth of one and a half miles, off Bermuda, speeds of up to three miles a day were recorded. These high speeds are now known to be due to mesoscale eddies. Although the wind-driven currents of the warm gyres do not extend down to the deep water, the mechanisms that produce surface eddies also transmit energy to the deeper layers, producing eddies up to 100 miles across traveling westward at about three miles per day. Understanding of these deep-water movements puts the marine disposal of radioactive waste in a new perspective. Whereas it had been assumed that any leakage would remain localized it is now known that contamination from a leaking container would quickly spread over a wide area.

The classic way of measuring ocean currents is to first measure the temperature and salinity structure of the water, from which density and pressure may then be calculated. Then, in the same way that a meteorologist calculates wind speed from charts of atmospheric pressure, the oceanographer may calculate the direction and strength of the currents from the pressure differences within the ocean. In deeper waters, where this method is unsatisfactory, temperature, salinity and other parameters are used as tracers.

In recent years current meters have been developed that can be used even at great depth. They are usually tethered on the seabed, sometimes for many months, measuring and recording temperature, current speed and direction, and may then be released by a sonar signal from a collecting ship. Other techniques involve the use of floats, weighted to remain at a predetermined depth in the ocean. The floats send out sonar signals, which may be tracked over great distances by ships and shore stations as the float drifts with the prevailing water movement.

WIND WAVES AND TSUNAMIS

The awesome power of the ocean waves cannot be appreciated until put in context. Each day thousands of waves pound against the coast releasing an amount of energy equivalent to a 50-megaton hydrogen bomb. This tremendous force of nature does considerable damage to the works of man, but if harnessed would be of infinite benefit.

The waves described above are called wind waves because they are generated by the wind. They are only one of a large variety of wave phenomena that pervade the oceans. Each type is generated differently and has quite different characteristics. The members of the wave family can be grouped according to their wavelength, that is the distance between successive wave crests, and their period, the time interval between successive passages of wave crests. Tides are the most commonly occurring long-period waves, having periods of either 12 or 24 hours. Waves generated by earthquakes and storm systems are not so common but can have even longer periods. At the other end of the scale are ripples or capillary waves that have periods of less than a second and wavelengths of less than 1.74 centimeters. In general wind waves fall between these two extremes but can vary from a few feet to almost a mile in wavelength and between one and 25 seconds in period. Wave height is the vertical difference between the trough and the crest and is determined by three things; the fetch, that is the distance over which the wind blows, the duration of the wind, and the wind speed. The largest waves occur in the Pacific, which has the greatest possible fetch of any ocean.

Of all phenomena in the oceans, wind waves have the greatest effect on man's fishing industry, shipping and coastal structures. Breakwaters and lighthouses must be able to stand up to the enormous force of crashing breakers. In the early part of this century a 65-ton concrete block making up part of the Cherbourg breakwater was moved 60 feet by storm waves. The Tillamook Rock Light on the Oregon coast is over 139 feet above sea level, but has to be protected by steel bars as the sea at this point is known to hurl rocks of over 100 pounds weight up as high as the lighthouse.

Wind waves are generated in a way that is only partially understood. A gusting wind pushes down harder on some parts of the sea than on others and the resulting distortion of the surface is seen as ripples. These quickly grow into waves that affect the flow of the wind, producing a stronger push on the windward side and a weaker one on the lee. The waves are blown along in much the same way that a sailing boat is propelled across the water. Once wind energy has been supplied it can be transferred from one wave to another in a way that is analogous to how motion would be transmitted between pendulums linked together by weak springs. In storms, waves receive so much energy that they are whipped into a frenzy such that waves with many different periods, lengths and directions of propagation exist simultaneously. The resulting chaotic wave pattern is generally termed a "wind sea."

Wind blowing across the water sets up small capillary waves with rounded crests and pointed troughs. Wave shape is determined by surface tension.

Once wavelength exceeds 1.74 centimeters, gravity takes over from surface tension as the dominant force on wave form. The crests become more pointed; the troughs rounded. The wind reinforces the wave shape by pressing down on the windward side and eddying over the crest to reduce pressure on the leeward side.

As the waves grow, their crests steepen until they reach an angle of 120°, at which point they become unstable and break, producing whitecaps.

Waves in the process of generation are called "forced waves." As they disperse from the source area they travel as long-crested swell waves.

The orbital movement of water particles at the surface has a diameter equal to the wave height, but reduces to zero at a depth equal to half the wavelength.

How big the waves get in the heart of great storms is not really known; 40- to 50-foot waves are considered monstrous, but the highest documented wave measured 112 feet. Freak waves of this magnitude are known to occur where storm waves are driven up against the continental shelf. Off the southeast coast of Africa the fast-flowing Agulhas Current runs at right angles to storm waves generated in the Indian Ocean, making these waters particularly hazardous. A ship encountering one of these waves may either be overwhelmed by water breaking over it, or plunge into the yawning trough preceding it.

After waves have been generated they propagate away from the storm site and undergo a transformation in shape. Instead of the sharp, ragged edges and many whitecaps that characterize the wind sea, the waves now become smooth, long-crested swells. These usually low undulations of the sea surface can travel great distances without appreciable attenuation. In one case swells were observed to travel from the Indian Ocean, past the Antarctic ice sheet, through the islands of the tropical Pacific Ocean, finally expending their energy on the coast of Alaska some 12,000 miles away from the site of their origin.

As the waves approach shore and their eventual destruction, they again undergo an unusual transformation. Their wavelength becomes less and their height increases as the water shoals until they become unstable and spill over as crashing breakers or "surf."

Another type of ocean wave that affects man, sometimes dramatically, is the seismic sea wave, or tsunami—a Japanese word. These are cataclysmic waves generated by undersea earthquakes or volcanic eruptions. They are popularly, and mistakenly, called tidal waves, although they have nothing to do with tides, which are yet another kind of ocean wave. Once generated, the tsunamis can travel across whole oceans at an extremely high speed—up to 450 mph. In the open ocean the wave crests are typically 100 miles apart and the interval between each may be 15 minutes or more. Their amplitude is very low and they frequently pass under ships unnoticed. These waves generally occur in the Pacific, where earthquake and volcanic activity is greatest.

The tsunamis expend their energy on the continental margins, usually without too much effect. However, there are certain regions where the sea floor can focus the wave energy much as a simple magnifying glass focuses the sun's rays. The resulting effects of the focused wave energy upon coastal structures and cities can be devastating as the numerous disasters in the Hawaiian islands demonstrate.

In recent years a sophisticated network of measurement stations has been set up around the Pacific Ocean to guard against the surprise assault of tsunamis. When an earthquake occurs, the presence of a potentially disastrous tsunami can be detected within a matter of hours and civil-defense warnings are flashed to imperilled coastal regions.

On 1 November, 1755, Lisbon experienced an earthquake that was followed by one of the most severe tsunamis ever recorded. Loss of life was heavy and the city was devastated by the shock and the ensuing waves. Tsunamis are generated when a submarine earthquake causes a sudden shift in the seabed. The upheaval of the overlying waters creates a bulge that breaks down into a series of waves that travels away from the earthquake center at up to 450 mph. The map plots the hourly position of a tsunami originating just south of Alaska.

In shoaling water, of depth less than half the wavelength, the waves heighten and steepen and the wavelength shortens. The particle movements become more elliptical until they can no longer maintain their orbits and the wave breaks.

Breakers on a gently sloping shore may either surge up the beach, *above left*, or break gradually, *above*, as water spills down the wave front. Where the shore steepens abruptly, *above right*, the wave overturns as a plunging breaker.

When waves approach the shore at an angle, the landward wing enters the shallow water first and is slowed down, allowing the seaward wing to overtake it—the whole wave-front gradually swinging round. As the waves break the swash carries sand particles up the beach at an oblique angle, but the backwash carries them straight back down, resulting in a net movement along the shore.

The first waves to reach the shore steepen ahead of the rest and produce a longshore current running in the surf zone from areas of high breakers to areas of low breakers. Water traveling in this way returns to the sea in localized rip currents that may surge more than half a mile out to sea and persist for between a few minutes and several hours. Rip currents are common in areas with sandbars.

THE SURGING TIDES

The rising tide entering the River Severn in England is funneled into a tidal bore three feet high. The bore travels upstream at 13 .mph., running 21 miles inland before losing its momentum.

High tides at Lake Harbor, Northwest Territories, raise and lower floating sea ice against the sheer cliff of grounded shore ice.

The ebb and flow of the tide in the Bay of Fundy in Nova Scotia sets up an oscillating wave which seesaws from one end of the bay to the other during each tidal cycle. This action amplifies the tidal range, resulting in the highest tides in the world—44 feet at spring tide. Stacks and cliffs around the bay are undercut by wave erosion throughout the entire tidal range.

The island of Mont-St. Michel is surrounded at low tide by sands stretching 10 miles into the English Channel. When the tide rises, it rushes in at a rate of 210 feet per minute, completely surrounding the island. Although at 41 feet the tides in the Bay of St. Michel are among the highest in Europe, their great range is disguised by their being spread over so vast an area.

Semidiurnal
Diurnal
Mixed

Semidiurnal tides occur twice every day (literally half-daily). **Diurnal tides** occur once daily. They are very rare and are due to local coastal configuration. **Mixed tides** are an amalgam of the above types—there are two tides per day, but one is very much stronger than the other.

It would be almost impossible to visit the seashore anywhere in the world without witnessing the regular twice-daily ebb and flow of the tide or, over a longer period, the monthly cycle of spring and neap tides, varying in amplitude with the phases of the moon. The Ancient Greeks were the first to record the relationship between the tides and the moon's monthly passage around the earth, but it was not until Newton presented his gravitational theory nearly 2000 years later that this relationship could be explained.

Everything in the universe exerts a gravitational force on everything else. For a small object like a grain of sand the force is immeasurably small; for a planet or star the force is enormous, tending to pull every other object into its own center of gravity. It is gravity that holds the planets in their orbits around the sun, and gravity that keeps the earth tied to its companion the moon.

Gravity tries to pull the earth and moon together, but they are kept apart by the centrifugal force of the lunar orbit. At the earth's center, these forces are in perfect equilibrium, but at the surface one or other predominates slightly. The tides are the oceans'

response to these unbalanced forces. On the side of the earth nearer the moon the net force is toward the moon; on the other side it is directed away from it. If the earth rotated much more slowly than it does, the result would be a bulge of water on both sides of the earth—one facing the moon, the other on the opposite face. As the earth turned on its axis, any given point would normally experience two tides each day—equal in magnitude when the moon is positioned over the equator, but markedly different when the moon is north or south of the equator. In these extreme positions many places would experience a pronounced once-daily tidal effect.

Similar tide-producing forces are generated by the sun, but although it is 27 million times heavier than the moon, it is 390 times farther away, and its tidal forces are only about two-fifths as strong as those caused by the moon. The variations in position of the sun and moon in relation to the earth produce the familiar range of tides, from the high spring tides to the lower-than-average neap tides. In reality, however, the two-bulge system described above is a gross oversimplification. The presence of continents and

midocean ridges, the frictional drag between watermass and seabed, and the Coriolis force created by the earth's spin, combine to produce a complex pattern of standing and rotating wave systems, oscillating and revolving around nodal points. Each system is restricted to its own ocean basin by the continents. Within these basins the rise and fall of the water surface varies from zero at the nodal points to 50 feet or more in some locally resonating basins like the Bay of Fundy in Nova Scotia. More typically, the tidal rise and fall in the open ocean is between three and ten feet. The Atlantic and Indian oceans generally resonate to the twice-daily tides, but respond only feebly to the daily tide component. Hence the tidal pattern familiar to Europeans is predominantly twice-daily. The Pacific Ocean responds to both tidal periods, but in such a way that one tide each day is normally much larger than the other.

The great tidal wave systems generated in the oceans spill over into the shallow seas of the continental shelves. Here, the tidal currents, very weak in the deep oceans, are magnified to three feet per second or faster as the water pours across the continental margins,

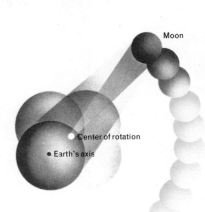

Earth and moon are locked together by their gravitational attraction. Not only does the moon orbit the earth but the earth also moves in a small circular orbit—both bodies rotating around a common center lying within the earth. The earth's motion may be compared with that of a man swinging a heavy weight (the moon) around his body. In order to counteract the force of the weight pulling away from him, he is forced to walk in a circle, the center of which lies in front of his feet.

The moon's gravity pulls the oceans on the moon side of the earth toward it. This is balanced by the centrifugal force of the earth's spin throwing the water on the opposite side outward away from the moon. If the earth rotated slowly enough these forces would produce two equal and opposite bulges in line with the moon. The earth, however, exerts a frictional force on the watermass, pulling the bulges around as it spins, so that high tides occur later in time, that is, slightly ahead of the moon's position.

producing the familiar tidal ranges of several feet amplitude.

The surging oceanic tides permanently contain about 700,000 million million (10^{18}) joules of energy—equivalent to the amount of electrical energy supplied to England and Wales over a period of seven months. About one-third of this is "potential" energy due to the vertical rise of the enormous masses of water; the remaining two-thirds is "kinetic" energy locked in the ceaseless movement of the tidal currents. Energy is dissipated by friction at the rate of five million million joules every second—one thousand times the output of a large power station. The energy balance is made good from the rotational energy of the earth, causing the day to lengthen by a few thousandths of a second each century. As the total momentum of the earth–moon system must remain constant, the slowing down of the earth is associated with a steady increase in the distance of the moon by about 2.5 inches a year. But one great puzzle remains; the rate of energy loss by the tides, as calculated from changes in the moon's orbit, is more than twice that calculated from direct studies of the tides themselves.

Each line on the map joins places that have high tide at the same instant. Every line is one hour later than that immediately behind it and the resulting pattern indicates how the tides move around the central nodes every 12 hours. The diagrams above give an idealized picture of the water surface behavior as it responds to the tide's movement around the node points.

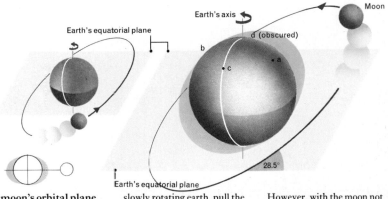

The moon's orbital plane reaches a maximum angle of 28.5° with the earth's equator every 18.6 years. When in this position the moon moves from 28.5° north of the equator through 28.5° south and back again each lunar month, and would, on a slowly rotating earth, pull the "tidal bulges" around with it. As the earth turned on its axis, every point would experience two high and two low tides each day. With the moon over the equator the tides would be equal in amplitude, *above left*.

However, with the moon not over the equator, all points would have two tides, but of unequal magnitude. Point (a), *above*, would have a "high" high tide; (b) a smaller high tide; while (c) and (d), at 90° to the earth–moon axis, have low tides.

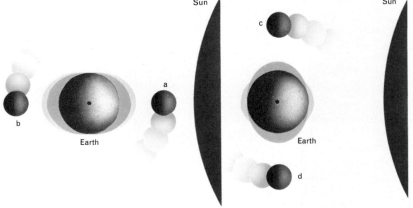

Spring tides have the largest range between high and low tide in the monthly cycle. They occur when the sun and moon are both pulling together, at new moon (a) and full moon (b). However, when the moon is in the first quarter (c) or last quarter (d) these two tide-producing forces are pulling at right angles to each other, and the consequent reduction in pull produces the much lower-ranged neap tides.

MAN'S OCEANIC QUEST

More than 50 feet beneath the surface of the Arctic Ocean at the Geographic North Pole, a member of the 1974 Arctic IV Expedition is photographed against the impressive bulk of a huge pressure ridge keel projecting nearly 70 feet below the surface. This remarkable photograph was taken by available light transmitted through the natural window of a recently frozen lead. Divers taking part in the North Pole Project—one of eighteen research projects undertaken by members of the expedition—were airlifted to the North Pole from their operational base at Resolute Bay in the Canadian Arctic.

FIRST ENCOUNTERS

Rock carvings at Kalnes in Norway, believed to be 4000 years old, clearly show boats with a ribbed construction, very similar to the skin-covered boats common in Europe in later periods.

The dugout is an ancient and widely distributed craft, made by hollowing and shaping a log using fire and simple tools.

The reed boat, constructed of bundles of reeds lashed together, is common in lake regions and areas where wood is scarce.

Hundreds of carved stones illustrating familiar themes were made by the Vikings as memorials to the dead. This eighth-century stone depicting a boat and voyagers comes from Gotland in Sweden.

Bark canoes are constructed of sheets of thin bark, often birch, sewn together with root fibers, over a wood frame.

The North American Indian bull boat, one of the family of skin boats, is made of buffalo hide on a framework of willow.

Odysseus and the legendary sirens, who lured sailors into peril by their charming songs, are illustrated on this fifth-century Greek vase, which exemplifies classical interest in ships and sea legends.

The double canoe used in the Pacific was developed to carry bulky cargo or large numbers of passengers. To avoid building larger hulls, two dugouts were joined together by crossmembers.

The Cheops ship, the world's oldest extant vessel, was discovered near the Pyramid of Cheops, where it was buried 4600 years ago. The ship supports the evidence of wall paintings and texts describing the sea-going skills of the Egyptians.

The Oseberg ship, a Viking craft probably built about A.D. 800, was excavated in Norway in 1905. This elegant ship was built entirely of oak and could have been propelled by sail or oars according to conditions.

EARLY NAVIGATIONAL AIDS

The first navigational aids probably did little more than complement the mariner's already formidable knowledge, for the effectiveness of navigation unaided by instruments is vividly illustrated by the colonization of the Pacific islands—a remarkable undertaking largely accomplished by A.D. 500.

The ancient Greeks were among the many people to systematize their knowledge of the winds for direction finding, building such structures as the Tower of the Winds in Athens, and their familiarity with the lead-weighted sounding line is recorded by Herodotus in the fifth century B.C. The lead line gave a rough indication of distance from land by water depth and by the nature of bottom sediments adhering to tallow on the base of the weight. Other early techniques for locating land included the observation of swell-wave patterns and cloud formations, and the release of land birds—a method described in the biblical tale of Noah.

By the fourth century B.C. written directions, possibly supplemented by maps, summarized the knowledge gained on many voyages, but genuine sea charts did not appear until the thirteenth century. The *Carta Pisana*, made in about 1275, is the oldest known chart and gives both compass bearings and scale distances. The first independent nautical direction-finding instrument was the magnetic compass, the outcome of technical refinements begun long before its first recorded appearance in the twelfth century; this was soon joined by the sandglass timekeeper, but more precise instruments did not appear until the Renaissance.

The Tower of the Winds in Athens displays eight personified winds.

The sandglass, listed in ships' inventories from 1295, was the standard marine time-keeper and was used with log and line to measure distances.

Some Micronesians navigated with a stick chart, or mattang, depicting ocean-swell patterns.

The sea has probably played a part in man's life and experience from the very earliest times, and even his prehuman ancestors are likely to have included shellfish, gathered along the shore, in their diet. As man expanded his territory to accommodate his rapidly growing population, new seas and straits, rivers and estuaries must have been discovered—some providing him with a source of food and water, others simply representing an impassable barrier to his onward movement.

Little trace remains of the earliest maritime activities as the materials most commonly used in primitive boat-building—wood, reeds and skins—are rapidly decomposed, while many coastal communities were located in areas subsequently inundated by rising sea levels. Nevertheless, some evidence has survived and conclusions may be drawn about man's earliest seafaring ventures.

Watercraft were used in the colonizing of Australia between 20,000 and 50,000 years ago as, despite lower Ice-Age sea levels, which elsewhere exposed land-bridges such as those between Japan and mainland Asia and between Siberia and Alaska, a channel 25 miles or more in width always existed between Australia and her northern neighbors. Earlier still, by the end of the Pleistocene period, about 10,000 years ago, continental western Europe had been extensively colonized, almost certainly via the Strait

of Gibraltar, which was never less than six miles wide. Use of water transportation is thus virtually established for Lower Paleolithic man.

Widely distributed cultures of Upper Paleolithic and Mesolithic age exploited the seas for food, and middens of shells and fishbones marking ancient shorelines testify to a diet of seafood. Occasional remains of deep-sea species suggest that boats may have been used.

The distribution of artifacts from the Neolithic period onward reflects a pattern of production, trade and exchange inconceivable without the use of boats. About 5000 years ago seafarers in the Aegean and central Mediterranean areas were distributing objects made of obsidian, a volcanic glass, from identifiable sources to destinations hundreds of miles away.

While there are no physical remains of boats to reliably predate European Neolithic dugouts, there is indirect evidence, both written and pictorial, for a variety of craft made of skin, bark or reeds. Among preindustrial societies, four main types of boats were used; dugouts of various types, reed craft, split sections of bark with internal supporting ribs, and skin-covered wooden-framed boats. None is confined to a single continent and the distribution of boat types usually reflects the local availability of materials.

Rock carvings found at Kalnes in Norway, and believed to be about 4000 years old, have been

interpreted as representing skin boats, and comparable craft are known to have been used in classical times in France. Coracles, kayaks and curraghs are modern equivalents of these simple craft. Other boat types show similar continuities in time: in the ancient Near East, pictures and texts provide evidence of skin and reed craft during the third millennium B.C. and a wooden-planked ship, the Cheops ship, actually survives from this period.

Whatever the type of boat, lakes and rivers probably functioned as the nursery for seafaring activities. Likewise, archipelagoes such as Indonesia, and heavily indented coastal areas such as Scandinavia, have served as the starting points for seafaring traditions. However, the spectacular maritime achievements of the Greeks, ancestral Pacific Islanders and Vikings were probably in response to social stimuli such as population pressures or economic incentives, rather than an automatic consequence of their environment.

The results, including the colonization of vast new areas, achieved by these early ocean ventures are probably even more exceptional than the voyages themselves. Sailing on the open sea may often be less hazardous than sailing close inshore, where the effects of tides, currents and weather are often magnified by the form of the seabed. If this is so, it is possible that the oceans were crossed far earlier than existing evidence or preconceptions suggest.

THE OCEAN PATHFINDERS

Lost to Europeans from the fifth century, the *Geographia* of Ptolemy, A.D. 140, *left*, was rediscovered in 1400 when a Byzantine Greek manuscript was brought to Florence. The Ptolemaic maps, comprising a world map and 26 regional maps, profoundly influenced European geography. This map is from the edition printed in Ulm in 1486.
Martin Waldseemüller, a German cartographer, published a world globe in twelve gores, *right*, in 1507. While individual countries were based on Ptolemaic maps, he included Africa and America as charted by the Portuguese and Spaniards. Waldseemüller first suggested that America should be so called after the explorer Amerigo Vespucci.

Portuguese seamen were the true pioneers of European oceanic exploration. Sent out by Prince Henry in the 1420s to find a seaway to the source of transsaharan gold, they discovered the Madeiras and Azores and, in 1434, rounded Cape Bojador at latitude 26°N, hitherto the southern limit of seafaring, and returned. To achieve this the clockwise circulation of the winds in the North Atlantic—the key to oceanic sailing-ship transportation—must have been discovered, for the North East Trade Winds off the Saharan coast enabled ships to sail south but prevented their return. Sailors found that by sailing due west into the ocean, they encountered winds from the south and then from the west which brought them back to Portugal.

The Portuguese, who charted their discoveries with considerable skill, had learned their navigation and hydrography from the Italians, who had developed the portulan chart in the thirteenth century for use with the then recently developed magnetic sea compass and sandglass for direction and distance finding in all weathers. These aids, with written sailing directions, made reliable year-round navigation practicable for the first time in the Mediterranean.

When exploring the Atlantic in the fifteenth century, however, the Portuguese experienced unknown currents that falsified their reckonings and made landfalls unpredictable and dangerous. About 1460 they devised a system of nautical astronomy to improve navigational accuracy. Variation in the altitude of the North Star, later of the sun at noon, measured with a quadrant and multiplied by the number of miles in a degree, gave an independent check on estimated distances sailed in a northerly or southerly direction. By the 1480s simplified astronomical rules and tables enabled the pilot to calculate his latitude. The explorer Bartolomeu Dias, so navigating, rounded the Cape of Good Hope in 1488 after first sweeping to the west in the South Atlantic to find favorable winds. He landed in Natal and returned to Lisbon having found a seaway to the East. Ten years later Vasco da Gama, also using the anticlockwise wind circulation in the South Atlantic and Indian oceans, reached and returned from India in his two specially constructed three-masted square-rigged ships. The three-masted ship evolved in Europe about 1450 and, armed with cannons and navigated by a pilot skilled in nautical astronomy, it gave Europe mastery of the oceans for close on four centuries.

The early sixteenth century saw many developments in marine expertise and exploration. At the beginning of the century the sea astrolabe and plane charts with a latitude scale came into use. At this time longitude could not be measured, so "running down the latitude" was practiced—that is, sailing to the latitude of a landfall, but three to four hundred miles seaward, then sailing due east or west to the landfall. After crossing the Atlantic in 1492 to reach the Indies, Columbus used this method of navigation on his return voyage from what was to prove to be a New World.

The continental nature of America, and the pattern of the North Atlantic currents which facilitated transatlantic voyaging, were established by the Spaniards in the sixteenth century. In Lisbon and Seville official hydrographers were charting discoveries and developing navigational techniques. From such charts up-to-date world maps were produced by European cartographers, notably by Waldseemüller, whose map of 1516 was the first to reject virtually all Ptolemaic geography in preference to the charted discoveries. The vast extent of the Pacific was disclosed during the circumnavigation of 1519–22, led initially by Magellan and completed by Del Cano after Magellan's death in the Philippines.

The seventeenth century saw the beginning of the search for a method of determining longitude. Galileo, who invented the pendulum-controlled clock and astronomical telescope, discovered that the planet of Jupiter has satellites and suggested that these might be used to measure longitude. Research at the Paris Observatory, founded in 1667, led to the accurate measurement of the length of a degree and the development of a method of determining longitude on land by observing the eclipses of Jupiter's satellites. The method, however, was not practicable at sea and the continuing search for a solution led to the foundation of the Royal Observatory at Greenwich, England, in 1675 with a special brief to solve this problem. In the 1760s John Harrison's fourth chronometer and the "lunar distance" method of calculating longitude provided the answers to the problem of longitude measurement at sea. The latter was made practicable by the publication of Maskelyne's annual *Nautical Almanac* from 1767 which gave lunar distances from the sun and certain stars for every three hours at Greenwich. John Hadley's invention of the reflecting quadrant in 1731, later improved into the sextant in 1757, enabled lunar observations to be made on board.

In the course of his three voyages between 1768 and 1780 Captain Cook explored the Pacific Ocean using the lunar distance method and his accurate charts opened the Pacific to economic exploitation. The accurate determination of position at sea was also the prerequisite to the exploration of the ocean's depths which followed in the next century.

Meridional tables published in 1599 by the mathematician Edward Wright enabled hydrographers to construct charts mathematically on what has become known as the Mercator projection after the cartographer Gerhardus Mercator. The first sea chart to use these tables was also published in 1599; above is a later edition dated 1655. Such charts allow positions to be plotted in terms of latitude and longitude, and direction and distance to be accurately charted.

Magnetic variation was known to compassmakers and mariners by about 1450, but was thought to be constant wherever it was observed. Its cause was unknown. The annual change in variation was discovered, and in the late 1690s the Admiralty commissioned an astronomer, Edmond Halley, to measure variation in the North and South Atlantic. He published the first isogonic—lines of equal variation—chart in 1701, later extending it to the Indian Ocean.

The three-masted ship was developed in the mid-fifteenth century and made oceanic navigation practicable. The engraving by an unknown artist, c. 1470–80, shows a three-masted ship in full sail.

NAVIGATIONAL INSTRUMENTS

The quadrant was used to measure the altitude of the North Star on departure and on passage. The difference, multiplied by the number of miles in a degree, provided a check on estimated north–south distances.

From about 1480 onward, Portuguese pilots were taught to determine their latitude by observing the sun's meridian altitude with an astrolabe. The cast brass sea astrolabe was developed by the Portuguese at the beginning of the sixteenth century to facilitate solar observations on board ship.

The cross-staff, developed by 1514, consisted of a bar that was slid along the staff until the top of the sun on the meridian was covered by the top of the bar while the bottom was on the horizon. The altitude was read from a scale.

John Harrison's marine timekeepers first solved the problem of determining longitude at sea. His fourth chronometer was successfully tested in 1762 and 1764 and this copy, made by Larcum Kendall in 1769, was used by Captain Cook on voyages to the Pacific.

The reflecting quadrant, first described by John Hadley in 1731, used the principle of double reflection and made altitude observations at sea sufficiently accurate to enable ships' local time to be determined.

The compass is a direction-finding instrument based on the discovery that a needle magnetized by a lodestone will direct itself toward magnetic north. The compass above dates from the eighteenth century.

The sextant was developed in the 1750s from Hadley's quadrant to measure the angular distance between the sun and either a star or the moon to find longitude by lunar distance. It measured angles up to 120 degrees.

EVOLUTION OF A SCIENCE

The **first map** to be made of an ocean basin, this charting of the bed of the North Atlantic, by Matthew Fontaine Maury, appeared in 1855 in his book *The Physical Geography of the Sea*. Maury used soundings made with a lead and line to prepare his map and demonstrated that some previous, very deep soundings were inaccurate or exaggerated, although some errors still remain on this map.

James Rennell, a British geographer, produced this chart of the currents of the Atlantic Ocean for his book *Investigations of the currents of the Atlantic Ocean* published in 1832. He believed that there were two types of currents: drift currents, movements of water caused by winds and stream currents, brought about by a drift current being deflected by a landmass. Although it is a remarkable work, modern research has modified the chart: for example the Southern Connecting Current and the North African and Guinea Current are no longer recognized. The true Guinea Current, an extension of the Equatorial Counter Current, was not known to Rennell.

THE VOYAGE OF THE CHALLENGER

The *Challenger* expedition of 1872 to 1876, perhaps one of the most important scientific voyages ever made, laid the foundation for modern oceanography. Two biologists, W.B.Carpenter and Wyville Thomson, persuaded the British government to equip the expedition to study deep-sea circulation and the distribution of life in the seas. A converted warship, H.M.S. *Challenger* was staffed by experienced naval surveyors and carried a team of civilian scientists on the four-year circumnavigation of the world. The voyage set a pattern for the oceanographic expeditions of the late nineteenth and early twentieth centuries and the Expedition Report, packed with data and illustrations, was a model presentation of scientific results.

Not until the late nineteenth century was the need felt for a name, oceanography, to describe the science of the sea. Yet as early as the fourth century B.C., Aristotle studied the life of the Aegean Sea and discussed theories of still earlier philosophers explaining such phenomena as the salinity of the sea. Information on tides and currents, learned from seafarers, was recorded by some medieval Arab and European writers, but most were content to speculate. It was during the seventeenth-century scientific revolution that scientists first attempted to combine their method with maritime expertise, hoping to learn more about the sea and make sea travel less hazardous.

In 1665 the Royal Society issued *Directions for seamen*, a pamphlet giving instructions for the collection of information about the depth of the sea, its salinity, its tides and currents. Tidal data thus obtained were later used by Sir Isaac Newton to illustrate his theory of gravity. Robert Hooke contributed ideas for apparatus, including depth-sounding

machines, water samplers and a deep-sea thermometer. Considerable interest was generated among professional men such as Richard Bolland and Sir Henry Sheeres who studied water movements in the Strait of Gibraltar, but practical difficulties and changing scientific fashions caused a decline toward 1700.

Scientific as well as political and economic motives led to the renewal of voyages of exploration during the eighteenth century. The solution of the longitude problem meant that a ship's position could be accurately fixed at sea, a prerequisite for the collection of scientific data. Information collected on the voyages of Cook, and others, was of such significance to the developing earth sciences that leading scientists such as Sir Joseph Banks and Alexander von Humboldt looked to the sea to enlarge these disciplines. Growing realization of the interest and importance of marine science in its own right led to the production of several major pieces of work in the early nineteenth century. They included Swiss-born Alexander Marcet's study of the

salinity of the world ocean, James Rennell's charts of the currents of the Atlantic, and Emil von Lenz's research on variation in temperature and salinity in the deep ocean, made on the Russian voyage of circumnavigation commanded by Kotzebue between 1823 and 1826. Lenz's results seemed to confirm the contemporary belief that ocean currents might be caused by density differences in the ocean rather than by action of wind at the surface. Opportunities to extend such work were, however, severely limited—not least by the enormous labor of retrieving apparatus from deep water, and interest again waned.

One person to combat this decline was Matthew Fontaine Maury. His wind and current charts, intended to assist sailing ships facing growing competition from steam, led him to a general interest in marine research. By the 1860s the increasing use of steamships, the development of sounding gear, and of engines for retrieving apparatus from the ocean bed in connection with submarine cable-laying, supplied the means for

One of the major objectives of the *Challenger* expedition was to examine the mysterious life of the deep sea. This involved dredging the depths for samples at regular intervals.

Much of the labor of dredging for samples was undertaken by the ship's crew. Life was found down to depths of 4500 fathoms (27,000 feet) where previously no life was thought to exist.

Deep-sea deposits, and specimens dredged from the sea bottom on the expedition, are among the hundreds of subjects meticulously documented by artists for the subsequent Expedition Report.

The contents of the dredge were then passed to the naturalists on board for examination and identification. The *Challenger* had well-equipped laboratories for scientific work.

the effective study of the deep ocean. Until the middle of the nineteenth century most people believed that no life could survive in the sea below 400 fathoms because of the harsh conditions, but gradually marine biologists extended the limit and eventually began to question whether a limit existed at all. In 1869 a British scientist, Wyville Thomson, dredged creatures from 2500 fathoms during a voyage in H.M.S. *Porcupine*. This work led to the voyage of H.M.S. *Challenger*, 1872–6, the first truly oceanographic expedition. Many nations followed this example. Some polar expeditions also contributed important work, while studies of deepwater movements by German ships, culminating in the *Meteor* cruise of 1925–7, led to the first accurate model of the circulation of the Atlantic.

By 1900 oceanography was recognized as an important science, but at first it developed unevenly in different parts of the world largely through lack of funds for permanent institutions: few governments were as enlightened as that of Prince Albert of Monaco,

who established institutes at both Paris and Monaco. Many of the early foundations were small seaside stations, specializing in biology and catering mostly for students on a seasonal basis. Some of these have since developed into national centers for oceanographic research. The first aspect of marine science to attract widespread government support was fisheries research. As early as the 1870s the decline of fish stocks was causing concern, and in 1925 Britain established the *Discovery* Investigations in an effort to conserve whale stocks in the Southern Ocean.

The decisive change came with World War II. For the first time scientists with mathematical and technical skills, needed for such pioneer work as wave forecasting and underwater acoustics, were attracted into oceanography on a large scale and governments of all persuasions began increasing funds for scientific research. The combination of new skills and resources has revolutionized oceanography during the last 30 years. Not only the size and scope but also the nature

of operations has changed. Echo sounding and continuous sensing devices linked to computers, and improved positioning due to satellite navigation have enabled scientists to learn about the physical properties of the ocean and the character of the seabed in far greater detail, making necessary a corresponding elaboration of theory. Since 1960 marine geophysicists have brought about a general revolution in the earth sciences with their theories of plate tectonics.

The depths of the sea, so long less well known than the heavens, no longer interest only the scientist, now that their military and commercial potential have been realized. Free-swimming divers using aqualung equipment devised by Cousteau and others during World War II can now explore the fringes of the ocean; submersibles can take man to the greatest depths, as Jacques Piccard showed in the bathyscaphe *Trieste* in 1960; and the oil and mineral resources of shallow seas are now being exploited with every likelihood of soon being extended to abyssal areas.

PROBING THE DEEPS

Tow rope

Gear box

Rollers for transport
of gauze strip

CF147

Propeller

Propeller guard

Plankton
entrance

Tank of preservative

Stabilizing fins

Diving plane

The Hardy continuous plankton sampler is typical of the devices used to collect small animals and plants on the move. Its shape ensures that it travels along at a depth of about 30 feet, and the flow of water past the propeller works the system of rollers, which carry a strip of gauze on which the samples are collected. The strip is rolled up in a tank of preservative and forms a record of the plankton encountered.

Messenger

Rigid ring to
keep the net open

Net bridles

Tube of fine
mesh material

Draw string

Sample collector

Trigger mechanism

A ring net is used to collect plankton from slow-moving vessels. It is clamped to a wire and suspended below the ship. Once it is in position a weight called a messenger is slid down the wire and trips off a release mechanism that closes the net. When a number of nets are used on the same wire to collect samples from different depths the trigger releases another messenger that activates the next net down.

Frame

Net

Sample collector

Flexible sheet to
protect the net

Skis

Pacer
wheel

Tow cable

Distance
recorder

Counter

Dredges are used to collect samples of organisms on or near the bed of the sea. The type shown here consists of a net mounted on a heavy steel frame carried along the seabed by a pair of skis. The fauna is caught by the net and passed into a container at the cod end. The amount of water filtered is important for statistical analysis and so the dredge usually incorporates a device that measures the distance covered.

In 1876 H.M.S. *Challenger* left port on a three-year voyage that was to mark the birth of oceanography. Much of the oceanographic instrumentation carried was brand new and completely unproven, and although it would appear primitive by present-day standards, the basic design of today's water samplers, corers, dredgers and current meters is much the same as that of 100 years ago.

Oceanographic instruments fall into two basic groups—those that bring back samples for further study in the controlled conditions of the laboratory and those that take readings in situ.

Sampling devices include water bottles and plankton nets that can work at any depth in the ocean, and corers, dredges and drills that take specimens from the seabed.

Plankton nets have their origins in the more conventional nets used by generations of fishermen. They are generally smaller, however, and usually have a finer mesh. Moreover they incorporate numerous modifications that reflect the scientific nature of their work. Since the depth at which a sample is taken is important, there may be an arrangement whereby the net only opens when it is lowered to the required depth. This may be achieved by attaching a number of nets at fixed distances on a cable and operating the whole system by dropped weights called messengers. The quantity of water that has passed through the net to give the sample is also important, and so some nets incorporate a flow meter to show how far it has traveled while operating. More sophisticated plankton samplers, such as the Hardy sampler, store and preserve plankton as soon as it has been caught and can be operated while the ship is under way. Such samplers have the advantage of being able to catch some of the larger animals that would avoid a slow-moving system.

Bottom samplers can be lowered or towed at the end of a cable or can be tossed overboard, to return to the surface once their work is done. It is not easy to retrieve a sample of bottom sediment without damaging it in some way and so a number of different systems have been evolved to minimize the risk. Grab samplers with hinged jaws "bite" samples at random from the bottom sediment. They have two jaws, as in the Peterson grab, or four, as in the orange-peel sampler. As grabs take only a small quantity of unconsolidated seabed material at a time, larger samples or rocks are brought up by dredges. These consist of heavy chain nets or basketlike structures that are dragged along the bottom. As they frequently become snagged on obstacles, the towing system usually incorporates a weak link that enables the dredge to break free of the main cable while still remaining attached to a safety line. The dredge has an advantage over the grab in that

Sampler sinks

Flag and flashing
light to locate
sampler on the
surface

Sampler returns
to the surface

Floats

Weights
dropped off

Weights

Jaws

Lower float
pulls jaws
closed

The boomerang grab sampler is taken to the seabed by the weights attached to the jaws. There the weights are jettisoned, the jaws close on a sediment sample and the device floats to the surface.

it can be used while the ship is in motion, albeit slowly.

Most seabed samples are taken by coring. This entails dropping a weighted tube vertically into the seabed so that a cylinder of sediment is trapped inside it and pulled to the surface. The simplest form of corer is lowered to the seabed, where a trigger mechanism allows the device to drop for the last few feet. The core is usually held by a core catcher—an arrangement of brass fingers that allows the sediment to enter the tube but prevents it from falling out. An advance on the simple gravity corer is the piston corer, which incorporates a moving plunger that passes up the tube as it enters the sediment. This creates a partial vacuum in the tube and allows longer cores—up to 60 feet in length—to be retrieved. The piston corer is usually triggered off by a small gravity corer, which is able to take an undisturbed core of the surface sediment that would otherwise have been deformed by the main corer. The ultimate in corers is the research ship *Glomar Challenger*, a drilling ship that has brought up cores from 4265 feet beneath the bed of the sea.

Grabs and corers are sometimes worked on the boomerang principle. The device is allowed to sink freely to the seabed, where it takes its sample. Once it has done so the weights that have taken it to the bottom are jettisoned and floats built onto it carry it to the surface, where it is retrieved with the help of flashing lights and indicator flags.

In situ recorders are used to study water conditions such as temperature and pressure. A reversing thermometer is used to measure temperature at a specific depth. It is lowered to the depth required and is then inverted so that the mercury thread breaks and preserves the reading that was being registered at that time. The thermometer is usually mounted on a reversing water bottle so that the two are operated simultaneously. A bathythermograph is a device that records changes in temperature and pressure as it is towed along at depth behind the survey vessel. Neutrally buoyant floats are employed to measure subsurface currents. They can be made to float at any depth and are allowed to drift with the current. They are tracked by monitoring radio signals emitted by battery-operated transmitters carried by them, and can be followed from a distance of several miles. Recording devices can be worked on the boomerang principle, but when they are required to remain at great depths for a period of time the weights are released by means of a sonar signal transmitted by the ship when it returns to the area.

Other retrieval and recording devices are continually being devised as new researchers with fresh and inventive minds enter the field.

The deep-sea reversing thermometer is used to measure the temperature of the water at depth. The principle of operation is simple, but the mathematical calculations involved tend to be complex. The protected deep-sea reversing thermometer is insulated from the pressure of the sea by a jacket of mercury. At its depth of operation it is inverted and the mercury thread breaks at the appendix. This quantity of mercury falls to the other end of the thermometer, preserving the reading. On the return to the surface this reading will have altered slightly because of the change of temperature and this is corrected by using the reading on the auxiliary thermometer. The unprotected deep-sea reversing thermometer is basically the same instrument, but its bulb is exposed to the sea pressure so that the reading recorded is determined by both the temperature and the pressure. This is usually mounted alongside the protected thermometer and the difference between the two readings obtained gives the pressure and hence the depth at which the reversal took place. This technique is very accurate and can record temperatures with an accuracy of within 0.01°C and the depth of the reading can be calculated to within six feet.

A bathythermograph is an instrument that records water temperature and pressure continuously as it is towed at depth behind a survey vessel. A stylus is moved by the change in temperature, and the slide on which the readings are inscribed is moved by the change in pressure. The slide then records variations of temperature with depth as the instrument travels through the water.

A box corer takes a broad, shallow core of the seabed sediment. A tube is pushed into the sediment and the pulleys swing down a spade to cut off the sample and hold it while it is brought up.

Long cores are retrieved by a piston corer that is dropped into the seabed. A piston inside the core barrel creates a partial vacuum that enables long cylinders of sediment to be collected.

PENETRATING THE DARK

Oceanography has been compared to a blind man feeling his way across the bottom of a deep puddle with a white stick three and a half miles long. This comparison is still quite apt, although the white stick has undergone many refinements in recent years.

Underwater photography is the most obvious technique for studying the bottom of the ocean. Cameras, both photographic and television, are taken to the seabed in pressure-proof cases, and below depths of about 200 feet electronic flash equipment is used. At great depths, where no light penetrates, the cameras need not incorporate any conventional shutter mechanism but can be exposed by the flash of the light equipment. Stereoscopic photographs are made with two cameras mounted side by side in a cradle with lights. A bottom-finding pinger operates the equipment when the required depth is reached. Television cameras are connected to the equipment on the survey vessel by means of the towing cable. This system has the advantage of allowing the scene to be viewed on a screen at the same time as it is recorded on tape. With such a system the camera can be directed according to what is being observed. Undersea visual work such as this is hampered by a number of disadvantages. The refractivity of the water means that a much narrower field of view is obtained than can be achieved in air. The water absorbs a great deal of the light produced and this has an adverse effect on the final image. Scattering of light from suspended material in the water means that the picture is very hazy and only closeup images are clear. Consequently underwater photography is used mainly for observation of life forms or for very small bottom features such as ripple marks and for the investigation of the extent and density of beds of manganese nodules.

The factors that reduce the distance that light waves travel in water do not generally affect sound waves, and hence systems based on the propagation and reflection of sound are increasingly used for large-scale surveys of the ocean floor.

Echo sounding, in which the length of time that a pulse of sound takes to echo back from a surface to its point of origin is used to determine distances, was developed in 1922, but did not become precise enough for oceanographic work until 1954. Today's equipment can measure depths to an accuracy of about six feet in 18,000. Sub-bottom echo sounding has now been developed in which sediment and rocks several thousand feet below the seafloor can be studied by using low-frequency high-energy acoustic pulses.

Side-scan sonar uses the same principles as echo sounding, except that short pulses are transmitted and received sideways from the ship or from a towed "fish." The first application of this took place in 1957, but since then great advances have been made, and today it is possible to produce sonographs of wide tracts of the seafloor that are as visually impressive as photographs. The pulses are sent out at very short intervals in very narrow bands—the narrower the band the better the resolution—as the ship cruises along. The echo pattern received is traced out on paper by a stylus, and the image is built up a line at a time, like the image on a television screen. The more powerful models can give images of features some 15 miles away. Because of the graphic nature of the results side-scan sonar is popular for geologic investigations, engineering surveys, plotting navigational hazards and for fish finding.

Seismic profiling is used extensively in seabed geologic surveys and is particularly important in the search for oil. Explosions are set off in the water, sending shock waves travelling through it into seabed rocks and to be reflected in part by each different layer of rock that they meet. The reflected shock waves are picked up and analyzed by a string of hydrophones towed behind the survey vessel and a profile of the seabed geology is obtained. An air gun is being used increasingly as a pulse source, as this has less of an effect on the animal life of the sea.

These techniques are seldom used in isolation, but are often combined in a general survey to produce a comprehensive picture of seafloor conditions.

Oceanographic submersibles are used to give scientists a first-hand view of conditions at the seafloor. Underwater photography is used extensively on their dives as the operators can select the features to be photographed and kept as a permanent record.

Oceanographic research vessels use a number of different observational techniques and deploy a variety of devices on their voyages. The equipment used can collect samples, record observations or build up pictures of the seafloor. Although all the techniques illustrated would be used on one voyage they would not all be used at the same time. The exact position of every observation made is important and so several navigational aids are used to locate the ship, including positioning by stars, satellites and radio beacons.

Seabed profile beneath "fish"

Shadow areas where beams do not overlap

Rock outcrop

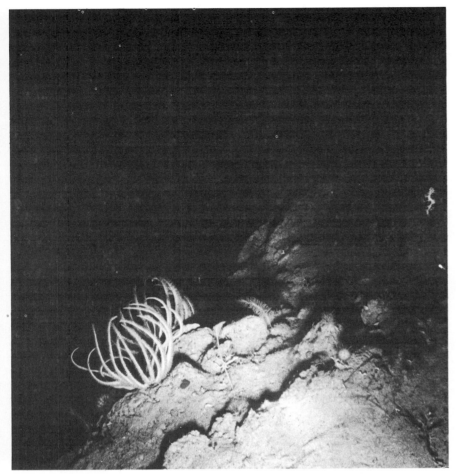

The limitations of underwater photography stem from the fact that light is easily absorbed and scattered by seawater, giving the camera a very short field of view.

Side-scan sonar uses the reflection of sound waves from obstacles to build up a three-dimensional picture of the seabed. A transmitter on a towed device, called a "fish," sends out a narrow beam of acoustic signals. The time taken for the echo to return from the various parts of the seabed struck by the beam is measured and plotted as a line of varying densities on a readout on board the survey vessel. As the "fish" moves it transmits its beams continuously and the readout is built up line by line to produce an image that is as visually satisfying as a photograph. Seabed elements that are hidden from the "fish"—those that lie in the acoustic shadow—register as white on the sonograph, giving the impression of a photographic negative. In practice a number of beams are transmitted at different angles from the "fish" to give as big a coverage as possible. The beams do not overlap and hence long-ranging sonographs show light bands at the top. These features are visible on the sonograph of the rocky outcrop on the seabed off SW England. Signal beams are sent out from both sides of the "fish" and so the full sonograph consists of two pictures as shown on the lower example. A submerged pipe is shown on the upper track and an anchor drag mark on the lower.

Submerged pipe

Path of survey vessel and "fish"

Anchor drag mark

10,000–20,000 ft

Armored coaxial cable

200 ft

Depressor platform

Instrument platform carrying cameras and lights

50–100 ft

Drogue

20–30 ft

Remotely controlled underwater cameras are mounted on sleds along with their lights. They are towed along at the required depth with the help of weights and drogues.

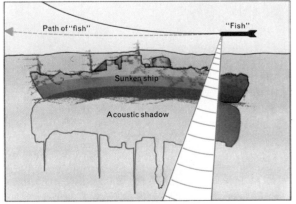

Path of "fish"

"Fish"

Sunken ship

Acoustic shadow

The principle of the side-scan sonar can be easily appreciated when a recognizable object such as a sunken ship is recorded. The sonograph, here shown as a photographic negative, portrays the seabed hidden from the signals from the "fish" as an acoustic shadow.

Gloria (Geological LOng Range Inclined Asdic) was the side-scan sonar fish used until recently by Britain's Institute of Oceanographic Sciences. It housed the transmitter and receiver and passed the signals to the survey ship via the towing cable.

MAN BENEATH THE WAVES

1690 Halley's
diving bell   60 ft

1715 Lethbridge's
armoured diving suit   72 ft

1828 Deane: earliest
diving helmet   80 ft

1872 Rouquayrol/Denayrouze:
development of the
demand valve and the back
air tank supplied from
the surface   100 ft

1878 Fleuss: earliest
self-contained
breathing apparatus   60 ft

1943 Cousteau/Gagnan:
development of the
aqualung   200 ft

1918 Ohgushi's
Peerless Respirator:
air was supplied at the
correct pressure
through the diver's
inflatable belt   300 ft

The development of diving apparatus has allowed the diver to become more mobile and has eventually freed him from the dependence on surface-supplied air. H. A. Fleuss developed the first practicable self-contained diving apparatus. It was able to filter out the carbon dioxide from the exhaled air and replace it automatically with the equivalent amount of oxygen.

In Japan pearl diving is an entirely female occupation. Before the appearance of diving equipment, women, relying only on the air in their lungs, could stay submerged much longer than men.

The traditional hard-hat gear is still used in underwater construction and salvage jobs. But the heavy brass helmet is being substituted for a much lighter fibreglass equivalent.

After diving to depths greater than 33 feet, at which the pressure is twice that on the surface, divers who have been breathing compressed air must ascend slowly to allow the nitrogen dissolved in their blood

Man's exploration and exploitation of the world's oceans has in the past been severely limited by his inability to remain underwater for any length of time. Man's desire to penetrate the deeps is evident in the large number of designs and descriptions of diving equipment—mostly entirely impractical—and the many accounts of submarine activities both factual and fanciful that can be found throughout recorded history. Perhaps the earliest record of a diving operation is that of the Greek Scyllis and his daughter Cyane, who succeeded in cutting the anchor cables of the Persian fleet immediately before the battle of Salamis by swimming underwater to evade the attention of sentries with little more than hollow reeds as snorkels.

The diving bell was the first successful piece of diving equipment to be developed. It took the form of a hollow conical vessel open at the bottom and weighted to prevent the air escaping. Until the invention of Dr Edmund Halley's bell in 1690 the divers were restricted to the amount of air contained in the bell at the time of submersion. Halley's bell was supplied with air through a leather pipe leading from a weighted, air-filled barrel. As one barrel was exhausted, another was lowered from the surface to take its place. At the end of the eighteenth century diving suits were developed, fed with air pumped from the surface.

The invention of the diving helmet in the early nineteenth century led to the development by Augustus Siebe of the open suit in 1819. This suit functioned in much the same way as a diving bell, being open at the waist to allow the escape of excess air. Although the diver had to be careful in his movements lest his suit should fill with water, the suit proved highly successful and was used in salvage work on the *Royal George* in the 1830s. In 1837 Siebe produced the first enclosed suit, which was to remain with subsequent modifications the standard diving equipment for nearly 100 years.

The traditional "hard-hat" equipment consists of a metal helmet with breast plate, heavy weighted boots and a watertight suit. The diver is supplied with a constant flow of air from the surface pumped through his suit and released through a valve in his helmet. As the air pressure at the diver's mouth, that is inside the helmet, determines the air pressure in his lungs, the pressure of the air supplied to the diver must be equal to that of the water in which he is working, otherwise his breathing will be restricted by the higher pressure of the water on his chest.

In 1943 Jacques Cousteau and Emile Gagnan carried out successful tests on a system known as Self-Contained Underwater Breathing Apparatus (SCUBA), in which the diver, wearing only lightweight rubber suiting, carries his air supply in cylinders on his back, thus releasing him from his airlines and heavy, cumbersome gear and allowing him to swim about freely. The air is supplied through a demand valve that operates only when he breathes. The system may be open so that the diver exhales directly into the water or closed so that the air is recycled and no bubble trail is seen. At shallow depths pure oxygen may be breathed, recycled through a carbon dioxide filter; however, below 25 feet pure oxygen is toxic and must be mixed with nitrogen or some inert gas. Air may be breathed safely down to depths of 200 feet, below which nitrogen, which makes up four-fifths of air by volume, becomes narcotic. At greater depths a mixture of oxygen and helium are breathed.

As the diver breathes air or a gas mixture at the same pressure as the surrounding water, nitrogen or the inert gas in the breathing mixture becomes absorbed into the bloodstream. If the diver ascends rapidly, insufficient time is available for this gas to be expelled through the lungs in the usual way and bubbles form in the blood, impeding its circulation. In mild cases this causes pains in the joints, a condition known as the "bends." More severe cases result in unconsciousness or even death. The deeper the dive and the longer the period spent at a particular depth, the greater the decompression time required, and at great depths a decompression time of several days is required. To avoid lengthy decompression periods every time a diver completes a spell of work, the diver may be saturated with inert gas for 24 hours in a pressurized chamber before commencing a dive, and then kept under pressure until he completes the job, resting between spells in the pressurized chamber on the ship's deck. The advantage of this technique is that no matter how long the diver remains at depth he will not absorb any more inert gas and will require only one lengthy decompression period, normally at the rate of one day per 100 feet.

The discovery of oil and other minerals under the seabed has resulted in an enormous increase in the demand for divers, particularly in connection with offshore rigs in areas such as the North Sea.

to be harmlessly released. Exercising the limbs and breathing oxygen at shallow depths aids its expulsion. Divers often use the anchor chain to find their bearings when surfacing.

The acceptance of saturation diving techniques has led to long-period experiments at depths of several hundred feet in which the divers are based in a "habitat" at the same pressure as the surrounding water. On board are sleeping, cooking and living accommodation, enough stores of food, water and oxygen for the duration of the experiment, as well as scientific facilities.

SUBMERSIBLE CRAFT

A small, light submersible, the Johnson *Sea Link*, *right*, is capable of descending to depths of 1500 feet with the aid of a specially equipped surface support ship, *above*. The submersible has an interesting design: at the front is an acrylic dome, which affords the pilot and observer exceptionally good visibility. Lockout facilities and a pressurizing chamber at the back of the craft enable divers to work from *Sea Link*.

The *Pisces* submersible being launched into the water by its support vessel, *left*, is a popular commercial machine used for a wide range of work such as seabed surveys, geological work and pipeline positioning. This hardworking submersible normally carries two men and can descend to depths of at least 2000 feet. This model is for observation purposes only, as it does not have lockout facilities. *Pisces* has recently taken part in experimental rescue operations from submarines.

An early wooden submersible, the *Turtle*, was built in 1776 for military purposes. It was manually operated by one navigator, who also organized the fixing of explosives to the enemy ship.

Underwater exploration has depended on the development of complex technical devices that help man to overcome the physical difficulties of spending prolonged periods of time under the sea. Attempts at producing such apparatus date back as far as the fourth century B.C. when Alexander the Great is believed to have descended beneath the Mediterranean Sea in a vessel resembling an early diving bell. Underwater craft were first used for military purposes in the eighteenth century, when a small submersible, the *Turtle*, built by David Bushnell in 1776, was used against the British in the American War of Independence. In 1863 the submersible *David* was used in the American Civil War and actually succeeded in sinking an enemy ship. Thirty years later Simon Lake constructed the *Argonaut First*—a true submersible in which atmospheric pressure could be maintained and which could move around the seabed on hand-powered wheels. Such machines were among the first to take man with his normal atmospheric environment beneath the sea.

The breakthrough of exploration into the ocean deeps occurred in 1934, when William Beebe and Otis Barton descended to a depth of 3028 feet in Barton's revolutionary bathysphere. This was a heavy steel sphere, which was lowered to the depths of the ocean by a cable payed out from a surface support ship and could not be independently maneuvered. A later version, the bathyscaphe invented by Professor Auguste Piccard, was free of surface cables and overcame the limitations of the earlier bathysphere. The bathyscaphe *Trieste* was used by Piccard for a dive 10,392 feet down off the coast of Italy in 1954 and in 1960 Piccard's son, Jacques, led the ultimate deep dive when *Trieste* touched the ocean bed of the Marianas Trench in the Pacific, about 35,800 feet down. The greatest depths had at last been conquered.

Undoubtedly the most influential concept in underwater exploration has been that of the military submarine. Following the pioneering examples of the *Turtle* and the *David* in the eighteenth and nineteenth centuries respectively, submarines have been developed by many navies to travel faster, at greater depths and farther afield, thus increasing the military strength of their countries. There are two basic types of submarine in existence today: first, the conventional submarine, which uses diesel power while traveling on the surface and battery power while submerged, and second, the nuclear submarine, which is powered by a nuclear engine and can operate for several months at a stretch without the need to refuel. In the future it is likely that this military technology will be used for peaceful purposes to exploit the natural resources of the ocean.

Like the military submarine, the mini-submarine, or submersible, was originally developed for aggressive purposes. However, because submersibles are relatively inexpensive and are very adaptable, scientific and commercial organizations have begun to use great numbers of them in recent years. They are employed in a wide variety of general activities, such as biological, geological and archaeological research and also for specialized tasks, such as the discovery and salvage of an unexploded nuclear bomb, or for seabed surveys of offshore oil fields. In a typical working situation two or three men live, in relative comfort, within a sphere approximately six feet in diameter and work for periods of about eight hours. The depth to which a submersible can descend varies according to the design and type, but different machines go to depths ranging from about 1000 feet to well over 10,000 feet.

Submersibles are very versatile vehicles. Some types, known as diver lockout submersibles, are equipped with a special pressure chamber from which the divers can exit to perform their work and then return to for gradual decompression. A wide range of other specialist equipment can be placed in and around a submersible such as television and still cameras, and remote control manipulators. These features enable the crew to carry out an extensive range of exploratory and mechanical work. The *Ben Franklin* is an example of a submersible specifically designed and equipped for oceanographic research work. With a crew of six it made a voyage which took 32 days, drifting 1444 nautical miles down the Gulf Stream of the Atlantic Ocean in 1969.

The atmospheric diving suit is an even more com-

Nuclear submarines, used mainly for military work, are capable of traveling at great speed underwater for considerable distances and usually accommodate large crews. The submarine has the advantage of being invisible from the surface as it operates independently with no support vessel.

A submersible for deep-sea divers, the *Perry* chamber provides the diver with a base to which he is attached by a line, and with breathing gas. The support ship has a deck compression chamber onto which the *Perry* locks; this can be used for slow decompression or for waiting between dives.

pact method of enabling a man to work underwater, with the added advantage that the diver can surface without having to undergo decompression. The robot-like suit has pressure-tight walls and specially designed articulated joints, which allow flexing of the diver's arms and legs within the suit. Early designs did not function successfully below about 300 feet because the joints became jammed, but in 1930 J. S. Peress developed an efficient suit, which attained fame when used in dives 360 feet down to the wreck of the *Lusitania*, sunk by a German submarine in 1915. The atmospheric diving suit in use today, known as JIM, is based on Peress's concept.

Underwater habitats, where men can live and work for prolonged periods, were once regarded as useful for observation purposes only. However, there is now a new and important role for underwater habitats in offshore oil fields. Wellheads on the seabed are enclosed in a pressure-proof habitat in which men can work. When maintenance work is required on the wellhead the workers are brought down in a freeranging chamber, which locks on to the habitat. The men then transfer and carry out their duties. More such systems to enable technical work to be carried out underwater are being developed.

Diving suits, submersibles, habitats and many other systems are all part of the search to develop better techniques for man to live, work and explore underwater. The necessity to exploit the resources of the world's oceans is increasing and in order to discover and use these resources there must be methods of taking people in safety and comfort deep into the oceans. Scientists, archaeologists and those in search of the important mineral resources must all have the freedom to explore the ocean which submersible technology can provide.

WORKING UNDER THE SEA

The atmospheric diving suit, JIM, is a pressure-resistant, articulated suit made of magnesium alloy. The operator can use this suit at depths of up to 1500 feet and while underwater can perform a large variety of practical tasks.

The first of its type, this system allows heavy equipment such as this cable-burying tractor to remain on the seabed until its work is finished or repairs are needed rather than having to be hauled up and down to the surface. It is operated by a free-ranging command module, which descends and locks on.

A projected system for connecting pipelines on the seabed is illustrated. A spherical habitat is placed around the pipes to be joined; a submarine then descends, locks on to the working habitat and the men transfer. An advantage of such a system is that it could be used at depths beyond the range of divers.

THE LAW OF THE SEA

The limits of maritime jurisdiction have remained a source of conflict between seafaring nations for many centuries. In the seventeenth century two areas of jurisdiction were broadly accepted; the territorial sea, subject to the jurisdiction of the adjacent coastal state, and the high seas, which were regarded as open to all states. The former was a narrow belt between three and six miles wide, sufficient to protect the state from attack but through which foreign vessels had the right of "innocent passage" so long as they in no way threatened the security of the coastal state. Beyond this zone, all states had freedom of navigation and fishing.

The Industrial Revolution brought a great intensification of trade and fishing. Some species, notably some of the whales, began to decline in the nineteenth century—soon to be followed by a growing number of commercial fish species. Fisheries commissions were instituted in an effort to manage the marine fish resource, but, being based on voluntary consent, generally failed to restrict catches to the levels necessary to protect the species. Member states not in agreement with the proposed catch quotas simply withdrew from the agreements. In 1930 the League of Nations attempted to secure agreement for a three-mile territorial sea, but the proposal failed when some states refused to accept the proposed "Contiguous Zone" beyond, in which the coastal states would have exercised limited controls.

Technological advances made during and after World War II vastly increased man's knowledge of the seabed and rapidly made possible the economic exploitation of seabed mineral deposits. The growing awareness of the potential value of offshore deposits resulted, in 1945, in President Truman's proclamation of the United States' exclusive right to exploit its continental shelf.

The First United Nations Conference
In 1958 the newly established United Nations convened a Conference on the Law of the Sea (UNCLOS 1) in Geneva at which the 86 participating states adopted four important conventions.

The Convention on the Territorial Sea and Contiguous Zone did not fix a limit for the territorial sea, but the principles on which baselines were drawn were laid down and a 12-mile contiguous zone was permitted in which customs, sanitary, and fiscal regulations could be enforced. The traditional right of innocent passage was retained.

The High Seas Convention codified four freedoms of the seas: the freedoms of navigation, fishing, overflight and the laying of pipelines and cables, and required that all freedoms be exercised "with reasonable regard for the interests of other states." Any state could register ships with which they could claim a "genuine link" under the exclusive jurisdiction of their flags, but the link was not defined—a vagueness which permits the issuance of flags of convenience.

The Convention on Fishing and the Conservation of the Living Resources of the Sea recognized the interest of a coastal state in maintaining fish stocks beyond its territorial sea. Other states fishing in such regions would be obliged to cooperate in the observance of conservation measures—failing which, the coastal state could impose nondiscriminatory scientifically based measures. While the other three conventions were ratified by about 50 states, this proposal proved more contentious and was accepted by only 34.

The fourth convention confirmed the right of a coastal state to explore and exploit, exclusively, the natural resources of "the submarine areas" on the continental shelf to a depth of 660 feet—and beyond that where the water depth "admits of exploitation." This seaward limit was, therefore, left open—dependent only on the advance of technology in deep-water exploitation. A wide interpretation of this limit was encouraged by the International Court of Justice's pronouncement, in the 1969 North Sea Case, that a coastal state has a right to exploit "the natural prolongation of its landmass under the sea"—a view that encouraged many states to claim the whole of their continental margins on a variety of geophysical and topographical grounds.

The continental margins
The 1958 Continental Shelf Convention confirmed the sovereign rights of coastal states to exploit the submarine areas off their shores, up to, and beyond, 660 feet depth where feasible. No outer limit was defined and many states claim rights over the whole continental margin, including the shelf, slope and rise, on the grounds that it is a natural prolongation of their landmass. This benefits the advanced nations, whose superior technology and financial resources make deep-sea mineral extraction possible.

Straits states
A 12-mile territorial sea would limit 100 straits less than 24 miles wide to right of innocent passage only since they would no longer retain a free high sea corridor. Submarines would be required to navigate on the surface and the states might insist on consent for warships, tankers and dangerous cargoes on the grounds of threats to their security. Maritime powers are consequently demanding free transit through straits.

— Nauru
— W. Samoa
— Tonga

Fishing states
This group includes states with important coastal fisheries and those with distant-water fleets; some, notably Japan and the USSR, have both interests. The former want exclusive rights within a 200-mile Economic Zone with the right to determine the total catch, permitting other states to take only that part of the total not required by their own markets. States with major distant-water interests want to retain historic rights.

Island states
If 200-mile Economic Zones, and rights to exploit the seabed off continental margins, are accepted, some oceanic island states will control vast areas of sea and seabed out of all proportion to their land areas. Anxious to preserve their coastlines from pollution, most press for rights of control over shipping passing through their Economic Zones —a move which is strongly resisted by many of the nations with major shipping investments.

Maritime states
Some states, including Greece and Liberia, register large tonnages of shipping; others, shown on the map above, are themselves dependent on seaborne trade. Most of the maritime states are anxious to preserve the freedom of navigation and are opposed to the enclosure of international straits within 12-mile territorial seas unless freedom of transit is guaranteed. Many also oppose coastal state pollution control.

Shelf-locked states
Some states, both developed and developing, find the seaward extension of their shelf areas blocked by the shelf claims of other states lying either to one or other side of them, or facing them across a sea. These states regard themselves as geographically disadvantaged and therefore entitled to compensation in the form of a share in the revenue derived from the continental margin and from the maximum international area.

Conflicts of Interest
Powerful multinational companies have now evolved the technology of deep seabed exploitation to the point where it is feasible to extract seafloor nodules containing valuable deposits of manganese, cobalt, copper and nickel. Not surprisingly, many less developed states having land-based deposits of these minerals are fearful of the effects on their economies of uncontrolled seabed production. Such states are naturally anxious to secure an agreement under which states lacking the technological resources to exploit the deep ocean floor should nevertheless receive some share of the return on such developments, or be compensated should their own land-based extractive industries suffer from the competition.

In other areas, too, the developing countries demand new international agreements. The advanced technology of distant-water fishing has resulted in the depletion of stocks off many coasts with drastic effects on local fisheries. As the world's sea-lanes have become more congested, the threat of pollution has grown, particularly with the advent of the supertanker, the liquid gas transporter and other specialized ships carrying hazardous chemical cargoes, many of which must pass through narrow straits.

The Third United Nations Conference
Following its establishment of a Seabed Committee to examine the Law of the Sea, the General Assembly of the United Nations called for a moratorium on the exploitation of the seabed beyond the continental shelf and adopted unanimously a Declaration of Principles proclaiming the seabed "the common heritage of mankind," to be exploited under an international regime. Thus, in 1973, the UN convened UNCLOS III with the priority of giving "consideration to ocean space as a whole." A single treaty was called for, based on a "package deal" approach and encouraging states to bargain among themselves—giving way perhaps on some issues in order to secure agreements on others. In a very short time, these negotiations clearly identified a large number of special interest groups—the landlocked states, the geographically disadvantaged states, the maritime states and so on.

Land-locked states
Having no natural access to the sea, the land-locked states are doubly disadvantaged; many are already considered poor and in addition they must secure transit agreements with other states in order to have access to the sea. The states are opposed to proposals to limit them to living resources only of their area and demand a large international area, in which they would be able to participate through membership of the Enterprise.

Archipelagic states
These states, consisting of groups of islands in proximity to each other, propose that the baselines from which their territorial seas and EEZs are drawn up should be lines around the outer limits of the archipelago as a whole. This would enclose vast areas of sea and seabed and would define the enclosed waters as "internal" without even the right of innocent passage. Not surprisingly, the maritime states demand rights of free passage.

In recent years the subdivision of the North Sea has highlighted many of the problems associated with the territorial claims of states grouped around the margins of a partially enclosed sea. The states involved are all shelf-locked, and the delineation of the boundaries has required long and detailed negotiation. The north-south boundary between the British Isles and Europe posed little problem; it is a simple boundary equidistant from both coastlines. The eastern sector, however, posed more difficult problems. Lines of equidistance from the coast would have reduced the German sector to a triangle blocked by the shelf claims of Denmark and the Netherlands lying to either side. Negotiation finally increased the German sector, as shown above, to a more reasonable size with boundaries regarded by the countries concerned as equitable in view of known and estimated resources.

Narrow-shelf states
States may claim to be disadvantaged if their offshore resource zones are less than 40,000 square miles in extent. Their interests are similar to those of the shelf-locked states and they too claim compensatory participation in the exploitation of the continental margins of neighboring states, and in exploitation of the international zone. Many have demanded reduction of areas under national jurisdiction.

Deep seabed exploitation
Several companies, including a number of consortia registered entirely in the developed states of the world, are now capable of exploiting deep-sea deposits. Major international groups include the Kennecott Consortium; Summa Corporation; Deep Sea Ventures; DOMA; Sumitomo; INCO and the AMR Group. Such international groups prefer national licensing or liberal international regulation and oppose tight control.

The developing states
Most developing states are members of the "Group 77"—a special interest group which, confusingly, comprises more than 100 states that consider themselves poor. Within the group the UN has identified 24 states, shown above, as being the least developed. Most are geographically disadvantaged, being land-locked, shelf-locked or limited in coastline. All expect to be specially compensated by the I.S.A.

Problems of pollution
States bordering narrow straits, enclosed seas, main oil tanker routes or offshore oilfields, or with areas that are ecologically or oceanographically fragile, are specially vulnerable to pollution. Canada alone has declared a unilateral Pollution Control Zone of 100 miles for the Arctic. Other states have demanded pollution control within the EEZ with mandatory higher standards for specially vulnerable areas.

The complexity of the task facing the Law of the Sea Conference may be gauged from the numbers taking part; 148 states, each with its own political and economic priorities, are faced with an agenda of nearly one hundred items—many of which are subject to several alternative proposals. The conference established three main committees to consider an international regime to control the exploitation of the seabed beyond the limits of national jurisdiction; to consider issues arising from the Geneva Convention; and to consider preservation of the marine environment, scientific research and the transfer of technology.

Five sessions have been held to date and by 1975 a four-part Informal Single Negotiating Text had been produced. This is not a treaty and is not binding on any state; it does, however, provide a basis for negotiation and was further refined in 1976 to form the Revised Single Negotiating Text—the basis of the most recent, and continuing, negotiations.

Part I of the RSNT proposes an International Seabed Authority which would itself exploit the "common heritage" area in parallel with states and companies under contract to it. Work would proceed under the control of an Enterprise Board and half of each area requested by a state or company would be retained by the Board. Developing states adversely affected by seabed production would be compensated. The proposed ISA would have an Assembly, a Council to balance group interests, a Secretariat and a number of Specialist Commissions. Some of the developed nations already object to the proposed extent of ISA control, while the developing land-locked states would prefer exclusive exploitation by the International Enterprise Body.

Part II proposes an Exclusive Economic Zone 200 miles wide with an inner 12-mile territorial sea. The coastal state would have wide jurisdiction over living and mineral resources of the seabed and water column in the EEZ. The Zone would not have the status of high seas but the traditional freedom of navigation and overflight, and rights of cable-laying and pipe-laying, would be retained. The outer limit of the continental shelf remains undefined, but the shelf is held to include the "natural prolongation" of the landmass beneath the sea, even beyond the 200-mile limit.

The controversial Part III proposes limits on the control to be exercised by coastal states over vessel-source pollution; higher standards for ecologically special areas, and "port state jurisdiction" under which, in certain circumstances, an offending vessel might be prosecuted at its next port of call irrespective of the zone in which the violation occurred. The final part of the RSNT includes a proposal for a Law of the Sea Tribunal for the settlement of disputes.

Future Prospects
The key to progress in these complex international negotiations lies in the nations coming to some agreement on who should exploit the international area and under what terms. That done, many of the other issues would rapidly be resolved. Though the fifth session of the conference appeared to make little real progress on the central deadlocked issues, the recent informal proposal by the United States, that methods of funding the Enterprise Body should now be explored, and that the regime should be reviewed in 25 years, may provide the basis for compromise.

The Law of the Sea is in a state of turmoil; old freedoms have been called into question without, as yet, being replaced by any firm international treaty. The legal status of the Revised Single Negotiating Text is obscure, despite attempts by many nations to clarify its standing, but many of the participating nations are already implementing some parts of the text—notably the proposed 200-mile fishery zone—in the belief that concensus has been effectively achieved.

Though frustrating, and at times apparently divisive, the importance of the Law of the Sea Conference must not be underestimated: the future of man's exploitation of the seas, and indeed the harmonious relations of those nations who depend on them, may depend on the acceptance, by all, of a Law of the Sea.

THRESHOLD OF THE FUTURE

City dwellers of the future might well find themselves living, working and relaxing in a totally new environment—at sea—if the futuristic design concepts represented by Sea City ever become a reality. The model city is the product of several years' research by Pilkington Bros. of the U.K., and was undertaken as an investigation of the design criteria and materials science involved in building a city at sea. A number of suitable sites were designated in the southern North Sea off the coast of East Anglia.

Marine engineering and technology are on the threshold of a new era in which the concept of terrestrial engineering simply transferred into water is giving way to a completely new approach. The dense fluid medium of the sea and its waves subject structures to powerful accelerative forces, which act on the entire volume of the structure rather than just on its surface as does a wind or current. Ordinary breakwaters depend on surface effects to destroy or reflect waves: the dynamic breakwater consists of very light spherical buoys tethered just below the surface and forced to move by volume forces—dissipating between 50 and 500 times as much wave energy as they would if they were held rigidly against the wave motion.

Natural land areas
Polder areas
Sand dunes
Fresh water
Sea water
● Major towns
━ Primary sea dykes
─ Canal or river
▪ Pump station

Heavy erosion of the soft lake banks threatened the rich towns of western Holland and prompted the Dutch, as early as the 17th century, to drain many of the lakes and so gain back from the sea land lost over a period of many hundreds of years. In the 20th century, however, this essentially defensive attitude has changed to a more aggressive approach. Plans were made to reclaim part of the Zuiderzee and gain, in one major operation, more land than had ever been inundated by the sea. In order to protect the newly reclaimed areas, and the vulnerable coast, a huge barrier dam more than 18 miles long was constructed to separate the Zuiderzee from the North Sea. This dam, and the smaller dykes used to isolate the polder areas, are constructed from sand and clay with a protective outer sheath made of brush matting and stone. All stages in the construction of a dyke can be seen in the photograph, *left*. Most of the early polders were for agricultural use, but recently the emphasis has changed to housing and industry to take the overspill from the West Holland conurbation.

The great oceans covering the face of our planet form a common link between the continents, compromising their environmental isolation and today seriously testing the sovereignty, laws, institutions and philosophies of all coastal and island nations. Future decades will witness a continuing struggle to resolve and reshape human codes to accommodate these vast, featureless realms for which law must eventually provide a framework of order for human actions.

In much the same way the oceans link the islands of man's intellect—the specialized disciplines of science, technology, politics and morality—testing their sovereignty, laws, dogmas, institutions and purposes. Now that the human race has become a force almost as powerful as many of the great natural planetary forces, ocean scientists must learn how the many different disciplines of the oceans fit together in order to understand and control the emergence of man as a geochemical, geophysical and geobiological force. The lesson that is being learned is that the physical forces, the tides, currents, sediments and seafloor, the chemicals, atmosphere, spinning earth and countless living creatures of the sea, act and interact with complete disregard for those artificial islands onto which man has fragmented his knowledge and understanding.

Thus both the science and politics of the sea will necessarily advance toward a growing realization that it is interaction on this planet, rather than the components of this planet, that constitute the vital problems—that the whole is not only vastly greater than, but also totally different from, the sum of its parts and that it is absolutely vital for human survival that the entire immense picture be viewed as a whole.

Present uses of the oceans too often suffer from single-minded intentions and viewpoints without regard for the interactions or the whole. Marine fishery studies, for example, are commonly conducted as though the species of fish involved were a population in isolation and as if controls can be based on the statistics alone with scant attention to the activities and responses of the prey, predators, competitors and parasites sharing the same environment. Future studies and regulations must come from an understanding of the broader picture, yet in the few current attempts to do so, the broader picture is frequently one transplanted from observations of processes on land—a concept fraught with pitfalls.

The living and physical systems of the seas and those of the land have evolved under the same natural laws, from the same initial bequest of cosmic material, and in response to the same broad episodes of solar and planetary evolution. Yet, as we now view these two systems, they most often strongly differ in the way they respond to man's actions. When these differences are better understood, the utilization of the marine resource will proceed with far fewer cases of environmental damage, and economic waste, and with many more examples of overall benefit.

For example, it will be better recognized that the sea is a hungry realm, overall not exceptionally productive, and that its food economy is highly dependent on—and specialized for—the recycling of organic waste material as food. Consequently the domestic wastes from coastal cities judiciously discharged offshore may be thought of as food for the sea's inhabitants rather than as pollutants—a partial recompense to the sea for the vast quantities of food taken from it. In similar fashion, the cooling water intakes of power plants situated on steep coasts may be so designed that they enrich the surface waters with the chemical fertilizers normally generated and trapped deep below the sunlit zone, far out of reach of the mass of marine life.

In order to evaluate the human impact on the ocean it is necessary to know the extent of natural changes and fluctuations. Special sedimentary deposits record the history of climate, currents and the populations of many creatures year by year for millennia. When more of these deposits have been studied and decoded there may emerge a meaningful understanding of the nature, range and perhaps the causes of natural fluctuations. The oceans appear either to control long-term weather patterns or to predict them. Already, spectacular long-range weather forecasts are emerging from the study of temperature changes in the sea. As these interrelationships become better understood, and as we can look back on their records over thousands of years, it should become possible to forecast those seasons, years and decades that will depart from the norm. Periods of drought, cold or flood—of dearth or abundance of crops or fishes—will be forecast: the seven fat years and seven lean of Joseph's time repeated in future terms. Studies of sedimentary records may finally yield that most vital piece of knowledge for the future welfare of mankind—the time scale, events and even the causes involved in the termination of an interglacial period.

Like our faulty understanding of the living systems of the seas, the engineering and technology of the marine realm suffers from the delusion that it is little more than land technology appropriately baptized with seawater. Yet there are many fundamental differences. Unlike forces acting on structures on land, those acting on objects in the sea are often dominated by effects that stem from changes in the velocity of the medium rather than from steady pressures. For large objects in the sea, these rapidly fluctuating forces are dominant. As this difference becomes more widely appreciated, marine structures will be more safely designed—often in totally new and unconventional ways. New and better ways of controlling storm waves, even in the deep open seas, and vast projects for transporting materials, will become more common. Dynamic breakwaters will protect coasts and harbors and offshore structures. Tabular icebergs transported from the Antarctic will supply fresh water to needy coastal areas, so removing the agelong ravages of drought.

The last decade has brought three new perspectives relating to the future of mankind.

First, the planet earth is a unique environment and alone in the solar system in possessing an abundance of living things. The human race must learn to solve its problems alone without any example of superior technology from extra-terrestrial civilizations.

Second, the most vital of environmental conditions, a viable sun, will undoubtedly provide a steady source of energy for at least 4000 million years. Our present foresight in planning, and the period of stability of our institutions, appear ridiculous in the light of this vast span. It is interesting to speculate on the possibility of an intelligent civilization elsewhere in the universe, at roughly our present level of understanding of astrophysics, finding themselves faced with a sun in the final stages of senescence.

Third, the new knowledge of continental drift,

As man progresses into ages of increasingly advanced technology his interest in the past history of his own race grows apace and that same technology that may feed, clothe and house him in future generations has provided the tools with which his past can be decoded.

Diving technology, underwater photography and techniques for dating and preserving antiquities have opened a rich new field of underwater archaeological research. In this photograph an ancient wreck off Kyrenia is marked out for detailed study.

seafloor spreading and plate tectonics presents us with a hitherto totally unprecedented level of certainty about the behavior of the surface of the earth over the next several million years. This knowledge emerges at a time when man is also confronted with the necessity to plan for just such a period of time, the time involved in the safe disposal of his most perilous substances— long-lived radioactive wastes. It may now be possible to show that, if injected far below the sediments of the ocean basins, these substances might be held out of range of living things until decay has neutralized them.

Just as the sea is a challenge to science as we now know it, so is it a challenge to our institutions as they now exist. Understanding of the seas, and the welding together of fragmented disciplines into a comprehensive science, should reflect upon other sciences, education and our social institutions. Education will come

to discover how to nurture and develop attributes of the intellect still too often neglected—conceptualization, intuition, curiosity, judgement and perhaps even intellectual fervor. With these examples, our social sciences will come to recognize the necessity of assembling their own disciplines into a coherent whole for the guidance of mankind.

It was largely the challenge of the sea that brought medieval man out of the dark ages and into the modern world. His discoveries of the oceans and continents, his development of navigation instruments and ships, gave him a new confidence in his ability to surpass the achievements of the ancients, the darkness of his times, and the inadequacies of his institutions. The sea again challenges our sciences and our institutions and presents again those same opportunities to guide ourselves out of the present age into the future.

LIFE IN THE OCEANS

Schooling is an important feature of the life-style of many species of fish, here illustrated by the silversides of the family Atherinidae. The schooling instinct is most prevalent among smaller species, often prey species forming the primary food source for predatory species higher in the food chain. By contrast, many predatory fish like the barracuda tend to live solitary lives. The schooling instinct and behavior have been closely studied in a number of species, but while their manifestations are well known, the reasons for them are not fully understood. Protection in numbers would seem to be one obvious advantage; an ever-present breeding population not dependent on chance meetings another. Recent research has also suggested that individuals tend to feed more readily and learn more quickly in the school environment.

PLANKTON:THE BASIS OF LIFE

Noctiluca scintillans, dinoflagellates (0.06 in)

Ceratium tripos, dinoflagellates (90 microns)

Biddulphia sinensis, diatoms (200 microns)

Phytoplankton are the minute plants, usually single celled, that drift passively with the movement of the oceans. As primary producers they have a key role in the ecosystems of the sea, but large masses of plant plankton can only occur in the upper zone of the ocean as light is necessary for the photosynthetic process. Diatoms and dinoflagellates dominate the phytoplankton—diatoms in cold waters and dinoflagellates in tropical and subtropical areas.

Dinoflagellate plants caused this remarkable discoloration of the water, known as a red tide, when a combination of favorable conditions produced a massive bloom of a species, resulting in concentrations of over 500,000 cells in every two pints of water. The toxic effects of such bloom can affect the area's animal life.

The clear blue water of the oceans and the green of the coastal seas may appear lifeless to us, but floating within them, at all depths from the surface to the deep ocean floor, are complex communities of tiny plants and animals on whose activities the life of all larger oceanic animals depends: these are the plankton communities drifting with the movements of the water.

In the open oceans the source of energy for the ecosystem is fundamentally different from that for terrestrial ecosystems. On land the ecosystem is dominated by large plants, but only a fraction of their production of organic material is consumed by herbivores, usually sizable animals; most of the organic production rots away by the action of fungi and bacteria. Only along the margins of the sea, where large fixed seaweeds and other algae occur close to the beach, do marine ecosystems resemble those on land. The ecosystems of the open ocean are fueled solely by the energy fixed from sunlight by myriad microscopic plant cells, known as phytoplankton, which float freely in the upper, lighted surface waters. Almost all of the organic matter they produce is rapidly grazed and digested by hosts of tiny herbivores, ranging from flea to mosquito size. Thus, the biomass

of herbivores, at any one time, in relation to plant biomass, can be very much higher in the ocean than it is on land, and hence the whole production process is more direct and efficient.

So, oceanic plankton ecosystems are dominated numerically by many species of single-celled plants, some passive and others highly mobile, and small colonies or "chains" of similar cells, which are fed upon by a host of herbivorous planktonic animals of many different animal groups, the most abundant being the small crustacea known as copepods. Feeding in turn on these herbivores is a wide range of carnivorous creatures, from the great baleen whales and basking sharks, which strain plankton directly from the water, to tiny planktonic animals that hunt and capture other zooplankton. These two feeding styles—straining, or filtering, and capturing—are predominant, and a great diversity of filtering mechanisms to remove small particles of food suspended in the water has evolved. All of these mechanisms demand energy, therefore it is critical to filter feeders that their food particles should be in a sufficiently high concentration to supply more energy after digestion than is expended in capturing them. Crustacean filtering mechanisms generally comprise a set of fanlike appendages armed with closely

set radiating hairy spines, which sweep particles from a current of water set up by the other appendages. The remarkable gelatinous salp, an inch or so long, constantly produces a rolling curtain of mucilaginous net, which is reingested for the sake of the phytoplankton cells it traps; this relatively large herbivore is thus capable of feeding on the very smallest individual plant cells. Many planktonic carnivores are armed with clawlike grasping organs, some with no parallel on land; the pelagic siphonophores, both those which float upon the surface and those which actively swim in midwater, trail below them long transparent tentacles, which are able to retract toward the mouth when prey is stunned and captured.

Few planktonic organisms are long-lived and life turns over rapidly in the pelagic realm: the plant plankton would double in quantity by simple cell division in one or two days if they were not continually being strained out and digested by herbivores. Copepods have a generation time of a few weeks in low latitudes throughout the year, and in midlatitudes during summer. The salps, on encountering suitable conditions, grow at a fantastic ten percent each hour, so that a new generation occurs every few days and a vast swarm can develop within a few weeks.

Sagitta sp., an arrowworm (3.5 in)

Physophora hydrostatica, a siphonophore (2 in)

Doliolum denticulatum, a salp (0.3 in)

Thysanopoda, a euphausiid (1.2 in)

Acanthometron, a radiolarian (0.08 in)

The term "zooplankton" describes the vast assemblage of animals that floats passively with the movements of the water. These creatures, from a wide variety of animal groups, include the main herbivores of the ocean converting plants into animal protein. Thus, they form a key link between the primary producers, phytoplankton, and larger marine life. Some zooplankton, such as arrow-worms, Chaetognatha, are carnivorous, feeding on other planktonic animals. Crustaceans, notably copepods and euphausiids, are the most important and abundant group.

Temora longicornis, copepods (0.05 in)

Cavolina tridentata, a pteropod (0.3 in)

There is no way to hide in the open ocean except by becoming invisible—a defense adopted by a great many planktonic animals; their bodies are as transparent as the clearest glass and often only their eyes, which require the presence of visual pigment in order to be functional, can be seen. Characteristically, small planktonic plants and animals tend to have a grotesque form because of the wealth of spines and long appendages attached to their bodies. Formerly thought to assist flotation, these features are now believed also to protect the owner from capture and filtration by other organisms to whom a spiny plant cell appears to be a larger particle than it actually is.

That the plankton ecosystem is effective in utilizing its living space is attested to by the great abundance of organisms that under some circumstances can color the ocean green, brown or even red; the clearer and bluer seawater appears, the less planktonic life it contains. Although difficult to calculate satisfactorily, it seems probable that planktonic plants produce at least as much plant material as the total production of land plants, wild as well as cultivated. As on land plant production is very variable and the high or low fertility of an area can determine the type of zooplankton community it supports.

Copepod

Medusa

Mysid

Lateral transportation of plankton is an almost entirely passive process depending on the current and eddy systems of the oceans, but in the vertical plane very active migrations occur both daily and seasonally. At dusk, almost everywhere in the deep ocean, a dense layer of planktonic animals, such as copepods and euphausiids, rises from a depth of 660–1600 feet to join the abundant plankton in the surface layers, passing through depths where little plankton occurs; at dawn it again descends, thus remaining always in the dark. Within the surface layers, and in shallower seas, similar but shorter migrations take place each night: the animals follow darkness upward to the zone of rich plant food, lighted by the sun during the day. In high latitudes, many species overwinter at as much as 3300 feet down to rise into the productive, lighted zone again each spring. The benefits that each species obtains from daily and seasonal migrations are complex, poorly understood and the subject of much scientific debate among biologists studying the basic processes of marine life.

FEEDING AND BREEDING

No bigger than a grain of rice, *Calanus finmarchicus* is still one of the largest of the planktonic copepods. Currents of water are swept through the filter chambers, where tiny food particles are extracted.

The queen scallop, *Chlamys operculus*, filters incoming water over the gills; fine food particles are removed and passed to the labial palps for sorting before they pass into the mouth.

The entire body of the sponge is used as a food filter. Water is continuously pumped in through a network of minute pores, *right*; microscopic food particles are extracted and the water expelled.

Five teeth, controlled by a complex set of muscles, ring the mouth cavity on the underside of the common sea urchin, *Echinus esculentus*. Spines, hydraulically operated tube feet and sensitive pedicellariae project from the shell.

Gliding over the surface of algal growths, herbivorous sea snails scrape their food from the rocks using a tough filelike radula, which protrudes from the mouth. The similarly equipped carnivorous whelk, *Buccinum undatum*, *left*, uses the foot to hold its prey while boring a hole in the shell.

The traveler flying over, or sailing across, any of the world's great oceans will gain little idea of the teeming life they contain. Sea travelers are often impressed by this apparent barrenness, but could they pause and closely examine the water they would find that in general it is just as productive as the land. Certainly some areas are less rich in life than others, but at best the ocean's turnover of energy is comparable with that of a tropical forest.

The oceans hold many advantages for life. First, they offer the dimension of depth, enabling resident life forms to move vertically as well as horizontally. On land, only birds, bats and insects have this degree of freedom and even they are tied to the land surface by their ultimate dependence on plant food growing in the soil. Second, the dense waters of the ocean offer physical support. Within the protective medium of the sea, a rigid structure is quite unnecessary and many marine organisms are so delicate that their bodies collapse if they are removed from the water. Sea water also supports great bulk; giant squid may reach lengths of 98 feet or more, while the giant clam, Tridacna, may grow to four feet in width and weigh as much as 510 pounds. Third, the seas contain all the elements essential to life. Generally these are taken up by microscopic plants, which then form the base for the ocean food chain, but some organisms are able to absorb their mineral needs direct from the water. Last, the sea acts as a buffer. Marine animals are spared the rigors of temperature change found on

land, or the abrasive effect of windblown dust; consequently few marine creatures require a tough outer skin.

As food in the open sea occurs mainly in the form of small particles, complex food chains develop, based on microscopic plants taking their energy direct from sunlight. These are combed from the water by countless millions of tiny animals, smaller in size than the head of a pin, which are in turn eaten by the next rank of feeders, and so on. Each species has its own feeding technique, often highly specialized. The food particles are too small to be caught individually, so many organisms strain their food from the water using filtering methods. Some, like the herbivorous copepods, achieve this by rowing movements of the limbs, which, being densely covered with fine hairs, trap diatoms and other minute plants as they swim. The water movements created by this action also ensure a constant supply of oxygen to the animal, which therefore feeds, swims and breathes by the same action. Larger carnivorous euphausiid shrimps feed on the copepods, combing them from the water using similar techniques. At each level in the feeding web there are divergent species— carnivorous copepods that feed on minute larvae and even parasitic forms that may be almost as large as their hosts. At the uppermost level huge squid pursue and devour fast-swimming fish and are themselves preyed on by toothed whales, notably the sperm whale.

The bodily forms of sea creatures reflect their ways of

life. Beautifully streamlined squid shoot through the water by jet propulsion, sweeping aside the myriad tiny creatures suspended in the water. Many of the minute organisms are covered with spines, which may be partly protective but also act like water skis—spreading the animal's weight and so reducing its tendency to sink through the water. Animals of the seabed, whether in deep or shallow water, are designed for a sedentary existence. They may be radially symmetrical, a sure sign of a low level of activity, and may hunt their food in a leisurely fashion like the echinoderms or simply wait for the currents to carry it within range. A great variety of burrowers and crawlers inhabits the seabed sediments, constantly reworking them to extract the minute food particles they contain.

Many of the tiny creatures of the sea lead a double life. The minute hatchlings from the countless eggs and spores released into the water may be quite unlike their parents. They spend the first few weeks or months of their lives as members of the plankton, carried far and wide by the ocean currents. In contrast, all levels of parental care may also be found, from the crabs which carry their eggs until they hatch as larvae, to the starfish and brittle stars, which incubate their young in special brood pouches until they emerge as miniature versions of the adults. Few, however, can match the devotion of the female octopus, who guards her eggs without pause even for food until she expires through starvation and exhaustion at about the time her young emerge into the marine environment.

Virtually sessile, the beadlet anemone, *Actinia equina*, extends the range of its feeding activity by means of tentacles armed with stinging cells. These tentacles, which surround the mouth at the top of the stout body, ensnare passing prey and cram it into the anemone's central digestive cavity. The anemone, *left*, is eating a goby.

Starfish will frequently open and feed on bivalves. Attaching its battery of tube feet to the prey, the starfish operates them in relays until the shells are forced apart. Its narrow stomach is immediately everted through the opening to digest the flesh inside.

METHODS OF REPRODUCTION

Invertebrates reproduce in many different ways. Very simple animals can reproduce by a process known as "budding"; a part of the parent body is reorganized to form another individual. Seaslugs, the Opistho-branchia, are among the most prolific of invertebrate egg layers, depositing huge numbers of eggs in feathery coils, in wide ribbonlike bands, or in twisting spirals. Some animals, such as crabs, lobsters and starfish, lay eggs which pass through an intermediary planktonic stage. These larval creatures are an important constituent of zooplankton.

Seaslug, *Doto fragilis*, and egg spirals

Larva of corysteid crab

Budding of soft coral, *Alcyonium* sp.

Ribbonlike bands of seaslug eggs

Larva of starfish, *Asterias rubens*

LIVING FOSSILS OF THE SEA

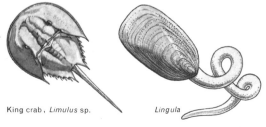

King crab, *Limulus* sp.   *Lingula*

Despite the constant motion of the seas, the marine environment is one of great stability. The geologic record does, certainly, disclose temperature fluctuations in the past, which may have caused the extinction of some animal groups, but a number of creatures flourishing today appear to be among nature's greatest successes. Perhaps the best-known example is the Coelacanth—a fish thought to have been extinct for more than 65 million years until it was rediscovered in 1939 in the Indian Ocean. The invertebrates, however, provide a number of even more dramatic survival stories. The horny shelled brachiopod *Lingula* survives in great abundance in a few locations in the Indian and Pacific oceans, especially where sewage outflow from the land provides a plentiful food supply. Fossils of almost identical species are known from rocks of the late Cambrian period, about 525 million years ago. King crabs, *Limulus*, which today inhabit the warm waters around the coasts of Australia and North America, and come inshore to spawn in such numbers that in some areas they are collected for use as fertilizer on the fields, have remained virtually unchanged since the Carboniferous period, about 380 million years ago. These, and many other species, have survived far beyond the expectation of life of most animals.

METHODS OF MOVEMENT

Locomotion is a characteristic of all animals, but the creatures of the sea display far greater variety in their methods of movement than is found on land. Some sea animals may be totally sedentary during their adult lives, cemented to the seabed and incapable of shifting their position in the least degree, but even these inactive creatures will have spent the juvenile or larval stages of their lives as active members of the marine community.

Many of the smaller animals, living as they do in the slowly moving currents of the ocean, allow themselves to be carried passively in the water. Such movements as they make serve mainly to allow them to keep station and not be swept to some entirely unsuitable area. Some creatures are propelled passively, by the wind. Flotillas of Portuguese men-of-war and By-the-wind sailors may be encountered in the warmer oceans, supported at the surface of the water by a gas-filled float, which also acts as a sail to transport them across the sea. Occasionally they may be blown off course to be cast up on cool temperate shores, where they quickly perish. Flotation by means of gas-filled bladders is used by some siphonophores, but these are mainly for the

maintenance of hydrostatic balance below the surface of the water. Some fish eggs float, but their buoyancy is generally achieved from enclosed oil droplets rather than gases.

A far more important method of locomotion among small animals is by the use of cilia. These short and usually densely packed hairlike structures beat in unison to draw the animal through the water. Sometimes they cover the creature completely, but more often they are arranged in bands, as in the larvae of annelids or mollusks. In the ctenophores, the cilia are fused to make eight rows of plates, which flicker rhythmically—often glowing with the colored light of their luminescence, which makes them some of the most beautiful animals of the sea. In other organisms one or two long threadlike flagellae beat frenetically, in some cases drawing, in others pushing, the tiny living organism through the water. Among invertebrates, sinuous movements like those of a swimming fish are very rare, although they are found in the "tadpole" larvae of ascidians.

Jet propulsion is a recent invention as far as man is

Pulsating gently through the warm waters of Florida and the West Indies, the jellyfish *Cassiopeia* demonstrates a method of locomotion common to many members of the group. The flattened, round bell, which may grow to more than three feet in diameter, is relaxed and opened to fill with water and is then contracted to force the water out and "lift" the animal through the water. *Cassiopeia* does not have a single main mouth, as do most jellyfish, but feeds in an unusual manner—turning over onto its back and exposing to the food-bearing surface currents a mass of bushy arms equipped with countless minute mouthlike openings.

The file shell, *Lima scabra*, swims by rhythmically contracting the valve-closing muscle. Each time the shell closes, water is expelled, sending the animal backward. At rest, the shell always lies on the right, or lower, valve. *Lima* has a double row of slender tentacles, which always protrude from the shell aperture.

Streamlined body and jet propulsion make the squid *Pyroteuthis* one of the most successful and abundant mollusks. The muscular mantle fills with water then contracts powerfully, sending a stream of water from the tubelike siphon and shooting the squid at high speed in the opposite direction.

concerned, yet many marine invertebrates were using a similar method of locomotion more than 600 million years ago. However, in contrast with the gas-propelled man-made machines, the propellant is always a jet of water. Some bivalve mollusks can exert themselves briefly in this manner to hop out of danger, but jellyfish and the medusa stages of some of their smaller relatives swim in this way all the time, and can be seen pulsating gently through the water. Squid and their relatives have strong, muscular bodies and they swim powerfully and fast by jet propulsion, in some cases moving fast enough to rise out of the water and skim for some distance across the surface. On the seabed, limbs and limblike appendages are often used for locomotion, but perhaps the most extraordinary way of walking is that employed by the echinoderms. These animals use small extensible bladders, called tube feet, which protrude through the hard outer body wall when seawater is pumped into them.

Most of the small invertebrates of the open seas are colorless; transparent as glass, they may, if plant feeders, show a green or yellow streak of gut crammed with colorful algae. Among larger animals the colors have a camouflaging effect when the creatures are seen in their natural environment, although sometimes bright colors act as a warning to would-be predators that their owner is unpalatable or poisonous. In the surface waters of the sea many animals are counter-shaded—darker above than below—a simple device that makes them match the dark waters when seen from above and indistinct against the light when viewed from below. Many middle-water crustaceans are red, and so appear black against a background from which red light is absent, while creatures of the greatest depths may be pale in color or even black; in the eternal darkness of the abyss, color is immaterial.

The senses of creatures of the sea are akin to those of land animals. Many small organisms have an allover smell-taste sense, which tells them of the general presence of food, but most have well-developed sense organs beyond this. Long antennae are organs of touch or smell and together with hairs or spines on the body may act as pressure receptors to inform of the presence of food or foes. Some may even act as sound receptors, for water transmits sound very well and many crustaceans in particular are noisy, making creaking or snapping sounds according to their kind. Inhabitants of the twilight zone often have large, well-developed eyes adapted to utilize every scrap of light in the near darkness. The eyes of squid are very similar to those of mammals and the large brains and complex nervous systems of cephalopods are probably the main reason for their abundance and success in the oceans.

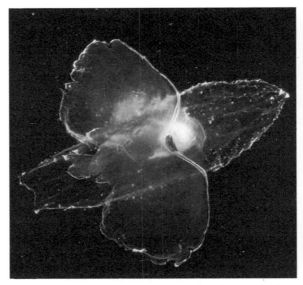

The tiny pteropod *Cymbulia peroni* is a member of the gastropod, or snail, group of animals, but the characteristically muscular foot, instead of being used for walking, is expanded into two winglike flaps with which the snail "flies" through the water. Of the several species of "flying" snail, some have lost their shells during their evolution; others retain a vestigial shell.

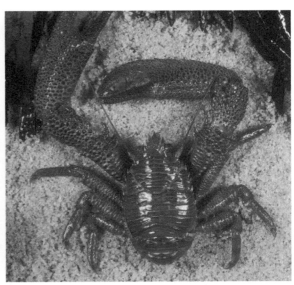

The squat lobster, *Galathea squamosa*, is a member of the group arthropoda, whose name, meaning "jointed limbs," reflects their most characteristic feature. The limbs may be specialized in a variety of ways, but in *Galathea* they are adapted to a predatory existence, crawling among rocks and weeds on the seabed and shore. The forelimbs carry massive pincers with which the lobster grips its prey.

Comb jellies, also graphically called seagooseberries, are delicate, transparent, pelagic organisms widely distributed throughout the world's oceans. Eight rows of fine comblike plates traverse the body from the broad upper surface, where a small cavity encloses a sense organ, to the narrower lower end, where the mouth is located. The combs alternately rise and then beat strongly down in a continuous undulating rhythm, which propels the animal through the water. Two long sticky tentacles may be withdrawn into sheaths at either side of the body, or be extended to gather food.

Gaudy colors and strange forms mark the seaslugs, or nudibranchs, as some of the most bizarre mollusks. All have lost their shells entirely and in compensation have evolved a variety of defensive devices. In many species, bright colors warn predators that the slug is poisonous or distasteful due to acid secretions in the body. Members of the Aeolid group feed on coelenterates, digesting the animals' bodies but retaining their stinging cells intact and incorporating them into the surface tissues of their own bodies. Other slugs repel attackers by regurgitating their internal organs—quite able to retire and grow them anew. *Chromodoris quadricolor, above left*, seeks protection in its conspicuous coloring, but the sea hare, *Aplysia, above*, relies on subdued, mottled colors to render it barely visible against the seabed. Others have evolved even more bizarre body forms to escape the attentions of predators, and the branching seaslug, *Dendronotus frondosus*, is so ornately frilled and branched that it can hardly be distinguished from the irregular background of the marine vegetation and seaweed-encrusted rocks among which it browses.

The five arms of the starfish *Asterias rubens* are linked by a vascular system in which water is drawn into the body and then pumped into the tube feet. The animal feeds, moves and rights itself, *above*, using the sucker action of the feet.

DESIGN FOR SURVIVAL

The term "fish" is commonly used to describe three very different groups of marine creatures. The hagfish and lampreys, most primitive of all vertebrates, are simple wormlike animals that lack the paired fins common to all other fish. Their internal skeleton is cartilaginous and, although they have a well-developed skull, the mouth is not supported by a lower jaw. Instead, the horny teeth are set in a plate at the front of the head and the animals feed with a rasping action, which restricts them to the role of scavengers or to a parasitic way of life.

Sharks and their relatives form a larger and more important group containing about 500 species, some of which are extremely abundant in tropical seas. They too have cartilaginous skeletons, only occasionally hardened with calcium salts, but many other differences exist between them and the third group—the true fish, or bony fish. They are immediately distinguished by their skin, which, instead of scales, carries dermal denticles—toothlike structures of bone and enamel. They have up to seven pairs of unprotected gill openings and their paired fins stand out from the body like hydroplanes. The hind fins of the male shark bear "claspers"—grasping organs that hold male and female together during mating to ensure the internal fertilization of the eggs.

Some sharks lay a small number of large yolk-filled eggs, often protected by horny cases; others retain the eggs in the uterus and produce live young, which may be nourished before birth on a diet of egg yolk. In some species the strongest of the young may survive by cannibalizing the weaker embryos in the uterus, while in others a placenta similar to that of a mammal is developed and the embryo is fed directly by the female. All members of the shark group are carnivores, although some, like the skates, are specialized to feed on mollusks and the mantas on plankton. Typically, however, they feed on medium- or large-sized prey, which they slash with their sharp triangular teeth. The smallest sharks grow to about one and a half feet in length, but most are considerably larger. Contrary to popular belief, man is not a significant element in the shark's diet: that sharks do attack man is undeniable, but the reason is obscure, as human flesh in general appears unpalatable to most species. The two largest sharks, the basking shark and the whale shark, which may grow to 59 feet in length, are both filter feeders, the former straining minute plankton from the water while the latter filters small fish.

The bony fish, which make up by far the largest

group, are characterized by a fully ossified skeleton, that is, one consisting of bone rather than cartilage. They are generally protected by overlapping scales set in the skin and the gills are covered by a bony plate. The fins vary greatly in size and shape, but are all much more flexible than those of the sharks and can be folded back against the body. Above all, in nearly all fish, swimming ability is greatly enhanced by the presence of a swim bladder. This gas-filled bag is adjusted to make the fish weightless at its natural swimming depth; the fish can rest or "hover" motionless in the water, whereas the shark, lacking any such buoyancy device, sinks as soon as it stops moving forward through the water.

Most bony fish produce vast numbers of eggs, which are fertilized externally by the male and, with the exception of a few shallow-water species, parental care of the young is unknown. The largest bony fish rarely exceed ten feet and most are very much smaller than the majority of sharks. Their smaller size, however, and their variety of shape have enabled the fish to exploit a great range of niches in the ocean. Most marine fish are carnivores and occupy the higher levels of the food chain. Some grub on the sea floor for worms and mollusks; others catch small invertebrates in midwater, sometimes straining them from the water by means of horny combs called gill rakers, attached to the gill bars. Some of the most specialized feeders are found in coral reef environments, where they gnaw the polyps from their stony homes with tough, protuberant mouths. Fast-moving predators of the upper waters, like the tuna, marlin and mackerel, are perfectly streamlined and have crescent-shaped tail fins. Slower-moving species like the cod inhabit lower levels, while the most extreme forms of bodily modification are found in the flattened bottom-dwelling species like plaice and halibut and, even more bizarre, in the strange and alien forms of the deep abyssal fish.

THE CARTILAGINOUS FISH

Cartilaginous fish, the Chondrichthyes, include two major groups; the sharks, skates and rays (Elasmobranchii) and the chimaeras (Holocephali). There are about 500 species—varied in form and in life-style, but all characterized by the cartilaginous skeleton.

"TRUE," OR BONY FISH

The bony fish, Osteichthyes, are possibly the most numerous of all vertebrates, with between 20,000 and 25,000 species. They may be flesh eaters, plant eaters or omnivorous and a bewildering variety of forms exists, developed to equip the fish for many different life-styles. As well as a bony skeleton, most share certain other characteristics: respiration through gills protected by external covers, a scaly skin, paired pectoral and pelvic fins and an air-filled bladder rendering them weightless in water.

Epineural spine

Operculum or gill cover

The gill system of the bony fish differs structurally from that of the cartilaginous fish. During respiration, water is taken into the mouth and expelled through slits at either side of the head. These external openings are kept closed—and protected—by bony plates.

There are four gill arches on each side, equipped with fine gill filaments; water passes over the gill filaments, where 80 percent of the dissolved oxygen is extracted, and then into a common chamber, the opercula cavity, the outer wall of which is formed by the external gill cover.

The sea lamprey, *Petromyzon marinus*, is a member of the primitive group of jawless fish. The circular mouth and the tongue are set with sharp rasping teeth by which the lamprey attaches to, and feeds from, its host. An anticoagulant in the lamprey's mouth secretions prevents the host's blood from clotting and interrupting the supply of food. Sea lampreys begin life in fresh-water streams, taking to the sea after four years.

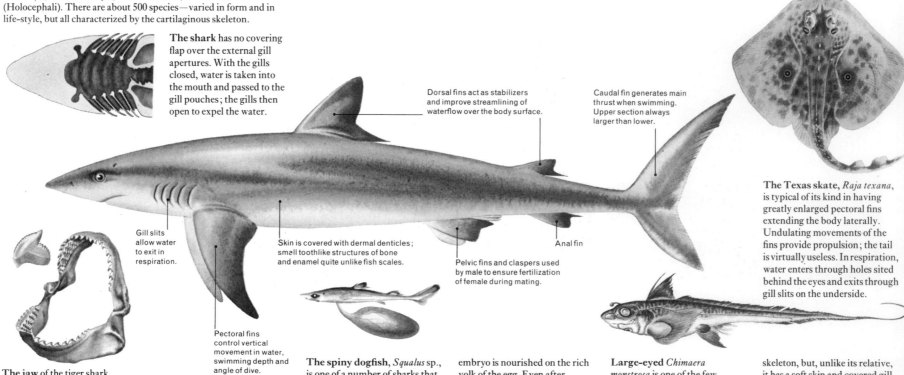

The shark has no covering flap over the external gill apertures. With the gills closed, water is taken into the mouth and passed to the gill pouches; the gills then open to expel the water.

Dorsal fins act as stabilizers and improve streamlining of waterflow over the body surface.

Caudal fin generates main thrust when swimming. Upper section always larger than lower.

Gill slits allow water to exit in respiration.

Skin is covered with dermal denticles; small toothlike structures of bone and enamel quite unlike fish scales.

Anal fin

Pelvic fins and claspers used by male to ensure fertilization of female during mating.

Pectoral fins control vertical movement in water, swimming depth and angle of dive.

The Texas skate, *Raja texana*, is typical of its kind in having greatly enlarged pectoral fins extending the body laterally. Undulating movements of the fins provide propulsion; the tail is virtually useless. In respiration, water enters through holes sited behind the eyes and exits through gill slits on the underside.

The jaw of the tiger shark, *Galeocerdo*, is set with rows of serrated teeth. New teeth continually replace the old.

The spiny dogfish, *Squalus* sp., is one of a number of sharks that give birth to live young. Fertilized eggs are retained in the uterus, where the developing embryo is nourished on the rich yolk of the egg. Even after birth, the young shark carries the yolk sac for some time—in a bag attached to the body.

Large-eyed *Chimaera monstrosa* is one of the few remaining members of a formerly abundant group. Like the shark it has a cartilaginous skeleton, but, unlike its relative, it has a soft skin and covered gill apertures. The body, tapering to a ratlike tail, is nearly 6.5 feet in length.

Deep-sea species like the hatchet fish, *Argyropelecus*, inhabit a zone where life, and therefore food, is relatively scarce. The sharp backward-pointing teeth ensure that victims do not escape. The hatchet fish's fierce appearance belies its small (3.5-inch) size.

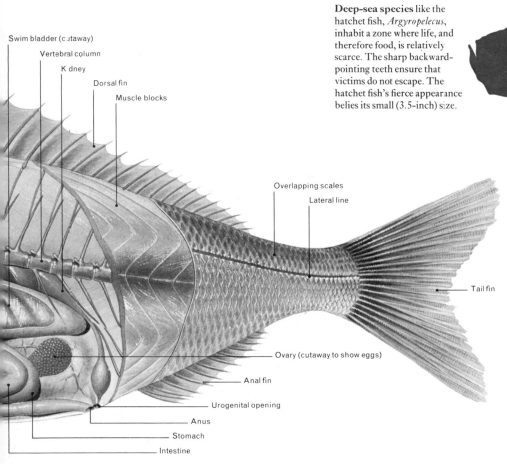

Swim bladder (cutaway)
Vertebral column
Kidney
Dorsal fin
Muscle blocks
Overlapping scales
Lateral line
Tail fin
Ovary (cutaway to show eggs)
Anal fin
Urogenital opening
Anus
Stomach
Intestine

The gray mullet, *Mugil* sp., lives in shallow waters, usually over muddy or sandy sediments. Here it feeds, head downward, grubbing up decomposing animal and vegetable material from the bottom. The mullet is equipped for this life-style with a thick-lipped mouth fringed with minute teeth; a muscular stomach then grinds the food before it passes to the intestine.

Herbivorous fish show a number of adaptations that distinguish them from hunters. The rabbit fish, *Siganus*, lives in coral reef formations, grazing on algal growths. Its lips are tough and the mouth is equipped with many tiny sharp teeth with which the fish can detach its plant food. It is slow moving, generally grazing in the protection of its rocky home.

The herring, *Clupea*, feeds on plankton—primarily copepods. The mouth is small and weak, as food is strained from the water by a filtering system of long bristles known as gill rakers. A slender, highly mobile fish, the herring must roam in search of plankton-rich waters, and consequently enormous shoals may congregate in areas where waters are rich in nutrients.

Marlin are large, aggressive, fast-moving fish measuring as much as 14 feet in length. They are voracious predators and their role as hunters is clearly displayed in their perfectly streamlined body form and slender, crescent-shaped tail fins. The long spearlike bill can be used to maim prey species as the marlin shoots through a shoal of slower fish.

ypical of its family in ving dazzling coloring, the ngnose butterfly fish, *Chelmon stratus*, attracts little attention its coral reef habitat. The elike spot is a defensive daptation. A predator will tack the spot thinking it ilnerable, and the fish is able to ccelerate away in the opposite irection from that expected.

Countershading, as exemplified by the mackerel, *Scomber scombrus*, is an important type of defensive camouflage seen in fish that habitually swim near the surface. The mackerel has a dark back shading to silvery underparts. To a predatory bird the fish is indistinct against the dark water, but from below it merges with the bright surface.

One of the most poisonous of fish, the southern puffer, *Sphaeroides nephelus*, has an unusual method of defending itself. It can distend its body dramatically, thus erecting the small spines which replace scales on the skin. Predators learn to avoid these creatures, which have poison in their flesh and internal organs.

The tuna, *Thunnus*, is one of the fastest and most elegantly streamlined of fish. A hungry carnivore, its capacity for speed is signaled by its crescent-shaped tail fin and fins, which can be folded back, thus offering no resistance to the water. Its red flesh denotes high muscular activity and distances of 150 miles a day have been recorded.

The cod, *Gadus morhua*, is a well-built, round-bodied fish that moves and captures its food at lower levels than the swift tuna, and therefore does not have to compete in speed. The blunt tail fin is characteristic of the slower mover and the cod does not have a sleek, streamlined body. It feeds on worms, mollusks and starfish.

The plaice, *Pleuronectes platessa*, exemplifies the slow-moving and sluggish bottom dweller. The flattened body is well adapted to life on the sea-bed; both eyes are positioned on the upper side and the mouth is twisted so that the more developed part is on the lower surface. The top is usually colored to blend with the habitat.

MARINE-LIFE PARTNERSHIPS

In the sea, as on land, nothing lives in isolation but as part of a web of dependent species. In some instances, known as symbiotic relationships, this dependence is total; the animals cannot live without each other. One such example is found in the reef-building corals, which contain, in their tissues, vast numbers of microscopic plants. In return for the coral's waste products, the plants generate oxygen, which the corals need in order to breathe. Less complete dependence, commensalism, is far more common and often represents a mutual, or even one-sided benefit rather than a dependence. Large sea anemones are commonly accompanied by clown fish, which are quite unharmed by the host. Wrasse and several shrimp species act as cleaners to larger fish, who tolerate their presence even within the mouth and gill openings; sharks are similarly often attended by remoras. In colder waters hermit crabs are adorned with hydroids or anemones growing on their shells; these "passengers" benefit from the crab's untidy eating habits and the crab in turn gains protection from its enemy, the octopus, deterred by the anemone's sting.

Cardinal fish sheltering among sea urchin spines.

Reef fish of many species shelter, unharmed, among sea anemones.

Hermit crab camouflaged and protected by a sea anemone.

Cleaner wrasse in attendance on a flame dwarf angelfish.

Remoras attend a sand shark, cleaning debris from the host.

RETURN TO THE SEA

Arctic shores and waters are the home of the polar bear, *Thalarctos maritimus*, and this harsh environment is reflected in the animal's physical adaptations. The soles of the feet are hairy, affording a secure footing on slippery ice, while the thick creamy coat protects the bear against the elements and provides camouflage while hunting. Longer limbed than other bears, *Thalarctos* swims powerfully.

Almost all vertebrates are able to swim, but the problems facing a land animal returning to the sea are such that few have overcome them, and the small group of reptiles and mammals that have made the transition back to the sea share a common restriction on their way of life. Unable to extract oxygen from the water, they must return frequently to the surface in order to breathe and must be able to hold their breath for long periods while submersed—a restriction that confines most species to the surface waters of the oceans. Marine reptiles rarely stray from the warm surface waters of tropical coasts, where they can still function efficiently despite their cold-blooded systems, while mammals, which are found throughout the colder seas as well, have evolved efficient methods of insulation to conserve their vital body heat. Reproduction, geared as it is to land life in mammals and reptiles, presents great difficulties in the sea and many otherwise aquatic animals return to the land to bear their young.

Among the marine reptiles, the iguanas of the Galapagos Islands are adept swimmers, but, when not feeding on submerged weeds, spend much of their time basking on the rocky shores. The sea snakes of the Indo-Pacific region are much more truly marine, for many species never come to land during their lives. They grow up to five feet long and many are brightly colored, possibly as a warning to predators, as they include some of the most poisonous of all known snakes. A few species return to land to lay their eggs, but generally, after mating in the sea, the females give birth to one or two well-grown young—already able to swim off and hunt for food.

Marine turtles are the only other marine reptiles. With limbs transformed into efficient flippers they swim powerfully and unexpectedly gracefully. Alas, though they mate in the sea, the females must return to land every year in order to lay their eggs in holes, which they excavate in beach sand, and here vast numbers fall prey to their chief enemy—man.

With the exception of the polar bear, the sea otter, which spends its life in the kelp beds off California and Alaska, shows the least physical adaptation to its aquatic way of life. Although its feet are webbed it still has four well-defined limbs, suggesting that in the timescale of evolution it has only recently taken to the sea. The other three groups of marine mammals, the sirenians, seals and whales, have occupied the marine environment for much longer and all are profoundly modified to suit their adopted habitat.

The sea cows are herbivores, grazing chiefly on eelgrass and similar plants close to the shore, or in river estuaries. They are slow-moving creatures, gaining their propulsion from a broad, rounded tail fluke and never leaving the water. The one cold-water species, Steller's sea cow, was exterminated soon after its

Sea otters, *Enhydra lutris*, live among beds of kelp in coastal waters rich in shellfish life. Skillful swimmers, they rarely leave the water and eat and sleep lying on their backs at the surface. They will use a stone as a tool to pound shellfish off the rocks underwater or to open them while eating. Pups are born at sea and sleep, secured by kelp strands, on the mother's chest.

discovery early in the eighteenth century. The present-day tropical species could easily suffer the same fate, as, throughout their range, they are persecuted by man either directly or through destruction of their estuarine and shallow inshore water habitats.

The two main groups of seals, the true seals and the eared seals, are both carnivorous, feeding on a variety of fish, mollusks and crustaceans. Despite their names, the two seal groups are not distinguished solely by the presence or absence of an easily visible external ear, but by their limb structure and locomotion. In the true seals, the hind limbs are turned back at the ankles and when swimming are used in a lateral sweeping movement like the tail of a fish. These animals are nearly helpless on land and must haul themselves forward using their small forelimbs alone. In contrast, the forelimbs of the eared seals are large and may be used for propulsion in slow-speed swimming. The hind feet, which are relatively small, can be turned forward under the body and on land the animal is able to move quite swiftly with a galloping gait. In high-speed swimming the power of the muscular body is transmitted to the tail flippers in strong vertical movements comparable with those of the whale. All seals are protected against the extreme cold of their habitat by a thick layer of blubber beneath the skin, while some members of the eared seal group also have a heavy coat of fur—an effective adaptation, but one which made them an easy and lucrative target for sealers in the past.

Despite their mastery of the water, seals have to mate and produce their young on land, or on floating ice in the southern oceans. Young of the true seals are born in an advanced stage of development and some are able to take to the water within hours of birth, but young eared seals are less well developed and may not venture into the water for many months. Most seals are polygamous, gathering in enormous colonies, sometimes numbering thousands of animals, during the mating season. The colonies are very highly structured, with young males roaming around the margins or trying to establish territories at the edge of the colony, while the huge mature bulls, the "beachmasters," rule over the prime territories along the water's edge.

Colonies of northern fur seals, *Callorhinus ursinus*, members of the sea lion group, haul out in spring to mate and breed. Each male establishes a territory and collects a harem of females.

Gregarious animals, walrus are often seen in huge colonies lying on the shores of the Arctic seas. They are large thick-necked animals weighing as much as 3300 lb and are distinctive for the long tusks, which have developed from the canine teeth in the upper jaw. These tusks, and the powerful neck muscles, enable walrus to uproot their main food—shellfish—from the bed of the sea.

An adept swimmer, the California sea lion, *Zalophus californianus*, has four paddlelike limbs. In water, when swimming slowly, the hind limbs trail behind, while the forelimbs give swimming power. On land, the animal moves with the hind limbs turned under the body.

The crabeater seal, *Lobodon carcinophagus*, is the most abundant seal in the world. It has developed highly specialized teeth, which are used to strain its food, planktonic krill, from the water.

Harbor, or common seals, *Phoca vitulina*, are widely distributed coastal animals. Like all seals they are perfectly adapted to underwater life, but are never at ease on land. Their hind limbs do not turn under and the seal must drag itself forward in a prone position. Seals breed on land; the female normally giving birth to one pup each season. A thick layer of blubber under the skin protects seals from the cold.

UNDERWATER EXPERTISE

Marine mammals normally collect their food underwater and therefore it is vital for them to be expert swimmers and divers. Individual performances, however, vary considerably.

The sea otter spends virtually its whole life in the water. When diving for food it may remain submerged for five minutes.

The sea lions, like the seals, display great expertise in water. The California sea lion, *Zalophus californianus*, has been trained to dive to depths of 820 feet in the Pacific.

Seals generally make repeated short dives lasting about ten minutes, but much greater accomplishments have been recorded: the Weddell seal, *Leptonychotes weddelli*, may dive to 2000 feet and remain at depth for up to 45 minutes.

The walrus dives to collect mollusks for food and has been observed diving 300 feet, staying under for ten minutes.

The manatee dives for about five minutes' duration and only to shallow depths. It normally breathes every two minutes.

The American manatee, *Trichechus manatus*, is a slow, timid creature that frequents shallow waters and estuaries, living on a diet of plants and waterweed. Its broad head merges with a plump, shapeless body ending in a paddle-shaped tail. The manatee habitually lies almost submerged in muddy water with only the eyes and nostrils above water. In many areas the species is protected by law.

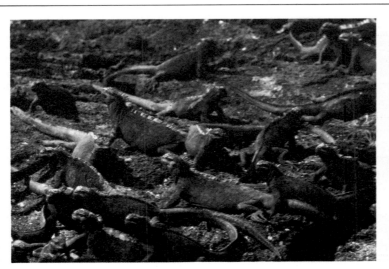

The squat marine iguana, *Amblyrhynchus cristatus*, lives on the rocky shores of the Galapagos Islands. The search for food brought them to the water, where they now feed on submerged weed. Keeping their limbs to their sides, they swim well with movements of the body and flattened tail. Iguanas still reproduce on land, where they lay their eggs in tunnels in the sand.

Turtle grass, *Thalassia* sp., is the food of the herbivorous green turtle, *Chelonia mydas*, one of five species of marine turtle. It is well adapted to marine life; limbs have modified into flippers and the domed shell of the land tortoise has become flatter and lighter to facilitate movement in water. Females lumber ashore to lay large clutches of leathery shelled eggs in deep pits excavated in beach sands.

WHALES AND DOLPHINS

THE SPERMACETI WHALE
Beale

The baleen, or whalebone, whales, Mysticeti, are a race of giants, the smallest being the pigmy right whale, *Caperea marginata*, at 15 feet. Baleen whales have no teeth and feed on planktonic organisms known as krill, which they strain from the water with huge fringed plates suspended from the roof of the mouth. These filter plates vary greatly in size according to the species—the longest being found in the right whale, *Eubalaena*, *above*, which has a bizarre highly arched upper jaw, set with plates 12 feet long. The huge skull of the baleen whale may account for one-third of its length.

Though legends and tall stories abound among whalers, there is no doubting the grim realities of an industry in which hundreds lost their lives. *Above*, whalers close on a harpooned sperm whale in order to despatch the stricken animal with their hand-held lances.

The group of animals to which the whales belong is known as the Cetacea and includes a large number of species ranging in size from the four-foot-long common porpoise to the enormous blue whale, which may reach a length of 120 feet. All share a number of important features. They are all legless, streamlined aquatic animals, swimming by means of boneless, horizontally set tail flukes. All are warm blooded and give birth to well-developed live young, which are carefully tended and suckled by the females. They are hairless except for a few bristles around the snout, but are well insulated against the cold of their aquatic environment by a thick layer of blubber lying immediately below the skin. This layer of oil-rich blubber—up to ten inches thick in some of the larger whales—covers the entire body but for the flippers, fin and tail flukes, and was the prime reason for their decimation by the profit-hungry whaling fleets of the world. The whale's vulnerability to the whaler's harpoon gun is also increased by its dependence, like all mammals, on air. All whales breathe at the surface, through nostrils situated on the top of the head, and the characteristic cloud of vapor from the whale's exhaled breath gives the animal little chance of escaping detection.

There is no doubt that the ancient ancestors of today's whales were land animals. However, the group must have taken to the water by the beginning of the Tertiary era, some 65 million years ago, for their physical adaptations to the marine environment are now so complete that they cannot survive out of the water. The members of the Cetacea fall naturally into two major subdivisions—the toothed whales, called scientifically the Odontoceti, and the whalebone whales, the Mysticeti. The Odontoceti is by far the larger group and contains all the small species, the dolphins and porpoises, and a number of the larger forms, including the killer whale and, largest of all, the sperm whale, which may attain a length of 60 feet. As their name implies, these species have teeth, but, unlike the teeth of most mammals, which are few in number and vary in shape according to their location in the mouth, whale teeth are invariably conical. Some species have very few teeth, but dolphins have up to two hundred, making their elongated jaws exceptionally efficient fish-catching devices. All toothed whales feed

on moderate- to large-sized prey, chiefly fish and squid, and the titanic struggles which take place in the ocean depths are borne out by the remains of the giant squid found in the stomachs of dead sperm whales and the deep scars left in the whales' skin by the squid's clawed suckers.

The second group, though smaller in number of species, contains the largest animals living today. Even the smallest member, the pigmy right whale, is 15 feet in length, while the blue whale is the largest animal ever to have lived on earth. These giant animals all feed on planktonic shrimps, or krill, which they strain from the water. The Mysticeti are all totally toothless, but hanging from the roof of the mouth they have a row of triangular plates of baleen—a horny material—finely fringed on the inner edge. The polar waters in which these baleen whales feed are rich in plankton and the whale feeds by swimming through a dense shoal of the tiny organisms with its mouth open. Closing the enormous gape, the whale then raises its tongue, forcing the food-laden water through the filtering curtain of the plates. Water is expelled through the sides of the mouth, leaving a mass of organic food on the inner surface of the plates. Each mouthful may yield no more than a few pounds of krill, but a large whale may gather two tons in a single day.

It is a sad reflection on man's integrity that despite the wealth of information now available on the biology of whales, their breeding behavior, population densities and their role in the marine ecosystem, whaling still continues—and to the extent that several species are now so reduced in numbers that their very survival is in danger. Very few whale products are without viable alternatives and yet the pelagic industries continue to operate in the face of growing world opinion. The arguments for conservation of whale stocks are overwhelming. If action is not taken, the loss of these animals may have disastrous long-term repercussions on the balance of the marine food web; a group of remarkable creatures may be lost for all time, and—perhaps more selfish and yet potentially just as important—man may lose forever a food resource which, if harvested carefully, could provide a future hungry world with an estimated sustainable yield of about two million tons of protein annually.

The killer whale, *Orcinus orca*, measures up to 30 feet and has a prominent dorsal fin. A fast swimmer and voracious predator, the killer whale feeds on seals, penguins, fish and even other whales.

All toothed whales, Odontoceti, as their name suggests, possess at least some teeth—some as many as two hundred, others as few as a single pair. There are many more species of toothed whales than of baleen, but with the exception of the 60-foot sperm whale, *Physeter catodon*, they are smaller individuals. Carnivorous predators, they feed on fish and the larger invertebrates, such as squid, which they take one at a time. All have acute hearing and produce high-frequency clicks used in a system of echolocation to help them judge distances.

The sperm whale, or cachelot, *Physeter catodon*, is the largest of the toothed whales—measuring at least 60 feet. The massive head, where the colorless fluid known as spermaceti is stored, accounts for about one-third of the total length. Cachelots are the deepest-diving whales; their drowned bodies have been discovered tangled in submarine cables at depths of 3600 feet.

Whales are mammals and must therefore return to the surface between dives to obtain oxygen. While the average man can dive for about one minute, most whales' limit is about 40 minutes. These feats

are accomplished by storing oxygen in the muscles and blood as well as in the lungs; the air is utilized economically by shutting down circulation to all but essential parts until surfacing again.

The harbor, or common porpoise, *Phocaena phocoena*, is a small cetacean reaching a maximum length of five to six feet. Found in temperate seas, it tends to stay in shallow coastal waters and will occasionally swim up rivers. It feeds on squid and fish.

The blue whale, *Balaenoptera musculus*, is not only the largest whale but the largest animal ever to have existed on earth. Individuals may exceed 100 feet in length and weigh 150 tons. In summer, the whale may eat three tons of krill every day.

The triangular horny plates of baleen have a fringed inner edge of brushlike bristles on which food particles are trapped. Though now of little importance, baleen was once a byproduct of the whaling industry.

Shrimplike krill form the main food of the baleen whales and, in antarctic waters, one of the most abundant species is the 2.5-inch *Euphausia superba*. Krill are permanent members of the marine animal plankton.

The minke whale, *Balaenoptera acutorostrata*, is rarely more than 30 feet long and has a characteristic white patch in the middle of each flipper. Minke inhabit temperate and polar seas of both hemispheres—the northern species being smaller than the southern.

The sei whale, *Balaenoptera borealis*, is a slender whale which may reach a length of about 60 feet. The distinctive white fringe on the baleen plates is a very fine sieve, which enables the sei to trap plankton smaller than the more usual euphausiids.

The greenland right whale, *Balaena mysticetus*, inhabits the arctic seas, traveling south in the winter. It is a medium-sized species that grows to a maximum length of 65 feet. The right whale has a very distinctive head shape with dramatically arched jaws.

The humpback whale, *Megaptera novaeangliae*, is about 50 feet long and less streamlined than many whales. It is remarkable for its long, narrow flippers measuring up to one-third of the body length. Flippers and head carry characteristic irregular lumpy growths.

Sowerby's beaked whale, *Mesoplodon bidens*, lives in the temperate waters of the North Atlantic and is about 16 feet long. It has a small head with a long pointed beak and is equipped with a single tooth on each side of the jaw. Beaked whales feed primarily on squid.

The upper and lower jaws of the killer whale are both set with about 12 strong, sharply pointed conical teeth, which interlock as the jaws close to provide a secure grip on the prey. The killer whale is a major predator on seals in the Antarctic.

The bottle-nosed whale, *Hyperoodon ampullatus*, may reach a length of 30 feet. It lives in the North Atlantic, migrating southward in winter. At most it possesses two pairs of teeth and feeds mainly on squid. The color becomes lighter as the whale ages.

The pilot whale, *Globicephala melaena*, is found in the Atlantic, Pacific and Indian oceans and is about 22 feet long. A gregarious whale, it moves in large schools feeding on squid and fish. It has a very distinctive rounded forehead and a deep dorsal fin.

The common dolphin, *Delphinus delphis*, can grow to about eight feet in length; it has a distinct beak and the astounding total of 200 teeth. Distributed throughout warm and temperate waters of the world, many have been successfully kept and trained in captivity.

The narwhal, *Monodon monoceros*, has a single pair of teeth, one of which, in males, grows out to form a long spiral tusk. Females do not generally develop a tusk. The arctic area of the North Atlantic is the narwhal's home and it can reach a length of 18 feet.

Unlike most mammals the whale is born tail first. The calf must arrive in a well-developed state, as it has to swim up to the surface of the water immediately and take its first breath. The mother and other "midwife" whales solicitously assist its progress.

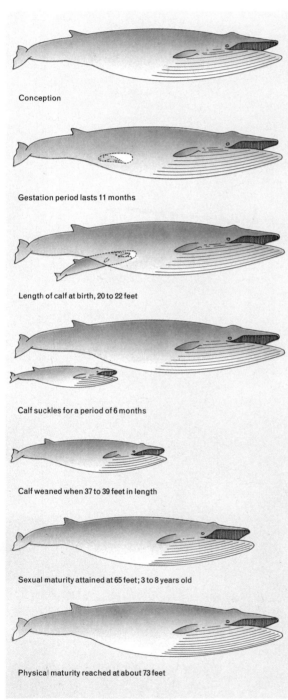

Conception

Gestation period lasts 11 months

Length of calf at birth, 20 to 22 feet

Calf suckles for a period of 6 months

Calf weaned when 37 to 39 feet in length

Sexual maturity attained at 65 feet; 3 to 8 years old

Physical maturity reached at about 73 feet

A whale usually gives birth to one calf at a time, which is born tail first. Different species have different cycles of growth, but, in general, toothed whales have a gestation period of more than one year; baleen whales of about 11 months. The fin whale, *Balaenoptera physalus*, is typical in having a gestation period of 11 months. The calf is about a third of the length of the mother at birth and is suckled for about 6 months, by which time is has grown about 17 feet. Growth continues after sexual maturity.

The age of a baleen whale can be estimated by counting the number of layers laid down in a horny plug found in the external ear.

BIRDLIFE OF THE OCEAN REALM

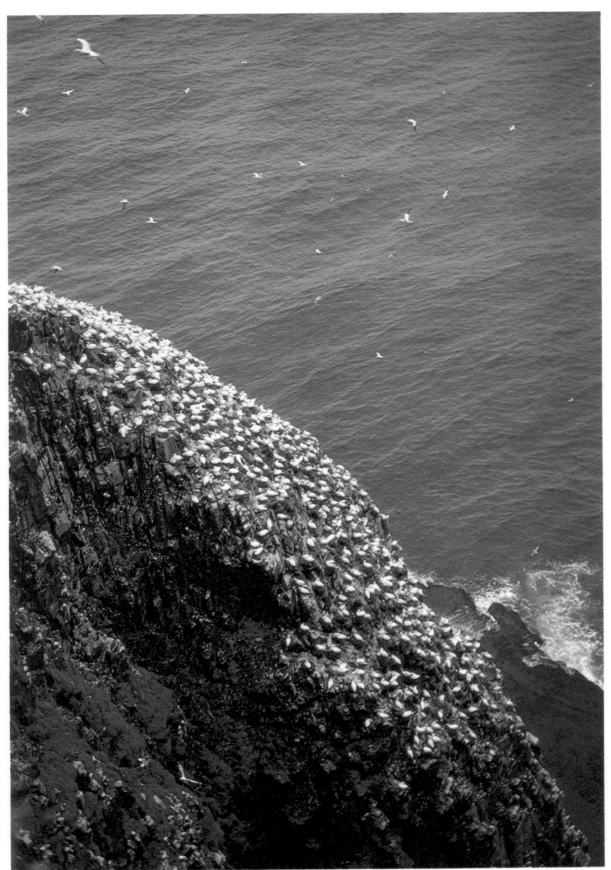

Colonial breeding is characteristic of most seabird species and some, notably the gannets, are extremely tenacious in their use of nesting sites. The gannetry, *above*, on St Mary's Cape, Nova Scotia, has been occupied every year, January through August, since 1897.

Black-footed albatrosses, *Diomedea nigripes*, demonstrate the powerful stiff-winged glide typical of their family. They are among the largest albatrosses, having a wingspan of nearly seven feet, and are able to achieve airspeeds of up to 60 mph.

Superstitious or not, the mariner's respect for the true ocean-wandering birds is well placed. It was ingenious enough that creatures evolved the ability to fly; even more so that some birds learnt to sustain life in the harsh conditions of the oceans. In answer to its demands, the 285 seabird species have between them developed a remarkable range of adaptations.

Albatrosses are the most uncompromisingly oceanic of birds. Some species spend up to nine months of the year at sea; on land they can hardly walk. But with narrow wings of great length in proportion to the body and too stiffly constructed to maintain flapping flight for any length of time, they wander all over the oceans of the southern hemisphere. Rising against the wind for maximum lift, turning downwind in a powerful dive, skimming inches above the heaving surface, where wind resistance is least, they seem effortlessly to wring impossible extra yards from every glide. These birds are not so much powerful fliers as perfectly adjustable sailplanes. When there is no wind, they have difficulty in taking off, but the more savage the gale, the more at home they are.

Scarcely less accomplished, but with a different flight technique, are the petrels, which, according to most dictionaries, derive their name from St. Peter, who walked on the water. They are small birds, at their best when feeding in heavy swell, flitting like swifts just above the surface, navigating in the shelter of the troughs with astonishing nicety. To maintain this performance for long periods it is likely that albatrosses, petrels and some other seabirds are capable of sleep of a sort while on the wing.

Oceans may be rich in food, but to seek it out above or below the surface there is a general requirement of seabirds to have exceptionally acute senses, most obviously of vision, but also of smell. In the case of penguins, there is also an ability to detect prey in the dark at depths of several hundred feet by a kind of sonar, listening to echoes of the noise made by bubbles collapsing in their wake.

Penguins have in fact adapted to aquatic feeding so completely that their wings are reduced to flippers. Consequently, they can pursue fish underwater at considerable speed. Auks have a similar, but not such total, underwater adaptation. Half-open wings with primaries closed are the main source of propulsion. Webbed feet, placed far to the rear of the body, act as rudders. This group, today comprising the razorbills, guillemots, murrelets, auklets and little auk, have, as might be expected, diminished powers of flight. In times past, various species of auk adapted so completely to underwater feeding that, like penguins, they became flightless. Their distribution in the northern hemisphere, comparatively near human habitation, made them more vulnerable; the last to become extinct (in 1844) was the great auk, slaughtered wholesale for consumption by fishermen and seal-hunters.

Diving for fish from the air is a feeding skill to which some seabirds, especially boobies and gannets, have adapted to a great degree. The birds may plunge vertically from as high as 100 feet. Their skulls are strengthened to withstand the impact and the body is protected by a layer of fat and a cushion of pneumatic air sacs. Probably the most singular maritime feeding adaptation is displayed by the skimmers: the adult's beak has a short upper but long lower mandible, which is scooped through the water by the bird in flight just above the surface, collecting small fish and invertebrates.

Sophisticated adaptations do not alter the fact that collecting food at sea is laborious, and this is one reason why seabirds tend to rear few young. Most in fact, like fulmars, raise one at a time. Another reason is that suitable nesting sites are limited and easily overcrowded. Most seabirds are conspicuously colonial nesters, the social stimulation of the colony leading to synchronized hatching and thus to an earlier and shorter, and therefore more successful, breeding season. Similar advantages apply to winter flocks. Many individuals can be on the watch for food; when prey is sighted, the first birds dive in pursuit and the others follow.

One of the most essential and universal seabird adaptations is for freely drinking seawater. A gland situated above the eye enables birds to secrete excess salt through the nostrils. There may also be a fold of skin in the nostrils to prevent entry of water during dives. Most birds have a gland, situated at the base of the tail, which secretes oil. During preening the oil is spread over the feathers to make them waterproof; seabirds repeat this routine several times a day. Some species, however, are notable for imperfect oil glands: cormorants and shags, for example, have to spread their wings to dry in the breeze after diving. Frigate-birds, perhaps the most aerial of seabirds, simply avoid getting wet. Prey is snatched from below the surface, or, if it happens to be flying fish, in mid-air.

In recent years ornithologists have tended to concentrate on the question of seabird survival at the expense of the more fascinating, less gloomy study of life-cycles and skills. This change in emphasis is well justified. Man's impact on seabird numbers is much greater than that of disease or predation. His activities may not be exclusively destructive—fulmars and gannets have in particular benefited through the increased quantities of offal jettisoned by modern deep-sea fishing fleets—but the balance is against the birds. Tens of thousands die after being caught in oil slicks; thousands more perish when they become entangled in nylon fishing nets. Very few seabirds escape contamination by toxic chemicals discharged into the sea by shore-based industries. Natural selection, with marvellous ingenuity, has made seabirds among the most resilient of creatures; unnatural causes could now reduce many to extinction.

The Arctic tern, *Sterna paradisaea,* is, like the gannet, a master of the technique of plunging onto its prey from the air—but is far more graceful. Its long pointed wings and streaming tail feathers confer a beautifully buoyant maneuverability. Terns quarter their hunting area only a few feet above the waves, hovering momentarily on sighting a fish before plunging vertically. They are nervous, capricious birds, screaming with excitement after a catch or when an intruder approaches. The Arctic tern is one of the most sensational migrants, covering 20,000 miles each year between its Arctic breeding grounds and Antarctic summer quarters.

Penguins can swim at speeds of up to 25 mph, leaping clear of the water like porpoises. Insulation and streamlining in the cold Antarctic water is provided by a layer of blubber beneath the skin and an undercoat of down overlain by short, dense contour feathers.

Fish offal is an important food for gulls and other seabirds, but the gull's versatility as a scavenger, exploiting refuse tips as readily as carrion, makes it equally successful on land.

The pelican scoops its prey into the unique pouchlike extension of its lower mandible as a fisherman uses a scoop net. The birds may drive fish into shallows by beating their wings.

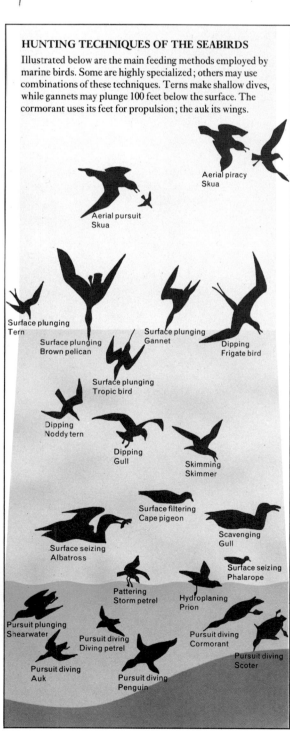

HUNTING TECHNIQUES OF THE SEABIRDS

Illustrated below are the main feeding methods employed by marine birds. Some are highly specialized; others may use combinations of these techniques. Terns make shallow dives, while gannets may plunge 100 feet below the surface. The cormorant uses its feet for propulsion; the auk its wings.

Aerial piracy Skua

Aerial pursuit Skua

Surface plunging Tern

Surface plunging Brown pelican

Surface plunging Gannet

Dipping Frigate bird

Surface plunging Tropic bird

Dipping Noddy tern

Dipping Gull

Skimming Skimmer

Surface filtering Cape pigeon

Scavenging Gull

Surface seizing Albatross

Surface seizing Phalarope

Pattering Storm petrel

Hydroplaning Prion

Pursuit plunging Shearwater

Pursuit diving Diving petrel

Pursuit diving Cormorant

Pursuit diving Auk

Pursuit diving Penguin

Pursuit diving Scoter

THE WEB OF LIFE

In order to build the cells of which it is composed, the plant life of the oceans and coastal seas elaborates complex organic materials from simple inorganic elements such as carbon, hydrogen, nitrogen and calcium. To do this the plants utilize energy captured from sunlight by photosynthetic pigments, the most important of which is chlorophyll—the green pigment responsible for the characteristic green color of many plants. By a complex set of pathways this plant material is captured, digested and transformed by a host of small herbivorous animals who use it both as a raw material for building new cell tissue and as a source of energy for their life processes. Predatory species subsequently capture the herbivores to obtain the material and energy they themselves need.

It is generally possible to trace a simple food chain of this kind for several further stages as larger, higher-level carnivores devour the smaller creatures of the primary feeding level. At each level of any such food chain the expenditure of energy reduces the amount of material available for transfer onward up the chain to only a very small proportion of that originally ingested. Hence in general the total biomass of predators is less than that of the herbivores, which is in turn much smaller than the biomass of the plant material at the base of the chain.

However, so simple a food chain hardly ever exists in reality anywhere in the ocean; more commonly a web of feeding relationships links the members of an ecosystem and where simple feeding chains appear to exist, closer analysis will generally reveal that these are being artificially isolated from a more complex food web. A good example of this situation is provided by the apparently simple food chain that occurs in the upwelling area off the coast of Peru, where abundant phytoplankton is fed upon by teeming shoals of anchovy, which themselves are preyed on by vast flocks of boobies, cormorants and pelicans. The birds in turn produce the vast deposits of guano, consolidated droppings, found on the offshore islands and mined as a valuable source of fertilizer. While it is true that the plankton–anchovy–seabird chain is probably the major pathway for the transfer of energy through this system, anchovies are also an important food source for marine mammals, including fur seals, sea lions and dolphins, as well as for carnivorous fish like the bonito and hake. Direct feeding links also exist between many of these predatory animals.

The place of a particular species in the food web

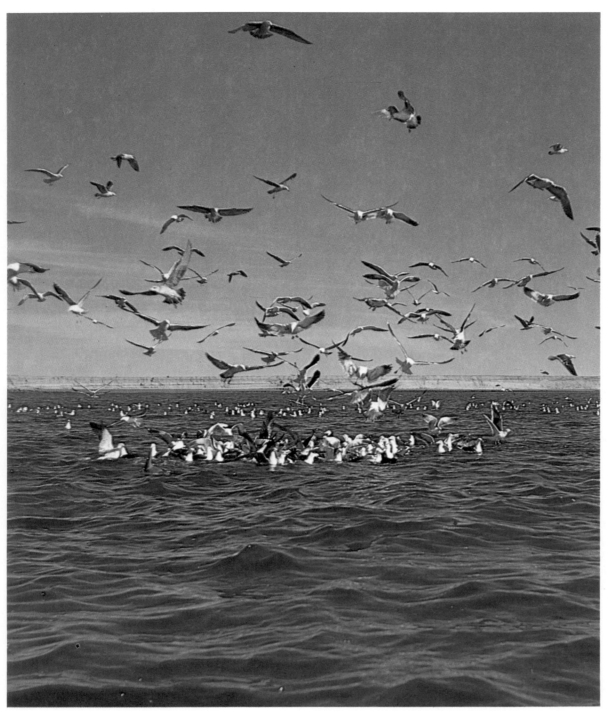

The presence of seabirds swooping down to feed indicates a high level of productivity in the ocean's surface waters.

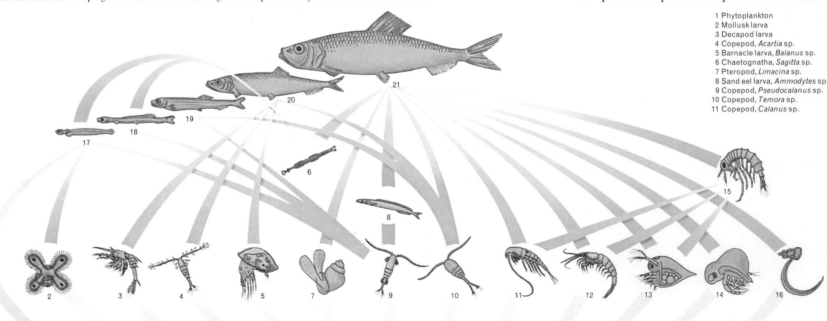

1 Phytoplankton
2 Mollusk larva
3 Decapod larva
4 Copepod, *Acartia* sp.
5 Barnacle larva, *Balanus* sp.
6 Chaetognatha, *Sagitta* sp.
7 Pteropod, *Limacina* sp.
8 Sand eel larva, *Ammodytes* sp.
9 Copepod, *Pseudocalanus* sp.
10 Copepod, *Temora* sp.
11 Copepod, *Calanus* sp.

12 Euphausiid, *Nyctiphanes* sp.
13 Cladocera, *Evadne* sp.
14 Cladocera, *Podon* sp.
15 Hyperiid amphipod
16 Appendiculate, *Oikopleura* sp.
17 Young herring, ¼–½ in
18 Young herring, 1¼ in
19 Young herring, 1¾ in
20 Young herring, 1½–5 in
21 Adult herring, up to 16 in

The feeding habits of the herring change with the different stages of its development. As the young herring grows, the diversity of its diet increases rapidly; the varied selection of food taken by the adult herring includes other small predatory creatures.

of an ecosystem is not necessarily constant; as an organism grows its feeding requirements change, often quite fundamentally. Thus the larval anchovies off Peru probably require large motile phytoplankton at the earliest feeding stage, yet after a few days only they must change to feeding on zooplankton of increasing size in order to survive. Finally, as adults, they may switch from straining food from the water to capturing individual large plankton as occasion demands. The herring at different stages of its development will select different types of food—mainly zooplankton and larval animals. It even occurs that an important element in the diet of some species is their own young. The cannibalizing of young by adults of the same species is a relatively common feature of the feeding behavior of many fish and is regarded as a means of providing the adults with a reserve food resource not otherwise available to them. A minority of species on the other hand do have very specialized and restricted diets. For instance, the adults of one small deep-sea pelagic fish eat only members of a single species of copepod selected from among the multitudes of similar-sized copepods living in close proximity.

Ashore, a single plant—such as an oak tree—may provide shelter and food for a characteristic and varied assemblage of animals linked into a complex food web. In the oceans this situation is less common, but does occur in relation to some of the larger seaweeds, one of the best examples being the giant kelp beds of the eastern Pacific. Here a great variety of animal life is supported within the kelp bed, interrelated in a complex food web, but, like the upwelling areas of Peru, dominated by one primary food chain: sea otters, which rest among the supporting strands of the kelp, feed on sea urchins, which in turn graze on the kelp fronds.

In general food webs are simpler, and contain fewer links, and the overall ecosystem is less diverse in areas where the natural environment is very variable. Such is the case in the polar seas, where plants can grow only in the brief summer season, and in the seasonal coastal upwellings off the coasts of Peru, California, Namibia and Morocco, where, for short periods of the year, plant nutrients are supplied to the surface by upwelling waters. In areas where conditions are stable, however, and where plant production occurs throughout the year with rapid recycling of nutrient material, the food web is at its most complex. A highly diverse ecosystem will evolve in which feeding relationships are complex and where no single food chain is dominant. The same pattern may be found in benthic food webs: in the relatively unchanging tropical seas there are complex feeding links between the organisms inhabiting the coral reefs and the ecosystem is extremely diverse. Similarly the ecosystem of the abyssal plains, where conditions are again very stable, tends to be diverse even though life on the deep ocean floor is very sparse. Both the tropical and abyssal food webs are more intricate and varied than the high-latitude, shallow-water communities such as are found around the shores of northwest Europe.

The fundamental pattern of feeding relationships may be considerably modified by the geography of the oceans and by the recent geologic and climatic history of an ocean basin. Because the tropical Indo-Pacific region has had such a long evolutionary history the fauna is much more varied, and the food web more intricate, than in comparable habitats in the Atlantic, where, in comparatively recent times, the tropical fauna was reduced to only a few remnant species confined mainly to the Caribbean.

Man's utilization of the oceans must also be taken into account. Most of our major ocean fisheries are based on species that occupy the higher levels of the food chain—thus making our use of the oceans very inefficient. For every step backward down the food chain in our selection of species to be taken for human food, the catch could theoretically be increased by 90 per cent. If krill were harvested in the Antarctic instead of whales, the total output of food from the ocean could be vastly increased without seriously upsetting the balance of oceanic life.

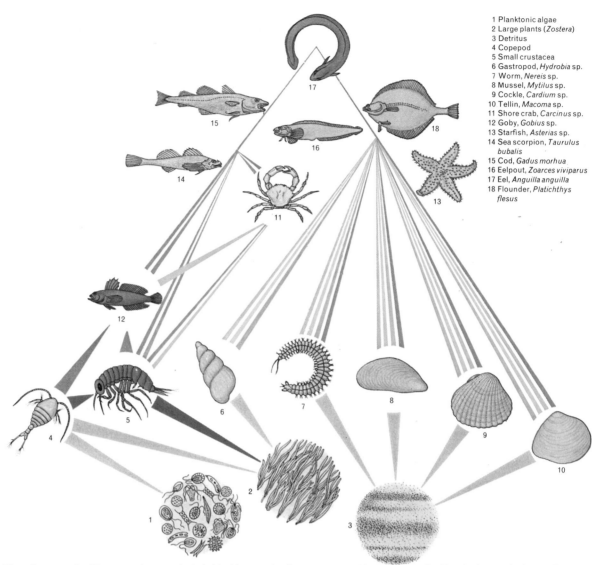

1 Planktonic algae
2 Large plants (*Zostera*)
3 Detritus
4 Copepod
5 Small crustacea
6 Gastropod, *Hydrobia* sp.
7 Worm, *Nereis* sp.
8 Mussel, *Mytilus* sp.
9 Cockle, *Cardium* sp.
10 Tellin, *Macoma* sp.
11 Shore crab, *Carcinus* sp.
12 Goby, *Gobius* sp.
13 Starfish, *Asterias* sp.
14 Sea scorpion, *Taurulus bubalis*
15 Cod, *Gadus morhua*
16 Eelpout, *Zoarces viviparus*
17 Eel, *Anguilla anguilla*
18 Flounder, *Platichthys flesus*

Many bottom-dwelling organisms are included in this example of the complex type of food web that might exist in Danish coastal waters. This web, based not only on phytoplankton but also on detritus and larger marine plants such as eelgrass, *Zostera* sp., supports a wide range of species. Zooplankton and other small invertebrates are able to feed on the detritus as well as on phytoplankton and provide an ample and varied food supply for the larger creatures of the web, like the starfish, crabs and fish.

Red-winged blackbird
Dragonfly
Winkle, *Littorina* sp.
Clapper rail
Raccoon
Plant-hopper, *Prokelisia* sp.
Grasshopper, *Orchelimum* sp.
Mud crab, *Eurytium* sp.
Gray mullet, *Mugil* sp.
Mussel, *Mytilus* sp.
Fiddler crab, *Uca* sp.
Fiddler crab, *Sesarma* sp.
Oligochaete
Streblospio sp.
Capitella sp.
Manayunkia sp.

The salt-marsh environment blends land and sea together in an area of grassy mudflats and creeks flooded twice each day by the tide. The system is dominated by the tough grass *Spartina*, which densely covers all the available land. *Spartina* supports the life of the marsh in two ways: first, insects such as plant-hoppers and grasshoppers feed directly on the grass; second, many more creatures, including crabs, worms and mussels, feed on the rich detritus produced by decomposed *Spartina*. Carnivores —raccoons, clapper rails and mud crabs—come to the marsh to prey on detritus feeders, while birds and dragonflies hover to feed on herbivorous insects.

MIGRATION:THE INSTINCTIVE JOURNEY

Migration is a movement from place to place. When applied to animals it implies a seasonal movement between areas used for specific functions such as feeding and breeding. Many animals migrate and examples of migrating species are to be found among all the major groups of animals that have representatives living partly or wholly in the sea. Regular seasonal movement enables a species to make the best use of particular areas at different times of the year and at various stages in its life cycle—thus ensuring the most efficient use of food supplies and the optimum population to exploit them.

The homing instinct, which is the ability to find the way back to a particular area favorable for a certain activity, such as breeding or feeding, is an important part of migratory behavior and increases survival rate. For example, only those fish spawned in a favorable area will survive to grow into adulthood and their ability to find their way back to that area is crucial for the survival of the next generation.

Migration is an adaption to abundance, and the fact that most of the species forming the basis of the world's fisheries are migratory illustrates the advantages of this behavior. These species are fished simply because they are abundant and they are abundant because they are migratory.

Migration of fish, and for that matter other animals, conforms to a simple pattern: breeding takes place on the spawning grounds from which the young fish travel, usually drifting passively on the prevailing ocean currents, to a nursery area and later joining the adult fish on their feeding ground. On maturity the young adults swim back to the spawning ground and the cycle repeats itself. The complete cycle may be thought of as a triangle with spawning ground, nursery and feeding ground forming the three corners.

This migration cycle often takes place within an oceanic current gyre. The group of fish of a particular species living within a current gyre forms a geographically distinct breeding community known as a stock. There are stocks of cod off Newfoundland, Greenland, Faroe and in the North Sea, to give only a few examples. Any fish that strays outside the gyre is lost reproductively to the stock and is termed an emigré.

Migration takes place along clearly defined routes and is precisely timed to coincide with the oceans' cyclic production of plankton, the basic food supply of all fish. In temperate and arctic waters this production is restricted and spawning of fish such as the cod and plaice must be timed to coincide with periods of abundant food. In tropical waters many fish take advantage of the periodic upwelling of nutrient-rich water and their migrations must be regulated to exploit them efficiently. The regulation is so precise that over a period of years the spawning peak of arctic and temperate fish recurs within the same range of 14 days. The locations of spawning, nursery and feeding areas remain constant over a long period, a fact closely related to the fish's homing instincts. The sockeye salmon of Cultus Lake in British Columbia provides the best-documented evidence of homing in fish. It has been shown that of those fish returning to spawn in fresh water more than 90 percent do so in their own parent stream and many even spawn in the same gravel bed in which they were hatched. It is thought that many

marine species home with the same degree of precision, but difficulties in marking the young fish and identifying older fish that have spawned in particular areas have made it difficult to provide direct evidence.

It is not clear how fish find their way back to particular areas. Once in the vicinity of a spawning ground local landmarks may be used to recognize its precise location. In the case of salmon the chemical characteristics of its native spawning ground are thought to be important. Having spent much of its early life in a particular river it becomes imprinted with these characteristics and on entering coastal water it is literally able to smell its way home. This principle is well established for salmon, but as yet has not been shown to be true for purely marine fish. The migration that the green turtle is believed to accomplish between its feeding grounds off the Brazilian coast and its nesting site on the beaches of Ascension Island, in the mid-Atlantic, is a feat of navigation as remarkable as that of any fish. The island is so very small that the slightest error in the course followed by the turtles will result in their missing the island completely.

Young fish making the migration from spawning ground to nursery area within a current gyre do so by merely drifting passively with the current. However, the migrations of adult fish are not so easily explained and many hypotheses ranging from random movements to the use of temperature gradients, geomagnetic fields and star patterns as navigational aids have been suggested.

The distances covered by different fish on their yearly migratory cycles vary enormously from species to species. The migrations of littoral species such as blennies and gobies are essentially short seasonal journeys of only a few miles to and from the coast. Some fish such as herring and cod make annual journeys of hundreds of miles between feeding and spawning grounds. Others like the tuna make enormous trans-oceanic migrations of several thousand miles across the Atlantic and Pacific. The annual migration of the gray whale is worth mentioning in this context. Each year it travels from the Bering Sea in the North Pacific to breed in the warm water off the coast of Baja California, a round trip of 10,000 miles.

Very little is known about the movements of fish at sea and this lack of data is a major problem in formulating theories of migration. Experiments using acoustic equipment have been carried out on several species, including bluefin tuna, cod, eels, plaice, salmon and shad. Acoustic tags are attached to the fish, enabling them to be tracked for several days over distances up to 90 miles. More sophisticated instrument packages developed recently may be placed within the fish's body to provide details of body temperature and muscular activity by radio transmission to a closely following ship.

As the world's major fishing stocks are at present contracting, detailed knowledge of their movements is now more than ever necessary to ensure their exploitation is regulated at levels that will both provide adequate catches and ensure their survival. Using techniques now being developed, the next ten years are expected to bring a significant advance in our understanding of the behavioral basis of migration and hence a more efficient and controlled utilization of the world's fish reserves.

Marine turtles come ashore to lay eggs. On hatching, the young head unerringly toward the sea no matter in which direction it may lie. Green turtles hatched on Ascension Island have been found along the coast of Brazil and although no turtles tagged on the Brazilian coast have been detected on Ascension Island, it is believed that the mature adults make the 1400-mile trip against the South Equatorial Current to nest on the island's beaches.

In the tropics (a) production of minute plankton on which young fish feed is more or less continuous and fish living within a tropical current gyre may spawn successfully at any time and at any place within the gyre. In temperate waters (b) the production cycle is not

continuous and the fish may spawn only where there is sufficient food to ensure the survival of their young. The young fish must also mature fast enough to be able to survive on other food by the time they drift out of the area of plankton production. In Arctic waters (c) the gyre

may be broken by an environmental barrier such as a polar front, preventing the fish from swimming on to the spawning area. They must swim back again, either against the current near the surface or in a deeper-lying countercurrent.

The North American and European eel both spawn in the Sargasso Sea. On hatching, the larvae are carried by the Gulf Stream toward the shores of North America and Europe, where they enter the rivers as young eels, or elvers. On reaching maturity the eels reenter the sea and swim back to the Sargasso Sea to spawn and die. It has been suggested that only the North American eel returns to the spawning ground and that it is its larvae that drifts round to the European coasts.

North American eel

European eel

1 Years from hatching

0   2000km
0   1000mi.

Salmon spend their entire adult life in the sea, only returning to their native river to spawn. Atlantic salmon may make two or even three spawning migrations, but the Pacific salmon spawns once only, dying soon after. In the North Pacific there are three distinct stocks of salmon: Asian, Bristol Bay and Gulf of Alaska-Oregon, all of which return to the rivers of Asia and North America to spawn. How they are able to find their way back to their respective coasts is at present a matter of debate.

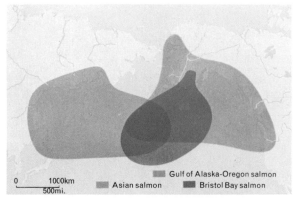

0   1000km
0   500mi.

Gulf of Alaska-Oregon salmon

Asian salmon

Bristol Bay salmon

THE VERTICAL DISTRIBUTION OF LIFE

The properties of seawater, generally thought to determine the nature and abundance of living organisms, change almost everywhere in the ocean very much faster in the vertical plane than in the horizontal. This fact determines the environment of the planktonic animals dispersed in the water column and also of the benthic animals associated with the seafloor. Radiation of both light and heat from the sun are rapidly absorbed in seawater and, depending on the amount of particulate material including plankton contained in the water, light penetrates to only a few hundred feet at most in the open ocean and to as little as a couple of feet in turbid coastal waters. Below this lighted zone all is dark for the remainder of the thousands of feet to the seafloor. Similarly, temperature changes very sharply across the thermocline, which typically separates the upper waters, mixed by winds and heated by the sun, from the colder water below.

Oxygen and nutrient salts such as nitrates and phosphates can also vary considerably with depth, especially in the upper 1000 feet, but this variability is an effect of plant production, which can only occur within the lighted upper zone. It is also in this upper zone that the greatest abundance of animals, both herbivores and carnivores, occurs. The only source of energy below the lighted zone is the organic material, such as feces and dead organisms, which sinks down from above, or river-borne material reaching the deep ocean floor as a mudslide down the continental slope.

Because there is a similarity between the environmental changes related to increasing depth and the changes between tropical and polar seas within the surface layers, it is no surprise that many organisms living near the surface in polar seas should also occur at greater depths in low latitudes. Examples abound in both plankton and benthos communities: the distribution of a large transparent copepod, *Eucalanus bungii*, abundant near the surface in the Bering Sea and Gulf of Alaska, extends southward at increasing depths until just north of the equator the copepod is found at more than 2500 feet; and the black Greenland shark is common at a depth of several thousand feet off California, while at polar latitudes in the North Pacific and Arctic Ocean it occurs in quite shallow water.

The form, behavior and color of animals changes strikingly with depth so the animals of each zone tend to have common characteristics. At the surface, in the upper inches of the open seawater column, there is a range of predatory blue crustaceans, mollusks and siphonophores which are almost invisible in the blue world they inhabit. As one passes downward through the lighted zone, transparent forms of invertebrates give way in the twilight depths to scarlet and black animals, invisible in the small amount of light which does penetrate so far down. Eyes become large and extraordinarily efficient to catch the last rays of light and carnivores are dominant. In the totally dark zone, down to the abyssal depths, the only light existing is that provided by a bewildering variety of luminous organs and exudations possessed by deep-sea fauna

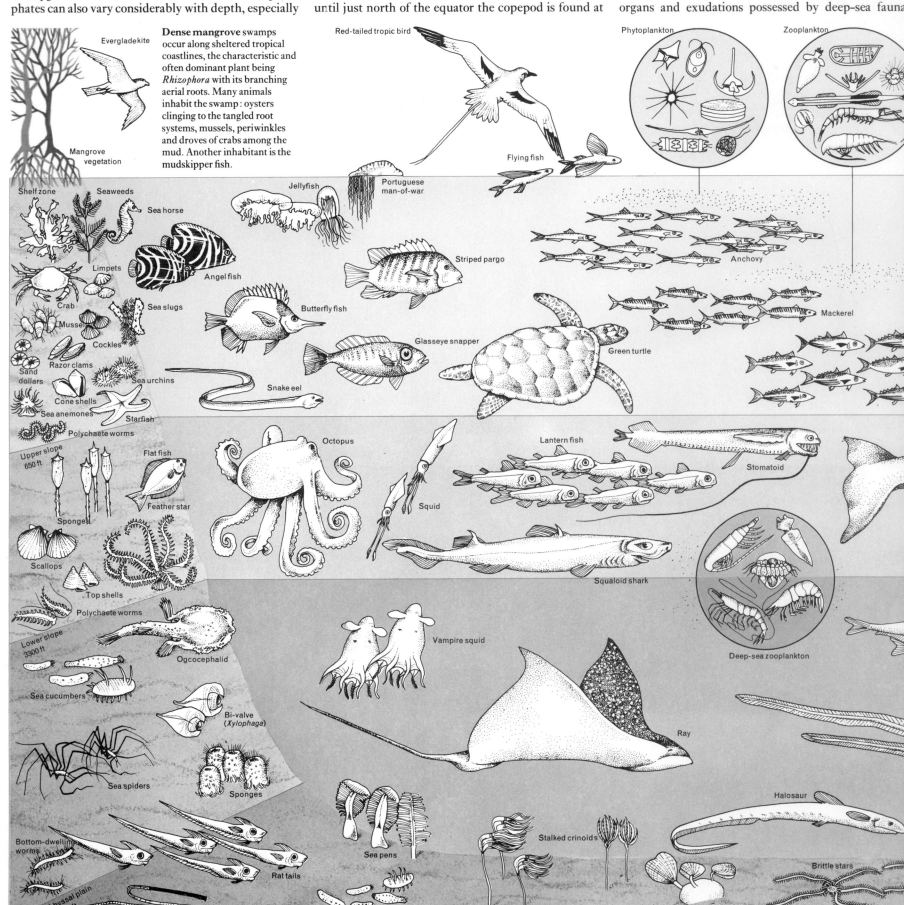

Dense mangrove swamps occur along sheltered tropical coastlines, the characteristic and often dominant plant being *Rhizophora* with its branching aerial roots. Many animals inhabit the swamp: oysters clinging to the tangled root systems, mussels, periwinkles and droves of crabs among the mud. Another inhabitant is the mudskipper fish.

Everglade kite

Mangrove vegetation

Red-tailed tropic bird

Flying fish

Phytoplankton

Zooplankton

Jellyfish

Portuguese man-of-war

Shelf zone

Seaweeds

Sea horse

Striped pargo

Anchovy

Limpets

Angel fish

Crab

Sea slugs

Butterfly fish

Mackerel

Mussel

Cockles

Glasseye snapper

Green turtle

Razor clams

Sand dollars

Sea urchins

Cone shells

Snake eel

Sea anemones

Starfish

Polychaete worms

Octopus

Lantern fish

Stomatoid

Upper slope 650 ft

Flat fish

Feather star

Squid

Sponge

Scallops

Squaloid shark

Top shells

Polychaete worms

Deep-sea zooplankton

Lower slope 3300 ft

Ogcocephalid

Vampire squid

Sea cucumbers

Bi-valve (*Xylophaga*)

Ray

Sea spiders

Sponges

Halosaur

Bottom-dwelling worms

Sea pens

Stalked crinoids

Brittle stars

Rat tails

Abyssal plain 19,500 ft

Pogonophora

Sea cucumbers

Lamp shells

such as squid and lantern fish. These luminous devices are used to lure prey, to signal to others of the same species for reproductive purposes, for camouflage and for a variety of other purposes. One remarkable use of bioluminescence is that a fish in the twilight zone can direct light downward from the light organs on its lower surface; thus the fish matches the radiance above and is camouflaged instead of appearing from below like a conspicuous black body against a lighted backdrop.

The strongest zonation with depth, however, occurs along the coastline in the benthic realm, especially in the intertidal zone, where the areas exposed at low tide, inhabited by both plants and animals, are well known to all seashore naturalists. From the spray zone high on the rocks to the sublittoral fringes of seaweeds, each zone is inhabited by a characteristic assemblage of animals and plants. The shallow waters of the benthic realm contain the most spectacular of all marine ecosystems: the coral reefs that border some tropical

coasts and form atolls in midocean, and the forests of giant kelp bordering the cold-water coasts on the western side of the American continent.

Below these shallow communities the life of the sea bottom progressively changes with depth across the continental shelf and down the slope to the deep ocean floor beyond. Burrowing animals predominate on mud bottoms, but on the softest oozes of the deep ocean there are creatures such as fish, crustaceans and sea cucumbers that have extraordinarily elongated appendages to enable them to support themselves on this surface. Animals that filter suspended particles from seawater to obtain their food decline in abundance with depth, while those that simply eat the bottom deposits for the content of organic material continue to be found to the greatest depths. Although both invertebrates and fish extend to the deepest regions, the numbers of animals of all sorts progressively decreases. The early naturalists' myth of the lifeless deeps did not long survive scientific exploration and

further evidence was provided when submarine cables were found to be covered by encrusting growths when recovered for repair from the deep ocean floor.

Few animals other than man possess the power of moving over great depth ranges and none can match our ability—aided by technology—to penetrate from the surface to the bottom of the abyssal trenches. However, as well as the daily and seasonally migrating plankton, which move over a range of 500 to 1000 feet, a few vertebrates do make spectacular feeding dives: the great sperm whales, although required to spend much of their time at the surface in order to breathe, nevertheless make regular forays to as much as 6500 feet down in order to hunt their quarry, the giant squid. A surprising encounter at great depths between the research submersible *Alvin* and a swordfish, a species usually thought to make its living close to the surface, showed that other surface-living carnivores may at times travel to the depths of the ocean in their continuous pursuit of food.

An imaginary profile of the typical coastal and oceanic zones is shown in the diagram below with a selection of the life forms that might occur in the waters off the Pacific coast of Central America. The animals illustrated are not drawn to scale as the range of sizes is too great. Plant and animal plankton, the basis of life in the ocean, occur in great quantities: their presence has been indicated, therefore, and examples of the major types have been illustrated. The density of life in general is very high in the upper sunlit zone so, in order to accommodate a reasonable selection of the vast numbers of inhabitants, the depth of the body of the diagram has been distorted; the true relationship of the depths of all the zones is indicated in the side panel.

Blue-footed booby
Great frigate bird
Gulls

Albacore
White-tip shark
Dolphin
Porpoise
Swordfish
Bonito
Marlin
Sei whale

Sunlit zone
650 ft
3300 ft

Squid
Sperm whale
Hatchet fish
Alepocephalid
Melamphid

Twilight zone

Bathypelagic zone
19,500 ft

Bristlemouth fish
Angler fish
Deep-sea eels
Gulper eel
Amphipod
Isopod
Brotulids
Giant isopod
Short-armed starfish
Venus flower baskets
Tripod fish
Trench zone
Sea cucumbers
Actinarians
33,000 ft

LIFE BETWEEN THE TIDES

The **seashore** is a rich and varied habitat providing food and shelter for many animals and plants. Though pebble beaches are unusually barren, rocky, muddy and sandy shores each have their own characteristic populations adapted to the prevailing conditions.

Upper zone Channeled wrack Kelp

The **rocky shore** is a heavily populated region, having a wide variety of attractive environments where plants and animals may live. Rocks bare of seaweed are often encrusted with huge clinging colonies of barnacles and limpets. More sheltered rocks are covered with seaweed where periwinkles, *Littorina*, hide. The sides and roofs of dark caves provide damp homes, well sheltered from the drying sun, for such creatures as sea anemones. The chitons, *Loricata*, with their flattened shells, are examples of the inhabitants of narrow crevices in the rocks, and crabs and worms will hide under boulders and stones. Rock pools harbor a large number of animals, some of which cannot survive the temporary dryness of the beach at low tide. In the absence of rock pools, such species would normally live below the low-water mark.

Channeled wrack, *Pelvetia canaliculata*, grows on rocks on the upper section of the shore.

A brown seaweed of the kelp family, *Laminaria digitata*, is found in the lowest shore zone.

Every type of beach—whether rock or pebble, sand or mud—has its own characteristic assemblage of animals and plants, all of which have become adapted for survival in a complex and often harsh environment lying between land and sea. It is a world of transition, washed by the ebb and flow of the tides and subject to constant change. The upper reaches are covered by seawater only briefly at high tide, while the lower parts of the beach are rarely exposed. Consequently the resident animal and plant species vary from top to bottom of the beach, those at the top having little tolerance of salt water, while those lower down are unable to survive for long without it.

Plants and animals living on the upper part of the beach must be adapted to life circumstances that may change drastically within minutes. They must be capable of being submerged in salt water yet be able to stand the desiccating forces of sun and drying winds at low tide. Those living in pools near the top of the beach must be able to stand the increase of salinity of the water as it evaporates on a hot day, or a decrease as it is diluted by rain. They must be able to stand drastic changes of temperature as the warm pool is suddenly cooled by the invading tide, and must withstand varying acidity of the water, for during a bright sunny day when the plants are photosynthesizing, the water will become highly alkaline, while at night, when they as well as the animals are taking up oxygen, the acidity will increase greatly. Perhaps most taxing of all they must be able to withstand the battering force of the waves, which may come crashing in with unbelievable force in times of storm.

The seaweeds of the seashore are fundamentally different from the flowering plants of the land. Possessed of no roots, stems, leaves, flowers or fruit, they are abundantly successful in the intertidal and sublittoral zones. As almost all are totally lacking in rigidity they cannot support themselves in the air, and at low tide hang dankly over rocks and breakwaters. Yet they have the strength to resist the sea, and it will be seen that when they are torn from their anchorage it is usually the rock that breaks and not the plant. Lacking any hard covering, they produce copious mucilage, which protects them against desiccation. Seaweeds reproduce in a variety of ways and some have complex life histories with alternating free and fixed generations of more than one physical form. They are virtually indigestible to most higher animals, which perhaps accounts for their absence from the inter-tidal zone; however, some invertebrates, particularly some mollusks, are able to feed on them.

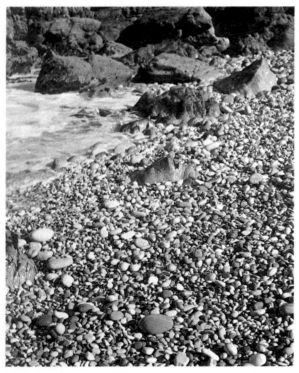

The **barren deserted pebble beach** is formed from rocks that have been constantly pounded, rolled and polished by the action of the waves until they are reduced to smooth fragments. Few plants or animals can survive in this environment as the pebbles are too large to trap and hold water, as does sand or mud, while the incessant shifting of the pebbles would crush the stoutest shell.

Upper zone Sandhopper
Middle zone Mole crab Unarmored worm Tellin
High water
Lower zone Sea cucumber Blue crab
Low water

A sandy beach is formed by the relentless action of the water breaking down fragments of rocks and boulders to fine particles. These are augmented by tiny pieces of the shells of animals. The sand provides no anchorage for seaweeds, and no inviting crevices, but it can hold water between its minute particles and, beneath the surface, the environment is not affected by the vagaries of weather. Thus many inhabitants of the sandy beach spend much of their lives below the surface giving the beach a barren look although it is in fact rich in life. Highly specialized burrowers such as the mole crab and the clams have mechanisms for filtering planktonic food from the water. Debris and seaweed are constantly thrown up onto the beach by the waves and tides and provide rich sources of food for small scavenging creatures including crabs and sandhoppers.

Large numbers of sandhoppers, *Orchestia* spp., scavenge among the debris on the beach.

The mole or sand crab, *Emerita talpoida*, has become modified for its life burrowing in sand.

Unarmored worms of the *Nereis* genus are found under stones and weeds, or in burrows.

The thin tellin, *Tellina tenuis* lives in the sand and feeds through an extended siphon.

Sea cucumbers, *Holothuroidea*, feed on the organic particles contained in the sand.

The blue crab, *Callinectes sapidus*, an edible variety, is an active and agile swimmer.

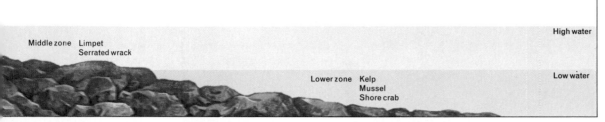

Middle zone Limpet
Serrated wrack

High water

Lower zone Kelp
Mussel
Shore crab

Low water

The sea slater, *Ligia oceanica*, is one inch long and lives in crevices or beneath stones.

The limpet, *Patella vulgata*, has a rough, ribbed shell and lives in dense colonies on the rocks.

The common mussel, *Mytilus edulis*, is a widely distributed animal living on sheltered rocks.

The shore crab, *Carcinus maenas*, is about 1.6 inches long and lives under stones or in rock pools.

Seaweeds such as the serrated wrack, *Fucus serratus*, are fundamentally different from land plants. They have no roots, leaves or flowers yet are perfectly adapted to the coastal environment.

Many groups of animals are found on the shore, protecting themselves against their capricious environment in three main ways: by being armored, by burrowing or by living in the shelter of crevices in the rocks or among the seaweeds. Obvious among the armored forms are the gastropod mollusks. Limpets, which appear totally immobile at low tide, graze the algae from the rocks when they are covered with water. The zigzag marks of their wanderings can often be traced on the rocks, and the scars left by their horny teeth may sometimes be seen in the tiny round holes they bore in the shells of their prey. Other carnivores include the shore fish, many of which lie in wait for small creatures of the rock pools. Sea anemones are also flesh feeders, for they paralyze any small animal unlucky enough to brush against their tentacles, which then pull the helpless prey into the anemone's mouth. This same

technique is used by the anemones' tiny relatives, the hydroids, which trap minute floating creatures of the shore. Tiny organic particles also form the diet of the myriad filter feeders, many of which are sedentary, armored animals. They include the hosts of barnacles on the beach, the multitudes of bivalves that lie hidden beneath the sand, and many species of worms. Some of these lie hidden in burrows; others are protected by sandy, limy or horny tubes into which they retreat at the least sign of danger.

No community is complete without its refuse collectors and an army of scavengers is present as an important part of the seashore food web. Many crustaceans are included among them, from crabs, which feed on dead or moribund fish, to sandhoppers, which appear in their millions to deal with the seaweeds thrown onto the shore by storms.

Upper zone Algae
Eelgrass

Middle zone Fiddler crab

High water

Lower zone Soft-shelled clam
Otter shell
Rag worm

Low water

A **muddy shore** is composed of the finest particles of both organic and inorganic matter often carried down by rivers. The land must be almost flat in order to allow the mud to accumulate sufficiently. The particles are so fine that there is little if any air space between them. Eelgrass, *Zostera*, is an important and abundant feature of these areas and helps to stabilize the shore by trapping and binding the loose silt. It also affords protection for animals living on or around it. Most of the inhabitants of the muddy shore are highly specialized and spend much of their lives beneath the surface, where the coherence of the mud allows them to build permanent burrows. The abundant and well-adapted siphon-feeding clams such as *Mya arenaria*, and burrowing worms, are examples of animals living and feeding in muddy environments.

The green alga, *Rhizoclonium*, a tangled, threadlike seaweed, grows high on the muddy shore.

Eelgrass, *Zostera*, is one of the few flowering plants that have adapted to a marine habitat.

The rag worm, *Nereis diversicolor*, is able to move about on the surface or burrow into the mud.

The soft-shell clam, *Mya arenaria*, is a deep-burrowing species with a long siphon.

The common otter shell, *Lutraria lutraria*, has a siphon twice the length of its shell.

The fiddler crab, *Uca* sp., digs a burrow in the mud into which it retreats if in danger.

SHORELINE ADAPTATIONS

Shore animals have evolved special ways of coping with the physical restrictions of their environments. Those living in exposed rocky situations have tough shells as protection against the buffeting of waves and weather, while creatures of sandy and muddy shores take refuge beneath the surface.

The mussel, *Mytilus edulis*, lives in large, dense colonies forming great mats or beds of animals on the surface of rocks. In order to withstand the battering of waves, the mussel fixes itself to its habitat by means of strong threads, formed from a fluid secreted by a gland near the foot. The fluid strands are attached to the rocks and rapidly harden into exceptionally tough, resilient anchors.

The common limpet, *Patella vulgata*, has two ways of protecting itself from damage from the pounding seas: first a broad-based, strong shell; second, the ability to cling to its rocky home at low tide with the adhesive muscular foot on its underside. When covered by the tide, limpets graze on algae on the surface of rocks, leaving zigzag marks as evidence of their wanderings.

Acorn barnacles, *Balanus balanoides*, are sessile animals constantly exposed to the pounding of the waves. They are protected by a strong shell firmly cemented to the rocks. The shell comprises six overlapping plates and has an upper opening covered by hinged plates; when submerged, the animal opens these plates and extends the long feathery feeding arms in search of food.

Attractive headlet anemones, *Actinia equina*, are among the many anemone species living on the shore. Some live on the rocks; others are adapted to live in deep cavities in the sand. When the tide withdraws, the tentacles can be retracted into the body, which is then contracted into a rounded mass of jelly in order to reduce water loss. The anemone has an adhesive base.

The lugworm, *Arenicola marina*, one of the most common sand worms, lives in a curving tubelike burrow and breathes by means of water currents drawn in at the upper, or tail, end of the burrow and passed to the head end. The worm feeds by swallowing sand and digesting the tiny organic particles it contains. Waste material is passed out of the burrow to form castings on the beach.

The common cockle, *Cardium edule*, is a specialized burrowing species, perfectly adapted for living in mud or sand. One of many plankton feeders, the cockle burrows into the sand using the muscular foot, and then lies with the two feeding siphons projecting above the surface. Water is drawn in through the lower siphon, food is filtered out and the water expelled via the upper siphon.

The unique razor shell can rapidly move under the sand to escape danger. *Ensis siliqua*, the largest at eight inches, has a straight shell. Its huge foot occupies half the shell space when retracted. If disturbed by vibration, it immediately extends the foot into the sand. The foot swells and grips the sand and the powerful muscle contracts to pull the animal down to safety.

THE LIVING REEF

The deep blue of a tropical sea may be broken in some places by patches of paler, greenish color, flecked by the white crests of wavelets breaking where coral reefs reach the surface of the water. Sometimes they surround islands; sometimes they form broken circles of low-lying reefs enclosing shallow lagoons. In either case these obstructions to the great expanse of the ocean are formed by the growth of countless millions of tiny creatures, whose limy skeletons form the rock which rises to the surface of the sea.

Living reefs are among the most brilliantly colored of all environments. The skeleton of most corals is white, but in life this is clothed with a soft tissue, which may be bright green, orange, pink, purple or yellow. Other animals, both vertebrate and invertebrate, are equally vivid in hue and only such skulking predators as the stonefish, which imitates a piece of dead coral, are dull colored. Corals are related to the familiar sea anemones of the shoreline, but they secrete an internal supporting skeleton of hard calcareous material. They are known from all the seas of the world, but those of colder and deeper waters are solitary: only where the water has an average temperature of not less than 68°F can the colonial species flourish, and it is these which are the main reef builders. But not any warm water will do: reef-building corals can thrive only in shallow seas, for their tissues contain minute plants, flagellates, which in order to photosynthesize must have plenty of light. Even in the clearest of tropical waters, light is filtered out below 165 feet to an extent lethal to plants. Therefore, living corals must always be in water of less than this depth. Where they appear to be growing from great depths they provide evidence of steady ocean bed subsidence, matched by upward growth of the corals. Only the surface of the reef is composed of living coral.

A reef-building coral starts life as a minute planktonic larva, which settles on a suitable warm, shallow spot. As it grows, the polyp does not increase greatly in size,

The idyllic island of **Raiatea** in the Pacific Society Island group is surrounded by a fringing reef—one of the three main types of reef. As the island is eroded, the enclosed lagoons will become larger and eventually the island will disappear to leave an atoll.

A reef-building colony consists of a vast number of coral polyps—individual minute anemonelike animals—each of which secretes a hard external skeleton. Layers of the limy secretion build up to form the reef structure. Corals reproduce asexually—forming new individuals by budding.

Platform coral—a species of *Acropora*

Brain coral—*Meandrina*

A gorgonian coral

Golden tubeastrea, *Tubeastrea aurea*, with the polyps exposed

The reef-building, or stony, corals, of which there are many species, totally dominate the coral landscape. *Acropora* is an important fast-growing coral, while the remarkable brain coral, *Meandrina*, although slow to increase, will eventually form large masses having a strong resemblance to the human brain. Gorgonians, or horny corals, do not produce lime and are not reef builders, but have a protein skeleton and are distinctive members of the reef. Vividly colored, they produce graceful, branching colonies interspersed with sea whips and sea fans.

but at a certain stage it divides, budding off another, similar polyp, which remains attached and then buds and divides for itself. Soon there is a colony of hundreds of separate but attached individuals, whose common skeleton forms the basis of the reef. As the colony grows upward, the founder members die, but their calcareous skeletons survive, often changing their crystalline form under pressure and the effect of percolating minerals from above. The strongest coral growth is usually at the outer edge of the reef, where currents of clear water constantly supply minute food particles to the hungry mouths of the polyps. Different species of corals are found in the various areas of the reef and as many as two hundred species have been recorded from a single reef, occupying microniches that vary only slightly in their degree of exposure, turbulence or silting. Their varied shapes offer footholds and homes for many creatures. Some, like the soft corals, sea fans and sea whips are related to the corals themselves. Others, such as the sponges, make impressive growths, which may vie with the corals, while many others are small creatures occupying the richness of living places within the reef. Many are filter feeders, combing the water so efficiently that it has been estimated that over 90 percent of plant plankton and 60 percent of animal plankton is removed from the reef area by them.

Echinoderms are important inhabitants of the reef. Brittle stars occupy every crevice in some shallow areas—their waving arms a trap for tiny floating creatures. In deeper places sea urchins may be abundant, some of them feeding on the coral polyps themselves. Throughout the reef, sea cucumbers are to be found and these inert-looking creatures are important in the development of the reef, for they feed on detritus and fragments of sand and shell—passed through their bodies—sift down to consolidate the loose structure of dead corals. Starfish are generally

not common, but recently one species has assumed great importance in the Indo-Pacific region. Known as the Crown of Thorns, this spiny predator feeds on the living coral polyps and in some areas has caused untold damage to reef structures.

Many varieties of mollusks inhabit the coral reef. Large sea snails, such as the Triton or the Tiger Cowrie, are abundant where their numbers have not been reduced by collectors attracted by their decorative shells. Bivalves, including the giant clam *Tridacna*, occur widely, but may lie almost engulfed by the growth of coral around them. Brilliantly colored sea slugs vie with the brightest corals and tube worms spread their elaborate tentacles to trap the minute food particles which sustain them.

Most colorful of all in this vivid environment are the fish, which find abundant niches in the coral reefs. Some are strongly territorial and will take refuge, whenever danger threatens, in the same clump of coral—even if this is lifted out of the water. Many are deep bodied, but narrow from side to side—an ideal shape for darting through the crevices in the living coral. Some are carnivores, often with extreme specialization in their feeding techniques. Thus long-snouted butterfly fish and surgeon fish feed on coral polyps, which they nip from their cup-shaped homes. Parrot fish are also coral feeders, but they have powerful jaws with which they crunch the coral skeleton as well as the polyps and a band of feeding parrot fish makes a noise which can be heard for some distance through the water. Damsel fish, trumpet fish and wrasse, eels and cavallas, along with a host of others, all have their place in this most colorful and complex of environments. Sharks may patrol on the edge of the reef, but these, along with the barracuda and bonito, flying fish and sailfish that may occasionally be seen there, are really inhabitants of the wide world of the open ocean rather than the closed microcosm of the reef.

Clown surgeon fish, *Acanthurus lineatus*

A sleeping parrot fish—*Scarus* sp.

The twin-spotted wrasse, *Coris angulata*

Electric-blue damsel fish, *Pomacentrus coeruleus*

An abundance of animal life is supported by the coral reef, which provides bases for attachment, hiding places and food. Starfish, sea urchins and mollusks such as the attractive tiger cowrie are important inhabitants, but the most eye-catching are the many varieties of fish. Their bright colors, so outlandish in isolation, become quite inconspicuous against the vivid coral. Many have specially adapted flattened bodies, which allow them to slip easily through gaps in the reef structure. Some are herbivores feeding on algae, while others eat coral polyps.

Sweetlips—*Plectorhynchus cuviera*

The tiger cowrie, *Cyprea tigris*

One hundred square miles of the Great Barrier Reef have already been killed by a predatory starfish known as the Crown of Thorns, *Acanthaster planci*. Once a rare species, its numbers have greatly increased and up to nine individuals per square yard have been recorded. A single animal may measure up to 16 inches across and may consume 16 square inches of coral in 24 hours, leaving a trail of destruction across the reef.

THE LIGHTED ZONE

0–50 g C/m² /yr
50–100 g C/m² /yr
100–200 g C/m² /yr
over 200 g C/m² /yr

0–100 g C/m² /yr
100–400 g C/m² /yr
400–800 g C/m² /yr
over 800 g C/m² /yr

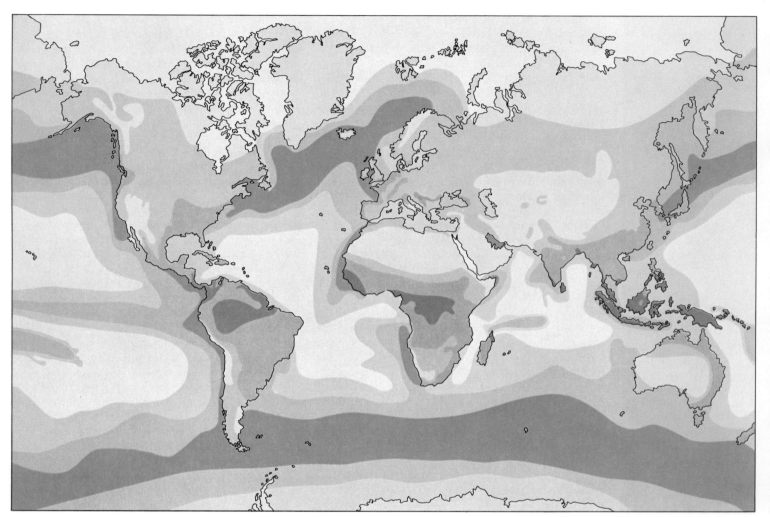

The term primary productivity describes the creation of organic matter by plants from inorganic elements, using the sun's energy captured by the photosynthesis process. The material produced is then available for use by animals. The primary productivity pattern of the world for both land and sea, measured in grams of carbon per square meter per year, is shown on the map. The oceans cover about 70 percent of the earth's surface, but only the sunlit surface waters can support plant life. Marine plants are of two main types: seaweeds, which grow in coastal regions, and single-celled floating plants known as phytoplankton elsewhere in the oceans. Their abundance is determined by such factors as circulation, current systems and upwellings of nutrient-rich water. The fertility of a region affects the type of plant and animal community it supports.

Seasonal cycles of plankton production vary according to the environment. The characteristic Arctic cycle has a single peak in the summer—the only period of sufficient light for plant production. In the North Atlantic temperate zone, zooplankton increase must await the spring bloom of phytoplankton, which grazing pressure then quickly reduces. In the North Pacific, however, zooplankton overwinter as a shallow layer of subadults and thus can take immediate advantage of phytoplankton, absorbing any spring increase. The tropical cycle shows only a series of minor increases and reductions in plankton stocks occurring throughout the year.

Phytoplankton
Zooplankton

J F M A M J J A S O N D
Arctic

J F M A M J J A S O N D
North Atlantic

J F M A M J J A S O N D
North Pacific

J F M A M J J A S O N D
Tropical

High-productivity assemblage

Low-productivity assemblage

1 Chaetoceros holsaticum
2 Rhizosolenia habetata
3 Limacina helicina
4 Calanus finmarchicus
5 Euphausia sp.
6 Chaetoceros furca
7 Coscinodiscus radiatus
8 Rhizosolenia castracanii
9 Planktoniella sol
10 Ceratium palmatum
11 Ceratium reticulatum
12 Dinophysis schutti
13 Thalassicolla
14 Bougainvillea ramosa
15 Sarsia prolifera
16 Sagitta serratodentata
17 Sagitta enflata
18 Stylocheiron elongatum
19 Salpa fusiformis
20 Euchaeta norvegica
21 Eucalanus attenuatus
22 Pontella atlantica
23 Calocalanus plumosa
24 Corycaeus gracilis

Animal and plant plankton communities in high-productivity areas of the ocean are dominated by large numbers of few species, while low-productivity areas support very diverse communities.

Sunlight, because it is scattered and absorbed rather rapidly, can only penetrate to a limited depth in seawater. Within the resulting narrow sunlit zone of the oceans are found assemblages of animals with common characteristics, all dependent on the fact that it is only in this lighted zone that plants are able to obtain energy from the sun and grow; therefore it is only here that the plant–herbivore–carnivore food chain can develop.

The nature of the life forms that inhabit the lighted zone is determined by the circulation patterns of the superficial watermasses of the oceans and by the diverse processes which serve to bring nutrient-rich water from the deeps up into the lighted zone. These nutrients help the populations of plant plankton to develop and produce the green turbid water which contrasts so strongly with the clear blue water of less dynamic regions. A number of different oceanographic processes serve to bring deep water to the surface. Off the coasts of Oregon–California and Peru–Chile in the Pacific and Mauritania and Namibia in the Atlantic, wind-driven coastal upwellings occur between the coast and the main boundary currents, while, in a broad band stretching along the equator from the Americas almost to the western side of the Pacific, divergence of watermasses due to the interaction of the trade winds and Coriolis force results in midocean upwellings. In high latitude regions of both Northern and Southern hemispheres, deep water may be brought to the surface by the intense mixing caused by winter storms and it is these upwellings, combined with the effects of the increasing spring sunshine, that form the basis for the spring bloom of plankton in these regions. Localized combinations of submarine topography and currents may also result in vertical mixing of watermasses: strong vertical eddying may occur in the wake of an island or headland projecting into a strong current, and even the shearing force between two opposing

currents in the open ocean can create vertical eddying sufficiently strong to raise deep nutrient-rich waters into the surface layers. The sum of all these processes determines the quantitative distribution of plant material as phytoplankton throughout the oceans and corresponds to the familiar maps of worldwide distribution of terrestrial vegetation. The difference between oceanic areas with rich and poor plant life is at least as great as that between forests and deserts on land.

The organization of the life forms that inhabit the enriched areas of the ocean differs strikingly from that in the areas with sparse plant populations and hence highly transparent water. In the enriched areas the diversity of both plant and animal plankton is reduced so that the communities of organisms are dominated by large numbers of very few species and food chains are relatively simple. Animal plankton in such areas is dominated numerically by herbivores, the percentage of carnivores rising gradually as the distance from the enriched area increases. Copepods, usually of the genus *Calanus*, and euphausiids are the most abundant animal plankton and are fed upon by large populations of fish and birds—again not as diverse in species as in the clearer, poorer waters of the central watermasses of the ocean. The populations of enriched areas, often dominated by clupeid fish—anchovies, sardines and herrings—are the basis of the great fisheries, such as those of California and Peru and of Morocco and Namibia, which contribute such a high percentage of the total world catch of fish from the sea. The highly diverse plankton communities, away from the direct influence of the enriched zones, support quite different fishery resources based upon the predatory; highly migratory tunas, bonito and sword-fish.

Imposed upon this pattern of high and low plant production, the main current systems have their own effect upon the distribution of organisms in the surface layers of the ocean. By controlling the manner in which

Subarctic assemblage

Central assemblage

1 *Eukrohnia hamata*
2 *Tomopteris pacifica*
3 *Euphausia pacifica*
4 *Sagitta elegans*
5 *Clione limacina*
6 *Parathemisto pacifica*
7 *Globigerina quinqueloba*
8 *Limacina helicina*

9 *Stylocheiron suhmi*
10 *Sagitta pseudoserratodentata*
11 *Euphausis brevis*
12 *Euphausia mutica*
13 *Clausocalanus paululus*
14 *Cavolina inflexa*
15 *Styliola subula*
16 *Limacina Lesuerii*

The **Pacific Ocean** has eight major plankton communities, the distribution of which is controlled by the current systems of the ocean. The map illustrates the extent of the "core" zones of all these communities and their relationship with the main current systems: the outermost contour of each zone extends farther and may overlap with other zones. The boundaries of each "core" include the distribution of all species associated with that zone. The assemblages illustrate examples of zooplankton species characteristic of the subarctic and central zones of the Pacific.

organisms can be transported from one place to another, the currents control the patterns of species distribution.

Recent studies of the distribution of planktonic species over the great area of the Pacific Ocean have shown that there are eight major plankton communities, the distribution of which is controlled by the current systems. The superficial watermasses and currents are symmetrical in the Northern and Southern hemispheres, except where they are modified by landmasses, therefore so are the plankton communities. For example, there is a subarctic community between about 50 and 60 degrees latitude in each hemisphere, but, because of the small extent of land in the Southern Hemisphere, the community is much less restricted in the South than it is in the North Pacific. These eight communities each cover a vast area of ocean, far exceeding the area of any terrestrial ecological community, and research has shown that there is relatively little mixing where their edges meet. The species composition of each area changes very little from one place to another thousands of miles away, and because the general form of the Pacific Ocean is so ancient— equatorial current systems can be traced back at least to the Miocene period 26 million years ago—it can be assumed that these communities are the oldest now existing on our planet. They are also among the least disturbed by man's impact on the ecosystems of the planet: in fact it would take an engineering work of the scale of the proposed sea-level canal at Panama to seriously disrupt these patterns of animal distribution.

A special category of marine organisms—the tunas and billfish—remains independent of these communities. These fish, which have high metabolic rates and a capacity for sustained high-speed swimming, perform routine transpacific and transatlantic migrations each year. In this way they place themselves in areas of abundant food supply at the appropriate times of the year.

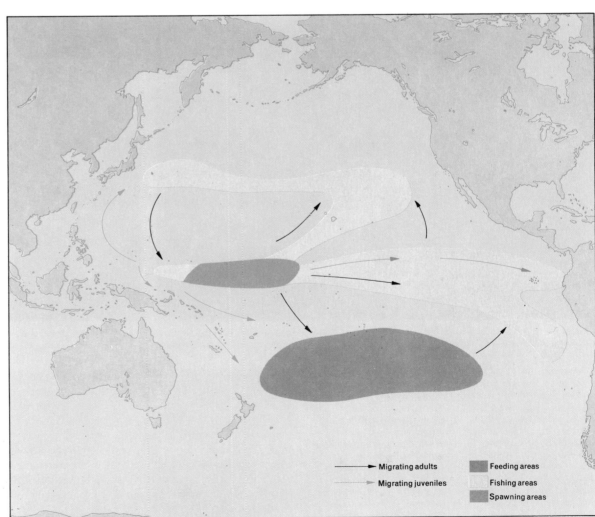

→ Migrating adults
→ Migrating juveniles

Feeding areas
Fishing areas
Spawning areas

Many other creatures inhabit the Pacific Ocean besides the zooplankton communities. The fast-swimming tunas are a special group as, because of their speed, they are not obliged to remain attached to one particular planktonic community. The bigeye tuna make long migrations across the ocean to place themselves in the optimum feeding or spawning areas for the time of year.

REALMS OF PERMANENT DARKNESS

Below the shallow surface layers illuminated by sunlight, and below the reach of the main surface current systems, great regions of permanent darkness stretch over all oceans virtually from pole to pole. This zone of permanent darkness extends to the ocean floor and thus encompasses about 90 percent of the whole water column in most places beyond the continental shelves, and about 95 percent of the water column over the greatest ocean depths. Within this region, which thus comprises so large a part of the total volume of the oceans, there is great uniformity: temperature varies relatively slowly with depth, remaining almost stable over great horizontal distances, and the seasons are almost imperceptible as are, of course, day and night. Water circulation, and hence current speeds, are generally very slow and must be trivial as an ecological factor except in certain places close to the bottom,

where bottom topography causes currents to be discernible. The abyssal plain itself is a vast, largely featureless expanse of soft ooze derived from the skeletons of planktonic organisms, which live in the superficial lighted zone. Only where midocean ridges, banks and coral atolls give structure to the ocean floor is there any important variability in the abyssal environment.

In these conditions it is not surprising to find that the fauna is correspondingly unchanging over great distances, for instance in the Atlantic there is great similarity between widely separated communities occurring on the continental slopes at about 1500 feet below sea level.

Of the 11 species of invertebrates that characterize the upper-slope community off tropical West Africa, no less than eight are also important in the equivalent

community off western France, a phenomenon made less surprising by the fact that the two environments differ by less than one degree centigrade in average temperature, although they are separated by nearly 40 degrees of latitude. Although biological exploration at such great depths is still in a very early stage, it is reasonable to suppose that these similarities may extend over very much greater distances on the Atlantic continental slopes, and that the same principle may apply in other oceans.

On the abyssal plains beyond the foot of the continental rise the situation has been better explored by the far-ranging Soviet exploratory oceanographic voyages of the 1950s and 1960s. The Soviet scientists found that each ocean has its own characteristic fauna of deep seafloor invertebrates with less than a quarter of all known species from these regions being common

The bizarre viper fish, *Chauliodus* sp., has very specialized jaws, studded with curving fangs that are capable of gaping to a huge extent—thus enabling the fish to consume large prey.

Orange or even bright scarlet bodies are a characteristic of the deep-sea varieties of copepods and euphausiids such as *Benteuphausia* sp., *above*. The lighted-zone species are usually transparent.

The cranchid group of deep-water squid have silvery translucent bodies and are able to hover in midwater by means of an ammonia-filled gland with which they maintain neutral buoyancy.

The abyssal plain, blanketed with layers of sediment built up from the skeletons of planktonic organisms, over many thousands of years, appears stark and desolate and in fact the density of animal life is extremely low. However, there are creatures that have adapted to life on the deep-ocean floor: some live burrowed in the ooze, from which they can also derive nourishment; some lurk to prey on the life that exists. Other animals, living attached to the seafloor, feed on the fine particles of

organic debris in the water. Sea pens, crinoids and glass sponges, like the exquisite Venus flower basket, live in this way. Echinoderms—starfish, urchins and sea cucumbers—are the most abundant animals of the abyssal landscape. Sea cucumbers are particularly numerous and leave characteristic trails in the soft ooze of the seafloor. Fish also live on the abyssal plain, one of the most remarkable being the predatory tripod fish, which can stand in silent ambush on its slender fins.

Deep-sea polychaete worm

Sea pen (Pennatulid)

Deep-sea crabs living on sponge

Brittle stars (Ophiuroids) and trails

to all oceans. They also discovered that the more ubiquitous species tended to be those inhabiting the greatest depth ranges—animal life being at its most restricted in horizontal distribution in the greatest depths of oceanic trenches.

The pelagic and planktonic animals—both fish and invertebrates—appear to be even more widely distributed than the bottom-dwellers and many occur in all oceans within a very wide range of latitudes: there appears to have been a much greater interchange of pelagic organisms than of benthic during the geological history of the oceans.

The energy expended by the organisms in the dark zone depends on the arrival of basic food material from the surface waters: phytoplankton cells and dead zooplankton gently settle from the lighted zone above, the bodies of larger organisms sink more rapidly to the bottom, and partly decomposed organic material of terrestrial origin slides down the submarine canyons cut into the continental edges. Food supplies decrease with depth and there is a corresponding decrease in the abundance of animal life. Near the division between the lighted and dark zones, where the separation between the abundant surface life and the sparse fauna of the deeper water occurs, the decrease is very fast, and from this critical depth animal life continues to decrease gradually to the greatest ocean depths. It has gradually come to be realized, however, that the sparse abyssal fauna, both planktonic and benthic, is highly diverse—at least as diverse as the shallow-water fauna of tropical seas. Paradoxical as it may seem, it is now understood that such high diversity of animal species is related to the stability and unchanging nature of the abyssal habitat.

The very low temperature of abyssal water, between two and five degrees centigrade even at the equator, combined with the scanty food supply, results in the abyssal fauna having an exceedingly low metabolic rate; each individual grows very slowly and tends to live for a very long time indeed. Bivalve mollusks, living on the ooze at 10,000 feet off the east coast of North America, are known to be up to 250 years old, though still only an inch or so long. Thus, though the fauna of the abyssal regions covers almost exactly half the surface of our planet, it is clear that its biological productivity holds no promise for commercial exploitation to supplement our failing fisheries. Moreover, the abyss must be extremely vulnerable to the effects of pollution such as the dumping of industrial wastes in the deep ocean as, because of the slow growth rates, damage to this ecosystem is repaired very slowly.

A widely distributed deep-sea jellyfish, *Atolla* sp., with its subtle colors, is one of the more beautiful creatures of the deeps.

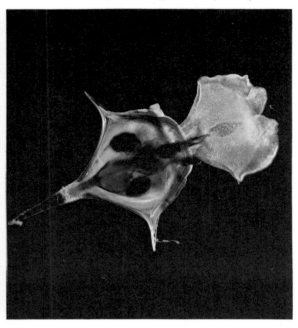

The deep-sea species of pteropods, such as *Diacria* sp., have varying amounts of dark, brownish coloration.

Seemingly an iridescent monster, the hatchet fish, *Argyropelecus* sp., would in fact fit on the palm of your hand. It has a laterally compressed coin-like body and its bulging upturned eyes and huge gaping mouth help to make it a successful predator.

The aptly named snipe eel, *Nemicthys* sp., is distinguished by the diverging beaklike jaws used to collect its crustacean food.

Rat tails, Macrouridae, with their large heads and whiplike tails, are among the most common fish at the greatest depths of the ocean.

The example above is a pelagic species, but many macrourids live close to the abyssal floor, where they graze for food.

is bigelowi

Deep-sea starfish, *Porcellanaster* sp.

Stalked and free-living crinoids

Sea spider, *Colossendeis* sp.

Venus flower basket, *Euplectella* sp.

Sea cucumber (Holothurian) and trail

Sea urchin, *Porocidaris* sp.

THE GREAT RESOURCE

Lake Maracaibo is the largest and richest of the three main oil-producing regions that between them make up Venezuela's known reserves of 18,000 million barrels. The lake covers 8296 square miles and is linked to the Caribbean by a narrow channel flowing north into the Gulf of Venezuela. In the early 1970s production was running at 3,700,000 barrels a day, and in 1976 oil exports accounted for nearly 97 percent of the country's foreign exchange income. Between 1974 and 1976 the Venezuelan government took the unusual step of reducing the rate of oil extraction in order to conserve reserves.

THE INSHORE FISHERMAN

During the present century, a way of life which took thousands of years to evolve has been largely extinguished. The spread of mechanized fishing vessels powered first by steam and later by oil has sadly reduced the rich variety of local coastal fisheries in all parts of the world. Many of the very successful and skillful West African inshore canoe fisheries have been destroyed by competition from cheaper imported frozen fish, while in Europe many of the traditional fishing techniques have simply been abandoned in favor of newer and more profitable methods.

The variety of techniques used prior to the impact of twentieth-century technology is almost endless. Rafts were floated far out to sea, attracting shoals of fish into their shade—and into the nets of the waiting fishermen. Great circular nets of woven palm fiber were cast from the bows of canoes to fall fully extended over shoals feeding in clear shallow waters; men of the Kru tribe of Liberia worked far out to sea in their tiny dugouts, trolling with lures on short lines to take the fast-swimming tuna, cavalla and barracuda; and in the Mediterranean great permanent fish traps, probably unchanged for thousands of years, were built on

prominent capes to intercept the schools of migrating tuna.

The boats, too, were wonderfully diverse and as perfectly adapted to their work as were the fishing techniques themselves. Each region had its own characteristic vessel, well suited to local conditions and often showing the influence of historical connections with other regions. Thus, the canoes of tropical West Africa do not have stabilizing outriggers, and planked boats are built on patterns learned from Portuguese mariners of the sixteenth century; boats of the eastern coast of Africa, where there is no historical connection with Europe, are almost entirely of the typical Indo-Pacific type. Even in Europe today, the shape of the early sailing boats is recognizable in the hull shapes of diesel-powered fishing boats working out of small ports like Brixham and Buckie.

Because coastal fisheries operate almost entirely with small boats, coastal fishermen have always been limited in their ability to follow the fish on their migrations. Consequently coastal fisheries for many, though not all, species are seasonal in nature and are very vulnerable to long-term changes in the distribution

and behavior of the target species. The Swedish herring fisheries suffered four major periods of failure between 1400 and 1950, each due almost certainly to the diversion of the shoals into the Norwegian area—far beyond the range of the Swedish fleets—in response to climatic changes. In each of these periods the rich herring fisheries suffered a period of decline lasting for more than 75 years.

Increasingly in recent years coastal fishermen have been in conflict with the larger vessels of the distant-water fleets; a situation keenly felt by the tropical fisheries, where trawlers from distant ports have overfished inshore waters with disastrous repercussions on local fisheries. Similarly, the inshore fleets of Europe and North America have been increasingly threatened by the operations of huge fleets of factory trawlers and, in some areas, the severe depletion of fish stocks in the main fishing grounds has been reflected in an almost total loss of fish stocks from neighboring inshore areas.

It is almost impossible to assess accurately the contribution of the coastal fisheries to the total world harvest from the seas, but in two respects the traditional inshore fisheries are of great importance. In many regions of the tropical Third World they have developed as an integral part of the local peasant economy, often on a seasonal or part-time basis, so that fishing and farming activities alternate in the local village calendar. The disruption of part of this fabric, before the evolution out of subsistence economy of the remainder, may destroy the whole structure of the society. And even within the much stronger and diverse economies of industrialized nations, many products of the inshore fisheries, including lobsters, crabs, shrimps, octopuses and shellfish, have a very high commercial value and cannot be provided by the far-ranging and mechanized deep-water fleets.

Fijian rock-wall traps were built on gently sloping shores between high and low water in order to strand shoals of fish above the receding tide. This is one of the most primitive of fish-trapping techniques, used since prehistoric times.

Fish species that commonly swim parallel to the coast may be deflected into the fisherman's hands by strategically placed fences. The seaward end of each fence leads into a heart-shaped trap, so constructed that once inside the fish cannot escape.

Barbed hooks, and gorges made of bone or wood, are among the many devices used to prevent a fish from escaping after striking at a baited line. The sharp gorge is hidden within the bait so that when swallowed it rotates and lodges in the fish's gullet.

Small shoals swimming close inshore may be encircled with a beach seine paid out from a small boat. Fish are frightened into the central bag by shouting and splashing, after which the net is hauled onto the beach by the teams of fishermen.

To escape the attention of predators, bottom-dwelling fish spend much of their time among rocks and reeds. The fisherman exploits this behavior by placing bundles of brushwood in the water, hoping that they will be mistakenly adopted as refuges.

The spear fisherman faces a problem not encountered by the hunter on land. Due to the refraction of light at the water surface his prey is not where it appears to be. To strike a fish he must aim at a point nearer than its apparent position.

In shallow muddy water, where neither fish nor fisherman can see each other clearly, or where the seabed is too rough to use nets, fish are often caught using cover pots. The fishermen work slowly forward, trapping the fish under hand-held pots.

Fyke nets consist of a series of conical nets leading one into the next and ending in a cylindrical chamber. The net is usually set to catch fish swimming with the current. Wings of netting are spread out from the entrance to increase the catchment area.

In shallow water, where the seabed is smooth, a net may be skimmed across the bottom to catch shrimps and small fish. Bobbinlike objects on the ends of the frame ensure that the net glides easily over muddy areas as the user pushes it before him.

Lobster pots are generally made of heavy netting or basketwork on a stout wooden frame—the darker and more claustrophobic the better, as lobsters like to hide in dark crevices. The pots are usually baited with crabmeat.

A springy branch, bent over and held by a quick-release device, may be used to activate a wide variety of traps and automatic fishing lines. The triggering mechanism of this Congolese trap is dislodged by the fish tugging at the bait.

The lift net is used to catch small surface-swimming fish, often for use as bait. The net is lowered into the water either by hand or by a derrick. When the fish swim over it, the net must be raised swiftly from the water before the shoal can swim on.

Dredges are used for harvesting shellfish from muddy or gravelly areas. When towed behind a boat the teeth on the leading edge of the dredge prise loose clams and other burrowing creatures. This particular dredge is designed to be used in cowrie fishing.

The interest created by the fishermen landing their catch at the Lake Edward fishing village of Vitshumbi, Zaire, is an indication of the economic importance of this activity to the local inhabitants. Fishing at a small-scale subsistence level makes an important contribution, often equal to that of agriculture, to the economies of many developing countries.

Traps such as these being set off the coast of Martinique are designed to catch crabs and lobsters, and are used in one form or other for this purpose all over the world. The traps are weighted to ensure they sink, and strung together on lengths of line to make them easier to locate. The end of the line is attached to a brightly colored marker buoy.

Brazilian fishermen haul in their catch in the early morning.

The sailing canoes of the Caroline Islands are among the most graceful of fishing boats.

Throwing a cast net 30 feet across, so that it opens to its maximum extent as it hits the water, requires a high degree of skill. The weighted outer edge pulls the net down over the fish, entangling them and pinning them to the bottom. The net lines are then hauled in, closing the net like a purse around the catch. More sophisticated nets have a number of pockets around the edge, which are similarly closed as the lines are tightened. The cast net is ideally suited to regions of clear, shallow water, where the bed is free of rocks.

Gill nets have the advantage of restricting their catch to fish of one size and therefore the harvesting of a particular area can be strictly controlled. The nets are made of fine cord, which when immersed in water is invisible to approaching fish.

The trammel net consists of two coarse outer nets suspended at either side of a fine entangling net. It is bulky and conspicuous and would normally be avoided by the fish. However, when alarmed by noisemakers, the fish swim blindly into the mesh.

Fish traps that do not depend on a mechanical triggering system must incorporate some form of nonreturn device to prevent the fish from escaping. In the case of the pound net, the fish are led up a ramp of netting, which takes them well above their normal level. They emerge into the top of a deep baglike compartment in which they are free to swim back down to their usual swimming depth. Because the fish do not normally leave their accustomed level unless forced to, they remain at this level—totally unaware of the

escape route some feet above them. Traps of this type are used in Japan for catching sardine; wide netting wings being added to funnel shoaling fish into the foot of the ramp. The large nets, however, are very easily damaged by rough weather.

FISHING THE DEEPS

In the fifteenth and sixteenth centuries, the discovery of rich stocks of fish on distant banks and coasts impelled the more adventurous inshore fishermen to take advantage of the great advances that had been made in the sciences of boat-building and navigation. The lure of great herring shoals drew Dutch, Swedish and British fishermen to the farthest corners of the North Sea, and their countries into armed conflict over the commercial prizes to be gained from these resources. The demand for oils and skins in the eighteenth century stimulated a search for seals and whales in the North Atlantic. These stocks were rapidly overfished, until by the early nineteenth century they had declined below profitable levels. The Yankee whalers now came into their own, sailing to all parts of the globe from the coasts of New England in vessels that were among the most seaworthy and beautiful that have ever been built.

As early as the seventeenth century Devon fishermen made the transatlantic voyage to the Newfoundland cod fisheries: in the nineteenth century the Portuguese made the same crossing in large sailing ships laden with small single-man dories. Once on the grounds, individual dorymen spread out from the mother ship to fish with hand-held baited lines under the most arduous conditions. The salted "bacalao" from these fisheries became a staple food in Spain and Portugal and remained so almost until the present day.

The introduction of steam and diesel propulsion accelerated the exploitation of distant fishing resources, and during the present century trawlers have probed northward into the Arctic Ocean in search of haddock and cod, carrying ice as a preservative. Voyages of three weeks to the coasts of Greenland, with only a few hours in port between voyages, became commonplace by the 1930s. Crewing was possible under such harsh conditions only because of the economic depression then prevailing. After World War II the economics of the industry were further improved by a series of important innovations: modern refrigeration enabled catches to be preserved in good condition for long periods at sea and electronic navigational aids and acoustic locating devices made it possible to operate economically a new generation of large fishing vessels far from their home ports.

Three main types of new vessel were developed at this time: the giant purse seiner, evolved for distant waters from the small Norwegian mackerel and herring ring netters; oceanic long-liners capable of fishing for tuna over the whole extent of the tropical oceans, and the factory trawlers. This last type, pioneered in Britain, was taken up by many European and Asian countries, but above all by the socialist states of Eastern Europe, whose massive fleets, built up in the sixties, have fished the continental shelves of the world as much as 10,000 miles from their home ports. The housewife in Moscow is offered fish from Antarctica, Pacific America, the African coasts and Europe.

The use by the Americans of highly sophisticated purse seiners in pursuit of tuna on the high seas has proved to be so profitable that these ships, though based in California, are to be found in the Atlantic and Indian oceans as well as the Pacific. Their large nets are capable of enclosing a whole school of tuna at one set and the ships have the capacity to carry 1500 tons of frozen fish in their holds.

In competition with the purse seiners are fleets of pelagic long-liners, mainly originating from Japan and South Korea. Each vessel lays behind it between one and three floating long-lines, each more than twenty miles long and bearing baited hooks every few feet. The main target species are far-ranging predatory fish such as marlin, sailfish and tuna.

The future of many of these highly capitalized fisheries is in serious doubt as more and more nations declare wide zones off their coasts to be restricted fisheries areas and as the resources on which they have worked in the past become increasingly unprofitable due to overfishing. Already, many distant-water vessels have been laid up and a return to local exploitation of offshore fisheries with small vessels seems to be a highly probable trend for the future.

The rapid growth of European populations in the nineteenth century produced an increased demand for food. The fishing industry responded in a period of dramatic expansion—the number of trawlers at Grimsby, England, grew from 24 in 1855 to 600 in 1877. Increased competition forced fishermen farther offshore into new waters such as the North Sea. Fishing was initially confined to the south, but by 1900 the whole sea was being exploited to meet demand.

Bridge

The Hammond Innes is a wet-fish trawler, that is, it does not freeze its catch at sea but transports it on ice, "wet," back to port. Wet-fish trawlers are used on short and medium trips to the North Sea and off the coasts of Norway and Iceland, where they are in easy reach of their home ports of Hull and Grimsby. On a good three-week trip a ship like this will make seventy or eighty hauls and catch over 200 tons of fish. On each haul the net is winched up the stern chute onto the deck, the cod end is untied, and the fish are sent down the fish hatch into a large tank, where they are fed by conveyor through the gutting and washing machines and into the fish hold to be stored in ice until the catch is landed.

Engine room: The main engines develop 2500 bhp at 500 rpm.

Crew accommodation

Trawl winches: Two hydraulic winches haul the 4-ton trawling gear with catch on deck.

From 1880 onward, steam and then diesel dominated sail as a means of propulsion for offshore fishing vessels. As fishing was no longer dependent on the presence of favourable winds, it could be carried out more confidently farther away from home. European trawlers ventured northward into the Arctic Ocean to exploit its rich stocks of cod and haddock. In this period there was very little mechanization, either on board or at major fishing ports such as Grimsby.

Stern trawlers have gradually replaced the older side-working trawlers since the 1950s. The ability to tow fishing gear directly astern greatly increases the maneuverability of the vessel and the size of the nets that can be used. The catch, as much as 80 tons, is hauled up over the stern and released onto the deck. Many stern trawlers are able to freeze their catch on board or, in the case of a factory trawler, to refine the waste materials, such as bone and skin, into fish meal.

Fish are detected by sonar equipment operated on board fishing vessels. A detector, located in the ship's hull, emits pulses of sound and measures the time taken for them to be echoed back by the seabed; when a shoal of fish swims within range, the sound waves are echoed back in a shorter time. The shoal appears on the screen of a recorder as a hyperbola, rising above the seabed. A second monitor, located within the net itself, indicates whether the net is correctly set to catch the fish detected. This information is relayed to the ship by a receiver towed astern.

Hydraulic net drum

Gutting machines: "Shetland" type designed for small round fish such as cod.

Fish washers

Fish hatch

Fish hold: 19,500 cubic feet of space, capable of holding 250 tons of wet fish.

Ice pounds: The catch is kept on ice to prevent deterioration.

Cod liver oil tank

World commercial catch in thousand metric tons (1974)

13,731
12,697
4,587
3,621
3,312
2,449
1,875
1,178
749
558

A B C D E F G H I J

A   Shark, ray, chimaera
B   Shad, milkfish
C   Flounder, halibut, sole
D   Tuna, bonito, billfish
E   Salmon, trout, smelt
F   Jack, mullet, saury
G   Mackerel, snook, cutlassfish
H   Redfish, bass, conger eel
I   Cod, hake, haddock
J   Herring, sardine, anchovy

THE NEW RESOURCE

The new resource of the ocean realm could affect man's future approach to world food supplies in a number of dramatic ways. Already the "battery farming" of some marine species has reached a high level of sophistication with bizarre-looking laboratory apparatus, *above*, being used to culture algal growth as an enriched food for developing oysters. Turtles are also farmed intensively, *right*, in many parts of the world and, in common with most of the mariculture techniques currently in use, produce low-bulk, high-value produce for the world market. Detailed study of the genetic makeup of mangroves, *left*, may eventually make possible the development of salt-tolerant strains of traditional food crops and hence make salt-water irrigation practicable.

The food webs of the open ocean differ dramatically from those on land, and man's efforts to feed himself by fisheries are very different from his approach to hunting for food on land. On land the food animals have nearly always been herbivores—animals that live on vegetation, nuts, seeds and fruit, or at least omnivores—those that consume a wide range of foods. No society ever conceived of attempting to feed itself on tigers. Yet at sea most herbivores are microscopic, and most often the creatures at the relative food web level of tigers or higher are the object of the marine fisheries. Potential food supply at such levels will ever be a factor of at least ten less than that of the creatures that feed directly on the microscopic plants and other fine particles of food in the sea.

It is immediately clear that the direct use of marine plants for human food will remain a rather minor contribution to world requirements. Seaweeds large enough to be used as food sources are of low nutritional value and represent only a very small part of the sea's productivity. Also, the areas in which they grow most prolifically are far removed from the main centers of population. Almost all of the sea's production is contained in a thin broth of single plant cells in the surface water of the ocean.

A simple consideration will show how inaccessible these cells are as a direct source of food for man. If a large ship were to steam at its most efficient speed through the richest part of the sea, and all of the food particles in the waters that it displaced in its motion were miraculously to appear in its hold, the cost of the catch would still be some hundreds of dollars per ton—many times its value as a food source. For the major part, the sea will continue to provide only animal food for humans.

In order to consider the future course of the development of the sea and marine animals as a food source, we should briefly review the steps by which modern animal husbandry has come into being.

Following the hunting and gathering stage, there is frequently a herding or ranching development. At this stage the preferred herbivorous livestock is semi-domesticated and guided in its grazing on a more or less natural range, while some burning, deforestation and predator control is exercised. It should be noted that much advanced animal husbandry is still conducted in this way where the quality of the range is too poor for man to collect the crop by his own efforts, with machine or otherwise. Rather, he continues to depend on his herds of livestock to collect the sparse vegetation, using the energy of that vegetation, rather than diesel oil, for its harvesting. It is precisely this mode of culture that is most broadly promising for marine animal husbandry.

Farming, the next stage of husbandry, is developed where land and crops are more abundant. Here there is a high degree of control of vegetation, and protection of the animals from weather and predators. Feed crops, most often gathered through the husbandman's efforts, are fed directly to the animals.

Where prices and economic development warrant, farming develops into its most advanced form, known as battery culture or feed-lot culture. In its final development this involves complexly formulated food materials purchased from whatever sources are economically feasible, even foreign if necessary. In each of these stages, disease control becomes increasingly necessary, and the selection of animals for qualities that are disadvantageous in the wild, such as rapid growth, inactivity and passivity, becomes important.

In our marine animal husbandry, we are attempting to condense this long land development and leap rapidly into a marine equivalent of battery culture, yet each of these phases has its place at sea, with peculiar advantages and differences unique to the sea.

In sea ranching, for example, there are great advantages in utilizing those animals with a homing instinct. The salmon, shad and smelt can be raised as young and then sent out to range freely until they return as adults. No land ranching ever enjoyed the advantage of an instinctive "roundup." The variety of organisms available for ranching, while not great, is still considerable and fortunately includes a number that feed rather primitively in the ocean—the shad and

Fish farming techniques have for many years been the subject of intensive study by teams of marine biologists and food scientists. High-value fish may be raised from spawn to maturity without ever being released into the sea; others may be raised through the vulnerable young stages and then released to boost natural stocks.

THE CLAUDE CONDENSATER

The power available in the thermal gradient of the ocean is almost unlimited but difficult to utilize efficiently. A possible solution is to use the power directly at source as a means of generating freshwater supplies. In the Claude condensater, very cold deep water (a) is pumped to the surface and used to cool the surface of a spray chamber (b). Moisture condenses (c) from the warm humid air drawn through the apparatus and is drawn off into tanks (d). The coolant water, warmed in the chamber, is passed through a heat exchanger (e) after use so that its temperature is reduced before it is returned to the sea. An added advantage of the system is that nutrient-rich deep water is cycled into the upper layers—so enhancing surface-water productivity.

smelt for example—rather than high in the food web—as do the salmons—where the total food and total potential crop are considerably less.

A ranching system in the sea would consist of large raising and harvesting pens—possibly involving the release of some attractant chemical to reinforce the chemical memory, and clues for adults seeking to return home. Some predator and competitor control might also be exercised. This would easily take the form of a cooperative commercial fishery. In one of our present sea-ranching efforts—the raising and release of salmon young—this aspect seems to be overlooked. In Puget Sound in British Columbia and Washington, systems are employed to avoid catching the dogfish, a small shark and both a predator and competitor to the salmon. Clearly the living room and food for salmon is being reduced by the increasing populations of dogfish. Future sea-ranching cannot be conducted so simple-mindedly. Other fisheries must be employed, by subsidy if necessary, for a judicious control of predators and competitors in the open sea range.

The analogy of farming at sea enjoys advantages of which no land farmer ever conceived, for food is effortlessly brought to the farmer's charges. The mussel and oyster and other filter feeders have no analogy on land, unless it be the spider with her nets spread to the breeze. It is this aspect of shellfish culture that caused it to be so spectacularly productive. No

other harvest approaches the same 100 tons of organic productivity per hectare per year of some mussel beds. Of course, this is not the initial productivity of only one hectare, for the food is elaborated in, and derived from, much greater areas and swept through or across the shellfish bed by currents.

Holding schools of young fish in floating pens anchored in coastal currents also appears to be a meaningful technique of farming. The pens allow the food organisms to enter but not the predators and competitors, and the Japanese have raised yellowtail and other fish in this way with excellent success.

The battery culture of marine animals for food is receiving considerable attention—and some success. In such a system, rather high-quality feed must be supplied, and this must be obtained on the world market often at considerable expense. General operating expenses may therefore always restrict such systems to the raising of relatively high-value luxury foods.

A continuing harvest of fish at the hunting level will, of course, continue and there will be further discoveries and developments of unfished stocks. For example, the total population of the small midwater fish of the open sea most probably greatly exceeds the weight of all other fish stocks. Deep seafloor scavengers are also a potential source of future fisheries, and these fish are surprisingly abundant: the total population of sablefish off the southern California coast in depths of a

half-mile or more is estimated as about a million tons.

Possibly the greatest potential for the further development of conventional commercial fisheries lies in the harvesting of the small herringlike species. Some traditional fisheries appear to be becoming more productive and that of the North Sea, almost doubled over the past ten years, has been attributed to the beneficial effects of the increased discharge into the sea of organic waste material. It is highly likely therefore that as we learn to dispose of our domestic waste carefully, avoiding harmful local side effects, productivity of many other areas may be similarly increased.

Beyond the development of fisheries, however, the future development of the marine resource holds many fascinating possibilities for a world hungry for food and raw materials. The study of salt-tolerant plants like the coastal mangroves may provide the necessary genetic information that will enable plant biologists to develop salt-tolerant strains of traditional food crops and hence open up the possibility of direct saltwater irrigation. The chemical harvest of the oceans may be yet another valuable new resource: all plants produce chemicals to combat disease, but marine plants have developed a number of chemicals not found on land and many which were thought not to exist at all in nature. Some have controlling effects on bacteria, viruses and even on leukemia, and their presence opens an entirely new field of marine pharmacology.

POWER FROM THE SEA

The tidal power station built across the mouth of the Rance estuary in France is the world's first fully operational system utilizing the power resource of the ocean. A dam spanning the estuary, *above*, contains turbines housed in tunnels below the waterline: as the tides ebb and flow, the turbines drive banks of generators. Lock gates incorporated at the western end of the dam, *right*, allow the passage of shipping, while six huge sluice gates at the eastern end allow the water levels at either side of the dam to be equalized quickly. A possible future development of the tidal power concept, illustrated below, avoids the problem of storing energy between tides. Tidal flow is used to drive air compressors that force air into underground storage chambers. This reservoir of compressed air may then be tapped at times of peak demand and used to drive gas turbine generators.

As mankind becomes aware of the present increasing consumption of energy and the ultimate limitation of conventional power sources the oceans are being studied more closely in an attempt to find long-range solutions to the problems.

Clearly the sea is important to conventional and nuclear power generation in a number of marginal but none the less important ways. For example, thermal power plants frequently use seawater for cooling. Such systems, properly designed, can have a small and perhaps beneficial effect on the environment. As another example, the floor of the deep ocean basins may constitute an appropriate site for the disposal of nuclear wastes—the most perilous substances known to man. These materials, solidified and buried deep below the ocean floor, could only reenter the sphere of living things after the passage of millions of years when the radioactivity would have been dissipated to inconsequential levels.

Of greater interest is the idea of the ocean as an active source of power and many potential sources exist that are largely unique to the marine realm. The total reserves of petroleum that lie in the sediments beneath the seawater are undoubtedly great and as yet only partly evaluated, but it is the power from the sea itself that will be of increasing importance in the future.

As a primary resource the ocean contains a number of sizeable potentials for power production. Potentials for mechanical, thermal, organic and nuclear power exist in a number of different forms.

Various reservoirs of extractable energy are present in the ocean, for example heat, thorium fission, uranium fission, deuterium fusion and hydrogen fusion, and estimates have been made of how long each would supply a level of power of 30 million megawatts —the estimated power requirements of the world at the beginning of the twenty-first century. Of these the lifetime of the energy resource represented by deuterium fusion approaches that of the sun and that represented by hydrogen fusion actually exceeds it. On the other hand the energy supplied by ocean thermal power would last only a thousand years or so. Clearly the development of practical fusion devices will solve all human power problems for the imaginable future, the fuels being in abundant supply.

The use of these techniques, apart from ocean thermal power, would be equivalent to "mining" the resource as the raw materials used would not be renewed to any substantial extent. Renewable power sources consist of ocean currents, tides, waves, salinity

gradients and temperature gradients. Of these only two—temperature gradient power and salinity gradient power—are of an order of magnitude that would supply a large part of the vast eventual human needs. Wave power is the most immediately attractive of these renewable resources as any energy extracted would be immediately made good by the constant addition of more energy by the wind. Also the regenerated waves would be of a higher frequency and hence more readily converted into power.

Fairly conventional machines could be used on each of these renewable sources of energy except in the case of salinity power. This power is represented by the osmotic pressure between two solutions with differing concentrations of dissolved material. Such solutions show a number of differences in physical properties such as vapor pressure and electrical potential and the technology can be developed to make use of these differences. However, the successful machine for tapping the vast power in the salinity gradients of the oceans may need to involve some fundamentally novel, clever and unconventional approach. Marked differences in salinity exist between seawater and salt pans along desert coasts and between the waters of rivers and brine lakes into which they flow (such as the Dead

OTEC plant

1000 ft

2000 ft

3000 ft

4000 ft

Double-acting pumps

Rocker vanes

Floating turbogenerator station

Low-pressure return pipe

High-pressure water pipes

Deck house

Ammonia tank

Separators

Generator

Evaporator

Condenser

Warm water inlet

Cold water exhaust

Warm water exhaust

Cold water pipe; 50 feet in diameter and 4000 feet long

Temperature difference between surface water and deep water would be about 39 F degrees (21.6 C degrees)

An enormous pump-action wave device has been proposed in which rocking motion imparted to huge floating vanes would be used as a primary source of power generation. The rocking action would activate banks of nonreturn valves forcing specially treated water through small-bore pipes to drive the turbines in a series of generator stations. After use, the water would return at low pressure along the large-diameter pipe forming the axis of the assembly. A system of this type could be ideal for use in the Atlantic approaches to Britain and has been estimated to be capable of providing the total energy requirement of the U.K.

Ocean thermal energy conversion (OTEC) is a development project recently undertaken in the United States by a number of leading engineering groups working under contract to the Energy Resource and Development Administration. This floating offshore installation would utilize the great temperature difference between deep ocean water and surface water to drive a closed evaporation–condensation cycle based either on ammonia or on another fluid with comparable thermal properties. Cold water would be used to condense the vapor—which would then be cycled through evaporators utilizing warm surface water and would drive turbines linked to banks of generators.

Sea or the Great Salt Lake). Here the energy density is immense and can be compared to the energy provided by the flow of water over a 10,000- to 15,000-foot-high dam. Innumerable "dry" holes drilled in search for oil have encountered brines and brackish water and these also represent a potential energy source of immense but unknown dimensions.

Salinity gradient energy could be extracted by using the principle of osmosis—the movement of water from a low-concentration solution to a high-concentration solution through a semi-permeable membrane—or directly in the form of electricity using the solutions as a sort of battery in a process called inverse electrodialysis. Both of these processes involve the use of membranes that can be manufactured by present technologies. Nevertheless much more research and experimentation is needed before any of these ideas can become practicable.

One of the main difficulties in using salinity energy is that the main salt in the oceans—sodium chloride—has a number of unique properties. One of these is the tendency of its solution to maintain a steady temperature when it is diluted. If sodium chloride solution were to change its temperature as solutions normally do much energy could be harnessed in this way.

Another possibility of extracting energy from the sea is the energy-farm concept in which marine plants are cultivated and harvested for fuel.

Considerable problems exist in transferring the power obtained by these techniques from the point of extraction—usually far from land or on remote and stormy coastlines—to the normal power-distribution systems and the point of consumption. One answer would be to use the energy to produce hydrogen from seawater on the site and transport it by tankers to the point of use, where it would be burned as fuel. Until the hydrogen–handling systems are developed ammonia could be synthesized on the site instead, ammonia being a valuable commodity that can be easily transported and used with existing equipment.

There have been other schemes proposed that would use natural power sources to accomplish tasks that already consume conventional power. Small man-made water currents can interact with tidal currents to influence the direction of sediment transport. If this can be controlled the costs of dredging and of keeping shipping lanes clear of sandbanks will be greatly reduced. On oceanic crossings it has been proved that the wave power involved in the up and down motion of a ship greatly exceeds the power required to propel it.

A simple and ingenious scheme may be used to convert this wasted wave power into propulsive power for a ship. Such a scheme might make practical the long-distance transport of low-value materials, such as low-grade ores and aggregates that are too expensive to transport at the moment.

All these schemes can be thought of as the utilization of solar energy, since the energy involved comes ultimately from the sun. The sun's gravity is involved in tide production, its radiation causes the winds that whip up the waves and its heat gives rise to the temperature differences between surface and deep waters.

The practical application of these ideas still lies in the future. The Rance tidal power station in northern France is the only large-scale ocean energy emplacement working at the moment. However, active research is taking place in all areas and full-scale prototypes of thermal-energy machines are currently being constructed. The wave energy conversion scheme will probably be the next to receive serious interest.

The oceans are so vast that they probably contain many more power sources than have yet been imagined. Clearly there is a great need for considerably more research to be done on the subject and undoubtedly great strides will be made in the near future.

OFFSHORE MINERAL DEPOSITS

Man may be distinguished from other animals as being the only one to be dependent on minerals. As he turned to the sea to augment his food supply from very early times, he may also have reflected on the possibility of obtaining minerals from the same source. Yet with one old exception—salt—the seabed has become an important source only very recently. The nature of the sea itself had proved an insurmountable obstacle; its opacity and its hostility demand relatively advanced techniques to enable mineral deposits on or under the seabed to be discovered and exploited. A mineral deposit, wherever it is, can be described as a "resource" only if it is likely to be exploited in the foreseeable future. The parts of resources that can be worked in the locally prevailing current economic circumstances are described as "reserves." Minerals on the seabed can be regarded as reserves and worked only when all of the costs involved are comparable with the costs of recovering the same minerals from land.

The earliest recovery of these minerals therefore proceeded to a fully marine environment via the generally shallow and protected waters of estuaries and lagoons. This is well illustrated by the offshore petroleum industry, which, in the last 20 or 30 years, has moved from such shallow, sheltered water as Lake Maracaibo, Venezuela, to the very high-cost operations in the North Sea. The cost of recovering salt from seawater is very low and transport costs are an important element. Seawater therefore remains an important source of salt in countries with a suitable climate that are a long way from other sources. Relative transport costs have also determined the growth of the marine sand and gravel dredging industry. The economic viability of marine mining for such high-value commodities as diamonds and tin ore, however, depends upon the grade, size and cost of mining deposits on the seabed compared with those on land, as transport costs are a small component of the total. Thus, although the average grade of diamond deposits off Namibia was at least three times higher than on land, the cost per cubic yard screened was almost always three to five times higher per carat than on land and marine mining was suspended in 1971. Similarly exploitation of marine gold placer deposits has not so far been commercially feasible.

Nevertheless, the winning of minerals from the continental shelf is now a major industry. This is in response to higher costs associated with meeting demand from land-based sources.

Marine mineral deposits can be classified on the basis of their origin and the methods used to recover them. First, minerals that are present as unconsolidated deposits resting on, or comprising the top few feet of, the seabed. These include sediments derived from adjacent land or precipitated chemically. This category includes sand and gravel, the value of which exceeds that of any mineral other than petroleum recovered from the seafloor; the aragonite deposits in the Bahamas; placer deposits in which the valuable heavy minerals are only a very small part of the sediment; and phosphate nodules. All of the deposits in this category can be recovered by dredging.

Second, there are minerals that can be recovered only by mining hard rock. These were deposited by the same processes as in the unsubmerged portions of the continental crust. Except for a single operation off Alaska, in which a barytes deposit is drilled, blasted and then recovered by dredging, recovery of solid minerals from hard rocks is restricted to mining beneath the seabed from shafts on land or, exceptionally, artificial islands. The most notable example is coal.

And last, there are minerals that are present as, or that can be converted to, liquids or gases. By far the most important is petroleum, but sulfur is recovered in a molten form and salt and potash may be recovered in solution. All may be won by means of boreholes.

Almost all of these marine mineral deposits are linked closely to continental crust, either because they are derived directly from it or this is the only environment in which they are likely to be found. Although there may be concentrations of metals in oceanic crust it is most unlikely that they will be exploited.

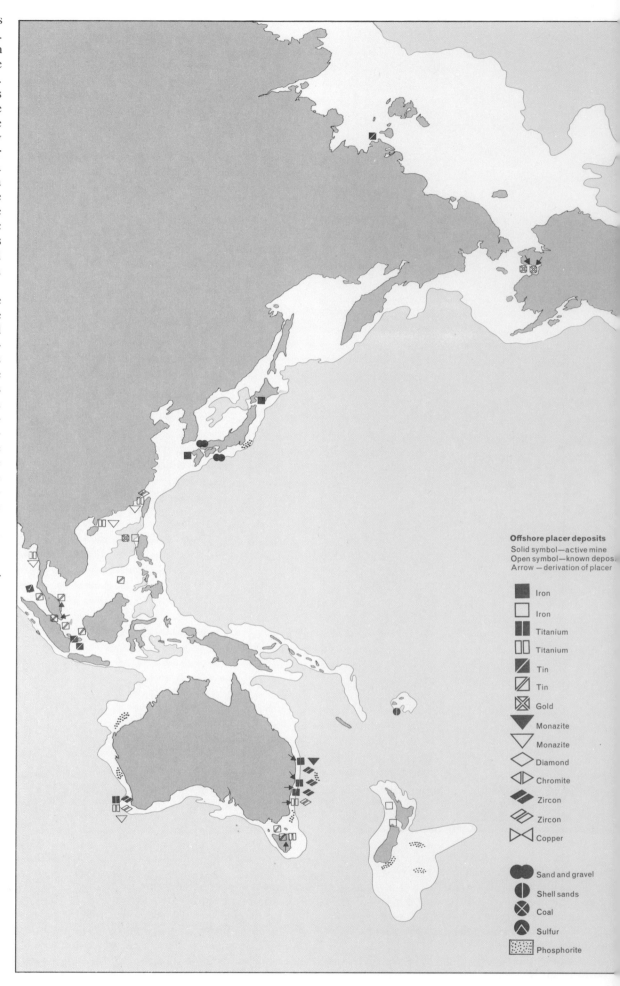

Offshore placer deposits
Solid symbol—active mine
Open symbol—known deposit
Arrow—derivation of placer

◼	Iron
◻	Iron
◼	Titanium
◫	Titanium
◪	Tin
◪	Tin
⊠	Gold
▼	Monazite
▽	Monazite
◇	Diamond
◁	Chromite
◪	Zircon
◪	Zircon
⋈	Copper
●	Sand and gravel
◖	Shell sands
⊗	Coal
⊘	Sulfur
▦	Phosphorite

Minerals have been won from the sea since the beginning of history. Common salt represents about three-quarters of the dissolved mineral content of seawater and has always been extracted by simply allowing the water to evaporate in shallow pans. The thin layers of salt precipitated onto the pan floor are scraped up every week where the climate is variable, but are allowed to form into thick beds over a number of years in more stable areas. Modern processes concentrate the brine first. The example shown is at Enfeh in the Lebanon, where the water is pumped to the pans by windmills.

Most offshore metals are
found as placer deposits. A
metal-bearing rock on land is
weathered and the debris
produced is washed to the sea
by rivers. There it is sorted by
the currents, waves and tides so
that the heavy metal particles
accumulate to form deposits
of mineral sand. These are
typically beach deposits, but
where the sea level has changed
they can be found well out on
the continental shelf. The sands
are lifted by dredgers and the
metal concentrated even further
by settling techniques that
reflect the winnowing conditions
of the placer's formation.

Ore body

Weathered
material
carried by river

Debris sorted by
longshore drift
and wave action

Heavy particles
settle out

MINERAL WEALTH OF THE DEEPS

The *Report on the Scientific Results of the Exploring Voyage of the H.M.S. Challenger*, 1873–6, records that "the dredges and trawls yielded immense numbers of more or less circular nodules and botryoidal masses of manganese oxides of large dimensions. To mention all the regions where manganese was observed would take up too much space. . . ." These were the first manganese nodules ever collected. There was little further scientific interest in them until the late 1950s, but it is not surprising that there was no industrial interest as deposits with their relatively low concentrations of nickel and copper would not have been considered as ores even if readily accessible on land.

Since the end of the Second World War the rapid increase in oceanographical research has revealed that in some areas the nodules are characteristically abundant. This stimulated academic research on their chemical composition, mineralogy, distribution and origin. The average grade of copper deposits being worked on land in the USA had fallen from about 2.6 percent in 1900 to 0.7 percent in 1965 and the nickel content of the ore being mined in New Caledonia was about 2.8 percent compared with about 7 percent in 1900. Demand for copper and nickel was increasing exponentially and projections of this growth indicated that still lower grade deposits would have to be mined on land to meet future demand. The scope for further technical development that had enabled lower grade ore to be mined at costs comparable to higher grades seemed limited so that future costs were likely to be higher. If the technology could be developed to recover nodules and extract the nickel, copper and perhaps other metals from them at costs comparable to those then applying to winning the same metals on land, commercial mining would be feasible. By the mid-1960s it seemed possible that the economic criteria might be satisfied so that concurrently with the burgeoning of scientific interest, industrial research and development programs were initiated. These were addressed to the three main problems that had to be solved: identification of potentially workable deposits, devising systems for their recovery from the seabed and methods of extracting the metals.

The diameter of most nodules is between one and two inches, but the size ranges from micro-nodules to six inches or more and the same material also occurs as encrustations. The shape varies from almost spherical to discoidal and the surface may be relatively smooth or lumpy. They are composed mainly of manganese and iron hydroxides with variable amounts of silicates derived from sediments and in some cases calcium carbonate. Copper, nickel and cobalt are present in appreciable amounts in some nodules, which also contain very small quantities of other metals, including zinc, molybdenum, lead and vanadium. "Manganese" nodule is thus a misleading term; the French "polymétallique" is more appropriate. The composition varies from layer to layer within the nodule. The copper and nickel occur within the manganese dioxide rather than as separate minerals. Physical separation is thus ruled out and of the alternatives a hydrometallurgical route is most likely to be used. This involves solution of part if not all of the nodule followed by further complex processes to separate the metals.

There is increasing evidence that the metal-rich nodules have grown at a much slower rate than the others and that they are associated with slowly accumulating red siliceous muds. The deposition of calcareous debris and terrigenous sediments inhibit the formation of metal-rich nodules. Thus although manganese nodules are widespread, potentially ore-grade nodules are restricted in occurrence; they are far from land and generally at depths of more than 13,000 feet. Nearly all are in the Pacific Ocean, most occurring in the area between the Clarion and Cliperton fracture zones.

The population (the proportion of an area occupied by visible nodules) of manganese nodules is also very variable. However, fewer data are available on a population and its distribution and the reasons for its wide variation over small distances has received less attention than research on nodule composition and origin. There is some evidence to suggest that nodules are present on about 15 percent of the seabed and that they are as abundant as will be necessary for mining by the first generation of equipment in perhaps about half of that area.

The companies now involved in research and development programs, all in consortia to share the enormous financial risks, are developing nodule recovery systems. In the future manganese nodules may by supplying a significant proportion of man's ever-increasing needs for some of the metals they contain.

Apart from phosphate nodules, which seem unlikely to be competitive with sources on land in terms of cost and grade for a very long time, the only other mineral deposits likely to be won in the foreseeable future are mineralized muds. These were first discovered in the deeps in the Red Sea beneath hot, concentrated and metal-rich brines by the *Atlantis II* in 1965. Although abnormal concentrations of minerals have been found associated with other divergent plate boundaries, for example in the rifts in the Mid-Atlantic ridge and in the East Pacific Rise, the concentrations are well below what can be regarded as potentially workable and it is most unlikely that such deposits will ever be of economic interest.

● Manganese nodules

⊗ Metal-bearing muds

COMPOSITION OF MANGANESE NODULES (air-dried, % by weight)

Element	Northeast Pacific Ocean	South Pacific Ocean	West Indian Ocean	East Indian Ocean
Manganese	22.33	16.61	13.56	15.83
Iron	9.44	13.92	15.75	11.31
Nickel	1.080	0.433	0.322	0.512
Cobalt	0.192	0.595	0.358	0.153
Copper	0.627	0.185	0.102	0.330
Lead	0.028	0.073	0.061	0.034
Barium	0.381	0.230	0.146	0.155
Molybdenum	0.047	0.041	0.029	0.031
Vanadium	0.041	0.050	0.051	0.040
Chromium	0.0007	0.0007	0.0020	0.0009
Titanium	0.425	1.007	0.820	0.582

The origin of manganese nodules is not yet fully understood. Seawater is more or less saturated with manganese ions contributed by rivers, volcanoes and from the seabed by the leaching action of seawater. The manganese in solution may attract other metals and they become attached to foreign bodies on the ocean floor building up around them in concentric layers. They are very porous and 30 percent of their weight is water. The different sea floor conditions give rise to a variety of nodule compositions—only a small proportion being rich in copper and nickel or cobalt. Investigation of nodule distribution is based on widely spaced seabed photographs and samples retrieved by dredges and grabs.

MINING THE SEABED

Any proposed scheme for harvesting manganese nodules will involve two processes—gathering the nodules from the seabed and bringing them to the surface. The collecting device may be either dragged along by the ship or be self-propelled, and it may incorporate a system for lifting the dredgings to the surface or may only accumulate them in manageable piles on the seabed to be lifted later by some other means. The technological difficulties involved, although not impossible to overcome, are very great. The machinery must be able to work at the great pressures encountered at these depths and must be reliable enough to avoid frequent costly returns to the mining ship.

A dragnet may be used to gather together the nodules over a wide track. Unwanted mud would be filtered out by the gauge of the steel mesh and the nodules concentrated for lifting.

Settling tank

Power room

Control room

A towed sled could scrape up the nodule-covered surface of the seabed and pass the nodules to the lower end of a suction pipe.

A self-propelled tracked device is envisaged as sweeping the seabed with a suction pipe, heaping the nodules into easily collected strips.

Intermediate stations would be useful for supplying the suction power and for processing the nodules before transfer to the surface.

A continuous line-bucket system involves a line of dredging buckets that would continuously scoop up the nodules and lift them to the ship.

103

THE SEARCH FOR OIL

The year 1896 marked the birth of the offshore oil industry when it was realized that the Summerland field in California extended beyond the coast, and wells were drilled from piers extending up to 800 feet from the shore. In the 1920s and 1930s wells in the Baku region of Russia were being drilled from trestles running out into the Caspian.

At about this time tentative moves were made into the waters of Venezuela's Lake Maracaibo after the discovery of the giant Bolivar Coastal field onshore, and in the late 1940s the first specifically designed steel offshore drilling structure was set in 23 feet of water in the Gulf of Mexico, heralding the start of the great development of the offshore oil industry.

Gradually techniques have been developed to overcome increasingly great water depths and harsher conditions of sea and weather, and drilling has now reached out into the stormy waters of the northern North Sea. By the end of 1975, 77 wells had been drilled in waters more than 600 feet deep round the world, and in 1976 wells were drilled from floating ice-islands in the Canadian Arctic and from a dynamically positioned drill-ship in over 3000 feet of water off the coast of Thailand.

In the oceans it is the continental shelf and, to a lesser extent, the continental slope that are prospective for oil and natural gas. Indeed the continental shelf is relatively more promising than the land. Continental shelves occupy only about 10 million square miles, but of this about 5.8 million square miles consists of sedimentary basins. The total land area of the world is 6 times as large (60 million square miles), but the sedimentary basin area is only about four times that of the continental shelf (20 million square miles).

Both onshore and offshore, explorers for oil and natural gas are looking for the same types of rocks and structures: a source rock rich in the organic remains from which the oil and natural gas are generated; a reservoir rock into which the oil and gas can migrate, typically a sandstone or limestone—porous to hold the oil or gas and permeable to let them pass through; an impermeable seal or cap-rock for the reservoir, typically shale or salt; and a structure such that the cap-rock can trap oil or gas in the reservoir and prevent them from escaping to the surface.

The most important technique in determining the structure of the rocks beneath the seafloor is the seismic reflection method, whereby sound waves from a controlled explosion on the surface are reflected from the boundaries between different types of rock beneath the seabed and are picked up by hydrophones trailed behind the survey vessel.

In the last few years rapid improvement in seismic techniques and skilled interpretation of the results have enabled increasingly accurate pictures of structures to be built up. But there is only one way to find out if a likely feature contains oil or gas and that is to drill a well into it. The great majority of structures are found to contain only water or uneconomic quantities of oil.

The first offshore drilling rigs were confined to shallow waters. Later, from 1953 onwards, they were able to go out into increasingly deeper water, up to perhaps 300 feet, by lowering legs down onto the seabed, then jacking up the platform containing the drilling rig out of reach of the waves. In 1962 came a breakthrough with the semisubmersible rig, which has pontoons to give buoyancy to a floating but partly submerged structure moored to the seabed. More recently in 1971 came the first commercial dynamically positioned drill-ship. Drill-ships anchored to the sea bottom had been in use for nearly 20 years, but this advanced type is able to maintain itself over a well in deep water by using directional propellers.

The number of offshore drilling rigs is growing rapidly. In 1965 there were about 70; the late sixties saw a great increase in jack-ups, the seventies a great increase in semisubmersibles. By 1976 the fleet of mobile drilling rigs had increased to over 350, and was deployed all over the world. Whereas in 1960 over 90 percent of the offshore rigs were drilling off the USA, today only a quarter are off the USA, and offshore exploration, both seismic exploration and drilling, is taking place off more than 100 countries.

Already one-fifth of all the oil discovered has been found offshore and this proportion is likely to increase as more onshore areas pass their exploration peak and the offshore search is intensified.

A little over one-fifth of the known offshore reserves has already been produced (about 5500 million tons) amounting to about one-tenth of the total world production. The offshore fields are now contributing nearly one-fifth of this total and as the offshore oil industry increases in importance its share of total output could rise to nearly one-third by the mid-1980s.

Flare stack

Drilling derrick

Main oil-line turbine exhausts

Skimmer tank for removal of oil from water

Radio tower

Cyclone unit for removal of sand from oil

Oil and gas separators

Mud-storage tanks

Main oil-line pumps

Strainers for removal of dirt from oil

Jacket

Main oil pipeline to shore terminal

Reef Thrust fault Unconformity Fault Anticline Sand lens Pinch-out Salt dome

Sandstone   Limestone   Oil   Gas   Water

Petroleum is formed by the decomposition of organic material in sedimentary rocks. Once formed it migrates, along with the gas produced at the same time, until it is trapped by an impermeable layer. There it accumulates to form a reservoir with the gas and oil floating above the water, the gas remaining at the top. Reservoir rocks such as sandstone and limestone are porous and permeable, allowing the free movement of fluids within them, and are capped by impermeable rock such as shale or anhydrite. Certain geological structures that bring reservoir and cap rocks together create oil and gas traps and it is these structures that are sought by the exploration teams.

Shot

Hydrophone array

Sea level

Radar reflector

Reflected waves

Seabed

Geologic structures that would make suitable oil and gas traps are detected by seismic profiling. A shock wave is set up in seawater by either an explosive charge or an air gun. This shock wave travels through the seabed rocks and is partially reflected from each layer. The reflected waves are picked up and recorded by a series of hydrophones towed by the survey vessel and the variations in the reflections, *left*, show the rock structures beneath the bed of the sea.

A production platform for the Forties oil field in the North Sea weighs 57,000 tons and is worked by 96 men. There are three decks measuring 175 by 170 feet and the top of the drilling derrick is 690 feet above the seabed. It is supported by four legs and from each of these 11 piles are driven 250 feet into the sea bottom to anchor the structure. External steelwork is protected against corrosion by seawater by a number of techniques, including coating by plastic. Each platform carries the equipment for drilling 27 wells, cleaning the oil as it is produced and pumping it to the oil refinery at Grangemouth on the Firth of Forth, 236 miles away. The lowest deck is 77 feet above sea level and the whole structure is designed to withstand wave heights of 94 feet with winds of 130 mph—conditions that are found to occur on average only once in a hundred years.

EXPLORATION RIGS

Template rig
Shallow/medium water

Semisubmersible rig
Deep-water operation

Jack-up rig
Medium water operation

Tension-leg rig
Experimental development

Drilling ship
General survey

Track for mobile derrick

Pedestal crane

Pipe racks

Offices

Well-logging unit

Helicopter deck

Water tank

Fuel tank

Wellheads spaced at 8-foot intervals

Lifeboat

Elevator shaft

Incoming pipelines from satellite platforms

285 feet

420 feet

1000 feet

500 feet

Production platforms are sited so that most of an oil field can be exploited by as few units as possible. The Forties field in the North Sea is worked by four platforms, each of which can drill 27 wells to 11,500 feet. Each well can be drilled out at an angle to reach a radius of 9000 feet and tap a wide area of oilbearing rocks. Only the top part of the reservoir need be drilled as the continuous pressure of water below the oil in the rock will push the oil up toward the wells.

Exploration rigs are used to find whether promising geologic structures contain oil. The template rig is the simplest but is difficult to move. Semisubmersibles travel to new sites on their floats and are stabilized by partial submergence. Drill-ships are held on location by propellers, while the tension leg design, still being developed, is buoyant and anchored over the site by a system of steel cables.

Once an economic field has been proven, production platforms are erected on the site to extract the oil or gas. These have been built to work in deeper water in the last few years as the search for hydrocarbons has reached into more inaccessible areas. The largest yet built—1163 feet from the seabed to the top of the derrick—has been installed near Santa Barbara, California.

PRODUCTION PLATFORMS

Sea level

500 feet

1000 feet

1 Leman Bank
North Sea 1966

2 Ekofisk
North Sea 1972

3 Brent B
North Sea 1975

4 Brent A
North Sea 1975

5 Hondo Field
Santa Barbara 1977

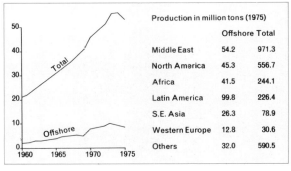

Production in million tons (1975)		
	Offshore	Total
Middle East	54.2	971.3
North America	45.3	556.7
Africa	41.5	244.1
Latin America	99.8	226.4
S.E. Asia	26.3	78.9
Western Europe	12.8	30.6
Others	32.0	590.5

The increase in world demand for oil over the past few decades has led to the rapid development of offshore exploitation so that it now represents more than 15 percent of the total production. Traditional oil-producing nations such as the USA and Saudi Arabia have moved to offshore production as an extension of their land-based activities. Others such as Norway have begun production with offshore oil.

THE FALTERING HARVEST

The fish resources of the oceans represent a renewable resource that could, given adequate management, be harvested indefinitely. However, during the great expansion of the world fishery industry that took place between the end of World War II and the early 1970s, global fish catches increased at an almost constant rate of seven percent per year. When this rate is compounded it represents a doubling of the world catch every ten years—a rate of increase that many predicted could be sustained until the end of the century.

By the end of the 1960s, when the annual world catch had reached 50 million tons, it was realized that the stocks then being fished would be unable to regenerate fast enough to sustain this growth rate and that a number of important species were being seriously overexploited. Some reductions were made and, in 1972, the world catch fell, for the first time ever, below that of the previous year.

As this evidence suggests, the management of the world fisheries has been by no means successful, in fact satisfactory management has been the exception rather than the rule. A fishery that has not been properly regulated goes through a "boom-and-bust" cycle. When a new fishery is discovered, fishing boats and gear are rapidly evolved to exploit it; fishermen crowd in to take advantage of the resource for as long as demand for the product remains high and for as long as the catch can be maintained. If entry to the fishery is unrestricted, it rapidly becomes overcapitalized with too many boats in search of too few fish: the fishery is quickly exhausted and soon crashes. The Californian sardine fishery of the 1930s is a classic example of this cycle. Its enormous growth rate of 50 percent per year could be maintained for only a few years before it crashed to extinction in the early 1950s.

Fisheries are regulated by a large variety of controlling bodies. The Californian sardine industry, for example, was controlled by a state organization having responsibility within a federal system. Other fisheries, such as that based on the Peruvian anchovy, are nationally controlled. For many fisheries there are internationally agreed quotas. These agreements may be made between individual nations for a particular fishery—such as that existing between the USA, Japan and the Soviet Union covering the North Pacific—or they may be made within the framework of an international commission, in which any interested nation may participate. The tropical tuna and halibut fisheries are controlled in this way.

It is impossible to demonstrate that any controlling body has been any more successful than any other. Failure or success is more dependent on the presence

The Peruvian anchovy is found close to the shores of South America, where the cold nutrient-rich Peru Current rises to the surface. Every few years a mass of warm, low-salinity water, originating in the Pacific Undercurrent, swamps the upwelling. The anchovies are compelled to remain at greater depth than normal, where they are out of reach of fishing nets. The warm surface water promotes rapid plankton production, which quickly exhausts the oxygen supply. High concentrations of poisonous dinoflagellate plankton are also commonly produced. The last appearance of this phenomenon, in 1972, brought economic disaster to Peru. In 1970 Peru produced 45% of the world's fish meal; by 1973 the proportion had fallen to 5.2%. The anchovy has not yet recovered its position—mainly because continued overfishing has not allowed the stock to recover sufficiently. The number of seabirds relying on anchovies for food was seriously reduced at this time. The consolidated droppings of the birds, guano, was at one time used extensively as fertilizer.

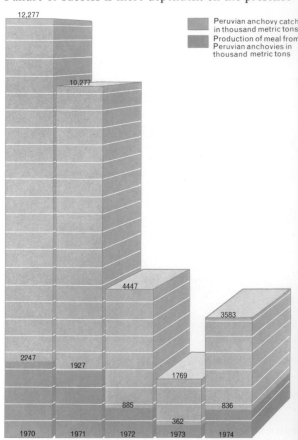

■ Peruvian anchovy catch in thousand metric tons
■ Production of meal from Peruvian anchovies in thousand metric tons

Year	Anchovy catch	Meal production
1970	12,277	2247
1971	10,277	1927
1972	4447	885
1973	1769	362
1974	3583	836

or absence of external political pressures than on the nature of the controlling body. Failure is certainly not due to any lack of scientific understanding of what is required for good management.

No more than five percent of all fish species are exploited commercially. Six species—cod, pollack, mackerel, herring, sardine and anchovy—make up more than half the total landings and about 35 species account for more than 70 percent of the world catch. The world fishery industry is therefore extremely sensitive to the fluctuations of individual fisheries. An extreme example is that of the Peruvian anchovy fishery, which in 1970 accounted for about 20 percent of world landings by weight. During 1971–2, when the normal upwelling off Peru failed to occur, the fishery contracted dramatically—yielding less than ten percent of its normal catch and producing a marked dip in the graph of total world landings.

Several other important species have in recent years shown evidence of overfishing. The Atlantic herring catch has fallen from nearly four million tons to just over one million tons and the major Atlanto–Scandian stock of this species has completely collapsed; Norwegian and Icelandic catches have fallen from two million tons to only 200,000 tons.

Fishery crises have in some cases made it possible for governments to impose unpopular measures on their national fishing industries. When, in 1972, the whole Peruvian fleet of anchovy seiners was temporarily made idle, the government was able to solve the over-capitalization problem by reducing the number of vessels licenced for the fishery—a measure long overdue but impossible to implement until then.

Unless it is possible to control fisheries rationally and reduce the economic and commercial pressures at present placed upon them, the future of the world fishing industry is bleak. The atmosphere of optimism prevalent in the 1960s, as the world catch increased steadily year by year and investment in the industry continued to yield profitable returns, has been replaced by one of uncertainty. It is unfortunate that the present period of growth has coincided with a natural decline in the fish population, which appears to be part of a long-term fluctuation cycle.

It is probably not too late for remedial action to be taken, and although the restrictions placed by many countries in the form of limits to the number of foreign vessels that may operate within their fishing area are designed to serve national economic interests rather than those of global conservation, the actual existence of controls provides hope for the future survival of the world's fish resources.

Despite several attempts to limit the numbers of whales caught, many of the 90 species are nearing extinction. Japan and the Soviet Union are the only countries at present catching baleen whales, of which fin, bottlenose and minke are the main prey.

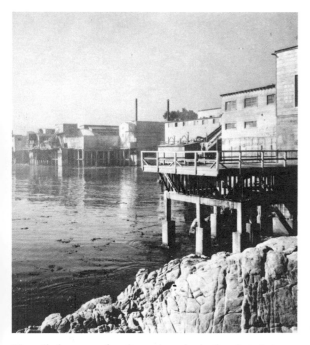

The mile-long complex of canneries and reduction plants that made up Cannery Row was built in the 1920s and 1930s to process the huge quantities of sardine caught by the Monterey fishing fleet, which, at its height, had as many as 80 purse seiners. By 1947 the number of canneries and reduction plants had grown to 31. From 1950 onward, the size of the sardine catch dwindled rapidly and after attempting to survive on outside stocks of pilchard and squid the canneries were eventually compelled to close down.

The sight of large numbers of fishing boats sweeping up huge shoals of fish is rapidly becoming a thing of the past. Although a great many factors have contributed to the demise of the world's fish stocks, overfishing is the root cause. The British herring industry, which for many years enjoyed large catches, is now faced with steadily contracting herring stocks. Attempts are being made to conserve what remains; the whole industry is now under review and total bans have been imposed in certain areas in the short term.

United Kingdom herring catch in thousand metric tons					
146	147	149	157	148	113
1970	1971	1972	1973	1974	1975

THE THREAT OF POLLUTION

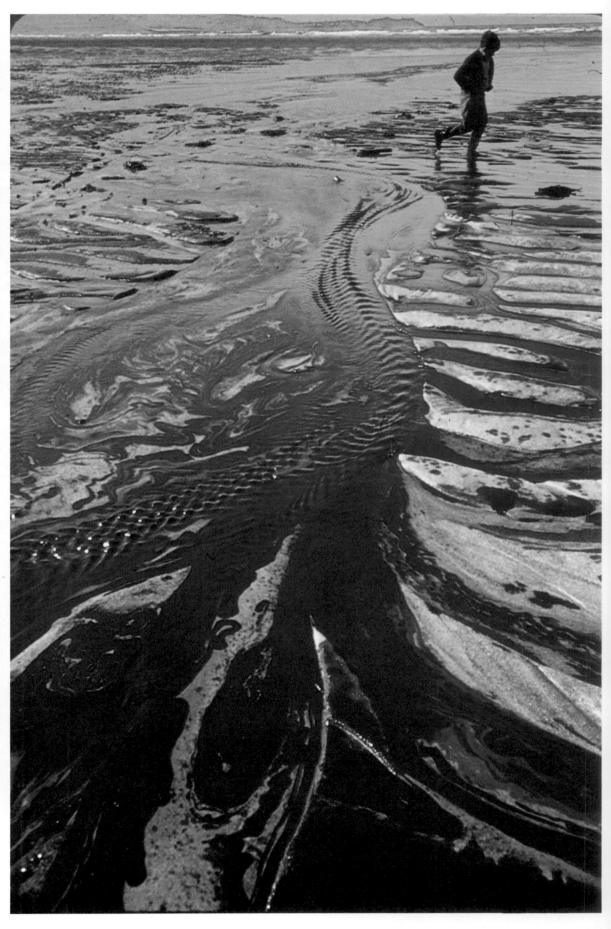

An accident at sea involving an oil tanker constitutes an immediate threat to the ecology and amenity value of all coastal areas in the vicinity. The oil is carried ashore by wind and currents, fouling rocky and sandy shores and killing wildlife. Attempts may be made to avoid coastal destruction by bombing and burning stricken ships, *upper photograph*, or by containing the oil within floating booms, *above*. Detergent treatment, *right*, can create problems, as some detergents are themselves toxic to marine life.

Changes in the marine environment are constantly being brought about by the activities of man. Some changes, such as the decimation of commercial whale species, are the direct consequence of a deliberate course of action; others, for example the accidental spillage of oil, are unintentional. Certain changes are however predictable. The increase in concentrations of radioactive particles from atmospheric and oceanic testing of nuclear devices and from nuclear reactor discharges, could be seen well in advance. Other changes, such as the widespread accumulation of halogenated hydrocarbons, including DDT, in marine organisms have surprised even the scientists.

Of the many thousands of millions of tons of raw materials and fossil fuels consumed by the world each year a major proportion of the waste material resulting from their use finds its way into the sea. However, only a small proportion of this consists of pollutants. Pollutants are defined as substances that by their presence or because of their involvement in marine processes bring about a loss, cause damage to or result in the restricted use of an ocean resource. Some pollutants interfere with the life processes of marine organisms and may also affect unfavorably the biological productivity of the oceans. Others, for example oil and litter, detract from their beauty and interfere with man's recreational activities in addition to being physically dangerous.

Clearly the complete cessation of pollution flow into the oceans in impossible. The real issue concerns the level of pollutants society is willing to accept, noting that even with controlled levels a risk of damaging marine resources will always exist. The answer to this question is essential to those concerned with management of the oceanic resource.

Five groups of pollutants causing international concern have been identified: petroleum, heavy metals, radioactive particles, halogenated hydrocarbons and litter. In addition organic pollutants deriving mainly from domestic sewage are troublesome. They contain high levels of nutrients, which promote rapid plankton growth using up all the available oxygen in the water and upsetting the ecosystem. Many coastal areas, notably along the northern Mediterranean coast, have been contaminated with this type of effluent.

The mass movement of oil from one part of the globe to another in response to man's ever-increasing demand for fuel has resulted in the spread of hydrocarbons throughout the world's oceans. The oil floats on the surface cutting out light and oxygen and impedes evaporation. The logs of many transoceanic voyages undertaken by small vessels record the presence over much of the oceans' surface of a fine film of oil and it has been discovered that even minute marine organisms carry a body burden of petroleum hydrocarbons.

In 1971, 1355 million tons of oil, including 100 million tons of crude, were transported across the oceans in a total of 6000 tankers. It is estimated that more than six million tons of this oil found its way into the ocean, much of it due to the practice of washing out the cargo tanks at sea. A new procedure known as Load on Top (LOT) is being adopted, which should drastically reduce this problem. In LOT the seawater used to wash out the tanks is retained on board and its oil content allowed to separate out in a holding tank, after which it is incorporated with the next shipment.

The risk of blow-out from offshore drilling platforms is a relatively new oil pollution hazard. In the Bravo rig blow-out in the North Sea in April 1977, between 3000 and 4000 tons of oil per day gushed out uncontrollably for over a week, producing a slick covering over 2500 square miles. The Norwegian government, in whose North Sea sector the blow-out occurred, prohibited the use of chemical oil dispersants because of the risk of damage to their fishing grounds and mechanical skimming equipment proved ineffectual in the rough conditions that prevail in the open sea.

Some metals are being liberated into the sea and air in amounts similar to those produced by natural weathering processes. For example, the combustion of fossil fuels and the manufacture of cement introduce mercury and barium into the ocean at rates comparable to that due to river discharge, so effectively doubling the natural rate of accumulation of waste materials.

So far there have been no reports of an increase in the heavy metal content of the oceans on a global scale, but serious local concentrations have occurred in coastal areas, sometimes with disastrous consequences. In Japan, between 1953 and 1970, 111 people were diagnosed to be suffering from severe neurological disorders caused by mercury poisoning. On investigation it was discovered that all the victims had eaten either fish or shellfish caught in Minimata Bay in southwest Kyushu. Mercury, used as a catalyst in the production of formaldehyde, had been released into the bay from processing plants and had been subsequently absorbed by the fish.

Of the thousands of organic compounds synthesized industrially those that contain the halogen atoms—chlorine, fluorine, bromine and iodine—are regarded as among the most potentially dangerous to marine life. The compounds fall into two main groups, those of high molecular weight such as the pesticides DDT, dieldrin and aldrin, and the polychlorinated biphenols; and those of low molecular weight used as aerosol propellants, solvents, refrigerants and cleaning agents. DDT is known to cause reproductive failure in some marine birds: high concentrations cause an abnormal calcium metabolism resulting in the production of thin eggshells, as has been shown in studies of the brown pelican.

Until recently most radioactive particles present in the ocean have been due to fallout from the atmospheric detonation of nuclear devices since the end of the Second World War. As many countries are now embarking on energy programs involving the construction of nuclear power stations and fuel-processing plants, more radioactive pollutants will enter the oceans from these sources in the future. Already the reprocessing plant at Windscale, on the west coast of the United Kingdom, has raised the amount of radioactivity present in coastal fish and on some beaches to between three and seven percent of the tolerable exposure levels.

Marine litter is made up of the solid refuse of society discarded at sea or discharged into the sea from inland waterways. Surface waters, beaches and even the deep ocean floor are littered with this debris, much of it consisting of package materials—plastic, metal, cloth, wood and glass—that cannot be broken down and readily reabsorbed into the environment. It has recently been estimated that a staggering 6.4 million tons of litter is dumped into the oceans every year, nearly 5.6 million tons of which comes from merchant shipping. Much of the merchant fleet refuse consists of lumber used to pack and secure cargo and its release into the oceans constitutes not only a hazard to small inshore craft but also a danger and source of damage in dock and harbor areas.

Garbage-strewn beaches are an all-too-common feature of our consumer society. Even the shore of the Ross Sea in Antarctica has not escaped pollution.

Some areas of the seabed are used as dumping grounds for noxious waste materials. Highly radioactive materials are encased in concrete and dropped into ocean deeps, where water mixing is weak enough to prevent excessive spreading even if a leak should occur. An acid dump off New Jersey, *left*, shows as a bright yellow stain on this satellite photograph: greenish patches extending to the north and south indicate mixing of the waste with sediment-laden waters of the Hudson River flowing in from the northwest.

A GLOBAL CONCEPT

The ethereal beauty of the coral reef is perfectly displayed in this aerial view of the barrier reef surrounding Bora Bora in the Pacific. Coral reefs are among the most fragile of marine habitats, sensitive to subtle changes in their environment and particularly vulnerable to pollution. Without urgent conservation measures many of the world's finest reefs may be doomed.

With an uncanny and tragic accuracy, waste material from an Italian metal refinery is being dumped in the one part of the Mediterranean where, summer after summer, migratory fin whales come to feed. The dumping has been linked to ship collisions with dead and incapacitated whales and to discoveries of dead, stranded whales—all of which have been found with large areas of skin destroyed or loaded with sulfur and heavy metals.

The whales feed in this particular locality, off the coast of Corsica, because it is one of the most productive areas in the Mediterranean. Tiny floating plants multiply explosively in regular blooms and these blooms support equally dramatic increases in the shrimp-like creatures that form the bulk of the whales' food. Like many sea creatures, whales are dependent on periodic plankton blooms and these are regulated largely by temperature changes in the water mass. In the spring and early summer, for example, Pacific fin whales feed on minute planktonic animals called copepods. When the waters warm to more than 8°C the copepods migrate down to levels the whales are unable to reach and the fin whales react by migrating north to colder feeding grounds.

Areas of regular or prolific plankton blooms, meadows of seagrasses, beds of seaweeds and coastal wetland habitats such as mangroves, salt marshes, lagoons and estuaries, are all known to conservationists as critical marine habitats. They are critical for the marine creatures living within them—and critical also for man, whose long-term welfare depends at least in part on the continuing stability and productivity of the entire marine food web.

Highly productive areas like coastal wetlands and offshore nutrient-rich upwellings, diverse communities of animal life like the coral reef and mangrove, and the feeding, resting and breeding areas of whales, seals, seabirds and turtles are all critical habitats. If too many are destroyed or damaged, then the vital harvest of the seas will inevitably diminish and eventually disappear. Many of these sensitive areas are already being wrecked by man's greed or thoughtlessness. Reefs in Thailand are being plundered of their finest corals and most beautiful shells for sale in the tourist shops of Southeast Asia; the reefs off the coast of Sri Lanka are being systematically quarried as a source of building material, and coastal wetlands in the United States of America are being drained, filled, polluted or otherwise damaged at an annual rate of between half and one percent of their total area. Reefs are among the most sensitive of all marine environments and the tiny polyps are particularly sensitive to the amount of sediment in the water. To some extent the corals can cope with a rain of particles falling through the water, but ill-considered forest clearance, arable and pastoral land use can lead to sudden and dramatic increases in soil erosion—often ruining the land in addition to killing offshore reefs.

A global network of marine parks and reserves is essential for the protection of critical habitats, but its establishment faces two enormous obstacles. First, most nations continue to regard the sea as a combined cornucopia and waste disposal facility of limitless capacity and are reluctant to set areas aside for apparently nonproductive and noneconomic purposes. Second, the seas themselves and the life they contain have no regard for national sovereignty. Potential marine parks often lie within the territorial waters of more than one country. Golfo de Fonseca for example spans the territories of El Salvador, Honduras and Nicaragua; Waddenzee similarly falls within the jurisdiction of Denmark, Germany and the Netherlands. The effective setting up and control of protected areas would therefore involve an exceptional degree of international cooperation.

Even if one country did take action to declare an adequate number of coastal and marine reserves, their effectiveness would be totally dependent on other countries taking supportive action. Many marine animals depend on a number of quite different habitats often thousands of miles apart. If the gray whales of the Pacific are to continue to flourish, their calving

Mangrove swamps are among the least popular of natural habitats, having little in their expanses of mud and their tangled masses of rotting vegetation to appeal to the public imagination. They are, nevertheless, fascinating and complex living communities providing a home for a wide variety of wildlife and, perhaps even more important, playing a vital role in the balance of the marine food web.

Research carried out in recent years in the Florida swamps has shown that almost 95 percent of all the leaf litter shed by the locally prolific red mangrove finds its way into the warm, shallow coastal waters. Here the litter is distributed by currents to form the basis of a complex food chain, the higher members of which include commercially valuable fish species.

The beluga, or white whale, *Delphinapterus leucas*, inhabits the Arctic seas off Canada, Alaska, Greenland, northwest Europe and the USSR, but enters river estuaries, particularly those with a relatively warm runoff, in order to breed. Diversion of major rivers by dams, and pollution by power stations and industrial complexes, robs the white whale of its breeding environment.

lagoons in Mexico must be protected from the effects of industrial development and excessive disturbance by tourism; their feeding grounds in the Bering Sea far to the north must remain productive and available to them, and the migration route they travel must not be made intolerable by shipping and pleasure craft operating without control.

Many shorebirds migrate extraordinary distances every year—for example from the Arctic through western Europe to sub-Saharan Africa. Their flyways link numerous island and coastal wetland habitats, most of which are important—some essential—as overwintering, moulting or breeding grounds, or simply as staging posts where the birds can rest and replenish their reserves of energy during the long journeys north and south.

Internationally agreed marine parks, reserves and protected areas are an urgent necessity, but in isolation they are not enough. Reefs, seagrass meadows, islands and coastal wetlands are not self-contained entities but parts of a continuum extending from the land to the open ocean and from one part of the ocean to another. The oceans have their boundaries, but they are subtle and do not always correspond with popular conceptions of them. Currents, upwellings, salinity and temperature differences may all act as barriers; the coast, by contrast, more often unites rather than separates land and sea.

As the continental uplands are eroded and washed down to the sea, the streams and rivers of the world carry in suspension enormous loads of minerals, much of which is deposited at the river mouths. These minerals fertilize the salt marshes, mangroves and estuaries on whose decaying vegetation and resident animal and insect life, birds, fish and sea mammals ultimately depend for food. In the USA alone the final market value of estuarine and associated fish has been estimated to be more than 1000 million dollars. Careless manipulation of rivers can therefore be economically counterproductive by greatly reducing the productivity of the seas. It can also disturb sensitive marine life in less direct ways. Each spring

belugas, or white whales, which spend much of the year in the cold Arctic waters off Alaska, Canada, Greenland, Norway and the USSR, enter the river estuaries of the northern continents to breed. They are attracted particularly to rivers with a relatively warm runoff; if the rivers are diverted by a dam, or polluted by industrial effluent, the belugas simply do not return.

Rational use of the seas depends on recognition that the life of the oceans has its own peculiar dynamic and that one sea area may be linked with another in dramatic and occasionally unsuspected ways. The life of the Bering Sea for instance is geared to a gigantic gamble of nature in which the stakes are a maximum of two plankton blooms in any one year. Egg-laying by many fish species is synchronized with the blooms—the eggs drifting with the currents toward the bloom areas so that by the time the larvae hatch and need food they are over the area of prolific food supply. Not surprisingly the failure rate is high and yet sufficient fish survive to support an estimated 450,000 tons of marine mammals and 14,500 tons of oceanic and coastal birdlife.

One of the many birds that depend on the hospitality of the Arctic shores is the bristle-thighed curlew, which breeds in Alaska and winters in the South Pacific. From the coastal waters of the Bering Sea the bristle-thighed curlew obtains the energy it requires for one of the most remarkable of all migrations—2500 miles in a single soaring flight to Hawaii, the first of the bird's staging posts on its way to the islands of the tropical South Pacific.

Unhappily human activities now threaten to undermine the delicately balanced system of the Bering Sea by competing directly for the available fish stocks. Already most food-fish stocks are fully or even overexploited and harvests of pollack—the most important commercial fish species—have exceeded the maximum sustainable yield every year since 1970. Competition for food is wasteful and destructive in the natural world and consequently most animals are adapted, either physically or behaviorally, to avoid it. The place of narwhals in the Arctic Ocean is taken by ice-

dwelling ringed seals only when the onset of winter forces the narwhals to move south down the Greenland coast. In the northwest Atlantic fin whales and harp seals both feed on capelin fish, but they take it in turn to do so—the whales utilizing the capelin stocks in summer, the seals in winter.

Remorselessly, as man fishes the conventional food species to the brink of extinction he turns instead to the natural food of the seals and whales. The recently established capelin industry now takes 500,000 tons of fish annually—as much as is taken each year by the entire population of fin whales and harp seals—and the industry is as yet only in the early stages of development.

Until the seas are managed for what they really are—dynamic systems of interacting physical and biological processes—they will continue to be managed badly. Management authorities with powers and interests confined either to a small number of species or to geographically small areas are no longer sufficient. Today national boundaries are being extended far out into the oceans, but for as long as marine animals cross those boundaries or occupy the diminishing areas of international free waters, and for as long as man remains unwilling or unable to adopt procedures recognizing the special needs of these animals, the potential for control by international authorities will remain limited.

In May 1975, at the International Conference on Marine Parks and Reserves held in Tokyo, the government of the Cook Islands in the southwest Pacific announced the establishment of the first World Marine Park. In this imaginative gesture, challenging the international community to take more direct action and formulate more substantial long-term policies, the Cook Island government presented the island of Manaue "to world science and for the benefit of mankind." Manaue is just one small coral island, a little more than eight square miles in extent, but its new status as the first totally protected marine environment represents a welcome step forward in man's approach to the ocean world.

THE FACE OF THE DEEP

The vast ocean realm covering nearly three-quarters of the surface
of our planet has many moods; lashed by storms or placid and
serene, fast-flowing or virtually motionless, teeming with life or
almost barren. Temperature may vary from nearly two degrees below
zero in the Antarctic to more than 35°C in the Persian Gulf in summer.
Here the United States icebreaker *Glacier* noses her way past a large
flat ice floe on the fringes of Antarctica. The ship is making its way
along the edge of the fast ice, held against the margin of the continent
throughout the Antarctic winter. Beyond lies a broad zone of pack
ice varying in density and constantly moving under the influence of
winds and currents.

THE WORLD OCEAN

ATLANTIC: BATHYMETRY

The Atlantic Ocean, though much smaller than the Pacific, has a far larger drainage area—four times that of the Pacific.
Area 31,660,000 square miles; 82,000,000 square kilometers.
Average depth 10,930 feet; 3330 meters.
Volume 77,235,000 cubic miles; 321,930,000 cubic kilometers.
Max. depth (South Sandwich Trench) 30,000 feet; 9144 meters.

The topography of the Atlantic Ocean floor is dominated by a central S-shaped ridge extending from north of Iceland to Bouvet Island on the edge of the Southern Ocean, where it bends eastward to join the ridge system of the Indian Ocean. Discovered more than 100 years ago, this immense mountain range—the Mid-Atlantic Ridge—divides the Atlantic into two broadly parallel troughs, which are in turn subdivided into smaller basins by transverse ridges. Iceland, the Azores, Ascension Island and Tristan da Cunha are among the few emergent parts of the Mid-Atlantic Ridge, the crest of which generally lies between one and two miles below sea level.

A characteristic feature of the ridge crest is a deep axial rift valley between 15 and 30 miles in width. The rift lies almost exactly along the median line of the ocean and is frequently displaced by east–west transform faults topographically expressed by narrow ridges and deep linear clefts that can be traced for more than 1250 miles in some places. The transverse fractures are particularly important as structural elements in the equatorial region, shifting the ridge axis a total distance of more than 1800 miles to the east between latitude 10°N and 10°S. Between the fracture zones, the bottom topography is often lineated in a direction parallel to the ridge axis—the north–south grain and the transverse fractures imparting a coarse trellislike texture to the flanks of the ridge.

The geology of the Atlantic islands and studies of submarine sediment samples attest to the fact that the Mid-Atlantic Ridge is a product of igneous processes. Crustal age steadily increases with distance from the central rift valley, leaving little doubt that the ridge has evolved by seafloor spreading associated with the movement of the Americas away from Europe and Africa. The rate of movement—roughly 0.4 to 0.8 inches a year on each flank—is appreciably slower than that measured on the East Pacific Rise, but generally comparable with motions determined on the Carlsberg

Ridge in the northwest Indian Ocean.

Coupled with the horizontal movement is a gradual subsidence of the crust, the slope of the ridge flank reflecting the contraction of the oceanic lithosphere as it cools. Recent volcanic eruptions, such as that heralding the birth of Surtsey off the southern coast of Iceland in 1963, provide dramatic evidence of the continuing geologic activity along the crest of the Mid-Atlantic Ridge. At several sites unusually copius outpourings of volcanic material have occurred over a protracted period of time and have produced, as seafloor spreading took place, some of the broad transverse ridges of thickened oceanic crust such as the Greenland–Iceland–Faeroe Ridge in the North Atlantic and the Walfisch Ridge in the South Atlantic. Recent volcanic activity in the Azores, and the development of complex topography to the east of the islands, appears to be related to movements taking place along the boundary between the Eurasian and African plates.

Between the Mid-Atlantic Ridge and the edges of the continents lie the vast sedimentary aprons of the continental rises and the abyssal plains. Here the volcanic basement has been obscured by rapidly deposited sediments brought down from the adjacent continents by dense bottom currents. Numerous canyons cutting deep into the continental slopes provide transportation routes for the sediment-laden currents. In several basins the pattern of bottom-water circulation has closely controlled the distribution of sedimentary material. The Argentine Rise, for example, is a thick mass of land-derived sediments shaped predominantly by the flow of deep water of Antarctic origin. Near the continental slopes the sediment thickness often exceeds three miles, in marked contrast with the blanket of pelagic ooze and clay, usually less than half a mile thick, covering the younger rocks close to the Mid-Atlantic Ridge. Drilling has revealed that the sedimentary record of the continental rise off North America and North Africa stretches back into the Jurassic period, 170 to 160 million years ago.

In marked contrast to the Pacific Ocean, only two trenches are found along the margins of the Atlantic and both are of relatively small dimensions when compared with the enormous arcuate submarine deeps off the Aleutians, Japan or the west coast of South America. The Puerto Rico Trench, near 20°N, appears to have been formed as a result of predominantly horizontal movement between the American and Caribbean plates, while the South Sandwich Trench in the South Atlantic is associated with a localized subduction of material of the American plate.

Incandescent lava pours into the sea from Surtsey—a new island born on the Mid-Atlantic Ridge, south of Iceland, in 1963.

THE EVOLUTION OF THE ATLANTIC OCEAN

Theodor Christoph Lilienthal, an eighteenth-century theologian, was one of the earliest writers to comment on the neat geometric fit of the coastlines of South America and Africa. His observations provided the first hint of the theory of continental drift, and later plate tectonics, which was to revolutionize the earth sciences in the twentieth century. Recent studies, aided by computer models, have shown that the fit of the continental margins around the Atlantic is indeed remarkably exact and it is now universally accepted that the Americas, Europe and Africa once formed a single landmass that fragmented to form the Atlantic Ocean basin. Evidence from deep-sea drilling and the study of magnetic anomalies has proved that rifting and separation of the Atlantic occurred in several distinct phases.

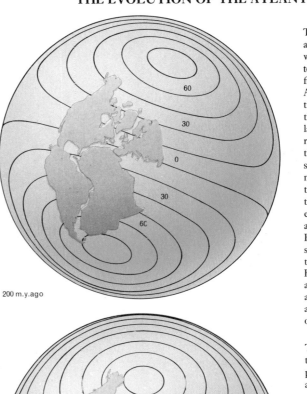

200 m.y. ago

The earliest phase of drifting took place during the Jurassic period, 195–135 million years ago, in what is now the central part of the North Atlantic. North America at this time drifted away from the combined landmass of Africa and South America with a separation rate of about three centimeters a year. By about 150 million years ago, the Central Atlantic had opened to roughly 30 percent of its final width, but the South Atlantic and the extreme North Atlantic remained fixed to Africa and Europe respectively.

150 m.y.ago

As the proto-Atlantic widened a narrow wedge of ocean floor extending northward to the continental margin of Ireland was formed by the rotation of Europe away from North America. At this time the Rockall Plateau, a small block of continental crust, probably became separated from Europe, but still remained attached to Greenland. South America and Africa began to drift apart during the Lower Cretaceous period, about 50 million years after the initial rifting took place, and during this phase the Bay of Biscay was created by the counterclockwise movement of the Iberian Peninsula.

105 m.y.ago

The last of the major ocean basins to be created—that lying between Greenland and the Rockall Plateau—was formed by a phase of seafloor spreading that began about 60 million years ago, at approximately the same time as the Norwegian Sea began to develop.

35 m.y.ago

Reconstructions of the global distribution of the continents show that all the landmasses have undergone large northward displacements during the last 200 million years. The shifts in latitude, and the incursion of a widening seaway through the interior of the pre-Jurassic landmass, brought about radical environmental changes on the continents and profoundly affected oceanic water circulation. One of the most significant changes to take place between 125 and 25 million years ago was the establishment of major connexions with deep basins at high latitudes, allowing, for the first time, large-scale interchange of water between the Atlantic and the polar regions.

ATLANTIC: MINERAL RESOURCES

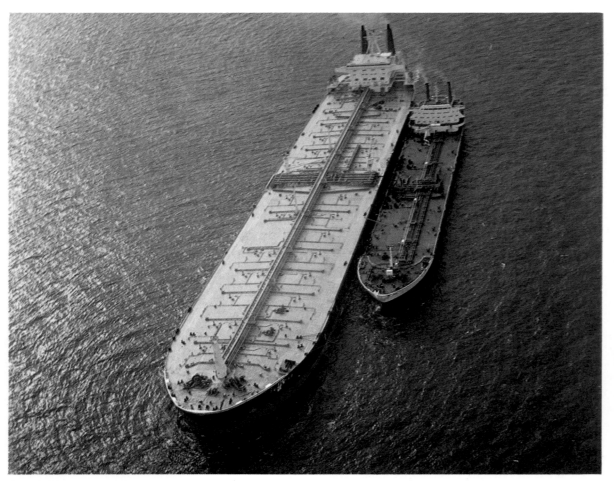

The **542,400-ton** *Batilus* is the world's largest tanker, measuring 1312 feet in length, 206 feet across the beam and having a draft of 93 feet. In order to enter the oil ports of Europe, she must first lighten her load by transshipping oil into smaller tankers.

Few of the mineral deposits of the Atlantic Ocean satisfy the economic criteria that determine whether or not they are worked, and those mined are restricted to shallow water on continental shelves. Apart from petroleum, the value of the sand and gravel won is greater than that of all other minerals combined, despite the fact that sand and gravel are among the lowest-value minerals exploited anywhere in the world. Production is concentrated on the shallow shelf of northwest Europe and, apart from the possibility of small-scale operations elsewhere, there is considerable interest in the winning of sand and gravel off the Eastern Seaboard of the United States to meet the demand for aggregates in coastal areas where local deposits are being depleted.

Although limestone is also a low-value commodity, alternative forms of calcium carbonate are also recovered from the seabed. The largest single offshore mining operation in the world is based on Ocean Cay, an artificial island created by dredging aragonite sand from the Great Bahamas Bank, big enough to provide harbor facilities and an aircraft landing strip. Ooliths of aragonite are precipitated from the warm water over these very extensive banks and have accumulated in unconsolidated deposits up to 20 feet thick, below which the aragonite has been converted into limestone. These deposits are recovered by a pumping system from below water about six feet deep. The aragonite, which contains about 97 percent calcium carbonate, is used for a variety of purposes, including the manufacture of Portland cement, glass and animal feed supplements, the regulation of the acidity of soil and in industrial acid neutralization processes. The main markets are in areas distant from deposits of suitable limestone on land, from Guyana to New Jersey, although most is delivered to ports in Florida. Some is supplied for use as fine aggregate in concrete where other sources of supply are more costly. The cement industry in Iceland is based on shell sand dredged from the continental shelf, some of which is also used as fertilizer and as an additive in animal foodstuffs. Small quantities of the calcareous algae *Lithothamnia* are dredged off the coast of Brittany for agricultural use.

Offshore prospecting, started in 1961, demonstrated that the valuable diamond deposits in Namibia (South-West Africa) extended offshore. Full-scale dredging started in 1962, but was suspended in 1971 as the operations were uneconomic, the higher grade of the deposits not compensating for the operating costs.

Phosphatic sediments (and glauconite, a potassium-rich mineral) on the seabed were discovered by H.M.S. *Challenger* on the Agulhas Bank off South Africa. Unconsolidated phosphate (or phosphorite) deposits, ranging from phosphatic mud through pebble-sized particles to encrustations, are now known to be relatively widespread, including off Namibia, northwest Africa, Florida and Georgia, where they extend down to the Blake Plateau, the Falkland Islands and on parts of the continental margin of South America. They occur from very shallow water to more than 10,000 feet, most occurring in the deeper water of the outer continental shelf. There is disagreement about the origin of many of these deposits, for example whether they are precipitated from seawater or are formed by the alteration of preexisting rocks, as most unconsolidated phosphate deposits are associated with phosphatic bedrock. Although some deposits are adjacent to areas of upwelling, most are relatively old, for example of Miocene age. These deposits have not been mined because reserves of higher-grade phosphate rock on land are large enough and can be recovered at lower cost. Rising transport costs have led to the exploitation of lower-grade land deposits rather than the high-grade deposits in the sea.

No manganese nodules of the grade regarded as necessary for first-generation mining have been recovered from the Atlantic Ocean. The highest recorded average (of four samples) is 1.45 percent combined copper and nickel from the Cape Basin.

Apart from the continuing recovery of salt from seawater, magnesium and bromine are recovered from the water of the Atlantic Ocean.

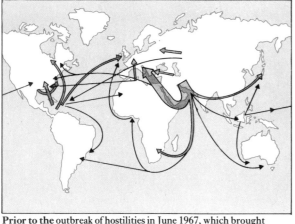

Prior to the outbreak of hostilities in June 1967, which brought about the closure of the Suez Canal, that crucial inland waterway carried the bulk of the world's traffic in crude oil.

Closure of the Suez Canal, and the rapidly escalating size of bulk oil carriers, several of which now exceed half a million tons, have made the Atlantic the main route for oil transportation.

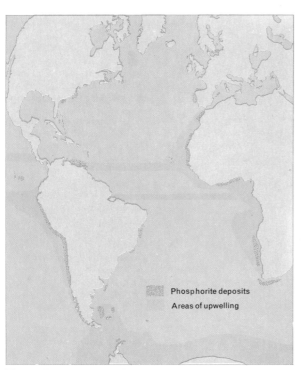

Phosphorite deposits

Areas of upwelling

The mode of formation of phosphorite concretions and encrustations is still a matter of scientific debate. Most known deposits are geologically fairly old, but others are known to be forming today, commonly in areas swept by strong currents and in areas of upwelling. Phosphorite is economically important as a fertilizer and as an active agent in the production of many other chemicals.

The world's largest single mining operation is the extraction of aragonite sands in the Bahamas. Sand is suction dredged onto an artificial island and then shipped out for a variety of uses.

Cement plant

Akranes

Iceland

Shell bank

FAXA BAY

Reykjavik

Keflavik

Faxa Bay, on the west coast of Iceland, is the site of a constantly replenished bank of shell sand, mined to feed primary raw material to the cement factory near Akranes. A rocky shoal lying to the west is home to a variety of shelled animals. Winter storm waves break the shells free, crush them, and the tidal currents sweep them onto the shell bank faster than the resource is extracted.

Offshore placer deposits
Solid symbol—active mine
Open symbol—known deposit

■	Iron
□	Iron
▮	Titanium
▯	Titanium

◪	Tin
◩	Tin
◼	Gold
▼	Monazite
▽	Monazite
◇	Diamond
●	Sand and gravel

◁	Chromite
◆	Zircon
◈	Zircon
⋈	Copper

◖	Shell sands
⊗	Coal
◐	Sulfur
▦	Phosphorite
●	Manganese nodules

▨	Major sedimentary basins
⊠	Oil and gas fields

200 meters

Though manganese nodules and encrustations are distributed widely over the deep floor of the Atlantic Ocean, the only commercially extracted minerals are oil, gas, gravel and shell sand from shallow shelf areas.

ATLANTIC OCEAN: CIRCULATION

Scattered cumulus clouds denote the meeting of cool and warm waters at the edge of the continental shelf off Cape Hatteras on the east coast of North America. Sediment-laden waters swirling from Pamlico Sound are swept north by the Gulf Stream.

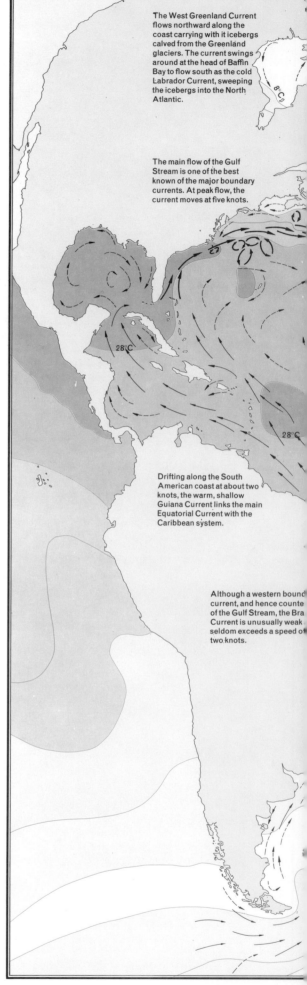

The West Greenland Current flows northward along the coast carrying with it icebergs calved from the Greenland glaciers. The current swings around at the head of Baffin Bay to flow south as the cold Labrador Current, sweeping the icebergs into the North Atlantic.

The main flow of the Gulf Stream is one of the best known of the major boundary currents. At peak flow, the current moves at five knots.

Drifting along the South American coast at about two knots, the warm, shallow Guiana Current links the main Equatorial Current with the Caribbean system.

Although a western boundary current, and hence counter of the Gulf Stream, the Brazil Current is unusually weak seldom exceeds a speed of two knots.

The current pattern of the North Atlantic is dominated by the great sweep of the North Atlantic Gyre, a roughly circular system of relatively warm waters driven by the North East Trade Winds between 10° and 30° north latitude and by the Westerlies between 40° and 60° north latitude.

In the southern part of the gyre, the North Equatorial Current carries surface waters toward North America, where the flow swings north to run along the coast as a narrow and intense current called the Gulf Stream. On reaching the latitude of the westerly winds, the Gulf Stream leaves the coast to become the North Atlantic Current—carrying warm waters toward northern Europe, where they exert a profound influence on the European climate. The return flow south to the equator is completed by a broad slow-moving current, the east side of which forms the relatively weak Canaries Current.

The speed of the main circulatory currents is usually about six miles a day, but the Gulf Stream, a classic western boundary current, may travel more than 80 miles in a single day. It has its origins where the Antilles Current is joined by the Florida Current sweeping out of the Gulf of Mexico, and then flows north as a strong, smooth and stable current. Off Cape Hatteras it reaches down to a depth of nearly 3300 feet and the core of the current has a width of about 40 miles. Farther north, the current moves away from the coast and becomes progressively less stable. Meanders form in the current, increasing in size downstream until they eventually break away from the main stream as Gulf Stream Rings, some 150 miles in diameter and containing current speeds as high as 60 miles a day. The rings break away and circulate back to rejoin the Gulf Stream near its source. Weaker rings, known as mesoscale eddies, are also produced. These contain current speeds of up to 15 miles a day and are found in all parts of the ocean.

In the region of the Grand Banks, the westerly airstream blowing across the meanders encounters, alternately, the warm waters of the Sargasso Sea on one side of the Gulf Stream and the cold waters of the Labrador Current on the other. These sudden and drastic changes in temperature produce the notorious fogbanks off Newfoundland—a hazard made even more treacherous by the icebergs swept down from West Greenland by the Labrador Current. It was precisely this combination of surface wind, currents and resultant fog which caused the tragic loss of the prestige liner *Titanic* in 1912.

A second warm water gyre in the South Atlantic is made up of the South Equatorial Current, the Benguela Current and the northern part of the Antarctic Circumpolar Current. The western boundary current of the gyre—the Brazil Current—is, however, unusually weak. One possible reason for this is that instead of forming the Brazil Current, part of the South Equatorial Current crosses into the North Atlantic Gyre as the Guiana Current, robbing the Brazil Current of a potential source of energy. But of greater importance is the substantial Equatorial Undercurrent, which flows to the east directly beneath the equator. This undercurrent is one of the world's most important; it is about 125 miles wide and flows at 50 miles a day, 330 feet below sea level—rarely breaking the surface but having sufficient energy in its upper layers to affect the steering of heavily laden supertankers.

Nearer the poles, the westerly winds drive two cold-water gyres. In the north, the subpolar gyre comprises the Irminger Current, the Greenland Current and the North Atlantic Current, while in the south a similar gyre is found in the Weddell Sea. Like the warm-water currents, these cold gyres are strongest near the surface, but while the warmer waters are markedly stratified, which restricts most currents to the upper 2000 feet of the ocean, the cold waters are much less stratified and the currents may extend down several miles. Thus the Antarctic Circumpolar Current carries deep Antarctic Bottom Waters at depths of nearly two and a half miles and sweeps it into the deep basins of the Indian and Pacific Oceans. The largest cold-water mass in the Atlantic is the North Atlantic Deep Water formed off Greenland. This great mass of dense cold water sinks and spreads out between 5000 and 13,000 feet, creating a south-flowing current along the western margin of the ocean.

Location of Atlantic water profiles

1 Gulf Stream at 66°W

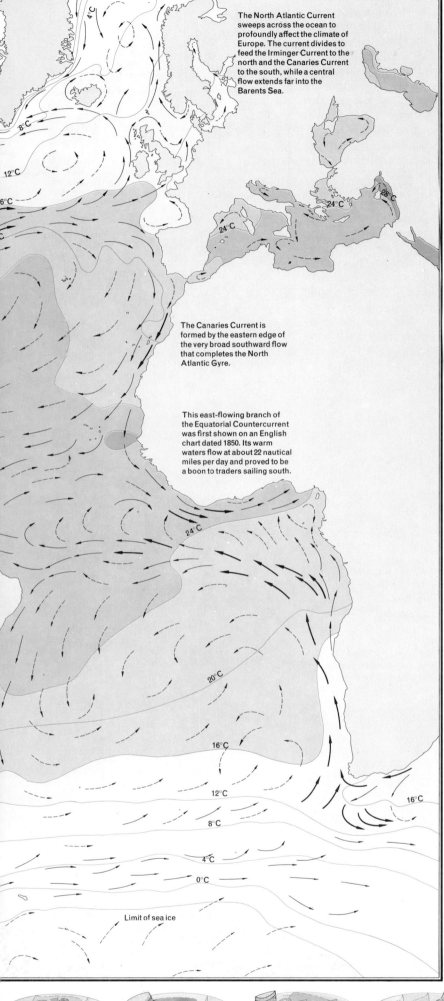

The North Atlantic Current sweeps across the ocean to profoundly affect the climate of Europe. The current divides to feed the Irminger Current to the north and the Canaries Current to the south, while a central flow extends far into the Barents Sea.

The Canaries Current is formed by the eastern edge of the very broad southward flow that completes the North Atlantic Gyre.

This east-flowing branch of the Equatorial Countercurrent was first shown on an English chart dated 1850. Its warm waters flow at about 22 nautical miles per day and proved to be a boon to traders sailing south.

Limit of sea ice

Major named currents of the Atlantic Ocean

Atmospheric circulation of the Atlantic Ocean

Swirling eddies and meanders in the Gulf Stream are vividly portrayed in this enhanced-color satellite photograph. Warm waters appear purple and red; cooler waters grade into tones of blue. The technique allows scientists to study the movement of heat energy across the world's oceans.

Growing instability causes Gulf Stream meanders to increase in amplitude (1–2) until they break away as independent eddies. If the cutoff occurs on the north side of the main stream (3A), the eddy has a warm core of Sargasso Sea water and rotates anticyclonically (4A). If the cutoff is to the south (3B), the eddy rotates cyclonically around a cold core of slope water (4B). North-side eddies progress westward to rejoin the Gulf Stream off Cape Hatteras, while south-side eddies make a long, irregular, southerly loop to rejoin near Florida. The eddies, which may be up to 200 miles across and more than a mile deep, may persist for two years and play an important role in the overall return flow of the Gulf Stream.

2 Grand Banks   3 Labrador Current   4 N. Atlantic Current   5 Benguela Current

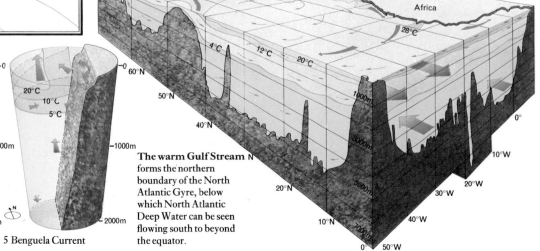

The warm Gulf Stream forms the northern boundary of the North Atlantic Gyre, below which North Atlantic Deep Water can be seen flowing south to beyond the equator.

ATLANTIC:LIVING RESOURCES

The Atlantic Ocean has been the cradle of many of the world's oldest oceanic fisheries. The herring, cod and flounder fisheries that originated in the North Sea and Norwegian Sea gave rise to modern distant-water factory trawlers and midwater trawling practices and also influenced the character of purse seining throughout the world.

Trawls have been in use since the end of the twelfth century. These large socklike nets look deceptively simple and yet more engineering expertise has been put into their design than into any other item of modern fishing equipment. Although trawls have been employed for centuries throughout the world, there is little doubt that they were originally developed in the North Sea and their high level of sophistication is a product of a series of innovations from French, British, German and Norwegian sources. Among the most important of these developments has been the technique of freeing the heavy trawl doors from the nets to allow them to be hauled on board with greater ease. Versatility of the equipment has also allowed the development of midwater trawling techniques.

Records of west European fishing activities date back well over 1000 years and the rise and decline of fisheries dependent on cyclic fluctuations of fish such as the herring has been well documented. In addition, fish played an important role in the economy of the west European nations during the time of the Hanseatic League and has also been significant in the economic history of Scandinavian countries, including Iceland.

Shortly after the discovery of the Americas in the fifteenth century, fishermen from many European ports crossed the Atlantic to harvest cod from the rich fishing grounds of the west Atlantic. Conflicts over fishing rights that have occurred during this century have their antecedents in the clashes over the rights to catch and salt fish caught off the eastern seaboard of North America and Canada in the 1500s.

The major part of the North Atlantic fish catch is taken on the rich continental shelf areas bordering northwest Europe, east Canada and the United States, where some of the world's largest and most important trawl fisheries are found. The most productive fishing grounds are those of the North Sea, the Norwegian Sea, the Barents Sea and those lying off the coasts of Newfoundland and New England. With the rapid development of trawling technology in the years following the Second World War, and the ever-increasing competition for fishery resources, trawl fishing has spread to areas off northwest Africa and to

The conventional bottom trawl (a) may only be used to catch fish such as cod and plaice that live directly on the seabed. For fish such as herring, tuna and capelin, which may be found at almost any depth, the midwater trawl (b) was developed. This gear may be used throughout the water column and can be guided up or down while actually in use. When towed by two vessels the net can be held open without the use of otter boards. Semipelagic trawls (c) are used to catch fish swimming just above the bottom.

Crustaceans	393
Mollusks	1,322
Diadromous fish	2,019
Marine fish	19,231

Atlantic total catch
22,965 thousand metric tons

	%
Others	8.1
Mediterranean	2.3
Caribbean	2.5
Indian	5.2
Atlantic	38.7
Pacific	43.2

World total catch
59,321 thousand metric tons

Fishing fleets operating out of New England and Canadian ports spend much of the winter off the Labrador coast, where the weather may be particularly severe. In the intense cold the ship's super-structure may become completely encrusted in frozen salt spray.

Fish belonging to the cod family, exploited mainly in the north Atlantic off the coasts of Norway, Iceland, Greenland and Canada, account for the largest single catch in the Atlantic. In tropical waters there is no similar dominant species group.

the Patagonian continental shelf off South America.

Forecasts of hitherto untapped fish resources have in some parts of the Atlantic not been realized: in the Brazilian town of Rio Grande a large fish-processing facility was built on the strength of estimates that indicated a potential resource far in excess of the local fleet's catching capability at that time. Sadly, several years of exploratory fishing eventually proved that the estimated rich stocks were simply not there. The seasonal appearance of the Falkland Current brings large stocks of hake, red porgy and blue fish into the area—but only for about four months of the year.

Large-scale fisheries for pelagic species occur predominantly in the North Atlantic, particularly in the North Sea, off Norway and off the northwest coast of the United States. The tuna fisheries of the Atlantic, although on a smaller scale than those of the Pacific, have in recent years become relatively important off northwest Africa. Catches of tuna in the Caribbean and off the coast of northeast South America have also been increasing.

The most important fisheries of the North Atlantic, rated by weight of catch, are those for the pelagic species—herring, sardine and anchovy—harvested by purse seiners; those for the demersal species, cod,

flounder and the Atlantic Ocean perch, exploited by trawlers, and those for hake found abundantly off the shores of south Europe, Africa and America.

Fishing for lobster, which commands a high market value throughout the world, occurs mainly off the northeast coast of the United States, in the Caribbean, off Brazil and along the South African coast. Most lobsters are taken from small craft using a variety of pots—though some are taken by large trawlers. Crab fishing in the Atlantic is an important industry on the east coast of the United States, while a less intensive fishery occurs in the North Sea and off the central east coast of South America. Like lobsters, the crabs are taken with a variety of pots, traps and ring nets.

Over the past decade the fisheries of the Atlantic have grown steadily even though the catches of some species have begun to show the effects of overfishing. Between 1965 and 1974 the total catch of Atlantic species rose from about 17 to more than 22 million tons—a figure only slightly below that for the very much larger Pacific Ocean. Based on catch per unit area, the Atlantic is the most intensively exploited ocean in the world and has a total catch estimated at about four thousand million dollars, which is an overall value of around 181.8 dollars per ton.

Atlantic cod stocks

- Stock areas
- Main spawning areas
- → Migration routes
- → Principal ocean currents

Cod

Demersal fish
- Areas of production

Pelagic fish
- ⟩⟩ Anchovy
- ⟩⟩ Sardine
- ⟩⟩ Herring
- ⟩⟩ Sprat
- ⟩⟩ Sardinella
- ⟩⟩ Capelin
- ⟩⟩ Tuna
- ⟩⟩ Mackerel
- ⟩⟩ Jack mackerel
- ⟩⟩ Mullet
- ⟩⟩ Menhaden
- ⟩⟩ Mixed

Northwest Europe

100m
200m
300m
400m
500m

Cod, haddock, whiting	Sole, flounder
Norway pout, saithe	Hake
	Plaice, rays
	Blue whiting

North Africa

100m
200m
300m
400m
500m
600m

Flatfish, surmullets	
Axillary breams, gurnards	
European hake, Norway pout, horse mackerel	
European hake	
Deepsea shrimps	

Demersal fish live on the areas of continental shelf that surround the oceans. Conditions of temperature, light intensity and pressure vary much more quickly with depth than they do geographically, limiting the vertical distribution of certain species.

Haddock

Saithe

Norway pout

Whiting

USSR	719,562
Norway	340,047
United Kingdom	316,994
Iceland	241,292
Spain	168,098
West Germany	161,901
Portugal	158,116
Canada	156,056
Denmark	138,908
France	97,898
Poland	97,589

Atlantic cod catch in metric tons

The cod is the principal member of a large group of commercially important species including saithe, haddock, Norway pout and whiting. They are essentially bottom-dwelling and carnivorous, feeding on small crustaceans, worms and the larvae of other fish. Cod are migratory and are divided into different stocks, or races, with different growth rates and spawning areas. Spawning takes place between January and March. The female lays several million eggs, hatching in 10 to 20 days.

CARIBBEAN: BATHYMETRY AND CIRCULATION

Temperature in °C

The Gulf of Mexico
Area 598,000 square miles;
1,543,000 square kilometers.
Volume 560,000 cubic miles;
2,322,000 cubic kilometers.
Av. depth 4960 ft; 1512 m.
Max. depth 13,218 ft; 4029 m.
The Caribbean Sea
Area 1,020,000 square miles;
2,640,000 square kilometers.
Maximum depth (Cayman
Trench) 25,216 ft; 7686 meters.

Although the bed of the Caribbean Sea has been mapped, probed and sampled more intensively than most other seabed regions, its geological development is still controversial. It is probably an ancient fragment of one of the Pacific plates, isolated by the formation of a trench along the west side of the Panamanian isthmus. Most of the old crust in the eastern Pacific has been dragged into the trenches of western America and destroyed; some has been thrust up onto the continental margins of California and Colombia, and only in the Caribbean does it persist as the floor of an ocean. The basin has been partly filled with sediment, most of the infill having been shed from the surrounding volcanoes and mountain ranges, for although the interior of the Caribbean is tectonically inactive, its margins have been sites of intense mountain building along the zones where Pacific and American plates slide past or beneath the relatively immobile Caribbean Plate. In the eastern Caribbean, Atlantic crust is being consumed beneath the Lesser Antilles, producing violent volcanic eruptions. One of the most devastating was the eruption of Mt Pelee, which incinerated the 30,000 inhabitants of St Pierre, Martinique, on 8 May, 1902. In the west, subduction beneath the isthmus causes the volcanism and most of the earthquake activity of Central America. Connecting the northern ends of these two zones is a giant fault along which the North American Plate is sliding westward past the Caribbean: this fault, with its narrow belt of earthquakes, passes north of Puerto Rico, south of Cuba, and through Guatemala to connect with the Middle America Trench. A movement of up to ten feet on this fault caused the destructive Guatemala City earthquake in February 1974. The southern tectonic connexion between the Pacific and West Indies is a complex zone of active faults in northern Venezuela and Colombia, along which South America is being shifted westward. The motion of South America welded that continent to Central America,

finally closing the Isthmus of Panama, only about three million years ago—an event that greatly altered the circulation of currents in the Caribbean Sea and throughout the North Atlantic.

The origins of the Nicaragua Rise, Beata Ridge and Aves Swell, which subdivide the Caribbean into separate deep basins, are geological mysteries. Beata Ridge is an upfaulted section of oceanic crust that may have formed at the same time as the isolation of the Caribbean Plate from the Pacific, while the ridge that parallels the arc of the Lesser Antilles is made partly of granitic rock, not typical of the ocean floor.

Water in the top few hundred feet of the Caribbean behaves as an extension of the North Atlantic Ocean. The Guiana Current and part of the North Equatorial Current flow past St Lucia almost unimpeded into the Caribbean and continue westward at a speed of nearly 20 miles a day. In the western Caribbean, the trade winds cause a surface flow of water northward, away from the coast of South America. This is replaced by nutrient-rich water upwelling from a depth of about 650 feet, and these extra nutrients support an important fishery industry.

Farther west, the main current turns north, through the Yucatan strait into the Gulf of Mexico, where the "Loop Current" channels the water toward the Florida Straits and back into the Atlantic to join the Gulf Stream. The turn that the Loop Current tries to make is sharp and it often becomes unstable, forming a large meander which may itself be cut off, leaving an eddy of warm surface water drifting westward across the Gulf of Mexico.

The basins of the Caribbean are up to 16,400 feet deep, as deep as much of the North Atlantic. However, the islands and connecting ridges of the Eastern Caribbean prevent any interchange of deep water: instead, the deep water of the Caribbean is all at roughly the same temperature, 4.85°C, the temperature of the Atlantic at a depth of 5,250 feet. It is thought that this Atlantic water occasionally spills over the ridges to form the deep Caribbean water.

The separation from the Atlantic is also observed in the tides, which are much smaller in the Caribbean and the Gulf of Mexico than in the Atlantic. In addition, the dominant tide of the Gulf of Mexico is the diurnal tide, giving one high and low water each day. In the Atlantic the dominant tide is the semi-diurnal or twice-daily tide. Rather more dramatic are the storm surges caused by hurricanes which can locally raise sea level by nearly three feet.

Sediment load, eddies and current paths show as tone variation in this Skylab photograph of Mobile Bay. Silt-laden water flowing into the Gulf of Mexico is swept westward by longshore currents.

ATLANTIC OCEAN

Jacksonville

Blake Plateau

Florida

Florida Escarpment

Straits of Florida

Miami

Great Bahama Bank

BAHAMAS

Caicos Bank

Havana

CUBA

Greater

Yucatan Channel

Yucatan Basin

CAYMAN IS.

Cayman Trough

Cayman Ridge

Antilles

JAMAICA

HAITI

DOMINICAN REPUBLIC

Puerto Rico Trench

PUERTO RICO

Virgin Is.

ANTIGUA

GUADELOUPE

DOMINICA

Nicaragua Rise

Beata Ridge

Venezuelan Basin

MARTINIQUE

ST. LUCIA

Aves Swell

Grenada Trough

ST. VINCENT

BARBADOS

HONDURAS

CARIBBEAN SEA

Colombian Basin

NICARAGUA

Managua

Los Roques Trench

NETHERLANDS ANTILLES

Lesser

Antilles

GRENADA

Tobago

TRINIDAD AND TOBAGO

Trinidad

Gulf of Venezuela

Barranquilla

Maracaibo

Lake Maracaibo

Caracas

COSTA RICA

CANAL ZONE

Panama

PANAMA

Cocos Ridge

COLOMBIA

VENEZUELA

Orinoco

GUYANA

meters

500
0
0
200
1000
2000
3000
4000
5000

0   100   200   300   400   500   600   700 km
0   100   200   300   400 miles

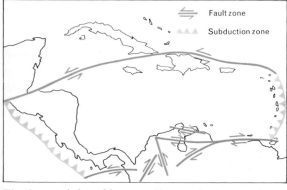

Fault zone

Subduction zone

The elongated plate of the Caribbean Sea is bordered to east and west by subduction zones, where major plates dip beneath the Caribbean basin. A simple fault zone across the northern margin and a complex fault system in South America absorb lateral movement.

Atchafalaya River

Lake Pontchartrain

Mississippi River

Birdfoot delta

Approximate ages of deltas

Teche	3800 yrs ago—2800 yrs ago
St Bernard	2800 yrs ago—?
Lafourche	1200 yrs ago—600 yrs ago
Plaquemines	1200 yrs ago—?
Modern	450 yrs ago—present

Since sea level stabilized 3500 to 4000 years ago, the Mississippi River has built a progressive series of deltas across the continental shelf. Beneath these recent deltaic complexes lies a vast thickness of earlier sediments filling a downwarped trough in the seabed.

Levee

Marsh

Mud diapir

Silt/sand

Silt/clay

Bar sands

Clay/mud

As the Mississippi outflow channels discharge into the sea, sands are deposited at the mouth of each channel, while finer sediments are carried farther to be deposited on the steep delta-front slope. Thus as the delta advances, the sands progressively overlie the earlier silts and clays. Compaction of these finer sediments can cause upward intrusion of mud diapirs, which may reach the surface and form mud islands in the distributory channels. The channels are bounded by levees of sand and silt beyond which lie broad marshy flood-plains.

125

CARIBBEAN: LIVING AND MINERAL RESOURCES

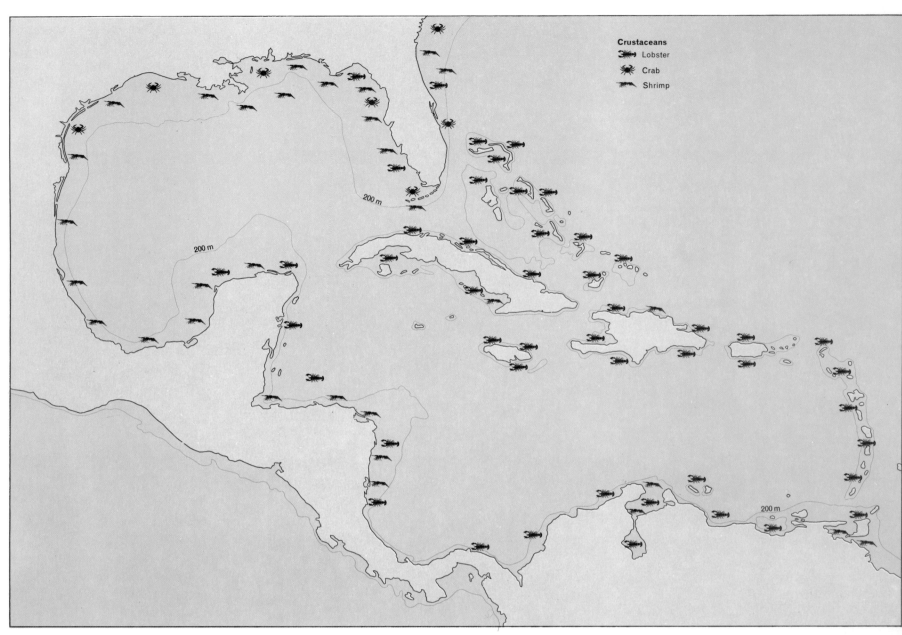

Crustaceans
- Lobster
- Crab
- Shrimp

Apart from mollusks and crustaceans, the most important fishery in the Gulf of Mexico is for industrial fish such as menhaden.

The fishery for both blue crabs and shrimps has been carried out in coastal and estuarine waters since prehistoric times.

Demersal fish
- Areas of production

Pelagic fish
- Anchovy
- Tuna
- Mackerel
- Jack mackerel
- Mullet
- Menhaden

Caribbean total catch
1498 thousand metric tons

Marine fish	1117
Crustaceans	222
Mollusks	157
Diadromous fish	2

World total catch			
59,321 thousand metric tons			
	%		%
Pacific	43.2	Atlantic	38.7
		Indian	5.2
		Caribbean	2.5
		Mediterranean	2.3
		Others	8.1

The dominant fishery of the region is that for shrimps, centered in the Gulf of Mexico. The Caribbean is generally less productive than the Gulf and much of its continental shelf is rough and unsuitable for trawl fishing. However, tuna are fished in the open sea and sardine and anchovy are caught off the Venezuelan coast.

The Caribbean region is generally less productive than many areas of the world ocean and with the exception of the northern part of the Gulf of Mexico most of the fisheries are small enterprises at a low level of sophistication. The relatively poor productivity of the region is due to three main factors: the lack of any major upwellings; the relatively narrow continental shelf, much of which cannot be fished because of coral reefs; and the lack of nutrient inflow to the surface waters. Nevertheless many of the island and coastal inhabitants are occupied with fishing activities and thousands of fishermen work the reefs and banks for shrimp, lobster, tuna, shark, red snapper and a wide variety of tropical fishes. The artisan fishery is, for the most part, conducted from small craft—canoes and rowboats—although in recent years many have been improved by the addition of inboard or outboard engines.

By far the most important fisheries of the area are those conducted for shrimp and menhaden, mainly in the Gulf of Mexico. In recent years shrimp fisheries have developed off Central America, Venezuela and the Guianas, but the largest and most mechanized fishery in the Caribbean is that based on the menhaden stocks in the northwestern Gulf of Mexico. Here, large carrier vessels up to 130 feet in length pump the catch taken by small seine boats into their holds and transport them to shore stations, where the catch is processed into fish meal. Production of menhaden from the Gulf has, in the last ten years, ranged between 500,000 and one million tons.

Of the island countries bordering the Caribbean, Cuba alone has made substantial efforts to modernize her fisheries. The Cuban catch, which has increased rapidly over the past decade, is composed of shrimp, lobster, demersal fish, tuna and mackerel. Most of the fish produce of the region south of the Gulf of Mexico is consumed fresh, but a small proportion is marketed smoked or dried for export.

The Caribbean Sea and the Gulf of Mexico have a long and complex sedimentary history and this, combined with the restricted nature of the water circulation within the partially enclosed basin complex, has given rise to a varied and valuable mineral resource.

The vast thicknesses of sediment underlying the present-day delta of the Mississippi River are rich in hydrocarbon deposits representing a valuable energy resource to a nation ranked highest among the world's users of energy. Nearly 1800 miles away to the south, on the southern margin of the Caribbean Sea, lies the region's other major hydrocarbon resource—the vast oil fields of Lake Maracaibo in northern Venezuela. In 1970 the Venezuelan oil fields were producing at the rate of 3.7 million barrels a day, making that country one of the world's leading exporters of crude oil and petroleum products.

The broad continental shelf areas of the north and west Gulf of Mexico contain thick sequences of evaporite deposits laid down in earlier marine phases. The sequences are rich in domes and plugs of salt that are locally favorable for the development of potash and magnesium deposits, while the anhydrite beds forming much of the evaporite sequence are favorable for the accumulation of sulfur—particularly as cap-rock formations over salt domes. The world's first offshore sulfur mine began operation in 1960, seven miles off the coast of Louisiana. Extraction of the sulfur is effected by the Frasch process in which hot water is pumped down the boreholes under pressure, melting the sulfur, which is then pumped out in liquid form.

Titanium, monazite and zircon deposits are known around the northern margins of the Gulf of Mexico; iron and titanium are present in continental shelf deposits off the coasts of Costa Rica and Colombia, and placer deposits of chromite, titanium and gold are probably present in the shelf sediments off Cuba and Haiti. At present none of these deposits are worked, but represent a potential future development.

Sulfur is extracted from below the seabed off the Louisiana coast, where it occurs in the cap rocks over salt domes. The sulfur is extracted by the Frasch process, which involves sinking three concentric pipes into the sulfur formation and pumping down super-heated water through the outer two. The sulfur at the base of the pipes melts and as the flow of water is continued down the outer pipe the melt rises through the inner. Compressed air is then pumped down the center pipe to lighten the liquid and help it to rise to the surface. The Grand Isle mine seven miles offshore is the largest steel island in the Western Hemisphere and stands in 50 feet of water. The power plant, which heats the water under pressure to 200°C, is sited some distance away to guard against subsidence.

The oil fields in Lake Maracaibo made Venezuela the world's third largest oil producer after the United States and the USSR. It has now fallen to about fifth place.

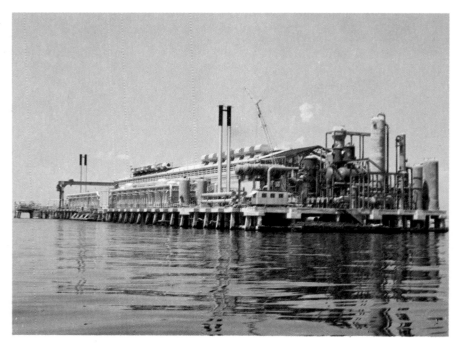

ARCTIC : BATHYMETRY AND CIRCULATION

The Arctic Ocean is the smallest of the major oceans with an area of only slightly more than one-sixth that of the Indian Ocean. Its basin is almost totally landlocked.
Area 4,700,000 square miles; 12,173,000 square kilometers.
Average depth 3,250 feet; 990 meters.
Max. depth (Pole Abyssal Plain) 15,091 feet; 4600 meters.

Prior to the middle of the twentieth century the Arctic Ocean was generally thought to consist of one large ocean basin, but research carried out in recent years, aided by the increasingly sophisticated tools of sonar, radar and deepwater sampling, backed up by ice-strengthened research vessels, aircraft and submarines, has proved otherwise. Though small in comparison with other oceans, the Arctic has a remarkably complex and varied seabed relief.

The basin is subdivided by three major submarine ridges. The Arctic Mid-Ocean Ridge is an active seafloor spreading center and part of the global system of major spreading ridges. It is offset from the northerly extension of the Mid-Atlantic Ridge by the Nansen Fracture Zone. The Arctic Mid-Ocean Ridge is separated from the great submarine mountain chain of the Lomonosov Ridge by the Pole Abyssal Plain—an elongated trough of deep water containing the greatest depth yet recorded in the Arctic—more than 15,000 feet, close to the geographic North Pole. The Lomonosov Ridge itself dominates the submarine relief of the Arctic basin, rising on average some 10,000 feet above the abyssal plain and reaching within a little over 3000 feet of the surface at its highest points.

On the Canadian side of the Lomonosov Ridge the ocean basin is again subdivided by the broad sweep of the Alpha Ridge, an irregular submarine mountain chain widely believed to be a now-inactive element in the global ridge system. Between the Alpha Ridge and the Canadian coast lies the Canada Abyssal Plain, by far the largest of the Arctic sub-basins, with an average depth of more than 12,000 feet.

The continental shelf areas of the Arctic form one of the ocean's most unique features, underlying almost one-third of the total area of the ocean. Off the

northern coastlines of Alaska, Canada and Greenland the shelf is of normal width, generally between 50 and 125 miles wide, but off the coast of northern Asia the shelf extends out for more than 1000 miles at its widest and is nowhere less than 300 miles in width. This vast shelf area is subdivided by island groups and peninsulas into a number of interconnected shallow seas, the largest of which are the Chukchi, East Siberian and Laptev seas. Though largely inaccessible throughout the severe Arctic winter, these shallow shelf seas have in recent years become the focus of intense geologic and geophysical investigation. In response to the ever-increasing world demand for oil and gas, governments and industry are turning to the continental shelves of the Arctic in search of future power resources.

The virtually enclosed nature of the Arctic Ocean, its varied submarine topography and its perennial cover of sea ice all combine to give the water movement and water budget of the ocean a character quite unlike that of any other ocean. The major part of the water inflow and outflow takes place through the Greenland Sea—the only deep-water connexion with the world ocean. Roughly 80 percent of the water entering and leaving the Arctic basin passes through this narrow channel between Greenland and Spitsbergen; less than 20 percent passes through the shallow Bering Sea.

The surface water circulation forms two easily identified systems; a broad clockwise gyre in the Canadian side of the ocean and a more direct flow sweeping in an arc over the shallower relief of the Asian side of the basin from the Chukchi Sea to the Greenland Sea. Heat exchange between the ocean and atmosphere is reduced by the ice cover to only a few percent of that found in an open ocean and the water directly beneath the ice is much more variable in temperature and density than is normal in surface waters. The variations are caused by ice melting, river inflow, freezing—which causes localized increases in salinity—and by the variable thickness of the insulating ice cover blocking out the heating effect of the sun. The thin, cold surface layer overlies a deep layer of slightly warmer, more saline water flowing into the basin from the North Atlantic. This midwater layer, extending from about 600 feet below the surface to about 3000 feet below, becomes colder and more dense as it traverses the deep ocean basins.

Icebergs calved from the glaciers of northern Greenland and the apronlike ice shelves of northern Ellesmere Island are carried westward along the Canadian Arctic coast and into the Beaufort Sea, where many are swept north and into the rotating current system. Thin tabular bergs from Ellesmere Island, often referred to as ice islands, are used as floating research stations.

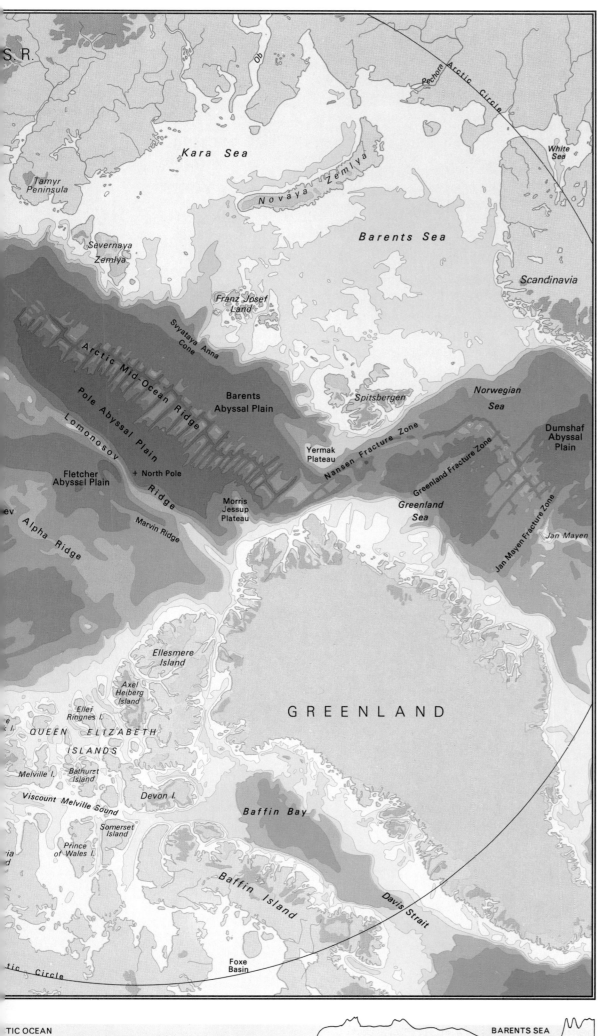

U.S.S.R.

Kara Sea

Tamyr
Peninsula

Novaya Zemlya

Barents Sea

White
Sea

Severnaya
Zemlya

Franz Josef
Land

Scandinavia

Arctic Mid-Ocean Ridge

Svyataya
Anna
Cone

Spitsbergen

Norwegian
Sea

Pole Abyssal Plain

Barents
Abyssal Plain

Dumshaf
Abyssal
Plain

Lomonosov

Yermak
Plateau

Nansen Fracture Zone

Greenland Fracture Zone

Fletcher
Abyssal Plain

+ North Pole

Greenland
Sea

Jan Mayen Fracture Zone

Ridge

Morris
Jessup
Plateau

Jan Mayen

Alpha Ridge

Marvin Ridge

GREENLAND

Ellesmere
Island

Axel
Heiberg
Island

Ellef
Ringnes I.

QUEEN ELIZABETH
ISLANDS

Melville I.

Bathurst
Island

Devon I.

Baffin Bay

Viscount Melville Sound

Somerset
Island

Prince
of Wales I.

Baffin
Island

Davis Strait

tic Circle

Foxe
Basin

Pechora

Arctic Circle

TIC OCEAN

Lomonosov
Ridge

Arctic
Mid-
Ocean Ridge

Pole A P

Barents
Abyssal
Plain

SPITSBERGEN

BARENTS SEA

NORWAY

Line of section

Drifting ships
— *Fram* (Norway) 1893–6
— *Maud* (Norway) 1922–5
Drifting "ice islands"
— Northpole I (USSR) 1937–8
— Fletcher's T3 (USA) 1952–present
— Arlis II (USA) 1961–5

Ever since the pioneer Norwegian explorer Nansen deliberately froze his ship *Fram* into the Arctic ice in 1893, scientists have sought methods of studying the movement of the Arctic sea ice. More recently, tabular icebergs between 90 and 150 feet thick, calved from the flat ice shelf of Ellesmere Island, have been utilized as drifting bases for scientific research stations.

°C   −1   0   +1   60°W   Ellesmere I.   Melville I.   120°W

Greenland

0°

Arctic Mid-Ocean Ridge

Lomonosov Ridge

Alpha Ridge

75°N   80°N   85°N   90°N   85°N   80°N   75°N

Surface current flow in the Arctic consists of two primary systems: a well-defined gyre occupies most of the Canadian side of the ocean basin, while a more direct transarctic current flow sweeps across from the Chukchi Sea toward the Greenland Sea.

Greenland

Baffin Island

Source of icebergs

Labrador

Newfoundland

Titanic sunk 1912

Treacherous conditions in the North Atlantic, southeast of the Newfoundland Banks, are caused by a combination of fog, due to humid winds blowing over the meeting of warm and cold currents, and icebergs carried out of the Davis Strait by the Labrador Current.

ARCTIC : LIVING AND MINERAL RESOURCES

Forging through the Arctic ice in 1969 the 150,000-ton tanker *S.S. Manhattan* made history by successfully penetrating the pack ice of the Northwest Passage. The 1005-foot ship had been specially converted from a merchantman to a combination tanker/icebreaker.

In response to the world's ever-increasing demand for energy, the search for oil and gas reserves has, in recent years, extended far into areas previously considered too hostile for exploratory operations. The continental shelves of the Arctic Ocean, of only average width on the Canadian side but of enormous width on the Asian side, represent the type of broad sedimentary basin locally favorable for the formation and accumulation of hydrocarbon deposits. Although the detailed exploration of the area is still in its infancy, two areas— one in the Laptev Sea, the other in the Canadian archipelago—are known to contain evaporite basins, a characteristic feature of which are salt domes and plugs that create ideal oil- and gas-trap structures.

Exploration activity is at its most intense in the Canadian Arctic, where large oil deposits have been discovered in the Beaufort Sea and several gas strikes made in the Melville Island area. The severe conditions experienced by the exploration crews—prolonged gale-force winds, extreme cold, icing of equipment and the fundamental problem of finding a secure base for a drilling rig in an ocean clogged with constantly moving ice—have brought forth many new approaches to drilling problems. Artificial islands have been built from seabed gravel and sand pumped onto the required location or simply dumped through holes cut into the seven-foot-thick winter ice, and one enterprising company has experimented with artificially thickened sea ice—repeatedly flooding the surface until the ice was strong enough to support a 500-ton drilling unit.

Two major problems face those involved in the exploitation of the Arctic reserves: transportation by sea has been proved possible by the voyage of the *S.S. Manhattan*, but its development would be costly and overland pipelines, despite the high costs and practical difficulties involved, may be more satisfactory. A second, and increasingly worrying, problem is that of a possible blowout; oil released in the Arctic would be trapped beneath the ice—with potentially disastrous effects on the ecology of the ocean.

Pioneering voyages by modern submarines could herald a new era in transportation. Already, engineers are considering the feasibility of submarine tankers equipped to navigate beneath the Arctic ice, so cutting thousands of miles off traditional routes.

The lure of the Arctic oil and gas fields has provoked a number of imaginative solutions to the problems of drilling in the far north. Artificial islands like Oilisland C–15, *above*, are built from gravel dredged from the seabed; in other operations the sea ice has been almost doubled in thickness by repeated flooding, making it strong enough to support a 500-ton drilling rig.

Barents Sea catch in thousands of tons					
	1969	1970	1971	1972	1973
Cod	1230	957	728	644	832
Haddock	147	86	80	188	294
Redfish	31	36	59	47	60
Capelin	680	1314	1392	1593	1336

Value of Barents Sea catch in thousands of dollars	
Plaice	2142
Cod	118,176
Haddock	28,020
Polar cod	129
Greenland halibut	3696
Redfish	11,075
Capelin	56,407

In 1973 the total catch of the most important fish caught in the Barents Sea was over 2.5 million tons. Plaice and Greenland halibut caught mainly for the fresh-fish market made up around 46 thousand tons, and cod and haddock for freezing and polar cod for the Russian market accounted for about 1.2 million tons. Most capelin were caught by Norway and converted into fish meal.

Within the Barents Sea there exist two main communities of fish; the cod, haddock and plaice living within the warm West Spitsbergen and North Cape currents, and the polar cod and capelin living in the cold water that flows over the Svalbard shelf. In response to long-term fluctuations in climatic conditions, the pattern of the currents is constantly changing and affecting the distribution of the fish. Although cod have been caught on their spawning grounds off the nearby Lofoten Islands since the twelfth century, cod and haddock were not taken in the open Barents Sea until around the 1920s, when the temperature of the North Atlantic reached a peak. The large catches of capelin that are being taken today are perhaps indicative of a period of climatic deterioration that started in the 1950s.

Since 1955, catches of arcto-Norwegian cod have fluctuated around a mean of 850,000 tons per year and those of haddock around a mean of 140,000 tons per year. Since 1969 the stocks of both cod and haddock have been showing signs of overfishing. All the major fisheries of the Barents Sea are seasonal. Those for cod, haddock and redfish take place mainly between February and September, whereas capelin are fished during the winter and early spring.

In 1973 the total catch yielded by the Barents Sea was valued at more than 430 million dollars, of which 70 percent was accounted for by catches of codlike fish. Although cod are plentiful in the North Atlantic and Arctic, they are in constant demand throughout the markets of Europe and North America and are therefore able to command a high value.

In 1974 and 1975 a sharp increase in fuel prices, and restrictions placed by the Canadian authorities on the fisheries under their control, diverted a considerable amount of effort from the Northwest Atlantic to the Barents Sea. A catch quota of 810,000 tons was imposed on the arcto-Norwegian cod stocks by the Northeast Atlantic Fisheries Commission in 1975 to limit their further exploitation.

Contrasting attitudes to the wildlife resource of the Arctic Ocean are illustrated in the photographs above and left. Each year thousands of Harp seals are killed on the Arctic ice simply to satisfy the international market in attractive animal furs. By contrast, the Eskimos of the far north have developed a close and balanced relationship with their harsh environment, taking enough to provide them with food and clothing, but never more than would insure the future survival of the population.

131

NORTH SEA:BATHYMETRY AND CIRCULATION

The North Sea is a shallow young sea formed by inundation of part of the continental shelf of northwest Europe.
Area 222,008 square miles; 575,000 square kilometers.
Average depth 308 feet; 94 meters.
Volume 12,955 cubic miles; 54,000 cubic kilometers.
Max. depth (in Skagerrak) 2297 feet; 700 meters.

The **continental shelf** of northwest Europe is, with the exception of the deep Norwegian Trough, without major relief features until the continental slope drops steeply to the Atlantic abyssal plain.

The North Sea is one of the few large sea areas to have been formed by inundation of an extensive tract of continental crust. Throughout its history this potential ocean has been subsiding and yet only in recent years has the extent of the subsidence been revealed. The rather featureless bottom topography conceals a deep depositional basin containing more than 20,000 feet of sediment deposited over approximately 250 million years.

The deepest feature on the North Sea floor is the Norwegian Trough, which skirts the coast of Norway from the Atlantic to the mouth of the Skagerrak, where it reaches its greatest depth of about 2300 feet. Although it is the most prominent feature, the trough lies to the east of the much deeper depositional basin of oil-bearing sedimentary rocks that runs down the center of the North Sea, hidden beneath the undulating banks familiar to fishermen. By contrast, the basins of younger sedimentary rocks to the west of the British Isles do roughly correspond to bathymetric deeps. They lie in a chain that extends north–south from west of the Shetlands through the Minches, the Sea of Hebrides, the North Channel, the eastern Irish Sea and St George's Channel to the Bristol Channel and the English Channel.

The seafloor topography we see today is probably very like that existing as dry land at the end of the last Ice Age. The ice covered most of the British Isles and flowed into the surrounding basins, reaching as far south as the Celtic Sea in the west and the Thames Estuary in the east. Glacier tongues cut down into old river valleys to produce the deep sea lochs of Scotland and the Norwegian fjords, and their seaward extensions in the Minches, the Sea of Hebrides and the Norwegian Trough. In the northern North Sea, vast thicknesses of glacial moraine were deposited by successive ice sheets, the most prominent being the Dogger Bank and the Jutland Bank. An inland lake was located over the Fladen Ground, surrounded on three sides by the edge of the ice sheet. Water flowing from the melting ice into this lake cut the long, deep channels, known as tunnel valleys, which still exist as the Fladen Gound Deep, the Buchan Deep and Devil's Hole.

As sea level rose with the retreat of the ice, waves and currents immediately began to redistribute the loose sediments in a process continuing today. The finest sediments travel northward in suspension, carried by the slow drift of the water, and are eventually deposited in the deeper parts of the northern North Sea, where currents are weaker. Sand is transported along the seabed by tidal currents, particularly in areas where strong currents coincide with large storm waves. The result is that sand is constantly removed from some parts of the seabed and deposited in others. Unfortunately for man, the approaches to the large ports of Liverpool, London and Hamburg are among the zones of sand accumulation. The Strait of Dover, one of the world's busiest shipping lanes, is also a site of sand deposition—despite the strong currents that flow through the narrow channel. Here the sand is swept into dynamic shapes, the largest of which are the long sandbanks, arranged parallel to the strongest currents, that partially choke the shallow southern North Sea and eastern English Channel. Sandbanks such as the Goodwin Sands and the Norfolk Banks have for centuries taken a heavy toll of shipping, and shifting bodies of sand are a constant hazard to navigation. The shipping lanes leading to the major ports of Europe require regular surveying—particularly in view of the ever-increasing draft of merchant vessels, many of which now exceed 60 feet. Wrecks are also a hazard to shipping; more than 14,000 are known to lie on the continental shelf of the British Isles alone. A static wreck may be clearly marked and present little danger, but if scouring of the seabed by currents causes a wreck to shift, or swing upright after lying on its side for many years, there is an immediate danger of collision. Scouring around seabed structures has in recent years assumed great importance with the development of the North Sea oil and gas fields. The shifting of sediments around pipelines, and the legs of drilling and production platforms, has added to the many environmental problems already facing the oil field engineers.

During the Permian period, some 250 million years ago, the North Sea area was a desert plain bounded by mountains. Inland seas and salt lakes were present and the rocks formed at this time were mainly sandstones and salt—important to gas trap formation.

The Upper Cretaceous, 100 million years ago, was a time when much of the lowlands of the northern hemisphere, including the North Sea basin, were flooded by shallow seas. Thick deposits of chalk are the characteristic rocks formed at this time.

During the Tertiary northern Europe was beginning to look rather as it does today. The shallow sea that still covered the North Sea basin received sediments from the rivers surrounding it and thick deposits of mud and clay were laid down.

Current flow in the North Sea is generated by the tides, the prevailing winds and by density differences in the watermass. The pattern is subject to great local and seasonal variation.

Mixed water *S. elegans*
Coastal water *S. setosa*
Oceanic water *S. dentata*

Indicator species may be used to identify the different watermasses present in a given area. In the North Sea, arrowworms of the genus *Sagitta* identify oceanic, mixed and coastal waters.

Summer currents

The English Channel current pattern shows a marked seasonal variation. In summer the main inflow from the Atlantic runs close to the French coast as far as Cherbourg then swings across to the north side of the channel; in winter the pattern is reversed.

Winter currents

NORTH SEA: MINERAL RESOURCES

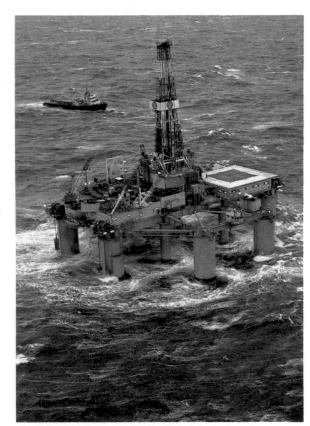

The self-propelled semisubmersible drilling platform *Ocean Voyager* operating in the North Sea during winter 1974.

The geologic history of the North Sea over the last 280 million years, from Permian to Recent times, is known with some certainty following the analysis of rock strata in the hundreds of boreholes that have been drilled in the search for oil and gas. The pre-Permian history, on the other hand, remains relatively obscure. The basement rocks that have been found are largely Carboniferous in age and consist of shales, sandstones and coals with some limestones. The Hercynian orogeny, the mountain-building activity that occurred at the end of the Carboniferous, cut deeply into them and into the older rocks beneath and constitutes a natural break between the varied history before the event and the history of more or less continuous deposition that has followed.

The earliest deposits to be laid down on the eroded Hercynian basement were Permian sands deposited in a desert basin extending from eastern England into northern Germany. They were interbedded with mud and salt deposited in lakes in the area. The gas discovered in the southern North Sea was trapped in the resulting sandstone and is a product of the underlying Carboniferous coals, from which it has been formed by a process of natural distillation. The gas is prevented from escaping by the presence of overlying nonporous carbonates, anhydrites and salt deposited in an inland sea, which occupied the desert basin following a marine inundation. The desert environment continued into the Triassic period, when several thousand feet of red sandstones and mudstones were deposited. In some areas, notably off the coast of East Anglia, the Triassic sandstones contain gas that has escaped, via a complex system of faults, from the Permian sandstones.

The onset of the Jurassic period saw the invasion of

northern Europe by seas that persisted throughout much of the remainder of geologic time. The Jurassic sediments have been deeply eroded in the southern North Sea, but in the north they are well developed and include thick marine shales, which are oil source-rocks, and porous sandstones, which now act as reservoirs for the oil. The oil-bearing Jurassic strata have been cut by numerous faults associated with a graben system that originated in Permian times, and extends from the extreme north, through the central North Sea into Holland. The faults have left a series of tilted blocks with oil trapped in their highest parts, in sandstone sealed in by later impermeable shales.

In the Cretaceous period, clear marine waters extended over the North Sea and much of Britain and continental Europe, forming chalk deposits of pure calcium carbonate in the south, grading through muddy chalk to pure mud in the northern areas.

The Tertiary period saw the elevation of the land areas around the North Sea and the subsidence of the basin as a whole. The sediments deposited in this basin are mainly clays with, in the north, local developments of sands. The Forties oil field is in such a sand.

After hydrocarbons, sand and gravel for aggregate are the main economic minerals obtained from the North Sea, and with the growth of the construction industry, and the deposits on land becoming increasingly scarce, the exploitation of marine gravel is rapidly increasing. In the North Sea more sand and gravel is being dredged from a marine environment than anywhere else in the world. Most of the coarser gravel occurs in the western part of the North Sea off the eastern coast of Britain, and the United Kingdom's production from it is almost ten million tons a year.

There is no common geologic origin for the gravel. North of 53°N much of it is glacial debris left behind by retreating Ice Age glaciers, whilst in the southern part of the North Sea, where the gravel has a high proportion of flint, chalk, sandstone and quartzite, it appears to have been deposited by Tertiary and

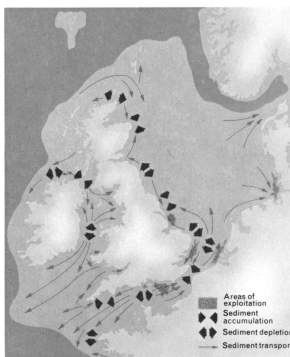

Areas of exploitation
Sediment accumulation
Sediment depletion
Sediment transport

Sand and gravel represented the most valuable mineral resource of the North Sea prior to the discovery of oil and gas. The deposits were carried into the area by ice sheets during the Ice Ages of the past two million years and have been supplemented by material from the surrounding river estuaries. The pattern of sediment movement by tides and currents is well known and certain areas are known to be accumulating sand and gravel while others are being depleted. Several areas in the south are currently being commercially exploited in a systematic manner by dredgers like the *Bowstream*, illustrated.

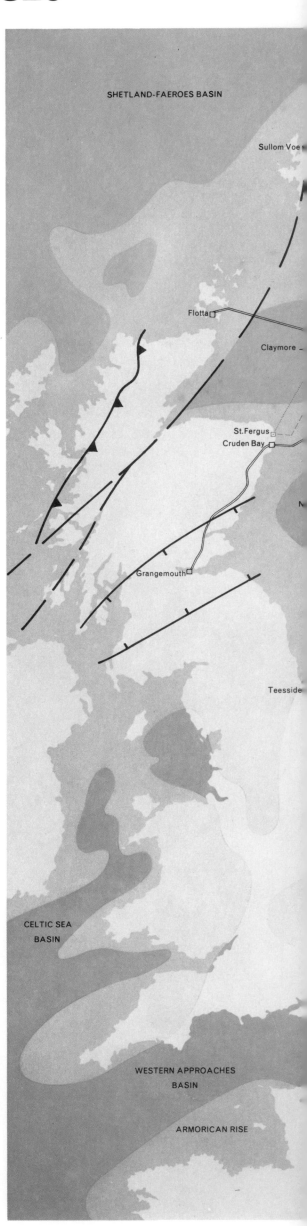

SHETLAND-FAEROES BASIN

Sullom Voe

Flotta

Claymore

St. Fergus

Cruden Bay

Grangemouth

Teesside

CELTIC SEA BASIN

WESTERN APPROACHES BASIN

ARMORICAN RISE

Quaternary rivers, perhaps representing the ancestral Scheldt and Thames, with the material largely derived from nearby chalk and Tertiary outcrops.

Though there are large areas of sand and silt on the seabed it is the gravel deposits that are in demand, and these occur only in restricted areas. The salt content of dredged material is small and has little effect on the properties of the concrete made from it, but a large quantity of shells may reduce its strength.

Most of the dredgers in the North Sea are suction dredgers operating in water less than 115 feet deep, with forward-facing pipes for working thick deposits while stationary, or trailing pipes for dredging surface gravels while in motion. Tidal considerations restrict operations to 75 miles from the port.

There are many constraints in exploiting the sand and gravel of the North Sea. Dredgers may be a navigational hazard in shipping lanes and dredging is usually prohibited within one mile of any hydrocarbon pipelines, well-head structures or telephone or power cables. Near the coast, dredging can cause coastal erosion. It can also have an adverse effect on fishing by leaving large holes or boulders on the seabed which can damage trawlers' nets, and by disturbing the spawning grounds of species like the herring, which lay their eggs on the seabed. The industry and government are however aware of these problems and much research is being carried out on the effects of dredging.

Hydrocarbons and sand and gravel are the main minerals being worked in the North Sea, though in Britain collieries in Northumberland and Durham extend nearly four miles offshore. Potash deposits that occur in the Permian rocks at a depth of 5000 feet in Yorkshire extend eastward beneath the North Sea and may one day be worked offshore.

The Brent oil field illustrates the unconformity trap. Oil-bearing sandstones of Lower and Middle Jurassic age are truncated and overlain by shale and clay formed during the Upper Jurassic and Cretaceous. Brent was the first of the northern group of fields to be discovered and was announced in 1972.

The Piper field is located in a fault-controlled structure. The reservoir consists of Middle Jurassic sandstones found in and around a faulted block. The cap-rock is of Upper Jurassic shale overlain unconformably by further shales of Lower Cretaceous age.

The Forties field is a straightforward anticline trap. Oil and gas produced from organic material in Jurassic rocks have risen through the strata and have been trapped in beds of sandstone of very early Tertiary age. The extent of the field is well mapped and it is being exploited by four carefully positioned platforms.

135

NORTH SEA: LIVING RESOURCES

The overall exploitation of fish stocks in the North Sea dates from immediately after the Napoleonic Wars, when the rapid growth of population, particularly in the London area, produced an increased demand for fish. The mid-nineteenth century saw the rise of large industrial towns and major movements in population. In the United Kingdom the population shift was largely northwards and to be near the new towns, the center of the United Kingdom fishing industry moved at this time to the Humber.

The first steam trawler was launched in 1881 and within a space of 20 years many hundreds, mainly from Britain and Germany, were working in the North Sea. The overexploitation of North Sea fishing stocks dates from this time.

The total catch of the more important species, defined as those yielding more than 10,000 tons per annum, was in 1973 just over three million tons. It comprised 150,000 tons of flat fish, such as plaice and

sole, 750,000 tons of cod-like fish, and 1,940,000 tons of industrial species such as Norway pout, sandeels, sprat, mackerel and herring used for fishmeal. The remainder was made up largely of dogfish, horse mackerel, crustacea and mollusks. These catches were not divided uniformly among all the North Sea fishing nations; most industrial species were caught by the Scandinavian countries, and the Netherlands caught most flatfish.

Some fisheries are highly seasonal. In 1973 catches of herring and Norway pout were highest between July and October and most sandeels were caught in May and June. In contrast catches of fish in the cod family, such as cod, haddock and whiting, showed very little seasonal variation in the same period.

The herring fishery is particularly noted for its seasonal variation. As herring are plankton feeders their abundance depends largely on the level of plankton production, and the constant movement of

herring shoals in search of food makes them difficult to track down and catch. The history of herring fishing in the North Sea is a long one, reaching back into the Dark Ages. In the past it had a much greater economic importance than today and many fishing ports in the Middle Ages were taxed in numbers of herring. Their abundance contributed greatly to the wealth of the Hanseatic League and the Netherlands—until the eighteenth century the greatest fishing nation in the North Sea.

The continuous exploitation of herring stocks over this long period, though particularly in the last 100 years, has resulted in their virtual exhaustion. In fact the situation was so bad in the spring of 1977 that all herring fishing in the North Sea was completely suspended.

Until recently herring were caught at night using drift nets, a method that is only successful during the hours of darkness, when the shoals rise to the surface.

Hours fishing, by types of gear, in 1973

Handline 21,602

Nephrops trawl 80,318

Midwater trawl 118,832

Danish seine 652,489

Beam trawl 1,155,802

Bottom trawl 2,122,942

Otter and beam trawls are the principal gear used for catching demersal fish, although hand-lines are occasionally used for cod. The drift net, at one time used extensively for herring, has given way to midwater trawls and purse seines, which are far more efficient methods of catching pelagic fish. The nephrops trawl is widely used throughout the North Sea for catching shrimps.

Species catch by weight and value for 1973

Cod
Herring
Plaice
Haddock
Sole
Mackerel
Norway pout
Saithe
Sandeels
Whiting
Sprat

100   200   Thousand tons   400   500   600

Million dollars
80
70
60
50
40
30
20
10

Grimsby is one of Europe's largest fishing ports and in the UK is second only to Hull. In 1974 over half the total landings of 133,962 tons were cod.

In 1973 the total value of the North Sea catch was around 500 million US dollars. Two-fifths of this figure is accounted for by catches of codlike fish, one-fifth by catches of flatfish, and the rest by catches of industrial fish. The value of fish used for industrial purposes is much lower than those used for human consumption, as the figures for sole and sprat illustrate.

More recently purse seines and midwater trawls which have a greater depth range have been employed.

Of the flatfish caught in the North Sea, plaice are the most heavily exploited and because of their importance their behavior has been carefully studied. Each winter the adults move south to spawn off the Dutch and Belgian coast. It is estimated that around 60 million plaice spawn in this area. Although the mature plaice are bottom-dwelling their eggs and larvae are not. The eggs are merely released into the water and allowed to drift with the current, in this case resulting in a general movement of a few miles per day along the Dutch coast toward Denmark. On hatching, the young fish assume a round-bodied shape. Only when they are between four and six weeks old do they take on the flat-bodied shape of the mature plaice. This southern spawning area is the most important one, however plaice also spawn off the east coast of England in the area between Flamborough head and the Dogger Bank

and in the German Bight north of the Friesian Islands.

Since 1955 three trends in fish catches have been noted. The catch of cod rose by a factor of three and extraordinarily large catches of haddock, spawned in 1962 and 1967, were taken during the 1960s. These rises are largely due to a natural increase in codlike fish over the same period. Catches of industrial species also increased, particularly that of Norway pout, which rose by a factor of four. On the other hand catches of herring and mackerel more than halved under the pressure of heavy fishing.

North Sea fishing stocks are protected by measures designed to maintain each stock at its maximum sustainable yield, thus protecting the fishing industry from collapse and any individual species from extinction. In the North Sea only plaice and whiting are being exploited at about this level. Cod and haddock are now being heavily overexploited and are unlikely to recover so long as the young fish continue to be

caught in small-meshed nets designed to take Norway pout. Herring have been overexploited for such a long time that their stocks are also in danger. Any recovery is being prevented by the young fish being caught in the large sprat fishery that operates in the same area occupied by the herring. Sole stocks are at present overfished by beam trawls which stir them out of the mud. The heavy chains that weight the bottom of the net disturb the seabed to such an extent that they are destroying the fish's habitat.

Conservation rests mainly on three measures: minimum landing sizes, which stipulate the smallest size of any fish of a particular species that may be landed in port; minimum mesh sizes for trawls and seines, which will prevent young immature fish being caught, and international catch quotas for each stock. Even so the continued expansion of fishing effort and the interference of industrial fishing with protected species is at present posing major conservation problems.

Haddock spawning ground
Cod spawning ground
Cod stock limit
Plaice spawning ground
Plaice stock limit
Herring spawning ground
Migration of cod

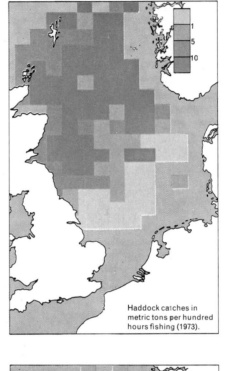

Haddock catches in metric tons per hundred hours fishing (1973).

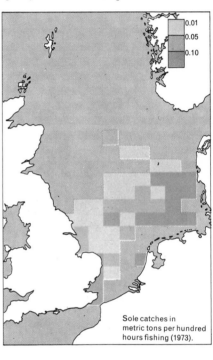

Sole catches in metric tons per hundred hours fishing (1973).

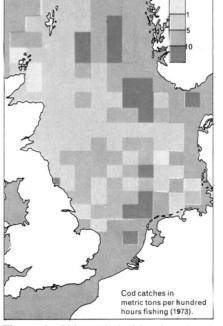

Cod catches in metric tons per hundred hours fishing (1973).

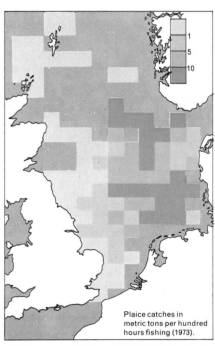

Plaice catches in metric tons per hundred hours fishing (1973).

The North Sea is a shallow basin of constantly mixing nutrient-rich water and high plankton production. It is ideally suited as a breeding ground for many commercially important fish species on which its valuable fisheries depend. Within the sea certain areas are favored by fish for spawning, and in the case of plaice and cod these are in three instances coincidental, the requirements of the spawn of both species being broadly similar.

The area in which a particular fishery is conducted broadly reflects the distribution of the species. Cod are found widely throughout the North Sea, whereas sole and plaice are largely confined to the south. Of all the fisheries in the North Sea, that of cod is the most valuable and the United Kingdom's share of 96,000 tons in 1973 was more than twice that of any other country. The plaice fishery is dominated by the Netherlands, which lands 44 percent of the total catch.

The otter trawl was developed from the beam trawl in which the mouth is kept open by a wooden beam. The otter trawl relies on two wooden paddles, or otterboards, to keep it open. The boards are attached to the net in such a way that they are forced apart when the net is drawn through the water. The boards may be extended on lines to increase their spreading effect.

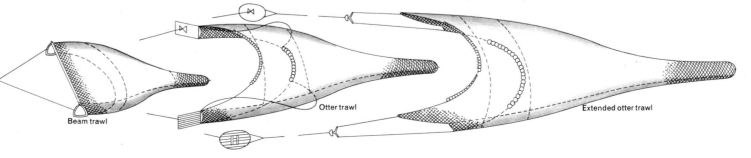

Beam trawl

Otter trawl

Extended otter trawl

MEDITERRANEAN:BATHYMETRY

The Mediterranean Sea is a
shallow elongated landlocked
sea holding detailed evidence of
a complex geologic history.
Area 1,145,000 square miles;
2,966,000 square kilometers.
Average depth 4921 feet;
1500 meters.
Max. depth (Hellenic Trough)
16,706 feet; 5092 meters.
Evaporation roughly three
times precipitation and runoff.

The Mediterranean Sea occupies a broad east–west
depression in the earth's surface wedged between the
African and Eurasian landmasses. It stretches for more
than 2500 miles from the Israel–Lebanon–Syria
coastline in the east to the Strait of Gibraltar, its only
link with the world ocean, in the west.

This inland sea is more than one million square
miles in extent, but is significantly shallower than most
major oceanic regions. Its water surface nevertheless
hides from view a complex system of ridges, troughs
and deep basins formed by seafloor movements that
are active even at the present day. Again in contrast to
the major oceans, continental shelf areas throughout
the Mediterranean are extremely narrow; the only
moderately wide shelf areas are found in the Adriatic,
off parts of the North African coast, and locally, where
the Rhône, Ebro and Nile rivers have built up great
wedges of sediment opposite their outlets. The
continental shelf throughout the Mediterranean Sea
is deeply incised by canyon systems.

The narrow constriction of the Strait of Sicily
effectively divides the Mediterranean seafloor into
distinct eastern and western basins. The Western
Basin is characterized by broad, generally smooth
abyssal plains in marked contrast with the Eastern
Basin, which is dominated by the Mediterranean
Ridge system. The two main depressions of the western
Mediterranean—the Balearic and Tyrrhenian Basins
—are separated by the island chain formed by Corsica
and Sardinia. The Balearic Basin has extensions into
the Alboran Basin, the Gulf of Valencia and the
Ligurian Sea: its floor is generally flat over large areas,
except where the Rhône and Ebro rivers have built
out their submarine fans and distribution channels
from the northern margin, or where clusters of knolls
mark the intrusion of underlying rock series. The
Tyrrhenian Basin, with maximum depths of nearly
12,000 feet, is the deepest part of the western Mediterranean. In this basin, the seafloor is dominated by a
large number of structural ridges and volcanic seamounts and only very small areas of abyssal plain. An
arc of major land, island and submarine volcanoes,
including the historically active Vesuvius, Etna and
Stromboli, occupies the southeastern part of the basin
and is linked to the zone of earthquake activity running
through Calabria.

The Mediterranean Ridge System is not, as was
earlier thought, comparable with the spreading ridges
of the major oceans. It is a feature developed by the
compression of a thick sedimentary rock pile between
Eurasia and Africa and comprises three main sections.
A large central arcuate ridge is located south of Greece,
Crete and Turkey, separated from them by a series of
narrow trenches representing the deepest parts of the
modern Mediterranean with maximum depths reaching
more than 16,000 feet. Two smaller arcuate ridges extend to west and east of the main ridge, one skirting the
toe of Italy and the other passing south of Cyprus.
Sediments of the Nile submarine fan and its distribu-
tary channels cover much of the deep seafloor to the
southeast of the Mediterranean Ridge. Seismic records
have shown that the relatively small abyssal plains in
this region must have formerly been much more
extensive, since their sediments have been caught up in
the building of the ridge system. Sands derived from
the Nile outflow about half a million years ago have
been identified in deep drilling cores from southern
parts of the ridge and bottom topography, and side-scan
sonar studies of the ridge crest show extensive recent
faulting and folding.

The Ionian Basin has the largest abyssal plain

Evidence from paleomagnetic
measurements on land followed
by deep-sea drilling studies
has shown that the western

Mediterranean basins were
formed over the past 25 to 30
million years. Rotational
displacement of the islands of

Corsica and Sardinia away from
the coast of southern Europe was
responsible for the formation of
the Balearic Basin.

The structural complexity of
the eastern Mediterranean Sea
contains ample evidence of a
long history of compressional

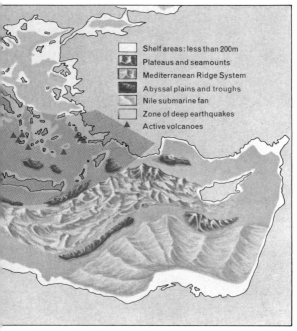

Shelf areas: less than 200m
Plateaus and seamounts
Mediterranean Ridge System
Abyssal plains and troughs
Nile submarine fan
Zone of deep earthquakes
▲ Active volcanoes

forces acting on the thick
sedimentary deposits of the
basin. The main arcuate ridge
is backed by a zone of deep

earthquake activity and a
matching arc of volcanoes. The
secondary ridge to the west is
similarly backed by volcanoes.

remaining in the eastern Mediterranean, but even this is subdivided into a number of separate areas by sea-mounts and submarine plateaus. Similar features are found in many other parts of the eastern Mediterranean and many of the plateaus rise to elevations well above those of the broad ridge system. Small abyssal plains occur in the southern Adriatic Sea and the Aegean Sea, but generally these seas are simply regarded as shallow extensions of the Mediterranean. The Adriatic consists mainly of shelf area, the northern parts of which are covered by the Po delta, while the Aegean is a generally shallow area with numerous islands linking the Mediterranean with the Sea of Marmara and the Black Sea. Many of the islands in the southern Aegean are active volcanoes, arranged in a volcanic arc linked to zones of earthquake activity. Studies of volcanic ashes found in deep drilling cores from the area have shown that one enormous eruption spread its ash over nearly 80,000 square miles of the eastern Mediterranean. The ash has been associated with an historic eruption of the volcano which makes up the island of Santorini: in about 1400 B.C. a colossal eruption blew apart most of the former, much larger island, destroying the Minoan civilization and perhaps giving birth to the legend of Atlantis.

The Alpine mountain ranges to the north of the

present-day Mediterranean Sea are thought to be the result of the African and Eurasian plates moving together and destroying a major equatorial ocean, known as Tethys, which had formerly separated them. The most recent Alpine mountain-building phase happened during the last two million years. Recent deep-sea drilling and seismic profiling has shown that the sediments built up in the eastern Mediterranean basins date back perhaps 70 million years, and that they are probably being compressed and crumpled into ridges even at the present day. Thus it is likely that the seafloor in that area is the result of a continuation of the Alpine mountain-building movements. Sediments in the present western Mediterranean basins date only from about 25 million years ago. Hence the earlier Tethyan seafloor was probably entirely taken up in the building of the Western Alps and new basins were formed by later extensional movements. Paleo-magnetic measurements show that the Balearic Basin probably developed by the rifting and rotation of Corsica and Sardinia away from Spain and southern France, beginning about 30 million years ago, while the Tyrrhenian and Aegean areas are considerably younger, their subsidence possibly being linked to seafloor spreading behind the still active Calabrian volcanic arc.

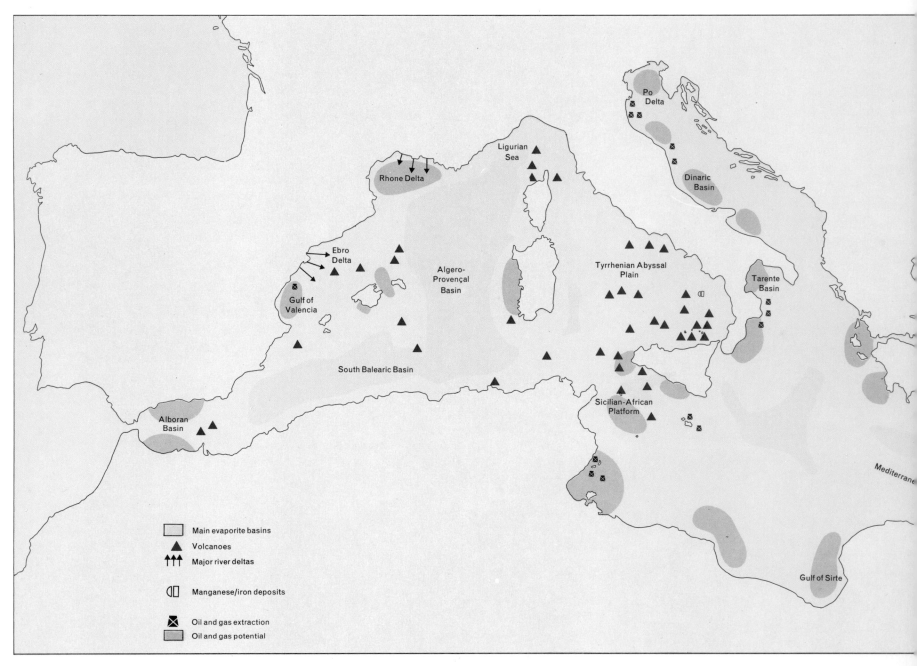

Po
Delta

Ligurian
Sea

Rhone Delta

Dinaric
Basin

Ebro
Delta

Algero-
Provençal
Basin

Tyrrhenian Abyssal
Plain

Tarente
Basin

Gulf of
Valencia

South Balearic Basin

Sicilian-African
Platform

Mediterrane

Alboran
Basin

Gulf of Sirte

☐ Main evaporite basins

▲ Volcanoes

↑↑↑ Major river deltas

◖▌ Manganese/iron deposits

⊠ Oil and gas extraction

▨ Oil and gas potential

The dramatic history of the Mediterranean was revealed in 1970 by deep drilling studies. Thick evaporite layers, known from earlier seismic profiles, were dated at five million years old — but were found sand-wiched between marine sediments laid down in deep water. The findings showed that at this time the Mediterranean virtually dried out, leaving a desert landscape thousands of feet below sea level. Even more surprising, to create the known thickness of evaporites the sea must have dried and flooded many times. The resource map, *above*, shows the extent of the deposits; the geologic section, *right*, illustrates their typical bed-form.

Line of section

A   B

Evaporite beds   Evaporite lense

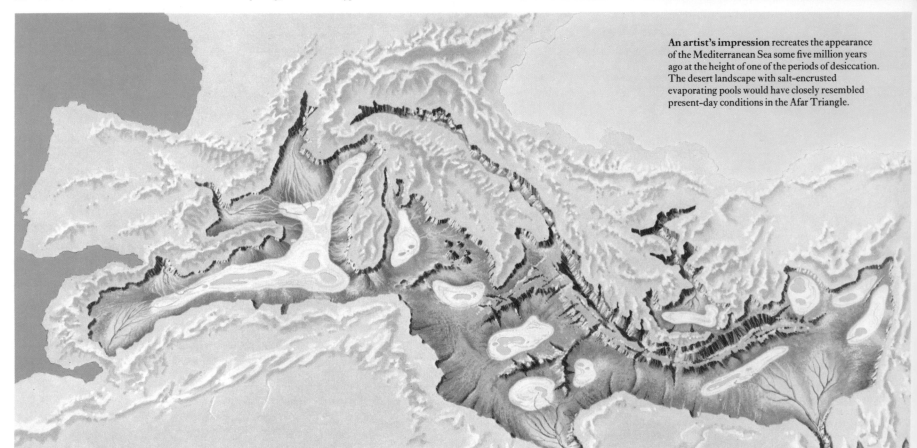

An artist's impression recreates the appearance of the Mediterranean Sea some five million years ago at the height of one of the periods of desiccation. The desert landscape with salt-encrusted evaporating pools would have closely resembled present-day conditions in the Afar Triangle.

Evaporite diapirs

Seismic profiles over the deep Mediterranean basins record the presence everywhere of a strongly reflecting rock unit, which is frequently seen to intrude upward in diapiric structures displacing the overlying sediments. Deep drilling studies in 1970 dated this rock at more than five million years old and identified it as a formation of evaporites: halite, anhydrite, gypsum and other minerals that accumulate from the evaporation of seawater. At its maximum the formation is more than 3000 feet thick and consists mainly of halite, or rock salt, which is capable of flowing under the pressure of overlying sediments to form the diapirs recorded on the seismic profiles.

These evaporite formations buried deep beneath the Mediterranean seafloor represent a huge potential source of rock salt, sulfur and potash salts—basic raw materials used in the chemical industries. The deposits are currently only mined where they outcrop on Sicily and other Mediterranean islands, but the buried resource of the seabed is conservatively estimated to be at least 240,000 cubic miles.

The Mediterranean region has considerable oil and gas potential: it possesses thick sequences of rapidly deposited sedimentary rocks rich in organic material and a generally high crustal heat flow conducive to hydrocarbon maturation. The deep evaporite formations are capable of acting both as a cap rock and, due to the richly organic sediments interbedded with the evaporite minerals, as a source rock. Exploration activity is currently intense, but restricted to offshore shelf areas, generally over geologic structures extending out from land. Potential oil and gas fields associated with the evaporite deposits would be beyond present extraction techniques since they are confined to deep basins, but highly porous traps in the limy rocks of the basin margins are comfortably within the range of present technology.

The Mediterranean has no major mineral provinces located on the seabed, as rates of sedimentation in this inland sea are generally too high to allow the formation of manganese nodule fields. However, hydrothermal solutions emanating from the current-swept crests of recently active submarine volcanoes have resulted in the formation of small manganese and iron-rich deposits that are both near to land and in relatively shallow and accessible areas.

In comparison with other oceans the Mediterranean is remarkable in that an abnormally high proportion of its fish species is economically important; about 120 out of a total of 500 are fished commercially. However, the stocks of these species are rather low due to the slow rate of plankton production throughout the sea. As plankton forms the basis of the fish food chain its rate of production is a major factor in determining the abundance of fish.

Production of plankton in the Mediterranean is inhibited by the low level of nutrients present in the surface water. The water of the Mediterranean is very stable and little mixing takes place between the surface and the nutrients contained in the deeper water. Also there are few rivers, particularly in the east, bringing down land-washed nutrients into the sea, a situation compounded by the building of the Aswan Dam, which has seriously reduced the amount of nutrient material entering the Mediterranean from the Nile. Plankton production is greatest in the west, where there are more rivers and where the beneficial effect of nutrient-rich surface water flowing in from the Atlantic is felt.

Despite these biologically unfavorable conditions the Mediterranean was estimated in 1970 to be able to support a fishery twice as valuable as that of any other ocean, and five times as valuable as the average for all the world's oceans taken together. This unusually high catch value is a product of cultural and traditional factors: fresh fish are considered to be a luxury in many Mediterranean countries and fishing boats are traditionally small, making short trips and landing small catches.

The high market price encourages overfishing. Nets are used with mesh sizes as small as 30–40 mm, which for some species does not allow even the smallest fish to escape. A large variety of fishing gear is used; trawls, gill and trammel nets, traps and long lines among others. Even such destructive techniques as dynamiting have been used, greatly increasing the fisheries' efficiency but depleting the resource still further. The coastal demersal fisheries along the southern coast of Europe have been the hardest hit. The stocks of sought-after fish such as hake, sole and red mullet have been sorely depleted and it has been suggested that fishing on the Castellon grounds off the Spanish coast should be reduced by two-thirds of the 1965 level. Along the African coast the situation is much better, but even here exploitation is approaching the optimum.

It is much more difficult to assess the stocks of pelagic fish such as tuna and mackerel because of their far-ranging, highly mobile nature, but it appears that at the moment they are underfished.

Because of the small-scale localized nature of the fisheries, statistics of catches and landings are often unreliable and as they frequently form the basis of tax returns they are also often understated.

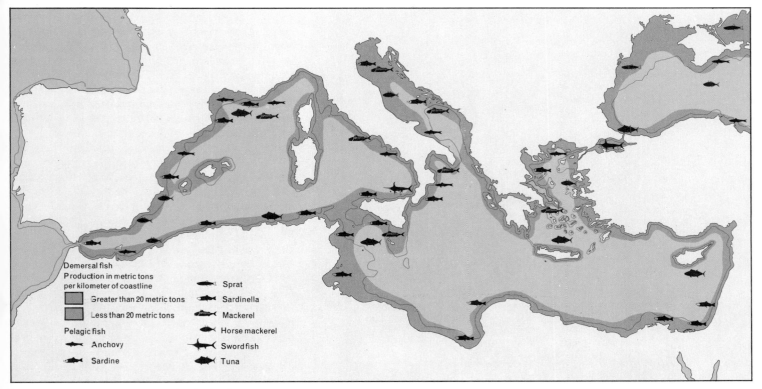

Demersal fish
Production in metric tons per kilometer of coastline
- Greater than 20 metric tons
- Less than 20 metric tons

Pelagic fish
- Anchovy
- Sardine
- Sprat
- Sardinella
- Mackerel
- Horse mackerel
- Swordfish
- Tuna

Mediterranean total catch
1351 thousand metric tons

Crustaceans 30
Diadromous fish 55
Mollusks 107

Marine fish 1159

World total catch
59,321 thousand metric tons

	%
Others	8.1
Mediterranean	2.3
Caribbean	2.5
Indian	5.2
Atlantic	38.7
Pacific	43.2

The fauna of the Mediterranean is closely related to that of the subtropical Atlantic, and many Atlantic demersal fish species such as hake, sole and red mullet are widely distributed throughout the sea. Some species such as poutassou and poor cod are, however, cold-water dwellers and are found only along the northwestern shore. Other demersal species have a very shallow depth range and are unable to survive below 30 feet. These fish—mainly gray mullet, sea bream, sea bass and some shrimps—are confined to shallow coastal waters. Although the pelagic species are largely independent of the seabed they are normally found in shallow coastal areas where plankton production is greatest. As these fish tend to move toward the shore in the summer in response to coastal upwelling, their fisheries tend to be seasonal.

MEDITERRANEAN:CIRCULATION

- Sediment transport by surface currents
- Sediment transport by undercurrent
- Sand ribbons
- Sand waves

- Smooth surface with thick sediment cover
- Mud waves
- Rock barriers
- Ridges

Side-scan sonar studies of the floor of the Gulf of Cadiz have revealed dynamic patterns of sedimentation formed by the Mediterranean Undercurrent. The relatively saline water pouring out from the Strait of Gibraltar creates the same sequence of sedimentary features as that found on continental shelf areas swept by tidal currents. As the undercurrent decreases in strength there is a progression from bare rock through sand ribbons to sand waves. Beyond the zone of sand deposition the weakening current deposits its load of fine mud, smooth where the undercurrent is in contact with the seabed but formed into waves up to 120 feet high where current/flow is irregular and contact with the bed is intermittent.

Vertical view of the Strait of Gibraltar taken from the Skylab space station.

The Mediterranean Sea is an almost totally land-locked basin, joined to the rest of the world ocean only by the narrow, steep-sided channel of the Strait of Gibraltar. Its pattern of water circulation, and its overall water budget, are therefore markedly different from most of the major oceans, being a delicate and constantly varying response to inflow from the surrounding river systems, evaporation into the atmosphere, seasonal changes in wind and pressure systems over the sea and the complex bottom topography of the sea itself.

The Mediterranean Sea loses by evaporation almost three times as much water as it receives through rainfall and runoff and this potential imbalance is compensated by a constant inflow of water from the Atlantic. The incoming water forms a surface current in the upper 250 feet of water flowing eastward along the coast of North Africa and into the eastern basin. It is the only well-defined current in the Mediterranean though minor branches feed the secondary counterclockwise circulations in the western basin, the Adriatic and Ionian seas and the eastern basin. The Mediterranean also receives a modest inflow from the Black Sea as a surface current through the Dardanelles.

As the main surface flow travels to the east it steadily loses momentum and is warmed by the sun. Evaporation causes the salinity to increase and the consequent increase in density causes the water to sink to greater depth. In winter, cold winds from the north cool the surface waters and produce additional sinking of dense water. The denser water of the deeper layers flows steadily back toward the Strait of Gibraltar, where it eventually spills over the sill at a depth of about 800 feet and flows out into the Atlantic. The water flowing from the Mediterranean is considerably more saline than that of the eastern Atlantic and the outflow can be detected as a horizontal tongue of relatively high salinity extending westward at a depth of about 3000 feet.

The circulation of the Mediterranean Sea is also affected seasonally both by the prevailing winds and by variations in sea level air pressure. Strong winds blowing to east or west may considerably alter the speed of the surface currents, while at times of very high atmospheric pressure, the surface of the Mediterranean may act rather like a diaphragm, forcing water out of the Mediterranean at depth and breathing it in at the surface at an increased rate.

The tides in the Mediterranean are small, the largest ranges being little more than twelve inches in amplitude. There is therefore little flushing of water from bays and inlets, and coastal waters tend to become stale and clogged with debris and chemical effluent. Water entering the sea from the Atlantic is also low in nutrients as most have already been removed by surface-living plankton. Consequently the basic biological productivity of the Mediterranean Sea is generally lower than that of most major oceans; it does not accumulate nutrients in its lower levels to any great extent due to the constant return flow to the Atlantic, and even when upwellings do occur they can only marginally improve marine productivity.

One of the most significant changes to take place in the Mediterranean Sea followed the completion of the Aswan Dam in 1970. For many centuries, the south-eastern area of the Mediterranean has supported a thriving fishery industry because the seasonal Nile outflow reduced the salinity of the water and added vast quantities of nutrient material. Completion of the dam removed this major source of nutrients and fresh water and, despite efforts to maintain stocks, productivity of the eastern Mediterranean is low.

THE POLLUTED SEA

Large-scale pollution from both industrial and domestic sources is seriously affecting the coastal environment of the western Mediterranean. The most heavily polluted areas are along the coasts of northwest Spain, France and around the Gulf of Genoa. Introduction of toxic materials, together with organic pollutants contained in domestic sewage, are both poisoning the coastal aquatic life and starving it of oxygen. It is estimated that more than 90 percent of all sewage entering the Mediterranean is untreated. Although the sea is virtually landlocked it receives a constant supply of oxygenated water from the Atlantic and as biological productivity is low, due to nutrient deficiency, sufficient oxygen is available for the biodegradation of the lower concentrations of these pollutants occurring away from the coast. More serious in the open sea is the practice of oil tankers discharging waste in specified "free zones." It is estimated that about 300,000 tons of oil enters the Mediterranean in this way each year. Thermal pollution, which so far has not been a problem, is expected to rise due to the increase in thermal generation of power along the Mediterranean coast.

A **three-dimensional** representation of the Mediterranean water circulation clearly illustrates the relationship between surface and subsurface waters. When surface water temperature is simply plotted on a map, areas of warm water assume an exaggerated importance; in sectional view they are seen to be little more than extensive shallow pools of relatively warm water lying in and above an enormous volume of much colder water. In the Mediterranean Sea, the warm surface layer varies between 250 and 1000 feet in depth and overlies a mass of cold water, in places up to 15,000 feet deep.

RED SEA:BATHYMETRY AND CIRCULATION

The Red Sea is a warm, highly saline sea extending some 1300 miles southeast from Suez to the Strait of Bab al Mandab.
Area 169,000 square miles; 438,000 square kilometers.
Width 90 to 190 miles; 145 to 306 kilometers.
Maximum depth (axial trough) 9580 ft; 2920 meters.
Evaporation more than 80 inches/year; 200 cm/year.

The concept of seafloor spreading at midocean ridges and destruction of oceanic crust at marginal subduction zones has enabled marine scientists to form a fairly comprehensive picture of the dynamics of the earth's crust and of the origins and evolution of ocean basins. Given that the major ocean basins present today—the Atlantic, Pacific, Indian and Arctic basins—are geologically fairly old, and that evidence of even earlier ocean basins is readily detectable in the uplifted mountains of the Himalayas and the mountain chains of America and northern Europe, it seems logical that somewhere on the earth's surface there should be an ocean, or oceans, in the earliest stages of formation.

The elongated rift of the Red Sea, gradually widening by seafloor spreading as the Saudi Arabian peninsula is carried away from the African continent, is considered to be one such embryonic ocean.

The topography of the Red Sea is dominated by two principal features; a broad, smooth continental shelf and a deep axial trough, which is itself split by an even deeper axial valley, at most about 15 miles wide. This axial valley, which plunges to nearly 10,000 feet at its deepest point, has clearly been formed by very recent spreading of the seafloor. Bottom photographs taken by a number of oceanographic survey vessels show fresh volcanic features, including cracks, fissures and recent lava flows. Seismic profiles taken across the width of the Red Sea disclose even more detail of the sea's recent history. The records clearly show a distinct acoustic reflecting layer beneath the continental shelf areas, covered by several hundred feet of sediments. When drilled in 1972 by the research ship *Glomar Challenger*, this reflecting layer was found to consist of a mixture of salt and anhydrite—minerals that are commonly deposited in shallow water in conditions of high evaporation. The deposits are five million years old and older and indicate that the Red Sea was an evaporating basin at this time—a discovery that correlates well with recent investigations into the drying up of the Mediterranean Sea. The complete absence of the reflecting layer in the axial valley simply reinforces other evidence, indicating that this deep gash in the earth's surface is of much more recent origin.

The exact mechanism responsible for opening the Red Sea is not yet completely understood. If the deep axial valley alone was formed by seafloor spreading, it could have been formed within the last two or three million years; if the entire Red Sea was formed in this way it must have happened in phases over a period of at least 20, and possibly nearer 30, million years. Studies of sediment distribution and thickness strongly support the theory that spreading occurred in two main phases. The layer of sediment overlying the reflecting evaporite layer was found to be of almost uniform thickness everywhere but in the axial valley—from which it is absent. If the Red Sea had been formed by continuous spreading of the basin, the sediment layer should be thickest close to land where the seabed is oldest, and gradually thin out toward the central valley. Thus the sediment pattern of the basin indicates that an initial phase of spreading was followed by a period of inactivity, during which the uniform layer of sediment was laid down. The pattern of magnetic stripes retained in the geologically recent lavas of the axial valley indicate that spreading restarted about two million years ago and has continued at the rate of about half an inch a year since then.

Roughly 200 million years ago the continental masses of Europe and Africa and the Americas must have been separated by a long, narrow, rifted ocean basin very like the present-day Red Sea. Evaporite deposits are found beneath the continental shelf off West Africa and Brazil, and drilling studies on the continental rise off the east coast of North America have revealed heavy-metal deposits very similar to those found in some of the deeper parts of the Red Sea axial valley. Today the Red Sea is barely 200 miles across at its widest point; at its present rate of spreading it could, in 200 million years, be as wide as the Atlantic we know today. We are witnessing the birth of a potential future major ocean.

Apollo 7 view of the Red Sea; the mountainous Sinai Peninsula separates the Gulfs of Suez and Aqaba.

Current flow in the Red Sea is very variable and almost entirely due to the prevailing winds. Between November and March the currents generally set to the northwest; between June and September the flow is generally southeasterly. During periods of change the currents are weak and variable. Flow patterns in the Strait of Bab al Mandab are mainly tidal.

RED SEA: STRUCTURAL GEOLOGY

The area around the Red Sea and the Persian Gulf is unique from a geological point of view as the entire process of plate tectonics can be seen at work within an area of just a few thousand square miles.

The first indication that this is so is the apparent fit of the opposing coastlines of the Red Sea. If these are brought together the match is almost perfect except for an area at the southeastern end, where the Yemen overlaps that part of Ethiopia known as the Afar Triangle. This would suggest that the Red Sea represents a widening rift in the earth's crust along which new crustal material is being formed, and that the sea itself is destined eventually to widen into an ocean. Studies of the rift valley along the floor of the Red Sea, where volcanic activity and areas of anomalously high heat flow are observed, confirm that this is so and the rift valley, after becoming rather confused off the Afar Triangle, continues out through the center of the Gulf of Aden to link up with the Indian Ocean ridge system. Crustal material formed in the center of the Red Sea is added to the African plate to the southwest and the Arabian plate to the northeast.

Less than a thousand miles away to the northeast lies the Persian Gulf, the deepest part of which lies along its northeastern shore quite close to the folded Zagros Mountains—a situation that suggests the major troughs and fold mountains of the Pacific margin. Here the floor of the Persian Gulf is returning to the mantle and being destroyed, crumpling up the edge of the adjacent Asian plate as it descends into the subduction zone. The seabed sediments are crumpled up by the compressional forces to form the oil traps that are so important to the economy of the area. The Arabian plate is one of the smallest of the earth's crustal plates and its continuing movement to the northeast will probably lead to complete closure of the Persian Gulf within only a few tens of millions of years.

The Afar Triangle lies at the triple-point junction where the rift valley of East Africa meets those of the Red Sea and the Gulf of Aden. This little-explored area is particularly interesting since it consists of oceanic crust that happens to be above sea level. It is bounded neatly by fault scarps on all three sides—the Ethiopian Escarpment, the Somali Escarpment and the escarpment on the coast of Yemen beyond the Red Sea. The evolution of the Afar Triangle can be thought

of as the raising of a blister on the earth's surface by upwelling mantle material beneath. As the blister rises, the tensions set up in the surface cause it to crack, forming three splits meeting at the center. The sides of the cracks move apart leaving the edges uplifted as the surrounding escarpments and the underlying surface raised above sea level as the Afar Triangle. The escarpments are in some places 13,000 feet high and have faulted and stepped profiles typical of graben structures. The land surface of the Afar Triangle is inhospitable desert, which, at some places in the north, lies 400 feet below sea level but rises to 3300 feet above sea level in the south. It is cut by a spectacular series of northwest–southeast trending faults, forming open fissures, horsts and grabens, that indicate a continuation of geological structure from the rifting in the centre of the Red Sea. Active volcanoes, hot springs and frequent earthquakes aligned parallel to the Red Sea axis show that the area is geologically unstable and even the most recent structures have been split open by large-scale faulting. The rocks of the grabens in the northern part of the area are typical of the rocks of the oceanic crust found on midocean ridges, and the region is lacking in the granitic rocks that are usually found in continents. Only in recent years has the geological importance of this area been realized and much detailed work remains to be done.

The unusual occurrence of this piece of oceanic crust as a dry land area may be only temporary. Indeed it can be shown that until quite recently it lay at the bottom of the sea. Young flat-topped volcanoes and volcanic ash rings that abound in the area could only have been formed by volcanic eruptions underwater. In some areas there are about 3000 feet of evaporite deposit that have been formed within the last two million years, suggesting an intermittent connexion with the Red Sea. These evaporites can still be seen forming as the scattered lakes and pools dry out. At the foot of the Ethiopian Escarpment a stone axe some 200,000 years old has been found. This axe was covered with seashells, showing that it had lain in the sea for some time since the days when it was used. At some time in the future this unique area may be submerged again as the continents continue to drift and the Afar Triangle will return to the bottom of the ocean to become a typical piece of submerged ocean crust.

The surface of the Afar Triangle was at one time below sea level—a fact proven by the presence of ash rings formed of fragments of volcanic glass erupted under water. Similar ash rings are seen developing today in Hawaii. The desert surface of the region is covered in places by thick deposits of salt formed by the evaporation of pools and lakes of saline water.

Faulting in the Afar Triangle attests to the intense geologic activity taking place there. This graben near Lake Abbe, with its dramatic faulted scarp slopes, was formed by extension of the earth's crust as the continental blocks gradually moved apart.

Flat-topped volcanic cones in the area were formed below the sea surface. They consist of shards of volcanic glass produced as hot lava exploded on contact with sea water and look very like the deep-sea guyots found in many of the world's oceans.

25 million years ago

3 million years ago

Present day

Red Sea

Yemen

Danakil Horst

Nubia

Gulf of Aden

Aysha Horst

Somalia

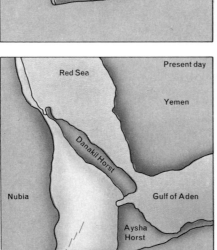

Tectonic activity in the Red Sea can be seen in the fresh volcanic structures of the central valley. They are typical of structures found in the rift valleys of the midocean ridges. The unusual structure, *left*, is a piece of basalt forced to the surface in a plastic state and extruded like toothpaste from a tube. A seismic reflection profile of the Red Sea, *below*, shows the central rift valley and the fault structures along its sides. A distinctive seabed layer can be seen at bottom depths of about 2000 feet. This is the so-called "S-reflector," which indicates the presence of a thick layer of evaporite. The deposit was probably formed when the spreading stopped for a time about five million years ago and the area partly dried out. It is not present in the much more recent central rift valley.

feet
0

Central trough

2000

Axial valley

4000

6000

Evaporite (S) layer

8000

0 miles   10   20   30   40   50   60

The Afar Triangle is the only part of the Red Sea margin that disrupts the geometric fit of the opposing coastlines. About 25 million years ago the Yemen fitted snugly between Nubia and Somalia, which started moving apart from two spreading centers at either side of a sliver of crust now forming the Danakil Horst. The area to the southwest became the Afar Triangle.

Dead Sea–Jordan Rift

ASIAN PLATE

Zagros Mountains

ARABIAN PLATE

Persian Gulf

AFRICAN PLATE

Red Sea

The Arabian Peninsula covers the area of one of the smallest plates on the surface of the earth. It is being formed in the Red Sea rift valley, traveling northeastward and being destroyed in a subduction zone in the Persian Gulf. All the classical features of plate tectonics can be seen in this area—the widening ocean with matching coastlines and axial rift, the deep-water trough at the other side and the folded mountains above the subduction zone. The sediments being deformed at the foot of the Zagros Mountains include deposits of salt that are pushed up into salt domes, giving rise to oil fields. In the southwest corner lies the Afar Triangle, an interesting area where the rift valleys of the Red Sea, the Persian Gulf and East Africa meet almost at a point and give rise to a number of geological features found nowhere else on the face of the earth.

Axial valley

Ethiopian Escarpment

Yemen

Afar Triangle

Lake Abbe

Gulf of Aden

Owen Fracture Zone

Somali Escarpment

East African Rift

147

PERSIAN GULF:LIVING AND MINERAL RESOURC

The main mineral resource of the Persian Gulf area is undoubtedly the vast reserve of oil lying beneath its desert surface. An almost uninterrupted sequence of sedimentary rocks has been laid down in the area since the beginning of the Mesozoic era, 280 million years ago. The assemblage consists mainly of limestones interbedded with organic-rich layers and some evaporites. During the Tertiary period these deposits were folded and forced upward by compression between the Arabian and Asian plates to form the Zagros mountains. Anticlines were formed in the sediments and the evaporites gave rise to salt domes, both structures providing ideal traps for the oil produced by decomposition of the organic matter in the sedimentary sequence. The oil reservoirs are found in Jurassic limestones and dolomites in Saudi Arabia, Cretaceous sands and limestones farther to the northeast, and Tertiary limestones, sometimes in reef structures, in the Iranian foothills. Iraq has the only oilfield in Triassic rocks, but it is of comparatively small size.

The first oil well was sunk in 500 B.C. at Shush in Iran during the reign of Darius the Great. Modern exploration began in Iran in 1890 and 1891, when three wells were drilled down to about 800 feet without striking any deposits. Another well in 1904 found a little oil, but greater success was achieved in 1908, when oil was discovered at a depth of 1180 feet. Oil seepages were noticed in 1914 in Kuwait and the British Admiralty recommended a program of shallow drilling. No oil was struck until 1937 and production of Kuwait oil did not start until 1946. Meanwhile, in Iran, the Naft-i-Shah field was discovered in 1923, but was not exploited until 1935.

Today the Persian Gulf area produces, at 1975 figures, 35.9 percent of the world's crude oil, at a rate of up to 23 million barrels a day. The area produced a total of 956 million tons in 1975.

The oil terminal at Das Island, Abu Dhabi, is typical of the oil installations in the Persian Gulf. From the air nothing is visible of this tiny sand island except an airstrip, a harbor and rows of oil tanks. The terminal brings ashore oil from the surrounding Umm Shaif, Zakum and El Bunduq fields by submerged pipelines up to 55 miles long. There the gas is removed from the crude oil and the cleaned oil is pumped to tankers at offshore loading berths.

The Red Sea, being a young ocean basin, is deficient in mineral resources and has no known oil deposits. A possible future resource of valuable metals exists, however, in pools of exceptionally hot brines found in the deepest parts of the central rift valley. Hot water, both juvenile and recycled, is circulated through the rocks of the rift, heated by the crustal activity associated with the seafloor spreading. These waters may have temperatures of 104°C when they erupt at the floor of the sea and they are rich in dissolved metals, including zinc and copper, which are deposited in the seabed muds. At some future date it may prove economic to extract these minerals, but at present the extraction costs would exceed the metals' value.

The Persian Gulf and the Red Sea also differ in their fisheries. The shallowness of the Persian Gulf allows light to penetrate to the bottom, promoting a high level of plankton production and hence a large and varied stock of fish. Sardine, anchovy, mackerel and barracuda are the main pelagic species, exploited mainly in the southeast. A variety of demersal fish is taken by trawl wherever the seabed is sufficiently flat.

The Red Sea, in complete contrast to the Persian Gulf, has no major fishery other than a sardine fishery in the north and a bottom trawl fishery in the south and, to a lesser extent, around Ghardaqa in the north. Sardines in the north and in the Gulf of Suez are caught using lamparas—large encircling nets used in conjunction with lights. The lights attract the fish to the surface, where they are swept into the nets. The low level of exploitation in the Red Sea is due partly to the poverty of the resource and partly to the presence of coral reefs, which restrict the activities of bottom trawlers. Among the fish commercially exploited are tiger fish, squirrel fish, soldier fish, puffer fish, bass, bream and mullet.

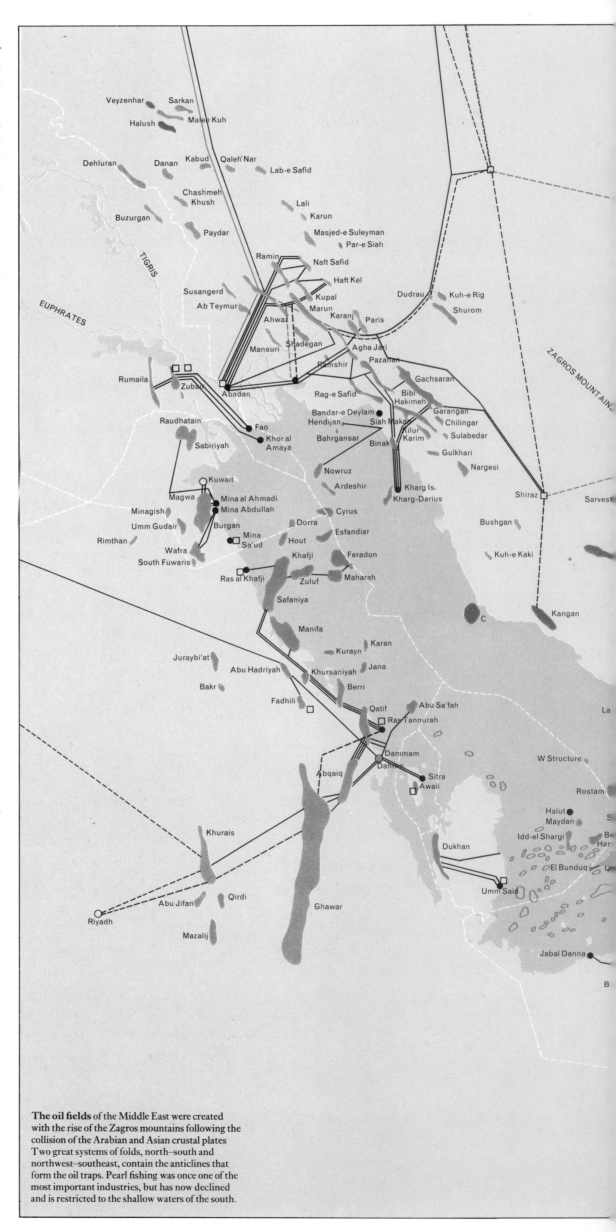

The oil fields of the Middle East were created with the rise of the Zagros mountains following the collision of the Arabian and Asian crustal plates Two great systems of folds, north–south and northwest–southeast, contain the anticlines that form the oil traps. Pearl fishing was once one of the most important industries, but has now declined and is restricted to the shallow waters of the south.

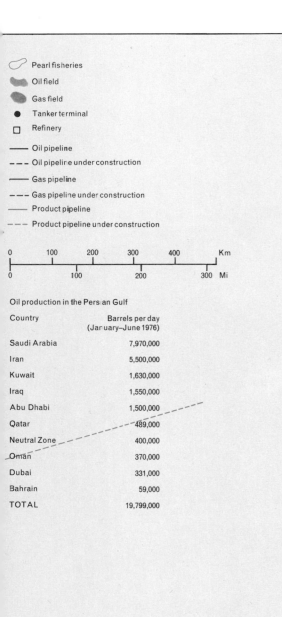

Legend

- 🦪 Pearl fisheries
- Oil field
- Gas field
- ● Tanker terminal
- □ Refinery

- —— Oil pipeline
- – – – Oil pipeline under construction
- —— Gas pipeline
- – – – Gas pipeline under construction
- —— Product pipeline
- – – – Product pipeline under construction

| 0 | 100 | 200 | 300 | 400 | | Km |
| 0 | | 100 | 200 | | 300 | Mi |

Oil production in the Persian Gulf

Country	Barrels per day (January–June 1976)
Saudi Arabia	7,970,000
Iran	5,500,000
Kuwait	1,630,000
Iraq	1,550,000
Abu Dhabi	1,500,000
Qatar	489,000
Neutral Zone	400,000
Oman	370,000
Dubai	331,000
Bahrain	59,000
TOTAL	19,799,000

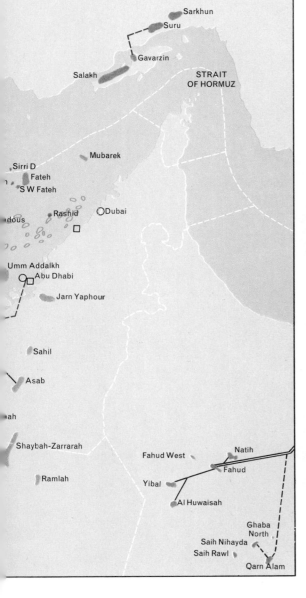

Sarkhun
Suru
Gavarzin
Salakh
STRAIT OF HORMUZ

Mubarek
Sirri D
Fateh
S W Fateh
Rashid
◯Dubai
ndous
Umm Addalkh
Abu Dhabi
Jarn Yaphour

Sahil
Asab
ah
Shaybah-Zarrarah
Fahud West
Natih
Fahud
Ramlah
Yibal
Al Huwaisah
Ghaba North
Saih Nihayda
Saih Rawl
Qarn Alam

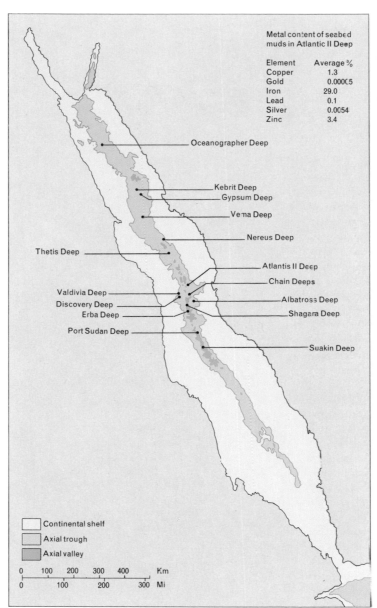

Metal content of seabed muds in Atlantic II Deep	
Element	Average %
Copper	1.3
Gold	0.00005
Iron	29.0
Lead	0.1
Silver	0.0054
Zinc	3.4

Oceanographer Deep
Kebrit Deep
Gypsum Deep
Vema Deep
Nereus Deep
Thetis Deep
Atlantis II Deep
Chain Deeps
Valdivia Deep
Albatross Deep
Discovery Deep
Erba Deep
Shagara Deep
Port Sudan Deep
Suakin Deep

- ☐ Continental shelf
- Axial trough
- Axial valley

| 0 | 100 | 200 | 300 | 400 | | Km |
| 0 | | 100 | 200 | | 300 | Mi |

| 0 | | 5 Km | Depth in feet |
| 0 | 3 Mi | | |

Seawater
Interface
5000
6000
Hot brine
7000

The axial valley of the Red Sea features a number of "pits" more than 6000 feet deep that contain hot brines, which have emerged from the seabed and are associated with the creation of new crustal rocks. The brine pools have temperatures of up to 60°C, suggesting that the brine is as hot as 104°C when it is extruded. Calculations indicate that the production of brine in some areas is 200 times greater than that of Old Faithful Geyser in the USA. The brines are rich in potentially valuable metals and these are subsequently deposited in the muds of the seafloor. The interface between normal seawater and brine shows clearly on echo-sounder traces.

Crude oil is now being stored in bell-shaped underwater tanks in the Persian Gulf. These are built on land and towed to their sites, where they are submerged. The water inside them is displaced through openings at the base as oil is pumped in at the top. Holding 500,000 barrels, the tanks are located in water deep enough to allow tankers to berth, and take on cargo, over them.

INDIAN OCEAN : BATHYMETRY

The Indian Ocean is the world's third largest water body and represents about 20 percent of the total world ocean area. **Area** 28,400,000 square miles; 73,600,000 square kilometers. **Average depth** 12,760 feet; 3,890 meters. **Volume** 70,086,000 cubic miles; 292,131,000 cubic kilometers. **Maximum depth** (Java Trench) 24,442 feet; 7450 m.

The most striking feature of the bed of the Indian Ocean is the great inverted Y of the midocean ridge system, one arm of which extends around southern Africa and connects with the Mid-Atlantic Ridge, while the other passes south of Australia to link with the East Pacific Rise. From the junction of the Y, the Mid Indian Ocean Ridge runs northward, then swings west as the Carlsberg Ridge to join the rift system of the Red Sea. This submarine mountain chain, extensively offset by fracture zones, is a belt of strong seismic and volcanic activity and represents the center for seafloor spreading in the ocean. Where it passes into the Red Sea, the northern part of Africa and Saudi Arabia have been actively spreading apart for the past 25 million years.

The Indian Ocean is also unusual in having a large number of relatively shallow submarine plateaus and ridges spread over its floor, draped with light-colored calcareous oozes. These shallower areas are not sites of earthquake activity and are clearly formed in manner very different from that of the geologically active midocean ridges. Most of the plateaus are thought to represent former microcontinents, left behind during seafloor spreading—to subside as the continents drifted apart. The linear, aseismic ridges have been shown by deep-sea drilling to have foundations of volcanic rock of the same age and composition as that below adjacent deeper areas of the seafloor. They are considered to have been formed by individual upstanding volcanoes on the midocean ridge which continuously extruded great quantities of volcanic rock as the seafloor moved away from them. Deep-sea drilling along the 1700-mile-long Ninety East Ridge shows that it must have been created from a point source at, or very near, sea level. The first sediments deposited on the newly created seafloor were low-grade coal and peat, or lagoonal sediments, indicating emerged land or extremely shallow water. Seafloor spreading subsequently caused the ridge to subside—to more than a mile below sea level in the north, where it is oldest and farthest from the point of formation.

The Central Indian, Wharton and Crozet basins—the major basins lying below a depth of 13,000 feet—are relatively remote from land and are sufficiently deep to preclude deposition of carbonate oozes. In these, the only sediments found are reddish-brown clays, or siliceous oozes in areas lying below the rich high latitude or subequatorial plankton productivity zones. In other areas, coarse sediments derived from the land encroach into these deep basins. Two of the world's largest river systems, the Indus and the Ganges-Brahmaputra, have built huge submarine fans into the Arabian Basin and the Bay of Bengal by stripping enormous quantities of sediment from the Himalayan mountain ranges. The Bengal Fan is by far the world's largest with a volume of about 1.2 million cubic miles of sediments.

The only major trench in the Indian Ocean, the Java Trench, lies south of the Indonesian arc of volcanic islands and attains a maximum depth of 24,400 feet. It is thought to mark the line of subduction of the Australian Plate below the Eurasian Plate, a process which has been active only for the past two million years. Related volcanic activity along the Indonesian arc has built up huge quantities of volcanic sediment and ash on the seafloor in this region. One of the best recorded of all historic eruptions was that of Krakatoa in 1883 in which about four cubic miles of mountainous island were blown away in one day as a result of four huge explosions—the largest of which was heard 3000 miles away in Australia.

THE EVOLUTION OF THE INDIAN OCEAN

Maps depicting the evolution of the world's ocean basins can be constructed from the distribution of magnetic lineations in the oceanic crust; from the paleomagnetism of adjacent continents; and from the proven increase in depth with age of the oceanic crust as it subsides away from the spreading centers. The Indian Ocean came into being when the ancient landmass of Gondwanaland began to fragment with the separation of Africa and Antarctica between 140 and 130 million years ago, followed by the separation of India from Australia and Antarctica about 110 million years ago.

70 million years ago India still lay south of the equator. A line of islands formed by the shallow Ninety East Ridge separated the 16,400-feet-deep Wharton Basin in the east from a shallower western region consisting of smaller basins bounded by ridges and plateaus.

53 million years ago the Ninety East Ridge formed a continuous barrier covering almost 30 degrees of latitude. The Wharton Basin and the western plateaus and ridges had become more extensive, and basins were forming off India and between Africa and Antarctica.

36 million years ago the Indian Ocean resembled its present-day shape. The eastern part of the midocean ridge, formerly north of Australia, now extended south of this continent and seafloor spreading was widening a seaway between Australia and Antarctica.

During the past 36 million years carbonate oozes have become more extensive and some areas of siliceous ooze have developed. The northern Indian Ocean is dominated by the Bengal and Indus fans.

151

INDIAN:LIVING AND MINERAL RESOURCES

Fisheries' development in the Indian Ocean has been much less intensive than that of either the Atlantic or the Pacific and it has been estimated that, on the basis of yield per unit surface area, the Indian Ocean yield of fish and fish products is only about one-fifth that of the Atlantic or Pacific. Total annual production from the Indian Ocean has, however, increased from about two million tons in 1965 to about three million tons in 1974 and this rate of fishery growth, measured in terms of weight of catch, currently exceeds that of any other major world ocean. Regardless, the production of fishery products from the Indian Ocean represents only five percent of the total world catch of marine fish and shellfish.

The small catches taken from the Indian Ocean can be attributed to a relatively low level of fishing effort; to the use in many areas of very primitive techniques, and in part to the availability of the fishery resource. Unlike the Atlantic and Pacific, there are few major contiguous shallow seas or extensive continental shelf areas in the Indian Ocean. The largest shelf areas are found in the Arabian Sea and the Bay of Bengal, but, on a comparative basis, the Indian Ocean has even less continental shelf area per unit surface area than either the Pacific or Atlantic. Moreover, much of the shelf area—particularly that lying off the coast of Africa—cannot be harvested because of extensive coral growth. Some scientists also believe that the seasonal wind patterns in the northern Indian Ocean may disrupt oceanic productivity and hence the availability of the fishery resource.

The fisheries conducted throughout much of the Indian Ocean are generally in close proximity to landmasses, and the fishing methods employed are often primitive. Nevertheless, the ocean fishery resources represent an important factor in the lives of many coastal communities, which rely on fish to provide much needed animal protein. Small-scale subsistence

Fishing methods in the Indian Ocean have changed little over the centuries

Estimates of the total fishery potential of the Indian Ocean are rather inaccurate. Surveys of demersal stocks have been hampered by the irregularity of the seabed, and the size of the stocks are only approximately known in a few well-fished areas, such as off the southern tip of India. The total fish resource may be around 13 million tons.

Indian total catch
3018 thousand metric tons

Marine fish	2636
Crustaceans	334
Mollusks	27
Diadromous fish	21

World total catch
59,321 thousand metric tons

	%		%
Pacific	43.2	Atlantic	38.7
		Indian	5.2
		Caribbean	2.5
		Mediterranean	2.3
		Others	8.1

Demersal fish
Fish production in thousand metric tons per fishing area

- Greater than 1000
- 500–1000
- 100–500
- Less than 100

Pelagic fish
- Anchovy
- Sardine
- Tuna
- Mackerel
- Mixed

Crustacea
- Shrimp
- Lobster

The continental shelf of any ocean is its most productive fishing area. At three million square miles, the Indian Ocean's continental shelf is 37 percent that of the Atlantic, but its total catch is only 13 percent of the Atlantic's catch. This low level of exploitation is due mainly to the small-scale nature of the fisheries and the primitive techniques employed. Studies of pelagic fish-stocks have revealed that they are being fished well within their limitations and that there is much room for expansion.

fisheries are particularly prevalent along the east coast of Africa, off some of the Arabian states and in the Bay of Bengal. The fishermen, who harvest a wide variety of tropical and subtropical species, carry out their operations from a great range of small craft, including dugouts and outrigger canoes, Arabian dhows and other craft. Fishing gear is very varied and includes drift nets, hand lines, spears, traps, a variety of set net systems and longline gear.

Modern techniques have, however, been introduced into the Indian Ocean fishery, particularly over the past few decades, and large-scale fisheries for tuna, shrimp and demersal fish occur in some areas. Japanese, Korean and Taiwanese longline vessels up to 165 feet in length range over large areas of the Indian Ocean in search of pelagic tuna, sailfish and marlin, while modern Soviet trawlers conduct intensive bottom-fishing in the Gulf of Aden and off the shores of the southern Arabian states. During the past 15 years important trawl fisheries for shrimp have developed in the waters off the coast of western India and Pakistan as well as off Kuwait and other Arab states. Most of the shrimp catch is exported to markets in the United States and Europe.

Although the fisheries of the Indian Ocean have not developed to the extent of those of the other major oceans, there has recently been a vastly increased effort on the part of a number of coastal states to utilize the untapped fishery resource of the region. Major efforts have, for example, been made by India to develop her coastal fisheries; harbor development programs have been initiated, exploratory fishing started and, on land, steps have been taken to extend modern processing facilities. There has also been a rapid growth of fisheries off Thailand, Malaysia and Indonesia. Future growth of the Indian Ocean fisheries is now assured as new areas are explored and new techniques introduced.

As with the other major oceans, the extraction of raw minerals from the seafloor of the Indian Ocean is still in its infancy. The immediate mineral resource potential of this ocean is largely tied to the exploration for oil and gas reserves, an activity currently restricted to offshore regions, and to the recovery of manganese or phosphate nodules from remote areas of the deep seafloor.

Critical evaluation of the sedimentary basins along its land margins, together with geophysical and drilling data from the deep ocean areas, has led to a rapid increase in hydrocarbon exploration interest in the Indian Ocean. Oil and gas extraction in Saudi Arabia and Iran has already been extended to offshore regions and particularly to beneath the Persian Gulf, and recently major submarine oil fields have been discovered off Western Australia.

Large areas of the Indian Ocean deep seafloor have been identified by marine geologists as manganese nodule pavements. Most extensive are those in the southern basins, swept by deep bottom currents emanating from the Antarctic. Techniques for the extraction of these nodules, rich in manganese, nickel, copper, titanium and lead, are currently being developed. In addition, an extensive field of phosphate nodules, representing a possible major new source of fertilizer, has been located on the Agulhas Plateau.

On the other hand, beach sands rich in heavy minerals, and offshore placer deposits, have been actively exploited around the margins of the Indian Ocean for up to 60 years. Monazite, ilmenite, rutile and zircon are mined from beach sands along the shores off Kerala state in southern India; sands rich in ilmenite, rutile, zircon and magnetite are extracted in northeastern Sri Lanka, and there is exploitation of beach deposits of glauconite—used in potash fertilizers—in eastern South Africa. Deposits of cassiterite are mined for their tin content from submarine channels up to five miles out from the shores of Burma and Indonesia, while barium sulfate concretions are today being dredged in waters 4050 feet deep off Sri Lanka.

Cassiterite, a major source of tin, was probably the first mineral to be exploited on the bed of the sea and is almost certainly predated only by salt as a nonliving marine resource. Marine production of tin is today concentrated mainly around the shores of Thailand and Indonesia, where it is dredged from submarine channels up to five miles from shore. Dredgers like that illustrated scoop sediment from the seabed and transfer it to land plants, where the tin is extracted. In 1970, tin concentrates valued at 8.2 million US dollars were produced by Thailand; Indonesia produced tin concentrates worth 33 million US dollars.

Offshore placer deposits
Solid symbol—active mine
Open symbol—known deposit

- Titanium
- Titanium
- Tin
- Tin
- Monazite
- Monazite
- Chromite
- Zircon
- Zircon

- Metal-bearing muds
- Phosphorite

- Manganese nodules

- Major sedimentary basins
- Oil and gas fields
- 200 m

The continental shelves of the Indian Ocean are rich in a variety of placer deposits of commercially valuable minerals. Monazite, ilmenite, rutile, zircon and magnetite are mined in offshore operations, while the cassiterite workings off Thailand and Indonesia account for nearly one-quarter of the world's offshore tin production.

INDIAN OCEAN:CIRCULATION

A satellite view of the Indian subcontinent in September shows stable conditions over the land with gentle onshore breezes around the coast. Beyond the clear sea-breeze zone, regular cells of cumulus cloud indicate even sea temperatures and lack of surface wind.

The North Indian Ocean is unique among the world's oceans in having a current pattern that changes twice during each year under the influence of the monsoon winds. Between November and April the North East Monsoon generates the North Equatorial Current, which carries water toward the coast of Africa. Here the current turns south and forms the western boundary current flowing along the coast of Somalia. On crossing the equator, the current joins with water of the South Equatorial Current and flows east as the Equatorial Countercurrent. In the region of the Indonesian Islands, this current divides, part turning north to rejoin the North Equatorial Current while the remainder continues to flow eastward as the Java Coastal Current or swings around to join the South Equatorial Current.

In April, in response to the changing pattern of high and low atmospheric pressure over the Asian landmass, the North East Monsoon ceases and is replaced by the South West Monsoon. The winds along the Somali coast are among the first to change their direction and these quickly generate a north-flowing Somali Current. Current flow in the rest of the ocean takes longer to react to the new wind pattern, but by July the Monsoon Current is flowing eastward everywhere north of the equator. This time, on reaching the Indonesian Islands the entire watermass turns south and returns westward as part of a much stronger South Equatorial Current, which in turn feeds the Somali Current—now a much intensified narrow western boundary current.

During the summer, when the South West Monsoon is blowing, not only is the circulation of the North Indian Ocean stronger, but intense upwellings can also develop, one of the most important occurring off the Arabian coast, where winds blowing parallel to the shore produce an offshore movement of surface water which is replaced by water from greater depth. A second important area of upwelling occurs where the Somali Current moves away from the coast, carrying warm surface water with it. In both regions, water wells up from a depth of 330 to 660 feet and can easily be tracked in satellite photographs, as the deeper water is considerably cooler than the surrounding watermass.

South of the equator, the Indian Ocean behaves in a much more conventional manner with the Trade Winds and Westerlies driving an anticlockwise gyre of warm water. The South Equatorial Current carries water toward Africa, where that part not connected with the Monsoon system turns south past Madagascar and enters the Agulhas Current. This is the strongest western boundary current in the Southern Hemisphere, reaching speeds of 112 miles a day along the edge of the South African continental shelf. At these speeds the southward-flowing current can more than double the height of the swell waves traveling north from storms generated in the Antarctic Ocean. The swell waves attain enormous proportions and in recent times

at least two ships each year have suffered serious damage from them. On reaching the southern tip of Africa, the Agulhas Current turns and meanders eastward with its energy much reduced. Occasionally meanders become cut off and form eddies that may travel westward into the South Atlantic, where they are incorporated into the north-flowing Benguela Current. Surprisingly—and in contrast with the South Atlantic and South Pacific—no well-developed current or upwelling region is found in the eastern part of the southern Indian Ocean. The return flow of the gyre is effected by the weak and poorly defined West Australia Current.

As in the other great ocean basins, the deep circulation of the Indian Ocean must be inferred from the apparent spreading out and diffusion of watermasses with known properties. This technique shows that

most of the water below 3300 feet in the Indian and Pacific oceans originates either as North Atlantic Deep Water or as Antarctic Bottom Water. On the western side of the ocean, the water properties sometimes indicate that deep currents could exist, though there are as yet few direct measurements to support this. Elsewhere, it is likely that water movement occurs through the mixing action of deep-water eddies.

Nearer the surface of the North Indian Ocean, warm saline water from the Persian Gulf is found at about 990 feet, and below this the even more saline water from the Red Sea can be detected at 2600 feet. The Red Sea, which itself reaches depths of 6550 feet, is remarkable for its deep pools of hot salty water found in the bottom 160 feet. The temperature of these pools reaches 56°C and their salinity may be as high as eight times that of normal seawater.

Northern Hemisphere summer

Captains of the sailing ships working the great trade routes to India and South East Asia were familiar with the yearly cycle of the monsoon current patterns. They would make the eastward crossing with the help of the South West Monsoon and then time their departure betwen November and March in order to capitalize on the winds and currents during the North East Monsoon period.

Warm, highly saline water from the Red Sea pours out through the Gulf of Aden and spreads out into the North Indian Ocean some 2600 feet below the surface. A similar outflow of water from the Persian Gulf is detected at about 990 feet.

The warm surface waters of the Agulhas Current flow south about 300 miles from the coast. Maximum flow is reached in winter when the current is reinforced by the South Equatorial Current driven by the monsoon wind system.

28°C
24°C
28°C
28°C
24°C
20°C
16°C
12°C
8°C
4°C
0°C
Limit of sea ice

24°C

28°C

28°C

28°C

24°C

Dramatic seasonal changes in the direction of flow of the surface currents are a unique feature of the northern part of the Indian Ocean. The main current map, *left*, shows the summer circulation pattern which should be compared with the generalized atmospheric pattern during the South West Monsoon. The winter circulation, *above*, should be read in comparison with the North East Monsoon chart.

The weak north-flowing West Australian Current provides the return flow for the South Indian Gyre. Though broad and poorly defined it appears to reach maximum flow during the Northern Hemisphere winter period.

LOW
1000 mb
1010mb

HIGH
1036 mb
1024 mb
1012 mb

South West Monsoon: heated air rising over the subcontinent in summer creates an intense low-pressure region. This in turn causes an inflow of air from the south that drives the surface currents.

North East Monsoon: in winter the pattern is reversed and a very strong high pressure area in northern Asia causes an overall outflow of air that drives the surface currents to the southwest.

Location of Indian Ocean water profiles

0°C 4°C 12°C 20°C

60°S 120°E 100°E Antarctica
40°S Australia 60°E 40°E
20°S
1000m
3000m
5000m
Africa
6

1 Agulhas Current

2 Somali Current

3 Gulf of Aden at 14°N

4 Bay of Bengal

5 Indian Ocean at 110°E

The southern Indian Ocean is dominated, at the surface, by the Antarctic Circumpolar Current sweeping west to east and forming the southern limb of the South Indian Gyre. Below the relatively shallow warm waters of the gyre, cold Antarctic Bottom Water sinks and spreads out at a great depth—circulating west to east like the surface current but also extending north to the equator at the bottom of the deep West Australian and Mid-Indian Ocean basins.

155

The Pacific Ocean is the largest by far of the world's oceans, covering approximately one-third of the earth's surface.
Area 64,000,000 square miles; 166,000,000 square kilometers.
Average depth 14,050 feet; 4280 meters.
Volume 173,625,000 cubic miles; 723,700,000 cu. km.
Maximum depth (Mariana Trench) 36,161 ft; 11,022 m.

The Pacific Ocean, still by far the largest of the world's oceans, is descended from Panthalassa, the great primordial ocean that surrounded the ancient supercontinent of Pangaea. Throughout its history the Pacific has decreased in area—an inevitable consequence of the opening up of the Atlantic and Indian oceans on a globe whose overall size has remained constant and whose continental area has not increased appreciably during the time taken for the fragments of Pangaea to disperse through the action of seafloor spreading.

Shrinking of the ocean basin has been accomplished by engulfment, or subduction, of the ocean floor at marginal trenches, where great slabs of oceanic crust plunge deep into the underlying mantle. The zone of violent volcanic and earthquake activity that surrounds the Pacific from New Zealand to southern Chile, and is known as the "Circle of Fire," is the modern manifestation of this ancient and continuing process. Intensely deformed fragments of oceanic crust have in some areas escaped remelting and have been plastered against the coasts of Japan, California and South America, retaining a record of destruction of the Pacific Ocean floor stretching back more than 100 million years. Subduction is faster on the margins of the Pacific than in other oceans and its trenches are considerably deeper. Both the Mariana Trench, where the Pacific crust plunges beneath the Philippine Sea at more than four inches a year, and the Tonga Trench north of New Zealand, have depths in excess of six and a half miles—more than twice the average depth of the ocean basin.

Although the trenches bordering most of the Pacific consume nearly a square mile of its crust each year, the basin is shrinking at only a quarter of this rate: as well as having the most active of the world's subduction zones, it also has the very active East Pacific Rise, where new oceanic crust is being created faster than at any other ridge crest. Here, crust that is being pulled toward the trenches of the western Pacific is separating at up to six and a half inches a year (about one mile in every 10,000 years) from crust bound for destruction in the trenches of Central and South America. This rate is more than five times that of the Mid-Atlantic Ridge. The crest of the East Pacific Rise is marked by an almost continuous eruption of lava as molten rock rises along fissures created by crustal separation.

The eastern half of the Pacific basin is relatively simple in structure. Its topography is dominated by the East Pacific Rise and two less active spreading ridges that branch eastward from it—the Galapagos Spreading Center near the equator, and the Chile Rise in the southeast of the basin. The regional slope of the seafloor is away from the crest of these rises. Between California and Hawaii the seafloor also deepens and increases in age from east to west, although the East Pacific Rise is absent except for a branch that is opening the Gulf of California by splitting Baja California away from the rest of the North American continent. A detached segment of ridge crest exists west of Washington and British Columbia: this was once continuous with the rest of the ridge, but most of the segments of spreading ridge that created the floor of the northeast Pacific have become extinct within the past 30 million years as they collided with the continent.

Apart from the rises and trenches, the most prominent features of the eastern Pacific are the great east–west fracture zones, narrow bands of high fault scarps and volcanic ridges many hundreds of miles long that are the inactive scars of transform faulting at the East Pacific Rise. There are also many submerged volcanoes—some isolated or in random clusters, others arranged in chains that probably grew by repeated eruptions at a fixed point as the plate moved over the "hot-spot". Prolific eruptions of lava along some of these chains have caused the volcanoes to merge into volcanic ridges such as the Cocos and Carnegie Ridges, which have the very active volcanoes of the Galapagos Islands at their ever-extending eastern ends.

The western half of the Pacific basin has a more complex structure and its geologic history is not yet fully understood. The crust is older than that on the flanks of the East Pacific Rise and much of the structural pattern inherited from the time of crustal formation has been obliterated by subsequent volcanic activity. Chains of volcanoes, like those forming the Gilbert and Ellice Islands and the Emperor Seamounts, are common. The western Pacific also has several large volcanic plateaus, such as the Shatsky Rise, Solomon Plateau and Manihiki Plateau, apparently formed by voluminous floods of lava very like those that created the continental plateaus of the Columbia River and the Deccan.

LOST PLATES OF THE PACIFIC

⊢ Active spreading center	20 Oldest sediments (m.y.)	100–135 million years old
Consuming plate margin	135 + million years old	65–100 million years old

22.5–65 million years old
0–22.5 million years old

100 million years ago the Pacific Ocean basin was larger than it is at present and although the exact geometry is uncertain the basin appears to have been made up of four major plates separated by spreading centers. These active ridges were connected to the ridge system of the Indian Ocean, whose activity was causing India to drift northward away from Antarctica. Trenches, or subduction zones, consuming oceanic crust, appear to have occupied most of the ocean margins and the granitic rocks now exposed in such ranges as the Sierra Nevada in California are traces of this activity.

Between 80 and 60 million years ago, seafloor spreading opened up the Tasman Sea separating New Zealand from Australia and subsequently, about 55 million years ago, Australia split away from the Antarctic plate to begin its drift north. The entire Kula plate was destroyed except for a fragment now forming the Bering Sea basin, while a similar cutoff fragment of the Farallon plate was isolated in the Caribbean. At 27 million years ago, shown above, the ridge between the Pacific and Farallon plates split into the smaller Gorda, Cocos and Nazca plates.

The age of the oceanic crust is known from deep drillings, but, due to our inadequate understanding of the mechanisms of plate motion, it is impossible to predict accurately the future of the basin. However, present trends may be expected to continue at least for the next few million years. Hence, the area of the ocean should diminish; Australia will continue to drift north, perhaps with more difficulty as it crashes past the East Indies; and Baja California will become increasingly remote from the coast of Mexico as it moves obliquely along the San Andreas fault.

157

PACIFIC: STRUCTURAL GEOLOGY

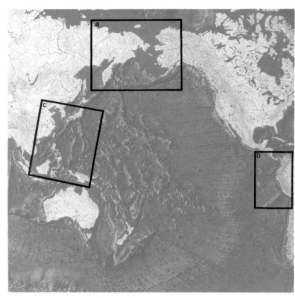

The Aleutian Arc and Bering Sea

Prior to 100 million years ago, the northernmost part of the Pacific Ocean seabed, then formed by the Kula plate, was moving toward the northwest and being consumed beneath the continental margins of Alaska and Siberia. However, at about 100 million years ago, and for reasons not yet understood, this huge oceanic plate developed a giant east–west fracture, which isolated a fragment of oceanic crust in the far north. The site of active subduction shifted south to this new fracture, which was to become the Aleutian Trench. The abandoned trench system was subsequently infilled and partly uplifted to form a fossil trench, whose rocks and structures are clearly exposed to view in the remote Koryak Mountains of eastern Siberia. The cutoff remnant of old Pacific crust stopped moving on its northwesterly path; subduction along the margin of Siberia ceased, and the crustal fragment became the tectonically stagnant floor of the deep Bering Sea Basin. Roughly half of the Bering Sea consists simply

of a slightly submerged continental shelf across which many species of animals, including early man, were able to migrate during periods of emergence, explaining the many similarities between the flora and fauna of the two areas.

Once subduction was established along the line of the new Aleutian Trench, a line of andesitic volcanoes developed north of, and parallel to, the trench above the down going slab of oceanic crust. This volcanic arc grew to become the still active arc of the Aleutian Islands. The ridge that was formed, connecting Alaska and Kamchatka in a sweeping curve some 2000 miles in length, formed a gigantic dam that ponded within the Bering Sea the entire sedimentary load shed from the surrounding continental landmasses. As a consequence, the oceanic crust plunging to destruction in the Aleutian Trench south of the island arc has only a very thin covering of pelagic sediment, while the oceanic crust beneath the Bering abyssal plain is buried beneath several miles of mud.

The South American Trench

At most of the trenches of the northern and western Pacific the oceanic crust is plunging beneath another plate of oceanic crust—either old, entrapped Pacific crust as in the Aleutians, or newly created marginal basin crust as in the Marianas Trench. In the eastern Pacific the seabed is plunging, at an equally fast rate (up to four inches a year), beneath the continental crust of South America. Instead of a festoon of island arcs, the volcanic manifestations of this process form a line of tall volcanoes in the Andes. The composition of their lava is very similar to the volcanoes of the western arcs and indeed this whole class of volcanic rocks associated with oceanic trenches is called andesite—after the mountain range.

In addition to the lavas, other components have melted out of the subducting ocean crust, risen through the continental crust and been exposed by erosion in

the high Andes. Some of these components have been segregated into ores of copper, silver, lead and gold, whose deposits were worked by the Incas and today form the mainstay of the economies of modern Peru, Bolivia and Chile. Other effects of the collision are not as beneficial. Many of the greatest ever recorded earthquakes have occurred in the trench off South America, or at greater depth beneath the Andes, and have wreaked great havoc on the densely populated continental margin. On May 31, 1970, a severe earthquake in the wall of the trench caused major landslides farther inland—including an avalanche from Huascaran mountain that killed more than 40,000 people.

Long-term studies of the geologic processes taking place in the South American Trench have two practical objectives. Better understanding may allow prediction of future earthquakes—with consequent saving of life, and location of new deposits of economic minerals.

Active trench

Active spreading center

Fossil spreading center

Historically active volcano

Active volcanic arc

Fossil volcanic arc

A

B

c

The Back-arc Seas of the West Pacific

Very soon after the revolutionary theories of plate tectonics and seafloor spreading became generally accepted by geologists and geophysicists, attention became focused once more on the unusual bathymetric character of the western Pacific region. In this area, the usual pattern of a single marginal trench and matching volcanic island arc is replaced by a widely separated pair of active trench systems between which lie a number of both active and inactive, or fossil, structural formations. The western Pacific is additionally interesting in containing some of the greatest depths recorded anywhere in the world ocean; 36,160 feet in the southern part of the great Marianas Trench, and 34,450 feet in the Philippine Trench.

Each of the main trenches in the western Pacific is accompanied by an inclined zone of earthquake foci, marking the line of the subducting oceanic plate, and an arc of active volcanoes responsible for the building up, above sea level, of an island arc. The broad Philippine Sea extends for more than 1000 miles from the Ryukyu Islands to the Mariana Islands, and the underlying crust of the ocean basin has been created in three distinct phases—each marked by a separate basin development. The oldest West Philippine Basin is thought to have been formed in a manner similar to that of the Bering Sea; about 50 million years ago a new trench developed within a section of old Pacific crust—probably along the line of a pre-existing fracture zone—and a volcanic ridge, analogous to the Aleutian Ridge, grew on its landward side, giving rise to the Palau-Kyushu Ridge.

Thereafter, the histories of the Aleutian and Philippine regions diverge. The Ryukyu and Philippine trenches remained active, consuming the Philippine Sea crust on its landward side. However, about 25 million years ago, new oceanic crust began to be formed by seafloor spreading that continued for some ten million years and created the Parece Vela Basin, which is itself now extinct and bisected by a fossil spreading center. This phenomenon of "back-arc" spreading, which begins with the splitting of a volcanic island arc, has been repeated in the past two to three million years. The Marianas Ridge was split into the still active volcanic arc next to the trench, and the West Marianas Ridge, which subsided below sea level once active volcanism had ceased there. The intervening Marianas Trench is today growing constantly wider by seafloor spreading, and this area is now being subjected to careful and detailed examination to see whether the mechanisms of crustal formation are the same as those known to occur on the midocean ridges.

50 million years ago

Ryukyu volcanic arc

China

Continental crust

Ryukyu Trench

Pacific crust fractures and starts new subduction trench

Subducting ocean crust

30 million years ago

Ryukyu arc still active

Philippine Sea starts to become narrower

New volcanic arc initiated above new subduction zone

Mariana Trench

Pacific crust

Subduction of oceanic crust continues

20 million years ago

Ryukyu arc still active

West Philippine Basin continues to narrow

Palau-Kyushu Ridge, split from Mariana Ridge by seafloor spreading, now inactive and subsiding

Mariana Ridge still active

Parece-Vela Basin widening by seafloor spreading

Mariana Trench

Subduction of West Philippine seafloor continues beneath Ryukyu arc

A

Today

Ryukyu arc still active

West Philippine Basin continues to narrow

Now inactive spreading center (Parece-Vela fossil spreading center)

Volcanically extinct West Mariana Ridge, split from Mariana Ridge by spreading of Mariana Trough

Mariana Trough widening by active back-arc seafloor spreading

Continuing andesitic volcanism

Mariana Trench (36,160 feet)

B

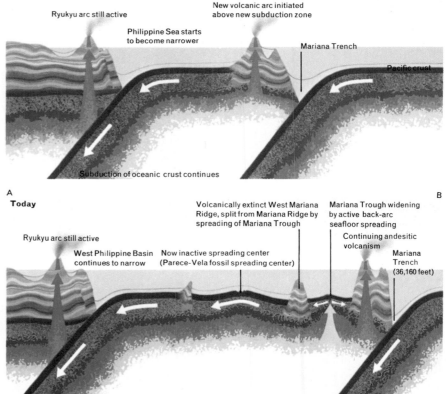

PACIFIC: REEFS AND ISLANDS

Quite apart from their outstanding natural beauty, one of the most striking features of the islands of the Pacific Ocean is that far from being scattered in a random pattern the majority are arranged in long, straight or gently curving chains. All true oceanic islands, as distinct from fragments, like New Zealand, that have broken away from continental masses, are volcanic in origin and those of the Pacific are of two distinct types. Most of the curved archipelagoes of the western margin, including the Kurils, Bonins and Marianas, have been built up by explosive eruptions of andesitic lava on the landward side of a deep oceanic trench—above the slab of oceanic crust that descends into the subduction zone. The volcanoes of the straight central Pacific chains have a very different, basaltic, composition and erupt much less violently. Their existence is less easily explained by the theory of plate tectonics, since they have evidently been built by fracturing and eruption deep within a supposedly rigid plate rather than at an active plate boundary.

A clue to the origin of the central Pacific islands lies in the fact that they become progressively older along the chain—a point recognized by James Dana, a geologist working with the United States Exploring Expedition, which visited the Hawaiian islands in 1840. His evidence was the increasing degree of erosion seen on the islands as the expedition traveled northwest along the chain from the fresh, active volcanoes of Mauna Loa and Kilauea on Hawaii. The age progression

has more recently been confirmed and quantified by isotope dating of rock samples; in the Hawaiian chain, the measured ages increase regularly to the northwest. The reason for the age spread is that the islands are formed by intermittent eruption from a lava source in the deep mantle. During the periods between island-building eruptions, the overlying lithospheric plate drifts with respect to the deep mantle so that a single point source—or hot-spot—eventually creates a chain of islands. The age of the Hawaiian islands increases from essentially zero at the still-active Kilauea to about five million years at Kauai, indicating that during their formation the Pacific plate drifted to the northwest at a rate of about three and a half inches a year.

Beyond the oldest volcanic island the chain may be prolonged by a line of submerged seamounts—the remains of still older islands that have sunk beneath the waves as a result of erosion, regional subsidence of the plate or local subsidence of the plate under the weight of the volcanic edifice itself. The straight line of the Hawaiian chain undergoes a major change of direction about 2175 miles northwest of Kilauea, where the volcanoes are about 40 million years old. The older seamounts beyond the bend, the Emperor Seamounts, are aligned roughly north–south, indicating an earlier direction of motion of the Pacific plate. Because most of the Pacific islands are built on the same plate, chains of similar age are generally parallel: young chains such as the Society Islands and the Australs trend north-

west–southeast like the Hawaiian islands, while older chains, including the Marshall Islands and Gilbert-Ellice Islands, trend north–south like the Emperors.

Once an extinct volcano has subsided below sea level an island may persist for some time due to the growth of coral reefs. The reef-building coral polyps require sunlight in order to survive and are therefore restricted to the shallow waters fringing the shore. As the islands subside, the corals build upward toward the light, constantly adding new growth over the dead remains of old coral. As the island is eroded, the reefs become barrier reefs and later, with the eventual disappearance of the island, parts of an annular atoll, which may have several thousand feet of coral limestone overlying the original volcanic basement. Charles Darwin, who first deduced the origins of reefs during his circumnavigation in H.M.S. *Beagle*, described the atolls as "shining white gravestones marking the sites of dead, sunken volcanoes."

As well as growing around oceanic islands, coral reefs develop along some continental shores, though their remarkable sensitivity to turbid waters, temperature variations and pollutants prevents their growth near the mouths of major rivers. The largest of such reefs is the Great Barrier Reef, which runs for more than 1250 miles along the down-faulted coast of northeastern Australia. The reefs of Australia, Southeast Asia and the Red Sea are among the most impressive and vulnerable of all marine habitats.

Fringing reef

Barrier reef

Coral atoll

Seamount

The evolution of an atoll begins as soon as the volcano is extinct and corals are able to colonize the shore and build fringing reefs. As the island subsides, the corals grow upward, becoming barrier reefs enclosing a shallow lagoon. The island eventually disappears leaving a ring of low coral islands, but if subsidence outpaces coral growth, the reefs die leaving a seamount.

Cape York

Cape Melville

Queensland

The Great Barrier Reef of northeastern Australia is not a simple continuous structure but a complex of several different reef types. The outermost elements are ribbon reefs, several miles long but seldom more than 1000 feet wide. In the protected waters within these reefs lie irregular patch reefs, ring-shaped atoll-like reefs, and small islands of coral sands and boulders.

Coral pinnacles
Lagoon · · Boulders

Reef crest

Outer reef
Ocean

1000ft

50

Less than
40 m.y.old
■ Islands
● Seamounts

More than
40 m.y.old
■ Islands
● Seamounts

Parallel chains of volcanic islands, and their extensions in the form of chains of submerged seamounts, are a distinctive feature of the Pacific. Young chains trend northwest–southeast while the older chains trend more nearly north–south. The change in orientation about 40 million years ago indicates a former direction of movement of the Pacific plate. The chains are formed, *right*, as the lithospheric plate drifts over a "hot-spot"—a point source of igneous activity in the mantle. The photograph, *top right*, shows the ropy surface appearance of the dark basaltic pahoehoe lava typical of the Hawaiian type of volcanic eruption.

THE SOCIETY ISLAND CHAIN

Atolls de l'Ouest

Seamount

Maupiti
"Almost-atoll"

Bora-Bora
"Almost-atoll"
4.0 m.y. old

Raiatea
Barrier reef
2.8 m.y. old

Huahine
Barrier reef

Moorea
Fringing reef
2.0 to 2.6 m.y. old

Tahiti
Fringing/barrier reefs
0.2 to 1.4 m.y. old

Meheita
No reef
Less than 0.5 m.y. old

Km 0   150
Mi 0   100

N

The Society Islands, *right,* provide a classic example of the increasing age of the islands in a volcanic chain. These islands show a progression from the youngest, Meheita, which has not yet developed a fringing reef, through large islands like Huahine with mature barrier reefs, "almost-atolls" like Bora-Bora, where a remnant volcano is surrounded by a barrier reef and small coral islands, to true atolls, lacking even a remnant island, in the northwest.

The island of Moorea, *above,* in the Society Island chain, is a relatively young volcanic island formed by eruption of basaltic lavas between 2.0 and 2.6 million years ago. The island has a well-developed fringing reef enclosing a narrow lagoon. Despite its youth, the island already shows signs of extensive erosion where torrential tropical rains have cut deep valleys into the weak flanks of the original volcanic cone.

Erosion has stripped away the soft rocks on the flanks of the original volcanic cone of Bora-Bora, leaving the more resistant rock of the central vent standing out as an isolated peak.

The island of Tetiaroa, lying some miles east of the main Society Island chain, has been reduced to an atoll—its roughly circular reef capped by arcuate and irregular coral islands.

161

PACIFIC OCEAN : CIRCULATION

The **mountainous peaks** of Guadalupe Island off Baja California rise 5000 feet above sea level, projecting through a typical layer of low-lying stratocumulus cloud and disturbing the southerly airflow to create a perfect series of eddies downstream of the island.

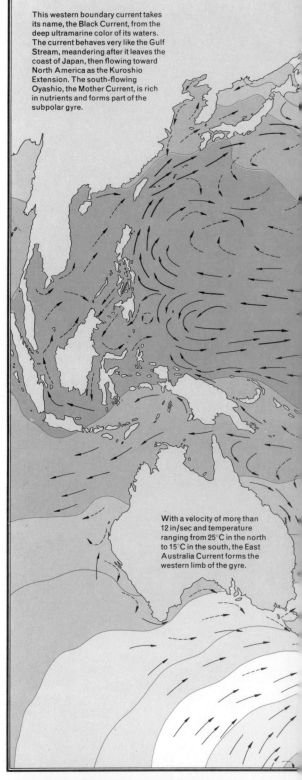

This western boundary current takes its name, the Black Current, from the deep ultramarine color of its waters. The current behaves very like the Gulf Stream, meandering after it leaves the coast of Japan, then flowing toward North America as the Kuroshio Extension. The south-flowing Oyashio, the Mother Current, is rich in nutrients and forms part of the subpolar gyre.

With a velocity of more than 12 in/sec and temperature ranging from 25°C in the north to 15°C in the south, the East Australia Current forms the western limb of the gyre.

The Pacific Ocean and its marginal seas comprise the world's largest body of water, covering roughly one-third of the surface area of the globe and exceeding in area the total land area of the planet. In area the Pacific Ocean is twice the size of the Atlantic, and because of its greater average depth contains more than twice the volume of water.

The overall pattern of circulation within this huge watermass is similar to that in the Atlantic, but the two main gyres are separated by a more complex system of equatorial currents and countercurrents. In the Northern Hemisphere, the warm North Equatorial Current carries water in an unbroken 9000-mile sweep across the full width of the ocean, representing the largest west-flowing current anywhere in the world's oceans. At its western extremity the flow turns north and is intensified into a narrow western boundary current called the Kuroshio, which flows northward at speeds of more than 93 miles a day. In the latitude of the islands of Japan, the Kuroshio meets the cold, south-flowing Oyashio Current and the two currents are deflected away from the coast to meander eastward across the North Pacific as the Kuroshio Extension. The northern gyre is completed in the east by a broad southward flow, the eastern margin of which forms the California Current.

North of the warm gyre lies a cold subpolar gyre formed in the east by the Alaska and Aleutian currents and completed in the west by the Oyashio Current. Because the cold waters are less subject to stratification than the waters of the warm gyres, their currents persist to great depths.

South of the equator, a second major gyre is made up of the South Equatorial Current, the East Australia Current, the Antarctic Circumpolar Current and the Humboldt Current. The latter is narrower and stronger than might be expected because of the influence of westerly winds deflected to the north by the Andes. On the opposite side of the ocean, the East Australia Current originates just south of the Coral Sea, and on reaching the latitude of Sydney turns eastward in a series of meanders to flow around the North Island of New Zealand. The Antarctic Circumpolar Current, driven by the westerly winds, generally has a surface speed of only 12 miles a day, but because it reaches down to depths of more than two miles, the total volume of water carried—more than 165 million tons per second—is greater than that transported by any other current in the world.

Over most of the ocean, pressure differences within the watermass are balanced by the Coriolis force due to the currents. At the equator the Coriolis force vanishes and this allows water from the North and South Equatorial currents to flow back to the east without traveling right around the gyre. The main resultant current is the Equatorial Undercurrent which flows eastward below the surface at up to 93 miles a day. The core of the current lies at about 660 feet in the west, rising to 160 feet beneath the surface in the east. On the surface, immediately above this undercurrent, local winds keep the Equatorial Current flowing in a westerly direction.

Most of the world ocean is like a terrestrial wasteland —a sterile expanse wherein little life can exist. The upper three hundred feet receives plenty of sunlight but often there are no nutrients present; 300 feet farther down there may be an ample supply of nutrients but a virtual absence of light. Hence, mixing of oceanic waters is of fundamental importance to marine life, particularly in areas where cold, nutrient-rich waters are brought up into the lighted zone. On continental shelves, tidal currents mix the waters from top to bottom and help to make the inshore zone biologically productive. In the deep ocean, sporadic upwelling occurs where the western boundary currents and mesoscale eddies hit the edge of the continental shelf. Vertical mixing of waters also occurs along the fronts separating watermasses of different properties. One such front occurs along the Antarctic Circumpolar Current and plays an important role in the productivity of the Southern Ocean.

The most dramatic of all upwellings occur on the eastern sides of the major oceans, where prevailing winds blow toward the equator. This occurs off Peru, California, South West Africa and North West Africa. Here, the force of the wind blowing toward the equator is balanced by an Ekman transportation of water away from the coast. This seaward movement of surface water is compensated by water welling up from about 500 feet, and as the colder, nutrient-rich waters are mixed into the surface layer, the productivity of the ocean is dramatically increased. In 1974, four million tons of anchovies were removed from the coastal waters of Peru; this represents one-seventh of the annual world catch of fish removed from only 0.02 percent of the ocean surface. Catastrophically, every few years, the undercurrent at the equator floods the coast region with a 500-foot-thick layer of warm unproductive water, which completely blocks the upwellings with disastrous effects on fisheries.

The **potential value of satellite photography** in ocean research is illustrated by this Gemini X photograph of the island of Taiwan in the West Pacific. The main current system in the area—the north-flowing western boundary current of the North Pacific Gyre—is parted by the southern tip of the island and the refraction of the incoming swell waves is clearly visible along the west coast of the island. Farther north, the two branches of the main flow are deflected away from the coast and this seaward transportation of surface water is compensated by the upwelling of deeper, colder water, which appears as the areas of darker blue in the photograph.

Temperature and salinity in the upper layers of the current are reduced by precipitation, though the main source of water is from the relatively warm Kuroshio Extension.

The poorly defined 600-mile-wide California Current forms the eastern limb of the North Pacific Gyre. Up to 100 miles from the coast, its waters flow northeast in winter and southeast in summer; farther from the coast the current always flows to the south.

8°C
12°C
16°C
20°C
24°C
28°C
28°C
28°C
24°C
20°C
16°C
12°C
8°C
4°C
0°C

Limit of sea ice

16°C
20°C
24°C
28°C

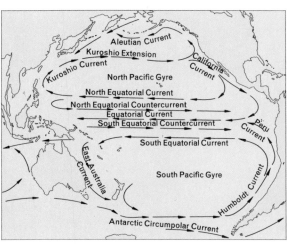

Aleutian Current
Kuroshio Extension
Kuroshio Current
California Current
North Pacific Gyre
North Equatorial Current
North Equatorial Countercurrent
Equatorial Current
South Equatorial Countercurrent
Peru Current
South Equatorial Current
East Australia Current
South Pacific Gyre
Humboldt Current
Antarctic Circumpolar Current

The current pattern in the equatorial region of the Pacific Ocean is rather more complex than that of the Atlantic Ocean, although to north and south similar enclosed circulatory gyres are formed. Recent research designates three west-flowing equatorial currents separated by two east-flowing equatorial countercurrents.

Water profiles of the Pacific Ocean

1 Kuroshio Current

2 Peruvian Upwelling

3 California Current

4 North New Zealand

Equatorial Undercurrent

24°C
22°C
22°C
Guayaquil
Peru Coastal Current
20°C
Callao
Peru Oceanic Current
18°C
Peru Current

Westerly flow   Easterly flow
50 30 10 0 10 30 50
Current flow in cm/sec

The Peru Coastal Current, cold and rich in nutrients due to local upwellings (see profile 4), is separated from the Oceanic Current by a tongue of warm, nutrient-poor water. Periodically, this tongue is boosted by the Equatorial Undercurrent, overriding the upwellings and destroying local fisheries.

The Equatorial Undercurrent in the Pacific Ocean lies directly below the west-flowing surface current, between 5°N and 5°S of the equator. It consists of a number of cells; the west-flowing outer units enclosing an east-flowing inner core, which rises from a depth of 660 ft in the west to 160 ft in the east.

PACIFIC:MINERAL RESOURCES

The main mineral resources of the Pacific Ocean, apart from manganese nodules, are placer deposits derived from the new mountain ranges round about.

Offshore placer deposits
Solid symbol—active mine
Open symbol—known deposit

Iron

Iron

Titanium

Titanium

Tin

Tin

Gold

Monazite

Monazite

Chromite

Zircon

Zircon

Metal-bearing muds

Sand and gravel

Shell sands

Phosphorite

Manganese nodules

Major sedimentary basins

Oil and gas fields

On 13 March, 1874, just south of Australia, the crew of H.M.S. *Challenger* hauled in from a depth of 15,600 feet a trawl containing many manganese nodules. This was the first of several such nodule recoveries recorded as the vessel transected the Pacific Ocean Basin in the first systematic sampling of sediment from the deep-sea floor. Analysis of the samples, reported in 1891 by John Gibson as an appendix to the famous *Report on the Deep-Sea Deposits* by Murray and Renard, showed the Pacific Ocean nodules to contain significant amounts of minor metals, particularly nickel, copper and cobalt, leading to the conclusion that the minerals had been formed in the sea.

It was more than 50 years later that systematic seafloor sampling demonstrated that manganese nodules were abundant throughout the deep regions of the Pacific. In the late 1950s the potential of these deposits as a source of nickel, copper and cobalt ore was finally appreciated. Between 1958 and 1968 numerous companies began serious exploration of the nodule fields to estimate their economic potential. By 1974, 100 years after the first samples were taken, it was well established that a broad belt of the seafloor between Mexico and Hawaii and a few degrees north of the equator was literally paved with nodules over an area of more than 1.35 million square miles.

Deep-sea mining will cause some disturbance to the marine environment, notably due to the stirring of fine-grained sediment particles into the water column, but the United States government has conducted a detailed study of possible effects and has found no significant problems related to open-ocean mining. Some scientists have even suggested that bringing nutrient-rich bottom water to the sea surface along with the nodules could promote increased biological growth in the vicinity of the mine site.

The periphery of the Pacific Ocean Basin abounds with mineral resources other than manganese nodules. Phosphate rock occurs in extensive areas along the western coasts of both North and South America. Some deposits are related to well-known coastal upwellings of nutrient-rich water and the resultant high biological productivity at the sea surface. Submarine plateau regions near New Zealand and Australia are blanketed with a crust of phosphate rock that was deposited many million years ago. The marine phosphate deposits are generally of poorer grade than many land deposits, so there has been little interest in exploiting them. However, consumption of land supplies, and the ever-increasing demand to improve agricultural yields, will undoubtedly force development of near-shore phosphate mining by the end of this century.

Near-shore geologic processes have concentrated many metals in placer deposits along the continental shelves around the Pacific. Gold has been mined for

Glomar Challenger, the 10,500-ton research ship of the Deep Sea Drilling Project, went into operation in 1968 and has drilled in more than 400 localities in water depths of up to four miles all round the world. Its deepest hole so far is 4265 feet. A reentry funnel located by sonar scanners and a system of directional propellors that keeps the ship on station enable the drill bit to reenter a previously drilled hole and obtain cores at great depths.

years off the beaches of Alaska; platinum is known to be present in the same general area, and substantial tin deposits exist in Indonesian waters. Mineral sands containing titanium, chromium and zirconium are present along the North American continent; iron ore is found throughout the western Pacific, generally associated with volcanic processes, and the Japanese have been mining offshore iron for many years.

Recent exploration has revealed metal-rich muds on the East Pacific Rise. The most studied of these deposits is just south of the Galapagos Islands. While no exploitation of these muds is presently contemplated, they do constitute a potentially important resource of the future.

Near-shore recovery of sand and gravel for the construction industry may prove to have a more direct impact on a greater number of people than any other marine mining operation, excluding perhaps the recovery of petroleum. Sand and gravel deposits, though often small in overall size, exist to some degree on nearly all continental shelves throughout the Pacific.

PACIFIC: LIVING RESOURCES

Since the earliest times, fishing has played a major role in providing food for the inhabitants of the continents bordering the Pacific Ocean, and the islands scattered throughout it. Fishing was important to the coastal Indians, Aleuts and Eskimo groups occupying Alaska and Siberia; to the peoples of Japan and the Philippines, and to the natives inhabiting the vast array of islands scattered throughout the South Pacific. The antecedent of many fisheries in the Pacific can be traced back several centuries and the roots of some fisheries predate current fisheries by well over 1000 years. Modern ocean fishing in the Pacific nevertheless largely followed technological innovations that occurred during the first half of the twentieth century. Chief among these manifestations were the development of the internal combustion engine, electronic navigation and detection devices, synthetic net fibers and modern food-processing technology.

The greatest portion of the harvest taken from the Pacific Ocean occurs within close proximity to land, usually within 150 miles, the exception being tuna fishing, which is conducted over vast reaches of the tropical, subtropical and temperate zones. The most important fisheries in the Pacific are concentrated in the productive shallow seas of the North Pacific or in areas where nutrient-rich upwelling occurs. Large-scale fisheries for bottom species (cod, flounder, rockfish, sea bass, croaker and snapper) occur on the continental shelf and upper slope areas between 1300 and 2600 feet deep in the eastern Bering, Okhotsk, Japan, Yellow and South China seas. Fisheries for herringlike species—sardines and anchovies—are

located off Peru, California and the northern coasts of Japan and Korea.

Although more than 1000 species are probably being taken by fishermen throughout the Pacific, less than 30 make up the bulk of the harvest. Chief among these are the Peruvian anchovy and the Alaskan pollock. The Peruvian anchovy fishery, which takes place off the coast of southern Peru and northern Chile, began to rise in a dramatic way in the 1960s and by the end of the decade had grown to be the largest single-species fishery in the world, making up almost 30 percent of the harvest by weight of fish from the Pacific and one-sixth of the total world catch of marine fishes between 1969 and 1971. The catch of Peruvian anchovy, which exceeded ten million tons in its peak years, is utilized almost entirely for manufacturing fishmeal—an essential protein additive in poultry and livestock feed. Unlike many fisheries conducted in the North Atlantic and North Pacific oceans, the harvest is almost all taken by small purse seine vessels less than 120 feet in length.

The Alaskan pollock is fished throughout most of the subarctic Pacific region, particularly in the Sea of Okhotsk off Kamchatka; in the Bering Sea and in the Gulf of Alaska. Catches of Alaskan pollock since 1970 have exceeded four million tons and, subsequent to the collapse of the Peruvian anchovy fishery in the early 1970s, have become the most important species from a weight standpoint harvested from the world's ocean. This ubiquitous species, along with other bottom fish—flounder, cod and rockfish—has been for the most part caught by trawl vessels operating out of northern Japan and Siberia. The fishing is carried out

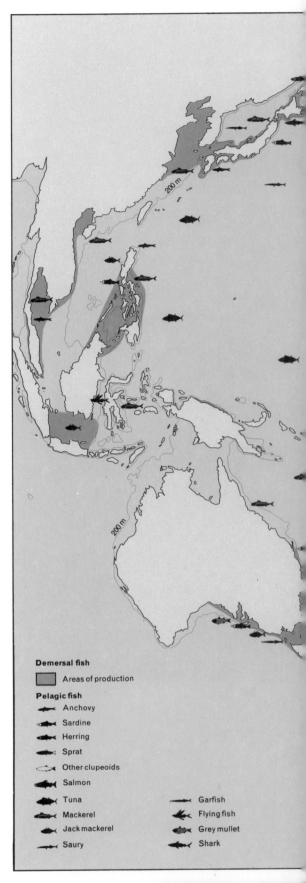

Demersal fish

▨ Areas of production

Pelagic fish

- Anchovy
- Sardine
- Herring
- Sprat
- Other clupeoids
- Salmon
- Tuna — Garfish
- Mackerel — Flying fish
- Jack mackerel — Grey mullet
- Saury — Shark

Bigeye

Albacore

Yellowfin

Tuna are large, fast-swimming fish closely related to the much smaller mackerel and found widely distributed throughout the tropical and subtropical waters of the world's three great oceans. They are sleek, far-ranging carnivores with voracious appetites. The most important members of the genus *Thunnus* caught in the Pacific are the yellowfin, albacore and bigeye. All three are closely related to the great bluefin tuna, which although found in the Pacific is mainly caught in the Atlantic. The albacore is highly prized for its

Although the Pacific Ocean is more than twice as large as the Atlantic, its continental shelf, which is the most productive fishing area, is only slightly greater than that of the Atlantic. The total catches of both oceans are therefore broadly similar.

Pacific total catch 25.604 thousand metric tons	
Diadromous fish	522
Crustaceans	907
Mollusks	1777
Marine fish	22,398

World total catch 59,321 thousand metric tons	%
Others	8.1
Mediterranean	2.3
Caribbean	2.5
Indian	5.2
Atlantic	38.7
Pacific	43.2

white meat and is easily distinguished from the others by its much longer pectoral fin. At one time tuna were caught, particularly by the United States, in the eastern tropical Pacific, using the pole and line technique whereby the tuna were attracted to the side of a boat by live baiting the water and then hauled out on the end of a line. Most tuna are now commercially caught by using either longlines or purse seines operated from fast long-range vessels and capable of working throughout the tropical waters of the world.

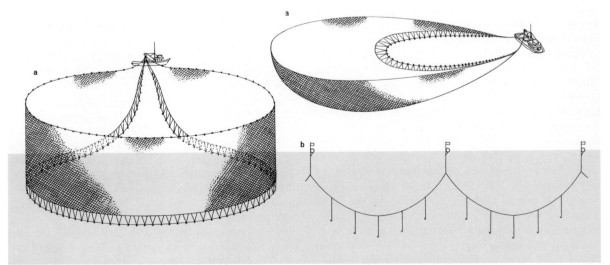

The purse seine (a) is probably the most important gear used for catching pelagic fish. It is essentially a wall of netting weighted at the bottom and buoyed up at the top which is set around the fish shoal. Especially fast-sinking nets have been developed for tuna to stop them from escaping underneath. When the shoal is surrounded,

the bottom of the net is drawn in until the net is completely pursed up and the catch may be hauled on board. These nets may be operated from either one or two boats. Longlines (b) are used principally for tuna. They may be a quarter of a mile long and have several hundred baited hooks suspended from them.

The shark occupies an ambivalent position in the pattern of world fishing. To some fishermen he is the basis of a livelihood while to others he is a competitor in the exploitation of the oceans' resources and a cause of damage to netting and other gear. In some parts of the world, shark meat is considered to be a delicacy and fetches a relatively high price, while in other parts it is sold in a dried state as a cheap form of protein. The processing of shark meat is a skillful operation; because of the quantities of urea present in the meat, the slightest deterioration in its condition results in the production of ammonia, which ruins the final product. Shark fishing is an important part of the Australian fishing industry, particularly in the state of Victoria, where the important varieties caught are the school shark and the gummy shark.

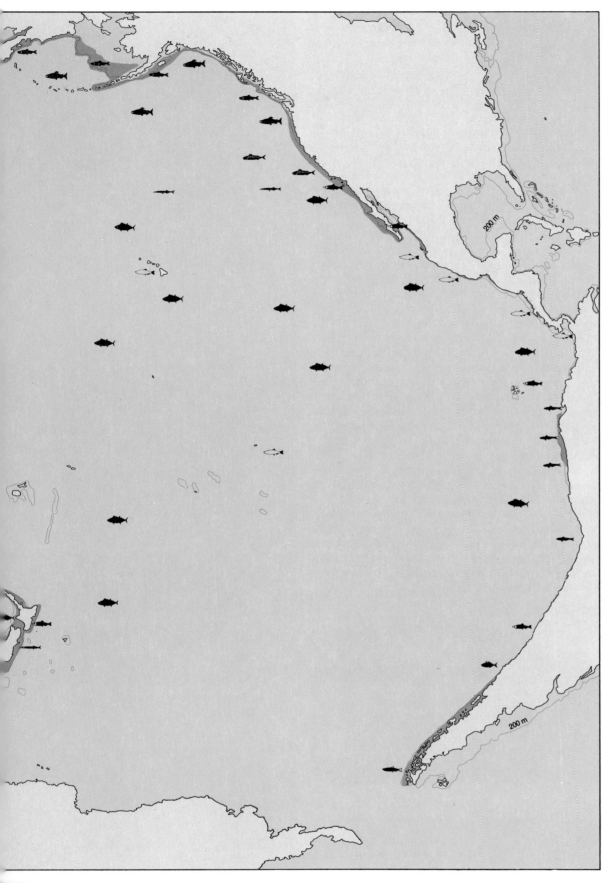

by catcher vessels up to 165 feet in length working with motherships, which process the catch on board, or by self-contained factory trawlers 200 to 300 feet in length equipped to both catch and process the harvest.

Species groups that are sought after because of their high market value include tuna and salmon. Tuna fisheries in the Pacific are largely carried out by vessels deploying floating line gear or large purse seine nets. Line operations are prevalent in the central and western Pacific, while purse seiner operations dominate the fisheries in the eastern tropical Pacific area. The salmon fisheries are generally carried out in close proximity to major rivers or streams using gill nets, purse seines or a variety of traps and weirs. Some high-seas fishing for Pacific salmon, however, is carried out in the western Pacific by Japanese fishermen.

The most important harvest of invertebrates includes fisheries for prawns, crabs, lobsters and squid. Prawn fisheries are particularly important in the Yellow and South China seas, off northern Australia, and in the Gulf of Alaska. Almost all shrimp are harvested by small vessels using otter trawl gear. Although crabs are taken widely over the Pacific, the most notable and exotic fishing is that done for king crab, a species which grows to a size exceeding three feet. The Alaskan king crab fishery occurs in the Gulf of Alaska along the Aleutian Islands and in the eastern Bering and Okhotsk seas off Kamchatka. The crabs are harvested either with pots or with tangle net gear. Lobsters, which are taken by pots deployed from small boats, are harvested over a broad area of the tropical Pacific, and squid, which are abundant in many areas of the Pacific, are fished extensively off northern Japan by vessels which fish at night and concentrate their quarry at the surface using banks of lights.

The annual catch of fish and shellfish from the Pacific has, over the last decade, exceeded that taken from any other world ocean. The largest production occurred in the 1970s when more than 32 million tons were harvested, but the catch of fish from the Pacific declined rather sharply after 1970, primarily as a result of the collapse of the Peruvian anchovy fishery. Regardless, annual catches from the Pacific over the past decade have constituted almost half the world catch of marine fish.

Fishing tactics related to fish behavior

Much of the fishing activity practiced throughout the world is highly dependent on the natural behavior patterns of the species sought. The vast majority of fish, some 90 percent, are taken in close proximity to land, where environmental factors are conducive to high concentrations of food and hence to large aggregations of fish. Many species have evolved behavioral patterns that ensure successful reproduction and protection from predators and knowledge of these patterns has greatly benefited inshore fishermen.

A classic example is the migratory and homing behavior of the Pacific salmon. The species spawns in the freshwater streams and lakes bordering the North Pacific; the young migrate to sea and the adults forage over vast areas of the temperate North Pacific. As the fish approach maturity, they return to their original streams and lakes—and into the traps and nets of the waiting fishermen.

This same technique has also been applied successfully to many strictly marine species. For example, many species of Pacific bottom fish migrate to deeper water during the winter months and subsequently to shallower waters in the spring and summer. Through experience, fishermen have come to understand these vertical migrations and use the knowledge to improve the efficiency of their methods.

Although the majority of fish are taken by conventional methods, a number of techniques have been developed to capitalize on specific responses to stimuli. Japanese fishermen exploit squid and saury using banks of lights. Lights are shown at one side of the ship until a sufficient number of fish congregate, then those lights are extinguished and those on the other side are switched on. The fish swim quickly beneath the ship and are scooped from the water with dip nets.

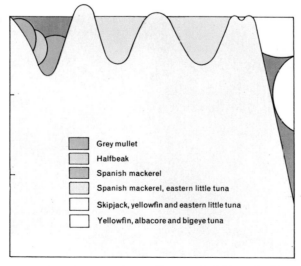

- Grey mullet
- Halfbeak
- Spanish mackerel
- Spanish mackerel, eastern little tuna
- Skipjack, yellowfin and eastern little tuna
- Yellowfin, albacore and bigeye tuna

Although the Great Barrier Reef is extremely rich in marine life it is of little value to the Australian fishing industry, as its highly irregular nature interferes with exploitation. However, Spanish mackerel, halfbeak and grey mullet are caught within the reef itself and tuna from the adjoining sea.

SOUTHERN OCEAN: BATHYMETRY AND CIRCULA

The Antarctic Ocean may be taken to include all oceanic areas lying south of the Antarctic Convergence, usually at about latitude 55° South.
Area 13,513,000 square miles; 35,000,000 square kilometers.
Sea ice 8,100,000 square miles, 21,000,000 square kilometers, freeze in winter: 1,540,000 square miles, 4,000,000 square kilometers, permanently frozen.

The continental shelf of Antarctica is narrower than that of most continents and generally much deeper, lying at between 1200 and 1600 feet deep compared with 600 feet around the coast of northwest Europe. Also there is generally a deep depression between the outer edge of the shelf and the final slope up to the land; the depressions are aligned parallel to the coast and may have been caused by fracturing of the crust due to downwarping under the tremendous load of ice on the continent. Other researchers have suggested that the outer lip itself may be a former moraine—bulldozed away from the continent by ice sheets of an earlier period.

Beyond the continental slope lie oceanic basins 13,000 to 16,500 feet deep bounded to the north by the midocean ridge system and subdivided into Atlantic, Indian and Pacific basins by submarine ridges between the Antarctic continent and America, Kerguelan and Tasmania. Further deep ocean basins exist north of the midocean ridge with deep channels leading into the West Atlantic and East Indian oceans.

As in all oceans the surface currents are determined primarily by the winds, but with northerly and southerly movements, due to oceanwide differences in density between warm and cold regions, or between regions of high evaporation and high rainfall, superimposed on the wind pattern. Between 40° and 50° South strong westerly winds are associated with a constant procession of atmospheric depressions moving from west to east around the circumpolar ocean. South of 50°S the winds become more variable and south of 60°S easterly winds predominate. North of 60°S the current flow at all depths is to the east; south of 60°S it is to the west, but superimposed on these currents there is a northward spreading of cold waters in the surface and bottom layers, compensated by a southward flow of warmer intermediate water, which maintains the balance.

In the northern half of the circumpolar ocean the southward movement of water is generally below 6000 feet, but on the threshold of the Antarctic zone it rises sharply to within a few hundred feet of the surface, overlying a column of cold water some 6500

to 10,000 feet deep. The sharp transition zone is called the Polar Front and determines the latitude at which Antarctic surface water sinks below warmer subantarctic water. The surface zone, or Antarctic Convergence, is marked by a sudden rise in surface temperature of two to three degrees centigrade and by the associated plankton species. Its dependence on some form of balance between deep and bottom currents fixes its position within narrow limits. Relatively small variations occur—probably in association with traveling eddies and meanders caused by passing atmospheric disturbances. North of the convergence there is a region of well-mixed water in which sinking Antarctic waters mix with warmer water intruding as a subsurface flow.

Some 10° farther north there exists another convergence between subantarctic and subtropical watermasses. Though seldom apparent as a sharp current boundary, it is generally sharply defined at the surface and represents the transition zone between waters of southern origin and warmer, more saline waters characteristic of lower latitudes.

The area of the Antarctic Ocean is approximately 13.5 million square miles. More than half—roughly 8 million square miles—freezes over each winter and some 1.5 million square miles remain unmelted at the end of the summer. Such large variations in ice cover must have a profound effect on the transfer of heat and moisture to the atmosphere, and therefore on winds, precipitation and climatic regimes. These complex interactions are however not yet known in detail. There is ample evidence of regional and general variations in ice cover from year to year, and some indication of apparent shifts in the extent of ice cover from one side of the continent to the other. The ice island technique of studying sea-ice conditions, used very successfully in the Arctic, is too hazardous in the remote Antarctic, where ice movements are more violent and unpredictable and where drifting manned stations would be insupportable for much of the year.

The Antarctic Circumpolar
Current completely dominates the surface water movement of the Southern Ocean as seen in the sectional view above taken along a line 10°E–170°W. Sinking of deep water beneath the sea-ice zone, and intrusion at mid-depth of Intermediate Water, are also clearly identified.

Antarctic volcanic activity has in recent years centered mainly on Deception Island in the South Shetland Islands. The island erupted in 1967 and 1969 throwing pyroclastic material and vapor high into the air, *left*, and covering the island with a layer of black ash. The locator map, *above*, shows the position of Deception Island off the Antarctic Peninsula.

OCEAN

SOUTH
AMERICA

Argentine Abyssal Plain

Rio Grande
Plateau

SOUTHEAST PACIFIC BASIN

Cape
Horn

Falkland Is.

Argentine
Rise

Falkland Plateau

Scotia Arc

Drake Passage

South
Shetlands Is.

West Scotia
Basin

ATLANTIC OCEAN

Bellingshausen

Peter I
Island

Adelaide I.

Sea

South
Georgia

Amundsen

Antarctic Peninsula

South
Orkney Is.

East
Scotia
Basin

Sea

Tristan da
Cunha

WEDDELL

South
Sandwich Is.

Gough Is.

SEA

South Sandwich Trench

ROSS

+ South Pole

SEA

ANTARCTICA

Maud
Rise

MID ATLANTIC RIDGE

Bouvet I.

ATLANTIC-INDIAN BASIN

SOUTHWEST INDIAN RIDGE

Agulhas
Plateau

AFRICA

Antarctic   Circle

SOUTH

Lena
Guyot

Crozet Plateau

Mozambique Ridge

INDIAN BASIN

Kerguelen Plateau

Crozet Is.

Heard I.

Madagascar
Plateau

AN RIDGE

Kerguelen

Crozet
Basin

INDIAN   OCEAN

SOUTHERN OCEAN : LIVING AND MINERAL RES

The rocks of Antarctica and its continental shelves were formed by the same geologic processes that shaped the neighboring continents. Iron and coal deposits have been found in its mountain ranges and the deep-drilling ship *Glomar Challenger* found evidence of natural gas beneath the sediments of the Ross Sea. By analogy with neighboring continents the continental rocks should contain nickel, copper, cobalt, chromium and other related minerals, but the enormous difficulties inherent in the extraction and transportation of minerals from the interior of the Antarctic place these deposits beyond current economic exploitation.

A general impression of the universal richness of the seas around Antarctica, based on dense catches of plankton and animal life, is being replaced by a more critical view. Although in the Antarctic spring and summer there is enormous productivity near land and near melting ice, in the open ocean, where the water is more exposed and subject to mixing by wind and waves, catches are less abundant. There is growing evidence that the richness near land and melting ice may be due to reduction in salinity and density of the surface waters, which lessens the chance of phytoplankton being carried down to depths below that at which there is sufficient light for photosynthesis.

The first whales to be hunted commercially were the northern right whales—so called because they could be taken with the primitive gear of the early whalers, and were the most profitable source of whalebone and oil. They, and the southern right whales, were reduced to unprofitable numbers by the middle of the nineteenth century. The large sperm whale industry declined at the same time, partly due to the introduction of mineral oil. The large blue and fin whales were too fast to be taken before the development of steam whalers and harpoon guns with explosive-tipped harpoons. Such whaling did not start in the Antarctic until 1904, when the first whaling station was set up in South Georgia. Factory ships moored near land, in sufficient shelter to allow whales to be flensed alongside, came into use soon after, and the early 1930s saw the introduction of floating factory ships capable of processing the whales on board without the need of a land-based factory.

In the 1930–1 season, nearly 43,000 whales were killed and although an International Whaling Commission exerted a measure of control, decline was inevitable. The present whale population is probably one-sixth to one-tenth of its pre-whaling numbers. Whaling is still practiced by the Soviet Union and Japan, but right, humpback and blue whales are now totally protected. Humpback whales were the most vulnerable species since they frequent coastal waters and, migrating north to breed and south to feed, they were taken by stations in South America, South Africa, Australia and New Zealand as well as Antarctica. Most of these stations are now inactive.

The Antarctic fur seal was practically exterminated in the 1820s after catches of several hundred thousand had been taken. They recovered to some extent; were again overexploited in the 1870s, and are only now recovering again. Elephant seal, which haul out onto land to breed, were exploited for their oil, but this industry has now ceased due to the cost of labor and transport, availability of alternative oils and through pressure of public opinion.

Too little is known about the fish and squid of Antarctic waters to assess whether they might be fished commercially. The most likely resource since the decline of whaling is krill—a Norwegian collective name for the small crustacea on which the baleen whales feed, and now almost synonymous with *Euphausia superba*, a small shrimplike crustacean between 1.9 and 2.4 inches long when adult. Five countries have recently sent pilot expeditions to test the practicability of its commercial exploitation and, if successful, krill harvesting could develop rapidly. Scientists are pressing for international investigations to increase our understanding of its reproduction and growth in order to assess the effect of exploitation on the Antarctic food web.

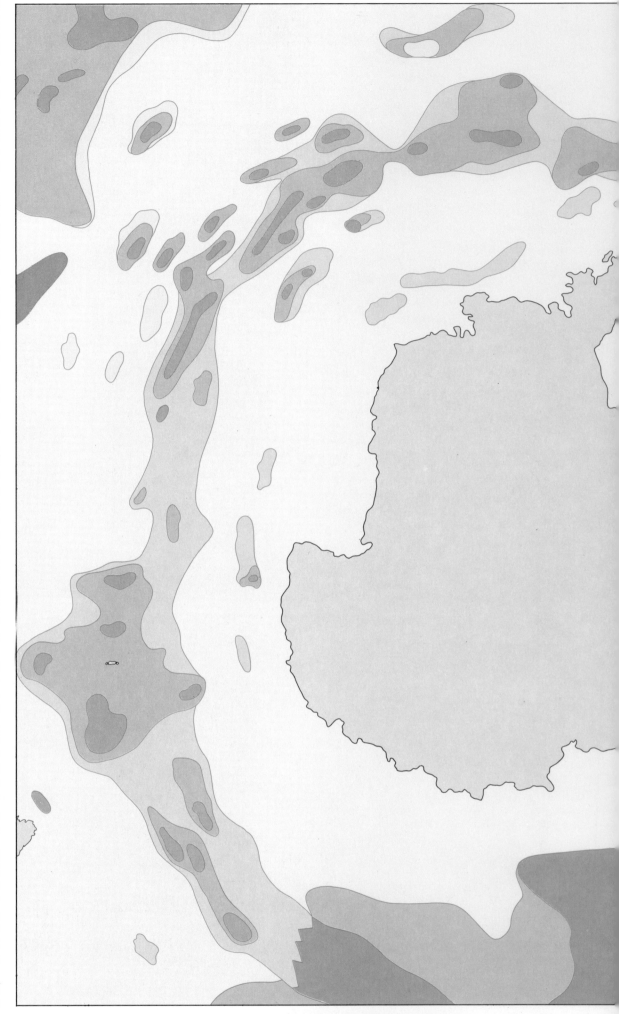

Ferromanganese deposits

Areas investigated by *Eltanin*

- Concretions and widespread mineral encrustations
- Closely spaced rounded nodules up to 10cm diameter
- Scattered nodules, pea-sized and larger; shape irregular

Areas likely to yield nodules

- High probability of nodules, concretions or encrustations
- High probability of fields of scattered nodules

The giant kelp, *Macrosystis*, reaches the surface from depths of up to 130 feet and, floating on the surface, may grow to a total length of more than 180 feet. It grows prolifically around Antarctic and subantarctic shores north of 60°S, and round the Falkland Islands. The kelp could be used as a source of alginates, used in the food industries, if the costs of collecting and processing the material in remote areas could be reduced.

Calcareous ooze consisting mainly of foraminifera.

Calcareous-siliceous ooze; both exceeding 30 percent.

Siliceous ooze; mainly diatoms, some radiolarians.

Clayey silts and silty clays; red, brown, gray and olive, often with volcanic debris. Calcareous or siliceous near oozes; sandy near land.

Shelf and coastal deposits; marine-glacial deposits around Antarctica; calcareous sands and gravels around New Zealand, Australia, Africa.

Thousands of whales

Right, bottlenose minke and others

Sperm 48ft/14.6m

Sei 50ft/15.2m

Humpback 41ft/12.5m

Fin 67ft/20.4m

Blue 79ft/24.1m

The changing composition of the Antarctic whale catch from the beginning of the century is illustrated, *left*. The humpback was the earliest prey, but from 1927–36 emphasis fell on the blue whale. In the post-war years the fin whale, and more recently the sei, sperm, *right*, bottlenose and minke have made up the bulk of the catch. In the photograph, *above*, a flenser starts work on cutting up a whale at the now-inoperative whaling station on S. Georgia.

40

30

20

10

1904–05 1909–10 1914–15 1919–20 1924–5 1929–30 1934–5 1939–40 1944–5 1949–50 1954–5 1959–60 1964–5 1969–70

ENCYCLOPEDIA OF MARINE LIFE

Zoologists and botanists considering the enormous diversity of living forms naturally first placed them in broad categories, grouping like with like. This system developed as scientific knowledge increased and is today reflected in the scientific naming of any individual animal or plant. Since Linnaeus' *Systemae Naturae*, published in 1758, introduced the binomial system of nomenclature, each animal or plant has been designated two names—the second signifying the individual species, while the first indicates the genus, or group of like species, to which the individual belongs. Thus herring and sprat both belong to the genus *Clupea*, the herring being *Clupea harengus* and the sprat *Clupea sprattus*.

Similar genera are grouped into larger divisions called families—in this case the Clupeidae—and then into orders and so on until a point is reached where larger and larger groups have been formed and a grouping is arrived at that contains all the animals having essentially the same fundamental structural plan. Of course, there will be different orders, classes and other less commonly used subdivisions within this largest grouping that will differ greatly from each other, but they will all share a fundamental similarity of basic organization. At this point, with no obvious links with other groups, the phylum level has been reached. The animals with backbones form one such phylum—the Chordates; although men and fishes are certainly superficially very dissimilar, they share a basic pattern of organization that is quite different from that shared by, say, squid and limpets, which belong to the phylum Mollusca. Ideally, at each level from genus to phylum, the groupings should be equivalent whether we are dealing with plants or animals, whales or fish.

In practice, few zoologists or botanists feel that the currently accepted schemes of classification achieve this ideal—and indeed there are good reasons why they should not. In most classifications the phylum Chordata is divided into a number of classes, among which are the Amphibia, Reptilia and Aves (the birds), but all zoologists agree that on the grounds of structural diversity the birds deserve no more than ordinal rank and should properly be placed as one order of the class Reptilia. Yet there are so many living birds, and for various reasons they have received so much scientific attention, that it is much more convenient to keep them in a class of their own. Again, botanists agree that the algae (and almost all marine plants belong to this group) are a heterogeneous assemblage grouped together for convenience as an interim measure until, hopefully, further work elucidates their relationships.

It is no wonder then that with the only fixed point in any classification being the individual species of animal or plant, different authors have different opinions about the larger groupings within the classifications they use. Therefore in different books there are sometimes different numbers of phyla, or groups considered as a family in one book but elevated to the rank of order in another.

It is important to realize that this apparent conflict simply reflects the different views currently held on the relationships between many groups; knowing this means that one should not be disturbed when classifications appear to differ in some areas. Classifications are simply systems of labelling animals or plants at the species level so that they can be clearly identified.

Even after death radiolarians are among the most breathtakingly beautiful of all marine creatures. Their delicate skeletons, formed of silica absorbed from the surrounding seawater, are remarkably strong and durable and form a supporting framework for the soft parts of the microscopic amoebalike animal. Many are globular or goblet shaped, perforated by hundreds of tiny regular apertures through which the mobile cytoplasm of the animal's body can stream in fine filaments in the endless search for food. The skeletons pictured here have been magnified more than 1400 times life-size and yet, over millions of years, the constant rain of these minute skeletons has blanketed some areas of the deep ocean floor with many hundreds of feet of fine radiolarian ooze.

GENERAL INTRODUCTION TO PLANTS

In the sea, as on land, the entire range of life is ultimately supported by the power of the sun, which is harnessed by plants and used to convert water and carbon dioxide into a carbohydrate—the fuel that drives the life processes of the cells. This reaction is known as photosynthesis. Plants absorb light energy from the sun in specialized membrane units called chloroplasts and it is here that the pigments which color plants occur. The most familiar is the green of chlorophyll, but this may be masked by additional red, yellow or brown pigments. Because all plants require sunlight to live, in the ocean they are either planktonic in the upper sunlit layers or occur attached to rocks or the seabed in the shallow areas of the coast. Although most marine plants are grouped in the superphylum Algae, this is more for convenience than as an indication of uniformity of basic structure or plan. The large littoral seaweeds are probably the most familiar algae, but the minute unicellular diatoms and flagellates that are present in such vast numbers are far more important in the productivity of the sea.

Besides the presence of an amazing variety of algae, the sea also has representatives of the flowering plants. These species appear to have adapted from terrestrial forms and have managed to cope with the problem of transferring pollen from one plant to another in the foreign medium of water. Marine fungi and bacteria do not require sunlight, but produce their energy by breaking down organic and inorganic substances.

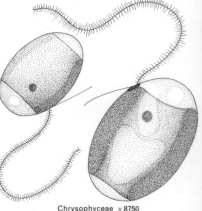

The diagram illustrates different types of seaweed. They are not drawn to scale. The seaweeds of the rocky European shores, on the left of the diagram, would not necessarily all occur in the same area. Zonation of seaweed varies with such factors as degree of exposure and boulder height. *Sargassum* is a floating seaweed and *Macrocystis* occurs off the Pacific coast.

SUPERPHYLUM ALGAE

This division is extremely broad and contains plants that range from microscopic unicellular organisms that reproduce by simple division to those that surpass even a thousand feet in length, have complex reproductive cycles and are multicellular with differentiated specialist tissues. Because of this wide variation in structure and habit a truly satisfactory way of classifying algae has not yet been established and species are still being changed from class to class as more becomes known. Recently an entire class, the blue-green algae, has been removed altogether and united with the bacteria. Seaweeds, however, are different colors and it is the pigments that they and the planktonic algae contain that are important in separating the various classes. All contain the basic green chlorophyll-a, but some contain additional yellow, brown or red auxiliary pigments, which may mask the green. Generally, there is a zonation of seaweeds on rocky coasts and the sequence of green, brown and red algae is common. This occurs because sunlight, which is essential for photosynthesis, is increasingly filtered as it travels to the seabed and, depending on how clear or murky the seawater is, darkness occurs at depths of between 50 and 65 feet. The long red rays do not penetrate as far as the short blue and green rays and, as complementary colors are absorbed and utilized, red and brown algae are more common at greater depths and in extremely clear water —some can survive at depths of up to five hundred feet. Not all algae, however, live on rocky shores, some preferring wooden piles of piers and the bottoms of ships, while others live as symbionts with other plants and animals and some are even parasitic. The free-floating planktonic forms are less obviously identifiable as plants without the aid of microscopic analysis, but they are, however, extremely important in the economy of the sea and represent the beginning of the complex food web that leads through fish and eventually to man. Direct cropping and consumption of algae is becoming economically more important, and more than 70 species are eaten by man, mostly in Japan and China. Other economic uses include the extraction of iodine, the production of soda and the manufacture of pectin for jelling agents in jams and ice creams.

Artificial fertilizers are manufactured from many algae and much research is at present being undertaken in this important economic area.

Class Phaeophyceae

These are the most abundant and conspicuous seaweeds, colored brown by fucoxanthin pigment. There is a wide range in form, from simple filamentous kinds to larger fucoids, such as *Laminaria*, and the most complex of all algae, the giant kelps of the Pacific.

The simplest are the small *Ectocarpus* and their relatives, some of which live as epiphytes attached to other algae. In some of these, for example *Cutleria*, there is a marked difference between sexual and asexual generations. The most familiar of the brown algae are the fucoids, which manage to live in the intertidal zone, coping with regular exposure to the air and partial desiccation. Most of these live for two to four years, but the slower-growing *Ascophyllum* may live for up to 19 years. Fucoids are zoned on temperate rocky shores that are partly sheltered from wave action, and clearing experiments have illustrated the delicate balance that maintains zonation and that it takes many years to reestablish. Grazing of young plants by winkles and limpets is a very important factor in limiting colonization by fucoids. Some shore fucoids, such as *Ascophyllum*, have air-filled bladders on the fronds and are related to the free-living fucoid *Sargassum*, which floats in enormous masses in the Sargasso sea.

Below the intertidal zone brown seaweeds are represented by the large kelps. These are attached to rocks by a rootlike holdfast, and have a thick stem and a large flattened frond. These are the asexual generation of these plants and alternate with a microscopic sexual stage. The largest kelps occur off the Pacific coast and are 200 feet long. They root in much deeper water than the European *Laminaria* and are of great importance in the ecology of the region, supporting a varied fauna that includes herbivorous fish. Kelps are cropped to extract alginates and when cut the giant *Macrocystis* will grow four feet a day! Because they are so large they are ideal experimental material and it has been shown that, like higher land plants, there are special cells in the stem which translocate food materials. Brown algae, however, never produce starch as an end product of photosynthesis, but mannitol, oil and laminarin— a commercially used polysaccharide. The mannitol that can be extracted from *Laminaria* accounts for up to 16 percent of the plant's weight and is a valuable addition to the sugar supplies of the world.

Class Rhodophyceae

These are the red seaweeds colored by phycocyanin and phycoerythrin pigments, and despite their name this class includes forms that are pink, red, mauve, violet and brown. Most live attached to rocks and wood or to other algae in the littoral zone and are filamentous or flattened.

There are, however, some unicellular planktonic forms, but these are poorly known. The life histories of the littoral red algae can be very complicated, and some forms are parasitic (though it is not entirely clear if they do much harm to the host algae). A number of different red algae ("Lithothamnions") form encrusting calcareous layers on the shores, and these are collected commercially and ground to produce fertilizer. The flattened *Porphyra* is cultivated and eaten in Japan, but the chief economic importance of red algae is as a source of Agar. Much research is being devoted to the cultivation of red algae for this purpose.

Class Chlorophyceae

Some of these are unicellular motile species with flagella and are found in the plankton; intertidally there are nonmotile forms, including the larger multicellular *Enteromorpha* and *Ulva*. Some of these larger forms are cropped for food, but the chief

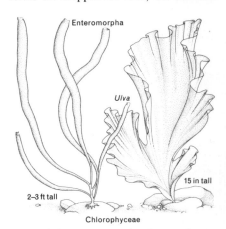

Enteromorpha

Ulva

2–3 ft tall

15 in tall

Chlorophyceae

economic importance and nuisance of green algae is that they are resistant fouling organisms on ship hulls. Green algae contain the pigments normal to most higher plants.

Class Prasinophyceae

These planktonic green algae are almost all unicellular, though some, such as *Halosphaera*, may form colonies within a ball of mucilage. They differ from Chlorophyceae by having scales on the flagella and sometimes over the body. Most species of this class are inhabitants of freshwater—only a few species are oceanic.

Class Chrysophyceae

These are golden brown microscopic unicellular forms, which often form into groups of cells and live on the seabed, alternating with planktonic motile forms. They are an important group in the nanoplankton. Sometimes motile and non-motile single cells

Chrysophyceae × 8750

alternate in the plankton. The motile stages are often covered with elegant scales, either siliceous or calcareous, and are at times abundant enough to turn the water milky. Chalk cliffs largely consist of the minute fossil scales of these coccolithophorids.

Class Xanthophyceae

These yellow green algae are mainly freshwater or terrestrial, but some are oceanic. The largest and most remarkable is *Vaucheria*, which makes mats of fine threads on mud in salt marshes and estuaries. Here they help to stabilize the soft upper layer of mud. Many species of *Vaucheria* have cell walls encrusted with lime and can give rise to small limestone deposits.

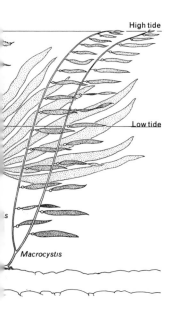

High tide

Low tide

Macrocystis

Class Euglenophyceae

These are small unicellular flagellates that are common in estuaries and live interstitially in sands and muds. Many have chloroplasts, which contain chlorophyll-a as well as xanthophyll and carotene. These species are photosynthetic, but others are colorless and are saprophytes. They make characteristic euglenoid wriggling movements, using the flagella like an oar, not like a propeller.

Class Cryptophyceae

These are estuarine flagellates, many of which live in symbiotic associations with animals, especially with corals. They contain varied auxiliary pigments and are many different colors. Few occur in the open sea, but in estuaries they are sometimes abundant enough to cause red tides. Cryptophyceae share with Dinophyceae small hairlike trichocysts that can be ejected from the body when the organism is stimulated, and this is an indication that they are saprophytes or even predatory in habit.

Class Dinophyceae

These are motile unicellular algae with two flagella, one lying in a girdle groove around the body. Some have thin walls, but others such as *Ceratium* have a thick, plated armor. Even in these species, it is possible that ingestion

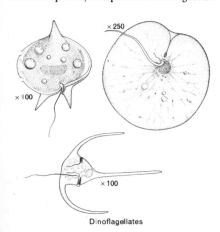

× 250

× 100

× 100

Dinoflagellates

of particulate matter occurs by opening of the plates. Many dinoflagellates (about half the species known) are colorless and sapro-

phytic, as is *Noctiluca*, which is brilliantly luminescent when disturbed. Some species are even parasites on fish and invertebrates.

Dinoflagellates, like diatoms, are relatively large cells and are abundant and important in the plankton; sometimes blooms will color the sea. Some species produce a toxin that acts on vertebrate motor nerves, and when these *Gonyaulax* and *Gymnodinium* species are filtered by oysters and other shellfish, the shellfish become highly poisonous and may prove fatal if consumed. These toxic species cause red tides, and since the toxins last for several months in the shellfish, when red tides occur there are legal prohibitions about selling shellfish in several countries.

Class Bacillariophyceae

These unicellular diatoms are one of the most important algal groups and are found in great abundance and variety in the plankton as well as on the seabed. Like some of the Chrysophyceae, they are an important food source for filter-feeding animals, but they are larger and are therefore accessible to copepods, which cannot trap smaller forms. Diatoms have a rigid silicified cell wall formed by two overlapping valves, which make an exquisitely sculptured little box with a closely fitting lid. Holes or slits in the valves permit entry of nutrients, and in a mysterious and little understood way effect some movement of certain diatoms.

× 40

Bacillariophyceae (Diatoms)

Like many landplants, diatoms are seasonal, and in temperate seas there is a massive spring outburst followed by decline in the population as the grazing animal filter feeders crop the diatoms and other planktonic algae. Diatoms divide by forming a new inner valve (or box) within each of the two present valves (which become the lids of the two new cells). As this process continues, half of the offspring each time will be smaller than the parent, and eventually spores are produced from which a new large pair of valves is formed. The silicified cell wall is much denser than seawater, and it is not surprising that most pelagic diatoms have spiny processes to increase drag and slow the sinking rate. Some have chitinous hairs for the same purpose, but it is still not clear how it is that healthy pelagic diatoms are neutrally buoyant. It is possible that they achieve this by regulating the ion composition of the cell sap.

SYMBIOTIC ALGAE

Several animal groups, notably cnidarians and giant mollusks, have entered into symbiosis with algae, which are usually called zoochlorellae or zooxanthellae, depending on their color. In the giant clam, *Tridacna*, the algae lie in blood sinuses surrounded by amoebocytes, and are protected by colored pigment filters in the outer tissues from too intense light. These are very large mollusks that weigh up to 300 pounds and owe their

success to farming the algae. The algae are now known to be dinoflagellates (*Symbiodinium*) and are recognized by their independent motile stages. Coral larvae usually do not contain algae, and the corals must therefore acquire the algae later in life. The mollusk and cnidarians benefit from oxygen and carbohydrates, and the algae obtain nitrogenous compounds, but some cases held to be symbiosis may be more one-sided. The flatworm *Convoluta* always contains the alga *Platymonas*, and cannot live without it, but sometimes may digest the algae it harbors. The symbionts of radiolarians and acantharians are sometimes cryptophyceans and sometimes chlorophyceans, apparently depending on which the protozoan finds available. Probably there is a wide range of relationships in different groups showing every grade from specialized symbiosis to commensalism.

ANGIOSPERMS

There are only some fifty marine flowering plants, all monocotyledons, and apparently all derived from terrestrial forms. They grow in shallow coastal and estuarine waters attached to the seabed by creeping rhizomes, often forming vast beds, which may be exposed at very low tides. Pollen is usually transferred in the water, and the flowers are either entirely underwater, or may be at the surface and pollinated by pollen drifting on the surface. Only one species (*Enhalus*) has aerial flowers and so aerial pollination.

These seagrasses are important as food for some marine mammals and reptiles, and their dense beds offer valuable shelter for many young animals of different groups. *Zostera*, the common temperate genus, was much reduced by disease in European

Zostera 1–2 ft

waters, but is now regaining its former abundance. Both tropical (*Thalassia*) and temperate forms show a discontinuous distribution, which can be accounted for on the basis of the geologic changes in the Paleozoic Tethys sea.

BLUE-GREEN ALGAE AND BACTERIA

Blue-green algae (*Cyanophyceae*) were once treated as algae, but it now seems more appropriate to ally them with bacteria since they are remote from algae of other kinds, and share certain fundamental characteristics with bacteria. Like bacteria they have no nuclei or organized chromosomes, and in some genera the cell wall is similar to that of bacteria. Blue-green algae vary in color from red and yellow to purple and black, as well as blue-green, and these colors are caused by pigments and by refraction of light. Some species, for example *Nostoc*, can fix nitrogen from the atmosphere in the same way as the root nodule bacteria of peas and lupins. Most marine blue-green algae are littoral, but a few are planktonic. They live attached to other plants or may bore into rocks. *Rivularia* joins with a fungus to form

Lichina, a common lichen intertidally.

Blue-green algae can reproduce at a remarkably fast rate, covering lakes and rivers with waterbloom within a matter of hours. The presence of *Oscillatoria erythrea* has given color, and hence the name, to the Red Sea. The capacity of blue-green algae to utilize atmospheric nitrogen and carbon dioxide as food, has allowed them to survive in very arid conditions. They can colonize recently cooled and bare volcanic surfaces and are important in forming the soil on the foreshore of new volcanic islands.

Marine bacteria are most abundant around the coasts, but in the open ocean they occur around phytoplankton and on surfaces of planktonic animals and detritus. Many are saprophytes, which can degrade every kind of organic material from chitin, celluloses, mucins and fats to crude oil. Although usually rather scarce in the ocean they are poised to exploit advantageous situations when they form blooms, as do algae. Others play an important role in the nutrient cycle, fixing atmospheric nitrogen and converting nitrite to nitrate. Their importance in the sea is as great as on land. Bacteria are too small for collection by most filter feeders, but the very special food-collecting mechanisms of larvaceans can cope with this and they are also held in check by antibiotics produced by diatoms.

With man continually pouring more and more industrial waste and effluent into the rivers and oceans, the role bacteria has in breaking down these potentially dangerous substances is now becoming critical if the ocean is to remain at least nominally clean.

FUNGI

Several quite different kinds of fungi are found in marine habitats, from free-living yeasts, which are saprophytic, to forms specializing in attack on polyurethane or attacking oyster shells and, in some cases, fish. *Ichthyophonus*, for example, is suggested to be a significant control of herring populations.

The role which saprophytic fungi play in the sea has not yet been assessed, but the parasitic forms, particularly those that live upon shellfish like oysters or crustaceans, are of considerable economic importance.

175

GENERAL INTRODUCTION TO ANIMALS

There is immense diversity of animals in the sea. Some members of every animal phylum are represented and about half of all phyla are exclusively marine. The land is richer in the actual number of different species, but this is because about 80 percent of all known animals are arthropods, and most of these are insects—a group which has almost completely failed to colonize the sea. As we should expect, the chemical and physical properties of seawater have determined the adaptions of animals living in the sea, so, for example, the largest animals that have ever lived exist in the sea, buoyed up by water, and some of the smallest, the planktonic forms, are able to take advantage of the chemical composition of the sea to exchange ions and lighten themselves. The rapid speed at which sound travels in seawater has also made it suitable as a means of navigation and communication.

Because the plants of the sea on which the food chains are based are generally much smaller than those of the land, the animals at the base of the food chain are those which are able to graze these small plants, and they are themselves small. The food chains are therefore usually longer than those on land, with many more steps between herbivore and the larger carnivores. Naturally, most is known of the marine animals that live conveniently on shores or in the shallow seas, but the adaptions of some groups for life in the deep sea, or in the ocean plankton, are so striking that they have stimulated numerous investigations.

As the world's population increases and as more people require food from less available agricultural land, the sea becomes of more economic importance. Overfishing has produced a decline in the populations of traditional commercial species, and it is now essential that all forms of life in the sea are closely monitored and understood if man is to continue getting food from the sea. Although at present the sea is teeming with life, the continued use of the sea as a dumping ground for chemicals and human waste could turn the oceans into watery deserts. All classes of animals need to be protected, however small, because food chains are long and complex and, like any chain, they are only as strong as the weakest links. Pollution striking at what may seem an insignificant animal may well tip the delicate balance that has taken millions of years to create.

PHYLUM PROTOZOA

These are single-celled animals, usually microscopic, but some are visible to the naked eye. They were originally thought to be derived from unicellular plants, but the distinction between phagotrophic protozoans and photosynthetic plant flagellates is not absolute, and protozoans represent a grade or organization that the different classes have reached (perhaps independently), and which one group has to some degree exceeded. Many marine protozoa build themselves shells or skeletons, and such has been their abundance over the millennia that these have accumulated to form layers of abyssal oozes and contributed to the formation of limestone and chalk.

Class Rhizoflagellates

Both amoeboid and flagellate forms are united in this class because, although they are very different in structure, there are stages in the life cycle of them both that are similar. There is, for example, an amoeboid stage in the life cycle of some zooflagellates. The most important marine rhizoflagellates are amoeboid forms with shells or skeletons—the foraminifera, the radiolaria and the acantharia.

Foraminifera live in little shells, which they make. These are usually constructed of chalk, although a few are made of silica, and penetrated by tiny holes through which the animal sends out thin branching strands of protoplasm that form a web for catching and digesting diatoms and other small planktonic organisms. The shell is chambered, and as the animal grows it adds larger chambers. Different species make a great variety of spirals, cones and other intriguing shapes. A few have only a single chamber, which grows as the animal grows.

The majority of foraminifera are either fixed or free bottom-living animals, but some important ones, such as *Globigerina*, are planktonic, and these have long, thin spicules which delay sinking. Their dead shells, which form *Globigerina* ooze, however, are simply rounded globules perforated

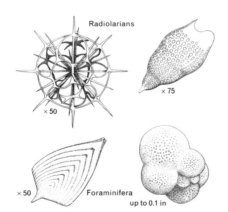

Radiolarians

×50

×75

×50   Foraminifera
up to 0.1 in

with many holes, since the long spicules are dissolved as the shells gradually sink to the bottom. These planktonic foraminifera contain symbiotic chrysophycean algae, as do the other planktonic rhizoflagellates. Foraminifera are very valuable fossils, for the group has been so abundant and varied since the early Cambrian, more than 550 million years ago, that they are important not only in paleo-ecological studies but also in the search for new petroleum reserves.

Radiolarians are all planktonic, and differ from foraminifera in that their protoplasmic processes are long, thin filaments that project from a central horny capsule. The capsule separates the inner mass of protoplasm, which contains the nucleus and oil drops, from the outer vacuolated

"flotation" layer. Like foraminiferans, radiolarians feed by collecting food particles on their protoplasmic processes. This food is then transported toward the center of the animal for digestion just outside the capsule. Many radiolarians have exquisite siliceous skeletons that are rather like three-dimensional snowflakes in their symmetrical form and variety of patterning. Almost all have spiny processes similar to other planktonic forms. The rain of dead skeletons to the bottom of tropical seas has produced the radiolarian oozes.

Acantharia are rather like radiolaria, but there is no central capsule and the protoplasmic filaments radiating from the animal are supported by axial spicules. At the outer ends of the filaments there are curious contractile processes that seem to be able to pull the filament up and down their spicules, possibly altering the buoyancy of the animal.

Finally, heliozoans are similar to acantharians in lacking a central capsule, but they have a rather different arrangement of radiating protoplasmic filaments from a central zone and sometimes curved siliceous spicules scattered around the outer region.

Heliozoans are carnivorous and are able to trap and cope with relatively large active prey and, for example, they can catch and subdue copepods and even nematodes! They do this by contracting the sticky elongate axopods, and probably also by secreting poison. Some heliozoans are spherical like radiolarians, but others may be semi-sessile and are fixed by a base at the end of a long stalk, which bears a "head" from which the axopods project. These are relatively large protozoa, and are of interest in understanding axopod movement.

Class Sporozoa

All sporozoans are internal parasites found in the gut of many invertebrates and in the gall bladder and other tissues of fish. Some sporozoans are multinucleate and during their life cycle seem to pass through a multicellular stage, so that they are very different from the usual unicellular protozoan condition. Sporozoan infestations may be common and comparatively harmless to the host, but in the crowded conditions of hatcheries and shellfish beds they may be very serious and commercially disastrous.

Class Ciliata

About half of all known protozoa are ciliates. Marine ciliates occur in the plankton, interstitially and as benthic forms. They are different from other protozoans in many features, such as having two different kinds of nucleus, and they are sometimes put in a

×360

0.1 in

Ciliates   ×230

separate subphylum. The simpler ciliates are covered with rows of cilia arranged in a particular pattern encircling a small mouth. The slipperlike freshwater *Paramecium* belongs to this group and there are many

marine ciliates of this kind that live between sand grains, among algae and in other similar places. Some ciliates are parasitic inside the gut of polychaetes and other invertebrates. One unmistakable group, the suctorians, has lost the cilia but developed poisonous tentacles. These live like small sea anemones stuck on the outside of crustaceans and prey on other ciliates. The more advanced ciliates have lost or modified most of the cilia on the body, and have evolved a specialized crown of membranelles around the mouth.

Tintinnids, which embrace approximately 900 species, are of this kind and are the most important planktonic forms. The houses they secrete are rather like wineglasses without feet, either transparent or covered with particles of debris. Each animal is attached by its foot, and leans out, braced by a few ciliary guy ropes, as it swims along.

PHYLUM PORIFERA

Sponges are sessile animals with a different inner and outer layer of cells. They filter feed by ciliary action. Water flows in through numerous pores and out by a common opening, while food particles are collected by the current-producing cells themselves. These are unusual in having a membranous collar around the cilia, rather like certain protozoans. The collar cells of the inner layer of the adult sponge can lose their cilia and become amoeboid or transform into genital cells.

Although they are multicellular, sponges are not exactly the same as other multicellular animals, and are sometimes placed in a separate subkingdom, the Parazoa, to distinguish their grade of organization from the Protozoa on the one hand, and the Metazoa on the other. All sponge cells retain some individuality and the sponge is more like a simple aggregation of cells than are other recognized multicellular animals. There do not seem to be either nerve or muscle cells. Several kinds of sponges can be dissociated into individual cells, and under appropriate conditions these cells will aggregate and recreate the sponge. There are three classes of Porifera, recognized by the differing construction of the skeleton.

Class Hexactinellida

These are the most primitive living sponges, built on a trelliswork of siliceous spicules, which have four, five or six branches. Today they are mainly deep-sea forms, but in the Jurassic and Cretaceous periods, between 195 and 65 million years ago, they were

16 in   Spicules

Hexactinellid

mainly littoral. Living rooted in ooze they have developed long basal anchoring spicules, up to nine feet long.

Deep-sea hexactinellids are rather disappointing to look at when first dredged up as they are almost always covered in mud, and felted, dirty spicules hide the inner trellis. After cleaning, however, they show the elegant engineering typified by the superb Venus' flower basket (*Euplectella*). Unlike other sponges Hexactinellids only have two kinds of cells, the usual outer layer of cells is missing.

Class Calcarea

These are small mainly littoral sponges, which often encrust rocks and are built on a skeleton of two-, three- or four-rayed calcareous spicules. These little sponges are more complex in structure than hexactinellids, for in most the collar cells are confined to pockets in the sponge and do not line all of its

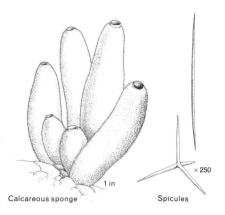

Calcareous sponge   Spicules

interior cavity. Examples of calcareous sponges are *Leucosolenia* and the purse sponge, *Grantia*.

Class Demospongiae

This is by far the largest class of the Porifera, characterized by complex canal systems and small collar cells, with a variety of cell types between inner and outer layers. If there is a skeleton it is built from siliceous spicules or from flexible spongin filaments, or from both mixed together. The traditional bath sponges

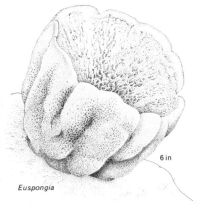

Euspongia

Hippospongia and *Euspongia* only have spongin filaments and are collected commercially. The sponges are allowed to rot, then washed and beaten and, finally, the bleached spongin skeleton can be used in the bath. Some Demospongiae are larger than bath sponges; *Hircinea gigantea*, for example, may weigh 110 pounds and measure three feet across. Many are brightly colored, possibly as a warning.

PHYLUM CNIDARIA

These remarkable radially symmetrical animals have achieved great diversity of form, size and habit, using only a two-layered structure—an inner and outer layer of cells separated by an amorphous zone secreted by the outer layer. This mesogloea (middle glue) differs a good deal in thickness and property in different cnidarians and, in the more advanced, it may be invaded by a variety of cells to give nearly the equivalent of the third cell layer of higher animals. The

phylum is named after the ingenious and still poorly understood stinging cells, or cnidae, which are arrayed among the outer layer on the tentacles. These are little harpoons or lassoes, which are discharged when stimulated, shooting out to immobilize and capture the small living prey on which many cnidarians feed. As they are discharged some kinds of cnidae secrete toxins, and in the most dangerous cnidarians these are capable of rapidly killing humans by causing cardiac failure.

Cnidae are manufactured in special regions of the body (just as are blood cells in vertebrates) and transported to their site of action by amoeboid cells. They were long supposed to be triggered by direct stimulus from the prey, but recently it has become clear that the cnidarian has some control over the sensitivity of the cnidae. After a meal, for example, the cnidae require much stronger stimuli to discharge than when the animal has been starved. Probably some kinds of cnidae discharge by turning inside out very rapidly, using osmotic forces, but it does not seem probable that this can be true for all types, and the way they work is still not entirely clear.

Physalia float 8 in

Charybdea

Dactylometra 3–4 ft long

bell 2.5 in

Obelia medusa .25 in across

Obelia

Strangely, some mollusks that browse on cnidarians swallow the cnidae of their prey and arrange for them to be transported, undischarged, to special organs on the back of the mollusk, where they are then employed in defending the mollusk against attack by predators.

All cnidaria are built on the same plan of a gut opening with a mouth that is surrounded by tentacles, and this plan has specialized in two directions. On the one hand, there are freeswimming, or rarely sedentary, medusae, and on the other there are sedentary, or rarely freeliving, polyps. In many cnidaria, for example Siphonophores, the two types alternate in different generations, and in some colonial forms modifications of the two types may both occur at the same time in the colony. All cnidarians are aquatic and most species are marine. The phylum includes jellyfish, sea anemones and coral.

The chief importance of the group is that some cnidaria form coral reefs in warm (20° to 30°C) shallow waters and that the very abundant pelagic Siphonophores form an important link in the food chain. The group was formerly divided into three classes, but it has recently been realized that there are in fact four classes of unequal size. The group is also classified under the name Coelenterata.

Class Hydrozoa

This class contains about a third of all living cnidaria, the simplest being the hydroid polyps with knobbed tentacles which alternate with the medusan sexual generation. The eggs hatch into a ciliated planula larva, which settles and gives rise to the new hydroid polyp generation. Sometimes hydrozoans of this kind omit the medusa phase, in which case there are special sexual polyps in the colony. Sometimes the polyp phase is omitted, and the eggs develop directly into a medusa—as does the beautiful little *Liriope*. *Liriope* and similar medusae are all only one or two inches across, probably because they are limited in size by the way that they swim using a velar collar. The majority of the common littoral hydrozoans are small forms, solitary or colonial, such as *Obelia* or *Hydractinia*, which lives on shells inhabited by hermit crabs. But in warm waters some hydrozoans, for example the milleporan corals, form stony calcified colonies contributing to coral reefs. Like the major coral-reef cnidarians of the class Anthozoa, milleporan corals harbor symbiotic algal cells, which color the tips of their knobbed tentacles. Milleporans show a pronounced difference between the feeding polyps, the handling polyps arrayed in a ring around each feeding polyp and the sexual polyps in the channels connecting the whole colony. This kind of polymorphism is at its most complex in the whole animal kingdom in the beautiful transparent pelagic Siphonophores, the most important hydrozoans. These have a medusalike form as a basic unit, which buds off a long chain on which there are feeding, excretory, protective and other kinds of polyp, as well as modified medusae forming bracts and other organs.

This is the arrangement in forms like *Hippopodius* (unique in its ability to vary its opacity when touched), which dart through the water and fish with their long tentacles. Some may be very large, up to 100 feet, but are rarely seen intact as they break up when caught in nets. The most spectacular Hydrozoan is the floating *Physalia*, the Portuguese man-of-war, with its blue–purple float filled with carbon monoxide which the animal periodically lays flat on the water to keep damp. *Physalia* drifts along fishing with long tentacles armed with batteries of cnidae sufficiently toxic to give extremely painful wounds to human beings. *Physalia* floats as asymmetrical, situated to the left and right, perhaps to prevent the loss of the whole group when adverse winds sail one kind ashore. The fragility and beauty of all Siphonophores masks their active predatory nature, which is well illustrated by the diphyids, which dash around with their fishing lines extended. It is their abundance and success in catching food that make the group so important in the open ocean.

Another siphonophore is *Velella*, popularly known as by-the-wind sailor, which lives floating on the surface of warm seas.

Class Cubozoa

Although cubomedusae have been known for a long time, only in the 1970s were they first reared from the egg in a laboratory. They were found to be so different in development to all other medusae that they have had to be placed in a class of their own more or less intermediate between Hydrozoa and Scyphozoa. The egg hatches into a planula that settles to form a curious little polyp with four tentacles. This then transforms directly to the four-sided squarish medusa. Cubomedusae are the most dangerously poisonous animals in the sea and contact with the tentacles can cause death within minutes, and even if not fatal, long-lasting painful wounds are inflicted by the cnidae.

Class Scyphozoa

These are the largest medusae, sometimes three or four feet across. They have a basic four-fold symmetry and a complicated sensory and nervous system. The active swimmers such as *Aurelia* feed on large copepods and fishes. Not all scyphozoans feed in this way, however, and some have an enormous multiple mouth that is used as a strainer, to feed on small organisms and detritus. Since the mouth in the medusae is ventrally situated some of them spend much of their time lying upside down on their backs in shallow water waiting for food material to fall into their mouths.

In Scyphozoa, the medusa is the dominant phase and, if present, the polyp generation is much smaller than the medusa. Sometimes the polyp phase buds off small medusae, which look like stacks of saucers breaking free. In one scyphozoan group, the Stauromedusae, there is, however, no medusa phase at all, and the medusoidlike polyp sits on its stalk and catches food with its clubbed tentacles. This small group of stalked jellyfish (55 species in all) seems likely to be important in showing very small ecological changes by its abundance and choice of sites.

Class Anthozoa

This is the largest and most important cnidarian class, containing approximately six thousand species. Medusae are lacking, and the polyps may be large and complicated, with internal divisions, special muscle tracts and a complicated set of conduction systems involving both nerves and sheets of epithelial cells. Sea anemones look, and mostly are, rather simple, sluggish animals, but although their time scale is slower than ours, some species, such as *Stomphia*, are capable of active swimming by lashing the column from side to side. Others, such as *Calliactis*, have evolved elaborate behavior patterns leading to protective associations with crabs or to

Coral 0.5 in diameter

Precious coral 6 in

Anemone 1.5 in tall

aggression against other anemones. It may seem hard to think of aggressive behavior in these sedentary and superficially plantlike animals, but in crowded situations, such as on coral reefs, anthozoans are competing for space and it is not surprising that some coral species such as *Acropora* dominate their neighbors on the reef and gradually destroy them.

Anemones and reef-forming corals have either sixfold tentacles and internal divisions or they are in multiples of six. The anthozoan group, which contains sea pens, precious coral and organ-pipe corals, has an eightfold symmetry and tentacles of the polyps are branched and feathery. In both groups symbiotic algae are abundant and, as in the giant clam *Tridacna*, the algae probably contribute glycerol to the diet of the animals as well as removing nitrogenous waste products.

Present-day reef-building anthozoans are limited around the world by the 21°C isotherm, and it has been shown experimentally that calcification of their skeletons is increased tenfold in light, when the symbionts are photosynthesizing, so that living reef-corals have to be in warm sunlit water.

Just as on the shore, where the large seaweeds are conspicuously zoned, so too in coral reefs the different anthozoans are zoned, forming a very complex community supporting an immense variety of animals. Some, such as *Caryophyllia*, are the only ones found in colder waters, but the colonial pennatulids can live in cold, deep waters rooted in mud. They are often strikingly luminous when stimulated and waves of luminosity pass over the colony. Fossil reef-corals differed from living anthozoa in having a fourfold symmetry. They have contributed to coralline limestones or rag, familiar as building stones and as decorative marbles.

PHYLUM CTENOPHORA

Superbly beautiful transparent pelagic animals luminous by night, ctenophores are related to cnidarians and sometimes grouped with them, but they have a different kind of lasso cell to the cnidae, elaborate apical sense organs and eight rows of comb plates formed by fused cilia. These comb plates beat rhythmically and drive the animal through the water as it trails its fishing tentacles. Ctenophores are among the most beautiful of all animals and no one who has ever seen a Venus' girdle, *Cestus*, insinuating its almost invisible way through the water could ever forget it.

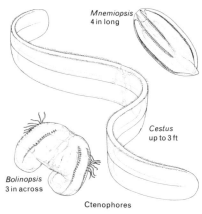
Mnemiopsis 4 in long
Cestus up to 3 ft
Bolinopsis 3 in across
Ctenophores

Remarkably enough, some ctenophores have abandoned pelagic life and live creeping around on the seabed. These forms perhaps show affinities of the group to the platyhelminthes. On the other hand, some unusual medusae, such as *Hydroctena*, have paired tentacles in pouches, somewhat similar to those of ctenophores. The ctenophores are specialized forms, but in their development and adult structure give some indications of a grade of organization a little higher than that of Cnidaria.

PHYLUM PLATYHELMINTHES

These are unsegmented flattened worms without a body cavity. They are bilaterally symmetrical and covered by a ciliated epidermis or by a resistant cuticle. In different classes digestive and reproductive systems are developed to different extents, but if there is a gut there is rarely an anus. Platyhelminthes are usually hermaphrodite, and cross-fertilization is the rule, leading to fertilized eggs within a shell. These eggs may hatch to yield a ciliated larva or development may be direct to the adult stage. There are parasitic and freeliving species.

The more advanced platyhelminthes are parasitic, and show remarkable modifications for the parasitic life, including special attachment organs and elaborate reproductive cycles. In Monogenea, as in many parasites, there are interesting relationships between the parasite and the host such that one attack confers immunity against another at the same site. Mucus from fish that have acquired immunity from a previous attack can kill flukes when added to seawater in which they are living, whereas mucus from fish that are heavily infested does not. Different fish subclasses are attacked by monogeneans to a different degree, so that teleosts are attacked by 12 families of flukes, elasmobranchs by five, holocephali by four and chondrosteans by two families only. Such data suggest that teleost fishes were the first group that monogeneans attacked, and show something of the interest of comparative parasitology. Non-marine species of platyhelminthes include disease-carrying human parasites.

The more primitive freeliving platyhelminthes are probably similar in structure to animals that gave rise to Aschelmintha on the one hand and to Nemertina, Mollusca and Annelida on the other. They represent a significant structural grade in animal evolution.

Class Turbellaria

These are mainly free-living carnivorous forms, which glide about using their body cilia for propulsion between grains of sand or among algae, corals or under rocks. The least developed have a very simple pharynx rather than a gut and some of these, such as

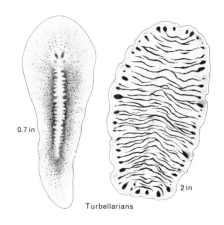
0.7 in
2 in
Turbellarians

Convoluta, contain algae symbionts, which may be so abundant as to color the sand green at low water.

The more advanced polyclads and triclads both have a well-developed gut—the polyclads' with many branches, and the triclads' with three branches, hence the names. They both also have more elaborate reproductive systems. Some turbellarians are several inches long and may be gaudily striped as a warning. Turbellarians are able to survive drastic cutting-up operations and have therefore been used a great deal in experiments on learning transfer, and on polarity in regeneration. A few turbellarians are endoparasites of such animals as echinoderms, crabs and mollusks.

Class Digenea

These are endoparasitic with at least two hosts in the complex life cycle, hence their name. A free-swimming ciliated larva enters a particular species of mollusk and multiplies until thousands of tailed swimming larvae emerge. Either directly, or via several more different host species, the end of the line is reached in a vertebrate host, where the adult flukes mature and the cycle begins again. Digeneans have two suckers as adults, a resistant cuticle and a bi-lobed gut, but as one might expect, most of the inside of the adult is taken up by the uterus. Digenean flukes are very important and dangerous parasites in freshwater and on land. Sheep liver flukes are digeneans and the disease Bilharzia is caused by one, but marine digeneans are not so harmful to man.

Class Monogenea

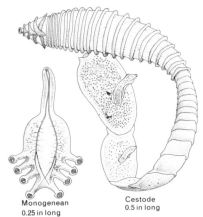
Monogenean flukes have a simpler life history than their digenean cousins. The adults are usually external parasites of fishes, feeding on blood or skin, and their larvae swim directly to another host. Monogenean adults often have a very complicated attachment organ at the rear end, exactly suited to clamp onto the gills of the host fish. A very few are internal parasites; one in particular is found in the hindgut of Holocephalan fishes.

Monogenean 0.25 in long
Cestode 0.5 in long

Class Cestoda

Adult tapeworms live in the gut of vertebrates, attached by fearsome suckers and hooks. The body may be divided into portions, but these are not segments equivalent to those of other worms. There is no gut, and much of the body is taken up by the uterus and larvae or eggs, which infect the next host. There are usually two or three hosts, for example crustaceans, fish and the final vertebrate host, which is the most narrowly specific. This host specificity has been ingeniously used by zoologists to throw light on the relationship between hosts, and has, for example, helped in the distinction between the two species of thresher shark.

PHYLUM NEMERTINA

Almost all members of this phylum are marine, although a few are terrestrial and some freshwater. They are elongated flattened worms with a retractable proboscis, usually living under stones, in rock crevices and in mud or sand, but sometimes inside other animals: they are sometimes parasitic. Some specialized nemertines are pelagic in the deep ocean. The sexes are always separate, and there is often a pelagic larva in the development of the adult. Structurally similar to flatworms, and certainly related to them, nemertines are more advanced in having a blood system, an anus and a rather complicated proboscis arrangement. They

6–20 in
average 15 ft
Nemertines

are the peak of development of animals without a body cavity, and it is only the absence of this body cavity that limits their diameter. The length of the body is not so limited, and the bootlace worm, *Lineus*, may be up to 98 feet long.

PHYLUM ASCHELMINTHES

Aschelminthes are all rather different in design, but they are grouped together because they share the same kind of body cavity. This is derived from the central space in the ball of cells during early development—a space different to the body cavity of annelid worms and other higher forms. Maybe this is a fortuitous resemblance, and zoologists are deceiving themselves in trying to associate such apparently unlike animals, but it is natural to try to associate animals in large groups. If the reader wishes to consider each of the aschelminth classes as separate phyla he is certainly at liberty to do so, and since fashions change, this may be the majority opinion in a few years' time. Most of the phylum are small animals, less than one millimeter long, but one class consists of much larger burrowing worms, and there is a single pelagic eight-inch worm in one class. The cell number is fixed in the embryonic stage, and as the cells of aschelminthes do not divide later on there is no asexual reproduction by budding nor regeneration of damaged parts.

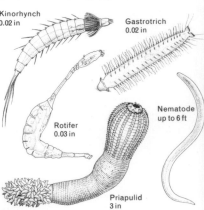
Kinorhynch 0.02 in
Gastrotrich 0.02 in
Rotifer 0.03 in
Nematode up to 6 ft
Priapulid 3 in

Class Nematoda

With 10,000 species this is by far the largest class of the Aschelminthes, and probably many more species are yet to be described. Nematodes are elongate thin worms, circular in section and covered by a tough cuticle. This makes them very resistant to any adverse conditions, and also allows them to parasitize the gut of other animals without fear of being damaged by the digestive enzymes of the gut. They have a complicated sucking pharynx, often armed with piercing stylets, and a simple but effective system of muscle cells for a writhing style of swimming. Internal fertilization and egglaying lead to larvae that resemble the adults and undergo four molts to reach the adult size. Marine free-living nematodes are most abundant in the upper layer of muds, but there are parasitic forms and they are found almost everywhere.

Class Rotifera

These are very different to nematodes, all microscopic and feeding on flagellates by means of a ciliated oral crown. Most are inhabitants of freshwater, but there are some 15 marine forms, including the elongated *Seison*, live on the gills of crustaceans, but there are a few free-swimming forms.

Class Gastrotricha

These are microscopic interstitial and pelagic forms which are like rotifers but without an oral crown. There is instead a sucking pharynx like that of nematodes. The head and ventral surface are ciliated, and gastrotrichs glide around feeding on diatoms, bacteria and protozoa. There are marine and freshwater species of gastrotrichs.

Class Kinorhyncha

Kinorhynchs are about the same size as gastrotrichs, but they have no cilia and the spiny body is divided into a number of segments. They feed on diatoms, using a suctorial pharynx, and live interstitially, moving by means of the segmental spines. The larvae resemble the adult and achieve maturity after only a single molt.

Class Priapulida

Priapulids are larger than any other Aschelminthes and range to three inches. They are sluggish sausage-shaped animals with a proboscis covered anteriorly with rows of hooks, and posteriorly with respiratory processes. They burrow in sand or mud, using the proboscis like a mollusk uses its foot, and feed on organic material. Priapulids are also able to capture slow-moving prey such as polychaetes and other priapulids.

PHYLUM ACANTHOCEPHALA

Adult Acanthocephala are small (half-inch) sausage-shaped worms living in the gut of fish and other vertebrates. They are named for the arrays of hooks on the proboscis that attach them to the gut wall of the host.

Acanthocephala up to 0.8 in

Although there is a body cavity that is mostly filled with gonads, it is not the same as that of Annelida or of the other small groups of wormlike animals, and the group is rather an isolated one, perhaps being distantly related to Nematoda. Larval stages are found in intermediate invertebrate hosts such as isopods, and sometimes there is a secondary host, so that *Corynosoma*, for example, enters an amphipod, changes to a larva in its body cavity, and is then ingested

by a fish that in turn is eaten by the final host, a seabird or seal. Sometimes present in great numbers, in the gut, acanthocephalans are dangerous parasites capable of killing their hosts.

PHYLUM ECTOPROCTA or BRYOZOA

These are abundant encrusting colonial animals of the shore and shallow sea, sometimes forming crinkled flat sheets or seaweedlike branching colonies created from many thousands of the chitinous or calcareous boxes in which each animal lives. The individuals are superficially rather like entoprocts, bearing a ciliated lophophore (a horseshoe-shaped fold of the body wall encircling the mouth), but are actually far more sophisticated. There is a body cavity equivalent to that in annelids and other groups, and a fairly complex muscular system that pushes the lophophore out hydraulically by deforming the little box that the animal occupies.

Not all the individuals in a colony need be

colony 2 in tall

animal 0.03 in

Ectoproct

feeding members, and there are others that form brood chambers, brooms to clean the colony and defensive snapping forms that stop other animals settling. Interestingly, sea urchins faced with a similar need for an antisettlement device, evolved the similar, snapping pedicellariae. There are various kinds of ciliated larvae in the different groups that arise, usually by ovoviviparity, since the eggs are brooded to a late stage. Bryozoans were more abundant in the past (15,000 fossil species) and are thus useful zonal fossils, but today, although important members of the sessile shallow-water fauna, are much less significant than the corals, which have a somewhat similar colonial habit.

PHYLUM ENTOPROCTA

Entoprocta are small polyplike animals with a ciliated crown of tentacles that collect diatoms and other particles. They may be either colonial or solitary and some live fixed upon other animals such as ascidians, sipunculids or sponges, and this association is strictly limited to specific species. The larvae are complicated, but vaguely reminiscent of the annelid trochophore larvae. There is a superficial similarity both to rotifers

and to bryozoans, but the real relationships of entoprocts are unknown.

PHYLUM PHORONIDA

These are small worms, usually only a few fractions of an inch long, which live in membranous tubes that they secrete attached to rocks and objects on the bottom in shallow water. Some species bore into mollusk shells and calcareous rocks by secreting an acid substance. At the anterior end there is a horseshoe-shaped lophophore bearing cilia that collects food particles from the water. This can be rapidly retracted into the tube when the worm is disturbed. Phoronids have a lophophore rather similar to that of the entoprocts and brachiopods, and are probably related to both phyla. Most phoronids have a curious planktonic larva that undergoes an extraordinarily sudden and drastic metamorphosis to the adult.

PHYLUM BRACHIOPODA

Brachiopoda are superficially rather like bivalve mollusks, and like some of them are filter feeders specializing chiefly on diatoms. But every detail of brachiopod structure is entirely different to that of any mollusk. The shell valves are made out of chitinous material which is strengthened with calcium carbonate, or calcium phosphate in some, with canals perpendicular to the surface. Between the two valves, one larger than the other and overlapping it, most of the space is taken up by the ciliated double spiral lophophore that collects food particles and transports them to the mouth. It was first imagined that this represented the molluscan foot, hence the name of the group. The valves are loosely held together by muscles in the more primitive living forms, such as *Lingula* (apparently identical to fossils known from the Ordovician, some 500 million years ago), but in the more advanced terebratulids the two are hinged together. The larger valve rests against the bottom, attached by a stalk passing through a hole at the end, except in *Lingula*, which lives vertically in a tube in sand, where the stalk can contract and pull the animal deeper.

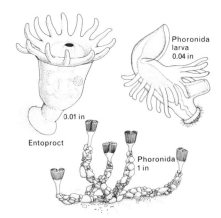

0.8 in across

Brachiopods 1 in across

Brachiopods were much more abundant in the past (30,000 species are known as fossils from the Cambrian period onward), and they radiated so widely that they are important zonal fossils. Living forms are of little significance, but they are important zoologically because they allow interpretation of the modes of life of fossil brachiopods and the conditions under which they lived.

PHYLUM ECHIUROIDAE

These are peculiar worms which feed on small particles using an enormously elongated ciliated grooved proboscis. This may be three feet long although the body is only

up to three inches in length. These animals have a large body cavity, but the proboscis cannot be retracted into it, although it can be shortened a little. Echiuroids live in various bottom deposits, from the intertidal zone to the abyssal floor.

Bonellia is remarkable because the males are minutely small compared to the females and are parasitic on her body. The ciliated larvae are attracted to the female proboscis, and caused to transform precociously into male worms one to three millimeters long, which then become attached to the three-foot-long female. They descend the proboscis, enter the female body and pass to the uterus, where internal fertilization is achieved. This strange pattern is not found in all species and external fertilization is generally the rule, leading to annelidlike larvae. Some adults bear a few bristles, and it seems that echiuroids are distantly related to annelids.

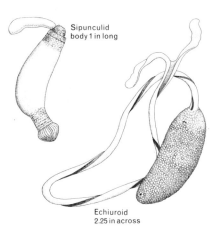

Sipunculid body 1 in long

Echiuroid 2.25 in across

PHYLUM SIPUNCULIDA

These are elongate or short sausage-shaped worms with a prominent long proboscis that ends in a ring of small tentacles around the mouth with which the animals collect small particles. The largest are around two feet long, but most are much smaller and they live buried in bottom deposits or hidden in crevices from the intertidal zone to depths of 13,100 feet. Some live commensally with corals and with other animals. They have a large body cavity, a long twisted gut and a fairly complex nervous system. The eggs are fertilized externally and a trochophore larva similar to that of annelids is found. Curiously some species harbor entoprocts around their basal ends. Probably sipunculids, like echiuroids, are distantly related to annelids.

PHYLUM CHAETOGNATHA

All marine, almost all planktonic, and all rather like each other, arrowworms are quite unlike other animals and are one of the most isolated phyla in the sea. They are elongate, bilaterally symmetrical, torpedo-shaped animals with a formidable set of spiny jaws and well-developed eyes and brain. Most are small, but some grow up to six inches. The body is covered by a thin cuticle, which is produced into fins, and the animals swim by rapid contractions of four longitudinal

0.8 in

Chaetognaths

1 in

bundles of muscle fibers. Most arrowworms are planktonic and glassily transparent, or if they live in the deep sea, an orange-red hue. All are efficient predators that prey mainly on copepods, but they also attack young fish,

179

medusae and anything else suitable in the plankton, which they swallow and rapidly digest. They are hermaphrodites, although there is usually cross-fertilization, and the pelagic eggs hatch directly into a miniature version of the adult.

Although some species are cosmopolitan, usually each species lives in a well-defined kind of water, so that its distribution is related to depth, salinity, temperature and light. Different species are therefore very good indicators of the kind of water, so that it is possible, by examining the arrowworms in a plankton sample, to tell the water type. In the Atlantic, for example, *Sagitta elegans* indicates oceanic water and *S. setosa* coastal water; both species are only taken together at the boundary zones, where the two watermasses are mixed. Conveniently, when preserved in formalin (as usual for the plankton sample), *S. elegans* remains transparent, while *S. setosa* becomes opaque. Because of their importance as indicator species, and their abundance in all oceans, even in the deep ocean, the systematics of arrowworms have been well worked out, but rather little is known of their physiology. They can occur in such great quantities that the surrounding waters take on a grayish appearance. This concentration usually indicates that the area is particularly rich in the phytoplankton, zooplankton and fish larvae on which chaetognaths feed. They are found in all oceans.

PHYLUM MOLLUSCA

Mollusks have been immensely successful in a wide variety of ways of life, and the phylum is second in size only to the Arthropoda. Most mollusks are marine (although land snails are only too widespread), and they occur in every part of the sea from the deep ocean floor to the plankton and littoral zones. Some squids can even take to the air for short jet-propelled excursions. Because they are soft-bodied, mollusks are extraordinarily varied in shape, and so the phylum is hard to characterize. Basically all mollusks are built on the same plan—an anterior head region with mouth and teeth borne on a radular file joins onto a muscular foot supporting a visceral mass covered by a hard shell. The shell is secreted and supported by a mantle, and between this and the visceral mass is a mantle cavity that shelters the gills and excretory ducts.

Respiratory and excretory currents in the mantle cavity are produced by cilia, but both the head and foot are muscular and controlled by a ganglionated nervous system. This simple plan has been exploited in all kinds of ways, and mollusks offer one of the very best examples of the plasticity and adaptive changes of a single group, giving rise to animals as superficially different as giant squids and shipworms.

Class Monoplacophora

First suggested as a class from Paleozoic fossils in 1940 (they were earlier thought to be fossil limpets), the first living *Neopilina* was dredged up in 1952 from muddy clay at 11,700 feet off the coast of western Mexico, and caused much excitement. This living fossil was just as interesting to zoologists as the coelacanth *Latimeria*, because it showed for the first time that mollusks might perhaps be segmented as are, for example, annelids or arthropods. Under the little four-centimeter-wide flat, saucerlike shell, *Neopilina* showed repetition of gills, muscles and excretory organs in a way not found in other living mollusks. But it is not sure yet how this is to be interpreted and argument continues. *Neopilina* probably feeds on radio-

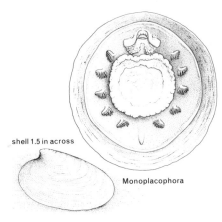

shell 1.5 in across

Monoplacophora

larians and detritus and, so far, has only been found off the coast of South America.

Class Amphineura

Two rather dissimilar small groups are joined in the amphineura because both show primitive features in the nervous and excretory system. The members of one group look rather like worms and have no shells. These wind around hydroids and feed on them or live in mud and feed on detritus. The other more familiar chitons (coat of mail shells) have eight plates along their back surrounded by a flexible girdle so that the animal is completely covered and flattened to the rocky surface on which it lives. Chitons are usually algal browsers, scraping the algal film off rocks, or chewing a path across coral

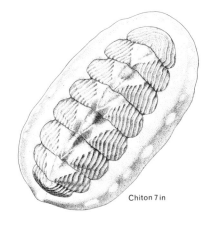

Chiton 7 in

rock. They behave sluggishly, rolling up slowly like wood lice if detached. Since they may be both abundant and up to 12 inches long, they have a significant effect on the algal cover. One chiton, *Placiphorella*, is able to trap and devour small active crustaceans by snapping down a raised flap at the front, just as mice are caught in a break-back trap. Others are sufficiently powerful to rasp entire barnacles from the rocks, and are at least in part carnivorous.

Class Gastropoda

These are by far the largest class of mollusks and have diversified in every direction, from sedentary grazing forms such as limpets to pelagic carnivorous heteropods and the tropical *Conus* species, some of which spear fish with poisoned darts and can even kill men. The gastropods are also the only mollusks, in the form of slugs and snails, that have managed to colonize the land.

Almost all gastropods have a large head that is well equipped with such sense organs as eyes and olfactory receptors. The shell is a single unit formed in a spiral or cone. Apart from the twisting or spiralling of the shell, all gastropods at an early stage of their lives undergo another quite separate twisting called torsion, which turns the mantle, and viscera through 180°. This extraordinary process seems to have been a larval adapta-

tion that has been taken over into adult life, but zoologists disagree about its significance. Still, it certainly has a profound effect on the adult gastropod, which has in consequence the gills and anus in front of the visceral hump.

The most primitive gastropods are animals such as limpets and topshells which crawl about grazing and, except for limpets, can retreat inside the shell and close the opening with a horny or stony lid, or operculum. More advanced gastropods are the slipper limpets, such as *Crepidula*, which

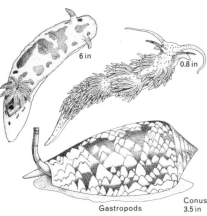

6 in

0.8 in

Gastropods

Conus 3.5 in

change sex as they age, the cowries, which in life cover their shells with the mantle, and the large tropical conch shells, which are capable of leaping along on the bottom. Several have adopted a planktonic carnivorous life, and some of these, such as both *Pterotrachea* and *Carinaria*, have reduced or lost both shell and mantle. The most advance gastropod carnivores are the conch shells, which slide a single tooth into the tip of the poison-filled proboscis, and use this weapon to harpoon other mollusks, worms and even fishes, which are eaten tailfirst. The conch, *Conus geographus*, has a sting lethal to man.

Janthina shell 0.8 in high

Pteropod shell 0.08–0.15 in

Heteropod 2.4 in

Pelagic mollusks

Gastropods have also taken other directions leading to often exceptionally beautiful sluglike forms and to the delicate pteropods, which keep afloat in the plankton by flapping their paired wings. Some have shells, but others have a sort of chitinous boat in which they anchor themselves as they flap along, and are among the most active of gastropods.

Class Lamellibranchia

Lamellibranchs are more sedentary than most gastropods, and seem to have had much less variety of structure. Even so they make the most of what they have, occupying many environments from the high littoral zones to burrows in various substrate (including wood and rock), and even changing the diet from filtering suspensions or deposits to eating large chunks of dead animals. Most, however, filter feed, using the gill cilia to produce the feeding current, and digest the collected particles using a crystalline rod that rotates in the stomach. This liberates enzymes and winds the mucus food-rope into the stomach like a windlass.

There are always two valves to the shell, which may be similar, or one may be flat and the other curved. Between these valves in the burrowing forms a muscular foot may protrude, which typically thrusts forward, anchors and pulls the animal along through the deposit. The head, buccal mass and teeth of gastropods are absent, and the mantle encloses the whole body as does the shell. In all lamellibranchs adductor muscles close the shell valves. These muscles are of a special kind and able to keep the shell closed for long periods without using much energy. The larvae attach themselves to the rocks, wood or sand by sticky threads, and in many of the simpler lamellibranchs, such as *Mytilus*, these form the byssus threads that hold the adult to its home. In scallops the byssus is absent and remarkably enough the animals swim by clapping their shells together.

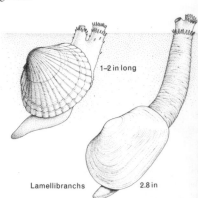

1–2 in long

Lamellibranchs

2.8 in

In lamellibranchs such as these, the adductor muscle is divided into two parts, a rapid-acting portion for snapping the valves together and a smaller portion for keeping it closed. Oysters also have an adductor muscle, but in these fixed forms its function is to clear silt from the mantle cavity.

Most of the giant clams (*Tridacna*) are also fixed, and live on, or embedded in, Indo-Pacific coral reefs. They can measure three feet across and weigh 300 pounds. Although the expanded siphons farm small algae, the usual equipment for ciliary feeding is still present. Probably the majority of lamellibranchs, such as cockles (*Cardium*), clams (*Anadora*) and razor shells (*Ensis*) burrow in bottom deposits. In all of these the mantle

Tridacna 3 ft

edges fuse to different degrees, forming siphon tubes through which water flows in and out of the mantle cavity. Many of these burrowing forms, such as oysters, are economically important as a food source, but one much modified burrower, the shipworm *Teredo*, was in Nelson's time a serious threat to ships on tropical station, using the much reduced shell as an auger bit.

Class Scaphopoda

This is a small group of burrowing mollusks with tubular shells like tiny elephant tusks. The animals live buried in the sand with the tip of the shell sticking out and at the other end an elongate foot with a rim (supposed to appear like the hull of a little boat) protrudes among an array of long ciliated tentacles. With these tentacles, which bear suckers, the animal catches diatoms and foraminiferans in the sand. The animals are popularly known as elephant-tusk shells.

Class Cephalopoda

Cephalopods are the most advanced and formidable mollusks. The development of elaborate eyes and a large brain, the transformation of the foot into tentacles around the mouth and the reduction of the shell have led to actively swimming predators capable of very rapid jet-propelled movements with extremely efficient hunting techniques. In many ways cephalopods have paralleled fish in their evolution, and oceanic squid both eat and are eaten by fish. Living forms are few compared to the legions of fossil ammonites and nautiloids, but they are very varied and certainly the most impressive invertebrate animals existing today. The primitive *Nautilus*, with its external chambered shell, pinhole camera eyes and no ink or hooks, is the remnant of a group dominant in the Paleozoic era and is plainly more primitive than other living forms. All other living cephalopods are much superior in activity and organization, and are divided into squids and cuttlefish with ten arms (two longer than the rest), an internal shell and fins on the body and the octopods, which have eight arms, no shell and no fins.

Squid 2 in

Octopus 3 ft

Cephalopods

Cuttlefish such as *Sepia* have an internal chambered shell (the cuttlebone), which acts as a buoyancy device the animal can adjust by pumping water in and out. They are also remarkable for a very complex color change mechanism. *Sepia* has such a varied repertoire of specific patterns that it is one of a very few invertebrates whose "feelings" can be inferred simply by looking at it. Cuttlefish prey on crustaceans, and use the two longer arms to catch the prey and draw it to the mouth, where it is bitten by the parrotlike beak and injected with poison. Squids have reduced the shell still further to a horny pen, and thus are lightened for a pelagic existence. Disappointingly, the giant architeuthids (up to 70 feet long including the tentacles) seem not to be so powerful as the voracious oceanic ommastrephids (up to six feet long), some of which have brilliant light organs. Angling for large ommastrephid squid in the open ocean is an unforgettable experience, as they are so active and wary, emit such vivid flashes when first hooked, and when brought aboard shoot powerful jets of water and ink in every direction. Many of the smaller less active pelagic squid have superb light organs and some secrete a luminous cloud instead of ink.

Octopods use all eight arms to catch prey, and to explore their surroundings and (in benthic forms) to build lairs. Not all are benthic, the paper nautilus *Argonauta* is pelagic and builds its papery house to carry the eggs; the bathypelagic Cirroteuthids

have the arms joined nearly to their tips by a web so that they swim rather like medusae. Octopods and squid are commercially important as food, but by far their greatest importance lies in the brilliant physiological work on their nervous systems, which have elucidated the way in which nerve fibers operate in all animals, and have explained much about the mechanism of learning.

PHYLUM ANNELIDA

Earthworms are the most familiar annelids and give a good idea of the general plan of the group—elongate segmented animals without a rigid skeleton, but instead a space filled with fluid between the gut and body wall which acts as a hydraulic skeleton against which the body wall muscles can operate. Few of the annelid class to which earthworms belong are marine, and almost all marine annelids belong instead to the Polychaeta (many bristles), recognized by their fans of bristles borne on fleshy lobes on each segment. There are also some marine fish leeches, and two small classes of mainly zoological interest. Polychaetes are an important food for fish, and some of the burrowing forms are so abundant that they play a similar role to earthworms on land, turning over and recycling the bottom deposits.

Class Polychaeta

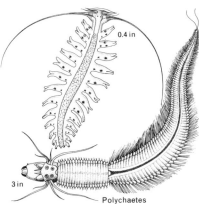

Almost all polychaetes are marine, and the class contains over 60 percent of all annelids. Most are small animals, and live on the shore, either free-living under stones, in crevices and temporary burrows in sand or mud, or living a sedentary life in permanent burrows or tubes. Sometimes these tubes are cemented together in large colonies forming massive sandy reefs, but more usually they are solitary or scattered, such as *Spirorbis* or *Pectinaria*. The body form and habitat of polychaetes depends very much on their diet, and most modifications of the head and body lobes are directly related to the method of feeding.

The free-living worms are often active carnivores that have an extendable toothed proboscis, up to six large eyes, sensory tentacles on the head and large paddle-shaped lobes along the body bearing large bristles. The nereid ragworms are of this

0.4 in

3 in

Polychaetes

kind, and some such as *Neanthes* may attain sizes up to two feet and *Marphysa*, of similar habit, may attain three feet in length. Both families reproduce by shedding gametes into the sea (like most polychaetes) and to ensure fertilization there are special structural and behavioral changes of a very striking kind. Nereids make changes to the posterior part of the body so that it is suited for swimming (the lobes enlarge on each segment, and the bristles are multiplied to make more effective paddles), and leave the bottom to swarm at the surface. There the sexes swim together and the eggs are fertilized to hatch as

ciliated trochophore larvae. The extraordinary regularity of the nuptial swim is best documented in the Polynesian Palolo worm (*Eunice virids*), where the adults cast off the gamete-filled posterior part of the body and this swims to the surface on its own, without a head. This spawning is regulated by the lunar cycle, and all the worms of the area send their rear parts to the surface in the morning of the seventh, eighth or ninth day after full moon in November or December. So numerous are these that they whiten the sea, and are, of course, a feast for the locals.

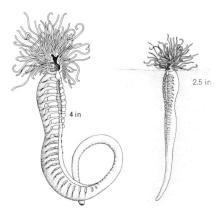

2.5 in

4 in

Mud-dwelling polychaetes

Tube-dwelling polychaetes are quite different to these free-living forms. They may make sandy tubes, such as the beautiful *Pectinaria* pipes, or tubes attached to algae (*Spirorbis*) that are white and calcified. Many have modified the anterior region into a tentacular crown that filters the water, and these filter feeders are extremely efficient. *Myxicola* filters about 11 fluid ounces of water per hour. The luminous *Chaetopterus* in its leathery tube filter feeds by making a mucus net, which is spread across its tube; this trap can cope with food particles down to four-millionths of an inch. Most filter-feeding polychaetes can only succeed in catching microorganisms one thousand times larger than this. Because the ciliated crowns are vulnerable and attractive food, such tube dwellers as *Myxicola* have developed a special nerve pathway for rapid retraction into the tube.

Burrowing polychaete 9 in

Many polychaetes live in sand or mud burrows, eating the substrate in the same way as earthworms on land. Large volumes of sand or mud need to be processed where the organic content is low and sand passes right through a lugworm (*Arenicola*) in 15 minutes. Its castings are familiar on all shores where there is muddy sand. A few polychaetes, such as the attractive transparent *Tomopteris*, are planktonic, and a few live in deep water, but the great radiation of the group has been on and near the shores so that it is hard not to see polychaetes when digging in sand or mud, or turning over stones and rock. There is a variety of ways of collecting particulate food that polychaetes can employ, either filtering particles from the water, digesting them off grains of sand or mud particles, or as do *Amphitrite* and

similar forms, collecting them from the substrate surface by ciliary action on numerous elongate processes spread out on the surface. As we should expect, each is most suitable for a given type of bottom and so the polychaetes we find when digging are very characteristic of different bottom deposits, just as are the burrowing mollusks.

As well as the habits mentioned, a number have joined forces with other animals to live commensally. There is *Arctonoe*, which lives in the mantle cavity of the keyhole limpet *Diodora* of the west coast of North America, or the nereid that shares the hermit crab's shell, or, indeed, the great variety which share the tubes of other species of polychaete in sand or mud.

Class Archiannelida

Archiannelids are a small group of tiny worms which live in surface mud and in the splash zone. Although a rather mixed group, some of them at least are probably survivors of archaic annelids, having, for example, external ciliation and simply arranged heads.

Class Myzostomaria

These are small, flattened, disk-shaped worms that live parasitically on or in echinoderms, especially crinoids. Their shape fits them to hold onto the arms of echinoderms and their role as internal parasites is only secondary. Crinoids react to the worms by enclosing them in cysts, which then affect the skeletal plates on their arms. As similar deformities are found in fossil crinoids it is clear that myzostomaria are ancient parasites of the echinoderm group.

Class Hirudinea

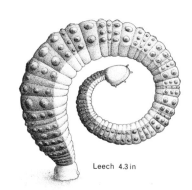

These annelids have few segments, a reduced body cavity and lack bristles. Marine leeches prey on fishes, remaining with a single host rather than operating as specialist predators as do the tropical terrestrial leeches. They suck blood, secreting an anticoagulant as they do so, and digest it by means of bacteria that live in gut pockets. Leeches copulate in the

Leech 4.3 in

same way as earthworms, and fish leeches lay a single egg in the cocoons that they produce. All fish leeches have two large suckers, one at each end of the body, and occur on both elasmobranch and teleost fish.

Class Oligochaeta

One oligochaete family, the enchytraeids, contains a few species that live under stones or amongst seaweeds in the upper littoral zones, but none have managed to descend below the tidemark and the group is insignificant in the sea, though abundant in freshwater. All oligochaetes are hermaphrodite and have a complex reproductive system to ensure cross fertilization.

PHYLUM POGONOPHORA

These are peculiar animals, mainly of the deep sea floor, where they live partly buried in deposits in the tubes that they secrete. Some species occur in water as shallow as 164 feet. These thin elongate wormlike metazoans (up to one and a half feet long) are unusual in that they lack both mouth and gut. Physiological studies suggest amino acids and other nutrients can be absorbed

Pogonophora 10 in long

through the skin directly. At first they were thought to be linked with the chordates, but embryological and fine-structural studies have shown close links with annelids.

PHYLUM ARTHROPODA

Most arthropods are recognizable by the combination of a jointed skeleton covering the limbs and body, large internal spaces filled with blood and an elaborate nervous system and sense organs. There are indeed a few, such as the much-modified parasitic copepods, which superficially appear different, but most arthropods, such as crabs and lobsters, or sandhoppers (amphipods) or king crabs (*Limulus*) are all easy to place in the phylum. The paired appendages—some claws, some walking legs—are one of the features that have made arthropods so successful, and have allowed rapid movement, handling of objects and the development of an elaborate nervous control system and sense organs. Next to cephalopods the higher crustaceans are the most active and aware marine invertebrates. Some, such as the mantis shrimp *Squilla*, or the ghost crabs of tropical sandy shores, are capable of extremely rapid movements, and others have most elaborate behavior patterns.

The Crustacea are the dominant marine class, as are the insects on land, but there are also in the sea a few chelicerates (pincer-bearing) and a few of the small primitive tardigrades (slow walkers). The arthropod outer skeleton is basically built of chitin, but over much of its area it is mineralized in different ways to give the rockhard lobster or crab shell, or thinner more yielding variants of this. At articulations in limbs or body there is no calcification and so the skeleton is flexible and the animal can move its body and limbs using muscles that insert onto infoldings of the outer skeleton. This rigid system, bending only in certain planes and at certain places, is simple to control using inner sensors that measure the amount and rate of bending across the joints. Much research has been done on this system.

The difficulty with the rigid outer skeleton is that it imposes the need for molting, and crustacean development is full of different stages. This typically begins with the nauplius larva, and then, in different groups, passing through a variety of different stages

and molts to reach the adult, which itself may molt, as lobsters do, at longer and longer intervals during its life. That molting is a drastic process can be appreciated when it is realized that the animals have to molt the lining of the stomach, the gill filaments, the rods to which the internal sensors are attached and the inpocketings that the muscles attach to.

Class Tardigrada

Tardigrades are small (less than one millimeter), plump animals looking rather like fat caterpillars with four pairs of fleshy legs ending in bizarre hooks or claws. All marine forms are covered with a cuticle made up of imbricated chitinous plates, which are often very spiny. All are herbivores, using stylets in the mouth to pierce algae, except for one species, which pierces the tentacles of holothurians and is parasitic.

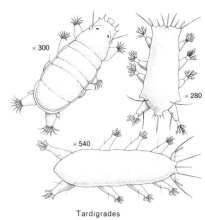

× 300

× 280

× 540

Tardigrades

In some ways intermediate between more normal arthropods and annelids, tardigrades are especially famous for their resistance to adverse conditions, and can survive desiccation for very long periods. The species *Echiniscoides*, which is found on beaches, has been placed in ether, absolute alcohol, hydrogen, helium, carbon dioxide, liquid helium at $-272°C$, dry air at $36°C$, and has survived these assaults and continued to live normally when returned to its standard conditions.

Class Chelicerata

In this class the first appendages on the heads of the animals have two or three joints and end in a pair of pincers, one jaw being immovable, the other closing against it like a pair of secateurs. The claws of crustaceans work in a similar way, but are not the most anterior appendages—crustaceans and other arthropods have antennae and various mandibular appendages.

From fossils it appears that chelicerates were large and dominant in the sea, but today

King crab 1.75 ft long

they are represented only by the curious mollusk-eating *Limulus*, which has a shield-shaped carapace, a triangular abdomen and a long, pointed tail. The animal is just under two feet long. King crabs can even swim

upside down, but can also crawl on the bottom in shallow water, where they burrow to some extent using the rear pair of feet to shift sand. There are rather simple eyes on the carapace (which have been much used in the neurophysiological investigation of vision), and underneath the abdomen there are serial platelike gills. King crabs lay externally fertilized eggs in scrapes in the sand of shallow water, and these hatch into larvae that look like little trilobites. After a series of no less than 16 molts in nine to 12 years, king crabs reach maturity.

King crabs are not of much importance today, but the living *Limulus* gives us an idea of the way early chelicerates lived in the Silurian to the Tertiary periods, when they were a most important marine group.

Class Pycnogonida

Pycnogonids are very curious small arthropods, which have reduced the volume of the body to such an extent that it is really almost only a tube on which four to six pairs of legs are inserted. The first appendages bear pincers, but unlike chelicerates there is a snout or trunk between them. The stomach passes into the legs, the

Pycnogonid 0.4 in

genital ducts open into the legs and ripe eggs are stored inside the fourth segment of the legs. Adult pycnogonids prey on sponges and hydroids, sometimes causing galls, which they use as a refuge. They are found in all oceans.

Class Crustacea

These are by far the most important class of marine arthropods, ranging from lobsters 24 inches long and the giant spider crab *Macrocheira*, whose legs span over 11 feet, to the minute interstitial cumacean copepods and anaspids. Some groups of the smaller crustacean have only been discovered recently. For example, both anaspids (1955) and mystacocarids (1943) were found between sand grains on American beaches.

These primitive little animals are interesting to zoologists, for they show something of the organization of crustaceans in the early Cambrian period, about 570 million years ago, but other crustacean groups are much more important. Barnacles are significant fouling organisms requiring costly countermeasures, while decapods are valuable as food. Several species are farmed commercially, but crustaceans are chiefly important not as food for man or slowing down his ships, but as an essential part of the economy of life in the sea. The group is sometimes compared to the terrestrial insects in abundance and variety, but this gives a false idea of the roles each group plays in the different environments. The pelagic copepods and other filter-feeding planktonic crustaceans graze the phytoplankton, and are then themselves preyed upon by small fish, jellyfish, arrowworms and other crustaceans. They are only one step from the base

of the food chain. On the bottom larger crustaceans form the chief food of a variety of fish and the group as a whole provides an immense food source, capable of supporting the largest animals that have ever lived. The baleen whales and the giant filter-feeding elasmobranchs live solely on crustaceans and it is easy to see that removal of all of them would have a more drastic effect on other living things than would the removal of terrestrial insects. The group is a very large one, so that it is convenient to divide it up into subclasses. Seven of these are marine, but as two of the subclasses only have three and four species, there are really five main divisions of the group.

Subclass Ostracoda Ostracods are small crustaceans, usually less than one millimeter in length, and remarkably modified to live inside what looks just like a small bivalve shell formed by the carapace. The animal living between the two valves beats its antenna to swim and to collect algae to feed on. Most are pelagic or live on the bottom, but some are interstitial, burrowing in sand or mud. The body is very short and unsegmented and about the same length as the

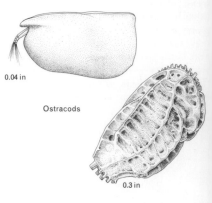

0.04 in

Ostracods

0.3 in

head. The largest ostracod known, *Gigantocypris*, about the size and shape of a cherry, is pelagic in deep water and has superb lensless eyes, which use parabolic mirrors to form images.

The abundance and wide distribution of ostracods make them good indicator species, and they have become of practical importance because as their valves are abundant fossils, being calcified to some degree, they have turned out to be useful zonal fossils in petroleum exploration.

Subclass Copepoda Originally free-living planktonic filter feeders like the present-day calanoids, copepods have radiated widely into all kinds of habit, including a variety of

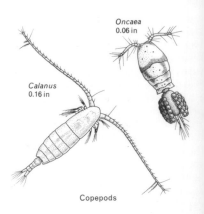

Calanus 0.16 in

Oncaea 0.06 in

Copepods

parasitic forms. Most are small, such as the well-studied *Calanus finmarchicus* on which herring feed, but some of the parasitic forms are much larger. The planktonic copepods often have elongate antennae with which they swim, and long branching appendages to slow their rate of sinking in the water. Many undertake extensive diurnal vertical migrations. Probably these migrations are related to different temperature regimes for feeding and digestion. These herbivorous small copepods of the plankton are by far the most important members of the subclass and, indeed, of the crustacea as a whole.

Others have become carnivorous, and there is a remarkable series of parasitic forms leading from slightly modified adults to the giant *Penella*, which as an adult is simply a long, thin body anchored in the blubber of whales.

Subclass Branchiura These are disk-shaped crustaceans up to one inch across that have become modified to attach themselves to the scales of teleost fish and feed on blood or mucus. They are attached by a pair of suckers at the front, and the limbs at the rear end are used for swimming. All are rather alike and seem to be temporary parasites, able to change hosts.

Subclass Cirripedia Most of this subclass are recognizable as barnacles, either stalked or without a stalk (as are the common barnacles of the shoreline), but there are also parasitic barnacles only recognizable by their development. Barnacles are usually hermaphrodites, like many completely sessile animals, and first give rise to a nauplius larva, which molts to a bivalved cyprid larva that looks rather like an ostracod.

The cyprid settles on its antennae and metamorphoses to the adult barnacle, feeding by sweeping a net of six-branched appendages to its mouth at regular intervals. The hard plates protecting the sedentary barnacle are often calcified and may become very thick. It is small wonder that barnacles are

Balanus 0.5 in diameter

Cirripedia

Lepas 1.2 in

able to resist not only desiccation at low tide, but also the pressure of storm waves. The muscle fibers holding the valves together and the cover down on top, are unusually large.

Two groups of parasitic barnacles (recognizable only by their cyprid larva) attack echinoderms and crabs, often causing castration of male crabs.

Subclass Malacostraca Most malacostracans are complicated, large, heavily armored crustaceans such as crabs and lobsters. There are small forms, the most primitive being the filter-feeding phyllocariids such as *Nebalia* of shallow water and *Nebaliopsis*, pelagic in the deep ocean.

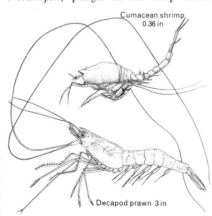

Cumacean shrimp 0.36 in

Decapod prawn 3 in

Larger and more complex, but still relatively primitive, are the mantis shrimps, or stomatopoda. These are elongate carnivores,

living in crevices in coral reefs or in burrows they dig in sand or gravel, where they wait for passing prey. The prey may be seized from the burrow or the stomatopod may stalk it then leap on it. In either case it is seized by the large pocketknifelike second thoracic appendages. The animal is aptly called a mantis shrimp, for it resembles in its rapidity of attack and form the terrestrial praying mantis, and has much the same way of capturing prey.

More important than either of these two groups are the euphausiids and decapods, which together form the eucarids. Euphausiids are prawnlike crustaceans up to three inches long, entirely pelagic and mainly oceanic, although a few species such as *Meganyctiphanes* live in coastal waters.

They have a series of light organs that can be moved by special muscles, and they possess lenses and filters. Their function is not yet established, although in *Meganyctiphanes* they have been observed to glow intermittently. Euphausiids are important because they can occur in dense swarms and form a major part of the diet of baleen whales. In the Barents Sea, almost a third of the diet of herring has been found to be euphausiids. Some decapods resemble euphausiids superficially, such as prawns and shrimps, some of which are farmed and are of considerable economic importance. Most decapods have many gills, protected by the wings of the carapace. In crabs this is tightly joined to the trunk, forming a more or less closed branchial chamber. This arrangement has allowed the crabs to come out on land, leading eventually to the completely terrestrial giant coconut crab *Birgus*, which returns to the sea only to shake off the young larvae attached to its legs. The large claws of crabs and lobsters are used both as powerful weapons and as signalling devices. *Birgus* can cut branches one inch in diameter as well as open coconuts. Crabs and lobsters are economically important as a food source for man, for fish and for cephalopods, and they are the largest and most advanced crustaceans.

Class Insecta

Only a few hundred species of the million or so known insects are marine or live in the intertidal zone, and none of these remain permanently submerged under the sea. Some, such as the seaskaters, are truly oceanic. These are related to freshwater gerrids, and prey on small organisms in the surface film. Others are littoral and there are many saltmarsh and mangrove species of mosquitos and flies, for example, and these are obviously bridging habitats toward the marine environment.

The most familiar marine insects are probably the seaweed flies (*Coelopidae*), which use the seaweed heaps on the shoreline for food and shelter, and occasionally are sufficiently abundant to be a nuisance to people on the beaches. The considerable variety of insects that has made the first steps to enter the marine environment proper include hymenoptera and parasitic anopluran and mallophagan lice, which attack seals and seabirds.

Insects are so successful on land and there are various suggestions for the relative failure of the class to make serious inroads into the marine environment. Among these are such ideas as competition with the already established crustaceans, or difficulties in osmotic regulation when submerged respiration is also needed.

PHYLUM ECHINODERMATA

This is the largest purely marine phylum, containing sedentary animals that are almost

all instantly recognizable by a combination of striking features such as fivefold symmetry and a calcareous skeleton of calcite plates within the skin. These may be fused together to make a rigid box, as in sea urchins, or may be variously articulated or scattered within the skin in more flexible groups. It is possible that the basic fivefold symmetry resulted from the arrangement of plates around the anus, as seen in some of the fossil echinoderms.

The most peculiar feature of echinoderms is their water-vascular system. This is a system of water-filled tubes that end in blind projections through the skin. The animal can operate these hydraulically, and in starfish the projections form tube feet on which the animal walks. In other echinoderm classes they are used to collect food and for respiration.

Very nearly all echinoderms are bottom-living, and most feed on particles, either by filtering them from the water or by collecting them off sand grains and mud that are eaten. Starfish, however, can feed on larger organisms, and some are economically important as predators of oysters and mussels. There are five classes of living echinoderms.

Class Crinoidea

Feather stars or sea lilies are familiar fossils, and while some living ones are cup-shaped animals set on top of a long pentagonal stalk with a holdfast at the base like the fossils, the most modern crinoids only remain stalked for a period in early life. They can creep around, and some may even swim by flapping their

Larva

4 in

3 in

Crinoids

arms. Crinoids feed on particles of detritus and small living organisms that fall on the arms. These are trapped in mucus and pass along grooves in the arms to the mouth.

Class Asteroidea

These are active echinoderms, burrowing or creeping on the bottom using tube feet. Many are predatory, feeding on mollusks, other echinoderms, corals and sea anemones. Starfish can open bivalves by combined hy-

2 in across

Asteroids

8 in across

draulic and muscular action, exerting more than six and a half pounds of pressure until

the bivalve gapes sufficiently for the starfish to insert its everted stomach. Both scallops and some sea anemones are stimulated to swim in an attempt to avoid starfish. Not all starfish have only five arms, some may have many more, such as *Solaster* (15 to 50), or the Crown of thorns, *Acanthaster*. Crown of thorns have greatly multiplied in certain areas and threaten some coral reefs. Starfish have striking powers of regeneration, and loss of arms and subsequent regeneration from single arms seems normal in certain species such as *Linckia*.

Class Ophiuroidea

Ophiuroids all have small disks and long muscular arms. They move by rowing movements of the arms, unlike the starfish, which move on their tube feet. These animals can be exceedingly abundant and densities of several thousand per square yard have been photographed on the seabed, with several layers of ophiuroids on top of each other.

4 in

Ophiuroids   in burrow

These are mainly filter feeders, but some feed on small organisms such as mollusks. Like starfish they have great powers of regeneration from fragments, and in *Ophiactis* splitting in two is a common method of asexual reproduction. Much the most spectacular ophiuroid is *Gorgonocephalus*, whose arms repeatedly divide so that when sitting on a coral the animal looks like a tangle of small snakes.

Class Echinoidea

Sea urchins are varied in shape, from more or less rounded forms such as *Cidaris* to the flattened and curiously shaped sand dollars (*Clypeaster* and *Rotula*). All share a rigid test covered with spines. Among the spines are tube feet and small pincerlike organs, which clean the animal, cover it with camouflage, or inject poison into attackers. All sea

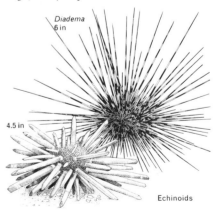

Diadema 6 in

4.5 in

Echinoids

urchins move using their spines, or spines and tube feet. Some burrow resting places in rock, while others live buried in sand, but most crawl over rock surfaces, scraping the algal film. Sea urchins are important algal browsers, using a complicated device for moving five rasping teeth. Sea urchins of temperate seas often seem sluggish animals, but tropical forms such as *Diadema* move rapidly and have long, sharp spines, which they shake and point at approaching objects in a remarkably alert manner.

Class Holothuroidea

Holothurians are sausage-shaped echinoderms with no arms. They usually burrow in sand or mud, or plow along the surface of the sea-bed, feeding with a treelike set of tube feet around the anterior mouth. The skin is toughened by large numbers of calcareous

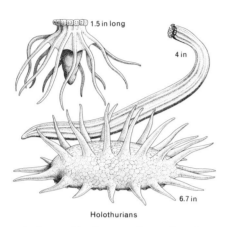

1.5 in long
4 in
6.7 in

Holothurians

spicules, and is often rough or spiny. Some holothurians can defend themselves by ejecting masses of thin sticky threads from the anus to entangle predators. Others eject the gut itself. Abyssal ooze-living holothurians are often strangely shaped, and there are few pelagic forms, one resembling a medusa. Sun-dried holothurians are eaten by man, but the chief importance of the class is in recycling organic matter of bottom sediments.

PHYLUM HEMICHORDATA

This phylum includes two classes. Enteropneusts (gut breathers) are fragile yellow or whitish worms, which burrow in subtidal sand or mud. The body, which is up to six and a half feet long, is divided into three parts and has a fat proboscis. This resembles an acorn and these animals are sometimes called acorn worms. A pouch in the proboscis opening to the pharynx has been supposed to be a notochord like that of chordata, but this is doubtful. The ciliated gill slits

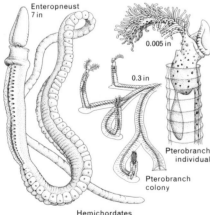

Enteropneust 7 in
0.005 in
0.3 in
Pterobranch individual
Pterobranch colony

Hemichordates

found serially in the second segment, and the tornaria larva, much like an echinoderm larva, suggest that these animals are implicated in the history of chordata, but their exact relationships are unclear.

The body is slimy and covered with cilia, all species smell strongly of bromoform, perhaps a chemical defense against predators.

The second class, the pterobranchs (wing gills) are quite different. They are much smaller colonial animals, living attached to shells and objects on the bottom in tubes they secrete. Each animal has a crown of tentacles, not unlike a bryozoan, but chordate affinities are indicated by the single pair of

gill slits and the tripartite organization. These little animals are probably the surviving relative of the extinct graptolites, an important group in the Ordovician period, but they are now of zoological interest only.

PHYLUM TUNICATA

These are filter feeders with a unique cellulose tunic and there is one sessile group and two pelagic ones.

Class Ascidiacea

These are common on the lower shore, where suitable sites for attachment occur, and are found down to the deep sea. Adults are completely sessile, often brightly colored and either solitary or colonial. Individuals of colonial species are usually small, although a colony may be much larger. Solitary species measure up to ten inches in length. Almost

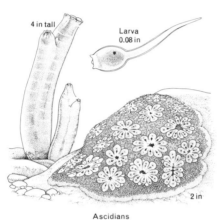

4 in tall
Larva 0.08 in
2 in

Ascidians

all feed by drawing water into a buccal siphon by ciliary action, trapping food particles on a gill network, and expelling water through an atrial siphon. Large ascidians may filter hundreds of pints of seawater a day. A few aberrant deepsea forms have abandoned filter feeding and are apparently carnivorous.

The free-swimming larval form resembles a minute amphibian tadpole, and its structure, with dorsal nerve cord, segmented muscular tail and notochord, gives the clue to the chordate relationship of the tunicates. Ascidians have simple brains that they can regenerate if damaged, and are rather unlike other chordates. The larval stage is short, and after choosing a settlement site the larva soon transform to the adult. A few adult ascidians are eaten, but the group is of chief economic importance in fouling of ships.

Class Thaliacea

Salps and doliolids are barrel-shaped transparent organisms that are jet propelled by contraction of muscle bands. In the small *Doliolum* these bands are completely circular and the animal resembles a small delicate wine barrel. In salps the tunic is much thicker and the muscles only extend half-way round the body. The gills in salps and doliolids are simpler than in ascidians, and food particles are caught on a mucus network. These animals are capable of very rapid reproduction and have a growth rate higher than that of any other metazoan, so they are able to exploit favorable conditions and are, with larvaceans, of considerable economic importance since they feed on the nanoplankton at the base of the food chain. Life cycles are complex, involving alternation of generations, and long chains of individuals may be formed.

Pyrosoma is essentially like a floating tube open at the rear end. The water that has been filtered passes to the hollow interior of

Pyrosoma colony 3 in
Salp 0.8 in
Doliolid 0.08 in
Thaliaceans

the tube, and the colony moves forward slowly by jet propulsion. Colonies may grow by budding to a large size and are found from the surface to deep water. Each individual has two special cell masses containing luminescent bacteria, and the entire colony lights up brightly when stimulated.

Class Larvacea

These are somewhat like ascidian tadpole larvae, and are thought to be derived from a larval form that has become precociously mature. They feed in bizarre gelatinous houses, which they secrete, complete with filters and food-collecting apparatus. Water is pumped through the house by periodic movements of the tail, and when the filters clog the house is abandoned, to serve as a small bacterial "greenhouse" exploited by other animals as a food source. Their houses are the most complicated objects made by any animals; the way in which they are secreted, pumped up and finally entered tail first is truly astonishing.

animal out of house 0.24 in long
0.02 in
Larvacean

Larvaceans are of considerable economic importance, for as well as utilizing the smallest nanoplankton they are the chief food of many fish larva.

PHYLUM ACRANIA

These are small yellow-white eellike animals without paired fins. They live buried in coarse sand and gravel deposits, mainly in shallow water. They may be extremely numerous in suitable bottom deposits, up to five thousand animals in each square yard. The backbone, or notochord, extends to the tip of the snout and there is no brain or ears. Light-receptive cells lie inside the nervous system all along the body. The mouth opens into an oral hood, which is fringed by a coarse sieve of stiff tentacles, and the animal filter feeds on small particles, drawing a current of water in through the mouth by means of the cilia on a long series of gill bars. The gill bars are enclosed and protected in an atrial cavity and the filtered water flows out through a ventral pore half-way back along the body. When feeding, amphioxus usually just pokes the tip of the snout out of the deposit, and if disturbed rapidly burrows deeper. Amphioxus swims by lateral oscil-

lations of the body brought about by contractions of the serial V-shaped muscle blocks along the body. It can swim either forward or backward. Usually, it makes short darting excursions from the bottom and then dives in again, head or tail first.

The chief interest of amphioxus is that it shows a remarkable mixture of fishlike and tunicatelike characters, the latter especially noticeable during development. Certainly, the group does show us something of the nature of early fishlike chordates, and for this reason has long been a favorite zoologists' animal, though unfamiliar to most people. Some species, however, such as the Amoy-amphioxus, are abundant enough to be used as a source of food.

Planktonic larvae are like the adult but lack the protective chamber enclosing the gill bars, which is not needed until the animal enters the bottom deposit and has to protect these delicate gills. The mouth of the larva is on the left side, not in the middle as in the adult, and a fairly complicated metamorphosis is undergone before the adult condition is reached.

LARVAL FORMS

Most groups of marine animals pass through a larval stage that acts as the distributory phase in the life cycle. The eggs hatch not into a miniature adult but into a minute transparent larva as different from the adult as a caterpillar from a butterfly. The larvae of several different groups share the same characteristics, because they face the common problems of keeping afloat in the plankton during the dispersal phase. They then need to select the site for settling and transformation into the adult. Larvae, therefore, are often ciliated, with cilia arrayed in rings or bands around the surface. They usually have eyespots to help direct them into the rich grazing of the upper sunlit layers, and simple equilibrium sensors to keep them upright. To aid ciliary or muscular effort to

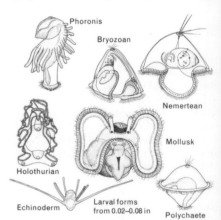

Phoronis
Bryozoan
Nemertean
Mollusk
Holothurian
Echinoderm
Larval forms from 0.02–0.08 in
Polychaete

maintain position, larvae often have long extensions of the body or limbs to slow the rate of sinking. Many may even lighten themselves by chemical means. One consequence of these adaptions to a pelagic life is that marine larval forms are often extremely beautiful. The shimmer of rapidly beating cilia in a glassily transparent animal just visible under the microscope is one of the most elegant sights in nature.

Change to adult form may be remarkably radical and rapid, or it may be a long gradual process, as in amphioxus and echinoderms. Most fish larvae are rather similar to the adults, and change to the adult is more or less linked to gradual increase in size. This is not true of all fishes, however, and larval swordfish and angler fishes, for example, are quite unlike the adult. Manifestly the larvae of groups that are absolutely sessile, such as barnacles or ascidians, bear the entire responsibility for selecting a site for the adult, and they are equipped with chemical sensors and patterns of testing behavior for this purpose. To a lesser degree this requirement falls on all larvae of inactive groups, and change to the adult may be long delayed if no suitable site presents itself. Different species (even within the same group) have adopted different strategies for their larvae which do not feed and only spend a short time in the plankton. Ascidian tadpoles and the larvae of chitons and scaphopods are of this kind. An entirely opposite idea is to produce many small eggs that hatch into small larvae that grow and feed in the plankton for months before transforming into adults. One edible mussel, *Mytilus*, can produce 12 million larvae, but of course success is much more dependent on good conditions in the plankton, so that this second strategy is good for exploiting a favorable year, but bad for riding out some failure of the plankton pastures.

PHYLUM CHORDATA

These are animals with a backbone, dorsal tubular nervous system and serial gills. Non-aquatic chordates do not have gills in the adult stage (we do not have them ourselves), but they are represented in development stages. The group sometimes includes acrania and tunicata, and has been divided in many ways. The different fish groups, for example, are sometimes given the rank of classes, but it is probably simplest to use the scheme below.

There are two major divisions of the chordata: the animals that do not have jaws, and those that do. By far the most successful chordates, in numbers of species as well as in numbers of individuals, are the bony fish, but we are fortunate in having alive today a number of different fish groups, such as the coelacanths, that show us other stages in chordate evolution. There are a few marine reptiles and a limited number of secondary marine mammals, but apart from fish, sea-birds are the other important chordates associated with the oceans.

SUPERCLASS AGNATHA

The earliest fish from the Ordovician period were agnathans. Jaws were lacking and the mouth was terminal or subterminal. Argument still continues about the precise numbering of the gill openings of these early fish. Present-day agnathans are included in two different groups, distinguished by their gill openings, by the number of nasal sacs and semicircular canals of the ear, as well as by their life history. Sometimes one of these groups, the hagfish, is linked to one of the fossil agnathan groups, and the other, the lampreys, to the other group.

Class Cyclostomata

Lampreys and hagfish are set apart from all other chordates because they lack jaws. The backbone consists of a gelatinous turgid tube, the notochord—there are no vertebrae like those of higher fishes. The mouth is more or less circular, terminal and suctorial. They feed by means of a rasping tongue while attached to the host. The gills are muscular pouches and water flows in and out through the same openings since the mouth is held against the host.

Hagfish seem to feed on dead or dying animals, but lampreys attach themselves to living fish and rasp sores from which they extract blood and tissue fragments. Sea lampreys, which are up to three feet long, also attach themselves to larger animals as hitchhikers, and both basking sharks and small cetaceans are commonly scarred by lampreys they have carried. Hagfish are entirely marine, but lampreys are like salmon,

they enter rivers to breed and the larva lives buried in mud for several years before it changes to the adult, which migrates down to the sea. Some lampreys are entirely fresh-

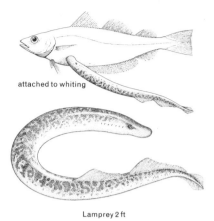

attached to whiting

Lamprey 2 ft

water and may do very considerable damage to freshwater fisheries, but in the oceans their attacks are probably not significant. Jawless vertebrates were abundant in the Ordovician, Silurian and Devonian periods, so their only descendents are of much zoological interest.

SUPERCLASS GNATHOSTOMATA

This second superclass contains all the other five classes of chordates, only four being marine since the amphibia have not succeeded in invading the sea. Gnathostomes are much more successful than the Agnatha; the development of jaws enabled them to occupy a wide variety of niches involving different diets, and allowed a more efficient method of collecting food. Once jaws had been evolved from the supporting elements

Chimaera 3 ft

Shark 6.5 ft

Skate 2 ft

Ray egg case 0.8 in wide

Electric ray 3 ft

Sturgeon 11 ft

of the gill apparatus, a long and fascinating series of steps has been traced in the gradual lightening and simplification of the skeletal elements and their articulations, until finally, as the remarkable comparative anatomical work of the last century showed, some of these elements became modified into the ear ossicles of the mammal.

Class Pisces

There are about 20 thousand known living fish, of which some 60 percent are marine. About a hundred new species are described each year. By far the greatest number of these are the bony teleosts, and most live in shallow warm seas. Fish have entered every environment in the sea and are found from the deep ocean floor to the surface layers. Adult fish range from 12 millimeters to 49 feet and show an extraordinary variety of ways of life. Bony fish in particular provide one of the best examples of adaptive radiation of an animal group into different niches. All fish groups, including the lampreys and hagfish, share certain special features that non-aquatic vertebrates do not possess. One of the most important of these is the lateral line system, a system of open canals containing sense organs that are responsive to water flow in the canals resulting from movements in the water outside the fish. It seems likely that fish use the lateral line system to detect other fish and to locate their prey. The system is enormously developed in some abyssal forms. Even more remarkable, but less widespread, are the different kinds of electrical generators and detectors found in some freshwater and marine fish groups. Like the lateral line system, these can be used

to locate objects in the surrounding water, or by the fish monitoring the electrical activity of its prey. Such specializations are peculiar to fish and directly related to the physical properties of the water in which they live.

Subclass Holocephali These are bottom-living fish of shallow waters and the deep sea which are distantly related to sharks. They have a very large head and a body that tapers to an elongate whip to increase the baseline of the highly developed lateral line system. The skeleton is cartilaginous and they resemble sharks in the urea content of tissues. Slow swimmers, they flap their pectoral fins like butterflies and near neutral buoyancy is achieved by very watery tissues and light oil stored in the liver. Holocephali feed on mollusks and have curious very characteristic tooth plates. Some species may be three feet or longer and a few are of commercial importance.

Subclass Elasmobranchi This is a small group of carnivorous fish with cartilaginous skeletons that are partly calcified in the larger forms. The skin is covered with an array of denticles that are specialized in the mouth to form rows of cutting or crushing teeth. Each gill opens to the outside separately as there is no operculum. The end of the backbone typically bends upward to form the upper lobe of the tail, an arrangement allowing lift to be provided to balance the lift from the anterior paired fins. Most elasmobranchs are denser than water, since a swim bladder is lacking, but some store oil to achieve neutral buoyancy.

All elasmobranchs have special electro-receptors, and some, such as the electric ray, *Torpedo*, can also generate stunning shocks. Like holocephali and the coelacanth, elasmobranchs store urea in the blood and tissues, making them nearly the same concentration as seawater. Fertilization is internal (the males have rather complicated intromittent organs) and some species lay eggs while others bear live young. The largest elasmobranchs are filter feeders, like the baleen whales, and the whale shark, basking shark and manta rays are the largest fish of any group. The white shark, *Carcharodon*, and the related porbeagle, *Lamna*, and the mako, *Isurus*, are warm blooded. Several species are known to have attacked man. Commercial and sport fisheries exist for several species, and data from these have shown that sharks undergo extensive migrations. Blue sharks tagged in Cornwall have been re-caught off the coast of South America and off Long Island.

Rays are usually bottom living, from shallow water down to the deep ocean floor, but some species are pelagic, and a very few enter freshwater. Sharks range also from shallow seas to the deep ocean, where the squaloid sharks have radiated into a variety of black, green-eyed corpulent fish, swollen with enormous livers containing oil for flotation.

Subclass Chondrostei The only marine chondrosteans are the isolated sturgeons, which live in the sea but migrate into freshwater to breed. The skeleton is nearly all cartilaginous, but there are some bony plates on the skin, and denticlelike structures between them. Sturgeons stir up mud on the bottom using the snout and swallow small invertebrates that are disturbed. They are commercially valuable for caviar, and isinglass is manufactured from the swim bladder.

Subclass Teleostei This is by far the most important fish group and much the hardest

Herring 10–12 in

Coelacanth 4 ft

to characterize, since there are so many different kinds and their adaptive radiation is relatively recent, so that clear divisions between the different teleost groups are not yet apparent. Consequently, teleost classification is still subject to changes, and many groupings appear in different books.

It is generally agreed that all came from herringlike fish known as fossils in the Jurassic period 195 million years ago, and that living herrings, tarpons, sprats and pilchards are rather like the ancestral teleost. From this fairly simple structural plan there soon came the immense diversity of living forms, resulting in fish as different as the seahorse and tuna, or garden eels and flying fish. The key advance seems to have been the development of the swim bladder, a gas-filled sac that allows the teleost to achieve neutral buoyancy, and so frees the fins from having to generate lift. Compared to sharks, teleosts are much more maneuverable and many can, for example, swim slowly backward. The gas in the swim bladder buoys up the skeleton, so this can be made of dense bone. The tail is symmetrical and scales are usually thin and light, or even absent altogether. The gills open into a common chamber covered by an operculum, and fins are flexible or stiffened by bony spines.

Internally, apart from the swim bladder, teleosts have an efficient heart and circulatory system, a kidney with a reduced filtration system in marine forms and a more complex brain than elasmobranchs. Few teleosts bear live young; fertilization is usually external, and the parents may either abandon millions of floating eggs to take their chance in the plankton (cod, turbot, ling) or take a great deal of care of few eggs laid in nests (wrasse) or kept in special pouches within the male (seahorses).

Some fish have bizarre reproductive cycles. The deepsea angler fish males live permanently attached to the females and a fairly large number of shallow-water reef fish change from female to male as they age, and are self-fertile hermaphrodites.

Teleosts often have complex and beautiful color patterns, and they can change these rapidly. Deepsea fish are usually dark brown or black, those in the upper layers silvery-sided, which camouflages them by reflection. Down to the limit of penetration of natural light into seawater, in the open ocean, fish have larger and larger eyes in order to hunt luminous prey, or to see prey that they may illuminate with their own headlight organs. Others rely on olfaction or vibration detectors and have reduced eyes.

Most teleosts are carnivores, catching prey either by rapid hunting, such as mackerel and tuna, or by lying in wait like barracuda and angler fish. A few, such as herring, filter

feed using a sieve attached to the gills, and many specialize, eating such invertebrates as worms, corals or sea urchins, having suitably modified mouths and teeth to deal with these quite different diets. The greatest numbers of teleost species are found in warm seas, around the coast and continental shelf. Fewer species occur in similar situations in cold seas, and the teleost fauna is still poorer in the deep ocean than in the surface layers. However, the teleosts that are most important economically—herring and cod species—live in cool-water shelf areas and the surface layers.

Subclass Crossopterygii There are three living lungfish in fresh water, but only one marine coelacanth, *Latimeria chalumnae*, found in deep water off the Comoro Islands near Madagascar. *Latimeria* is covered in bluish brown rough scales and has many of the features of the group known first from the Jurassic period fossil. The tail is three-lobed, the fins are lobed and the skull hinges at a median transverse joint. The backbone consists of a large notochord surrounded by skeletal elements which disappears in development in most fish groups. The swim bladder is filled with fat and the blood and tissues contain much urea, similar to those of sharks. *Latimeria* is a large fish that weighs up to 209 pounds and feeds on fish, which are swallowed whole. It produces very large white eggs the size of tennis balls, and bears live young. The importance of *Latimeria* lies in what it can show us of the early stock that gave rise to tetrapods. Unfortunately it has proved impossible to capture one in sufficiently good condition to understand how it uses the various puzzling features of the anatomy.

Class Reptilia

Reptiles were dominant in the sea throughout the Mesozoic Era, but today there is only a pale reflection of this assemblage of marine reptiles. Reptiles are not able to regulate their own body temperature as mammals do and therefore usually inhabit warm tropical seas. Most species reproduce by internal fertilization.

Living forms are placed in four groups: turtles, marine iguanas, sea snakes and a few ocean-living crocodiles.

Turtles have horny beaks and row themselves along with paired flippers. They have to come ashore to breed and are then at the mercy of human predators. Eggs are laid in holes dug in sand, but many young are lost when they hatch as they are eaten by sea-

birds before they can reach the sea. Some progress is being made in artificially rearing eggs and releasing young turtles. The green turtle feeds on *Thalassia*, but the other marine turtles, such as the leatherback, are carnivorous, salps and medusae both being items of their diet.

Marine iguanas such as those of the Galapagos Islands (*Amblyrhynchus*) are the only marine lizards, and are very like their terrestrial relatives. They feed on seaweed and live in large herds on the shore. Like seabirds they have nasal salt glands to rid themselves of excess salt.

Leatherback turtle 9–10 ft

Sea snakes are highly poisonous, related to cobras and kraits, and their tails are vertically compressed for swimming. Often warningly colored in red, black, yellow or white stripes, sea snakes are ovoviviparous and so do not need to come ashore to breed.

Class Aves

Seabirds range from waders, which live and feed in estuaries, to birds of the open ocean such as petrels and albatrosses, which come ashore only to breed. The emperor penguin breeds on sea ice in the Antarctic and is the only bird that never comes ashore. Seabirds feed mainly on fish and catch them by diving (gannets and pelicans), underwater swimming using the feet (most divers, cormorants) or underwater swimming with flipper-like forelimbs (penguins). They are thus at the top of the food chain, and vulnerable to chemical pollution.

King penguins 3 ft

Seabirds that search for food from the air (terns, gulls, gannets) are almost invariably white or pale gray, perhaps as a camouflage. Many nest in dense colonies, and it is thus economically feasible to collect their accumulated droppings, guano, as a source of phosphate.

Class Mammalia

Marine mammals vary in their degree of adaption to life in water. There are those such as the polar bear and sea otter that are little modified. The polar bear, *Thalarctos maritimus*, however, is different from most bears in

that it has long legs, which make it a powerful swimmer, and a thicker coat, which insulates it against the bitter cold of the ice-strewn seas where it feeds and breeds. The sea otter has webbed feet and is more adapted to an aquatic life, but still it only inhabits the coastal regions off California and Alaska, where it feeds on the giant kelp beds of those areas. The sea otter spends nearly all its life at sea, sleeping among the kelp and feeding on shellfish; even the young are born at sea.

The majority of marine mammals have, however, profoundly changed from their original terrestrial form. There are three groups—the sirenians, the seals and the whales. The sirenians, or sea cows, consist of two families—the dugongs and the manatees, both of which are distantly related to elephants and have become almost totally adapted to life in the sea. They have huge cigar-shaped bodies with the front limbs formed like paddles. There are no hind limbs and the tail is flattened. Both dugong and the three species of manatee live in coastal regions, grazing on the pastures of *Zostera* and *Thalassia*.

There are three groups of seals: earless, or true, seals; eared seals, or sea lions; and the walrus. They are all carnivorous and possess streamlined bodies and limbs modified to flippers. A layer of thick blubber beneath the skin protects them from the cold. As their name suggests the true, or earless, seals have no external ear flaps and also have the distinguishing feature that their tails cannot swing forward under the body; thus, on land, they can only clumsily haul themselves along with their short forelimbs. The sea lions have conspicuous external ear flaps and can turn the hind limbs under the body and move in a galloping fashion on land. The California sea lion, *Zalophus californianus*, is the most familiar and is often seen in zoos and circuses. The walrus, with its characteristic long tusks, is found in Arctic waters.

The most impressively adapted mammals are the whales and dolphins. They have tapering streamlined bodies; the front limbs have become broad paddle-like flippers and there are no hind limbs. The horizontal fluked tail makes whales immediately distinguishable from fish. A thick layer of blubber just beneath the skin insulates and protects the whole body. Whales cannot move at all on land and require water on their skin at all times. They lack a breastbone and often die when stranded on beaches because of pressure on their lungs. There are two distinct types of whale: toothed whales and whalebone, or baleen, whales. The toothed whales, including sperm whales, dolphins and narwhals, are generally smaller than baleen whales. They have conical pointed teeth in the lower or in both jaws or a single long, tusklike tooth in the upper jaw. The diet of the toothed whales consists mainly of fish and squid. The baleen whales are all large—the smallest reaching no less than 17 feet when fully grown and the largest, the Blue whale, *Balaenoptera musculus*, is the largest mammal that has ever lived, reaching a record size of 108 feet. The baleen whales do not have teeth but have instead plates of whalebone, or baleen, set on the upper jaw. These plates act as sieves to strain the whale's planktonic food from the water.

TABLES

CONTINENTAL SHELF AREAS (Seabed not deeper than 200m/656ft)

ATLANTIC OCEAN

Ocean/Subarea	Square kilometers	Square miles
Northwest Atlantic	1,260,000	486,360
W. Greenland	85,000	32,800
Labrador	100,000	38,600
Newfoundland	490,000	189,140
Nova Scotia & St Lawrence	310,000	119,660
New England	185,000	71,410
Middle Atlantic	90,000	34,740
Northeast Atlantic	3,011,000	1,162,250
Iceland	142,000	54,810
Barents Sea	1,300,000	501,800
North Sea	550,000	212,300
Skagerrak & Kattegat	40,000	15,440
British Isles	449,000	173,310
Baltic	420,000	162,120
Spain—Portugal—France	60,000	23,160
Southwest Atlantic	1,950,000	752,700
Guyana	160,000	61,760
Brazil	610,000	235,460
Uruguay	150,000	57,900
Argentina	1,030,000	397,580
Southeast Atlantic	no data	
Eastern Central Atlantic	480,000	185,280
Morocco coastal	65,000	25,090
Sahara ,,	65,000	25,090
C. Verde ,,	110,000	42,460
C. Sherbo ,,	70,000	27,020
W. Gulf Guinea	50,000	19,300
C. Gulf Guinea	65,000	25,090
S. Gulf Guinea	55,000	21,230
Western Central Atlantic	1,280,000	494,080
US east coast	110,000	42,460
Bahamas—Cuba	120,000	46,320
Gulf of Mexico	600,000	231,600
Caribbean	250,000	96,500
S. America	200,000	77,200
Total Atlantic	7,981,000	3,080,670

PACIFIC OCEAN

Ocean/Subarea	Square kilometers	Square miles
Northwest Pacific	995,000	384,070
Okhotsk Sea	610,000	235,460
Japan Sea	202,000	77,970
N.W. Pacific areas	183,000	70,638
Northeast Pacific	1,276,000	492,540
Bering Sea	1,000,000	386,000
Oregon—S.E. Alaska	96,000	37,060
Gulf of Alaska	100,000	38,600
Alaska Peninsula	80,000	30,880
Southwest Pacific	930,000	358,980
New Zealand	200,000	77,200
Australia	730,000	281,780
Southeast Pacific	177,000	68,320
Peru	87,000	33,580
Chile	90,000	34,740
Western Central Pacific	4,610,000	1,779,460
Yellow Sea—E. China Sea	950,000	366,700
Formosa Strait	280,000	108,080
Gulf of Tongking	200,000	77,200
Gulf of Thailand	305,000	117,730
S. China Sea	970,000	374,420
Java Sea	580,000	223,880
Gulf of Carpentaria	960,000	370,560
Islands	365,000	140,890
Eastern Central Pacific	450,000	173,700
Total Pacific	8,438,000	3,257,070

INDIAN OCEAN

Ocean/Subarea	Square kilometers	Square miles
East Africa	390,000	150,540
Arabian Sea	400,000	154,400
Bay of Bengal	610,000	235,460
Indonesia	130,000	50,180
Western Australia	380,000	146,680
South Australian coast	260,000	100,360
Red Sea	180,000	69,480
Persian Gulf	240,000	92,640
Madagascar	210,000	81,060
Oceanic islands	200,000	77,200
Total Indian	3,000,000	1,158,000

PRODUCTION BY FISHERY COMMODITY & CONTINENT (Thousand metric tons)

FISH: FRESH, CHILLED OR FROZEN

Continent/Area	1965	1966	1967	1968	1969	1970	1971	1972	1973	1974
Africa	22	20	18	18	19	25	25	23	34	36
N. America	435	443	412	457	483	482	465	491	549	466
S. America	67	58	85	94	94	106	141	106	172	179
Asia	1,642	1,488	1,592	1,883	1,779	2,220	2,562	2,735	2,838	2,706
Europe	607	636	688	738	856	957	967	992	1,067	1,102
Australia & Oceania	—	—	—	—	—	—	—	—	—	—
USSR	1,578	1,766	1,879	1,952	2,308	2,557	2,45C	2,607	2,891	3,085
Total	4,351	4,411	4,674	5,142	5,539	6,347	6,610	6,954	7,551	7,574

FISH: DRIED, SALTED OR SMOKED

Continent/Area	1965	1966	1967	1968	1969	1970	197˙	1972	1973	1974
Africa	147	155	154	232	268	306	283	344	325	318
N. America	103	96	129	98	97	99	104	96	71	80
S. America	70	79	94	87	64	65	63	72	82	69
Asia	988	1,064	1,047	1,348	1,398	1,350	1,374	1,434	1,360	1,404
Europe	753	730	716	625	598	614	575	603	547	544
Australia & Oceania	*	*	·*	*	*	*	*	*	*	*
USSR	873	794	786	797	735	721	658	632	735	700
Total	2,934	2,918	2,926	3,187	3,160	3,155	3,060	3,181	3,120	3,115

FISH: AIRTIGHT CONTAINERS (CANNED)

Continent/Area	1965	1966	1967	1968	1969	1970	1971	1972	1973	1974
Africa	145	145	157	124	121	141	108	143	182	217
N. America	345	390	331	378	335	409	424	487	499	488
S. America	104	90	90	96	94	116	116	126	124	132
Asia	1,188	1,337	1,420	1,664	1,735	1,756	1,901	1,923	1,965	1,934
Europe	562	584	600	573	614	676	711	685	727	732
Australia & Oceania	5	6	7	9	8	8	32	36	37	37
USSR	427	486	517	547	617	690	743	796	820	887
Total	2,776	3,038	3,122	3,391	3,524	3,796	4,035	4,196	4,354	4,427

CRUSTACEANS & MOLLUSKS: FRESH, FROZEN, DRIED, SALTED, ETC.

Continent/Area	1965	1966	1967	1968	1969	1970	1971	1972	1973	1974
Africa	9	9	9	14	14	16	17	20	23	22
N. America	138	144	147	172	179	178	185	190	200	197
S. America	30	26	27	33	37	46	49	53	56	55
Asia	338	400	576	698	648	505	482	530	643	649
Europe	118	118	117	121	126	115	119	140	119	118
Australia & Oceania	8	9	11	13	13	14	16	18	17	16
USSR	—	—	—	—	—	—	—	—	—	—
Total	641	706	887	1,051	1,017	874	868	951	1,058	1,057

CRUSTACEANS & MOLLUSKS: AIRTIGHT CONTAINERS (CANNED)

Continent/Area	1965	1966	1967	1968	1969	1970	1971	1972	1973	1974
Africa	1	1	1	*	*	*	*	*	*	*
N. America	62	65	66	63	61	67	71	70	73	77
S. America	3	3	3	2	3	2	3	2	2	3
Asia	58	49	60	60	58	66	57	73	69	61
Europe	27	29	29	30	36	39	34	38	40	42
Australia & Oceania	—	1	1	2	2	2	2	2	2	2
USSR	6	6	5	5	5	4	3	2	2	2
Total	157	154	165	162	165	180	170	187	188	187

Grand total	10,859	11,227	11,774	12,933	13,405	14,352	14,743	15,469	16,271	16,360

FISH OILS AND FATS

Continent/Area	1965	1966	1967	1968	1969	1970	1971	1972	1973	1974
Africa	68	61	78	139	117	95	68	72	99	73
N. America	116	101	85	117	114	122	150	105	123	126
S. America	137	171	310	328	224	335	472	238	53	243
Asia	38	37	42	54	71	106	89	104	124	144
Europe	379	465	544	401	338	316	311	332	336	331
Australia & Oceania	—	—	—	—	—	—	—	—	—	—
USSR	44	48	55	57	60	60	63	63	63	63
Total	782	883	1,114	1,096	924	1,034	1,153	914	798	980

FISH MEAL & SOLUBLES

Continent/Area	1965	1966	1967	1968	1969	1970	1971	1972	1973	1974
Africa	357	358	427	563	530	428	352	398	417	346
N. America	428	399	376	423	456	478	523	528	524	536
S. America	1,401	1,723	2,020	2,202	1,831	2,492	2,248	1,062	577	1,159
Asia	370	392	440	510	612	702	725	795	861	830
Europe	889	1,007	1,056	990	962	957	1,040	991	944	1,019
Australia & Oceania	1	1	1	2	2	3	3	3	2	2
U.S.S.R.	203	238	294	326	348	368	406	440	489	488
Total	3,649	4,118	4,614	5,016	4,741	5,428	5,297	4,217	3,814	4,380

Grand total	4,431	5,001	5,728	6,112	5,665	6,462	6,450	5,131	4,612	5,360

* = Less than 500 metric tons

LANDINGS OF FISH BY OCEANS (Thousand metric tons)

ATLANTIC OCEAN LANDINGS (including Caribbean)

Diadromous Fish	1965	1966	1967	1968	1969	1970	1971	1972	1973	1974
Sturgeon, etc.	*	*	*	*	*	*	*	*	*	*
River eels	9	10	9	10	9	10	11	10	13	12
Salmon, trout, etc.	323	597	552	658	892	1,547	1,623	2,008	2,085	1,969
Shad, milkfish, etc.	40	41	42	56	69	47	48	39	33	40
Miscellaneous	0	0	0	0	0	0	0	0	0	0
Total	372	648	603	724	970	1,604	1,682	2,057	2,131	2,021

Marine Fish	1965	1966	1967	1968	1969	1970	1971	1972	1973	1974
Flounder, sole, etc.	523	562	608	647	695	726	742	697	662	639
Cod, hake, etc.	5,470	5,718	6,186	6,956	6,903	6,932	6,548	6,767	6,657	7,111
Redfish, bass, etc.	1,301	1,405	1,500	1,432	1,392	1,822	1,762	1,863	1,855	1,992
Jack, mullet, etc.	659	629	650	710	784	1,057	1,387	1,393	1,647	1,514
Herring, sardines, etc.	6,992	6,936	6,894	6,848	6,052	6,056	5,776	5,863	6,269	6,165
Tuna, bonito, etc.	340	301	288	329	325	312	372	410	393	420
Mackerel, snoek, etc.	437	792	1,330	1,263	1,314	1,082	1,122	1,146	1,325	1,249
Sharks, rays, etc.	165	177	181	194	211	214	231	240	238	244
Miscellaneous	715	774	810	821	922	914	910	895	990	1,014
Total	16,602	17,294	18,447	19,200	18,598	19,115	18,850	19,274	20,036	20,348

Crustaceans	1965	1966	1967	1968	1969	1970	1971	1972	1973	1974
Crabs, etc.	105	114	102	98	116	118	124	122	122	139
Lobsters, etc.	100	99	90	100	108	100	107	110	109	107
Shrimps, prawns, etc.	273	262	279	287	289	319	315	352	334	355
Krill, etc.	0	0	0	0	0	0	0	0	0	0
Miscellaneous	5	6	19	24	31	28	28	11	23	14
Total	483	481	490	509	544	565	574	595	640	615

Mollusks	1965	1966	1967	1968	1969	1970	1971	1972	1973	1974
Winkles, conchs, etc.	12	13	12	11	11	11	10	12	13	14
Oysters	413	420	492	504	427	406	406	409	387	365
Mussels	245	228	206	259	271	275	289	335	330	281
Scallops, etc.	171	155	113	123	115	116	116	121	117	124
Clams, cockles, etc	235	243	246	232	263	259	264	261	310	323
Squid, cuttlefish, etc.	187	160	211	206	185	173	187	261	295	302
Miscellaneous	30	34	44	37	60	55	57	55	64	70
Total	1,293	1,253	1,324	1,372	1,332	1,295	1,329	1,454	1,516	1,479

	1965	1966	1967	1968	1969	1970	1971	1972	1973	1974
Grand total including Caribbean	18,750	19,676	20,864	21,805	21,444	22,579	22,435	23,380	24,323	24,463
Grand total excluding Caribbean	17,373	18,422	19,585	20,451	20,032	21,169	20,815	21,890	22,965	22,965

CARIBBEAN SEA LANDINGS

Diadromous Fish	1965	1966	1967	1968	1969	1970	1971	1972	1973	1974
Sturgeon, etc.	*	0	0	*	*	*	*	*	*	*
River eels	*	*	0	*	0	0	*	*	*	*
Salmon, trout, etc.	*	—	—	—	—	—	—	—	—	0
Shad, milkfish, etc.	8	2	2	2	2	4	2	5	2	2
Miscellaneous	0	0	0	0	0	0	0	0	0	0
Total	8	2	2	2	2	4	2	5	2	2

Marine Fish	1965	1966	1967	1968	1969	1970	1971	1972	1973	1974
Flounder, sole, etc.	4	2	1	—	2	2	2	3	3	5
Cod, hake, etc.	1	—	—	0	*	0	0	—	0	0
Redfish, bass, etc.	150	142	142	142	146	146	144	218	164	185
Jack, mullet, etc.	61	61	59	58	44	44	47	52	50	50
Herring, sardines, etc.	610	523	484	534	662	674	858	645	601	724
Tuna, bonito, etc.	61	51	46	43	41	38	46	42	45	42
Mackerel, snoek. etc.	1	1	1	2	5	1	2	2	1	3
Sharks, rays, etc.	9	10	10	11	10	6	7	8	11	12
Miscellaneous	67	72	89	98	87	71	80	90	103	96
Total	964	862	832	888	997	982	1,186	1,060	978	1,117

Crustaceans	1965	1966	1967	1968	1969	1970	1971	1972	1973	1974
Crabs, etc.	40	29	28	24	31	32	31	32	36	37
Lobsters, etc.	15	14	13	16	18	17	18	18	19	21
Shrimps, prawns, etc.	139	128	154	148	148	168	176	180	152	163
Krill, etc.	0	0	0	0	0	0	0	0	0	0
Miscellaneous	2	2	2	4	4	1	1	1	1	1
Total	196	173	197	192	201	218	226	231	208	222

Mollusks	1965	1966	1967	1968	1969	1970	1971	1972	1973	1974
Winkles, conchs, etc.	*	*	1	1	1	1	1	2	3	4
Oysters	196	197	228	260	193	177	179	157	138	127
Mussels	*	*	*	*	*	*	*	*	*	*
Scallops, etc.	5	13	12	3	5	11	12	11	11	6
Clams, cockles, etc.	6	4	4	4	9	11	6	9	12	12
Squid, cuttlefish, etc.	1	2	2	3	3	2	4	6	4	6
Miscellaneous	1	1	1	1	1	4	4	5	2	2
Total	209	217	248	272	212	206	206	194	170	157

	1965	1966	1967	1968	1969	1970	1971	1972	1973	1974
Grand total	1,377	1,254	1,279	1,354	1,412	1,410	1,620	1,490	1,358	1,498

* = Less than 500 metric tons

189

LANDINGS OF FISH BY OCEANS (Thousand metric tons)

PACIFIC OCEAN LANDINGS (Including Bering Sea)

Diadromous Fish	1965	1966	1967	1968	1969	1970	1971	1972	1973	1974
Sturgeon, etc.	*	*	*	*	*	*	*	*	*	*
River eels	0	0	0	0	0	0	0	0	0	0
Salmon, trout, etc.	448	458	415	408	397	444	458	354	419	362
Shad, milkfish, etc.	96	100	97	119	176	141	141	138	146	159
Miscellaneous	*	*	*	*	*	*	*	*	1	1
Total	544	558	512	527	573	585	599	492	566	522

Marine Fish	1965	1966	1967	1968	1969	1970	1971	1972	1973	1974
Flounder, sole, etc.	408	504	582	485	564	557	620	580	555	504
Cod, hake, etc.	1,284	1,567	2,147	2,620	2,996	3,566	4,090	4,649	5,244	5,542
Redfish, bass, etc.	1,497	1,378	1,325	1,460	1,332	1,530	1,501	1,592	1,693	1,892
Jack, mullet, etc.	1,362	1,342	1,259	1,134	1,048	1,220	1,462	1,310	1,607	1,572
Herring, sardines, etc.	9,108	11,042	11,970	12,756	11,260	14,604	12,882	6,498	4,094	2,266
Tuna, bonito, etc.	840	995	980	939	1,000	982	983	1,102	1,209	1,195
Mackerel, snoek, etc.	930	930	1,109	1,518	1,528	1,842	1,833	1,842	1,943	2,229
Sharks, rays, etc.	138	141	140	162	161	175	160	155	180	166
Miscellaneous	4,974	5,145	5,267	5,594	5,890	6,188	6,725	6,985	7,164	7,032
Total	20,541	23,044	24,779	26,668	25,779	30,664	30,256	24,713	23,689	22,398

Crustaceans	1965	1966	1967	1968	1969	1970	1971	1972	1973	1974
Crabs, etc.	208	238	246	278	232	271	244	261	259	272
Lobsters, etc.	24	23	32	33	39	51	47	42	34	35
Shrimps, prawns, etc.	289	324	363	377	392	437	474	491	561	572
Krill, etc.	0	0	0	0	0	5	10	2	0	1
Miscellaneous	14	24	28	25	30	24	23	29	31	27
Total	535	609	669	713	693	788	798	825	885	907

Mollusks	1965	1966	1967	1968	1969	1970	1971	19172	1973	1974
Winkles, conchs, etc.	29	31	31	34	32	32	36	38	44	35
Oysters	327	341	345	376	337	302	318	361	389	328
Mussels	29	34	42	36	36	42	60	62	56	45
Scallops, etc.	7	9	8	12	23	25	34	56	75	98
Clams, cockles, etc.	327	367	348	353	372	374	350	380	340	390
Squid, cuttlefish, etc.	625	626	709	954	744	727	671	792	712	705
Miscellaneous	141	182	179	176	202	279	246	243	145	176
Total	1,485	1,590	1,662	1,941	1,746	1,781	1,715	1,932	1,761	1,777

Grand total	23,105	25,801	27,622	29,849	28,791	33,818	33,368	27,962	26,901	25,604

INDIAN OCEAN LANDINGS

Diadromous Fish	1965	1966	1967	1968	1969	1970	1971	1972	1973	1974
Sturgeon, etc.	0	0	0	0	0	0	0	0	0	0
River eels	0	0	0	0	0	0	0	0	0	0
Salmon, trout, etc.	0	0	0	0	0	0	0	0	0	0
Shad, milkfish, etc.	18	19	16	14	14	22	24	29	25	21
Miscellaneous	0	0	0	0	0	0	0	0	0	0
Total	18	19	16	14	14	22	24	29	25	21

Marine Fish	1965	1966	1967	1968	1969	1970	1971	1972	1973	1974
Flounder, sole, etc.	11	9	8	13	14	15	13	11	16	23
Cod, hake, etc.	7	5	3	4	2	2	10	6	7	7
Redfish, bass, etc.	274	341	327	318	342	377	546	411	418	586
Jack, mullet, etc.	77	95	103	90	86	74	80	94	97	155
Herring, sardines, etc.	416	430	408	462	391	485	470	383	362	504
Tuna, bonito, etc.	166	174	224	273	242	183	226	207	231	237
Mackerel, snoek, etc.	100	100	80	63	149	200	275	185	143	129
Sharks, rays, etc.	85	100	99	100	111	111	112	147	177	136
Miscellaneous	573	604	608	642	662	722	737	766	904	859
Total	1,709	1,858	1,860	1,965	1,999	2,169	2,469	2,210	2,355	2,636

Crustaceans	1965	1966	1967	1968	1969	1970	1971	1972	1973	1974
Crabs, etc.	*	*	*	*	*	*	*	*	*	*
Lobsters, etc.	12	14	14	15	13	13	14	14	15	14
Shrimps, prawns, etc.	117	134	141	153	162	179	202	212	264	298
Krill, etc.	0	0	0	0	0	0	0	0	0	0
Miscellaneous	8	10	13	9	14	16	20	25	21	22
Total	137	158	168	177	189	208	236	251	300	334

Mollusks	1965	1966	1967	1968	1969	1970	1971	1972	1973	1974
Winkles, conchs, etc.	*	1	4	8	6	6	7	7	5	5
Oysters	0	0	0	0	0	0	0	*	*	*
Mussels	*	*	*	*	*	*	*	1	0	0
Scallops, etc.	11	13	13	13	5	3	6	8	13	13
Clams, cockles, etc.	—	—	—	*	*	*	*	0	0	0
Squid, cuttlefish, etc.	1	1	5	4	5	4	5	8	6	7
Miscellaneous	2	2	2	3	2	3	2	2	2	2
Total	14	17	24	28	18	16	20	26	26	27

Grand total	1,878	2,052	2,068	2,184	2,220	2,415	2,749	2,516	2,706	3,018

*= Less than 500 metric tons

GLOSSARY

Abyssal. Lying in the deep ocean.

Abyssal plain. The ocean floor below 12,000 feet but not including the ocean trenches.

Annular. Ring shaped.

Anticline. A fold of rock in the form of an arch.

Archipelago. A group of islands. Often used to denote an island chain.

Asthenosphere. A semimolten layer of the earth's upper mantle *see below* on which the crustal plates move.

Barrel. A unit of volume in the measurement of liquids. The unit is different in size for different liquids. 1 barrel of petroleum = 35 gallons (UK) = 42 gallons (US).

Bathymetry. The measurement of depths of water in the oceans.

Bathypelagic. Living in deep water below the level of light penetration but above the abyssal regions.

Bedding planes. A plane in a sedimentary rock parallel to the original surface of deposition. A sedimentary rock usually splits along such a plane.

Bedrock. Unweathered rock lying beneath the soil or surface sediment.

Benthic. Occurring at the bottom of the sea.

Cap rock. The rock formation above a salt dome or oil and gas trap that prevents the escape of fluids.

Continental Rise. The gently sloping part of the seabed leading down from the continental slope into the abyssal plain.

Continental Shelf. The part of the seabed, normally not deeper than 600 feet, adjacent to a landmass and forming a submerged part of the continent itself.

Continental Slope. The steeply sloping part of the seabed leading down from the continental shelf.

Crust. The outermost large scale division of the earth's structure. It is between 10 and 25 miles thick, the thinnest parts being beneath the oceans.

Cuticle. A superficial covering layer on either a plant or an animal.

Demersal fish. Fish living on or near the seabed.

Detritus. A mass of loose rock fragments.

Diadromous fish. Fish that migrate between fresh and seawater.

Diapir. The intrusion of relatively less dense material through the lower layers of more dense overlying rocks causing doming at the surface.

Dolomite. Limestone containing more than 15 percent magnesium carbonate.

Dory. A small high-sided flat-bottomed boat.

Drogue. A device towed behind an underwater instrument to regulate its speed or its direction of movement.

Earth's axis. The line about which the earth rotates.

Ecosystem. The relationship between a community of plants and animals and its environment.

Eddy. A small circular current.

Epeirogenic movements. The uplift or depression of large areas of land.

Epipelagic. Living in the upper lighted layer of seawater.

Euphotic zone. The upper layer of seawater having sufficient light to support plant life.

Eustatic changes. Changes in sea level.

Evaporite. A sedimentary rock produced by the evaporation of salt water.

Fault. A break in a rock along which displacement has occurred.

Thrust fault. A fault in which one block of rock is forced over another.

Transform fault. A fault occurring between crustal plates where the midocean ridge is offset.

Graben. A rift consisting of a downthrown block between parallel faults.

Guano. A deposit of seabird excrement.

Guyot. A flat-topped mountain occurring on the abyssal plain.

Gyre. Circular or spiral movement.

Horst. An upthrown block between parallel faults.

Hot spot. A postulated source of volcanic heat located in the earth's mantle. Such a spot tends to remain stationary while the plates move over it, giving rise to chains of volcanic islands.

Hydrothermal. Concerning natural hot springs.

Isostatic movement. The movement of a land mass to attain equilibrium.

Kinetic energy. Energy associated with movement.

Lagoon. A shallow lake at the edge of a deeper body of water, often separated from it by a reef.

Lithosphere. The outer rigid skin of the earth consisting of the crust and the topmost part of the mantle. This constitutes the "crustal plates," which move on the more fluid asthenosphere.

Littoral zone. The area of coast between high and low tide.

Magma. Molten igneous material.

Magnetic poles. The opposite ends, or poles, of the earth's magnetic field.

Mantle (biology). The material covering the body of a mollusk lying immediately inside the shell.

Mantle (geology). The large-scale division of the earth's structure lying between the surface crust and the innermost core.

Medusa. Jellyfish and the free-swimming stages of some other marine organisms.

Meridian. A line of longitude.

Metric ton, tonne. One thousand kilograms.

Nanoplankton. Minute planktonic organisms, too small to be caught in a plankton net.

Notochord. The axial skeletal support in chordates.

Oolith. A spherical rock particle formed by the accretion of calcite around a nucleus.

Orogeny. The process of mountain-building.

Ovoviviparous. Producing eggs that are hatched within the maternal body.

Pahoehoe. Lava having a ropey appearance.

Pedicellaria. Pincerlike spines occurring on the surface of sea urchins and starfish.

Pelagic fish. Free swimming fish inhabiting the open sea, independently of the seabed.

Placer deposits. Deposits of economic minerals eroded from a landmass and accumulated by waves, currents or tides under water.

Plate tectonics. The modern study of the large-scale features of the earth's surface involving the creation of "crustal" plates at midocean ridges and their destruction in the deep-sea trenches.

Polyp. The sedentary form of Cnidaria (corals sea anemones, etc.), some of which form colonies.

Potential energy. Energy latent in a body by virtue of its position or relation to other bodies.

Pyroclastic. Formed of igneous rock blown into the air by a volcanic explosion.

Rift valley. An elongated subsided block bounded by parallel faults in the form of a valley.

Seismic. Concerning earthquake waves and the artificial production of similar shock waves.

Sessile. Attached by the base. Normally refers to organisms fixed to the ground or seabed.

Setae. Bristlelike structures occurring on invertebrate animals.

Sonograph. A picture of the seafloor produced by means of sound waves and having the appearance of a photograph.

Spicules. Spines or needles of calcium carbonate occurring in the tissues of certain organisms, such as sponges.

Subaerial. On the earth's surface, i.e. below the air as opposed to *submarine*—below the sea.

Subduction zone. The area at the margin of a crustal plate where one plate is being destroyed beneath another. This coincides with a deep-sea trench.

Tectonics. The study of the large-scale features of the earth's surface and their evolution.

Thermocline. The layer in a stratified body of water in which the temperature changes most rapidly with depth.

Trench. An elongated depression in the seabed produced as one crustal plate slides beneath the other. The trenches are the deepest parts of the ocean.

Troll. To fish with hook and line drawn through the water, often behind a boat.

Turbidity current. The movement of a slurry of suspended material, such as silt or clay, in water.

Unconformity. A break in a sequence of sedimentary rocks. It is produced when the depositional process that laid down the sediments is halted and begins again after a pause. Bedding planes above and below the unconformity frequently lie at different angles.

CONVERSION FACTORS		
1 meter	= 3.281 feet	
1 centimeter	= 0.394 inches	
1 micron	= 0.039 thousandths of an inch	
(1 millionth of a meter)		
1 foot	= 0.305 meters	
1 kilometer	= 1000 meters	= 0.621 miles
1 mile	= 1.609 kilometers	
1 gram	= 0.035 ounces (dry)	
1 ounce (dry)	= 28.35 grams	
1 kilogram	= 1000 grams	= 2.205 pounds
1 pound	= 0.454 kilograms	
1 metric ton	= 0.984 long tons (UK)	= 1.102 short tons (US)
1 long ton (UK)	= 1.016 metric tons	= 1.120 short tons (US)
1 short ton (US)	= 0.907 metric tons	= 0.893 long tons (UK)
1 liter	= 0.220 gallons (UK)	= 0.264 gallons (US)
1 gallon (UK)	= 4.546 liters	= 1.201 gallons (US)
1 gallon (US)	= 3.785 liters	= 0.833 gallons (UK)
1 barrel (oil)	= 0.132 metric tons	= 0.134 long tons (UK)
	= 0.150 short tons (US)	= 159 liters
	= 35 gallons (UK)	= 42 gallons (US)

INDEX

Alphabetization is word by word
Italicized references are to maps,
tables and illustrations
Bold references are to *The
Marine Life Encyclopedia*

Ab Teymur oilfield *148*
Abadan *148*
Abbe, lake 146, *146*, 147
Abqaiq oilfield *148*
Absorption, light, seawater
  and 26, 27
Abu Al Bu Khoosh oilfield *148*
Abu Dhabi, Das Island, oil
  terminal 147
  oil production, barrels per
  day 149, *149*
Abu Ghuraib oilfield *148*
Abu Hadriyah oilfield *148*
Abu Jifan oilfield *148*
Abu Sa'Fah oilfield *148*
Abyss
  floor of **179**
  oil and mineral exploitation 47
  oozes **176**, **184**
  see also specific ooze
  water, temperature 89
Abyssal plain
  continental shelf *22*, 23
  ecosystem 77, 88
  fauna 80–1, 88–9, *88–9*
  see also specific plain
Abyssal trenches 81
Acantharia/acantharians **176**
  symbionts **175**
Acanthaster 85, *85*, **183**
Acanthocephala **179**
Acanthometron 63
Acanthurus lineatus 85
Acartia sp. 76
Acid dump, off New Jersey 109,
  109
Acidity, seawater 26, 82
Acorn barnacles 83, *83*
Acorn worms **184**
Acoustic reflecting layer, Red
  Sea 144
Acoustic shadow 51, *51*
Acoustics 47, 50, 51, 78, 94
Acrania **184**, **185**
Acropora 84, *84*, **178**
Actinarians **81**
Actinia equina 83, *83*
  feeding 65, *65*
"Actualism," continental drift
  and 13
Adductor muscle,
  lamellibranchs **180**
Adelaide Island *169*
Aden, Gulf of, *see* Gulf of Aden
Adriatic Sea
  features 138, 139, *139*
  Mediterranean current and
  142
Advection, water 30
Aegean Sea 46, 139, *139*

Aeolid group 67, *67*
Aerosol propellants, pollution
  and 109
Afar Triangle 146–7, *146–7*
Africa
  Agulhas current, storm waves
  and 37
  Atlantic hake fisheries 123
  calcareous sands around *171*
  continental drift 12
  Saudi Arabia and
  North American and 117
  continental shelf 152
  currents around 37, 154
  fisheries off 92, 123, 141
  history 13, *13*, 16, 17, 44, 117,
  151
  Indian Ocean and *155*
  invertebrates off 88
  Mid-Atlantic Ridge and 116
  North Equatorial Current
  and 154
  North West, tuna fisheries 123
  oil production, tonnage 105
  Saudi Arabia Peninsula and
  144
  surface waters, temperature 30
  tuna fisheries 123
African Plate 15, 116, 139, 146,
  147
Agar, red algae and **174**
Aggregates 99, 100, 118
Agha Jari oilfield *148*
Aghar oilfield *148*
Agnatha **185**
Agulhas Bank 118
Agulhas Basin *155*
Agulhas Current 154, *154*, 155
  circulation *33*
  storm waves and 37
Agulhas Plateau *117*, *150*, 153,
  169
Ahagar *117*
Ahmadi oilfield *148*
Ahwaz oilfield *148*
Aids, navigational, 44
Air
  diving and 52, 53
  masses, circulation 108
  sea and 30–1, *30–1*
Airborne radar 29
Airflow 30
Akranes 118, *118*
Al Huwaisah oilfield *149*
Alaska 37, *37*, 128, 158, 166
  fauna
  bristle-thighed curlew 111
  King crab 167
  pollock 166–7
  white whale 111
  fishery
  King crab 167
  pollock 166–7
  resource 70, 100, 167
Alaska Current
  circulation *33*
  sub-polar gyre and 162, *163*
Alaska-Kamchatka Ridge 158
Alaskan pollock 166–7
Albacore *81*, 166, *166*
Albatross 74, *74*, 75, **186**
Albatross Deep *149*
Alboran Basin 138, *138*, *140*
Alborz oilfield *148*
Albuskjell oilfield *135*
Alcyonium sp. 65
Aldrin, pollution and 109

Alepocephalid *81*
Aleutian Abyssal Plain *156*
Aleutian Arc 158, *158*
Aleutian Current *33*, 162, *162*,
  163
Aleutian Islands 30, 116, *156*
  King crab fishery 167
Aleutian Ridge 159
Aleutian Trench *156*, 158, *158*
Aleuts, fishing and 166
Alexander the Great 54
Algae 67, 77, 96, *96*, 118, **173**,
  174, **176**, **181**
  blue green **174**, **175**
  brown **174**
  chitons and **180**
  coral and **175**
  Dinophyceae **175**
  epiphyte seaweeds **174**
  green **174**
  kelps **174**
  ostracods and **182**
  red **174**
  sea urchins and **183**
  symbiotic **174**, **175**, **177**, **178**
  tardigrada and **182**
  turbellaria and **178**
Algero–Provencal Basin *140*
Alginates, kelp and 170, **174**
Alluvial plain, Mississippi *125*
Alpha Ridge
  bathymetric profile *128*
  current flow and *129*, *129*
Alps 12, 16, 17, *117*, 139
Altocumulus *31*
Altostratus *31*
Alula-Fartak Trench 145
Alumina *102*
Aluminium, seawater 27
Alvin 81
Alwyn oilfield *135*
Amazon, river 116
America
  charting 44
  erosion of coasts 18
  Mid-Atlantic Ridge and 116
  midocean upwellings and 86
  mountain chains and 144
  resource 81, 123
  submarine ridges and 168
  see also specific regions
American manatee 71, *71*
American Plate 116, 124
Amethyst gasfield *135*
Amino acids, *Pogonophora* **182**
Amirante Trench *150*
Ammodytes sp. 76
Ammonia 26, 99, *99*, 166
Ammonites **181**
Amoebocytes, algae and **175**
Amoeboid forms **176**
Amoeboid sponge cells **176**
Amoyamphioxus **184**
Amphibia 16, **173**
Amphineura **180**
Amphioxus **184**
Amphipods *81*, **182**
Amphitrite **181**
AMR Group 57
Amsterdam Fracture Zone *150*
Amsterdam Island *150*
Amundsen Gulf *128*
Amundsen Sea *169*
Amur, river *156*
Anadora **180**

Anal fin, shark 68, *68*
Anaspids **182**
Anatomy, marine animals,
  see specific animal
Anaximander Mountains *139*
Anchovy 76, *80*, 107
  Atlantic *122–3*, 123
  Caribbean 126, *126*
  Indian Ocean 152
  Mediterranean *141*
  North Atlantic 123
  Pacific 166, *166–7*
  Persian Gulf 148
  Peru 76, 106, *106*, 107, 166
  tonnage 162
  world catch, tonnage 95
Ancylus Lake, origin 21, *21*
Andaman Islands *151*
Andana Basin *139*, *140*
Andes 16, 22, *116*, *157*, 158,
  158, 162
Andesitic lava 160
Andesitic volcanism 158, *158*,
  159
Andrew oilfield *135*
Angel fish 69, *69*, *80*
Angler fish *81*, **185**, **186**
Anglo-Paris Basin *135*
Angola Abyssal Plain *117*
Anguilla anguilla 77
Anhydrite/s 104
  Arctic *130–1*
  Gulf of Mexico 127
  Mediterranean Basin 141
  North Sea oil/gas and 134, *135*
  Red Sea 144
Animal/s
  feed 118
  husbandry 96
  marine 66–7, *66–7*, **176–86**
  see also specific animal
  plankton 85, 86
  protein 63, 152
Annelida/annelids 178, **179**, **180**,
  181
  pogonophora **182**
  tardigrades and **182**
Annular atoll, formation 160
Annular zones 30
Anopluran lice **183**
Antalya Basin *139*, *140*
Antarctic
  bathymetry and circulation
  28, 35, 120, 153, 168–9,
  168–9
  bottom water 35, *35*, 121, *121*,
  154, 155
  continental shelf and *155*, 168
  fauna
  Arctic tern 75
  Emperor penguin **186**
  krill in 73
  minke whale 73
  penguins 73, 74, 75, *87*
  ice 28, *28*, 37
  icebergs 28, 59
  resource 170–1, *170–1*
  temperature 113
  whale stocks 47
Antarctic Circumpolar Current
  121, *155*, 162, *163*, 168, *168*
  Antarctic bottom waters and

  35, *35*, 120
  circulation *33*
  current pattern and 32
  route 35
  South Atlantic warm water
  gyre and 120
  Southern Indian Ocean and
  155
Antarctic convergence 168
Antarctic Peninsula *169*
Antarctic Plate 14, 157, *157*
Antarctica 35, *155*, 168–9, 170
  continental rise *151*, *156*
  continental shelf 35, 170, *171*
  history 13, *13*, 17, 151
  icefloe near 113, *113*
  resource 170
  Ross Sea, shore pollution 109,
  109
Antennae, marine animals 67
Anthozoa **177**
Antibiotics, marine bacteria and
  175
Anticlines 104, 148
Anticyclones 30
Antigua *125*
Antikythera Channel 21
Antikythera, Island of 21
Antilles *125*
Antilles Current *121*
  circulation *33*
  Gulf Stream and 120
Antipodes Islands *156*, 168
Aplysia 67, *67*
Appalachian Mountains 13, *13*,
  17, *116*, *157*
Appendiculate 76, *76*
Apulian Plateau *139*
Aqualung 52, 53
Aquatic life, pollution and 143
Arabia 16, 17, 148, 154
Arabian Basin 150, *150*
Arabian Peninsula 147, *147*
Arabian Plate 146, *147*, 148
Arabian Sea, continental shelf
  152
Arabian states, shrimp fisheries
  off 153
Aragonite 100, 118, *118*
Arch/es 19, *19*
Archaeology 20, 59, *59*
Archiannelida **181**
Archipelagic states, rights of 57
Archipelagos, Pacific 160
Architecture **181**
Architeuthids **181**
Arctic
  air 30, *30*
  Beaufort gyre and 28
  continental shelf 128, 130,
  130–1
  current flow 129, *129*
  fauna
  Arctic tern 75, *75*
  bristle-thighed curlew 111
  Greenland right whale 73
  Greenland shark 80
  minke whale 73
  narwhals 111
  shorebirds migration from
  111
  walrus 70
  white whale 111
  features 128–9, *128–9*
  ice 28, *28*, 29
  fish spawning 78, *78*
  fishing trawlers and 95
  plankton and 78, 86, *86*

Pollution Control Zone 57
  resource 104, 130–1, *130–1*
Arctic Basin 128, 144
Arctic IV Expedition, diver
  40–1, 41
Arctonoe **181**
Arcuate ridges 138, 139
Ardeshir oilfield *148*
Arenicola **181**
Arenicola marina 83, *83*
Argentine Abyssal Plain 116, *169*
Argentine Continental Rise 116
Argentine Continental Shelf 116
Argentine Rise 116, *117*, *169*
Argo Abyssal Plain *151*, *156*
Argonaut First 54
Argonauta, paper nautilus **181**
Argus aircraft, ice research 29, *29*
Argyll oilfield *135*
Argyropelecus 69, *69*, *88–9*, 89
Aristotle, Aegean Sea and 46
Arlis Plateau *128*
Arlis II (USA), drifting "ice-
  island" *129*
Armored animals, beach life 83
Armorican Rise *134*
Arrowworms **179**, **180**, **182**
  North Sea watermass identifi-
  cation and 133
  plankton and 63, *63*
Arsenic pollution,
  Mediterranean 143
Arthropoda/arthropods **176**, **180**,
  182
  chelicerates comparison **182**
  crustacea **182**
  squat lobster of group 67, *67*
  tardigrades and **182**
Asab oilfield *149*
Ascension Fracture Zone *117*
Ascension Island 78, *78*, 116, *117*
Aschelminthes **178**, **179**
Ascidiacea/ascidians **179**, **184**
  larval forms **185**
  movement 66
Ascophyllum **174**
Asexual reproduction, *see* specific
  animal
Ash cone, volcanic 146, *146*
Asia
  Arctic Basin and surface
  water 128
  continental shelf 128, 130
  factory trawlers 94
  history 12, 16, 17
  submarine route and *130*
  see also specific region
Asian Plate *147*, 148
Asian salmon 79, *79*
Asterias sp. 77
Asterias rubens, larva 65
  movement 67, *67*
Asteriodea **183**
Asthenosphere 14, *15*, 16, 17
Astrolabe 44, 45, *45*
Astronomy, nautical, history and
  44
Aswan Dam, Mediterranean
  and 141, 143
Atbara, river *144*
Atchafalaya, river *125*
Athens, Tower of Winds 43, *43*
Atherinidae, schooling and
  60–1, 61
Atlantic *125*, *169*
  bathymetry and evolution
  116–17, *116–17*

Caribbean water and 124
circulation 35, 46, 47, 116,
 120–1, *120–1*, 124, 163
coastal upwellings 86
coastline and ocean
 distribution 12
continental margin 22
continental shelf *119*, 122
crust 124
English Channel and 133
fauna
 continental slopes 88
 narwhals 73, *73*
 pilot whale 73, *73*
fish
 blue fin tuna 166
 catch 122
 salmon 79
 tuna migration and 78
fishery 122–3, *122–3*
 cod catch, tonnage *123*
 food web 77
 foraminifera remains *24*
GATE experiment 31
history 15, 17, 44, 46, *46*, 47,
 117
Mediterranean and 143
minerals and sediments *102*,
 118–19, *118–19*
Norwegian Trough and 132
Pacific and 157, 162
purse-seiner fishing vessel 94
salinity profile *34–5*, 35
submarine route *130*
submersible voyage 55
temperature 35, *35*, 124
tides and 38, 124
trailing margins of 17
wave power and 99
Atlantic Basin 12–13, 17, 117,
 117, 144, 168
Atlantic-Indian Basin *117*, *150*,
 169
Atlantis, legend 139
Atlantis Fracture Zone *117*
Atlantis II 102
Atlantis II Deep, Red Sea *145*,
 149
Atlanto-Scandian herring stock
 107
Atlas Mountains *117*, *138*
Atmosphere
 circulation 108, *121*
 depressions, Southern Ocean
 168
 hydrosphere and 10–11
 ocean's loss of heat to 30
 pressure 143
 sea ice and 28
 testing, radioactive pollution
 and 108
Atmospheric habitat 54–5, *55*
Atmospheric transportation,
 hydrological cycle and 27, *27*
Atoll/s 81, 84, 160, *160*, 161, *161*
Atolla sp. 89
Auk/s 74, *75*
Auk oilfield *135*
Aukland Isles 168
Aurelia 177
Auklets 74
Australia
 calcareous sands around *171*
 continental shelf *155*
 drift 157
 history 16, 17, 43, 151, 157
 Indian Ocean and 150

reefs 160
sea fauna
 humpback whale 170
 King crabs 65
 shark 166
 submarine plateau regions
 near 165
 whaling stations 170 *see
 also* specific region
Australian Basin 168
Australian Plate 150
Australs
 Pacific chains and 161, *161*
 trend 160
Aves 173, 186
Aves Swell 124, *125*
Awali oilfield *148*
Awash, river *145*
Axel Heiberg Island *129*
Axial shield volcano *25*
Axial trough, Red Sea *149*
Axial valley, Red Sea 144, *147*,
 149, *149*
Axillary breams *123*
Axis, earth *39*
Axopods 176
Aysha Horst *147*
Azores 44, 116, *117*

B

Bab oilfield *149*
Bab al Mandab *145*
Bab West oilfield *148*
Bacillariophyceae 175
Back-arc seas 159, *159*
Backboned animals, *see*
 Chordates
Backwash, waves and 37
Bacteria, marine **179**
 blue-green algae and *174*, *175*
 luminescent **184**
Bacton shore station *135*
Badlands 23
Baffin Bay 28, *120*, *129*
Baffin Island *116*, *129*
Bahamas Islands 100, *116*, *125*,
 157
Bahrein, oil production, barrels
 per day *149*, *149*
Bahrgansar oilfield *148*
Bait, lift net 92, *92*
Baja California 78, 157, 162
Bakr oilfield *148*
Baku region 104
Balaena mysticetus 73, *73*
Balaenoptera acutorostrata 73, *73*
Balaenoptera borealis 73, *73*
Balaenoptera musculus 73, *73*
Balaenoptera physalus 73
Balanus sp. 76
Balanus balanoides 83, *83*
Balearic Basin 138, *138*, 139
Balearic Islands *138*
Baleen whales 62, 72, 73, *73*, 170,
 186
Balleny Islands *156*, *168*
Baltic Ice Lake 21, *21*
Baltic Sea 20, *21*, *117*
Bandar-E Deylam *148*
Banks, Sir Joseph 46
Banks Island *128–9*
Bar sands, Mississippi delta
 125, *125*
Barbados *125*
Barchans 24
Barents Abyssal Plain *129*
Barents Sea 121, *121*, 122, *129*,
 131, *131*, **183**
Barium 100
 manganese nodule constituent
 102
 pollution 109
 Sri Lanka 153
 world reserves, tonnage *101*
Bark canoes 42, *42*
Barnacle/s **182, 183**
 chitons and **180**
 habitat 82, 83
 larva 76, *76*, **185**
Barracuda 61, 85, 92, 148, **186**
Barrier reefs 110, *110*, 160–1,
 160–1
Barrow *130*
Bars, offshore 19
Barton, Otis 54
Barytes, *see* Barium
Basalt
 earth's crust 11
 lava 25, 161, *161*
 Red Sea 147, *147*

rocks 15, 18, *18*
Basin, *see* Ocean Basin; specific
 basin
Basking shark 62, 68, **185**
Bass 95, 141, 148
Bath sponges **177**
Bathurst Island *129*
Bathymetry, *see* specific ocean/
 sea
Bathypelagic fish
 see also specific fish
Bathypelagic zone, sea fauna *81*
Bathypterois bigelowi 89, *89*
Bathyscaphe 54
Bathysonde *50*
Bathysphere 54
Bathythermograph 49, *49*
Batilus 118, *118*
Battery culture 96
"Battery farming" 96
Bay of Bengal 150, *150–1*, 152,
 155
Bay of Biscay 23, *23*, 117, *117*,
 138
Bay of Fundy 38, *38*
Baykal, lake *156*
Bays, beaches and 19
Beach/es
 cliff erosion and 19
 deposits 22, 101
 flies **183**
 formation 19, *19*
 life 82–3, *82–3*
 pollution 109, *109*
 sealevels and 20
 submerged 22
"Beach-masters", bull seals 70
Beach plains, formation 19
Beach sands, minerals 153
Beach seine-net 92, *92*
Beadlet anemone 65, *65*, 83, *83*
Beagle, HMS, Charles Darwin
 and 160
Beaked whale, Sowerby's 73, *73*
Beam trawls, North Sea, 136,
 137, *137*
Beata Ridge 124, *125*
Beaufort Gyre, Arctic drift
 pattern 28
Beaufort Sea 29, *29*, 128, *128*, 130
Bedding plane 18
Bedrock 23, *23*, 118
Beebe, William 54
Belgian coast, plaice spawning
 and 137
Bellingshausen Sea *169*
Belugas, *see* White whales
Ben Franklin 54
Bends, the 53
Bengal, Bay of, *see* Bay of Bengal
Bengal Fan 150, 151, *151*
Benguela Current 33, *120*, 121,
 121, 154, 155
Benteuphausia sp. 88
Benthos
 animals 25, *25*, 80, **176, 181**
 food webs 77
 geologic history 89
 zonation with depth 81
 see also specific ocean/sea
Bering Abyssal Plain *156*, 158,
 158
Bering Sea 128, *156*, 158, *158*
 continental shelf 158
 current flow and 129
 fauna
 bristle-thighed curlew 111

copepod 80
 gray whale 78, 111
King crab 167
fishery
 King crab 167
 Pacific 166
 submarine routes *130*
Bering Sea Basin 157, 158
Bering Strait *128*, 156
Bermuda 116
Bermuda Rise *116*
Berri oilfield *148*
Beryl oilfield *135*
Bibi Hakimeh oilfield *148*
Bicarbonate, seawater 27, *27*
Biddulphia sinensis 62
Bigeye tuna 166, *166*
 migrations 87
Bikini atoll *156*
Bilharzia **178**
Billfish 87, *95*
Binak oilfield *148*
Binomial system *173*
Bio-accumulation, seawater
 elements and 27
Bio-luminescence 81, **184**
Bird/s
 classification **173**
 DDT and 109
 feeding methods 74–5, *74–5*
 food web 77, 111
 see also Aves
Birdfoot Delta, Mississippi *125*
Birgus **183**
Biscay Abyssal Plain *117*
Bismarck Archipelago *156*
Bivalve mollusks, *see* Mollusks
Black Current, *see* Kuroshio
 Current
Black Sea *139*, *139*, 142
Blackbird, red-winged 77
Black-footed albatross 74, *74*
Blake Plateau *116*, 118, *125*, *157*
Blennies 78
Block Island Channel *23*
Block Island Shore *23*
Blowhole/s 19, *19*
Blow-out
 Arctic 130–1
 North Sea, Bravo Rig 109
Blubber 70, 71, 72
Blue crab 82, *82*, 126
Blue crustaceans 80
Blue fish, Falkland current and
 123
Blue-footed booby *81*
Blue-green algae **174, 175**
Blue mollusks 80
Blue Nile *144*
Blue sharks **185**
Blue whales 72, 73, *73*, 170, 171,
 171
Blue whiting *123*
Bluefin tuna 78, 166
Blueness, ocean water 26
Boats 42–3, *42–3*, 92, 141
Bolivar coastal oilfield 104
Bolivia, mineral deposits 158
Bombing, oil pollution remedy
 108, *108*
Bonellia **179**
Bonin Islands *159*, 160
Bonin Trench *151*, *156*, *159*
Bonito 80–1
 anchovies and 76
 fishery 86, *166–7*
 habitat 85

world catch, tonnage *95*
Bony fish, *see Teleostei*
 see also specific fish
Boobies 74, 76
Boomerang grab sampler 48,
 48, *50*
Booms, floating and oil pollution
 108, *108*
Bootlace worm **179**
Bora Bora Barrier Reef 110, *110*,
 161, *161*
Borates, gulf seawater and 27
Boreholes, North Sea 134
Boric acid, seawater constituent
 27
Borneo *151*, *156*
Boron, seawater constituent 26
Bosphorus *139*
Bothnia, Gulf of, *see* Gulf of
 Bothnia
Bottlenose whale 73, *73*, 107,
 171, *171*
Bottom trawl/trawlers 122, *122*,
 136, 148, 153
Bottom water 25, 35, *35*, 154, *165*
 see also specific ocean
Bougainvillea ramosa 86
Boulders 18, 160
Bounty Island 168
Bounty Trough *156*
Bourdon Tube *49*
Bowstream dredger 134, *134*
Box corer 49, *49*, *50*
Brachiopod/*brachiopoda* 65, *65*,
 179
Brae oilfield *135*
Brain coral 84, *84*
Branchiura **183**
Bravo rig blow-out 109
Brazil
 continental shelf 144
 fish catch 93, *93*
 Green turtles off 78, *78*
Brazil Current 33, *120*, *120*, 121
Breakers 36, 37, *37*
Breakwaters 19, *19*, 36, 58, *58*, 59
Bream *123*, 141, 148
Bream oilfield *135*
Breeding
 marine vertebrates 64–5, *64–5*
 migration and 78
 schooling instinct and 61
 see also specific animal
Brent oilfield *105*, 135, *135*
Brine 28, 102, *149*
 lakes, salinity 99
 pools, Red Sea 149
Brisling oilfield *135*
Bristlemouth fish *80–1*
Bristle-thighed curlew 111
Bristol Bay salmon 79, *79*
Bristol Channel 32, *132*
British Columbia 78, 97, 157
British Isles, *see* United Kingdom
Brittany, algae from 118
Brittle stars *80*, 88, *88*
 breeding 64
 coral reef habitat 85
Brixham 92
Broken Bank gasfield *135*
Broken Ridge *151*
Bromide, seawater constituent 27
Bromine 26, *101*, 109, 118
Bromoform **184**
Brood chambers **179**
Brooks Range *128*

C

Brotulids *80–1*
Brown algae *174*
Brown pelican *75*
Bruce oilfield *135*
Brushwood fish trap 92, *92*
Bryozoans **179**, **184**
Bu Hasa oilfield *148*
Buccinum undatum 64, *64*
Buchan Deep 132, *133*
Buchan oilfield *135*
Bucket system, harvesting manganese nodules 103, *103*
Buckie 92
Bul Hanine oilfield *148*
Bull boat 42, *42*
Bull seals 70
Burgan oilfield *148*
Burma, cassiterite deposits off 153
Burning, oil pollution remedy 108, *108*
Burrows/burrowers 82, *82*, 83, *83*
Bushehr oilfield *148*
Bushgan oilfield *148*
Bushnell, David 54
Butterfly fish 69, *69*, *80*, 85
Buzurgan oilfield *148*
Byssus **180**

Cable-burying tractor 55, *55*
Cachelot 72, *72–3*
Caicos Bank *125*
Calabria 138, *139*
Calanoids **182**
Calanus sp. 76, 86
Calanus finmarchicus 64, *64*, 86, **182**
Calcarea **177**
Calcareous algae 118
Calcareous debris 102
Calcareous ooze 24, *24*, 150, *171*
Calcareous rocks, worms and **179**
Calcareous scales, *Chrysophyceae* **174**
Calcium 26, 27, *27*, 76, *102*, 109, **179**
Calcium carbonate 102, 118, 134
Caledonian Mountains 16, 17
California
  continental blocks and 22
  continental margins 124
  drought 30
  ecosystem 77
  fisheries off 86, 106, 166
  kelp beds 70
  Pacific oceanic crust and 157
  purse-seiners based in 94
  sardines 106
  sea fauna
    Greenland shark 80
    sea lion 71, *71*
  Sierra Nevada and 157
  "staircase" beaches 20
  upwellings off 77, 86, 162
Californian Basin 22
Californian Current *33*, 162, 163, *163*
Callentsoog shorestation *135*
Calliactis **177**
Callinectes sapidus 82, *82*
Callorhinus ursinus 70, *70*
Calocalanus plumosa 86
Cambrian Period 16, *16*, 17, 65, **179**, **182**
Camille, Hurricane 31, *31*
Camouflage, marine animals 67, 69, 81
Campbell Island *156*, *168*
Campeche Bank *124*
Campeche Canyon *124*
Campeche Escarpment *124*
Campeche Knolls *124*
Canada
  abyssal plain 128, *128*
  Atlantic cod catch *123*
  continental shelf 128
  fishing off *122*, *123*
  Hudson's Bay region, isostatic uplift 20
  Pollution Control Zone 57
  western, fjord coastlines and 20
  white whale habitat 111
Canadian Arctic 41, 104, 128, 130
Canadian-British Ice Research 29
Canaries Current 32, *33*, 120, 121, *121*
Canary Abyssal Plain *117*
Canary Islands *117*
Canneries, sardine 106
Cannery Row 106, *106*
Cannibalizing 68, 77
Canoes 42, *42*, 92, 93, *93*, 126, 153
Canyons, submarine 22, *22*, 23, *23*, 138
Cap rocks 104, 127, 141
Cape Basin, manganese nodules 118
Cape Bojadore, rounding of 44
Cape Farewell *117*
Cape Guardafui *145*
Cape Hatteras 35
  continental shelf 120
  cumulus clouds off 120, *120*
  Gulf Stream and 120, 121, *121*
  salinity profile from *34–5*
Cape Horn *116*, *157*, *169*

Cape Melville 160, *160*
Cape of Good Hope 44
Cape pigeon *75*
Cape Verde Islands 33, *33*, *117*
Cape York 160, *160*
Capelin 111
  Atlantic *122–3*
  Barents Sea 131, *131*
  midwater trawl and 122
  whales, seals and 111
Caperea marginata 72, *72*
Capillary waves 26, 36
Capitella sp. 77
Carapace **182**, **183**
Carbon 11, 76
Carbon dioxide 27, 52, 53
Carbonates 27, 134, 151
Carboniferous Period 16, 17, 65
  mountains 13, *13*, 16
  North Sea 134
Carcharodon **185**
Carcinus sp. 77
Carcinus maenas 83, *83*
Cardinal fish 69, *69*
Cardium sp. 77, **180**
Cardium edule 83, *83*
Caribbean
  bathymetry and circulation 120, 124–5, *124–5*
  continental shelf 126, *127*
  Farallon Plate isolated in the 157
  fish catch *126*
  fishery 126, *126*
  food web 77
  Lake Maracaibo and 91
  resource 126–7, *126–7*
  surface water temperature 30
Caribbean Basin 124, *125*
Caribbean Current *33*, *121*
Caribbean Plate 116, 124, *125*
Carinaria **180**
Carlsberg Ridge 116, *147*, 150, *150*
Carnegie Ridge 116, *157*, *157*
Carnivore/s **176**, **180**, **183**, **186**
  feeding techniques 64
  fish, Atlantic 123
  food chain **176**
  habitats 77, 83, 85
  plankton 62, 86
  sea strata and 80, 81
  see also specific carnivore
Caroline Islands 93, *93*, *151*, *156*, 161, *161*
Carotene **175**
Carpathian Mountains *117*
Carpenter, W. B. 46
Carta Pisana 43, *43*
Cartilaginous fish 68, *68*
Caryophyllia **178**
Caspian oil wells 104
Cassiopeia 66, *66*
Cassiterite, *see* Tin
Castellon grounds, fishing 141
Cast-net 93, *93*
Catch, fish
  Atlantic *122*, 123
  Barents Sea 131
  Caribbean *126*
  Indian Ocean 152, *152*
  Mediterranean 141, *141*
  North Atlantic 122
  North Sea 136, *136*
  Pacific 166
  world 95
Caudal fin, shark 68, *68*
Cavalla 85, 92
Cave, formation 19, *19*
Caviar, sturgeon's **185**
Cavolina inflexa 87
Cavolina tridentata 63
Cayman Islands *125*
Cayman Ridge *125*
Cayman Trench *124*
Cayman Trough *116*, *125*, *157*
Celebes *151*, *156*
Cells, Equatorial undercurrent 163, *163*
Cells, marine animals, *see* specific animal
Celluloses, marine bacteria and *175*
Celtic Sea 132, *132*
Celtic Sea Basin *134*
Cement 109, 118, *118*
Cenozoic Period 17
Central America *80–1*, 81, 124, 126, 157

Central Atlantic, width 117
Central Graben *135*
Central Indian Basin 150, *150*
Central Pacific 30
Central Rift Valley 148
Cephalopoda/cephalopods 67, **181**, **182**, **183**, **186**
Ceratium **175**
Ceratium palmatum 86
Ceratium reticulatum 86
Ceratium tripos 62
Cestoda **178**
Cestus **178**
Cetacea 72–3, *72–3*, **186**
  see also specific cetacean
Chad, lake *117*
Chaetoceros furca 86
Chaetoceros holsaticum 86
Chaetognatha 63, 76, *76*, **179**
Chaetopterus **181**
Chagos Laccadive Ridge *150*
Chagos Trench *150*
Chain Deeps *149*
Chain nets, bottom sampling and 48
Chalk 18, *18*, 132, 134, *135*, **176**
Challenger, HMS 47, 48, 102, 118, 165
Challenger Fracture Zone *157*
Chelonia mydas 71
Channel, *see* specific channel
Channeled wrack 82, *82*
Charleston, South Carolina 19, *19*
Charting 44, *44*, 45, *45*
Chashmeh Khush oilfield *148*
Chatham Islands *156*
Chauliodus sp. 88
Chelicerata/chelicerates **182**
Chelmon rostratus 69, *69*
Chemical industries, Mediterranean resources and 141
Chemical pollution, seabirds 75
Cheops Ship 42, *42*, 43
Cherbourg breakwater 36
Chesapeake Channel 23
Chile 86, 157, 158, 166
Chile Rise *116*, *157*, *157*
Chilingar oilfield *148*
Chimaera monstrosa, 68, *68*
Chimaeras 68
Chitin **175**, **179**
Chitinous plates, *Tardigrada* **182**
Chitinous shell/s **179**, **182**
Chitons 82, **180**, **185**
Chlamys operculus 64, *64*
Chloride, seawater *27*
Chlorine 11, 26, 27, 109
Chlorophyceae/chlorophyceans **174**, **175**
Chlorophyll 27, 76, **174**, **175**
Chloroplasts **174**, **175**
Chondrichthyes 68, *68*
Chondrostei/chondrosteans **178**, **185**
Chordata/chordates **173**, **182**, **184**, **185**
Christmas Island *151*, *156*
Chromite/chromium
  Caribbean *127*
  Indian Ocean *153*
  Pacific *164–5*
  North American sands and 165
  placer deposits, offshore *100–1*
  world reserves, tonnage *101*
Chromodoris quadricolor 67, *67*
Chromosomes **175**
Chronometers 44
Chrysophyceae/chrysophycean **174**, **175**, **176**
Chukchi Plateau *128*
Chukchi Range *128*
Chukchi Sea 128, *128*
Cidaris **183**
Cilia, marine animal movement and 66
Ciliata **176**
"Circle of Fire" 157
Circulation, ocean 86, 88
  see also specific ocean/sea
Circumpolar Current, *see* Antarctic Circumpolar Current
Cirripedia **183**
Cirroteuthid **181**
Cirrus cloud 30, *31*
Cities, focused wave energy and 37

Cladocera, *Evadne* sp. 76
Clams 25, 83, *83*, 92, **180**
  see also Giant clams
Clapper rail/s 77, *77*
Clarion Fracture Zone 102, *156*
Claspers, shark 68, *68*
Claude Condensater 97, *97*
Clausocalanus paululus 87
Clay *125*, 132, 135, 150
  see also Red clay
Clay cliffs, erosion and 18
Clayey silts, Antarctica *171*
Claymore oilfield *135*
Cleaning agents, pollution and 109
Clefts, erosion and 18, 19, *19*
Cliffs *18*, 18–19, 20, 22
Climate 26
Climatic zones, continental drift and 13
Clione limacina 87
Clipperton Fracture Zone 102, *156*
Clipperton Islands *157*
Clouds 10, 27, 30, *30*, 31
Clown fish 69
Clown surgeon fish 85
Clupea 69, *69*, **173**
Clupea harengus **173**
  see also Herring
Clupea sprattus **173**
Clupeids 86, **173**, **186**
  see also specific clupeid
Clupeoids, Pacific fishery *166–7*
Clypeaster **183**
Cnidae **177**
Cnidaria **177**, **178**
Coal 12, 16, 100, 134, 150, 170
Coast/coastal 18–21, *18–21*, 26, 82–3, 108, 111, *135*
  fisheries 92–3, *92–3*
  plain *23*
  structures 36, 37
  upwellings 86
  water identification 133, **180**
  wetland habitats 110–11
Coastline/s 18, *18*, 20, 21, *21*
Cobalt 25, 56, *101*, 102, *102*, 165
Cobras, seasnakes and **186**
Coccolithophorids **174**
Cockle/s 77, *80*, 83, *83*, **180**
Coconut crab **183**
Cocos Island *151*
Cocos Plate 25, *25*, *157*, *157*
Cocos Ridge *116*, *125*, *157*, *157*
Cod 68, 69, *69*
  bottom trawl and 122
  commercial exploitation 107
  continental shelf *123*
  eggs in plankton **186**
  fishing
    Arctic 95, 131
    Atlantic 122, 123, *123*
    Barents Sea 131, *131*
    Grimsby and 136
    Newfoundland, history 94
    North Atlantic 123
    North Sea 136, 137, *137*
    Pacific 166
    world catch, tonnage 95
  migration 78
  overfishing 137
  research 78
  spawning 78
    Lofoten Islands 131
    North Sea 137
  stocks 78, *123*
  trawlers 94, 95, *95*
Cod-like fish, North Sea catch 136
Cod gasfield *135*
Coelacanth 65, **180**, **185**, **186**
Coelenterates 67, *67*, **175**
Coelopidae **183**
Cold front, depressions and *31*
"Cold" origin for earth 11
Collar cells **177**
Colombia 124, 127
Colombian Basin *125*
Colonial breeding 74, *74*
Colonial species, coral 84
Colonies, seal 70
Color
  marine animals 67, 80, **181**
  marine plants **174**

Comb jellies 67, *67*
Commensalism, marine 69, **175**, **179**, **181**
Commercial catch, fish, *see* Catch
Comoro Island 150, **186**
Compass 44, 45, *45*
Compressed air
  divers and 52–3
  tidal power scheme 98, *98*
Compressibility, water 26
Conch shells **180**
Concrete, aragonite and 118
Condensater, Claude 97, *97*
Cone shells 80
Conger, world catch 95
Congo, river *117*, *150*
Congo cone *117*
Congolese fish trap 92, *92*
Conservation, fish stocks 56
"Conservative" elements, seawater 26
Construction, coastal landscape 18
Constructive plate margins, earth's 15
Consuming plate margin *157*
"Contiguous zone," fishing limits 56
Continent/s *15*
  components of a 12, *12*
  earth's crust and 13
  mountain formation and a 16
  ocean formation and a 16
  rift valley formation 22
  seafloor spreading and 15
  sealevel 20, 26
  tides and 38
Continental crust
  earth's 11
  mineral deposits and 100
  North Sea formation of 132
  Pacific *158*, *159*
  Rockall Plateau and *117*
  South America 158
Continental drift 12–13, *12–13*, 47, 59
  Afar Triangle and 146
  Lilienthal observations and *117*
  mechanism 15
  oceans and 16
  see also specific subject
Continental margins
  active 22, *22*
  right to exploit 56
  South America 118, 158
  tidal ranges 38–9
  topography 23, *23*
  tsunami waves and 37
  types 22
Continental platform 22
Continental rise 22, *23*, 88, *116*, *151*, *156*
Continental shelf 22–3, *22–3*, *16*
  areas *188–90*
  1958 Convention 56
  currents and 24
  deposits 56, 100, *101*, *100–1*, *102–3*, *119*, *127*, 144, *153*, *165*, *171*
  fish/ing 94, 122, 123, 152, *152*
  marine life 81
  ocean darkness 88
  oil 128
  right to explore and exploit 56
  sealevel changes 20
  sediments 104, *119*, 142
  storm waves 37
  teleosts **186**
  tides 39
  wind on waters of 124
Continental slope 12, 22, *22*, *23*, 35
  Argentine Rise and *116*
  Atlantic 88, 132
  marine life and 81, 88
  Pacific fishery 166
Continental uplands 111
Contraction, water 26
Conus **180**
Conus geographus **180**
Convection process, earth's evolution 10–11
Convention on Fishing and the Conservation of the Living Resources of the Sea 56
Convention on the Territorial Sea and Contiguous Zone 56

Convoluta **175**, *178*
Cook, Captain 44
  Harrison chronometer used by
    45, *45*
Cooks Islands 111, *156*
Coolant water, demand for 143
Copepoda/copepods 64, 76, *76*,
  177, **182**
  arrowworms and **179**
  deep-sea 88, *88*
  distribution 80, 86
  feeding techniques 64
  fish and 69, 77
  generation time 62
  Heliozoans and **176**
  phytoplankton and **182**
  plankton ecosystem and 62
Copper 102
  Atlantic 118
  Atlantis II Deep 149, *149*
  Indian Ocean 153, *153*
  manganese nodules
    constituent 102, *102*, 118
  Pacific 158, *164–5*, 165
  placer deposits, offshore
    100–1
  Red Sea 148
  residence time, mineral
    formation 27
  seabed 25, 56, 148
  world reserves *101*
Coracles, origin of 43
Coral 65, 85, 152
  Asteroidea and **183**
  atoll 88, 160, *160*
  chitons and **180**
  Cryptophyceae and **175**
  hydrozoans and **177**
  island/s 161, *161*, *167*
  larvae **175**
  reef 69, 81, 84–5, *84–5*, 126,
    178
    Bora Bora 110, *110*
    Caribbean 126
    continental shores and 160
    ecosystem 77
    fauna 68
      Butterfly fish 69
      Cnidaria **177**
      Crown of Thorns **183**
      Giant clams **180**
      Malacostraca **183**
    fisheries, Red Sea 148
    Pacific *160–1*, *160–1*
    Thailand 110
  sipiniculoids and **179**
  teleosts and **186**
  Turbellaria and **178**
  zonal fossils comparison with
    179
Coral Sea *151*, *156*, 162
Corers 48, *48*
Coring 49
Coriolis force 32, *32*, 33, *33*, 162
  currents and 32
  midocean upwellings and 86
  wave systems and 38
Coris angulata **85**, *85*
Cormorants 75, *75*, 76, **186**
Cormorant oilfield *135*
Corner Rise *116*
Cornwall, blue sharks tagged in
  185
Corsica 110, 138, *138*, 139
Corycaeus gracilis 86
Corynosoma **179**
Corysteid crab, larva 65
Coscinodiscus radiatus 86
Costa Rica, continental shelf
  minerals 127
Côtes du Nord 98
Countercurrent, fish spawning
  and 78
Countershading, marine animals
  67, 69
Cousteau, Jacques 53
Cousteau/Gagnan, aqualung 52
Cover-pots, inshore fishing 92,
  92
Cowries **180**
  fishing dredge 92, *92*
Crabs *80*, **182**, **183**
  Anthozoans and **177**
  barnacles and **183**
  breeding 64, 65, *65*
  fishery
    Atlantic 123
    Caribbean *126*
    inshore 92
    Pacific 167

food web 77, 83
  habitat 77, 80, 82, 83, 88
  lobster bait 92
  species
    blue 82, *82*, 126
    deep-sea 88, *88*
    fiddler 77, 83
      Sesarma sp. 77
      Uca sp. 77, 83, *83*
    ghost **182**
    giant coconut **183**
    giant spider **182**
    hermit 69, *69*, **177**, **181**
    king 65, *65*, *167*, **182**
    mole 82, *82*
    mud 77, *77*
    sand 82, *82*
    shore 77, 83, *83*
    yellow 25
  traps, Martinique 93, *93*
  Turbellarians and **178**
Crabeater seal 71, *71*
Cracks, Red Sea, volcanic 144
Cranchid group, deep-water
  squid 88, *88*
*Création et ses Mystères dévoilés,
  La* 12
Crepidula **180**
Crest/s 13, 36, 37
  Crustal rift zone 25
Cretaceous Period 13, 17, 127,
  134, 135, *135*, 148, **176**
Cretan Basin 139
Crete 21, 138, *139*
Crinoidea/crinoids 88, 89, *89*,
  181, **183**
Croakers, Pacific fishery 166
Crocodiles **186**
Crops, forecasting supply 59
Crossopterygii **186**
Cross-staff 45, *45*
Crown of Thorns 85, *85*, **183**
Crozet Basin 150, *150*, *169*
Crozet Islands *150*, *169*
Crozet Plateau *169*
Crude oil, *see* Oil
Cruden Bay shorestation *134*
Cruiser Seamount *117*
Crust, earth's 11, 13, 14–15,
  14–15
  continental, minerals from 100
  formation 149, 159
  Mediterranean 141
  Red Sea 146, 148
  separation 25
Crustacea/crustaceans **176**, **182**
  blue 80
  camouflage 67
  catch
    Atlantic *122*
    Caribbean *126*
    Indian Ocean *152*
    Mediterranean *141*
    North Sea 136
    Pacific *166*
  deep ocean 81
  filter mechanisms 62
  fishery
    Caribbean *126*
    Gulf of Mexico 126
    Indian Ocean *152*
    Mediterranean *141*
  food chain 77, **182**
  fungi and **175**
  habitat 67, 83
  insects and **183**
  marine animals and 70, 89,
    123, **183**
    chelicerates **182**
    chitons **180**
    cuttlefish **181**
    Seison **179**
    zooplankton and 63
  plankton and 62
  tapeworms and **178**
Crustal plates 14, 15, 16, 17
Cryptophyceae/cryptophyceans
  175
Ctenophora/ctenophores 66, **178**
Cuba 124, 126, 127
Cubomedusae **177**
Cubozoa **177**
Cultus Lake, sockeye salmon 78
Cumacean copepods **182**
Cumulonimbus, depressions
  and 31
Cumulus clouds 30, 120, *120*,
  154
Curlew, bristle-thighed 111
Curraghs, origin of 43

Current/s 32–5, *32–5*
  Antarctic ice and 113
  Arctic 129, *129*
  Atlantic 44, 46, *46*, 120–1,
    120–1
  Barents Sea 131
  boundary, upwellings and 86
  Caribbean 124
  continental slope 23
  deep ocean 24
  energy source 98, 99
  English Channel 133, *133*
  fish spawning and 78
  fog creation and 33
  gyres and 32–3, *32–3*, 78
  heat control and 26
  history 44, 46
  life forms and 86–7
  mantle and 15
  Mediterranean 142, *142–3*
  Mobile Bay 124, *124*
  North Atlantic 44
  North Sea 132, 133, *133*
  Pacific 87, *87*, 162, 163, *163*
  placer deposits and 164
  plankton and 87, *87*
  Red Sea 145, *145*
  ripple marks 19, *19*
  sediments and 24
  shellfish culture and 97
  Southern Ocean 168
  speed at depth 88
  storm waves and Agulhas 37
  subsurface 88
  surface 142, 168
  vertical eddying and 86
  winds and 33, *33*
  see also specific current
Current charts, Maury's 46
Current gyre 78, *78*
Current meters 48
Cutlassfish, world catch 95
Cutleria **174**
Cuttlebone **181**
Cuttlefish **181**
Cyanophyceae **175**
Cyclones 30, 31, *31*
Cyclonic storms 30, *30*, 31, *31*
Cyclostomata **185**
Cymbulia peroni 67, *67*
Cyprea tigris 85
Cyprid larva **183**
Cyprus, arcuate ridge 138
Cyrenian Mountains *139*
Cyrus oilfield *148*

D

Da Gama, Vasco 44
Daedalus Reef *144*
Dahlak Islands *145*
Dahran *148*
Dam/s 58, 111
Dammam oilfield *148*
Damsel fish 85, *85*
Dan oilfield *135*
Dana, James 160
Danakil Horst 146, *147*
Danan oilfield *148*
Danish coastal waters 77
Danish seine, North Sea fishing
  136
Danube, river *117*, *139*
Darius the Great 148
Darwin, Charles 160
Das Island, oil terminal 148, *148*
David 54
Davis Strait 129, *129*, 130
DDT 108, 109
Dead Sea 99, *144*, *147*
Deane's diving helmet 52
Decapod/s 76, *76*, **182**, **183**
Deccan Plateau 157
Deception Island 168, *168*
Decompression time, diver's 53
Deep basins, high latitudes and
  117
Deep mantle, Pacific Islands 160
Deep ocean floor 13, 15, 22,
  24–5, *24–5*
Deep sea
  animals **176**
  drilling project 165
  eels 69, *69*, 77
  fish 69, *69*, 77
  minerals/mining 102–3,
    102–3, 165
  mollusks **180**
  Pogonophora **182**
  reversing thermometer 49, *49*
  trenches 10, 15
  zooplankton 80
Deep water 86, 97, 99, *99*, 124,
  154
Deep Sea Ventures 57
Dehluran oilfield *148*
Del Cano 44
Delaware Channel 23
Delphinapterus leucas, see White
  whale
Delphinus delphis 73, *73*
Delta/s 20, *23*
  see also specific delta
Demerara Plateau *116*
Demersal fish, catch tonnage
  Atlantic *122–3*
  Caribbean *126*
  Cuban 126
  Indian Ocean *152*, 153
  Mediterranean 141, *141*
  North Atlantic 123, *123*
  North Sea 136
  Pacific *166–7*
  Persian Gulf 148
  stocks 152
Demospongiae **177**
Denayrouze, Rouquayrol and,
  diving equipment 52
Dendronotus frondosus 67, *67*
Denmark 57, *57*, 110, *123*
Density, water 35, 133
Depositional basin, North Sea
  132
Depositional zone, deltas and 20
Deposits
  deep sea 47, *47*
  sealevels and 20
  see also specific deposit
Depressions 30, 31, *31*, 168
Dermal denticles, shark 68, *68*
Derrick/s, oil *104–5*, 105
Desert 17, 146
  coasts 99
  plain 132
Destruction zone, ocean basins
  and 17
Destructive plate margins 15, 22
Detergents, oil pollution and
  108, *108*
Detritus

Amphineura and **180**
Aurelia and **177**
  coral reef 85
  crinoids **183**
  deep ocean floor and 25
  food web 77, *77*
  marine bacteria **175**
  Neopilina and **180**
Deuterium fusion 98
Developing countries/states
  56, 57, 93
Devil's Hole, the 132, *133*
Devon Island *129*
Devonian Period 13, *13*, 17, **185**
Dhows, Arabian 153, *153*
Diacria sp. 89
Diadema **184**
Diadromous fish 122, 126, 141,
  152, 166
Diamantina Fracture Zone *151*,
  156
Diamond deposits 22, 100,
  100–1, 118, *119*
Diapirs 125, *125*, *140*, 141
Dias, Bartolomeu 44
Diatoms 24, 62, *62*, **175**, **176**, *179*,
  181
  antibiotic production **175**
  Bacillariophyceae **175**
  copepods and 64
  gastrotrica **179**
  marine bacteria and **175**
  oozes 24, *24*, 171
  plankton and **175**
  sea productivity and **174**
Dieldrin, pollution and 109
Digenea **178**
Dinaric Basin *140*
Dinoflagellates 62, *62*, 106, **175**
Dinophyceae **175**
Dinophysis schutti 86
Dinosaurs, evolution 17
Diodora **181**
Diomedea nioripes 74, *74*
Dip nets, Pacific fishery and 167
Diphyids **177**
Directional propellers, drill
  ships 104, 165
Directions for Seamen, Royal
  Society 46
Discovery, investigations, whale
  stock 47
Discovery Deep, Red Sea 149
Disease control 96
Distant-water fishing 94
Distillation, North Sea gas 134
Diurnal migration, copepods **182**
Diurnal tides 38, *38*, 124
Diver/s
  human 40–1, *41*, 52–3, *52–3*
  marine animals 71, *71*, 72, 74,
    75
Diver lockout submersibles 54
Diving apparatus 52, *52*, 53, 55
Diving petrel, feeding method 75
Djibouti *149*
  Republic of *149*
Dog-fish 68, *68*, 136
Dogger Bank 132, *133*
Doliolum/doliolids **184**
Doliolum denticulatum 63
Dolomite rocks *135*, 148
Dolphins 72–3, *72–3*, 76, *81*, **186**
DOMA 57
Dominica 125
Dories/dory men 94
Dorra oilfield *148*
Dorsal fins, shark 68, *68*
Doto fragilis, egg spirals 65
Dottie gasfield *135*
Dover sole *123*
Downfaulted continental slopes
  22
Downwarped trough,
  Mississippi deltas and 125
Downwellings 15, 30
Drag net 103
Dragonflies 77
Drake Passage *169*
Drakensberg Mountains *117*,
  150
Draught, merchant vessels 132
Drava, river *139*
Dredger/s *134*, *134*, 135, 153,
  153
Dredges
  fish trapping 92, *92*
  sampling 48, *48*, 50
Dredging 99, 100
  Challenger expedition 47, *47*

minerals and 100, 103
North Sea 134
Drift
  continental, *see* Continental
    drift
  currents, Rennell's theory 46
  nets 136–7, 153
Drilling
  Arctic 130–1
  deep sea 165
  Mediterranean sediments 139
  oil, *see* Oil
  platforms 22
  rigs, *see* specific rig type
Drill/s 48, 165, *165*
Drill ship 104, 105, *105*, 165,
  165
Drogues *51*
Drought, forecasting 31, 59
Dubai *149*
Dudrai oilfield *148*
Dugongs **186**
Dugout 42, *42*, 153
Dujaila oilfield *148*
Dukhan oilfield *148*
Dumping grounds, waste
  materials and 109, *109*
Dumshaf Abyssal Plain *117*, *129*
Dunes, coastal 19
Dunlin oilfield *135*
Durham colleries 135
Dutch coast, plaice spawning
  and 137
DuToit, Alex L. 13
Dyke construction 58, *58*
Dynamic breakwater 58, *58*, 59
Dynamiting, Mediterranean
  fishing and 141

E

Ear ossicles, mammal **185**
Eared seals 70
Earth
  age compared with ocean 16
  axis *39*
  crust 13, 14–15, *14–15*
  equatorial plane *39*
  formation 10–11
  rotation 32, *32*, 39
  tides and 39
Earth-moon system, tides and 38, *39*, 39
Earthquake/s
  Afar Triangle 146
  East Mediterranean Basin 139
  fracture zones and 15
  Grand Banks area 22, *22*
  Lisbon 1755; 37, *37*
  midocean ridges and 13
  Pacific 157, *158*, 159
  plate tectonics and 15
  ridge crests and 15
  sediment and 24
  South America Trench 158
  submarine 37
  transform faults and 15
  tsunami detection and 37
  undersea 37
  waves and 36
  Western Pacific 159
Earthquake belt/zone 22, 124, 138, *138–9*
Earthworms **181**
Easington shorestation *135*
East Africa 13, 16, 17, 146, *147*
East African Rift 16–17
East Anglia, Triassic sandstones, gas 134
East Australia Current *33*, 162, *162*, 163
East Frigg gasfield *135*
East Greenland Current *33*, 121
East Indian Oceans 168
East Pacific Rise *156–7*
  Indian Ocean midocean ridge and 150
  Mid-Atlantic Ridge comparison 116
  minerals 102
  oceanic crust and 157
  plates and plate margin at 14, *14*, 15
  spreading rate 25, *25*, 116
East Shetland Rise *134–5*
East Scotia Basin *169*
East Siberian Sea 128
Easter Island *157*
  Fracture Zone *157*
Easterly winds, Southern Ocean 168
Eastern Caribbean, deep water 124
Eastern little tuna *167*
Eastern Mediterranean Sea 138–9, *138–9*
Eastern valley 150
Eastern tropical Pacific, plankton community 87
Ebb and flow, tide 38
Ebro, river 138, *138*
Ebro Delta *138*, *140*
Echiniscoides 182
Echinodermata/echinoderms **183**, **184–5**
  barnacles and **183**
  food and 64
  habitats 85, 88
  movement of 67
  parasites and **178**, **181**, **183**
Echinoidea **183**
Echinus esculentus 64, *64*
Echiuroidea/echiuroids **179**
Echo
  location, toothed whale 72
  sounding 47, 50, 149
Ecosystem 62, *62*, 76, 89, 108
Ectocarpus 174
Ectoprocta **179**
Edda oilfield *135*
Eddy/eddies
  currents and 35
  deep water 154
  Gulf Stream 121, *121*

  meso-scale 162
  Mobile Bay 124, *124*
  South Atlantic and 154
Eddying, vertical 86
Edward, lake, landing fishing catch at 93, *93*
Eels 77, 78, 79, *79*, 80–1, 85, **186**
Eelgrass 70, 77, 83, *83*
Eelpout 77
EEZ 57
Effluent, *see* specific effluent
Eggs 109, 137
  laying 65, *65*, 111
Ekman current meter 34, *34*
Ekman spiral 32, *32*
Ekman transportation of water 35, *35*, 162
Ekofisk oilfield *105*, 135
El Bunduq oilfield 148, *148*
El Haba oilfield *148*
El Salvador, Golfo de Fonseca and 110
Elasmobranchi/elasmobranchs 68, **182**, **185**
  flukes and **178**
  leeches and **181**
  teleost comparison with **186**
Eldfisk oilfield *135*
Electric ray **185**
Electrodialysis, inverse 99
Electro-receptors, elasmobranchs **185**
Elephant seal, exploitation 170
Elephant teeth, Hudson River 23
Ellef Ringnes *129*
Ellesmere Island 128, *128*, 129, *129*
Ellice Islands, volcanoes 157
Eltanin, *170*
Elvers 79
Embayments 21, *21*
Emden shorestation *135*
Emerita talpoida 82, *82*
Emperor Islands 161, *161*
Emperor penguin **186**
Emperor Seamounts *156*, 157, 160
Enchytraids **181**
Endoparasites **178**
Energy
  currents and 35
  dissipation, sound waves and 26
  mesoscale eddies and ocean 32
  sea 98–9, *98–9*
    -air transfer 30
    ice and 28
  tides and 39
  waves and 36, 37
Energy Resource and Development Administration 99
Enfeh, salt pans 100, *100*
Engineering, marine 58, *58*
English Channel 98, 132, 133, *133*
Engulfment, Pacific Ocean Basin and 157
Enhalus **175**
Enhydra lutris 70, *70*
Ensis **180**
Ensis siliqua 83, *83*
Enteromorpha **174**
Enteropneusts **184**
Entoprocta/entoprocts **179**
Environment, pollution 108–9, *108–9*
Eocene Period, sealevel changes 20
Epeirogenic movements, land masses and 20
Epipelagic zone *81*
Epiphytes, seaweeds **174**
Equator
  Coriolis force at 162
  current gyre and the 162
  midocean upwellings along 86
  moon, tides and 39, *39*
  temperature profile 35, *35*
  trade winds and 32
Equatorial Countercurrent 46, 121, *121*, 154, 155
  circulation 33
Equatorial Current 120, *163*
Equatorial current systems, Pacific Ocean and 87
Equatorial plane, earth's *39*
Equatorial plankton community 87
Equatorial region 116, 163, *163*

Equatorial undercurrent 120, 162, 163, *163*
Eratosthenes Mountains *139*
Erba Deep *149*
Erben Guyot *156*
Erosion 18
  Bay of Fundy 38, *38*
  Bora Bora 161, *161*
  coastal landscape 18
  continental slopes and 22
  icebergs 28
  precipitated seawater and 26
  sea 18–19, *18–19*
  wave 22
Eruption, volcanic, *see* Volcano
Escarpments, Afar Triangle and 146
Esfandiar oilfield *148*
Eskimo/s 131, *131*, 166
Estuaries 19, 110, 111, **174**, **175**
Estuarine 111
Ethiopia 146
Ethiopian Escarpment 146, *147*
Etna 138
Eubalaena 72, *72*
Eucalanus attenuatus 86
Eucalanus bungii 80
Eucarids **183**
Euchaeta norvegica 86
Englenophyceae **175**
Eukrohnia hamata 87
Eunice viridis **181**
Euphausia sp. 87
Euphausia mutica 87
Euphausia pacifica 87
Euphausia superba 73, 170
Euphausians **183**
Euphausiids 63, *63*, 64, 73, 76, *76*, 86, 88, *88*
  sei whale and 73
Euphausis brevis 87
Euphausians **183**
Euplectella 89, **177**
Euphrates, river *148*
Euplectella 89, **177**
Europe
  factory trawlers and 94
  fish, cod markets 131
  history 12, 13, *13*, 17, 46
  inshore fishing fleets 92
  Mid-Atlantic Ridge and 116
  North Sea boundary 57, *57*
  Northern
    North Atlantic 120
    North Sea 132–3
    Urals formation 17
  Northwest
    continental shelf and 122, 132, 168
    fish catch 122
    North Sea formation 132
    tides 38
    white whale habitat 111
  ports of 132
  rotation away from North America 117
  shrimp catch exported to 153
  Southern
    Atlantic hake fisheries 123
    Balearic Basin formation 138
    demersal fisheries 141
    history 17
  Western
    oil production 105
    weather 30
European eel, migration 79, *79*
European hake *123*
Eurytium sp. 77
Eusponginia **177**
Eustatic changes, water levels 20
Evadne sp. 76
Evaporating basin, Red Sea and 144
Evaporation 10
  direct 27, *27*
  gulf seawater 27, *27*
  Mediterranean Sea 138, 142
  oceans and 26
  oil pollution, effect on 108
  Red Sea 144
  salinity and 26
  seawater and 26, 27, *27*
Evaporation-condensation cycle 99, *99*
Evaporite
  basins
    Arctic 130
    Mediterranean *140–1*
  deposits
    Afar Triangle 146

Gulf of Mexico 127
  gulf subsidence and 27, *27*
  Mediterranean 140, *140–1*
  North Sea oil/gasfields and *135*
  Persian Gulf 148
  Red Sea 144
Everglade kite 80
Evolution
  Atlantic Ocean 117, *117*
  terrestrial life and water 26
Exclusive Economic Zone 57
Experiments, air-sea interaction 31
Exploration 46, 141
  rigs, *see* specific rig type
Explosions, rock structure determination and 104
Explosives, disposal 22
Extinct volcano, coral reefs and 160
Eyes, marine animals 67

F

Factory ships/trawlers 92, 94, 95, 122, 167, 170
Fad *148*
Fadhili oilfield *148*
Fahud oilfield *149*
Fahud West oilfield *149*
Falkland Current *33*, 121, 123
Falkland Fracture Zone *117*
Falkland Islands *116*, 118, *159*, 170
Falkland Plateau *116–7*, *169*
Fallout, ocean pollution 109
False color photography, hurricane Camille 31, *31*
Farallon Plate 157, *157*
Farasan Bank *145*
Farasan Islands *145*
Farm Deeps *133*
Farming, land 96
Faeroe Islands 78, *117*
Fast ice 28, 113, *113*
Fateh oilfield *135*
Fats, marine bacteria and **175**
Fault/s 15, 18, 25, 134, 138, 146
  scarps 146, 157
  zone, Caribbean 125
Faulted block, North Sea oilfields 135, *135*
Fauqui oilfield *148*
Faxa Bay, shell sand mining 118, *118*
Feather stars 80, **183**
Feeding
  areas 78, *78*, 87, 110–11
  marine animals 64–5, *64–5*, 74, 75, *75*, 78, 110–11, 170
  methods 75, *75*
  migration and 78, 170
  relationships 77
  schooling instinct and 61
Feeding chains, *see* Food chains
Feed-lot culture 96
Fences, fish traps 92, *92*
Feradum oilfield *148*
Fernando Po Island *117*
Ferromanganese deposits 170
Fertility, regional 86
Fertilization, marine animals *see* specific animal
Fertilizer 59, 65, 118, 153, **174**
Fetch, wave height and the 36
Fiddler crab 77, 83
Fiji
  Islands *156*
  Plateau *156*
  rock-wall fishtraps 92, *92*
File shell 66, *66*
Filter
  chamber, *Calanus finmarchicus* 64, *64*
  feeders/feeding 69, 85, 179, 185
    beach life and 83
    marine ecosystem and 62
    technique 64
    see also specific animal
Fin whale 73, 107
  capelin fish and 111
  whale catch and 171, *171*
  whaling and 170
Fins, shark 68, *68*
First-year ice 28, 29, *29*
Firth of Forth, Grangemouth oil refinery 105
Fish 68–9, *68–9*
  Amphioxus and **184**
  Antarctic waters 170
  Bony, *see Teleostei*
  cannibalizing and 77
  catch
    Atlantic *122*
    Caribbean 126
    Indian *152*
    Mediterranean *141*
    Pacific *166*, 167
    Peruvian anchovy 166
    world commercial catch, tonnage 95
  class *Pisces* **185**
  detecting, sonar 95, *95*

dinoflagellates and **175**
  distribution 89
  farming 97, *97*
  feeding 76, 77, 85, 111, 141
  forecasting supplies 59
  fungi and **175**
  gut **179**
  habitat
    abyssal plain 88
    coral reef 85
    deep sea 81, 88–9, *88–9*
    herbivorous, kelps and **174**
    larva, larvaceans and **184**
    leeches **181**
    mercury, poisoning from 109
    migration 78–9
    offal, seabirds and 75, *75*
    poisonous 69, *69*
    prey of seal/whale 70, 72
    radioactive pollution 109
    schooling *60–1*, 61
    seabirds and **186**
    species 56, 108, 141
    stocks 56, *106–7*
      Bering Sea 111
      decline 47
      Eastern Mediterranean 143
      Indian Ocean 152
      inshore areas, loss of 92
      Mediterranean 141
      migration research and 78
      North Sea 136–7, *136–7*
      survival and 78
      tapeworms and **178**
      traps/trapping 92–3, *92–3*
      USA market value 111
  "Fish," sonar 50, 51, *51*
Fisheries Commissions 56
Fishermen 74, 167
Fishery/fisheries
  Atlantic 122–3, *122–3*
  Barents Sea 131
  Caribbean 124, 126
  clupeid fish and 86
  development 97
  food chains and 77
  freshwater, lampreys and **185**
  Indian Ocean 152–3, *152–3*
  local exploitation 94
  marine 58
  Mediterranean 141
  North Sea, distribution 137, *137*
  Pacific 166–7, *166–7*
  Persian Gulf 148
  Peru currents and 163, *163*
  Red Sea 148
  research 47
  upwellings and 162
  zone 57
Fishing
  areas 87
  continental shelves 94
  dredges and 135
  factory trawlers 94
  fleets, Labrador coast 122, *122*
  freedom 56
  history 94, 95
  hours and gear, North Sea *136*
  industry 36, 94–5, *94–5*, 121
  inshore 92–3, *92–3*
  Mediterranean 143
  methods 152
  nets 75
  rights 56
  tactics 167
  vessels, sonar equipment and 95, *95*
  wind waves and 36
Fish-farming activities 92
Fishmeal 95, 106, 136, 166
Fissures, Red Sea 144
Fjords 19, 20, *20*, 132
Fladen Ground 132, *133*
Flagellae/flagellates 66, 84, **174**, **176**, **179**
Flags of convenience 56
Flame dwarf angel fish 69, *69*
Flatfish 80, *123*, 136, *136*
Flats, sediment 19
Flatworm/s **175**, **179**
Flemish Cap *117*, 121
Flensing 170, 171, *171*
Fletcher Abyssal Plain *129*
Fletcher's T3 (USA), drifting "ice-island" 129
Fleuss, H. A. 52
Fleuss self-contained breathing apparatus *52*
Flint 134

Floating
 icebergs, Arctic 28
 line gear, Pacific fishery 167
Floats, current measurements
 and 35
Floe, ice, *see* Icefloe
Flood, forecasting 31, 59
Floor, deep ocean 13, 24–5, *24–5*
 see also Seabed
Florida 111, 118, 121
 Current, Gulf Stream and 120
 escarpment 125
 Straits, "loop current" and
  124
"Flotation" layer, radiolarians
 176
Flotta shorestation *134*
Flounder *77, 123*
 Atlantic 122, 123
 Pacific 166
 world catch, tonnage 95
Flounder oilfield *135*
Flow meter, water sampling 48
Flowering plants, marine 175
Flukes 178
Fluorates, gulf seawater and *27*
Fluoride, seawater *27*
Fluorine, marine life and 109
Fly/flies 183
Flying fish *80, 85, 166–7, 186*
"Flying" snail *67, 67*
Flyways, shorebirds migratory
 111
Focused wave energy 37
Fog 33, *33, 120, 121*
Fold mountains 12, *12,* 13, *13,* 19
Food chains 68, 76–7, 111, 174,
 176, 182, 184
 abundance 87
 Antarctic 170
 fish and 68, 141
 krill and 170
 larvae and plankton blooms
  111
 Mediterranean 141
 ocean 87, 96
 seabirds and **186**
 seashore 83
 siphonophores 177
 sunlit zone 86
 supply 87, 111
Foraminifera 24, **176, 181**
 oozes 24, 171
"Forced waves" 36
Forces, sea 59
 see also Coriolis force
Forests, submerged offshore 20
Formaldehyde, mercury
 pollution and 109
Formation of oceans, age and
 16–17, *16–17*
 see also specific subject
Forties oilfield *104–5,* 105, *135,*
 135
Fortune Shore *23*
Fossil/s 179
 Agnatha **185**
 ammonites **181**
 brachiopods **179**
 chelicerate **182**
 coalfields 12
 coccolithophorids **174**
 compasses 16
 coral reef **178**
 crinoid **181, 183**
 distribution 13
 echinoderms **183**
 fern 13, *13*
 fuels 108, 109
 limpets **180**
 living sea 65, *65*
 magnetism 16
 ocean floor *24*
 Ordovician **179**
 ostracods **182**
 Paleozoic **180**
 reptile 13, *13*
 sea levels and 20
 spreading center 159, *159*
 submerged beaches 22
 teleosts **186**
 trench 158, *158*
Foxe Basin *129*
Fracture zones 15, *117,* 150, 157
 see also specific zone
Fram 28, 129
France 88, *123,* 138, *138,* 139,
 143
Franklin Shore *23*
Frasch process 127

Frazil ice 28, *28,* 29
Freak waves 37
"Free waves" 36
"Free zones," oil waste
  discharge and 143
Freezing
 point 26
 seawater 28–9, *28–9*
Freshwater
 generating 97
 see also specific subject
Friction, tidal energy and 39
Frictional drag 26, 38
Frigatebird 75, *75*
Frigg gasfield *135*
Fringing reef 84, 160, *160*
Fronts, depressions and *31*
Fucoids 174
Fucoxanthin pigment **174**
Fucus serratus 83, *83*
Fulmars 74, 75
Fungus/fungi 175
Fur seal/s 70, *71,* 76, 170
Fusion, power development and
 98
Future use of ocean 58–9
Fyke nets 92, *92*

G

Gachsaran oilfield *148*
Gadids **186**
Gadus morhua 69, *69, 77*
Gagnan, Emile 53
 Cousteau and, aqualung *52*
Galapagos
 Fault Zone 25
 Islands 25, *116, 157,* 165
  marine iguanas 70, 71, *71,*
   186
  volcanoes 157
 Ridge *116,* 157
 Rift 25
 spreading center, Pacific
  Basin and 157
 Triple Junction 25, *25*
Galathea squamosa 67, *67*
Galeocerdo 68
Galileo, longitude determina-
 tion 44
Gall/s, pycnogonids and **182**
Gall bladder, sporozoa 176
Gambier Islands 161, *161*
Gametes, worms and **181**
Ganges, river *150*
 -Brahmaputra submarine fan
  150
Gannet/s 74, 75, *75,* **186**
Gannetry, Nova Scotia 74, *74*
Garangan oilfield *148*
Garden eels **186**
Garfish *166–7*
Garonne, river *138*
GARP Atlantic Tropical
 Experiment (GATE) 31
Gas natural 11, 26
 Antarctica 170
 Atlantic 119
 continental shelf prospects
  104
 Das Island oil terminal and
  148
 Indian Ocean 153
 Mediterranean *140–1,* 141
 North Sea 134
 pipelines, Middle East 149,
  149
 strikes, Melville Island 130
 trap, Arctic 130
Gasfields *100–1*
 Arctic *130–1*
 Atlantic *119*
 Caribbean 127
 Indian Ocean *153*
 Middle East 149, *149*
 North Sea *135*
 Pacific *164–5*
Gastropoda/gastropods 67, *67,*
 77, *77,* 83, **180**
Gastrotica 179
GATE experiment 31
Gavarzin oilfield *149*
Gear, fishing 136, *136,* 141
Gemini X, photograph 162, *162*
Genital cells, sponge 176
Genus, nomenclature **173**
Geographia of Ptolemy 44
Geographic North Pole, diver
 at *40–1,* 41
Geologic dating, sealevel
 changes and 20
Geological LOng Range
 Inclined Asdic (GLORIA) 51,
 51
Geology
 continental slope boundary 12
 drift arguments 16
 oceans basins and 13
 oil and gastraps 104
 seabed 50
 see also specific ocean/sea
Geo-magnetic fields 78
Geomorphology, sealevel
 changes and 20
Geophones 104
Georgia, phosphate deposits 118
Geostrophic flow 32, *32*
German Bight *133*
Germany, West 57, *57,* 110, *123*
Gerrids, freshwater **183**
Gestation period, whales 73
Ghaba North oilfield *149*
Ghardaqa, Red Sea, fishery 148

Ghawar oilfield *148*
Ghost crabs 182
Giant architeuthids **181**
Giant clam 64, *175, 178,* **180**
Giant coconut crab **183**
Giant crab **182**
Giant isopod *81*
Giant kelps 170, *170,* **174**
Giant sea anemones 25
Giant squid/s 64, 72, *81,* **180**
Gibbs Fracture Zone *117*
Gibraltar 35
 Strait of 142, *142*
Gibson, John 165
Gibson Desert *151, 156*
Gifford Seamount *116, 157*
Gigantocypris 182
Gilbert-Ellice Islands 160, 161,
 161
Gilbert Islands 157
Gill nets 93, *93,* 141, 167
Gill rakers 68, 69
Gills marine animals, 68, *68*
 see also specific animal
Glacial valleys 20, *20*
Glacier, US icebreaker 113, *113*
Glaciers 18, 20, 29, *132, 171*
Glass, aragonite and 118
Glass sponges 88
Glasseye snapper *80*
Glauberite, gulf seawater and *27*
Glauconite 118, 153
Glycerol, algae and **178**
Global Atmospheric Research
 Programme (GARP) 31
Globicephala melaena 73
Globigerina **176**
Globigerina quinqueluba 87
Glomar Challenger 49, 144, *165,*
 170
GLORIA 51, *51*
Glossopteris, fossils 13, *13*
Gnathostomata **185**
Gobi Desert *156*
Gobius sp. 77
Gobiusculus sp. 65
Goby 65, *65, 77,* 78
Gold deposits
 Alaska 100, 165
 Atlantic *119*
 Atlantis II Deep 149, *149*
 Caribbean 127
 continental shelf 22
 Pacific 158, *164–5*
 placer, offshore *100–1*
 world reserves, tonnage *101*
Golden tubeastra 84, *84*
Golfo de Fonseca 110
Gonads 179
Gondwanaland 12, 13, 16, 17,
 151
Gonyaulax 175
Goodwin Sands 132, *133*
Gorda Plate 157, *157*
Gorda Ridge *156*
Gorges, fish traps and 92, *92*
Gorgonian coral 84, *84*
Gorgonocephalus **183**
Gough Island *169*
Grab sampler/sampling 48, *48,*
 49
Graben 25, *134,* 146, *146*
"Gradualism," continental
 drift and 13
Grand
 Banks 22, *22, 116, 120, 121,*
  129
 Canyon 22
 Isle 127
Grangemouth shorestation *134*
Granitic rocks 146, 157
Graptolites **184**
Grasshopper/s *77, 77*
Gravel
 Arctic 130
 Atlantic 118, 119
 marine 100
 North Sea *134,* 135
 Pacific *164–5,* 165
 sand and *100–1,* 130
 stomatopods and *183*
Gravity 12, 32, **32,** 38, 39
 corer 49
Gray mullet 69, *69, 77, 141,*
 166–7, 167
Gray whale 78, 110–11
Grease ice 29
Great Auk 74
Great Bahamas Bank 118, *125*
Great Barrier Reef 85, *85,* 160,

 160, 167, 167
Great Bear Lake *128*
Great Bight Abyssal Plain *151,*
 156
Great Dividing Range *151, 156*
Great Fisher Bank *133*
Great Frigatebird *80–1*
Great Salt Lake 99
Greater Antilles *125*
Greece 21, 56, 138
Greeks, ancient 38
Green algae **174**
Green turtle 78, *78, 80,* **186**
Greenland
 Arctic current flow and 129,
  129
 conditions off *129*
 continental shelf 128
 fauna
  right whale 73, *73*
  shark 35, 80
  white whale 111
 fishing
  cod 78, 122
  halibut *131*
  history 94
  habitat 111
 history 13, *13,* 94
 icebergs 28, 128, *128*
 narrwhals migration 111
 North Atlantic deep water 120
 Northern, icebergs 128, *128*
 Rockall Plateau and 117
 shark 35, 80
 submarine routes and *130*
 transpolar drift stream and 28
 white whale 111
Greenland Current 120
Greenland Fracture Zone *129*
Greenland-Iceland-Faeroe
 Ridge 116
Greenland Sea 128, 129, *129*
Greenwich, Royal Observatory
 44
Grenada *125*
 Trough *125*
Grimsby, fish 94, 95, 136
Groningen gasfield *135*
Groundwater 10, 27
"Group 77" 57
Groynes, beach 19, *19*
Guadeloupe Island *125, 156,*
 162, *162*
Guam Island *151, 156*
Guano fertilizer 76, 106, **186**
Guatemala City, earthquake 124
Guiana Current 120, *120,* 121
 Caribbean and 124
 circulation *33*
Guianas, shrimp fisheries 126
Guillemots 74
Guinea Current *33,* 46, 121, *121*
Gulf of Aden *145, 147,* 155
 bottom fishing, Soviet
  trawlers 153
 rift system formation 16–17
 rift valley, Afar Triangle 146
Gulf of Alaska
 copepod in 80
 Oregon salmon 79, *79*
 Pacific fishery 166
 prawn fishery 167
Gulf of Aqaba, Apollo 7 view
 144, *144*
Gulf of Bothnia, uplifting and 21
Gulf of Cadiz, features 142, *142*
Gulf of California, East Pacific
 Rise and 157
Gulf of Gabes *139*
Gulf of Genoa, pollution and 143
Gulf of Mexico 18, 124, *124–5*
 currents and 120, 124
 resource 104, 126, 127
Gulf of Oman *145*
Gulf of Sirte *139, 140*
Gulf of Suez
 Apollo 7 view 144, *144*
 sardines 148
Gulf of Valencia *138, 140*
 Balearic Basin and 138
Gulf of Venezuela 91, *125*
Gulf seawater *27, 27*
Gulf Stream 120, *120,* 121
 Atlantic water profile 120
 circulation *33*
 Coriolis force and 32
 eel migration and 79
 Kuroshio Current comparison
  162
 "loop current" 124

 160, 167, *167*
North Atlantic gyre and 32
 rings 32, 120
 speed 32
 submersible voyage down 54
 temperature 30
 waters of Pamlico Sound and
  120
Gulkhari oilfield *148*
Gull/s 74, 75, *81,* **186**
Gulper eel *81*
Gummy shark 166
Gurnards *123*
Gut
 ciliates **176**
 cnidaria **177**
 fish, worms in **179**
 platyhelminthes **178**
 sporozoa **176**
Guyana, aragonite market 118
Gymnodinium **175**
Guyots, deep sea 146
 see also specific Guyot
Gypsum
 Deep, Red Sea *149*
 Mediterranean Basin 141
Gyres 33, *33,* 163, *163*
 Arctic Basin and 129
 Arctic surface water 128
 Atlantic 120
 cold water 120
 currents and 32–3, *32–3*
 fish migration and 78
 Indian Ocean and 154
 North Atlantic 120
 Pacific 162
 South Indian 155
 temperature distribution and
  35
 tropical current, spawning fish
  and 78, *78*
 warm water 120

Habitat
Insecta **183**
marine animals 82–3, *82–3*, 110, 137, 160
see also specific habitat
"Habitat," underwater working 53, *53*, 55, *55*
Haddock
Arctic 95
Atlantic 123, *123*
Barents Sea 131, *131*
North Sea 136, 137, *137*
overfishing 137
trawlers 94
world catch, tonnage *95*
Hadley, John 45
reflecting quadrant 44, 45, *45*
Haft Kel oilfield *148*
Hagfish 68, **185**
Haiti *116*, 127, *157*
Hake *123*
anchovies and 76
Atlantic fisheries and 123
Mediterranean stocks 141
world catch, tonnage *95*
Halat Al Mubarraz *148*
Halfbeak 167, *167*
Halibut 68
fishery agreements 106
world catch, tonnage *95*
Halieis 21
Halite, Mediterranean Basin 141
Halley, Edmund 44, 53
diving bell *52*, 53
Halocarbons, pollutant group 108
Halogen compounds, pollution and 109
Halosaur *80*
Halosphaera **174**
Halush oilfield *148*
Halut *148*
Hamaliyah oilfield *148*
Hamburg, port of 132
Hammond Innes, The 94, *94–5*
Handlines 136, 153
Hanish Islands 145
Hanseatic League 122, 136
Harbor/s 19, 20, 21, 22, 153
porpoise 72, *72*
seals 71, *71*
"Hard hat" diving gear 52, *52*, 53
Hardanger fjord *133*
Hardy Sampler 48, *48*
Harp seals 111, 131, *131*
Harrison, John 44, 45, *45*
Hatcheries, *Sporozoa* and **176**
Hatchet fish 69, *69*, *81*, 88–9, 89
Hatching, plaice 137
Hatchlings, plankton and 64
Hatteras Abyssal Plain *116*, *157*
Hawaii *156*
volcanoes 146, 160
Kilauea *8–9*, 9
Hawaiian Islands 15, 37, 160, 161, *161*
Hawaiian Ridge *156*
Headland/s *18*, *18*, 19, 86
Heard Island *150*, *169*
Hearing, toothed whales 72
Heat 13, 15, 26, 30, 98, 121
Heather oilfield *135*
Heavy metal deposits 144
Heavy minerals, continental shelf and 22
Hebrides, Sea of the *132*
Heezen Fracture Zone *156–7*
Height, wave 36, 37
Heimdal gasfield *135*
Heliozoans **176**
Helium, diving and 53
Hellenic-Roman harbor 21
Hellenic Trough 138, *139*
Helmet, diving 52, *52*, 53
Hemichordata **184**
Hemispheres 32, *32*, 33, *33*, 86, 87
Hendijan oilfield *148*
Herbivore/s
animal plankton 86
copepods **182–3**
feeding techniques 64
fish 69, *69*, 85, **174**

food chain 86, **176**
land/marine 62
plant life and 76
sea cow **186**
sea strata 80
Tardigrada **182**
zooplankton 63, *63*
Hercynian Mountains 12, 13, 17, 134
Hermaphrodites **178**, **180**, **181**, **183**, **186**
see also specific animal
Hermit crab 69, *69*, **177**, **181**
Herodotus Abyssal Plain *139*
Herring 69, *69*
ancestry **186**
Atlantic 107, 122, *122–3*
Barents Sea **183**
British industry and 107
Calanus finmarchicus **182**
catch 95, *107*
exploitation 107
filter feeding **186**
fishing industry 94
food chain and 69, 76, *76*, 77
fungi and **175**
genus **173**
history and 94
midwater trawl and 122
migration 78
North Atlantic 123
North Sea 135, 136, *136*
Norwegian fisheries 92
Pacific *166–7*
ring-netters 94
Swedish fisheries 92
United Kingdom catch, tonnage *107*
world catch, tonnage *95*
Hess Deep 25, *25*
Hess Guyot *156*
Heteropods **180**
Hewett gasfield *135*
Hexactinellida **176**
High seas
Convention 56
definition 56
High tide 38, 39, *39*
Highlands, Scotland 13, *13*
Himalayas 12, 16, *16*, 17, 144, 150, *150*
Hinge line, sealevels and 21
Hippopdius **177**
Hippospongia **177**
Hircinea gigantea **177**
Hirudinea **181**
HMS *Beagle* 160
HMS *Challenger* 46, *46*, 48, 102, 118, 165
oceanographic expedition 47
HMS *Sovereign* 29, *29*
Hod oilfield *135*
Holland, *see* Netherlands
Holocephali 68, **178**, **185**
Holothuria/holothurian 89, *89*, **182**, **184**
Holothuroidia, habitat 82, *82*
Homing behavior/instinct 78, 96–7, 167
Hondo oilfield *105*
Honduras 110
Hooks, barbed, fish traps 92, *92*
Horny corals 84
Horse mackerel *123*
Mediterranean tonnage *141*
North Sea catch 136
Horseshoe Seamounts *117*
Horst/s *25*, 146
see also specific horst
Hot brines, Red Sea 148, 149, *149*
Hot pools, ocean origin and 10
Hot spot 15, 157, 161, *161*
Hot springs 25, 146
Hout oilfield *148*
Huahine Island 161, *161*
Huascaran Mountain 158
Hudson Bay 20, *116*, *157*
Hudson Canyon 23, *23*, *116*, *157*
Hudson Channel 23, *23*
Hudson Delta 23, *23*
Hudson river 23, *23*, 109, *109*
Hull, fishing 94, 136
Humber, fishing industry 136
Humboldt, Alexander von 46
Humboldt Current 33, 162, *163*
Hummock ice *29*
Humpback whale 73, *73*
breeding 170
protection 170

whale catch and 171, *171*
Hurricane/s 30, *30*, 31, *31*, 124
Husbandry, animal 96
Hutton oilfield *135*
Huwaila oilfield *148*
Hydractinia **177**
Hydraulic dredging, minerals 100
Hydrobia sp. 77
Hydrocarbon/s 134, 135, 141, 153
deposits 127, 130
oil exploration and 105
pollution by 108–9
Hydroctena **178**
Hydrogen
fusion 98
plant life and 76
seawater 26
sulfide 25
Hydrographers, early 44
Hydroid/s **180**
feeding techniques 83
hermit crabs and 69
polyps **177**
pycnogonids and **182**
Hydrological cycle 26, 27, *27*
Hydrophones, oceanography using 50
Hydrosphere 10–11, 13
Hydrothermal solutions 25
Hydrozoa **177**
Hymenoptera **183**
Hyperiid amphipod 76, *76*
Hyperoodon ampullatus 73, *73*

Iberian Peninsula 117, *117*
Ice 13, 26, 28–9, *28–9*, 168
Age 13, 20, 21, 132, 134
bergs 28, 59, 120, *128*, *129*
breaker 130, *130*
caps 12, 13, 20, 22, 28
cores 30
cover 128, 168
drift 28
floes 28, 29, 113, *113*
islands 128, 168
sheets 20, 28–9, *28–9*
Iceland 15, 116, 118, *118*
fish/fishing 94, 122
cod 122, *123*
herring 107
Icelandic Low 30
Ichthyophonus **175**
Idd-el Shargi oilfield *148*
Identification, water, North Sea 133, *133*
Igneous activity 161
Igneous rock, fossil magnetism 16
Iguanas, marine 70, *17*, *71*, **186**
Ilmenite, Indian Ocean 153
INCO 57
Indefatigable gasfield *135*
India
drift 12, 151, 157
history 13, *13*, 16, 17, 44
subcontinent satellite view 154, *154*
trade routes to 154
Western, shrimp fisheries off 153
Indian Ocean 145, 150–1, *150–1*, 154, *169*
Antarctic Circumpolar Current and 35, 120
Atlantic Ocean Ridge and 116
circulation 154–5, *154–5*
continental shelf 152, *153*
continents bordering 15
fish catch 152, *152*
fishery 152, *152*
history 17, 44, 151, *151*, 154
lingula and 65
North 154
Pacific Ocean size and 157
pilot whale and 73
purse-seiner and 94
resource 152–3, *152–3*
ridge system and 146, 157
storm waves 37
swells from 37
tides and 38
wind circulation, history 44
Indian Ocean Basin, age 144
Indians, fishing and 166
Indicator species
arrowworms **180**
North Sea 133, *133*
ostracods **182**
Indies, Columbus crossing to 44
Indigirka, river *128*
Indonesia 150, 154
resources 153, 165
Indonesian Arc *151*, *156*
Indo-Pacific Region
coral reefs **180**
food web 77
inshore fishing 92
seasnakes 70
Indus, river *150*
fan 150, *150*, 151
Industrial pollution, breeding environment and 111
Industrial Revolution 56
Industrial species, fish 136, 137
see also specific fish
Industrial wastes, disposal 22
Inert gas, divers and 53
Inflow
English Channel, current pattern 133, *133*
gulf salt water 27
Mediterranean 142
Informal Single Negotiating Text, UNCLOS III; 57
Inland Seas, North Sea, Permian Period 132
"Innocent passage" 56, 57

Insecta/insects 111, **176**, **183**
Inshore fisherman 92–3
Inshore fishing 92–3, *92–3*
Inshore water, turbidity 26
Inshore zone, currents and 162
Institute of Oceanographic Sciences 51
Intercontinental telegraph 46
Intermediate water *35*, 162, 168, *168*
International Conference on Marine Parks and Reserves, 1975 111
International Court of Justice, North Sea case 56
International Enterprise Body 57
International Ice Patrol 28
International Seabed Authority (ISA) 57
International Whaling Commission 170
Interstitial animal forms **179**, **182**
Intertidal
plants, *see* specific plant
sediment flats 19
zone 82, **179**, **183**
depth and 81
Intracontinental mountain ranges 16, *16*
Inverse electrodialysis 99
Invertebrates, marine **175**
ciliates and **176**
distribution 89
feeding and breeding 64–5, *64–5*
movement of 66–7, *66–7*
Pacific fishery and 167
sea strata and 81
Investigations of the Currents of the Atlantic Ocean 46
Iodine 109, **174**
Ion/s, seawater 27, *27*, **176**
Ionian
Basin 138–9, *139*
Sea *139*, *142*
Iran, oil and gas 148, 149, *149*, 153
Iraq, oil 148, 149, *149*
Ireland 117
Irish Sea 132, *132*
Irminger Current
circulation 33
North Atlantic Current and 121, *121*
sub-polar gyre and 120
Iron/deposits
Antarctica 170
Atlantic *119*
Atlantis II Deep 149, *149*
Caribbean 127, *127*
earth's core of nickel and 14, *14*
manganese nodule constituent 102, *102*
Mediterranean *140–1*, 141
offshore *100–1*
Pacific *164–5*
seawater 27
Western Pacific 165
ISA 57
Isinglass **185**
Island/s 86, 111
arcs *15*, 16, 22
states maritime law and 56
Isle of Man *132*
Isobars, depressions and *31*
Isogonic chart 44, *44*
Isopod *81*, **179**
Isostatic movement 20
Isostatic uplift, Baltic Ice Lake 21, *21*
Isotherm, anthozoans and **178**
Isotope dating, Pacific Islands 160
Isthmus of Panama, closure 124
Isurus **185**
Italians, portulan chart and 44
Italy, arcuate ridge 138

Jabal Danna *148*
Jack mackerel
Atlantic *122–3*
Caribbean *126*
Pacific *166–7*
world catch, tonnage *95*
Jack-up (rig) 104, 105, *105*
Jaham oilfield *148*
Jan Mayen
Fracture Zone *129*
Ridge *148*
Jana oilfield *148*
Japan
fish 27, 109, 166, 167
trap 93, *93*
fisheries 106, 166
fishermen, tactics 167
fishing vessels 94, 153
islands of 162
Kuroshio Current and 162
long-liners 94
maritime law and interests 56
mercury poison 27, 109
Minimata 27, 109
North Pacific fishery 166
agreement 106
offshore iron 165
Pacific Oceanic crust 157
Porphyra consumption **174**
Sea of *151*, *156*, 166
storms from 30
submarine deeps and 116
Trench *156*
whaling 107, 170
Jarn Yaphour *149*
Java *151*, *156*
Coastal Current 154, *155*
Trench 150, *151*, *156*
Jaw, *Gnathostomata* **185**
Jawless
fish 68
vertebrates **185**
Jellyfish 66, *66*, *80*, **177**, **182**
deep-sea 89, *89*
movement 67
Jersey 98
Jet propulsion, marine animals 66–7, **184**
Jet stream 30, *30*
Jiddah *149*
JIM diving suit 55, *55*
Johnson *Sea Link* 54, *54–5*
Joints, rock 18, *18*
Josephine oilfield *135*
Juan de Fuca Ridge *156*
Juan Fernandez Island *116*, *157*
Jupiter, planet of 44
Jurassic Period
Atlantic 116, 117
coelacanth **186**
events 17
Gondwanaland 13
North Sea 134, 135, *135*
Persian Gulf 148
sponges **176**
teleost fossils **186**
Juraybi'at oilfield *148*
Jurisdiction, maritime, *see* Law, maritime
Jutland Bank 132, *133*
Juvenile water 10

K

Kabud oilfield *148*
Kalahari Desert *117, 150*
Kalnes, Norway, rock carvings 42, *42*
Kamchatka *156*
  Alaska-K. Ridge 158
  Pacific fishery 166, 167
Kane Fracture Zone *116–17*
Kara Sea 129
Karan oilfield *148*
Karanj oilfield *148*
Karun oilfield *148*
Kauai, Pacific, age of 160
Kayaks, origin of 43
Kebrit Deep, Red Sea *149*
Kelp 82, *82*, 174
  America 81
  Antarctic 170, *170*
  fauna and 174
  food chains 77
  Pacific 77, 174
  sea otter habitat 70
Kelvin Seamounts *116*
Kenchreai 21
Kendall, Larcum, Harrison chronometer by 45, *45*
Kennecott Consortium 57
Keratin plates, marine mammals **186**
Kerguelen
  Island *150, 169*
  submarine ridges and 168
  Plateau *150, 169*
Kermadec Trench *156*
Keyhole limpet **181**
Khafji oilfield *148*
Kharg-Darius oilfield *148*
Khor al Amaya *148*
Khurais oilfield *148*
Khursaniyah oilfield *148*
Kifl oilfield *148*
Kilauea volcano *8–9*, 9, 160
Killer whale 72, 73, *72–3*
"Kinetic" energy, tides and 39
King crab 65, *65*, 167, **182**
Kinorhyncha **179**
Kirala state, beach sand minerals 153
Kolyma, river *128*
Kolymskoye Mountains *156*
Korea
  fisheries off 166
  fishing vessels 153
Koryak Mountains 158, *158*
Kraits **186**
Krakatoa *151, 156*
  eruption 150
Krill
  fishing and 77, 170
  food chains 77
  plankton and 71
  seal and 71
  whales and 72, 73, *73*
Kru tribe, Liberia, inshore fishing 92
Kuh-E-Kaki oilfield *148*
Kuh-E Rig oilfield *148*
Kula Plate 157, *157*, 158
Kupal oilfield *148*
Kurayn oilfield *148*
Kuril/s
  structure of 160
  Trench *156*
Kuroshio Current 162, *162*, 163, *163*
  air-sea interaction and 30
  circulation *33*
  Coriolis force and 32
  fog creation and 33, *33*
  speed 32
Kuroshio Extension 162, 163, *163*
  circulation *33*
Kuwait 148
  oil production 148, 149, *149*
  trawl fisheries for shrimp off 153
Kyrenia, wreck off 59, *59*
Kythera 21
Kyushu, Minimata Bay, mercury poisoning 109

L

Lab-E-Safid oilfield *148*
Laboratories, HMS *Challenger* 47, *47*
Labrador 122, *129*
  Current 120, *120, 121*
    Atlantic water profile *121*
    circulation *33*
    Gulf Stream and 120
    icebergs and 120
    North Atlantic conditions and 129
Lafourche, Mississippi delta *125*
Lagoons 84, *84–5*, 110, 150, 160
Lake/s
  dykes 58
  Harbor, high tide 38, *38*
  ocean origins and 10
  salt pan *27*
  see also specific lake
Lake, Simon 54
Lali oilfield *148*
Lamellibranchia **180**
Laminaria **174**
  digitata 82, *82*
Laminarin **174**
Lamna **185**
Lamp shells 80
Lamparas 148
Lamprey 68, *68*, **185**
Lancaster Sound *130*
Land animals returning to the sea 70–1, *70–1*
Land erosion, precipitated seawater and 26
Land fall, history and finding 44
Land forms, Quaternary Ice Age and 20
Land longitude, determination 44
Land outbuilding 19
Land, primary productivity and 86, *86*
Land, reptile fossil 13, *13*
Land, sealevels and 20
Land, temperature of sea and 30
Land, world total area 104
Landing sizes, fish, North Sea 137
Landlocked seas, salinity 26
Landlocked states, rights of 57
Landscapes, sealevels and 20
Lantern fish 80, 81
Larva/larvae, marine animals 65, *65*, 66, 123, **179, 184, 185**
  anchovies, food requirements 77
  eel 79
  green turtle *78*
  plaice 137
  plankton blooms and 111
Larvacea/larvaceans **175, 184**
Laser profilometer 29, *29*
Lasso cell 177
  see also Cnidae
Lateral line system, fish **185**
Latimeria **180**
Latimeria chalumnae **186**
Latin America, oil production, tonnage 105
Latitude/s 16, 20, 44, 45, 117
Lau Ridge *156*
Laurasia 12, 13, *13*, 17
Laurentian Cone *116*
Lava 9, 25, *25*, 144, 158
Lavan Island *148*
Law, maritime 56–7, *56–7*
Law of the Sea Tribunal 57
Lead/deposits
  Atlantis II Deep 149, *149*
  Indian Ocean 153
  manganese nodule constituent 102, *102*
  Pacific 158
  pollution, Mediterranean 143
  residence time 27
Lead, frozen 29, *29*, 41
Lead-line, ancient Greeks and 43
League of Nations, territorial sea and 56
Lebanon, salt pans 100, *100*
Lee, wind flow and 36
Leeches, marine **181**
Leman Bank
  gasfield *135*
  production platform *105*
Lena, river *128*
Lena Guyot *150, 169*
Lenses, evaporite *140*
Lenz, Emil von 46
Leptonychotes weddelli 71
Lesser Antilles 124, *125*
Lethbridge's armored diving suit 52
Leukemia, marine plants and 97
Levantine Abyssal Plain *139, 140*
Levees, sand and silt 125, *125*
Liberia
  Kru tribe, inshore fishing 92
  registered shipping 56
Lice **183**
Lichina **175**
Lift-net, bait and use of 92, *92*
Light
  absorption, water and 26
  arrowworms and **180**
  fish behavior to 167
  marine plants and **174**
  oil pollution, effect on 108
  organs **181, 183**
  penetration, wavelength and 27
  seawater and 80
  underwater photography and 50, 51, *51*
Lighthouses, windwaves and 36
Ligia oceanica 83, *83*
Ligurian Sea 138, *138, 140*
Lilienthal, Theodor Christoph 117
Lima scabra 66, *66*
Limacina 76, *76*
  helicina 86, *87*
  lesuerii 87
Lime
  muds *100–1*
  producing coral 84
Limestone
  Atlantic 118
  coral 160, **178**
  formation **176**
  North Sea 134, *135*
  oil, gas and 104, *135*
  Persian Gulf 148
Limpet 80, **180**
  binomial system and **173**
  Diodora **181**
  fossil **180**
  habitat 82, 83, *83*
  rocky shore and 82
  seaweeds and **174**
Limulus sp. 65, *65*, **182**
Limy rocks, Mediterranean Basin 141
Linckia **183**
Line gear, Pacific fisheries 167
Linear dunes 24
Lineus 179
Ling, eggs in plankton **186**
Lingbank *133*
Lingula 65, *65*, **179**
Linnaeus **173**
Liriope **177**
Lisbon 37, *37*, 44
Lithosphere 14, *15*
  Atlantic Ocean 116
  Gondwanaland 17
Lithospheric Plate
  drifts, Pacific islands 160
  "hot-spot" and 161, *161*
Lithothamnia/lithothamnions 118, *174*
Litter, marine 108, 109
Little auk 74
Little Fisher Bank *133*
Littoral zone **180, 181**
  blue-green algae **175**
  hydrozoans **177**
  migrations 78
  mollusks **180**
  seaweeds **174**
  sponges **176**
Littorina sp. 77, 82
Littorina Sea, origin 21, *21*
Liver
  flukes **178**
  oil **185**
Liverpool, port, sand deposition 132
Livestock feed, fishmeal 166
Load on Top (LOT), oil tank washing 109

M

Mabel oilfield *135*
Mackenzie, river *128, 156*
Mackerel 80
  Atlantic *122–3*
  Caribbean 126
  commercial exploitation 107
  countershading 69, *69*
  Cuban catch 126
  Horse 123, *123*, 136, *141*
  Indian Ocean 152
  Mediterranean 141, *141*
  North Sea catch 136, *136*, 137
  Norwegian, purse-seiners and 94
  Pacific fishery *166–7*
  Persian Gulf 148
  prey catching 186
  Spanish, Great Barrier Reef fishery 167, *167*
  tuna relationship 166
  upper water fish 68
  world catch, tonnage 95
M'Clure Strait *129*
Macoma sp. 77
Macrocheira **182**
Macrocystis 170, *170*, 174
Macrouridae 89, *89*
Madagascar *150*
  Jurassic deposits 13
  latimeria off 186
  Plateau *150, 169*
  South Equatorial Current and 154
Madeira 117
  discovery of 44
Magellan, Pacific circum-navigation 44
Magma, 10
Magnesium
  Atlantic 118
  Gulf of Mexico 127
  gulf seawater and 27, *27*
  manganese nodule constituent *102*
  seawater constituent 26, *27*
Magnetic
  compass 43, 44
  field, earth's 15
  lineations 16, 151
  North, compass and 45
  Pole 13, *15*
  "Signature" 15
  variation 44
Magnetism, rock 12, 13, 16
Magnetite 153
Magnetization, oceanic crust 15
Magnus oilfield *135*
Magwa oilfield *148*
Maharah oilfield *148*
Mahzam oilfield *148*
Mako **185**
Malacostraca **183**
Malaysia, fisheries 153
Maleh Kuh oilfield *148*
Mallophagan lice **183**
Malpelo Island *116, 157*
Mammalia/mammals **186**
  classification **173**
  marine **175**
  support by fish 111
Man, sharks and 68
Manatee 71, *71*, **186**
Manaue, World Marine Park on Island of 111
Manayunkia sp. 77
Mandous oilfield *149*
Manganese
  nodules 24, 25, 102
    Antarctica 170
    Arctic *130–1*
    Atlantic 118, 119
    composition and harvesting *102–3*, *102–3*
    HMS *Challenger* and 165
    Indian Ocean 153, *153*
    Mediterranean *140–1*, 141
    Pacific *164–5*, 165
    rights to extract 56
  ore, lowgrade *102*
  residence time 27
  rights to extraction 56
  world reserves, tonnage 101
Mangrove 80, 96, *96*, 97, 111
  habitat 110
  Insecta **183**
  swamps 80, 111, *111*
Manhattan, S.S. 130, *130*
Manifa oilfield *148*
Manihiki Plateau *156, 157*
Mannitol, brown algae and **174**
Mansuri oilfield *148*
Manta rays 68, **185**
Mantis shrimp **182, 183**
Mantle, earth's 10, 14, *14*, 15
  deep 160
  East Pacific Rise 14
  material 14, 16
  mollusks **180**
  oceanic plate and 14
  Pacific 157, 158, 160
  Persian Gulf 146
Maquarie
  Island *168*
  Ridge 156
Maracaibo, lake 91, *91, 125*
  oil and 100, 104, 127
Marcet, Alexander, salinity, world ocean 46
Marcus Island *156*
Margin/s, continental 17, 22, *22*
Marginal
  crust, Pacific 158
  trenches 15, 157
Mariana Islands 159, *159*
  structure 160
Marianas
  Pacific crust and 157
  Trench *151, 156*, 158, *159*
  depth 159
  the *Trieste* and 54
  Trough 159, *159*
Mariculture techniques 96
Marine life
  animals **176–86**
  Challenger expedition 46
  encyclopedia **172–86**
  nutrients 162
  plants **174–5**
  pollution 108
  tonnage of 109
  see also specific subject
Maritime
  air, Icelandic Low and 30
  law 56–7, *56–7*
  States 56
Marjan oilfield *148*
Marlin 68, 69, *69*, 81
  Indian Ocean 153
  long-liner fishing fleets and 94
Marmara, Sea of 139, *139*, 142
Marphysa **181**
Marquesas Islands *156*
Mars, surface 10
Marsh, Mississippi delta 125, *125*
Marshall-Gilbert-Ellice Islands *156*
Marshall Islands 160, 161, *161*
Martinique 125
  fishtraps 93, *93*
  St. Pierre, incineration 124
Marun oilfield *148*
Marvin Ridge *129*
Mascarene Plateau *150*
Masjed-e-Suleyman oilfield *148*
Maskelyne's *Nautical Almanac* 44
Massawa *149*
Mastodon, fossilized remains 22
Mating, shark 68
Mattang 43, *43*
Matto Grosso *116*
Maud (Norway), drifting ship 129
Maud Rise *169*
Mauna Loa, Hawaii volcano 160
Mauna Ulu vent, Kilauea *8–9*, 9
Maupiti, "Almost-atoll" 161, *161*
Maureen oilfield *135*
Mauritania, coastal upwellings 86
Mauritius *150*
  Trench *150*
Maury, Matthew Fontaine 46
Maydan oilfield *148*
Mazalij oilfield *148*
Meadows, sea-grass 110
Meander/s 32
  Gulf Stream 120, 121, *121*
Meandrina 84, *84*
Measurement stations, Pacific 37
Measuring

currents 35
equipment *34–5*
Mechanical power, sea and 98
Medina
  Bank *139*
  Mountains *139*
Mediterranean
  Ridge *117*, *150*
    System 138–9, *138–9*, 140
  Sea *144*
    abyssal plains 138, *139*
    Atlantic salinity profile 35, *35*
    bathymetry 138–9, *138–9*
    circulation 142–3, *142–3*
    continental shelf 138, 141,
      142
    drying up of 144
    fauna 141
    Fish catch 141, *141*
    Fishery 141, *141*
      traps 92
    pollution 108, 110
    resources 140–1, *140–1*
    rock cliffs and 19
    salinity 26
    structure 138–9, *138–9*
    submersible 54
    Undercurrent 142, *142*
Medusa 67, **177**, **180**, **181**
  Holothurian **184**
  turtle prey **186**
Meganyctiphanes **183**
Megaptera novaeangliae 73, *73*
Meheita Island 161, *161*
Mekong, river *151*, *156*
Melamphid *81*
Meltwater, formation 28
Melville Island
  Arctic current flow and 129,
    129
  gas strikes 130
Membranelles **176**
Menard Fracture Zone *156–7*
Mendeleyev Abyssal Plain *129*
Mendocino Fracture Zone *156*
Menhaden
  Atlantic *122–3*
  Caribbean 126, *126*
Mercator, Gerhard 44
Mercator's projection 44
Mercury
  pollution 109
    Mediterranean 143
  surface of planet 10
Meridian, continent position 16
Meridional tables 44, *44*
Mesh size, fishing nets 137, 141
Mesogloea **177**
Mesoplodon bidens 73, *73*
Mesosaurus, fossils, freshwater
  reptile 13, *13*
Mesoscale eddy 32, 35, 120
Mesozoic Period 148, **186**
Messenger/s, sampling devices
  48, *48*
Messina Rise *139*
Metal/s
  Atlantis II Deep 149, *149*
  East Pacific Rise and 165
  Indian Ocean *153*
  marine organisms concentra-
    tion 108
  mud *24*, 25, *102–103*, 153,
    164–5, 165
  nodules and 102
  offshore 101
  Pacific Ocean *164–5*
  pollution and 108, 109
  Red Sea 149
  seafloor muds and 25
  seawater 27
  waste, dumping 110
Metalliferous muds *24*, 25,
  102–3, *153*, *164–5*, 165
Metazoa/metazoans **176, 182,**
  184
Meteor cruise, Atlantic circula-
  tion and 47
Meteorites 11, 25
Meteorology, air–sea interactions and 30
Methoni, port 21
Meuse, river *133*
Mexico
  Gulf of, *see* Gulf of Mexico
  gray whales 110
Micro-continents, Indian Ocean
  and 150
Micronesians, early navigational
  aids 43

Mid-Atlantic Ridge 13, 116, *117*,
  128, *169*
  crustal separation 157
  formation 116
  Indian Ocean, midocean
    ridge and 150
  minerals 102
  Nansen Fracture Zone and
    128
  Reykjanes Ridge and 15
  spreading rate *25*
Mid-Indian
  Basin 155, *155*
  Ocean Ridge 150, *150–1*, *155*,
    168, *169*
Midocean ridge/s *15*, 159
  abyssal environment and 88
  African plate and 15
  currents and 24
  formation 15, *15*
  Indian Ocean 150, 151
  ocean basin and 16
  origins 15
  plate tectonics and 15
  seafloor spreading at 144
  shape of 25
  system, Antarctic 168
  tides and 38
Midocean upwellings 86
Mid-Pacific Mountains *156*
Mid water
  currents 24
  trawl 122, *122*
    North Sea 136, 137
Middle America Trench 116,
  124, *157*
  Caribbean fault and 124
Middle East, oil 104, 105
Middle Jurassic Period 135
Midway Island *156*
Migration 78–9, *78–9*, 87, 167,
  182
  behavior, fish 167
  feeding grounds 110
  marine animals
    Arctic tern 75
    bristle-thighed curlew 111
    cod *137*
    eels 79, *79*
    gray whales 110–11
    humpback whales 170
    salmon 79, *79*
    tuna 87
    turtles 78, *78*
    whales 110–11, 170
  routes
    cod *123*
    gray whales 111
Milkfish, world catch, tonnage
  95
Milleporan coral **177**
Milwaukee Seamount
  156
Mina Abdulla *148*
Mina Al Ahmad *148*
Mina Sa'ud *148*
Minagish oilfield *148*
Minches, the 132, *132*
Mineral oil, sperm whale
  industry and 170
Minerals
  Antarctica 170
  Arctic *130–1*
  Atlantic 118–19, *118–19*
  Caribbean 127, *127*
  deep sea 102–3, *102–3*
  Indian Ocean 153
  offshore 100–1, *100–1*
    continental shelf rights 56
    placer deposits
      Atlantic *119*
      Caribbean *127*
    Pacific, segregation 158
  polar ice and 28
  river 25, 26, 111
  shallow seas and 47
  stream 111
Mines
  Caribbean *127*
  Indian Ocean *153*
  Pacific *164–5*
Minimata Bay, mercury poison-
  ing 27, 109
Mining 118
  Atlantic 118–19, *118–19*
  Indian Ocean 153
  marine viability 100
  Pacific Ocean 165
  seabed 103, *103*
  sulfur 127

Minke whale 73, *73*, 107
  whale catch and 171, *171*
Miocene Period 20, 87, 118
Mississippi, river 127
  continental shelf 125, *125*
  delta 116, *124–5*, 125, *157*
  subsidence and 20
Missouri, river *116*, *157*
Mixed tides 38, *38*
Mixed water, identification by
  S. elegans 133
Mixing time, ocean 27
Mobile Bay 124, *124*
Moçambique Channel *155*
Mole crab, feeding technique
  82, *82*
Molecular viscosity, seawater 26
Mollusca/mollusks **178, 179, 180,**
  181, 183
  bivalve 67, 83, 89, **179, 183**
    see also specific subject
  blue 80
  catch
    Atlantic *122–3*
    Caribbean *126*
    Gulf of Mexico *126*
    Indian Ocean *152*
    Mediterranean *141*
    North Sea *136*
    Pacific *166–7*
  cnidarians and **177**
  cod and 69
  endoparasites and **178**
  food of marine animals 68, 69,
    70, 71
  Gastropoda **180**
  giant, algae and **175**
  habitat
    abyss 89
    coral reef 85
    seashore 83
  Holocephali and **185**
  larva 66, 76, *76*
  marine animals and 68, 69, 70,
    71
  seal and 70
  seaweed and 82
  shells **179**
  skate and 68
  turbellarians and **178**
  walrus and 71, **186**
  worms and **179**
  Yoldia Sea 21
Mollusks, *see* Mollusca
Molokai Fracture Zone *156*
Molt/molting 74, **179, 183**
  crustacean **182**
  shorebirds and 111
  see also specific animal
Molten rock, water storage and
  10
Molybdenum 102
  manganese nodule constituent
    102
Monaco, oceanography research
  and 47
Monazite *100–1*
  Atlantic *119*
  Caribbean *127*
  Gulf of Mexico *127*
  Indian Ocean 153, *153*
  Pacific *164–5*
Monocotyledons, angiosperms
  175
Monodon moniceros 73, *73*
Monogenea **178**
Monoplacophora **180**
Monsoon/s 154, 155
  currents 154, *154*, 155
  drift, circulation *33*
  wind system, Agulhas Current
    and 154
Mont Forel *117*
Mont-St. Michel 38, *38*
Monterey fishing fleet, sardines
  and 106
Montrose oilfield *135*
Moon, earth and 11, 38
  formation theory 13
  orbital plane *39*
  surface 10
  tides and 38, *39*
Moorea Island 161, *161*
Moraine 132, 168
Moray Firth *132*
Morocco 77, 86, *142*
Morris Jessup Plateau *129*
Mosquito/s 62, 183
Mother Current, *see* Oyashio
  Current

Mt. Aconcagua *116*
Mt. Cameroon *117*
Mt. Cook *156*
Mt. Djaja *151*, *156*
Mt. Everest *151*
Mt. Irazu *116*, *157*
Mt. McKinley *156*
Mt. Pelee, eruption 124
Mt. Venus 25
Mountain/s 12, *12*, 16, 25
  belt 15, 17
  chains 22
  range/s 14, 124
Movement,
  earth's 14–15, *14–15*
  marine invertebrates 66–7,
    66–7
  water 32, *32*
Mozambique
  current, circulation *33*
  ridge *150*, *169*
Mubarek oilfield *149*
Mubarraz oilfield *148*
Mucilage, seaweed and 82
Mucins, marine bacteria and **175**
Mud/s
  bottoms, burrowing animals
    81
  cliffs in, erosion and 18, *18*
  crab 77, *77*
  diapirs 125, *125*
  East Pacific Rise 165
  fauna of mangrove 80
  flats, formation 19
  Indian Ocean *153*
  islands 125
  metalliferous 25, *153*, *164–5*
    165
  mineralized 102
  North Sea 134
  Pacific Basin 132, *164–5*
  phosphatic 118
  skipper fish 80
  stones, North Sea and 134
  waves, Mediterranean *142*
Mugil sp. 69, *69*, 77
Mullet
  Atlantic *122–3*
  Caribbean 126
  food web 77
  gray 69, *69*, 77, 141
    Great Barrier Reef fishery
      167, *167*
    Pacific fishery *166–7*
  red 141
  Red Sea 148
  salt marsh 77
  world catch, tonnage 95
Multiyear ice, Arctic 28, 29, *29*
Murchison oilfield *135*
Mures, river 139
Murray Fracture Zone *156*
Murrelets 74
Mussel/s *80*
  habitat 80, 83, *83*
  harvesting, farming 97
  larvae **185**
  mangrove swamp 80
  Mytilus sp. 77, **180, 185**
  Spartina algae and 77
  starfish and **183**
Mya arenaria 83, *83*
Mystacocarids **182**
Mysticeti 72
Mytilus sp. 77, **180, 185**
  edulis 83, *83*
Myxicola **181**
Myzostomaria **181**

N

Naft I-Shah oilfield *148*
Naft Safid oilfield *148*
Nahr Umr oilfield *148*
Namibia 77, 86, 100, 118
Nanoplankton **174, 184**
Nansen
  bottles 34, *34*
  Fracture Zone 128, *129*
Nansen, F. 28, 129
Nares Abyssal Plain *116*
Nargesi oilfield *148*
Narrow-shelf states, rights 57
Narwhals 73, *73*, 111
Nasr oilfield *148*
Nasser, Lake *144*
Natal, Dias exploration and 44
Natih oilfield *149*
Natural gas
  Antarctica 170
  Atlantic 119
  Continental shelf prospects
    104
  Das Island oil terminal and
    148
  Indian Ocean 153
  Mediterranean *140–1*, 141
  North Sea 134
Nautical Almanac 44
Nautical astronomy 44
Naturaliste Plateau *151*, *156*
Nauplius larva **182, 183**
Nautiloids **181**
Nautilus (Cephalopod) **181**
Nautilus *Argonauta* **181**
Nautilus (submarine) route *130*
Navigation
  aids 43, *43*, 44–5, *44–5*, 50,
    50, 94
  history 44–5, *44–5*
  pollution and 109
  rights to 56, 57
Nazca
  Plate 25, *25*, 157, *157*
  Ridge *116*
Neanthes **181**
Neap tides 38, 39
Nebalia **183**
Nebaliopsis **183**
Nematoda/nematodes **178, 179**
  heliozoans and **176**
Nemertina **178, 179**
Nemicthys sp. 89
Neopilina **180**
Nephrops trawl 136
Nereid **181**
Nereis sp. 77, 82, *82*
  diversicolor 83, *83*
Nereus Deep, Red Sea *149*
Nesting site, Green turtle 78
Net/s
  fishing 92–3, *92–3*
    Mediterranean 141
    North Sea 137, *137*
  Sampling 48, *48*
Netherlands 20, 58, *58*, 134, 137
  Antilles *125*
  flatfish catch, North Sea 136
  North Sea boundaries and 57,
    57
  plaice fishery 137
  Waddenzee and 110
Neutral buoyancy floats 35, 49
Neutral Zone, Persian Gulf 149,
  149
New Britain Trench *156*
New Caledonia, nickel 102
New England
  fishing fleets 122, *122*
New Guinea *151*, *156*
  "staircase" beaches 20
New Hebrides Trench *156*
New Jersey
  acid dump off 109, *109*
  aragonite market 118
New Orleans *125*
New Siberian Islands 128
New World discovery 44
New Zealand *163*
  calcareous sands around 171
  "Circle of Fire" 157
  East Australian Current 162
  humpback whale 170
  islands 160

phosphate rock 165
Plateau *156*, *168*
"staircase beaches" 20
submarine plateau regions
  near 165
Tasman Sea separation 157
Tongue Point, Wellington 20,
  20
Newfoundland
  Abyssal Plain 22
  Banks, weather conditions
    129, *129*
  cod 78, 94
  conditions off *129*
  continental shelf 22
  fishing ground 122
Newton, *Sir* Isaac 38, 46
Nicaragua
  Golfo de Fonseca 110
  Rise 124, *125*
Nickel
  Atlantic 118
  earth's core of 14, *14*
  Indian Ocean 153
  manganese nodules and 102,
    102, 118
  Pacific 165
  residence time 27
  rights to extract 56
  seabed 25, 56
  world reserves, tonnage *101*
Niger, river 20, *117*
Nilas 29
Nile, river *117*, *139*, *144*, *150*
  Aswan Dam and 141
  cone *140*
  continental shelf areas 138
  delta *139*, *140*, 144
  fishing industry 143
  sediments 138
Nimbostratus, depressions and
  31
Ninety East Ridge 150, 151, *151*,
  155
Ninian oilfield *135*
Nintoku Seamount *156*
Niobium, tunicates and 27
Nitrates
  marine bacteria **175**
  sea strata and 80
  seawater 27
  upwellings and 154
Nitrite, marine bacteria **175**
Nitrogen
  diving and 52, 53
  fixation **175**
  marine bacteria **175**
  meteorites and 11
  plant life and 76
  waste **178**
Noctiluca **175**
  scintillans 62
Noddy tern 75
Node points, tides and 39
Nodule, root bacteria **175**
  see also Manganese nodules
Nomenclature, binomial
  system 173
Norfolk
  Banks 132, *133*
  Island *156*
North Africa 17, 116, 138, 142
North African Current 46
North America
  cod markets 131
  Continental Rise *116*
  continental shelf 23
  currents and 120, *162*, 163
  drifting, Jurassic Period 117
  earthquake 22, *22*
  East coast 22, 144
  eel 79, *79*
  fish/ing 92, 122, 131
  Grand Banks area 22, *22*
  metal deposits 144
  mountains 13, *13*, 17
  North Equatorial Current
    and 120
  oil production, tonnage 105
  phosphate rock off 165
  Proto-Atlantic Ocean and 17
  resources 12, 105, 144, 165
  rotation of Europe and 117
  sedimentary record 116
  submarine routes and *130*
  temperature of coast 30
  see also specific region
North American Indian bull
  boat 42, *42*
North Atlantic

Arctic Basin and 128
  Caribbean water and 124
  Current 33, 120–1, *121*, *129*
  deep water 120, 121, *121*, 154
  fauna 73, 122, 123, 131
  fisheries 122, 123, 131, 166
  gyre 32, *33*, 120. *121*
    currents and 32, 120, 121
    Gulf Stream and 121, *121*
  icebergs 28, 124
  temperature 131
  weather conditions 129, *129*
North Cape Current 131, *131*
North Channel 132, *132*
North Equatorial Counter-
  current *163*
  circulation *33*
North Equatorial Current *121*,
  155, 162, *163*
  Caribbean and 124
  circulation *33*
  North Atlantic Gyre and 32,
    120
  North East Monsoon and 154
North Indian Ocean 154
North Magnetic pole *15*
North Pacific
  fauna 80, 167
  Gyre *33*, 162, *162*, 163, *163*
  resource 102, 166
North Pole *129*
  Geographic *40–1*, 41, 128
  Project 41
North Pole 1 (USSR), drifting
  "ice-island" 129
North Sea *117*, *133*
  Basin *135*
  bathymetry and circulation
    132–3, *132–3*
  boundary, British Isles and
    57, *57*
  continental shelf 132
  fish/fisheries 122, 123
    breeding ground 137
    cod 78
    crab 123
  fishing 94, 136–7, *136–7*
  mineral resources 134–5,
    134–5
  oil 100, 104–5, *104–5*
  oilfields *135*
  Zuiderzee and 58
Northwest Africa 13, *13*, 118,
  122, 162
  Atlantic 32, *32*, 111, 131
  Indian Ocean 116
  Pacific 13, 30, 33, *33*
  Territories, high tide, Lake
    Harbor 38, *38*
Northumberland collieries 135
Northwind Escarpment *128*
Norway
  Arctic, fish catches 131
  Atlantic, cod catch 123
  bathymetric profile and *129*
  fisheries off 94, 122, 123
    cod fishing 122, 123
  fjord 20, 132
  herring 92, 107
  history 13, *13*, 17, 132
  Norwegian Trough and coast
    of 132
  oil production and 105
  pout 123, *123*
    North Sea catch 136, *136*,
      137
Norwegian
  herring 92, 107
  Sea *117*, *129*
    fisheries 122
    history 117
  Trench 132
  Trough 132, *133*
Nostoc **175**
Notochord **184**, **185**
  See also specific animal
Nova Scotia
  Bay of Fundy 38, *38*
  Sable Island 19, *19*
Novaya Zemlya *129*
Nowruz oilfield *148*
Nubia, Yemen 146
Nuclear
  devices/reactors, pollution by
    98, 108, 109
  submarine/s 54, 55, *55*
Nuclei **175**, **176**
Nudibranchs 67, *67*
Nullabor Plain *151*, *156*
Nursery ground, fish 78

Nutrient/s
  Caribbean 126
  deficiency, Mediterranean 143
  hot springs 25
  marine bacteria **175**
  North Sea plankton 137
  Oyashio Current and 162
  Pacific 165
  photosynthesis and 27
  plankton and 137, 141
  plants and 27, 86
  Pogonophora and **182**
  pollutants and 108
  Salts, seastrata and 80
  seawater 27
  Sunlit Zone and 86
  upwelling 78
Nyctiphanes sp. 76

Ob
  river *129*
  Trench *151*
Obelia **177**
Observatories 44, 46
Obsidian 43
Occluded front, depressions and
  31
Ocean
  age and formation 16–17,
    16–17
  banks 88
  basin/s
    continental margins and 22
    depth of 12
    enclosed, salinity 26
    history 15, 16, 46, *46*, 144
    seafloor spreading rates 15
    shape, changes in, 20
    wave systems and 38
    see also specific basin
  Cay, offshore mining 118
  crust
    Afar Triangle 146
    destruction 144
    earth surface 11
    mantle material 16
    metal in 100
    origin 15, 16, 151
    Pacific *157*, 158, 160
    rock magnetism and 16
    sealevel 146
    thickness of 13
    volcanoes and 10
  current/s 32–3, *32–3*, 34–5,
    34–5
  floor
    darkness 88–9, *88–9*
    deep 24–5, *24–5*
    sampling techniques 13
    see also Seabed
    origin 11, 16–17, *16–17*
    plates 14, *14*
    see also specific plate
    ridge/s 16
    see also specific ridge
    ridge crests 15
  Thermal Energy Conversion
    (OTEC) 99, *99*
  trenches, animal life 89
    see also specific trench
  Voyager, North Sea drilling
    platform 134, *134*
Oceanograph, evolution 46–7,
  46–7
Oceanographer Deep, Red Sea
  149
  Fracture Zone 117
Octopods **181**
Octopus 80
  anemone, crab and 69
  breeding 64
  inshore fisheries and 92
Odin gasfield *135*
Odontoceti 64, 72
Odysseus, sea legends 42
Ogcocephalid 80
Oikopleura sp. 76
Oil 47, 118
  brown algae and **174**
  divers and 53
  exploration 28, 50, 105, **182**
  fields 54, 55, 100–1, *100–1*
    Arabian Peninsula 147
    Arctic 130, *130–1*
    Atlantic 119, *119*
    Beaufort Sea 130
    Caribbean *127*
    Indian Ocean 153, *153*
    Iran 153
    Lake Maracaibo 91, 127
    Mediterranean *140–1*, 141
    Middle East 148–9, *148–9*
    North Sea 134, *135*
    Pacific *164–5*
    Persian Gulf 148–9, *148–9*,
      153
    Saudi Arabia 153
  gland, seabirds 75
  marine bacteria and **175**
  pollution 108–9, *108*
    Mediterranean 143
    seabirds and 75

  production 104–5, *104–5*
    Iraq 148
    North Sea 134, *134*
    Persian Gulf 148–9, *148–9*
      barrels per day 149, *149*
    see also Oilfields
  refinery, Grangemouth 105
  rig/s, *see* specific rig
  shorestation, *see* specific
    shorestation
  terminal, *see* specific terminal
  transportation 118, *118*
  traps
    Arctic 130
    Brent 135
    Mediterranean 141
    Middle East 148
    Persian Gulf 146
  rock structure and 104, *104*
    see also Oilfields
Oilisland C-15; 130, *130–1*
Okhotsk
  Abyssal Plain *156*
  Sea *156*
  fishery 166, 167
Old Faithful Geyser, USA 149
Oligochaeta 77, **181**
Oman, oil production 149, *149*
Ommastrephids **181**
Ooliths, aragonite 118
Ooze
  abyssal 88, **176**
  Antarctica **171**
  calcareous 24, *24*, 150, *171*
  deep ocean floor 24–5, *24–5*
  Globigerina **176**
  Indian Ocean 150
  radiolarian **173**, **176**
  sea fauna 81
  sponges **176**
  siliceous 24, *24*, 150, 171
Open-ocean mining, Pacific 165
Operculum **180**
Ophiactis **183**
Ophiuroidea/ophiuroids 88, *88*,
  183
Opisthobranchia, egg-laying 65
Optical properties, seawater 26
Orange, river *117*, *150*
Orange peel sampler 48
Orbital
  movement, water 36
  plane, Moon's *39*
Orchelimum sp. 77
Orchestia sp. 82
Orcinus orca 72, *72–3*
Ordovician Period 17
  Agnatha **185**
  fossils **179**
  graptolites **184**
  jawless vertebrates **185**
Ore/s 99, 102, *102*
Oregon, Tillamook Rock Light
  36
Oregon-California, coastal
  upwelling 86
Organic
  pollutants 108, 143
  power, sea and 98
Organisms, marine
  heavy metals concentration
    108
  petroleum hydrocarbons in
    108
  see also specific organism
Organization, binomial system
  and 173
Organ-pipe corals **178**
Orinoco, river 116, *125*
Orkney Islands *132*
Orogeny, Caledonian and
  Hercynian 17
Oseberg Ship 42, *42*
Osmosis 98, *99*
Ostracoda/ostracod **182**, **183**
Osteichthyes 68
OTEC 99, *99*
Otter shell 83, *83*
Otter boards 122
Otter trawl
  North Sea 136, 137, *137*
  shrimp fishery gear 167
Otters, seas, food chain 77
Outer Hebrides *132*
Outer Silver Pit 132, *133*
Outriggers 92, 153
Overfishing 94, 106
  anchovy 106
  Arctic 131
  Atlantic 123

  inshore waters 92
  Mediterranean 141
  North Sea 136, 137
  species 107
Overflight, rights to 56, 57
Overhang, erosive waves and 18,
  18
Ovoviviparity **179**, **186**
Owen Fracture Zone *147*, *150*
Oxidic nickel ore *102*
Oxidization, plants and bacteria
  27
Oxygen, seawater 26, 27
  current measurements 35
  diving and 52, 53
  oil pollution and 108
  plankton growth 108
  sea strata and 80
Oyashio Current 162, *162*, *163*
  fog creation and 33, *33*
Oyster/s **180**
  farming 96, 97
  fungi and **175**
  mangrove swamps and 80
  parasite fungi and **175**
  poisonous **175**
  shells, fungi and **175**
  starfish and **183**
  zinc absorption 27

P Q

Pacific Ocean *124*, *156–7*, 157
  Antarctic Circumpolar
    Current and 35, 120
  Antarctica and *168–9*
  barrier reef 110, *110*
  bathymetry 156–7, *156–7*
  circulation 162–3, *162–3*
  continental margins 22
  continental shelf 165, 166
  crust *158*
  eastern kelp beds 77
  energy budget *30*
  fauna 80–1, 81
    California sea lion 71
    clams **180**
    fin whales 110
    Lingula 65
    pilot whale 73
    salmon 79
    tuna 78, 87
  fish
    catch 166, *166*
    fishery 166–7, *166–7*
      salmon 79
      tuna 78, 87, 123
    fishing vessel and 94
  geology 158–9, *158–9*
  giant kelps **174**
  history 44, 154
  margins 10, 17, 22
  minerals 164–5, *164–5*
    manganese nodules 102, *102*
  Northwest 30, 33, *33*
    ridge system 13
  plankton communities 87, *87*
  reefs 160–1, *160–1*
  storm system 31, *31*
  submarine route *130*
  tectonic connection with
    West Indies 124
  tides and 38
  tsunami waves 37
  undercurrent 106
  upwellings 86, 106
  water/land hemisphere
    comparison 12
  waves and fetch 36
Pacific-Antarctic Rise *156*, *168*
Pacific Basin 13, 144, 168
Pacific islands 37, 160–1, *160–1*
  mountain chains, formation
    theory 12
  swell 37
  trend 160
Pacific Plate *157*, *157*
  Caribbean and 124
  Galapagos Triple Junction 25,
    25
  movement of 161
Pack ice 28, *28*, 29, *29*, 35, *35*,
  113, *113*, 121
Pahoehoe lava 9, 161, *161*
Palau–Kyushu Ridge 159, *159*
Paleomagnetism 138, 139, 151
Paleontology, "tide marks" and
  20
Paleozoic Period *134*, *175*, *180*,
  181
Palolo worm **181**
Pamlico Sound 120
  isthmus 124
Panama, sea-level canal 87
Pancake ice 28, *28*, 29
Pangaea 12, 17, 157
Panthalassa 157
Paper nautilus *Argonauta* **181**
Paramecium **176**
Parana, river *117*
Parasites **179**
  algae **174**
  barnacles **183**
  copepods **182**
  dinoflagellates **175**
  fungi **175**
  Myzostomaria **181**
  red algae **174**
  worms **178**
Parathemisto pacifica 87
Parazoa **176**
Par-E Siah oilfield *148*
Parece Vela Basin 159, *159*
Parece Vela Trench *159*
Paris

Observatory 44
oceanography research 47
oilfield, Persian Gulf *148*
Parks, marine 110, 111
Parker Seamount *156*
Parrot fish 85, *85*
Passive continental margins 22, *22*
Patagonia 123
Patella vulgata 83, *83*
Pathfinders, ocean 44–5
Pavlo harbor 21
Paydar oilfield *148*
Pazanan oilfield *148*
Peake Deep *117*
Pearl
    diving 52, *52*
    fisheries 149, *149*
    fishing 148
Peas, nitrogen fixation 175
Peat 20, *23*, 150
Pebbles 18, 82, *82*
Pechora, river *129*
Pectin manufacture, algae and 174
Pectinaria 181
Pectoral fins, shark 68, *68*
Pedicellariae 64, 179
Pelagic
    animals 89
    ctenophores 178
    fish 180
        Atlantic *122–3*
        Caribbean 126, *126*
        copepod and 77
        Indian Ocean 152, *152*
        Mediterranean 141, *141*
        North Sea 136
        Pacific *166–7*
        purse seines and 136, 166
        long-liners and 94
        malacostracans 183
        nemertines 179
        organisms 67, *67*
        sediments 158, *158*
        siphonophores 62, 177
        species, fisheries 123, 148
        worms 178
Pelican 75, *75*, 76, 186
    brown 75, 109
Pelvetia canaliculata 82, *82*
Pelvic fins, shark 68, *68*
Penella 183
Penguins 72, 74, 75, *75*, 186
Pennatulids 88, *88*, 178
Pens 97
Pepper, J. H. 12
Perch, Atlantic 123
Percolation 10
Peress, J. S. 55
Periods, wave 36
Periwinkle 21, 80, 82
"Permanency," continental drift and 13
Permian Period 13, 17, 132, 134, *135*
Pernambuco Abyssal Plain *117*
Perry 55, *55*
Persian Gulf *145*, 147, 148–9, *148–9*
    Arabian Peninsula formation 147
    Asian Plate and 146
    currents 145, *145*
    fisheries 148
    iceberg towing to 28
    Indian Ocean and 154
    oil 148–9, *148–9*, 153
    plate tectonics 146
    temperature 113
Peru
    anchovy 106, *106*, 107, 166
    ecosystem 77
    food chain 76
    mineral deposits 158
    sea-surface temperature anomalies 30
    upwellings off 76, 77, 86, 162, *163*
Peru Current 163, *163*
    anchovy and 106
    circulation *33*
Peru–Chile Trench *116*, *157*
    crustal plate 14, *14*
Pesticides 109
Peter I Island *169*
Peterson Grab Sampler 48
Petrels 74, *75*, 186
Petroleum, *see* Oil
Petromyzon marinus 68, *68*

Phaeophyceae 174
Phagotrophic protozoans 176
Phalarope 75
Phalasarna harbor 21
Pharmacology, marine 97
Philippine Sea 157, 159, *159*
Philippine Trench *151*, *156*, 159, *159*
Philippines 30, *151*, *156*, 166
Phoca vitulina 71, *71*
Phocaena phocoena 72, *72*
Phoenix Islands *156*
Phoronida 179
Phosphate/s 118, 165
    guano and 186
    nodules 100, 102, 153
    rock 165
    sea strata and 80
    seawater and 27
    sediments 118
    upwelling and 154
    world reserves *101*
Phosphorite 100–1, 118, *118*, *119*, *164–5*
Phosphorus 102
Photography, underwater 50
Photosynthesis 174
    Antarctic 170
    beach life 82
    green algae 174
    phytoplankton 170
    pigments 76
    plant life and 74, 176
    productivity and 86
    symbionts 178
    water and 26
    zones, plants oxidation 27
Phycocyanin 174
Phycoerythrin 174
Phylocariids 183
Physalia 177
Physeter catodon 72, *72–3*
Physophora hydrostatica 63
Phytoplankton 62, *62*, 76, *76*, *80*, 89
    anchovies and 77
    Antarctic and 170
    distribution 86
    foodweb 77, *77*
    marine bacteria and 175
    marine ecosystem and 62
    North Atlantic 86, *86*
    North Pacific 86, *86*
    Peru, coast 76
    seawater and 26, 27
    surface water and 86
    zooplankton and 63
Piccard, Auguste 54
Piccard, Jacques 54
Pigmy right whale 72, *72*
Pilchard 106, 186
Piles, wooden 174, 184
Pilot whale 73, *73*
Pinch-out, oil traps 104
Pinna 180
Pinnacles, coral 160, *160*
Pioneers, ocean 44–5
Pipelines
    continental shelf 22
    freedom to lay 56, 57
    Middle East 149, *149*
    North Sea *135*
Piper oilfield 135, *135*
Pisces 185
Pisces (submersible) 54, *54*
Piston corer 49, *49*
Placer deposits 100, 101, *101*
    Atlantic *119*
    Caribbean 127, *127*
    Indian Ocean 153, *153*
    Pacific *164–5*, 165
Placiphorella 180
Plaice 68, 69, *69*, 122, *123*
    Barents Sea 131, *131*
    bottom trawl and 122
    migration research 78
    North Sea catch 136, *136*, 137, *137*
    spawning 78, 137
Plane charts 44
Planetisimals 11
Planets 11, 38
Planked boats 92
Plankton
    abyssal plain 88
    algae 77, *174*, 175
    animals 89, 175, 176
    Antarctic 170

arrowworms 179, 180
    blooms 111
    Chrysophyceae 174
    ciliates 176
    communities 86, 87
    copepods 182
    current system 87
    diatoms 175
    ecosystems 62–3, *62–3*, 108
    food 82, *82*
    growth 108
    hatchlings 64
    invertebrates 65
    larval forms 84–5, 179, 184, 185
    Mediterranean 141, 143
    migration route and 78
    mollusks and 180
    nets 48
    oozes and 24
    Persian Gulf 148
    plants and 85, 86, 174
    productivity zones 150
    sampler/sampling 48, *48*
    seasonal cycles 86, *86*
    seawater and 80
    species 168
    teleost eggs and 186
    upwellings and 86
Planktoniella sol 86
Plants, marine 76–7, *76–7*, 86–7, *86–7*, *174–5*, 176
    energy source 99
    flagellates 176
    food resource 24
    growth 27
    sea strata and 80
    sediment flats and 19
Plant–herbivore–carnivore food chain 84
Plant-hopper, *Prokelisia* sp. 77
Planula 177
Plaquemines *125*
Plate/s 15
    boundary 17, 22
    Caribbean 125
    crustal 16
    growth 15
    lost Pacific 157
    margins 14, *14*, 15
    motion 157
    mountain formation 16
    Pacific 157
    size 15
    tectonics 15
        Arabian Peninsula 147
        continental margin and 22
        future and 59
        Lilienthal observations 117
        ocean basin formation 16
        Pacific volcanoes 160
        Persian Gulf and 146
        Red Sea and 146
        theories 47
Plateau/s 22, *138–9*, 150, 157
    see also specific plateau
Platform/s, erosion and 18, 19, 20
Platform coral 84, *84*
Platichthys flesus 77
Platinum
    Pacific *164–5*, 165
    placer deposits *100–1*
    world reserves *101*
Platyhelminthes 178
Platymonas 175
Plectorhynchus cuviera 85
Pleuronectes platessa 69, *69*
Plugs, salt 127, 130
Po, river *139*
Po Delta 139, *139*, *140*
Podon sp. 76
Pogonophora 80, 182
Poland, Atlantic cod catch *123*
Polar
    bear 70, *70*, 186
    cod 131, *131*
    front 31, 78, 168
    regions 35, 117
    seas 26, 28–9, *28–9*, 73, 77, 80
    wandering curve 13
Polarity, magnetic field 15
Polders, Dutch 58, *58*
Pole/s
    Abyssal Plain 128, *129*
    Coriolis force and 32, *32*
    magnetic 15
    star 44, 45
    westerly winds and 32

Pole and line fishing 166
Pollack
    exploitation 107, 111
Pollen, marine flowering plants 175
Pollutants 108, 143, 160
Pollution 108–9, *108–9*
    abyssal regions 89
    breeding, marine animals and 111
    cargoes, hazardous, and 56
    island states and 56
    Mediterranean 143
    seabirds and 75, 186
    white whale and 111
Pollution Control Zone 57
Polychaeta/polychaetes 179, 181
    ciliates and 176
    commensal 181
    tube dwelling 181
    worms 80, 88
Polychlorinated biphenols 109
Polyclads 178
Polyhalite *27*
Polymetallique 102
    see also Manganese nodules
Polymorphism 177
Polynya 28, 29, *29*
Polyp/s 84–5, 177
    see also specific animal
Polysaccharide, brown algae and 174
Polyurethane, fungi and 175
Pomacentrus coeruleus 85
Pontchartrain, lake 125
Pontella atlantica 86
Poor cod, Mediterranean 141
Porbeagle 185
Porcellanaster sp. 89
Porcupine Bank *117*
Porgy, red 123
Porifera, see Sponges
Porocidaris sp. 89
Porphyra 174
Porpoise 72, *72*, *81*
Ports, approaches 22
Port Sudan *149*
Portland cement 118
Portugal 44, *123*
Portuguese
    explorers 44
    man-of-war 66, 80, 177
Portulan chart 44
Postglacial rebound 21
Potamos, port of 21
Potash
    Atlantic *119*
    Caribbean *127*
    fertilizers 153
    North Sea 135
    Gulf of Mexico *127*
    Mediterranean 141
    placer deposits *100–1*
    recovery of 100
    world reserves, tonnage *101*
Potassium 26, 27, *27*, *102*, 118
"Potential" energy, tides and 39
Pots, fishing 123, 167
Poultry feed, fishmeal 166
Pout, Norway 123, *123*, 136, *136*, 137
Poutassou, Mediterranean 141
Power, *see* Energy
Prasmophyceae 174
Pratt Seamount *156*
Prawns 167, 183
Precambrian Period 13, 17
Precious coral 178
Predators, animal husbandry and 96, 97
Pressure ice 29, *29*
Pressure ridges 28, 29, *29*, *40–1*, 41
Pressure root 29, *29*
Pressure water 26, 35, 49
Pressurized chamber, divers and 53
Priapulida 179
Primary productivity 86, *86*
Prince Albert of Monaco 47
Prince Henry 44
Prince of Wales Island *129*
Prince Patrick Island *129*
Prion, feeding method 75
Production platforms, oil 105, *105*
Productivity, primary 86, *86*
Progressive erosion 18
Promontories, coastal landscape and 19

Propellers, drill ships 104, 105
Prospecting, offshore 118
Protected areas 111
Protected fish species 137, 170
Protein
    skeleton, Gorgonians 84
    whales and 72
Proto-Atlantic 17, 117
Protoplasm 176
Protozoa 176, 179
    comparison with sporozoa 176
    symbiosis and 175
Proxy indicators 30
Prudhoe Bay *130*
Pseudocalanus sp. 76
Pterobranchs 184
Pteropods 63, 67, *67*, 76, *76*, 180
    deep sea 89, *89*
    oozes 24, *24*
Pterotrachea 180
Ptolemaic maps 44, *44*
Ptolemy, the *Geographia* of 44
Ptolemaic maps 44, *44*
see also specific animal
Pteropus 180
Puerto Rico 124, *125*
    Trench 116, *116*, 125
Puffer fish, Red Sea 148
Puget Sound 97
Purse seine/seiner, fishing 122, 126
    anchovy 107, 166
    distant water 94
    herring 137
    Monterey 106
    North Atlantic 123
    North Sea 136, 137
    Pacific 167
    tuna 166, *166*
Pycnogonida 182
Pyramid of Cheops 42
Pyrenees *117*
Pyroclastic material, Deception Island 168
Pyrosoma 184
Pyroteuthis 66, *66*

Qaleh Nar oilfield *148*
Qarn Alam oilfield *149*
Qatar, oil production 148, *149*
Qatif oilfield *148*
Qird oilfield *148*
Quadrant 44, 45, *45*
Quartzite 134
Quaternary Period 20, *135*
Queen Elizabeth Islands *129*
Queen scallop 64, *64*
Queensland 160, *160*

R

Rabbit fish 69, *69*
Rachi oilfield *148*
Raccoon 77, *77*
Radar 29, *29*, *50*, 104
Radiation, temperature contrasts 30
Radio navigation *50*
Radioactive waste 35, 59, 98, 108, 109
Radiolaria/radiolarians 24, *24*, 63, 173, *173*, 176
    ooze 24, *24*, 171, *176*
    symbionts 175
Radiometric dating, sealevels and 20
Rafting, ice 28, 29
Rag coralling 178
Rag worm 83, *83*
Rag-E-Safid oilfield *148*
Raiatea Islands 84, *84–5*, 161, *161*
Rain/rainfall 10, 27, 31, *31*, 142
    seawater precipitation and 26, 27
Raised beaches 20, *20*
Raja texana 68, *68*
Rakhsh oilfield *148*
Ramin oilfield *148*
Ramlah oilfield *149*
Ramshir oilfield *148*
Rance Tidal Power Station 98, 99, *98–9*
Ras al Khafji *148*
Ras Tannurah *148*
Rashid oilfield *149*
Rat tails *80*, 89, *89*
Ratawi oilfield *148*
Randhatain oilfield *148*
Rays 68, *80*, *123*, 185
    electric 185
    manta 185
    world catch, tonnage *95*
Razor *80*
Razor shells 83, *83*, 180
Razorbills 74
Reactivity, residence time of elements and 27
Reclaiming land 19, 58, *58*
Record wave, highest documented 37
Recycled water 10, 27
Red clay 24–5, *25*
Red mangrove, leaf litter of 111
Red mullet, Mediterranean 141
Red porgy, Falkland current and 123
Red sandstones, North Sea 134
Red Sea 17, *144–5*
    bathymetry and circulation 144–5, *144–5*
    continental shelf 144, *149*
    fishery, sardines 148
    Indian Ocean and water from 154
    Midocean ridge and 150
    mineral resources 102, 148
    ocean formation and 16, *16*, 17
    outflow 154, *154*
    plate tectonics and 146
    reefs and the 160
    rift system and 17, 146, 150, *150*
    salinity 26
    structural geology 146–7, *146–7*
Red seaweeds 174
Red snapper 126
Red-tailed tropic bird *81*
Red tides 62, *62*, 175
Red-winged blackbird 77
Redfish *95*, 131, *131*
Reedboat 42, *42*
Reefs 111
    building 69, *84*, 84–5
    Caribbean 126
    coral *see* Coral reef
    fish 69, *69*
    habitats 160
    Malacostraca 183
    oil traps and 104
    Pacific 160–1, *160–1*
    structures 85
    Thailand 110

Reflecting quadrant 44, 45, *45*
Reflecting rock unit 141
Refraction, wave 162
Refrigerants, pollution and 109
Refrigeration, fishing industry and 94
Regeneration 183, **184**
Relationships, marine 69
Remoras 69, *69*
Rennell, James 46
Report on the Deep-Sea Deposits 165
Report on the Scientific Results of the Exploring Voyage of the HMS Challenger, 1873–1876 102
Reproduction, marine animals 65, *65*, 70, **178**
see also specific animal
Reptile 13, *13*, 17, 70, *173*, 175, **186**
Reservoirs, oil 104, 105
Residence time, seawater 27
Resolute Bay, divers from 41
Resource
  future 58–9, *58–9*
  new, food 96–7, *96–7*
  offshore minerals 100–1, *100–1*
  pollution and 108
  see also specific resource;
    specific ocean
Resting area, sea fauna 110
Retreat, cliff, England 19
Réunion, La 150
Reversing thermometer 49, *49*
Revilla Gigedo Islands *157*
Reykjanes Ridge 15, *117*
Rhine, river *133*, 134
Rhine–Meuse delta 20
Rhizoclonium 83, *83*
Rhizoflagellates **176**
Rhizomes 175
Rhizophora 80
Rhizosolenia castracanii 86
Rhizosolenia labetata 86
Rhodophyceae **174**
Rhône, river 138, *138*
Rhône delta 138, *138*
Ria coastlines 19, 20, 21, *21*
Ribbon reefs 160, *160*
Ridge
  activity 25
  Mediterranean *142*
  ocean 13
  shape 25
  submarine 150
  see also specific ridge
Ridge crest 15, 25
Ridge system 17, 25
Rift valley 25
  continental margin and 22
  formation of 16
  Mid-Atlantic Ridge and 116
  Red Sea 146, 147, 148
Rifting ice sheet 29, *29*
Right whale 72, *72*, 170, 171, *171*
Rigs, offshore drilling, *see* Oil production
Rimthan oilfield *148*
Ring net 48, *48*, 123
Ringkøping Fyn Rise *135*
Rio Grande 123, *124*, 157
  Fracture Zone *117*
  Plateau *117*, 169
Rip currents 37
Ripple marks 19, *19*, 36, 50
River 23, 109, 111, 160
  valleys 19, 20, 21, *21*
Rivularia 175
Riyadh *148*
Rock
  barriers, Mediterranean *142*
  carvings, Kalnes, 42, *42*, 43
  earth's 11
  erosion 26
  magnetism 16
  magnetization 15
  North Sea *132*, 134
  pools 82, 83
  salt 141
  samples 48
  sampling techniques 13
  shores 82
  strata, North Sea 134
  structure 104, *104*
  Unit, Mediterranean Basin 141
Rockall plateau *117*, *117*

Rockfish 166
Rocky Mountains 12, *157*
Rodrigues Island *150*
Roman port 21
Romanche Fracture Zone *117*
Root nodule bacteria **175**
Roques Trench, Los *125*
Ross Sea 109, *109*, 169, 170
Rostam oilfield *148*
Rotational movement 138, *138*
Rotifera/rotifers **179**
Rotula 183
Royal George, salvage 53
Royal Observatory, Greenwich 44
Royal Society, *Directions for Seamen* 46
Rumaila oilfield *148*
Runoff 10
  groundwater 27
  hydrological cycle and 27, *27*
  Mediterranean 138, 142
  rivers 27
  white whale breeding in warm 111
Russian circumnavigation 46
Rutile 153
Ryukyu Islands 159, *159*
Ryukyu Trench *151*, *156*, 159, *159*

S

"S-reflector," evaporite and 147
Saath al Raazboot oilfield *148*
Sabiriyah oilfield *148*
Sable fish 97
Sable Island 19, *19*
Safaniya oilfield *148*
Sagitta sp. *63*, 76, 133
Sagitta elegans 87, **180**
Sagitta enflata 86
Sagitta pseudoserratodentata 87
Sagitta serratodentata 86
Sagitta setosa **180**
Sahara
  coast, winds off 44
  Desert *117*
Sahil oilfield *149*
Saih Nihayda oilfield *149*
Sail Rawl oilfield *149*
Sailfish 85, 94, 153
S.S. *Manhattan* 130, *130*
St. Bernard, Mississippi delta 125
St. Fergus shorestation *134*
St. George's Channel 132, *132*
St. Helena Island *117*
St. Lawrence River *116*, *157*
St. Lucia 124, *125*
St. Mary's Cape, Nova Scotia 74, *74*
St. Paul Island *150*
St. Pierre, Martinique 124
St. Vincent *125*
Saithe 123, *123*, *136*
Sakhalin Island *156*
Salakh oilfield *149*
Salinity
  Aleutian Current and 163
  Antarctic productivity and 170
  Arctic water 128
  arrowworms **180**
  Atlantic *34–5*, 35
  Currents and 35, 163
  explanation of 46
  gradient power 99
  Mediterranean 140, *140*, 142–3
    ocean water 26, 35, 46, 111
    seawater 27, 99, 154
    surface water freezing and 35
    water and beach life 82
  "Salinity crisis," Mediterranean 140, *140*
Salmon
  acoustic and 78
  Asian 79, *79*
  behavior 78, 167
  homing instinct 78
  migration 78, 79, *79*
  Pacific 166–7, *167*
  Sea ranching 96–7
  Sockeye 78
  stocks 79
  world catch, tonnage *95*
Salp 62, *63*, **184**, 186
Salpa fusiformis 86
Salt
  Afar Triangle 146
  Atlantic Ocean 118
  cap rock 104
  deposits 146
  domes 127, *127*
    Arctic 130
    Gulf of Mexico 127
    oil traps and 104
    Persian Gulf 148
    Zagros Mountains 147
  lakes, North Sea 132
  marsh
    algae **174**
    environment 77
    formation 19, *19*
    habitat 77, 110
    Insecta **183**
    mineral fertilization and 111
    mud crabs 77
    plants 19
    sediment flats and 19
  North Sea 132, 135
    gas and 134
    oil/gas fields *135*
  pans 100, *100*
    Gulf *27*

salinity 99
  recovery of 100
  reflecting layer 144
  rocks 132
  seabirds and excess 75
  seawater 26, 27, 100, 153
    freezing and 28
    world reserves *101*
Salting fish 122
Salt-water irrigation 96, 97
Samawa oilfield *148*
Samoa Islands *156*, 161, *161*
Samplers, water 48
San Andreas Fault 157, *157*
San Felix Island *!16*, *157*
Sand
  beach 82, *82*, 153, 165
  calcareous *171*
  cliffs 18, *18*
  construction industry and 165
  currents and 22, 23, *23*, 142
  deposition 23, *23*, 132, 134, 142
  dunes 19, *58*
  erosion and 18, *18*
  glass, history 43, *43*, 44
  gravel and *100–1*
    Arctic 130
    Atlantic 119
    North Sea 135
    Pacific *164–5*
  lens 104
  marine, value 100
  mineral 153, 165
  mining 118, *118*
  Nile and Mediterranean Ridge System 138
  North Sea 132, 134, *134*
  Pacific 165
  Persian Gulf 148
  ribbons 142, *142*
  sea cucumber and 85
  structures 23, *23*
  turbidity current and 22
  waves 24, 142, *142*
Sandbanks 19, 99, 132
Sandbars 37
Sandhoppers 82, *82*, 83, **182**
Sandstone
  erosion and 18, *18*
  gas reservoir 104
  North Sea 132, 134, 135
    oil/gas fields *135*
  oil trap 104, *104*, 135
Sandy beach, 82, *82*
Sandy silts, Antarctica 171
Santa Barbara, California, oil 105, *105*
Santorini, Island of 139
Santos Plateau *117*
Sao Tiago 33, *33*
Saprophytes **175**
Sardine
  Atlantic *122–3*
  California 106
  Caribbean 126
  commercial exploitation 107
  Indian Ocean *152*
  Mediterranean *141*
  Monterey 106
  North Atlantic 123
  Pacific 166, *166–7*
  Persian Gulf 148
  pound net fish trap 93, *93*
  Red Sea 148·
  world catch, tonnage *95*
Sardinella *122–3*, *141*
Sardinia 138, *138*, 139
Sargasso Sea
  eels migration and 79
  Gulf Stream and 120, 121, *121*
  seaweed **174**
  water level 32
Sargassum **174**
Sarkan oilfield *148*
Sarkhun oilfield *149*
Sarsia prolifera 86
Sarvestan oilfield *148*
Sassan oilfield *148*
Satellite
  navigation 47, 50
  photography 162, *162*
Saturation diving techniques 53
Saudi Arabia 105, 144, 148, 149, *149*, 150, 153
Saury *166–7*
Scales, fish 68
Scallop 64, *64*, *80*, **180**, **183**
Scandinavia 18, 20, 122, 136
Scandinavian Rise *135*

Scaphopoda/scaphopods 18, **185**
Scattering, light, seawater and 27
Scavengers, beach life and 83
Scheldt, river 135
Schools/schooling, fish *60–1*, 61, 97, 166
Scomber scombrus 69, *69*
Scoter 75
Scotia Arc *116*, *117*, *169*
Scotland 13, *13*, 17, 132
Scott Fracture Zone *156*, *168*
Scott Island *156*, *168*
Scour, tidal 19, 23, *23*
Scouring, deep ocean floor 24
SCUBA 53
Scyphozoa **177**
Sea
  air and 30–1, *30–1*
  circulation, *Challenger* expedition 46
  fauna 80–1, *80–1*, 88–9, *88–9*
    movement of 66–7, *66–7*
  power 98–9, *98–9*
  ranching 96–7
  stacks 19, *19*
  strata 80–1, *80–1*
  surface 27, 30
  temperature 30, 154, *154*
  walls 19, *19*
Sea anemones *80*, 82, 84, **176**, **177**, **183**
  commensalism and 69
  feeding techniques 83
  giant 25
  hermit crab and 69, *69*
  reef fish and 69, *69*
Sea bass 141, 166
Sea bream 141
Sea city 58, *58*
Sea cows 70, **186**
Sea cucumbers *80*, *81*, 89, *89*
  habitats 81, 82, *82*, 85, 88
Sea fans 84, 85
Sea gooseberries 67, *67*
Sea hare 67, *67*
Sea horse *80*
Sea ice 28–9, *28–9*, 130, 131, 168, **186**
Sea lamprey 68, *68*, **185**
Sea Link 54, *54–5*
Sea lion 70, *70*, 71, *71*, 76, **186**
Sea of Hebrides 132, *132*
Sea of Marmara 139, *139*, 142
Sea otters 70, *70*, 71, *71*, 77, **186**
Sea pens *80*, 88, *88*, **178**
Sea scorpion 77
Sea slater 83, *83*
Sea slugs 67, *67*, *80*
  egg-laying 65, *65*
Sea snails 64
Sea snakes 70, **186**
Sea spiders *80*, 88, 89, *89*
Sea urchins *80*, 89, *89*, **179**, **183**
  cardinal fish and 69, *69*
  feeding mechanism 64, *64*
  food chain 77
  habitat 85, 88
  kelp and 77
  teleosts and **186**
Sea whips 84, 85
Seabed
  Committee to Examine the Law of the Sea 56
  frictional drag and 38
  geology 50–1, *50–1*
  muds 25
  placer deposits *100–1*
  rights to exploit 56, 57
  samplers 48–9, *48–9*
Seabirds 74–5, *74–5*, **186**
  anchovy and 106
  breeding 75, 110
  Corynosoma and **179**
  feeding 76, *76*
  lice and **183**
  pollution and 108, 109
  turtle eggs and **186**
Seafloor
  animal life 88–9, *88–9*
  Mediterranean Ridge 138
  research 50–1, *50–1*
  rock structure 104
  sampling 48–9, *48–9*
  spreading 15, 16–17, 25
    age of oceans and 16
    centers 24–5, *25*, 157, *157*
    future and 59
    metals and 25
    ocean and 16, *117*

rates 15, *25*
  sediment and 25
  see also specific ocean; sea
Seagrass meadows 110, 111, **175**
Seahorse *80*, **186**
Seal 70, **186**
  Arctic harp 131, *131*
  breeding 110
  common 71, *71*
  corynosoma and **179**
  fur 76
  great auk and 74
  harp 111, 131, *131*
  hunting 170
  lice and **183**
  ringed 111
  whale and 172
Sealevel 20–1, *20–1*
  Continental shelf and 22
  historical 21, 22
  hurricane and 124
  placer deposits and 101
  water pressure 26
Seamount/s 160, *160*
  currents and 24
  Ionian Basin 139
  Mediterranean 138–9
  Pacific 160, 161
  Society Island chains 161, *161*
  see also specific seamount
Sean gasfield *135*
Seaport buildings 20
Seashells, sealevel changes and 20
Seashore 82–3, *82–3*
Seaskaters 183
Seasnakes **186**
Seawater
  constituents 26, 27, *27*
  evaporation 141
  properties 26, 80
  Red Sea 149
  salinity 27, 99, 154
  seabirds and 75
Seaweed *80*
  beds of 110
  flies 183
  euchytroids and 181
  food chain 77, 96
  kelp, *see* Kelp
  marine iguanas and **186**
  pigments **174**
  seashore 82
  surface water and 86
  zoning **178**
Sediment
  air-sea interaction 30
  Atlantic 116, 118–19, *118–19*
  bottom water 116
  Caribbean 127, *127*
  continental drift and 12
  continental slope 22
  currents and 22, 99, 142
  deep ocean floor 24–5, *24–5*
  distribution *24*
  echo sounding studies of 50
  eroding waves and 18
  Gulf of Cadiz 142, *142*
  Indian Ocean 150
  Mediterranean 139, 142, *142*
  midocean ridges 13
  minerals and 100, 102
  Mobile Bay 124, *124*
  mountain belts and 17
  nodules and 102
  North Sea 132, 134, *134*
  ocean floor 24–5, *24–5*, 59
  oil traps 146
  oldest *157*
  Quaternary Ice Age and 20
  radioactive wastes and 59
  sampling techniques 13
  seabeds *24*, 27
  turbidity currents and 22
  water storage 10
Sedimentary Basins *100–1*
  Arctic 130, *130–1*
  Atlantic *119*
  Caribbean 127
  continental shelves 104
  Indian Ocean 153, *153*
  Pacific *164–5*
Sedimentary rock 16, 132, 138, 141
Sedimentation rates 141
Sedimentology, "tide marks" and 20
Sei whale 73, *73*, *81*, 171, *171*
Seine net fishing 92, *92*, 122, 126, 167

anchovy 107, 166
distant water 94
herring 137
Monterey 106
North Atlantic 123
North Sea 136, 137
Pacific 167
tuna 166, *166*
Seismic
activity 150
profiles 50, 104, 139, 141, 147, *147*
sea wave 37
trace *104*
zone, earth's 15
Seison **179**
Self-contained underwater apparatus (SCUBA) 53
Semi-diurnal tides 38, *38*, 124
Semi-pelagic trawls 122, *122*
Semi-sessile **176**
Semi-submersible/s 104, 105, *105*, 134, *134*
Senses, marine animals 67
Sensing devices 47
Sepia **181**
Serajeh oilfield *148*
Serrated wrack 83, *83*
Sesarma sp. 77
Sessile
animals 65, 83, *83*, **176**, **179**, **184**
barnacles **183**
groups **185**
tunicata **184**
Severn, river 38, *133*
Severnaya Zemlya *129*
Sewage 22, 143
Sextant 44, 45, *45*
Seychelles Islands *150*
Shadegan oilfield *148*
Shagara Deep *149*
Shags 75
Shah oilfield *149*
Shale 104, 134, 135
Shark 68, *68*, 166, *166–7*
breeding 68
Caribbean fishery 126
catching system 97
fishing importance of 166, *166–7*
habitat 85
lampreys and **185**
migration **185**
species
basking *62*, 68, **185**
blue **185**
Greenland 35, 80
gummy 166
sand 69, *69*
school 166
snapper 166
squaloid **185**
thresher **178**
tiger 68
whale **185**
white **185**
white-tip *81*
teleost, comparison with **186**
temperature affecting 35
world catch, tonnage 95
Shatsky Rise *156*, 157
Shaybah-Zarrarah oilfield *149*
Shearwaters 74, *75*
Shelf-locked states, rights 56
Shelf zone, sea fauna *80*
Shells 135, **180**
Crustacean **182**
sand *101–1*, 118
Atlantic 119, *119*
Caribbean 127
Mining 118, *118*
Pacific *164–5*
sealevel changes and 21
stromboid conch **180**
Shellfish
culture 97
dredges and 92
fisheries 92
Indian Ocean 152
mercury and 27, 109
Pacific 167
parasite fungi and **175**
poisonous **175**
sea otters and 70
walrus and 70
Shetland Islands 132, *133*
Shetland-Faeroes Basin *134*
Ship/s
algae and **174**

fouling of **174**, **184**
registration 56
three-masted 44, 45, *45*
Shipping 36, 132
Shipworm **180**
Shiraz *148*
Shoals, fish
inshore fishing methods 92
net traps 92, *92*, *93*
sonar detection 95, *95*
Shoaling water 37, *37*
Shock wave, gas and oil detection by 104
Shore crab 77, 83, *83*
Shore fish 83
Shorebirds 111
Shoreline 20, 23
Short-armed starfish *81*
Short-range weather forecasts 30
Shrimp **183**
Caribbean 126, *126*
catching methods 92, *92*
Cuban 126
deep sea *123*
exports 153
feeding techniques 64
Gulf of Mexico 126
Indian Ocean *152*, 153
inshore fisheries 92
Mantis **182**, **183**
Mediterranean 141
North Sea 136
Pacific 167
plankton and 72
seafarming and 97
species, cleaner role 69
trawl fisheries and 153
Shurom oilfield *148*
Shush oil well 148
Siah Makan oilfield *148*
Siba oilfield *148*
Siberia 28, 158, 166
Siberian Plateau *156*
Sicilian-African Platform *140*
Sicily 141
Side scan sonar 24, 50, 51, *51*, *142*
GLORIA 51, *51*
Siebe, Augustus 53
Sierra Leone Rise *117*
Sierra Nevada 157
Sigsbee Escarpment *124*
Sigsbee Plain 124
Silica/silicates 27, 102, *102*, *173*, **176**
Siliceous ooze 24, *24*, 150, 171
Siliceous scales **174**
Silt/s 124, *124*, 125, *125*, 171, *171*
Silurian Period 17, **182**, **185**
Silver deposits *100–1*, 149, *149*, 158, *164–5*
Silver pit 132, *133*
Simpson Desert 151, *156*
Sinai Peninsula 144, *144*
Sinanus 69, *69*
Siphonophore 62, *63*, 80, **177**
Sipunculida/sipunculids **179**
Sirenians 70
Sirri A/C/D/oilfields *149*
Skagerrak 132, *133*
Skate/s 68, *68*
Skimmer/s 74, *75*
Skin
shark 68, *68*
whales 110
Skua 75
Sledge, harvesting manganese nodules *103*
Sleet 26
Sleipner gasfield *135*
Slipper limpets **180**
Slugs **180**
Smelt/s 95, *96–7*
Snail/s 21, 64, 67, *67*, **180**
Snake
eel *80*
sea, reproduction 70
Snapper shark 166
Snappers, Pacific 166
Snider-Pelligrini, Antonio 12
Snipe eel 89, *89*
Snow 10, 26, 27
Society Islands 84, *84–5*, *156*, 160, 161, *161*
Sockeye salmon 78
Soda production, algae and **174**
Sodium/salts 26, 27, *27*, 99, *102*
see also Salt
Soft corals 84, 85
Sogne fjord *133*

Sohm Abyssal Plain *116*
Soil, evaporation from *27*
Solar system 11, 27, 28, 99
see also Sun
Solaster **183**
Soldier fish 148
Sole *123*
Mediterranean 141
North Sea 136, *136*, 137, *137*
World catch 95
Sole pit 132, *133*
Solomon Plateau *156*, 157
Trench 156
Solutions, gulf seawater 27, *27*
Solvents, pollution and 109
Somali
Abyssal Plain *150*
Current *33*, 154, 155
Escarpment 146, *147*
Somalia 146, *147*, 154
Somerset Island *129*
Sonar
current measurements 35
equipment, fish detection 95, *95*
"fish" 50, 51, *51*
record, ice and 29, *29*
scanners *Glomar Challenger* and 165, *165*
whales and **186**
Sonographs 23, *23*, 50, 51, *51*
Sound, seawater and 26, 27, 50, 104, **176**
South Africa
Agulhas Bank 118
Agulhas Current and 154
Atlantic lobsters and 123
continental shelf 153
glauconite deposits 153
phosphatic sediments 118
South America
Andes formation 22
continental margin 118
crab fishing 123
crust destruction and 157
drifting of North America and 117
fault system 125
Isthmus of Panama closure 124
movement of 124
Pacific oceanic crust and 157
Patagonia continental shelf 123
phosphate rock off 165
shark migration 185
trawl fishing and 123
tuna 123
water flow 124
west coast, submarine deeps and 116
whaling station and humpback whales 170
South American Trench 158, *158*
South Atlantic
Benguela Current and 154
Dias exploration 44
eddies and 154
formation of 17
history 17, 44, 117
magnetic variation 44
warm water gyre 120
wind circulation history 44
South Atlantic Gyre *33*, *121*
Benguela Current and 121
South Balearic Basin *140*
South Carolina 19, *19*
South China Sea 166, 167
Southeast Asia 105, 130, 154, 160
Southeast Trade Winds *121*
South Equatorial Counter-current *121*, *163*
South Equatorial Current 154, 155, 162, *163*
green turtles migration and 78, *78*
South Fuwaris oilfield *148*
South Georgia Island 117, 170, 171, *171*
South Indian Basin *151*, *156*, *169*
South Indian Gyre 155
circulation *33*
West Australian Current and 155
South Korea 94
South magnetic pole 15
South Orkney Islands *117*, *169*
South Pacific
Benguela Current and 154

Gyre *33*, *163*
South Pole 16, *168*, *169*
South Sandwich Island *169*
Trench 116, *117*, *169*
South Shetland Islands *116*, 168, *168*, *169*
Southwest Africa 118, 162
Southwest Fateh oilfield *149*
Southwest Indian Ridge *150*, 155, *169*
Southwest Monsoon 154, 155
Southwest Pacific Basin 168
Sovereign, HMS 29, *29*
Soviet Union, see Union of Soviet Socialist Republics
Sowerby's beaked whale 73, *73*
Spain *123*, 139, *142*, 143
Spanish mackerel 167, *167*
Spartina 77
Spawning
areas 78, *87*, 123, 131, 135, *137*
billfish 87
cod 123, *123*
off Lofoten Islands 131
eel 79
fish 78
see also specific fish
green turtle 78
King crabs 65
North Sea 137, *137*
plaice 137
salmon 79, *79*
tuna 87
worms 181
Spear-fishing 92, *92*, 153
Sport fish 92
Sperm whale 72, *72–3*, *80–1*
catch 171, *171*
feeding dives 81
industry 72, 170
prey of 64
whalers and 72, *72*
Spermaceti 72
Sphaeroides nephelus 69, *69*
Spicules **176**, **184**
Spider 97
Spider crab, giant **182**
Spirorbis **181**
Spits, formation 19
Spitsbergen 128, *129*
Sponges 80, 85, **176**, **179**
feeding technique 64, *64*
Sporozoa **176**
Sprat
ancestry **186**
Atlantic *122–3*
genus *173*
herring and 137
Mediterranean *141*
North Sea 136, *136*
Pacific *166–7*
Spreading, see Seafloor spreading
Spring tide 38, 39
Squaloid shark 80, **185**
Squalus sp. 68, *68*
Squat lobster 67, *67*
Squid 66, *66*, 80, 81, *81*, **181**
Antarctic waters and 170
Atlantic *122–3*
behavior to light 167
binomial system *173*
bottle-nosed whale and 73
canneries and 106
Caribbean *126*
commercial fishing 170
deep water 88, *88*
eyes of 67
giant 64, 72, 81, **180**
jet propulsion **180**
movement 66, *66*, 67
oceanic **181**
pelagic **181**
Pacific *166–7*, 167
porpoise feeding on 72
prey 64
sperm whales and 81
Vampire *80*
whales and 64, 72, 73, 81
Squilla **182**
Squirrel fish 148
Sri Lanka 110, 153
"Staircase" beaches 20
Stalked barnacles **183**
Stalked crinoids 80, **183**
Stalked jellyfish **177**
Star patterns, fish migration and 78
Starfish 80, **183**
abyssal habitat 88

Asterias sp. 77
breeding 64, 65
cod and 69
coral reef 85
deep sea 89, *89*
feeding technique 65, *65*
food web and 69, 77, *77*
Great Barrier Reef 85, *85*
habitats 85, *85*, 88, 89, *89*
larva 65
movement 67, *67*
Statfjord oilfield *135*
Stauromedusae **177**
Stavorten 58
Steam trawler, first, North Sea 136
Steam whalers, Antarctic 170
Stellar navigation *50*
Stellar's sea cow 70
Stereoscopic photographs, underwater 30
Stern trawlers 94, 95, *95*
Sterna paradisaea 75, *75*
Stick chart, Micronesian 43, *43*
Stimuli, fish response 167
Stock, fish, definition 78
see also specific fish
Stocks Seamount *117*
Stomatoid *80*
Stomatopoda **183**
Stompha **177**
Stonefish 84
Stony corals 69, *84*, *84–5*
Stony mantle 10, 14, *14*
Storm
air–sea interaction 30
development zone *30*
Gulf of Mexico hurricanes 124
systems 36
tail, hurricane *30*
track, hurricane *30*
waves, 22, 36, 59, 118
winter 86
Storm petrel, feeding method 75
Strabo Trench *139*
Strait of Dover *133*
Strait of Gibraltar 138, *138*
Mediterranean and 142
Strait of Hormuz 145, *149*
Strait of Sicily 138
Straits of Florida 125
Stratification, gyres and 162
Stratified water 35, 120
Stratocumulus cloud 162
Stream
beds, ancient 22
currents, Rennell's theory 46
mineral suspensions 111
Streblospio sp. 77
Striped pargo *80*
Strombid conch shells **180**
Stromboli 138
Strontium 26, *27*, *102*
Structure, rock, determination of 104
Sturgeons **185**
Styliola subula 87
Stylocheiron elongatum 86
Stylocheiron suhmi 87
Suakin Deep *149*
Subantarctic water 168
Subarctic 87, *87*
Subduction
Arabian Peninsula 147
Caribbean 125
marginal 144
mountain formation and 16
oceanic
crust 157, *158*
plate, Western Pacific 159
Pacific 157, 158, *158*, 159, 160
trench *159*
Sublittoral zone, seaweed and 82
Submarine
areas, right to exploit 56
cables 22, *22*, 46
canyons 22, 23
earthquake 37, *37*
fan, Nile 138
mountain chain, Mid-Indian Ocean Ridge 150
plateaus 139, 150, 165
ridges 128, 150, 168
Submarine
military 54
nuclear 55, *55*

routes 130, *130*
tanker routes, proposed *130*
Submerged beaches, relics of 22
Submergence, sealevel changes and 20
Submersible *50*, 54–5, *54–5*
Sub-polar gyre 120, 162
Sub-Saharan Africa, shorebirds migration to 111
Subsea mineral deposits 165
Subsidence
Aegean area 139
coral and 84, 160
deltas and 20
gulf 27, *27*
North Sea 132
Pacific Island seamounts and 160
sulfur mining 127
Subsistence fisheries, Africa 152–153
Subsurface currents, measurement 49
Suctorians **176**
Suez Canal 118, 144
Sulabedar oilfield *148*
Sulfur/sulfates
Atlantic *119*
Caribbean 127
Gulf of Mexico 127
gulf seawater and 27, *27*
Louisiana offshore extraction 127, *127*
Mediterranean 141
mine 127
placer deposits *100–1*
recovery 100
seawater constituent 26, *27*
whale skin, effect of waste on 110
world reserves *101*
Sullom Voe shorestation *134*
Sumatra *151*, *156*
Sumitomo 57
Summa Corporation 57
Summerland, Californian oilfield 104
Sun
energy source 59
ionized gases and 11
navigation history 44, 45
photosynthesis and 26
productivity and 86
Spring tides and 39
tides and 38, 39
Sunlight
coral and 160
life forms and 86
marine plants and **174**
penetration 27
upwellings and 86
world ocean nutrients and 162
Sunlit zone 59, 86,
see Fauna *81*
Supercontinents, Gondwana-land and Laurasia 13, *13*
"Surf" 37
Surface currents
Arctic 129, *129*
gulf 27
Indian Ocean 155, *155*
Mediterranean 142, 143
Surface tension, waves and 26
Surface water
Arabian Coast and 154
Arctic 128
Atlantic, effect on Mediterranean 141
freezing of 28
Mediterranean 141, 143, *143*
oscillations 18
OTEC plant 99, *99*
productivity 97
temperature 30
transportation 162, *162*
wind and flow of 32, *32*
Surgeon fish 85
Surmullets *123*
Surtsey 116, *116*, *117*
Suru oilfield *149*
Survey vessel, seismic shooting and 104
Survival, homing instinct and 78
Susangerd oilfield *148*
Svalbard shelf 131, *131*
Svyataya Anna Cone *129*
Swash, waves and 37
Sweden, herring fisheries

failures 92
Sweetlips *85*
Swell 37, 162, *162*
    waves 11, 36, 43
        Agulhas Current and 154
Swim bladder, marine animals
    185, 186
Swordfish *80–1*
    fishery recourse 86
    larval **185**
    Mediterranean 141
Sydney, East Australian Current
    and 162
Symbionts **178**
Symbiosis **175**
Symbiotic relationships 69, **174,
    175, 176, 177, 178**
    see also specific animal
Systemae naturae 173

T

Tabular icebergs 59, 128, 168
Tactics, fishing 167
Tadjura Trench *145*
Tagus, river *138*
Tahiti Island *156*, 161, *161*
Taiwan, Island of *151*, 153, *156*,
    162, *162*
Takla Makan Desert *150*
Tamyr Peninsula *129*
Tana, Lake *145*
Tangle net gear 167
Tankers/tanker routes 118, *118*,
    130, *130*, 149, *149*
Tapeworms **178**
Tardigrada/tardigrades **182**
Tarpons, ancestry **186**
Tartan oilfield *135*
Tasman
    Abyssal Plain *156*
    Plateau *151*, *156*, *168*
    Sea 157, *157*
Tasmania, Submarine ridges
    and 168
Taurulus bubalis 77
Taylor, F. B. 12
Teche, Mississippi delta *125*
Tectonics 20, 124, 147
    see also Plate tectonics
Teesside shorestation *134*
Teeth, whales and dolphins 72
Telegraph, intercontinental 46
Teleostei/teleosts 68, **185, 186**
    flukes and **178**
    leeches 181
Television, underwater
    photography 50
Tellin 82, *82*
    Macoma sp. 77
Tellina tenuis 82, *82*
Temora sp. 76
    longicornis 63
Temperate waters 78, *78*
Temperature, water
    air-sea interaction and 30
    Aleutian Current 163
    Arrowworms and **180**
    changes
        beach life and 82
    Currents and 35, 163
    depth and 49, *49*, 88
    fish migration 78
    Hurricane Camille and 31, *31*
    meander and 32
    depth and 88
    OTEC plant 99
    plankton blooms and 110
    power and 98
    recorders and 49
    saline pools, Red Sea 154
    sound signals and 26
Template Rig, oil 105, *105*
Tenchi seamount *156*
Tensional rifts, ocean basin
    formation and 16
Tentacles, marine animals **176,
    177, 178**
Teredo **180**
Tern **186**
    Arctic 75, *75*
Terrigenous deposits *24*, 102
Territorial sea, definition 56
Territorial waters, potential
    marine parts 110
Tertiary period
    Forties oilfield 134, 135
    King crabs and **182**
    North Sea 132, 134, *135*
    Persian Gulf 148
    Whales and 72
Tethys Sea 17, *139*, **175**
    Tetiaroa Island 161, **161**
Tetrapods **186**
Texas skate 68
Thailand 104, 110, 153
Thalarctos maritimus 70, *70*
Thalassia sp. 71, **175, 186**
Thalassicola 86
Thaliacea **184**
Thames estuary 132, *133*
Thar Desert *150*
Tharp Fracture Zone *156*, *157*
Thaw holes 28
Theddlethorpe shorestation *135*

Thermal
    pollution, Mediterranean 143
    power 98
Thermodine 80
Thermometer, reversing 49, *49*
Thetis Deep, Red Sea *149*
Thistle oilfield *135*
Thomson, 46, 47
Thomson, Wyville 46, 47
Thorium 98, *101*
Three-masted ship 44, 45, *45*
Thresher shark 178
Thrust
    fault, oil traps and 104
    Zone, North Sea oil/gasfields
        135
Thunnus 69, *69*, 166
    see also Tuna
Thysanopoda 63
Tibesti *117*
Tibet Plateau *151*
Tidal
    bore, River Severn 38
    bulges 38, 39
    currents 38, 118, 162
        cliff erosion and 19
        continental shelf and 22, 142
        sand structures 23, *23*
        sediment transport and 99
    force, continental drift theory
        and 12
    power scheme 98, *98*
    scour 19, 23, *23*
    waves, tsunami and 37
Tide/s 38, *38*, 39, *39*
    Caribbean 124
    current flow and 133
    diurnal 38, *38*, 124
    Mediterranean 143
    North Sea 133
    power 98
    red 62, *62*, **175**
    sea level and 20
    waves and 36
Tideless Seas, erosion band 18
"Tide-marks," past evidence 20
Tiger cowrie 85, *85*
Tiger fish, Red Sea 148
Tiger shark 68
Tigris, river *148*, *150*
Tillamook Rock Light, Oregon
    waves and 36
Time, local, ships 45
Tin/deposits
    Atlantic *119*
    Continental shelf 22
    dredger 153, *153*
    Indian Ocean 153, *153*
    Indonesia 165
    marine mining 100
    Pacific *164–5*
    placer deposits *100–1*
    production, dollars 153
    world reserves, tonnage *101*
Tintinnids **176**
Titanium
    Atlantic *119*
    beach sand 165
    Caribbean 127, *127*
    Gulf of Mexico 127
    Indian Ocean 153, *153*
    Manganese nodule,
        constituent 102
    North American sands and
        165
    Pacific *164–5*
    placer deposits *100–1*
    seawater 27
    world reserves, tonnage *101*
Tokelan Island *156*
Tokyo, International
    Conference on Marine Parks
    and Reserves 1975; 111
Tomopteris **181**
Tomopteris pacifica 87
Tonga Trench *156*
    depth 157
    plates and the 14, *14*
Tongue point, New Zealand,
    coastal uplift 20, *20*
Toothed whale 64, 72, *72–3*, 73
Topshells *80*, **180**
Tor oilfield *135*
Torpedo **185**
Torsion **180**
Tortoise, land 71
Tower of the Winds, Athens 43,
    43
Toxins **175, 177**
Trace elements, seawater *27*

Tractor, cable-burying 55, *55*
Trade routes 154
Trade winds 32, 54, 86, 124
Trammel net 93, *93*, 141
Transform faults/faulting 15,
    157
Transformation, waves 37
Transpiration, plant 27, *27*
Transpolar Drift Stream,
    Arctic 28
Transponder, radio 50
Transportation
    Ekman, of water 35, *35*, 162
    precipitated seawater 27
    Surface water 27
Trap/trapping, fish 92–3, *92–3*
    Crab 123
    Indian Ocean 153
    Mediterranean 141
    Pacific 167
Traps, oil
    Arctic 130
    Brent oiltrap 135
    Mediterranean 141
    Middle East 148
    Persian Gulf 146
    Rock structure and 104, *104*
    see also Oilfields
Trawl 122, *122*
    beam *137*
    bottom 122, *122*
    midwater *122*, *137*
    nets, North Sea 137, *137*
    Otter *137*
    semipelagic *122*
Trawler 122
    fishing industry and 94
    North Atlantic fisheries and
        123
    Pacific fishery 167
    wet-fish 94, *94–5*
Trawling
    Atlantic 122, 123
    Caribbean 126
    Mediterranean 141
    North Sea 136, 137
    Red Sea 148
Trench/trenches 15
    active *158*, *159*
    Aleutian 158
    formation 16, *158*
    history 16, 17, 157, 158
    oceanic, animal life 89
        crust and 15, 157
    Pacific *158*, *159*, *159*
    systems, Pacific 159
    zone, sea fauna *81*
    see also specific trench
Trent, river *133*
Triassic Period 13, *13*, 17, 134,
    135
Trichechus manatus 71, *71*
Trichocysts **175**
Triciads **178**
Tridacna 64, **175, 178, 180**
Trieste 54
Trilobites **182**
Trinidad *125*
Tripod fish *81*, 88, 89, *89*
Tristan da Cunha 116, *169*
Tropical
    current gyre, spawning fish
        78, *78*
    cycle, plankton production 86,
        86
    rain, Moorea Island and 161
    waters, fish migration and 78
Tropics, sea-surface
    temperature 30
Tropopause, hurricane and 30
Trough of Rhodes 139
Trough, wave 36
Trout world catch, tonnage 95
Trumpet fish 85
Tsunami 37, *37*
Tuamotu Archipelago/islands
    156, 161, *161*
Tuba oilfield *148*
Tube feet, echinoderms 67
Tubeastrea aurea 84, *84*
Tubuai Islands *156*
Tuna 68, 69, *69*, 166, **186**
    Atlantic *122–3*, 123
    Caribbean fishery 126, *126*
    Cuban catch 126
    fishery agreements 106
    fishery resources and 86–7
    Great Barrier Reef fishery
        167, *167*
    Indian Ocean *152*, 153

inshore fishery 92
    long-line fishing fleets and 94
    Mediterranean 92, 141, *141*
    Midwater trawl and 122
    migration 78, 86, 87
    Pacific *166*, *166–7*
    plankton communities and 87
    prey catching **186**
    purse-seiners and 94
    research 78
    species 166, *166*
        albacore *81*, 166, *166*, *167*
        bigeye 87, 166, *166*, *167*
        bluefin 78
        yellowfin 166, *166*, *167*
    world catch, tonnage 95
Tungsten *100–1*
Tunicata/tunicates 27, **184, 185**
Tunnel valleys 132
Turbellaria **178**
Turbid water 80, 162, *162*
Turbidity current 22, *22*
Turbot **186**
Turbulence, Tansan 162, *162*
Turkey, Mediterranean Ridge
    System and 138
Turtle 71, *71*, **186**
    breeding 70, 78, *78*, 110
    farming 96, *96–7*
    grass 71
    green *80*, **186**
        migration of 78
Turtle, The 54, *54*
Twilight zone, fauna *81*
Tyrrhenian Abyssal Plain *140*
Tyrrhenian Basin 138, *138*, *139*
Tyrrhenian Sea 139, *139*

U

Uca sp. 77, 83, *83*
Uithuizermeeden shorestation
    135
UK, *see* United Kingdom
Ulm, Ptolemaic maps 44
Ulva 174
UM Addalkh oilfield *149*
UMM Gudair oilfield *148*
UMM Said *148*
UMM Shaif oilfield 148, *148*
UNCLOS I, 1958 56
UNCLOS III 56–7
Uncomformity traps, oil 104,
    135, *135*
Undercurrent *142*, 162
Undersea earthquakes 37
Underwater
    acoustics 47
    apparatus 52–3, *52–3*
    oil tanks, Persian Gulf 149
    photography 50
    transmissions, frequencies 26
    see also Submarine
Union of Soviet Socialist
    Republics
    Arctic fishery, cod 131
    Atlantic cod catch *123*
    baleen whaling and 107
    cod and *123*, 131
    fisheries and 106, 123, 131
    maritime interests, law and 56
    North Pacific fishery
        agreement 106
    oil production 127
    polar cod fishery 131
    whaling 107, 170
    white whale habitat 111
United Kingdom
    Atlantic cod catch, tonnage
        123
    coastal landscape 18
    cod
        Atlantic catch 123
        Grimsby 136
    Cod fishery, tonnage 137
    continental shelf, wrecks and
        132
    energy requirement 99
    fishing industry *107*, 123, 136,
        137
    Grimsby, cod 136
    herring
        catch, tonnage *107*
        fleets, North Sea 136
    Humber, fishing industry 136
    North Sea
        boundary 51, 57
        herring fleets 136
        Ice Age 132
    oil production and 105
    pollution 109
    shell deposits 118
    Windscale, radioactive
        pollution 109
United Nations Conference on
    the Law of the sea, *see*
    UNCLOS
United States of America
    Atlantic
        lobsters 123
        sand and gravel for 118
    continental shelf, fish catch
        122
    crab fishing, east coast 123
    fish catch, N. Atlantic 122
    fisheries 106, 123
    lobsters 123
    North Atlantic fish catch 122
    North Pacific fishery
        agreement 106
    North west coast fisheries 123
    oil production and 104, 105,
        127
    Pacific tuna fishing 166
    sand and gravel for 118
    shrimp catch exported to 153
    tuna fishery, Pacific, and 166
    Wetlands and 110
    Winter weather 30
    see also specific region
United States Exploring
    Expedition 1840 160
United States icebreaker 113, *113*

United States Naval
  Observatory 46
Untreated sewage,
  Mediterranean 43
Upland area, erosive waves and
  18, *18*
Uplift, sealevel changes and 20
Upper Carboniferous Period 13
  Cretaceous Period 20, 132
  Jurassic Period 135
Uppermost mantle, earth's
  structure and 14
Upperwater, fish 68
Upwelling/s
  Afar Triangle 146
  anchovy fishery 107
  asthenosphere 16
  Benguela Current and 121
  Cape Verde Islands 33, *33*
  Caribbean 124, 126
  coastal 77, 86, 165
  currents and 15, 35, *35*, 121,
    162
  fish migration and 78
  food chain 76, 77
  habitat 110
  Indian Ocean 154
  Mediterranean 143
  midocean 86
  migration, fish 78
  North Indian Ocean 154
  Ocean
    action of 111
    currents and 162
    plant life and 86
  Peru 107
    food chains 76
  phosphate deposits 118, *118*
  plant life and 86
  ridges, new material of 15
  rift valleys and 16
  Satellite photograph
    showing 162, *162*
  Sea temperature contrasts and
    35
  western Caribbean 124
  winter storms and 86
Ural Mountains 16, 17
Uranium fission 98
Urchins, *see* Sea urchins
Urea
  elasmobranchs storage of **185**
  Holocephali and **185**
  Latimeria **186**
  Shark processing and 166
USA, *see* United States of
  America
USSR, *see* Union of Soviet
  Socialist Republics

Valdivia Deep, Red Sea *149*
Valerie Cuyot *156*
Valhalla oilfield *135*
Valley, glaciers, coastal
  landscapes and 19
Vampire squid *80*
Vanadium 27, 102, *102*
Variation, magnetic 44
Vaucheria **174**
Vegetation
  salt marsh 19
  wildlife dependence 111
Vema Deep, Red Sea *149*
Vema Fracture Zone *117*
Vema Seamount *117*
Vema Trench *150*
Venezuela
  faults 124
  Lake Maracaibo 91, 104, *125*
  Northern 124
  oil 91, 100, 104, 127
  shrimp fisheries 126
Venezuelan Basin *125*
Venus flower basket 81, 88, 89,
  89, **177**
Venus girdle **178**
Venus surface 10
Verkhoyansk Mountains *128*,
  156
Vertical migrations, fish 167, **182**
Vertical mixing, watermasses 86
Vespucci, Amerigo 44
Vesuvius 138
Veyzenhar oilfield *148*
Victoria Island *129*
  lake *150*
  shark fishing 166
Viking
  Bank *133*
  boat 42, *42*
  gasfield *135*
  Graben *135*
Viper fish 88, *88*
Virgin Islands *125*
Viruses, marine plants and 97
Viscosity, seawater 26
Viscount Melville Sound *129*,
  130
Vision, seawater 27
Volcanic
  Island Arc 159, *159*
  Islands 14, 15, 19, *159*
  plateaus 157
  see also specific plateau
  ridges 157
  rock *150*
  Seamount 138
Volcano/volcanoes
  activity 25, *158*
    Afar Triangle 146
    Deception Island 168, *168*
    earth's interior and 11
    fossil *159*
    Indonesian arc 150
    Mediterranean *138–9*
    Mid-Indian Ocean range
      150
    oceanic trenches and 15
    Pacific Ocean 157, *158*, 159
    Red Sea 146
    sediment and 25
    trenches 15
  Aegean 139
  Afar Triangle 146
  Antarctica 168, *168*, 171
  ash 25
  atoll evolution and 160
  Caribbean margins 124
  cones, Pacific *158*
  continental margins and 22
  debris, Antarctica 171
  earth's origin and 10
  eastern Pacific 157
  eruptions
    Caribbean 124
    plate tectonics and 15
    tsunami and 37
  glass, Afar Triangle 146
  Hawaiian *8–9*, 9
  hydrosphere origin and 10
  iron ore and 165
  Mediterranean 139, *140–1*

Pacific 158, *158*
  iron ore and 165
  structure 160
  submerged 157
  western 165
Red Sea 144
silts, Antarctica 171
structure, Pacific 160
submerged 157
tsunami and 37
Volume forces, breakwaters and
  58
Voring Plateau *117*

Waddenzee, potential marine
  park 110
Waders 186
Wafr oilfield *148*
Wake Island *156*
Waldseemüller, Martin 44, *44*
  map of 44, *44*
Walfisch Ridge 116, *117*
Wallaby Plateaus *151*, *156*
Walrus 70, *70*, 71, *71*, **186**
Wands Basin, Red Sea *149*
Warm front, depressions and *31*
Washington
  dogfish catching system of 97
  ridge crest west of 157
Waste products
  algae and **178**
  Coral's 69
  disposal
    metal 110
    nuclear 98
    domestic 59
    fisheries 97
    industrial 22
Water
  column 26
  convergences 168
  depth, tidal scour 19
  evaporation 27
  exchange, earth's interior
    and hydrosphere 10
  flow, ice drift and 28
  level, circulating currents and
    32
    ice caps and 20
  manganese nodule
    constituent *102*
  mass 38, 86, 133
  meteorites and 11
  mixing, dumping grounds and
    109
    Mediterranean 141
  movement 32, *32*
  oil traps and 104
  origin of earth's 10
  passive, marine animals and
    66
  planet 10
  primary productivity and 86,
    86
  profiles
    Indian Ocean 155
    Pacific Ocean *163*
  properties, physical and
    chemical 26–7
  samplers 48
  sedimentary rock and 16
  surface behavior, tides and 39
  temperature 30
  terrestrial life, evolution and
    26
Watercraft, history 43
Waterweed, manatee and 71
Wave
  beach life and effect of 82
  breakwaters and 58
  continental shelf and 22
  energy 58
  erosion 18–19, *18–19*
  forecasting 47
  forms 36–7, *36–7*
  Forties oilfield and height of
    105
  length 27, *27*, 36, 37
  power 98, 99, *99*
  refraction 162, *162*
  storm 22, 36, 59, 118, **183**
  systems, tides and 38
  water properties and 26
Weather 30–1, *30–1*, 33, *33*, 59
Weddell Sea 35, 120, *169*
  Gyre *121*
Weddell seal 71
Wegener, Alfred 12, *12*, 13
Welker Guyot *156*
Wellington, Tongue Point 20,
  20
Wells, oil, *see* Oil production
West Africa 13, 88, 144
West Atlantic 168
West Australian Basin 155, *155*
West Australian Current
  circulation *33*

Indian Ocean and 154
  South Indian Gyre and *155*
West Ekofisk oilfield *135*
West European drought 30
West Fateh oilfield *149*
West Germany, Atlantic cod
  catch 123
West Greenland
  Current *120*, 121
    circulation *33*
    icebergs from 120
    oldest rock 11
West Indies, tectonic connection
  with Pacific 124
West Mariana Ridge 159, *159*
West Pacific
  bathymetry 159
  satellite photograph 162, *162*
West Philippine
  Basin 159, *159*
  Trench *159*
West Scotia Basin *169*
West Sheba Ridge *145*
West Sole gasfield *135*
West Spitsbergen Current 131,
  131
Westerlies/westerly winds
  current pattern of North
    Atlantic 120
  Gulf Stream and 121
  Indian Ocean and 154
  Southern Ocean 168
Western Approaches Basin *134*
  Australia 28, 153
  Basin, Mediterranean Sea 138
  Caribbean 124
  Crete 21
  Mediterranean Basins 138,
    138
  Rift Valley *117*, 160
Wet-fish trawler 94, *94–5*
Wetland, coastal 110–11
Whale 70, 72–3, *72–3*, **186**
  Antarctic 170, 171, *171*
  breeding 78, 110, 111, 170
  capelin fish and fin 111
  catch, Antarctic 171, *171*
  see also Whaling
  decimation 108
  decline of 56
  feeding dives 81
  fishing, history and
    importance of 94
  see also Whaling
  metal waste dumping and 110
  plankton and 62
  population 170
  prey and 64
  shark 68, **185**
  song 186
  species
    baleen 62, 72, 73, *73*, 170
    beaked 73, *73*
    blue 72, 73, *73*, 170, 171,
      171
    bottle-nose 73, *73*, 107, 171,
      171
    fin 73, 107, 110, 111, 170,
      171, *171*
    gray
      habitat 110–11
      migration 78
    humpback 73, *73*, 170, 171,
      171
    narwhal 73, *73*, 111
    Northern right 170
    pilot 73, *73*
    right 72, *72*, 170, 171, *171*
    sei 73, *73*, *81*, 171, *171*
    Sowerby's beaked 73, *73*
    sperm 64, 72, *72–3*, *80–1*,
      81, 170, 171, *171*
    toothed 64, 72, *72–3*, 73
    whalebone 72, **182**, **183**, **185**
    white 111, *111*
  stock, *Discovery* investigations
    47
  whaling and 72, 107, *107*, 170
    baleen 73
    sperm 72, *72*
    Yankee 94
Whalebone whales 72, **182**, **183**,
  185
Whaling 72, 107, *107*, 170
  baleen and 73
  sperm whale and 72, *72*
  Yankee 94
Wharton Basin 150, 151, *151*,
  156
Whelk, feeding technique 64, *64*

White Nile *144*
White Sea *129*
White shark **185**
White-tip shark *81*
White whale 111, *111*
Whitecaps 36, *36*, 37
Whiting
  Atlantic 123, *123*
  North Sea 136, *136*, 137
Wind
  air-sea interaction 30
  Antarctic ice and 113
  coastal upwellings and 86
  Coriolis force and 32, *32*
  currents and 32, 33, *33*, 35, *35*,
    133, 168
  energy and 98
  erosion and 18, 26
  fishing history and 95
  fog creation and 33, *33*
  history
    circulation 44
    discovery 44
    fishing and 95
    Maury's charts 46
  hurricane 30, *30*
  ice, Antarctic and 113
  icesheet and 28
  marine animal movement and
    66
  Mediterranean Sea and 143
  Middle Atlantic Bight 22
  North Sea, current flow and
    133
  patterns 152, 168
  Persian Gulf 145
  sealevels and 124
  seawater and 26, 80
  speed
    Forties oilfield production
      platform and 105
    hurricane 30
  surface flow and 32, *32*
  terrestrial deposits and 16
  upwellings, coastal, and 86
  waves and 36
  "Wind Sea" 36
Wind waves 36–7
Windmills, salt extraction and
  100
Windscale Reprocessing Plant,
  pollution and 109
Winkle 77, *77*, **174**
Winter/s 30
  catch, fish, tonnage *95*
  see also specific ocean/sea
    for comparisons
  clupeid fish catch 86
  currents 33, *33*
  ocean 114–15
  oil
    demand 105
    production, tonnage *105*
    weather 33, *33*
Worm 80, **178**, **179**
  beach life and 82, *82*, 83
  burrowing 83, *83*
  cod and 69
  deep sea polychaete 88
  Enteropneusts **184**
  habitats 82, 83
  marine fish and 68, 69
  Myzostomaria **181**
  Nereis sp. 77
  polychaete *80*, 88
  rocky shore habitat 82
  sandy beach 82, *82*
  Spartina, algae and 77
  teleosts and **186**
Wrack
  channeled 82, *82*
  serrated 83, *83*
Wrangel Abyssal Plain *129*
Wrangel Island *128*
Wrasse **186**
  cleaning angel fish 69, *69*
  twin-spotted 85, *85*
Wreck/s 59, *59*, 132
Wright, Edward 44
Writers, early oceanography and
  46

Wust Seamount *117*

Xanthophyceae 174
Xanthophyll 175
Xylophaga *80*

Yablonovyy Mountains *156*
Yangtze, river *151*, *156*
Yankee whalers 94
Yap Palau Trench *151*, *156*
Yeasts 175
Yellow crabs 25
Yellow river 151, *156*
Yellow Sea 151, *156*
  Pacific fishery 166
  prawn fishery 167
Yellowfin tuna 166, *166*
Yellow-green algae 174
Yellowtail fish 97
Yemen 146, 147, *147*
Yermak Plateau *129*
Yibal oilfield *149*
Yoldia Sea, origin 21, *21*
Yorkshire, potash 135
Yucatan Basin *125*
  Channel *125*
  Strait 124
Yukon, river, *128*

Zagros Mountains *145*, 146, 147, *147*, 148
Zakum oilfield 148, *149*
Zalophus Californianus 71, *71*
Zambesi, river *150*
Zinc/deposits *100–1*
  Atlantis 11 Deep 149, *149*
  Indian Ocean *153*
  manganese nodule constituent 102, *102*
  Red Sea 148
  residence time, mineral formation 27
  seawater 27
Zircon
  Atlantic *119*
  beach sand 165
  Caribbean *127*
  Gulf of Mexico 127
  Indian Ocean 153, *153*
  North American sands 165
  Pacific *164–5*
  placer deposits *100–1*
  world reserves, tonnage *101*
Zoarces viviparus 77
Zonal fossils 179, 182
Zonation, marine plants 174
Zooflagellates 176
Zoo-geography, ocean 87
Zooplankton 63, *63*, *80*
  anchovies and 77
  Atlantic 86, *86*
  food web 77, *77*
  larva and 65
  marine ecosystem and 62
  North Atlantic temperate zone 86, *86*
  North Pacific 86, *86*
  overwintering 86
  Pacific 86, *86*
  species 87, *87*
  temperate zone 86, *86*
Zooxanthellae 175
Zostera 70, 77, *77*, 175, 186
  habitat 83, *83*
Zubair oilfield *148*
Zuiderzee 58
Zuluf oilfield *148*

ACKNOWLEDGEMENTS

A great many people and institutions have given advice and assistance in the preparation of the Atlas of the Oceans. *The publishers wish to extend their thanks to them all and in particular to the following.*

Erik C. Abranson.
Brazilian Embassy, London.
Dr. J. Birks, British Petrol Company, London.
Dr. A. L. Bloom, Cornell University, New York.
Charles Swithinbank, Miss Ann Tod, British Antarctic Survey, Cambridge.
Arthur Bourne.
Paul Bradwell.
John H. Burne, Department of Agriculture and Fisheries for Scotland.
G. P. R. Cobbett, British Sulphur Association.
Marianne Darling, Nuffield Institute, London Zoo.
Directie van de Visserijen, 's-Gravenhage.
Le Direction des Pêches Maritimes, Secrétariat Général de la Marine Marchande, Paris.
The Directorate of Sea Fisheries, Department of Industries, Cape Town.
Andrew Duncan.
William M. Dunkle, Chart and Map Librarian, Woods Hole Oceanographic Institution, Woods Hole, Massachusetts.
The Financial Times, London.
Dr. R. Fisher, Scripps Institution of Oceanography, La Jolla, California.
Freeport Minerals Company, New York.
French Embassy, London.
Friends of the Earth, London.
The Herring Industry Board, Edinburgh.
Keith Howell, The Editor, *Oceans Magazine*.
Mr. J. W. Hutchinson, UK, FAO National Committee.
A. Madgewick, P. Hunter, Institute of Oceanographic Sciences.
The Institute of Petroleum, London.
Kelvin Hughes, Equipment and Systems.
Jan Jones.
Dr. D. R. C. Kempe, British Museum (Natural History) London.
Lamont-Doherty Geological Observatory, New York.
M. Legand, Office de la Recherche Scientifique et Technique Outre-Mer, Nouvelle Caledonie.
Marsha Lloyd.
J. Mammerickx, Scripps Institution of Oceanography.
The Marconi International Marine Company Ltd.
Metallgesellschaft, Frankfurt.
Dr. B. J. Mason, G. A. Corby, D. E. Parker, The Meteorological Office, UK.
Mining and Transport Engineering N.V., Amsterdam.
Ministerie van Verkeer en Waterstaat, 's-Gravenhage.
Netherlands Embassy, London.
Mr. A. Northolt, Institute of Geological Sciences, London.
N. Otsuru, Fishery Agency, Ministry of Agriculture and Forestry, Tokyo.
Preussag Aktiengesellschaft, Hanover.
Vicki Pritts, World Data Center, Goddard Space Flight Center, Maryland, USA.
John Rae.
John W. Reintjes, National Marine Fisheries Service, US Department of Commerce.
Rio Tinto Zinc.
The Royal Geographical Society, London.
F. S. Russell, C. M. Yonge.
Dr. A. G. Smith, Department of Geology, Sedgwick Museum, Cambridge.
Dr. Haroun Tazieff, Directeur de Recherche au CNRS.
Dr. J. Ulrich, Institut für Meereskunde, Kiel University.
United States Information Center, London.
Helen Varley.
Venezuelan Embassy, London.
Sally Walters.
P. Warren, Inshore and Shellfish Laboratories, Ministry of Agriculture, Fisheries and Food.
Mrs. Althea Washington, Audio-Visual Department, NASA, Washington.
Jackie Webber
Whale Research Unit, British Museum (Natural History) London.
Dr. A. H. Woodcock, University of Hawaii at Manoa.
Professor J. D. Woods, Institut für Meereskunde, Kiel University.
Tom Wray, White Fish Authority Industrial Development Unit, UK.
Dr. J. J. Zijlstra, Director of Biology, Nederlands Instituut voor Onderzoek der Zee.
Zoology Library of the British Museum (Natural History) London.
Library of the Zoological Society, London.

SPECIAL ACKNOWLEDGEMENTS

The American Geographical Society for permission to use the maps of ferromanganese deposits and sediments on pages 170 and 171.

The Food and Agriculture Organization for information used in compiling the fish distribution maps on pages 122–3, 126, 141, 156, 166–7.

Dr. Helmut H. Lieth, University of North Carolina at Chapel Hill, USA, for the World Primary Production Map on page 86.

Dr. J. D. Phillips, Woods Hole Oceanographic Institution, and Dr. D. Forsyth, Brown University, Rhode Island, for the paleobathymetric maps of the Atlantic Ocean on page 117, first published in Volume 83 of the Geological Society of America Bulletin, 1972.

Mr. D. Privett and the staff of the library at the Institute of Oceanographic Sciences for their help and cooperation.

Dr. John G. Sclater for permission to use the paleobathymetric maps of the Indian Ocean on page 151.

Index prepared by Susan Wilson

PICTURE CREDITS

Credits read from left to right, in descending order on each page.
1 ZEFA. 2 ZEFA. 4 ZEFA. 6 Bildagentur Mauritius. 8 R Grigg. 11 Mats Wibe Lund/Bruce Coleman. 16 NASA; C Purcell/Photo Researchers. 17 J Amos/Photo Researchers. 18 John de Visser; S Gooders/Ardea; J R Brownlie/Bruce Coleman; G R Roberts; John de Visser. 19 John de Visser; A J McClane/Photo Researchers; H W Kitchen/Photo Researchers; John de Visser; M Pendrill/Bruce Coleman; Picturepoint; Picturepoint. 20 G R Roberts; G R Roberts; Paolo Koch. 21 G R Roberts. 23 The Institute of Oceanographic Sciences. 24 Oxford Scientific Films; Heather Angel; Oxford Scientific Films; Arbeitsgemeinschaft Meerestechnisch Gewinnbare Rohstoffe, Frankfurt. 25 Peter Lonsdale. 26 John de Visser. 28 M J Bramwell; Ian Collinge. 29 Fred Bruemmer. 31 NASA; NASA/GSCF. 32 This photograph was furnished by the NOAA Environmental Satellite Data Services through the World Data Center A for Rockets and Satellites. 33 NASA. 34 The Institute of Oceanographic Sciences. 36 Warren Bolster. 37 Ann Ronan Picture Library. 38 John de Visser; G Silk/© Time Inc. 1977; John de Visser; G Silk/© Time Inc. 1977. 40 Dr J B MacInnis/Undersea Research Ltd. 42 Jac Brun/Mittet Foto; Michael Holford; Michael Holford/Trustees of the British Museum. 43 Snark International/Bibliothèque Nationale, Paris; Michael Holford/Ann Mowlem; Michael Holford/National Maritime Museum. 44 Michael Holford/National Maritime Museum; Claus Hansmann Foto; National Maritime Museum; National Maritime Museum. 45 National Maritime Museum; National Maritime Museum; National Maritime Museum; National Maritime Museum; National Maritime Museum/on loan from Ministry of Defence – (Navy); National Maritime Museum; Michael Holford/National Maritime Museum; Michael Holford/National Maritime Museum.

46 Institute of Oceanographic Sciences; Institute of Oceanographic Sciences; Michael Holford; Michael Holford; Michael Holford. 47 Michael Holford/ National Maritime Museum; remaining photographs: Michael Holford. 50 F Schulke/Seaphot. 51 National Science Foundation and the Smithsonian Oceanographic Sorting Center; Oceaneering International Inc.; Oceaneering International Inc.; The Institute of Oceanographic Sciences; The Institute of Oceanographic Sciences. 52 A Giddings/The Sea Library; B Campoli/The Sea Library; P A Lake/The Sea Library. 53 M Church/The Sea Library. 54 D Clarke/Seaphot; John Bevan; Mary Evans Picture Library; D Clarke/ Seaphot. 55 B Campoli/The Sea Library; A Giddings/ The Sea Library. 58 Pilkington Bros. Ltd; Royal Netherlands Embassy/KLM Aerocarto. 59 Seaphot. 60 Allan Power/Bruce Coleman. 62 D P Wilson; D P Wilson; D P Wilson; Dr G Gerster/John Hillelson Agency. 63 Jacana; Heather Angel; Jacana; P David/ Seaphot; Oxford Scientific Films/Bruce Coleman; D P Wilson; P David/Seaphot. 64 D P Wilson; Jane Burton/Bruce Coleman; Ph F Winner/Jacana; Jane Burton/Bruce Coleman; Jane Burton/Bruce Coleman; H Genthe/The Sea Library; Heather Angel. 65 Jane Burton/Bruce Coleman; H Chaumeton/Jacana; H Chaumeton/Jacana; Heather Angel; Oxford Scientific Films/Bruce Coleman; H Genthe/The Sea Library; P Capen/The Sea Library; D P Wilson. 66 Nat Fain/ Natural Science Photos; Nat Fain/Natural Science Photos; Nat Fain/Natural Science Photos; Nat Fain/ Natural Science Photos; Nat Fain/Natural Science Photos; Jane Burton/Bruce Coleman; P David/Photo Researchers. 67 C Carré/Jacana; S C Bisserot/Bruce Coleman; C Carré/Jacana; Allan Power/Bruce Coleman; F Winner/Jacana; D P Wilson; D P Wilson. 69 Allan Power/Bruce Coleman; Ron Church/The Sea Library; S C Bisserot/Bruce Coleman; Jane Burton/Bruce Coleman; J C Hookelheim/The Sea Library. 70 S Gillsater/Bruce Coleman; J Foott/ Bruce Coleman; J Foott/Bruce Coleman; C Roessler/ The Sea Library; S Gillsater/Bruce Coleman; L Lee Rue/Bruce Coleman. 71 F Erize/Bruce Coleman; F Erize/Bruce Coleman; G Cubitt/Bruce Coleman; J Foott/Bruce Coleman; A Warren/Ardea; Fred Bruemmer; D Hughes/ Bruce Coleman; Bruce Coleman. 72 The Mansell Collection. 73 Marineland of Florida; The Institute of Oceanographic Sciences. 74 John de Visser; P Germain/Ardea. 75 David & Katie Urry; Dr H J G Dartnall; G Langsbury; P J K Burton/Natural Science Photos. 76 D Bartlett/Bruce Coleman; J. Dermid/Bruce Coleman. 79 D Hughes/ Bruce Coleman; M E Bacchus/Natural Science Photos; Bruce Coleman. 82 P Ward/Natural Science Photos; Heather Angel; Jane Burton/Bruce Coleman; P Steyn/ Ardea; R N Mariscal/Bruce Coleman Inc, New York; Heather Angel; J & D Bartlett/Bruce Coleman Inc, New York; Nat Fain/Natural Science Photos; D Schwimmer/Bruce Coleman Inc, New York; Nat Fain/ Natural Science Photos. 83 Heather Angel; S C Bisserot/Bruce Coleman; N Fox Davies/Bruce Coleman; Heather Angel; S C Bisserot/Bruce Coleman; Jane Burton/Bruce Coleman; Heather Angel; Heather Angel; D B Lewis/Natural Science Photos; Heather Angel; Jane Burton/Bruce Coleman. 84 N Devore/ Bruce Coleman Inc, New York; Diane Wayman/ Colorific!; C Petron/Seaphot; G Harwood/Seaphot; C Petron/Seaphot; Jane Burton/Bruce Coleman. 85 Allan Power/Bruce Coleman; Allan Power/Bruce Coleman; Jane Burton/Bruce Coleman; Jane Burton/ Bruce Coleman Inc, New York; Stan Wayman/© Time Inc. 1977; Allan Power/Bruce Coleman; Allan Power/Bruce Coleman. 88 Oxford Scientific Films. 89 Oxford Scientific Films; Oxford Scientific Films; Oxford Scientific Films; P David/Seaphot. 90 Dr G Gerster/John Hillelson Agency. 93 G D Plage/Bruce Coleman; Bill Levy/Colorific!; J Dowd/Bruce Coleman; N Devore/Bruce Coleman. 94 Mary Evans Picture Library. 95 The Mansell Collection; The British Trawler Federation; Her Majesty's Stationery Office. 96 M F Wood; Heather Angel. 97 Christian Zuber/ John Hillelson Agency; ZEFA. 98 C Delu/Explorer. 100 Paolo Koch. 102 Arbeitsgemeinschaft Meeres-

technisch Gewinnbare Rohstoffe, Frankfurt. 104 Seismograph Service Ltd. 106 Tony Morrison. 107 N Bonner; Photo Researchers; Fishing News. 108 Bill Eppridge/© Time Inc. 1977; J L Mason/ Ardea; John Reader/© Time Inc. 1977. 109 F Erize/Bruce Coleman; NASA. 110 Erwin Christian. 111 Heather Angel; G Laycock/Bruce Coleman. 112 Dr G Gerster/John Hillelson Agency. 116 Mats Wibe Lund. 118 Shell Photo Service; Alan Archer. 120 NASA. 121 The Nimbus 3 HR IR photograph has been provided by the National Space Science Data Center through the World Data Center A for Rockets and Satellites. 122 John de Visser. 124 NASA. 127 ZEFA. 128 Dr P Wadhams. 130 British Petroleum; Paolo Koch. 131 John de Visser; Paolo Koch. 134 Shell Photo Service; Aeromarine Fotos Ltd/British Dredging Aggregates Ltd; 136 M F Wood. 142 NASA. 144 NASA. 146 Dr Haroun Tazieff. 147 D Ross and R Young. 149 Chicago Iron and Bridge Co. Ltd. 152 Robert Harding Associates. 153 Alan Archer. 154 NASA. 160 NASA. 161 Dr Lee Tepley; Erwin Christian; Erwin Christian; Erwin Christian. 162 NASA; NASA. 163 NASA. 164 Deep Sea Drilling Project. 167 D Bartlett/Bruce Coleman. 168 M J Bramwell. 170 N Bonner. 171 N Bonner. 172 Oxford Scientific Films. **Jacket photographs: Front** Jane Burton/ Bruce Coleman Inc, New York. **Back** John Moss/ Colorific!; Erwin Christian.

ILLUSTRATION CREDITS

Credits read from left to right in descending order on each page.

10 Brian Delf. 12 Arka Graphics; Sidney Woods; Arka Graphics; Sidney Woods. 13 Arka Graphics; Sidney Woods; Dougal Dixon; Arka Graphics. 14 Chris Forsey. 15 Chris Forsey. 16 Sidney Woods. 17 Sidney Woods. 18 Chris Forsey. 19 Chris Forsey. 20 Mike Saunders. 21 Mike Saunders. 22 Pierre Charron; Mike Saunders; Arka Graphics; Mike Saunders. 23 Brian Delf; Mike Saunders; Brian Delf; Brian Delf. 24 Arka Graphics. 25 Arka Graphics; Chris Forsey; Chris Forsey; Chris Forsey. 27 Allard Graphics. 28 Mike Saunders; 29 Chris Forsey. 30 Mike Saunders; Mike Saunders; Mike Saunders; Brian Delf; Mike Saunders; Mike Saunders. 31 Mike Saunders. 32 Mike Saunders. 33 Arka Graphics. 34 Alan Suttie; Chris Forsey; Alan Suttie; Mike Saunders. 35 Arka Graphics; Arka Graphics; Mike Saunders. 36 Mike Saunders. 37 Mike Saunders. 38 Sidney Woods. 39 Mike Saunders. 42 Chris Forsey. 48 Chris Forsey. 49 Mike Saunders; Mike Saunders; Alan Suttie. 50 Alan Suttie. 51 Alan Suttie. 52 Chris Forsey. 55 Alan Suttie. 58 Sidney Woods. 63 Chris Forsey. 64 Michael Woods. 65 Michael Woods. 67 Michael Woods. 68 Brian Delf. 69 Brian Delf. 71 Michael Woods. 72 Michael Woods; Gordon Miles. 73 Gordon Miles; Chris Forsey. 75 Chris Forsey. 76 Sidney Woods. 77 Sidney Woods; Ayala Kingsley. 78 Sidney Woods. 79 Sidney Woods. 80 Chris Forsey. 83 Chris Forsey. 84 Chris Forsey. 86 Arka Graphics; Sidney Woods; Sidney Woods. 87 Arka Graphics; Sidney Woods; Sidney Woods. 88 Chris Forsey. 92 John Davis. 93 Sidney Woods. 94 Terry Collins. 95 Chris Forsey; Mike Saunders. 97 Mike Saunders. 98 Mike Saunders. 99 Mike Saunders. 100 Arka Graphics. 101 Brian Delf. 102 Arka Graphics. 103 Alan Suttie. 104 Chris Forsey; Mike Saunders. 105 Terry Collins; Alan Suttie; Alan Suttie; Alan Suttie. 106 Mike Saunders. 107 Mike Saunders. 114 Pierre Charron. 116 Sidney Woods. 117 Pierre Charron; Arka Graphics. 118 Mike Saunders; Arka Graphics; Mike Saunders. 119 Arka Graphics. 120 Arka Graphics. 121 Arka Graphics. 122 Sidney Woods; Arka Graphics; Arka Graphics. 123 Arka Graphics; Mike Saunders; Gordon Miles; Mike Saunders. 124 Arka Graphics; Sidney Woods. 125 Hunting Surveys; Mike Saunders; Mike Saunders; Mike Saunders. 126 Arka Graphics. 127 Arka Graphics; Mike Saunders. 128 Sidney Woods. 129 Hunting Surveys; Trianon; Mike Saunders; Arka Graphics; Mike Saunders. 130 Arka Graphics. 131 Arka Graphics. 132 Sidney Woods; Pierre Charron; 133 Hunting Surveys; Arka Graphics. 134

Sidney Woods. 135 Sidney Woods. 136 Mike Saunders. 137 Arka Graphics; Sidney Woods. 138 Sidney Woods; Mike Saunders. 139 Hunting Surveys; Mike Saunders. 140 Arka Graphics; Mike Saunders; Brian Delf. 141 Arka Graphics. 142 Brian Delf; Mike Saunders. 143 Arka Graphics. 144 Sidney Woods. 145 Hunting Surveys; Arka Graphics. 147 Trianon; Chris Forsey. 148 Arka Graphics. 149 Trianon. 150 Sidney Woods; Pierre Charron. 151 Arka Graphics. 152 Arka Graphics. 153 Arka Graphics. 154 Arka Graphics. 155 Arka Graphics. 156 Pierre Charron. 157 Sidney Woods; Mike Saunders. 158 Pierre Charron/Chris Forsey; Brian Delf. 159 Pierre Charron/Chris Forsey; Brian Delf. 160 Brian Delf; Mike Saunders. 161 Mike Saunders; Brian Delf; Mike Saunders. 163 Arka Graphics. 164 Arka Graphics. 165 Mike Saunders. 166 Gordon Miles; Arka Graphics; Sidney Woods. 167 Arka Graphics; Mike Saunders. 168 Sidney Woods; Arka Graphics; Mike Saunders. 169 Hunting Surveys. 170 Arka Graphics. 171 Arka Graphics; Mike Saunders. 174–186 Michael Woods.

Retouching by Sally Slight.

BIBLIOGRAPHY

Anikouchine, William A. & Sternberg Richard W. *The World Ocean* Englewood Cliffs, New Jersey: Prentice-Hall 1973. Arnold, Augusta Foote *The Sea Beach at Ebb-Tide* New York: Dover Publications, Inc. 1968. Badgley, Peter C. ed. et al. *Oceans from Space* Houston, Texas: Gulf Publishing Company 1969. Barnett, John & Yonge, C. M. *Collins Pocket Guide to the Sea Shore* London: Collins 1958. Barton, Robert *Atlas of the Sea* London: Heinemann 1974. Belderson et al. *Sonographs of the Sea Floor* Amsterdam: Elsevier Publishing Company 1972. Bodechtel, Johann & Gieloff-Emden, Hans Gunter *The Earth from Space* Newton Abbot, Devon: David and Charles 1974. Boney, A. D. *Studies in Biology: Phytoplankton* London: Edward Arnold 1975. Von Brandt, Andres *Fish Catching Methods of the World* West Byfleet, Surrey: Fishing News (Books) Ltd. 1964. Briggs, John C. *Marine Zoogeography* New York: McGraw Hill Book Company 1974. Buchsbaum, Ralph *Animals without Backbones* London: Penguin Books 1951. Buchsbaum, Ralph & Milne, Lorus, J. *The Lower Animals* New York: Doubleday Inc. 1972. Burton, Robert et al. *The Living Sea* London: Orbis Publishing Ltd. 1976. Campbell, A. C. *The Hamlyn Guide to the Seashore and Shallow seas of Britain and Europe* London: Hamlyn Publishing Group Ltd. 1976. Critchlow, Keith *Into the Hidden Environment* London: George Philip 1972. Cushing, David *The Detection of Fish* Oxford: Pergamon Press 1973. Davis, Sir Robert H. *Deep Diving and Submarine Operations* London: St. Catherine Press 1951. Deacon, M. *Scientists and the Sea* London: 1971. Dodd, S. H. *Polynesian Seafaring* New York: Dodd, Mead & Company 1972. *FAO Catalogue of Fishing Gear Designs*, West Byfleet, Surrey: Fishing News (Books) Ltd. 1972. Farner, D. S. & King, J. R. ed. *Avian Biology Vol 1* London: Academic Press Inc. 1971. Firth, Frank E., ed. *The Encyclopedia of Marine Resources* New York: Van Nostrand Reinhold Company 1969. Fraser, J. H. *Nature Adrift* London: Foulis 1962. Friedrich, H. *Marine Biology* London: Sidgwick Jackson 1969. Gaskell, T. F. *World Beneath the Oceans* London: Aldus Books 1964. *Geology Today* Del Mar, California: CRM Books 1973. Gulland, J. A. *The Fish Resources of the Ocean* West Byfleet, Surrey: Fishing News (Books) Ltd. 1971. Harden Jones, F. R. *Fish Migration* London: Edward Arnold Ltd. 1968. Hardy, Alistair *The Open Sea: Fish & Fisheries* London: Collins 1959. Harrison, R. J. & King, J. E. *Marine Mammals* London: Hutchinson 1965. Herald, Earl S. *Living Fishes of the World* London: Hamish Hamilton 1961. Heezen, Bruce C. & Hollister, Charles D. *The Face of the Deep* New York: Oxford University Press 1971. Hornell, James *Water Transport* Newton Abbot: David & Charles 1970. Idyll, C. P. *Exploring the Ocean World* New York: Thomas Y. Crowell Company 1969. Kinsman, Blair *Wind Waves* New Jersey: Prentice-Hall Inc. 1965. Kristjonsson, Hilman *Modern Fishing Gear of the World* London: Fishing News (Books) Ltd. 1971. Lieth H. & Whittaker, Robert H. *Primary Production of the Biosphere* New York: Springer-Verlag 1975. Macmillan D. H. *Tides* London: C. R. Books Ltd. 1966. Marshall, N. B. *Aspects of Deep Sea Biology* London: Hutchinson's 1954. Marshall, N. B. *The Life of Fishes* London: Weidenfeld and Nicholson 1965. Matthews, L. H. *The Whale* London: Allen & Unwin 1968. McConnaughey, Bayard H. *Introduction to Marine Biology* Saint Louis: The C. V. Mosby Company 1974. Miller, Robert C. *The Sea* London: Thomas Nelson and Sons Ltd. 1966. Mörzer Bruyns, W. F. J. *Field Guide of Whales and Dolphins* Amsterdam 1971. Murray, John, & Hjort, Johan *The Depths of the Ocean* London: Macmillan & Co. Ltd. 1912. Muus, Bent J. & Dahlstrom, Preben *Collins Guide to the Sea Fishes* London: Collins 1974. Newell, G. E. & Newell, R. C. *Marine Plankton* London: Hutchinson Educational 1963. Norman, J. R. *History of Fishes* London: Ernest Benn Ltd. 1975. Odum, Eugene P. *Fundamentals of Ecology* Philadelphia: W. B. Saunders Company 1971. Parsons, T. R. & Takahashi, M. *Biological Oceanographic Processes* Oxford: Pergamon Press 1973. Raymont, J. E. G. *Plankton and Productivity in the Oceans* London: Pergamon Press 1963. Russell, F. S. & Yonge, C. M. *The Seas* London: Warne & Co. 1928. Tait, R. V. *Elements of Marine Ecology* London: Butterworths 1972. Thorson, Gunnar *Life in the Sea* London: Weidenfeld and Nicholson 1971. Sainsbury, John C. *Commercial Fishing Methods* West Byfleet, Surrey: Fishing News (Books) Ltd. 1971. Wimpenny, R. S. *The Plankton of the Sea* London: Faber 1966.